Security Engineering: A Guide to Building Dependable Distributed Systems

Ross J. Anderson

Wiley Computer Publishing

John Wiley & Sons, Inc.

NEW YORK • CHICHESTER • WEINHEIM • BRISBANE • SINGAPORE • TORONTO

Publisher: Robert Ipsen
Editor: Carol A. Long
Managing Editor: Micheline Frederick
Text Design & Composition: Interactive Composition Corporation

Designations used by companies to distinguish their products are often claimed as trademarks. In all instances where John Wiley & Sons, Inc., is aware of a claim, the product names appear in initial capital or ALL CAPITAL LETTERS. Readers, however, should contact the appropriate companies for more complete information regarding trademarks and registration.

This book is printed on acid-free paper. ∞

Published by John Wiley & Sons, Inc.

Published simultaneously in Canada.

This publication is designed to provide accurate and authoritative information in regard to the subject matter covered. It is sold with the understanding that the publisher is not engaged in professional services. If professional advice or other expert assistance is required, the services of a competent professional person should be sought.

Library of Congress Cataloging-in-Publication Data

Anderson, Ross, 1956-
    Security engineering : a guide to building dependable distributed systems/Ross J. Anderson.
        p. cm.
    "Wiley Computer Publishing."
    Includes bibliographical references and index.
    ISBN 0-471-38922-6 (pbk. : alk. paper)
    1. Computer security. 2. Electronic data processing—Distributed processing. I. Title.
    QA76.9.A25 A54 2001
    005.8—dc21   00-068486

Printed in the United States of America.

10 9 8 7 6 5 4 3

To Shireen

Contents

Preface

For generations, people have defined and protected their property and their privacy using locks, fences, signatures, seals, account books, and meters. These have been supported by a host of social constructs ranging from international treaties through national laws to manners and customs.

This is changing, and quickly. Most records are now electronic, from bank accounts to registers of real property; and transactions are increasingly electronic, as shopping moves to the Internet. Just as important, but less obvious, are the many everyday systems that have been quietly automated. Burglar alarms no longer wake up the neighborhood, but send silent messages to the police; students no longer fill their dormitory washers and dryers with coins, but credit them using a smartcard they recharge at the college bookstore; locks are no longer simple mechanical affairs, but are operated by electronic remote controls or swipe cards; and instead of renting videocassettes, millions of people get their movies from satellite or cable channels. Even the humble banknote is no longer just ink on paper, but may contain digital watermarks that enable many forgeries to be detected by machine.

How good is all this new security technology? Unfortunately, the honest answer is "nowhere near as good as it should be." New systems are often rapidly broken, and the same elementary mistakes are repeated in one application after another. It often takes four or five attempts to get a security design right, and that is far too many.

The media regularly report security breaches on the Internet; banks fight their customers over "phantom withdrawals" from cash machines; VISA reports huge increases in the number of disputed Internet credit card transactions; satellite TV companies hound pirates who copy their smartcards; and law enforcement agencies try to stake out territory in cyberspace with laws controlling the use of encryption. Worse still, features interact. A mobile phone that calls the last number again if one of the keys is pressed by accident may be just a minor nuisance—until someone invents a machine that dispenses a can of soft drink every time its phone number is called. When all of a sudden you find 50 cans of Coke on your phone bill, who is responsible, the phone company, the handset manufacturer, or the vending machine operator? Once almost every electronic device that affects your life is connected to the Internet—which Microsoft expects to happen by 2010—what does 'Internet security' mean to you, and how do you cope with it?

As well as the systems that fail, many systems just don't work well enough. Medical record systems don't let doctors share personal health information as they would like, but still don't protect it against inquisitive private eyes. Zillion-dollar military systems prevent anyone without a "top secret" clearance from getting at intelligence data, but are often designed so that almost everyone needs this clearance to do any work. Passenger ticket systems are designed to prevent customers cheating, but when trustbusters break up the railroad, they cannot stop the new rail companies cheating each other. Many of these failures could have been foreseen if designers had just a little bit more knowledge of what had been tried, and had failed, elsewhere.

Security engineering is the new discipline, that is starting to emerge out of all this chaos.

Although most of the underlying technologies (cryptology, software reliability, tamper resistance, security printing, auditing, etc.) are relatively well understood, the knowledge and experience of how to apply them effectively is much scarcer. And since the move from mechanical to digital mechanisms is happening everywhere at once, there just has not been time for the lessons learned to percolate through the engineering community. Time and again, we see the same old square wheels being reinvented.

The industries that have managed the transition most capably are often those that have been able to borrow an appropriate technology from another discipline. Examples include the reuse of technology designed for military identify-friend-or-foe equipment in bank cash machines and even prepayment gas meters. So even if a security designer has serious expertise in some particular speciality—whether as a mathematician working with ciphers or a chemist developing banknote inks—it is still prudent to have an overview of the whole subject. The essence of good security engineering is understanding the potential threats to a system, then applying an appropriate mix of protective measures—both technological and organizational—to control them. Knowing what has worked, and more importantly what has failed, in other applications is a great help in developing judgment. It can also save a lot of money.

The purpose of this book is to give a solid introduction to security engineering, as we understand it at the beginning of the twenty-first century. My goal is that it works at four different levels:

- *As a textbook that you can read from one end to the other over a few days as an introduction to the subject.* The book is to be used mainly by the working IT professional who needs to learn about the subject, but it can also be used in a one-semester course in a university.

- *As a reference book to which you can come for an overview of the workings of some particular type of system.* These systems include cash machines, taxi meters, radar jammers, anonymous medical record databases, and so on.

- *As an introduction to the underlying technologies, such as crypto, access control, inference control, tamper resistance, and seals.* Space prevents me from going into great depth; but I provide a basic road map for each subject, plus a reading list for the curious (and a list of open research problems for the prospective graduate student).

- *As an original scientific contribution in which I have tried to draw out the common principles that underlie security engineering, and the lessons that people building one kind of system should have learned from others.* In the many years I have been working in security, I keep coming across these. For example, a simple attack on stream ciphers wasn't known to the people who designed a common antiaircraft fire control radar so it was easy to jam; while a trick well known to the radar community wasn't understood by banknote printers and people who design copyright marking schemes, which led to a quite general attack on most digital watermarks.

I have tried to keep this book resolutely mid-Atlantic; a security engineering book has to be, as many of the fundamental technologies are American, while many of the interesting applications are European. (This isn't surprising given the better funding of U.S. universities and research labs, and the greater diversity of nations and markets in Europe.) What's more, many of the successful European innovations—from the smartcard to the GSM mobile phone to the pay-per-view TV service—have crossed the Atlantic and now thrive in the Americas. Both the science, and the case studies, are necessary.

This book grew out of the security engineering courses I teach at Cambridge University, but I have rewritten my notes to make them self-contained and added at least as much material again. It should be useful to the established professional security manager or consultant as a first-line reference; to the computer science professor doing research in cryptology; to the working police detective trying to figure out the latest computer scam; and to policy wonks struggling with the conflicts involved in regulating cryptography and anonymity. Above all, it is aimed at Dilbert. My main audience is the working programmer or engineer who is trying to design real systems that will keep on working despite the best efforts of customers, managers, and everybody else.

This book is divided into three parts.

- The first looks at basic concepts, starting with the central concept of a security protocol, and going on to human-computer interface issues, access controls, cryptology, and distributed system issues. It does not assume any particular technical background other than basic computer literacy. It is based on an Introduction to Security course that I teach to second-year undergraduates.

- The second part looks in much more detail at a number of important applications, such as military communications, medical record systems, cash machines, mobile phones, and pay-TV. These are used to introduce more of the advanced technologies and concepts. It also considers information security from the viewpoint of a number of different interest groups, such as companies, consumers, criminals, police, and spies. This material is drawn from my senior course on security, from research work, and from experience consulting.

- The third part looks at the organizational and policy issues: how computer security interacts with law, with evidence, and with corporate politics; how we can gain confidence that a system will perform as intended; and how the whole business of security engineering can best be managed.

I believe that building systems that continue to perform robustly in the face of malice is one of the most important, interesting, and difficult tasks facing engineers in the twenty-first century.

Ross Anderson
Cambridge, January 2001

About the Author

Why should I have been the person to write this book? Well, I seem to have accumulated the right mix of experience and qualifications over the last 25 years. I graduated in mathematics and natural science from Cambridge (England) in the 1970s, and got a qualification in computer engineering; my first proper job was in avionics; and I became interested in cryptology and computer security in the mid-1980s. After working in the banking industry for several years, I started doing consultancy for companies that designed equipment for banks, and then working on other applications of this technology, such as prepayment electricity meters.

I moved to academia in 1992, but continued to consult to industry on security technology. During the 1990s, the number of applications that employed cryptology rose rapidly: burglar alarms, car door locks, road toll tags, and satellite TV encryption systems all made their appearance. As the first legal disputes about these systems came along, I was lucky enough to be an expert witness in some of the important cases. The research team I lead had the good fortune to be in the right place at the right time when several crucial technologies, such as tamper resistance and digital watermarking, became hot topics.

By about 1996, it started to become clear to me that the existing textbooks were too specialized. The security textbooks focused on the access control mechanisms in operating systems, while the cryptology books gave very detailed expositions of the design of cryptographic algorithms and protocols. These topics are interesting, and important. However they are only part of the story. Most system designers are not overly concerned with crypto or operating system internals, but with how to use these tools effectively. They are quite right in this, as the inappropriate use of mechanisms is one of the main causes of security failure. I was encouraged by the success of a number of articles I wrote on security engineering (starting with "Why Cryptosystems Fail" in 1993); and the need to teach an undergraduate class in security led to the development of a set of lecture notes that made up about half of this book. Finally, in 1999, I got round to rewriting them for a general technical audience.

I have learned a lot in the process; writing down what you think you know is a good way of finding out what you don't. I have also had a lot of fun. I hope you have as much fun reading it!

Foreword

In a paper he wrote with Roger Needham, Ross Anderson coined the phrase "programming Satan's computer" to describe the problems faced by computer-security engineers. It's the sort of evocative image I've come to expect from Ross, and a phrase I've used ever since.

Programming a computer is straightforward: keep hammering away at the problem until the computer does what it's supposed to do. Large application programs and operating systems are a lot more complicated, but the methodology is basically the same. Writing a reliable computer program is much harder, because the program needs to work even in the face of random errors and mistakes: Murphy's computer, if you will. Significant research has gone into reliable software design, and there are many mission-critical software applications that are designed to withstand Murphy's Law.

Writing a *secure* computer program is another matter entirely. Security involves making sure things work, not in the presence of random faults, but in the face of an intelligent and malicious adversary trying to ensure that things fail in the worst possible way at the worst possible time ... again and again. It truly is programming Satan's computer.

Security engineering is different from any other kind of programming. It's a point I made over and over again: in my own book, *Secrets and Lies*, in my monthly newsletter *Crypto-Gram*, and in my other writings. And it's a point Ross makes in every chapter of this book. This is why, if you're doing any security engineering ... if you're even *thinking* of doing any security engineering, you need to read this book. It's the first, and only, end-to-end modern security design and engineering book ever written.

And it comes just in time. You can divide the history of the Internet into three waves. The first wave centered around mainframes and terminals. Computers were expensive and rare. The second wave, from about 1992 until now, centered around personal computers, browsers, and large application programs. And the third, starting now, will see the connection of all sorts of devices that are currently in proprietary networks, standalone, and non-computerized. By 2003, there will be more mobile phones connected to the Internet than computers. Within a few years we'll see many of the world's refrigerators, heart monitors, bus and train ticket dispensers, burglar alarms, and electricity meters talking IP. Personal computers will be a minority player on the Internet.

Security engineering, especially in this third wave, requires you to think differently. You need to figure out not how something works, but how something can be made to not work. You have to imagine an intelligent and malicious adversary inside your system (remember Satan's computer), constantly trying new ways to subvert it. You have to consider all the ways your system can fail, most of them having nothing to do with the design itself. You have to look at everything backwards, upside down, and sideways. You have to think like an alien.

As the late great science fiction editor John W. Campbell, said: "An alien thinks as well as a human, but not like a human." Computer security is a lot like that. Ross is one of those rare people who can think like an alien, and then explain that thinking to humans. Have fun reading.

Bruce Schneier
January 2001

Acknowledgments

A great many people have helped in various ways with this book. I probably owe the greatest thanks to those who read the manuscript (or a large part of it) looking for errors and obscurities. They were Anne Anderson, Ian Brown, Nick Bohm, Richard Bondi, Caspar Bowden, Richard Clayton, Steve Early, Rich Graveman, Markus Kuhn, Dan Lough, David MacKay, John McHugh, Bob Morris, Roger Needham, Jerry Saltzer, Marv Schaefer, Karen Spärck Jones and Frank Stajano. Much credit also goes to my editor, Carol Long, who (among many other things) went through the first six chapters and coached me on the style appropriate for a professional (as opposed to academic) book. At the proofreading stage, I got quite invaluable help from Carola Bohm, Mike Bond, Richard Clayton, George Danezis, and Bruce Godfrey.

A large number of subject experts also helped me with particular chapters or sections. Richard Bondi helped me refine the definitions in Chapter 1; Jianxin Yan, Alan Blackwell and Alasdair Grant helped me investigate the applied psychology aspects of passwords; John Gordon and Sergei Skorobogatov were my main sources on remote key entry devices; Whit Diffie and Mike Brown on IFF; Steve Early on Unix security (although some of my material is based on lectures given by Ian Jackson); Mike Roe, Ian Kelly, Paul Leyland, and Fabien Petitcolas on the security of Windows NT4 and Win2K; Virgil Gligor on the history of memory overwriting attacks, and on mandatory integrity policies; and Jean Bacon on distributed systems. Gary Graunke told me the history of protection in Intel processors; Orr Dunkelman found many bugs in a draft of the crypto chapter and John Brazier pointed me to the Humpty Dumpty quote.

Moving to the second part of the book, the chapter on multilevel security was much improved by input from Jeremy Epstein, Virgil Gligor, Jong-Hyeon Lee, Ira Moskowitz, Paul Karger, Rick Smith, Frank Stajano, and Simon Wiseman, while Frank also helped with the following two chapters. The material on medical systems was originally developed with a number of people at the British Medical Association, most notably Fleur Fisher,

Simon Jenkins, and Grant Kelly. Denise Schmandt-Besserat taught the world about bullae, which provided the background for the chapter on banking systems; that chapter was also strengthened by input from Fay Hider and Willie List. The chapter on alarms contains much that I was taught by Roger Needham, Peter Dean, John Martin, Frank Clish, and Gary Geldart. Nuclear command and control systems are much the brainchild of Gus Simmons; he and Bob Morris taught me much of what's in that chapter.

Sijbrand Spannenburg reviewed the chapter on security printing; and Roger Johnston has taught us all an enormous amount about seals. John Daugman helped polish the chapter on biometrics, as well as inventing iris scanning which I describe there. My tutors on tamper resistance were Oliver Kömmerling and Markus Kuhn; Markus also worked with me on emission security. I had substantial input on electronic warfare from Mike Brown and Owen Lewis. The chapter on phone fraud owes a lot to Duncan Campbell, Richard Cox, Rich Graveman, Udi Manber, Andrew Odlyzko and Roy Paterson. Ian Jackson contributed some ideas on network security. Fabien Petitcolas 'wrote the book' on copyright marking, and helped polish my chapter on it. Johann Bezuidenhoudt made perceptive comments on both phone fraud and electronic commerce, while Peter Landrock gave valuable input on bookkeeping and electronic commerce systems. Alistair Kelman was a fount of knowledge on the legal aspects of copyright; and Hal Varian kept me straight on matters of economics, and particularly the chapters on e-commerce and assurance.

As for the third part of the book, the chapter on e-policy was heavily influenced by colleagues at the Foundation for Information Policy Research, notably Caspar Bowden, Nick Bohm, Fleur Fisher, Brian Gladman, Ian Brown, Richard Clayton—and by the many others involved in the fight, including Whit Diffie, John Gilmore, Susan Landau, Brian Omotani and Mark Rotenberg. The chapter on management benefited from input from Robert Brady, Jack Lang, and Willie List. Finally, my thinking on assurance has been influenced by many people, including Robin Ball, Robert Brady, Willie List, and Robert Morris.

There were also many people over the years who taught me my trade. The foremost of them is Roger Needham, who was my thesis advisor; but I also learned a lot from hundreds of engineers, programmers, auditors, lawyers, and policemen with whom I worked on various consultancy jobs over the last 15 years. Of course, I take the rap for all the remaining errors and omissions.

Finally, I owe a huge debt to my family, especially to my wife Shireen for putting up with over a year in which I neglected household duties and was generally preoccupied. Daughter Bavani and dogs Jimmy, Bess, Belle, Hobbes, Bigfoot, Cat, and Dogmatix also had to compete for a diminished quantum of attention, and I thank them for their forbearance.

Legal Notice

I cannot emphasize too strongly that the tricks taught in this book are intended only to enable you to build better systems. They are not in any way given as a means of helping you to break into systems, subvert copyright protection mechanisms, or do anything else unethical or illegal.

Where possible I have tried to give case histories at a level of detail that illustrates the underlying principles without giving a "hacker's cookbook."

Should This Book Be Published at All?

There are people who believe that the knowledge contained in this book should not be published. This is an old debate; in previous centuries, people objected to the publication of books on locksmithing, on the grounds that they were likely to help the bad guys more than the good guys.

I think that these fears are answered in the first book in English that discussed cryptology. This was a treatise on optical and acoustic telegraphy written by Bishop John Wilkins in 1641 [805]. He traced scientific censorship back to the Egyptian priests who forbade the use of alphabetic writing on the grounds that it would spread literacy among the common people and thus foster dissent. As he said:

> It will not follow that everything must be suppresst which may be abused... If all those useful inventions that are liable to abuse should therefore be concealed there is not any Art or Science which may be lawfully profest.

The question was raised again in the nineteenth century, when some well-meaning people wanted to ban books on locksmithing. A contemporary writer on the subject replied [750]:

> Many well-meaning persons suppose that the discussion respecting the means for baffling the supposed safety of locks offers a premium for dishonesty, by showing others how to be dishonest. This is a fallacy. Rogues are very keen in their profession, and already know much more than we can teach them respecting their several kinds of roguery. Rogues knew a good deal about lockpicking long before locksmiths discussed it among themselves . . . if there be harm, it will be much more than counterbalanced by good.

These views have been borne out by long experience since. As for me, I worked for two separate banks for three and a half years on cash machine security, but I learned significant new tricks from a document written by a convicted card fraudster that circulated in the U.K. prison system. Many government agencies are now coming round to this point of view. It is encouraging to see, for example, that the U.S. National Security Agency has published the specifications of the encryption algorithm (Skipjack) and the key management protocol (KEA) used to protect secret U.S. government traffic. Their judgment is clearly that the potential harm done by letting the Iraqis use a decent encryption algorithm is less than the good that will be done by having commercial off-the-shelf software compatible with Federal encryption standards.

In short, while some bad guys will benefit from a book such as this, they mostly know the tricks already, and the good guys will benefit much more.

PART

One

In this section of the book, I cover the basics of security engineering technology. The first chapter sets out to define the subject matter by giving an overview of the secure distributed systems found in four environments: a bank, an air force base, a hospital, and the home. The second chapter is on security protocols, which lie at the heart of the subject: they specify how the players in a system—whether people, computers, or other electronic devices—communicate with each other. The third, on passwords and similar mechanisms, looks in more detail at a particularly simple kind of security protocol that is widely used to authenticate people to computers, and provides the foundation on which many secure systems are built.

The next two chapters are on access control and cryptography. Even once a client (be it a phone, a PC, or whatever) has authenticated itself satisfactorily to a server—whether with a password or a more elaborate protocol—we still need mechanisms to control which data it can read or write on the server, and which transactions it can execute. It is simplest to examine these issues first in the context of a single centralized system (access control) before we consider how they can be implemented in a more distributed manner using multiple servers, perhaps in different domains, for which the key enabling technology is cryptography. Cryptography is the art (and science) of codes and ciphers. It is much more than a technical means for keeping messages secret from an eavesdropper. Nowadays it is largely concerned with authenticity and management issues: "taking trust from where it exists to where it's needed" [535].

The final chapter in this part is on distributed systems. Researchers in this field are interested in topics such as concurrency control, fault tolerance, and naming. These take on subtle new meanings when systems must be made resilient against malice as well as against accidental failure. Using old data—replaying old transactions or reusing the credentials of a user who has left some time ago—is a serious problem, as is the multitude of names by which people are known to different systems (email addresses, credit card numbers, subscriber numbers, etc.). Many system failures are due to a lack of appreciation of these issues.

Most of the material in these chapters is standard textbook fare, and the chapters are intended to be pedagogic rather than encyclopaedic, so I have not put in as many citations as in the rest of the book. I hope, however, that even experts will find some of the case studies of value.

What Is Security Engineering?

Out of the crooked timber of humanity, no straight thing was ever made

—IMMANUEL KANT

The world is never going to be perfect, either on- or offline; so let's not set impossibly high standards for online

—ESTHER DYSON

Security engineering is about building systems to remain dependable in the face of malice, error, or mischance. As a discipline, it focuses on the tools, processes, and methods needed to design, implement, and test complete systems, and to adapt existing systems as their environment evolves.

Security engineering requires cross-disciplinary expertise, ranging from cryptography and computer security through hardware tamper-resistance and formal methods to a knowledge of applied psychology, organizational and audit methods and the law. System engineering skills, from business process analysis through software engineering to evaluation and testing, are also important; but they are not sufficient, as they deal only with error and mischance rather than malice.

Many security systems have critical assurance requirements. Their failure may endanger human life and the environment (as with nuclear safety and control systems), do serious damage to major economic infrastructure (cash machines and other bank systems), endanger personal privacy (medical record systems), undermine the viability of whole business sectors (pay-TV), and facilitate crime (burglar and car alarms). Even the perception that a system is more vulnerable than it really is (as with paying with a credit card over the Internet) can significantly hold up economic development.

The conventional view is that while software engineering is about ensuring that certain things happen ("John can read this file"), security is about ensuring that they don't

("The Chinese government can't read this file"). Reality is much more complex. Security requirements differ greatly from one system to another. One typically needs some combination of user authentication, transaction integrity and accountability, fault-tolerance, message secrecy, and covertness. But many systems fail because their designers protect the wrong things, or protect the right things but in the wrong way.

In order to see the range of security requirements that systems have to deliver, we will now take a quick look at four application areas: a bank, an air force base, a hospital, and the home. Once we have given some concrete examples of the kind of protection that security engineers are called on to provide, we will be in a position to attempt some definitions.

1.1 Example 1: A Bank

Banks operate a surprisingly large range of security-critical computer systems:

- *The core of a bank's operations is usually a branch bookkeeping system.* This keeps customer account master files plus a number of journals that record the day's transactions. The main threat to this system is the bank's own staff; about one percent of bankers are fired each year, mostly for petty dishonesty (the average theft is only a few thousand dollars). The main defense comes from bookkeeping procedures that have evolved over centuries. For example, each debit against one account must be matched by an equal and opposite credit against another; so money can only be moved within a bank, never created or destroyed. In addition, large transfers of money might need two or three people to authorize them. There are also alarm systems that look for unusual volumes or patterns of transactions, and staff are required to take regular vacations during which they have no access to the bank's premises or systems.

- *The public face of the bank is its automatic teller machines.* Authenticating transactions based on a customer's card and personal identification number—in such a way as to defend against both outside and inside attack—is harder than it looks! There have been many local epidemics of "phantom withdrawals" when villains (or bank staff) have found and exploited loopholes in the system. Automatic teller machines are also interesting as they were the first large-scale commercial use of cryptography, and they helped establish a number of crypto standards.

- *Behind the scenes are a number of high-value messaging systems.* These are used to move large sums of money (whether between local banks or between banks internationally); to trade in securities; to issue letters of credit and guarantees; and so on. An attack on such a system is the dream of the sophisticated white-collar criminal. The defense is a mixture of bookkeeping procedures, access controls, and cryptography.

- *Most bank branches still have a large safe or strongroom, whose burglar alarms are in constant communication with a security company's control center.* Cryptography is used to prevent a robber manipulating the communications and making the alarm appear to say "all's well" when it isn't.

■ *Over the last few years, many banks have acquired an Internet presence, with a Web site and facilities for customers to manage their accounts online.* They also issue credit cards that customers use to shop online, and they acquire the resulting transactions from merchants. To protect this business, they use standard Internet security technology, including the SSL/TLS encryption built into Web browsers, and firewalls to prevent people who hack the Web server from tunneling back into the main bookkeeping systems that lie behind it.

We will look at these applications in later chapters. Banking computer security is important for a number of reasons. Until quite recently, banks were the main non-military market for many computer security products, so they had a disproportionate influence on security standards. Second, even where their technology isn't blessed by an international standard, it is often widely used in other sectors anyway. Burglar alarms originally developed for bank vaults are used everywhere from jewelers' shops to the home; they are even used by supermarkets to detect when freezer cabinets have been sabotaged by shop staff who hope to be given the food that would otherwise spoil.

1.2 Example 2: An Air Force Base

Military systems have also been an important technology driver. They have motivated much of the academic research that governments have funded into computer security in the last 20 years. As with banking, there is not one single application but many:

■ *Some of the most sophisticated installations are the electronic warfare systems whose goals include trying to jam enemy radars while preventing the enemy from jamming yours.* This area of information warfare is particularly instructive because for decades, well-funded research labs have been developing sophisticated countermeasures, counter-countermeasures, and so on—with a depth, subtlety, and range of deception strategies that are still not found elsewhere. Their use in battle has given insights that are not available anywhere else. These insights are likely to be valuable now that the service-denial attacks, which are the mainstay of electronic warfare, are starting to be seen on the Net, and now that governments are starting to talk of "information warfare."

■ *Military communication systems have some interesting requirements.* It is often not sufficient just to encipher messages: an enemy, who sees traffic encrypted with somebody else's keys may simply locate the transmitter and attack it. *Low-probability-of-intercept* (LPI) radio links are one answer; they use a number of tricks, such as spread-spectrum modulation, that are now being adopted in applications such as copyright marking.

■ *Military organizations have some of the biggest systems for logistics and inventory management, and they have a number of special assurance requirements.* For example, one may have a separate stores management system at each different security level: a general system for things like jet fuel and boot polish, plus a second secret system for stores and equipment whose location might give away tactical intentions. (This is very like the business that keeps separate sets of books for its partners and for the tax man, and can cause similar problems for the poor auditor.) There may also be intelligence systems and command systems with even higher protection requirements. The general rule is that sensitive information may not flow down to less-restrictive classifications. So you can copy a file from a Secret stores system to a Top Secret command system, but not vice versa. The same rule applies to intelligence systems that collect data using wiretaps: information must flow up to the intelligence analyst from the target of investigation, but the target must not know which communications have been intercepted. Managing multiple systems with information flow restrictions is a difficult problem that has inspired a lot of research.

■ *The particular problems of protecting nuclear weapons have given rise over the last two generations to a lot of interesting security technology.* These range from electronic authentication systems, which prevent weapons being used without the permission of the national command authority, through seals and alarm systems, to methods of identifying people with a high degree of certainty using biometrics such as iris patterns.

The civilian security engineer can learn a lot from these technologies. For example, many early systems for inserting copyright marks into digital audio and video, which used ideas from spread-spectrum radio, were vulnerable to desynchronization attacks, which are also a problem for some spread-spectrum systems. Another example comes from munitions management, in which a typical system enforces rules such as, "Don't put explosives and detonators in the same truck." Such techniques may be more widely applicable, as in satisfying hygiene rules that forbid raw and cooked meats being handled together.

1.3 Example 3: A Hospital

From food hygiene we move on to healthcare. Hospitals use a number of fairly standard systems for bookkeeping and the like, but also have a number of interesting protection requirements—mostly to do with patient safety and privacy:

■ *As Web-based technologies are adopted in hospitals, they present interesting new assurance problems.* For example, as reference books—such as directories of drugs—are moved online, doctors need assurance that life-critical data (such as the figures for dosage per body weight) are exactly as published by the relevant authority, and have not been mangled in some way, whether accidental or deliberate. Many of these safety problems could affect other Web systems in a few years' time. Another example is that as doctors start to access Web pages containing patients' records from home or from laptops in their cars, suitable electronic authentication and encryption tools are starting to be required.

■ *Patient record systems should not let all the staff see every patient's record, or privacy violations can be expected.* These systems need to implement rules such as, "nurses can see the records of any patient who has been cared for in their department at any time during the previous 90 days." This can be hard to do with traditional computer security mechanisms, as roles can change (nurses move from one department to another); and there are cross-system dependencies (the patient records system may end up relying on the personnel system for access control decisions, so any failure of the personnel system can have implications for safety, for privacy, or for both). Applications such as these are inspiring research in role-based access control.

- *Patient records are often anonymized for use in research, but this is difficult to do well.* Simply encrypting patient names is usually not adequate, as an enquiry such as "Show me all records of 59-year-old males who were treated for a broken collarbone on September 15, 1966," would usually be enough to find the record of a politician who was known to have sustained such an injury as a college athlete. But if records cannot be anonymized properly, then much stricter rules will usually have to be followed when handling the data, and this will increase the cost of medical research.

- *New technology can introduce risks that are just not understood.* Hospital administrators understand the need for backup procedures to deal with outages of power, telephone service, and so on, but medical practice is rapidly coming to depend on the Net in ways that are often not documented. For example, individual clinical departments may start using online drug databases; stop keeping adequate paper copies of drug formularies; and never inform the contingency planning team. So attacks that degrade network services (such as viruses and distributed denial-of-service attacks) might have serious consequences for medical practice.

We will look at medical system security in more detail later. This is a much younger field than banking IT or military systems, but as healthcare accounts for a larger proportion of GNP than either of them in all developed countries, and as hospitals are adopting IT at an increasing rate, it looks set to become important.

1.4 Example 4: The Home

You might not think that the typical family operates any secure distributed systems. But consider the following:

- *Many people use some of the systems we've already described.* You may use a Web-based electronic banking system to pay bills; and in a few years you may have encrypted online access to your medical records. Your burglar alarm may send an encrypted "all's well" signal to the security company every few minutes, rather than waking up the neighborhood when something happens.

- Your car may have an electronic immobilizer that sends an encrypted challenge to a radio transponder in the key fob; the transponder has to respond correctly before the car will start. Since all but the most sophisticated thieves now have to tow the car away and fit a new engine controller before they can sell it, this makes theft harder, and reduces your insurance premiums. However, it also increases the number of car-jackings: criminals who want a getaway car are more likely to take one at gunpoint.

■ *Early mobile phones were easy for villains to "clone."* Users could suddenly find their bills inflated by hundreds or even thousands of dollars. The current GSM digital mobile phones authenticate themselves to the network by a cryptographic challenge-response protocol similar to the ones used in car-locks and immobilizers.

■ Satellite TV set-top boxes decipher movies as long as you keep paying your subscription; DVD players use copy control mechanisms based on cryptography and copyright marking to make it harder to copy disks (or to play them outside a certain geographic area).

■ In many countries, households that can't get credit can get prepayment meters for electricity and gas, which they top off using a smartcard or other electronic key which they refill at a local store. Many universities use similar technologies to get students pay for photocopier use, washing machines, and even soft drinks.

The chances are that you already use many systems that enforce some protection policy or other using largely electronic mechanisms. Over the next few decades, the number of such systems is going to increase rapidly. Unfortunately, based on past experience, many of them will be badly designed. The necessary skills are just not spread widely enough.

The aim of this book is to enable you to design such systems better. To do this, an engineer or programmer needs to learn about current systems, how they work, and—at least as important—how they have failed in the past. Civil engineers learn far more from the one bridge that falls down than from the hundred that stay up; exactly the same holds in security engineering.

1.5 Definitions

Many of the terms used in security engineering are straightforward, but some are misleading or even controversial. Though there are more detailed definitions of technical terms in the relevant chapters, which you can find using the index, I point out here where the main problems lie.

The first thing we need to clarify is what we mean by *system*. In practice, this can denote:

1. A product or component, such as a cryptographic protocol, a smartcard, or the hardware of a PC.

2. A collection of the above plus an operating system, communications, and other things that make up an organization's infrastructure.

3. The above plus one or more applications (accounts, payroll, design and so on).

4. Any or all of the above plus IT staff.

5. Any or all of the above plus internal users and management.

6. Any or all of the above plus customers and other external users.

7. Any or all of the above plus the surrounding environment including the media, competitors, regulators, and politicians.

Confusion among these definitions is an extremely fertile source of errors and vulnerabilities. Broadly speaking, the vendor and evaluator communities focus on the first (and occasionally) the second of them, while a business will focus on the sixth (and occasionally the fifth). Ignoring the human components, and thus neglecting usability and liability issues, is one of the primary causes of security failure, so we will generally use definition 6 or 7. When we take a more restrictive view, the meaning should be clear from the context.

The next set of problems comes from lack of clarity about who the players are and what they are trying to prove. In the literature on security and cryptology, it's a convention that principals in security protocols are identified by names chosen with (usually) successive initial letters—much like hurricanes—and so we see lots of statements such as, "Alice authenticates herself to Bob." This makes things much more readable, but often at the expense of precision. Do we mean that Alice proves to Bob that her name actually is Alice, or that she proves she's got a particular credential? Do we mean that the authentication is done by Alice the human being, or by a smartcard or software tool acting as Alice's agent? In that case, are we sure it's Alice, and not perhaps Cherie to whom Alice lent her card, or David who stole her card, or Eve who hacked her PC?

By a *subject* I mean a physical person (human, ET, . . .), in any role including that of an operator, principal, or victim. By a *person*, I mean either a physical person or a legal person such as a company or government.

A *principal* is an entity that participates in a security system. This entity can be a subject, a person, a role, or a piece of equipment, such as a PC, smartcard, or card-reader terminal. A principal can also be a communications channel (which might be a port number or a crypto key, depending on the circumstance). A principal can also be a compound of other principals; examples are a group (Alice or Bob), a conjunction (Alice and Bob acting together), a compound role (Alice acting as Bob's manager), and a delegation (Bob acting for Alice in her absence). Beware that groups and roles are not the same. By a *group* I mean a set of principals, while a *role* is a function assumed by different persons in succession (such as "the officer of the watch on the USS Nimitz" or "the president for the time being of the Icelandic Medical Association"). A principal may be considered at more than one level of abstraction; for example, "Bob acting for Alice in her absence" might mean "Bob's smartcard representing Bob who is acting for Alice in her absence" or even "Bob operating Alice's smartcard in her absence." When I have to consider more detail, I'll be more specific.

The meaning of the word *identity* is controversial. When I am being careful, I will use it to mean a correspondence between the names of two principals signifying that they refer to the same person or equipment. For example, it may be important to know that the Bob in "Alice acting as Bob's manager" is the same as the Bob in "Bob acting as Charlie's manager" and in "Bob as branch manager signing a bank draft jointly with David." Often, the term identity is abused to mean simply "name," an abuse entrenched by such phrases as "user identity" and "citizen's identity card." Where there is no possibility of being ambiguous, I'll sometimes lapse into this vernacular usage in order to avoid pomposity.

The definitions of *trust* and *trustworthy* are often confused. The following example illustrates the difference: if an NSA employee is observed in a toilet stall at Baltimore

Washington International Airport selling key material to a Chinese diplomat, then (assuming his operation was not authorized) he can be described as "trusted but not trustworthy." Hereafter, I'll use the NSA definition that a *trusted* system or component is one whose failure can break the security policy, while a *trustworthy* system or component is one that won't fail.

Beware, though, that there are many alternative definitions of trust. A U.K. military view stresses auditability and fail-secure properties: a trusted systems element is one "whose integrity cannot be assured by external observation of its behavior while in operation." Other definitions often have to do with whether a particular system is approved by authority: a trusted system might be "a system that won't get me fired if it gets hacked on my watch" or even "a system that we can insure." I won't use either of these definitions. When I mean a system that isn't failure-evident, or an approved system, or an insured system, I'll say so.

The definition of *confidentiality* versus *privacy* versus *secrecy* opens another can of worms. These terms clearly overlap; but, equally clearly, they are not exactly the same. If my neighbor cuts down some ivy at our common fence with the result that his kids can look into my garden and tease my dogs, it's not my confidentiality that has been invaded. And the duty to keep quiet about the affairs of a former employer is a duty of confidence, not of privacy.

I'll use these words as follows:

- Secrecy is a technical term that refers to the effect of the mechanisms used to limit the number of principals who can access information, such as cryptography or computer access controls.

- Confidentiality involves an obligation to protect some other person's or organization's secrets if you know them.

- Privacy is the ability and/or right to protect your personal secrets; it extends to the ability and/or right to prevent invasions of your personal space (the exact definition varies quite sharply from one country to another). Privacy can extend to families but not to legal persons such as corporations.

Thus, for example, hospital patients have a right to privacy; in order to uphold this right, the doctors, nurses, and other staff have a duty of confidence toward their patients. The hospital has no right of privacy in respect of its business dealings, but those employees who are privy to them may have a duty of confidence. So, in short, privacy is secrecy for the benefit of the individual, while confidentiality is secrecy for the benefit of the organization.

There is a further complexity in that it's often not sufficient to keep the contents of messages secret. For example, many countries have laws making the treatment of sexually transmitted diseases secret, yet a private eye who could find out that you were exchanging encrypted messages with an STD clinic might well draw the conclusion that you were being treated there. So one may also have to protect metadata such as the source or destination of messages. *Anonymity* can be just as important a factor in privacy (or confidentiality) as secrecy. To make things even more complex, some writers refer to what I've called secrecy as *message content confidentiality*, and to what I've called anonymity as *message source (or destination) confidentiality*.

The meanings of *authenticity* and *integrity* can also vary subtly. In the academic literature on security protocols, authenticity means integrity plus freshness: you have established that you are speaking to a genuine principal, not a replay of previous messages. There is a similar idea in banking protocols. In a country whose banking laws state that checks are no longer valid after six months, a seven-month-old uncashed check has integrity (assuming it has not been altered), but is no longer valid. (Bankers would not use the word *authenticity* in this context.) The military usage of authenticity tends to apply to the identity of principals and orders they give, while integrity applies to stored data. Thus, we can talk about the integrity of a database of electronic warfare threats (it has not been corrupted, whether by the other side or by Murphy), but the authenticity of a general's orders (which has an overlap with the academic usage). There are also some strange usages. For example, one can talk about an *authentic copy* of a deceptive order given by the other side's electronic warfare people; here, the authenticity refers to the act of copying and storage. Similarly, a police crime scene officer will talk about preserving the integrity of a cheque that was not authentic but forged, by placing it in an evidence bag.

The last matter I'll clarify here is the terminology that describes what we're trying to achieve. A *vulnerability* is a property of a system or its environment, which, in conjunction with an internal or external *threat*, can lead to a *security failure*, which is a state of affairs contrary to the system's security policy. By *security policy* I mean a succinct statement of a system's protection strategy (for example, "each credit must be matched by an equal and opposite debit, and all transactions over $1,000 must be authorized by two managers"). A *security target* is a more detailed specification, which sets out the means by which a security policy will be implemented in a particular product—encryption and digital signature mechanisms, access controls, audit logs, and so on—and which will be used as the yardstick to evaluate whether the designers and implementers have done a proper job. Between these two levels we may find a *protection profile*, which is like a security target except written in a sufficiently device-independent way to allow comparative evaluations among different products and different versions of the same product. I'll elaborate on security policies, security targets, and protection profiles in Chapter 7 and Chapter 23. In general, the word *protection* will mean a property such as confidentiality or integrity, defined in a sufficiently abstract way for us to reason about it in the context of general systems rather than specific implementations.

Finally, it's worth noting that much of the terminological confusion in security engineering is somewhat political in nature. Security is a terribly overloaded word, and often means quite incompatible things to different people. To a corporation, it might mean the ability to monitor all employees' email and Web browsing activity; to the employees, it might mean being able to use email and the Web without being monitored.

1.6 Summary

I am reminded of a passage from Lewis Carroll:

'When I use a word,' Humpty Dumpty said, in a rather scornful tone, 'it means just what I choose it to mean—neither more nor less.' 'The question is,' said Alice, 'whether you can make words mean so many different things.' 'The question is,' said Humpty Dumpty, 'which is to be master—that's all.'

It is important for the security engineer to develop sensitivity about the different nuances of meaning that common words acquire in different applications, and to be able to formalize what the security policy and target actually are. That may sometimes be inconvenient for clients who wish to get away with something, but, in general, robust security design requires that the protection goals are made explicit.

CHAPTER
2

Protocols

It is impossible to foresee the consequences of being clever.
—CHRISTOPHER STRACHEY

If security engineering has a unifying theme, it is the study of security protocols. Rather than starting off with a formal definition of a security protocol, I will give a rough indication, then refine it using a number of examples. As this is an engineering book, I will also give several examples of how protocols fail.

A typical security system consists of a number of principals such as people, companies, computers, and magnetic card readers, which communicate using a variety of channels including phones, email, radio, infrared, and by carrying data on physical devices such as bank cards and transport tickets. The security protocols are the rules that govern these communications. They are typically designed so that the system will survive malicious acts such as people telling lies on the phone, hostile governments jamming radio, or forgers altering the data on train tickets. Protection against all possible attacks is often too expensive, so protocols are typically designed under certain assumptions about the threats. Evaluating a protocol thus involves answering two questions. First, is the threat model realistic? Second, does the protocol deal with it?

Protocols may be extremely simple, such as swiping a badge through a reader in order to enter a building; or they may be very complex. The world's networks of cash machines have dozens of protocols specifying how a cash machine interacts with customers, how it talks to the bank that operates it, how the bank communicates with the network operator, how money gets settled between banks, how encryption keys are set up between the various principals, and what sort of alarm messages may be transmitted (such as instructions to capture a card). All these protocols have to work together in a large and complex system.

Often, a seemingly innocuous design feature opens up a serious flaw. For example, in the past, a number of banks encrypted the customer's PIN using a key known only to their central computers and cash machines, and wrote it to the card magnetic strip. The idea was to let the cash machine verify PINs locally, which saved on communications and even allowed a limited service to be provided when the cash machine was offline. After this system had been used for many years without incident, a programmer (who was playing around with a card reader used in a building access control system) discovered that he could alter the magnetic strip of his own bank card by substituting his wife's bank account number for his own. He could then take money out of her account using the modified card and his own PIN. He realized that this also enabled him to loot any other customer's account, and he went on to steal hundreds of thousands over a period of years. The affected banks had to spend millions on changing their systems.

So we need to look systematically at security protocols and how they fail. As they are widely deployed and often very badly designed, I'll give a number of examples from different applications.

2.1 Password Eavesdropping Risks

Passwords are still the foundation on which much of computer security rests, as they are the main mechanism used to authenticate human users to computer systems. In the form of PINs, they are also used in many embedded systems, from cash machines through mobile phones to burglar alarms. They raise many problems, such as the difficulty people have in choosing passwords that are difficult to guess, or remembering passwords generated randomly by the system.

We discuss the "human interface" problems of passwords in the next chapter. For now, let us consider the limitations of embedded systems that use passwords. The typical application is the remote control used to open your garage or to unlock the doors of cars manufactured up to the mid-1990s. These primitive remote controls just broadcast their 16-bit serial number, which also acts as the password.

An attack that became common was to use a "grabber," a device that would record a code and replay it later. These devices, seemingly from Taiwan, arrived on the market in about 1995; they enabled thieves lurking in parking lots to record the signal used to lock a car door and then replay it to unlock the car once the owner had left.

One countermeasure was to use separate codes for lock and unlock. But this is still not ideal. First, the thief can lurk outside your house and record the unlock code before you drive away in the morning; he can then come back at night and help himself. Second, 16-bit passwords are too short. In the mid-1990s, devices appeared that could try all possible codes one after the other. A code would be found on average after about 2^{15} tries, which at 10 per second would take less than an hour. A thief operating in a parking lot with a hundred vehicles within range could be rewarded in less than a minute with a car helpfully flashing its lights.

Another countermeasure was to double the length of the password from 16 to 32 bits. The manufacturers proudly advertised "over 4 billion codes." But this only showed they hadn't really understood the problem. There was still only one code (or two codes) for each car, and although guessing was now impractical, grabbers still worked fine.

Using a serial number as a password has a further vulnerability in that there may be many people who have access to it. In the case of a car, this might mean all the dealer staff and, perhaps, the state motor vehicle registration agency. Some burglar alarms have also used serial numbers as master passwords; this is even worse, as the serial number may appear on the order, the delivery note, the invoice, and all the other standard paperwork.

Simple passwords are sometimes the appropriate technology, even when they double as serial numbers. For example, my monthly season ticket for the swimming pool simply has a barcode. I'm sure I could make a passable forgery with our photocopier and laminating machine, but the turnstile is attended and the attendants get to know the "regulars," so there is no need for anything more expensive. My cardkey for getting into the laboratory where I work is slightly harder to forge, as it uses an infrared barcode. Again, this is probably quite adequate—our more expensive equipment is in rooms with additional door locks. We'll discuss passwords in more detail in Chapter 3. But for things that lots of people want to steal, like cars, a better technology is needed. This brings us to cryptographic authentication protocols.

2.2 Who Goes There? Simple Authentication

A simple example of an authentication device is an infrared token used in some multistorey parking garages to enable subscribers to raise the barrier. This first transmits its serial number and then transmits an authentication block that consists of the same serial number, followed by a random number, all encrypted using a key that is unique to the device.

I will postpone discussion of how to encrypt data and what properties the cipher should have; here, I will simply use the notation $\{X\}_{KT}$ for the message X encrypted under the key K. Then the protocol between the access token in the car and the parking garage can be written as:

$$T \longrightarrow G : T, \{T, N\}_{KT}$$

This is the standard protocol engineering notation, and can be a bit confusing at first, so we'll take it slowly.

The in-car token sends its name, T, followed by the encrypted value of T concatenated with N, where N stands for "number used once," or *nonce*. The purpose of nonce is to assure the recipient that the message is *fresh*, that is, it is not a replay of an old message that an attacker observed. Verification is simple: the parking garage server reads T, gets the corresponding key, KT, deciphers the rest of the message, checks that the plaintext contains T, and, finally, that the nonce N has not been seen before.

One reason many people get confused is that to the left of the colon, T identifies one of the principals (the token that represents the subscriber), whereas to the right it means the name (that is, the serial number) of the token. Another cause of confusion is that once we start discussing attacks on protocols, we can suddenly start finding that the token T's message intended for the parking garage G was actually intercepted by the freeloader F and played back at some later time. So the notation is unfortunate, but it's too thoroughly entrenched now to change easily. Professionals often think of the $T \longrightarrow G$ to the left of the colon as simply a hint of what the protocol designer had in mind.

The term *nonce* can mean anything that guarantees the freshness of a message. A nonce may, according to the context, be a random number, a serial number, or a random challenge received from a third party. There are subtle differences between the three approaches, such as in the level of resistance they offer to various kinds of replay attack. (We'll discuss these later.) But in very low-cost systems, the first two predominate, as it tends to be cheaper to have a communication channel in one direction only.

Key management in such devices can be simple. A typical garage token's key KT is simply its serial number encrypted under a global master key, KM, known to the central server:

$$KT = \{T\}_{KM}$$

This is known as *key diversification*. It gives a very simple way of implementing access tokens, and is very widely used in smartcard-based systems as well. But there is still plenty of room for error.

At least two manufacturers have made the mistake of only checking that the nonce is different from last time, so that, given two valid codes A and B, the series $ABABAB \ldots$ was interpreted as a series of independently valid codes. In one car lock, the thief could open the door by replaying the last-but-one code. Another example comes from the world of prepayment utility meters. Over a million households in the United Kingdom, plus many millions in developing countries, have an electricity or gas meter designed so that they can purchase encrypted tokens to take home and insert into the meter, which then dispenses the purchased quantity of electricity or gas. One electricity meter widely used in South Africa checked only that the nonce in the decrypted command was different from last time. So the customer could charge the meter up to the limit by buying two low-value power tickets and then repeatedly feeding them in one after the other [39].

The question of whether to use a random number or a counter is not as easy as it might seem [195]. With random numbers, the lock has to remember a reasonable number of past codes. There's also the *valet attack*; someone who has temporary access to the token—such as a valet parking attendant—can record a number of access codes and replay them later to steal your car.

The problem with counters is maintaining synchronization. A key may be used for more than one lock, and may also be activated by jostling against something in your pocket (I once took an experimental token home where it was gnawed by my dogs). So there has to be a way to recover after the counter has been incremented hundreds or possibly even thousands of times. This can be turned to advantage by allowing the lock to "learn," or synchronize on, a key under certain conditions; but the details are not always designed thoughtfully. One common product uses a 16-bit counter, and allows access when the counter value that is deciphered is the last valid code incremented by no more than 16. To cope with cases where the token has been used more than 16 times elsewhere (or chewed by a family pet), the lock will open on a second press, provided that the counter value has been incremented between 17 and 32,767 times since a valid code was entered (the counter rolls over so that 0 is the successor of 65,535). This opens it to a replay attack, because someone only needs six access codes—say for values 0, 1, 20,000, 20,001, 40,000 and 40,001 to break the system completely.

So designing even a simple token authentication mechanism is not straightforward. There are many attacks that do not involve "breaking" the encryption. Such attacks are likely to become more common as cryptographic authentication mechanisms proliferate.

An example that may become contentious is *accessory control*. It is common for the makers of games consoles to build in challenge-response protocols to prevent software cartridges or other accessories being used with their product unless a license fee is paid. This practice is spreading. According to one vendor of authentication chips, some printer companies have begun to embed authentication in printers to ensure that genuine toner cartridges are used. If a competitor's product is loaded instead, the printer will quietly downgrade from 1200 dpi to 300 dpi. In mobile phones, much of the profit is made on batteries, and authentication protocols can be used to spot competitors' products so they can be drained more quickly. (I wonder how long it will be before the research that toner cartridge and battery manufactures will do to defeat these systems will hit the street in the form of better car theft tools?)

2.2.1 Challenge and Response

The most modern car door locks use a more sophisticated two-pass protocol, often called *challenge-response*. As the car key is inserted into the steering lock, the engine management unit sends a challenge, consisting of a random n-bit number to the key using a short-range radio signal. The car key computes a response by encrypting the challenge. In this way, writing E for the engine controller, T for the transponder in the car key, K for the cryptographic key shared between the transponder and the engine controller, and N for the random challenge, the protocol may look something like:

$$E \longrightarrow T : N$$
$$T \longrightarrow E : \{T, N\}_K$$

This is still not bulletproof. In one system, the random numbers generated by the engine management unit turned out to be rather predictable, so it was possible for a thief to interrogate the key in the car owner's pocket, as he passed, with the anticipated next challenge.

In fact, most of the widely used software products that incorporate encryption—including Kerberos, Netscape, and PGP—have been broken at some time or another because their random-number generators weren't random enough [340, 256]. The fix used varies from one application to another. It's possible to build hardware random-number generators using radioactive decay, but this isn't common because of environmental concerns. There are various sources of randomness that can be used in large systems such as PCs; for example, it's possible to use the small variations in the rotational velocity of the hard disk caused by air turbulence [225]. Practical systems for PCs often mix the randomness available from a number of environmental sources, such as network traffic and keystroke timing, and from internal system sources [363]; the way these sources are combined is often critical [447]. But in a typical embedded system such as a car lock, the random challenge is generated by encrypting a counter using a special key that is kept inside the device, and not used for any other purpose.

Locks are not the only application of challenge-response protocols. Many organizations—including most U.S. banks, many phone companies, and a number of defense agencies—issue their staff password generators that enable them to log on to corporate computer systems [808]. These may look like calculators (and even function as calculators) but their main function is as follows: When you want to log in to a machine on the network, you call up a logon screen and are presented with a random

Figure 2.1   Password generator use.

challenge of maybe seven digits. You key this into your password generator, together with a PIN of maybe four digits. The device encrypts these 11 digits using a secret key shared with the corporate security server, and displays the first seven digits of the result. You enter these seven digits as your password. (See Figure 2.1.) If you have a password generator with the right secret key, and you enter the PIN right, and you type in the result correctly, then the corporate computer system lets you in. But if you do not have a genuine password generator for which you know the PIN, your chance of logging on is small.

Formally, with S for the server, P for the password generator, PIN for the user's personal identification number that bootstraps the password generator, U for the user, and N for the random nonce:

$$S \longrightarrow U : N$$

$$U \longrightarrow P : N, PIN$$

$$P \longrightarrow U : \{N, PIN\}_K$$

$$U \longrightarrow S : \{N, PIN\}_K$$

(For a more detailed description of one of the more popular challenge-response products, see [15, p. 211 ff].)

The encryption in challenge-response protocols does not always need to be invertible, and so in general it can be accomplished using a "one-way function" or "cryptographic hash function," which has the property that it's less subject to export restrictions than are encryption algorithms. (For its technical properties, see Chapter 5, "Cryptology.")

2.2.2 The MIG-in-the-Middle Attack

There is an interesting attack on challenge-response systems that appears to have played a role in bringing peace to Southern Africa.

The ever increasing speeds of warplanes in the 1930s and 1940s, together with the invention of the jet engine, radar and rocketry, made it ever more difficult for air defence forces to tell their own craft apart from the enemy's. This led to a serious risk of "fratricide"—people shooting down their colleagues by mistake—and drove the development of *identify-friend-or-foe* (IFF) systems. These were first fielded in World War II, and in their early form enabled an airplane illuminated by radar to broadcast an identifying number to signal friendly intent. In 1952, this system was adopted to identify civil aircraft to air traffic controllers and, worried about the loss of security once it became widely used, the U.S. Air Force started a research programme to incorporate cryptographic protection in the system. Nowadays, the typical air defense system sends random challenges with its radar signals, and friendly aircraft have equipment and keys that enable them to identify themselves with correct responses.

U.S. aircraft use an IFF system called 'Mode XII,' and systems are under development for ground troops too. But the South African Air Force (SAAF) had been cut off from Western arms supplies by sanctions and had to design its own system.

In the late 1980s, South African troops were fighting a war in northern Namibia and southern Angola. The goals were to keep Namibia under white rule and to impose a client government (UNITA) on Angola. Because the South African Defense Force consisted largely of conscripts from a small, white population, it was essential to limit casualties. So, most South African troops remained in Namibia on policing duties while the fighting to the north was done by UNITA troops. The role of the SAAF was twofold: to provide tactical support to UNITA by bombing targets in Angola, and to ensure that the Angolans and their Cuban allies did not return the compliment in Namibia.

Suddenly, Cuban aircraft broke through the South African air defenses and bombed a South African camp in northern Namibia, killing a number of white conscripts. This proof that its air supremacy had been lost helped the Pretoria government decide to hand over Namibia to the insurgents—itself a huge step on the road to majority rule in South Africa several years later. The raid may have been the last successful military operation ever carried out by Soviet bloc forces.

Some years afterward, a former SAAF officer told me how the Cubans had pulled it off. Several MIGs had loitered in southern Angola, just north of the South African air defense belt, until a flight of SAAF Impala bombers raided a target in Angola. Then the MIGs turned sharply and flew openly through the SAAF's air defenses, which sent IFF challenges. The MIGs relayed them to the Angolan air defense batteries, which transmitted them at a SAAF bomber; the responses were relayed back in real time to the MIGs, which retransmitted them and were allowed through (see Figure 2.2). According to my informant, this had a significant effect on the general staff in Pretoria. Being not only outfought by black opponents, but actually outsmarted, was not consistent with the world view they had held until then.

I have no independent confirmation on this story from the Angolan or Cuban side. But the basic technique is at least as old as World War II, and illustrates the basic idea behind an attack known to the cryptographic community as the *man-in-the-middle* or (more recently) the *middleperson* attack. We will come across it again and again in applications

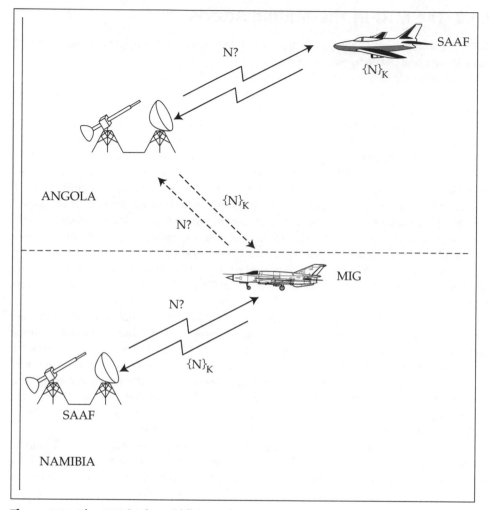

Figure 2.2   The MIG-in-the middle attack.

ranging from pay-TV to Internet security protocols. It even applies in online gaming. As the mathematician John Conway once remarked, it's easy to beat a grandmaster at postal chess: just play two grandmasters at once, one as white and the other as black, and relay the moves between them!

In many cases, middleperson attacks are possible but not economic. In the case of car keys, it should certainly be possible to steal a car by having an accomplice follow the driver, and electronically relay the radio challenge to you as you work the lock. But it would be a lot simpler to just pick the driver's pocket or mug him.

2.2.3 Reflection Attacks

Other interesting problems arise with *mutual authentication*, that is, when two principals have to identify each other. Suppose, that a simple challenge-response IFF system designed to prevent anti-aircraft gunners attacking friendly aircraft also had to be deployed in a fighter-bomber. Now suppose that the air force simply installed one of its air gunners' challenge units in each aircraft and connected it to the fire-control radar. But now an enemy bomber might reflect a challenge back at our fighter, get a correct response, and then reflect that back as its own response:

$$F \longrightarrow B : N$$

$$B \longrightarrow F : N$$

$$F \longrightarrow B : \{N\}_K$$

$$B \longrightarrow F : \{N\}_K$$

So we will want to integrate the challenge system with the response generator. It is still not enough for the two units to be connected and share a list of outstanding challenges, as an enemy attacked by two of our aircraft might reflect a challenge from one of them to be answered by the other. Likewise, it might not be acceptable switch manually from "attack" to "defense" mode, during air combat.

There are a number of ways of stopping this *reflection attack*. In many cases, it is sufficient to include the names of the two parties in the authentication exchange. In the previous example, we might require a friendly bomber to reply to the challenge:

$$F \longrightarrow B : N$$

with a response such as:

$$B \longrightarrow F : \{B, N\}_K$$

Thus, a reflected response $\{F, N\}$ (or even $\{F', N\}$ from the fighter pilot's wingman) could be detected.

This is a much simplified account of IFF but it serves to illustrate the different trust assumptions that underlie an authentication protocol. If you send out a challenge N and receive, within 20 milliseconds, a response $\{N\}_K$, then, because light can travel a bit under 3,730 miles in 20 ms, you know that there is someone with the key K within 2,000 miles. But that's all you know. If you can be sure that the response was not computed using your own equipment, you now know that there is someone *else* with the key K within 2,000 miles. If you make the further assumption that all copies of the key K are securely held in equipment that may be trusted to operate properly, and you see $\{B, N\}_K$, you might be justified in deducing that the aircraft with callsign B is within 2,000 miles. A clear understanding of trust assumptions and their consequences is at the heart of security protocol design.

By now you might think that the protocol design aspects of IFF have been exhaustively discussed. But we've omitted one of the most important problems—and one which the designers of early IFF systems did not anticipate. As radar returns are weak, the signal from the IFF transmitter on board an aircraft will often be audible at a much greater range than the return. The Allies learned this the hard way; in January 1944, decrypts of Enigma messages revealed that the Germans were plotting British and American bombers at twice the normal radar range by interrogating their IFF. So many modern systems authenticate the challenge as well as the response. The NATO mode XII, for example, has a 32 bit encrypted challenge, and a different valid challenge is generated for every interrogation signal, of which there are typically 250 per second. Theoretically there is no need to switch off over enemy territory, but in practice an enemy who can record valid challenges can replay them as part of an attack.

There are many other aspects of IFF which are less protocol related, such as the difficulties posed by neutrals, error rates in dense operational environments, how to deal with equipment failure, how to manage keys, and how to cope with multinational coalitions such as that put together for Operation Desert Storm. We'll return to IFF in Chapter 16. For now, the spurious challenge problem serves to reinforce an important point: that the correctness of a security protocol depends on the assumptions made about the requirements. A protocol that can protect against one kind of attack (being shot down by your own side) but which increases the exposure to an even more likely attack (being shot down by the other side) does more harm than good. In fact, the spurious challenge problem became so serious in World War II that some experts advocated abandoning IFF altogether, rather than taking the risk that one bomber pilot in a formation of hundreds would ignore orders and leave his IFF switched on.

2.3 Manipulating the Message

One kind of middleperson attack is often treated as a separate category of attack. This is where the attacker does not just reflect identification information, but manipulates the message content in some way. We saw an example at the beginning of this chapter: ATM cards designed for offline operation could be manipulated in order to steal money. In effect, the magnetic card acted as a store-and-forward communication channel between the bank's mainframe computer and its cash machines whenever the phone lines (or the mainframe) were down.

Another example is when dishonest cabbies insert pulse generators in the cable that connects their taximeter to a sensor in their taxi's gearbox. The sensor sends pulses as the prop shaft turns, which let the meter work out how far the taxi has gone. A pirate device, which inserts extra pulses, makes the taxi appear to have gone further. We'll discuss such attacks at much greater length in Chapter 10, "Monitoring Systems." Section 10.4.

However, many application-level message manipulation attacks are really just variants on the replay attack, which we saw previously. They aren't limited to low-grade systems, such as remote door locks that can be defeated by recording and replaying a fixed password. The Intelsat satellites used for international telephone and data traffic have robust mechanisms to prevent a command being accepted twice—otherwise, an attacker could repeatedly order the same maneuver to be carried out until the satellite ran out of fuel [617].

Another example is a key log attack, which defeats many pay-TV systems (it's also known as *delayed data transfer*, or DDT). Typical pay-TV equipment has a decoder which deciphers the video signal and a customer smartcard which generates the deciphering keys. These keys are recomputed several times a second using a one-way encryption function applied to various "entitlement control messages" that appear in the signal. Such systems can be very elaborate (and we'll discuss some more complex attacks on them later), but there is a very simple attack that works against a lot of them. If the messages that pass between the smartcard and the decoder are the same for all decoders (which is usually the case), then subscribers can record logs of all the keys sent by their cards to their decoders, and post them to the Net. Someone without a subscription, but who has video-recorded the enciphered program, can then download the key log and use it to decipher the tape.

Changing pay-TV protocols to prevent DDT attacks can be difficult. The base of installed equipment is huge, and many of the obvious countermeasures have an adverse effect on legitimate customers (such as by preventing them from videotaping movies). Pay-TV companies generally ignore this attack, since connecting a PC to a satellite TV decoder through a special hardware adaptor is something only hobbyists do; it is too inconvenient to be a real threat to their revenue stream.

2.4 Changing the Environment

A very common cause of protocol failure is that the environment changes, so that assumptions that were originally true no longer hold, and the security protocols cannot cope with the new threats.

One nice example comes from the ticketing systems used by London Transport. In the early 1980s, passengers devised a number of scams to cut the cost of commuting. For example, a passenger who commuted a long distance from a suburban station to downtown might buy two cheaper, short-distance season tickets—one between their suburban station and a nearby one, and the other between their destination and another downtown station. These would let them get through the barriers; on the rare occasions they were challenged by an inspector in between, they would claim that they'd boarded at a rural station that had a broken ticket machine.

A large investment later, the system had all the features necessary to stop such scams: all barriers were automatic, tickets could retain state, and the laws had been changed so that people caught without tickets got fined on the spot.

But then the whole environment changed, as parts of the system were privatized to create dozens of rail and bus companies. Some of the new operating companies started cheating each other, and there was nothing the system could do about it! For example, when a one-day travel pass was sold, the revenue was distributed between the various bus, train, and subway operators using a formula that depended on where it was sold. Suddenly, the train companies had a motive to book all their ticket sales through the outlet that let them keep the largest percentage. Chaos and litigation ensued.

The transport system's problem was not new; it had been observed in the Italian ski resort of Val di Fassa in the mid-1970s. There, one could buy a monthly pass for all the ski lifts in the valley. An attendant at one of the lifts was observed with a deck of cards, one of which he swiped through the reader between each of the guests. It turned out that the revenue was divided up between the various lift operators according to the number of people who had passed their turnstiles. So each operator sought to inflate its own figures as much as it could [730].

Another relevant example comes from the world of cash machine fraud. In 1993 and 1994, Holland suffered an epidemic of phantom withdrawals; there was much controversy in the press, with the banks claiming that their systems were secure, while many people wrote to the papers claiming to have been cheated. Eventually, the banks were shamed into actively investigating the claims, and noticed that many of the victims had used their bank cards at a certain filling station near Utrecht. This was staked out and one of the staff was arrested. It turned out that he had tapped the line from the card reader to the PC that controlled it; his tap recorded the magnetic stripe details from their cards while he used his eyeballs to capture their PINs [19].

Why had the system been designed so badly? Well, when the standards for managing magnetic stripe cards and PINs were developed in the early 1980s, by organizations such as IBM and VISA, the engineers had made two assumptions. The first was that the contents of the magnetic strip—the card number, version number, and expiration date—was not secret, while the PIN was [548]. (The analogy used was that the magnetic strip was the holder's name and the PIN their password. We will have more to say on the subtleties of naming later.) The second assumption was that bank card equipment would only be operated in trustworthy environments, such as in a physically robust automatic teller machine, or by a bank clerk at a teller station. So it was "clearly" only necessary to encrypt the PIN on its way from the PIN pad to the server; the magnetic strip data could be sent in clear from the card reader.

Both of these assumptions had changed by 1993. An epidemic of card forgery, mostly in the Far East in the late 1980s, drove banks to introduce authentication codes on the magnetic strips. Also, the commercial success of the bank card industry led banks in many countries to extend the use of debit cards from ATMs to terminals in all manner of shops. The combination of these two environmental changes undermined the original system design: instead of putting a card whose magnetic strip contained no security data into a trusted machine, people were putting a card that did rely on security data in the strip into an untrusted machine. These changes had come about so gradually, and over such a long period, that the industry didn't see the problem coming.

2.5 Chosen Protocol Attacks

Some people are trying to sell the idea of a "multifunction smartcard," an authentication device that could be used in a wide range of transactions to save users having to carry around dozens of different cards and keys.

This introduces some interesting new risks. Suppose that you use your card to sign bank transactions; a common way of doing this would be to have the card compute a digital signature on the transaction data. In fact, to save on computation, the signature is usually computed on a random-looking 20-byte digest of the transaction. (We'll discuss in Chapter 5 how to compute such digests.) Now suppose that this card can be used by any other application that anyone cares to design. How might the Mafia design a protocol to attack it?

Here's one example. At present people visiting a Web porn site are often asked for "proof of age," which usually involves giving a credit card number, whether to the site itself or to an age-checking service. If credit cards become able to do digital signatures, it would be natural for the porn site to ask the customer to sign a random challenge as proof of age. A porn site could then mount a *Mafia-in-the-middle* attack, as shown in Figure 2.3. The perpetrators wait until an unsuspecting customer visits their site, then order something resellable (such as gold coins) from a dealer, playing the role of the coin

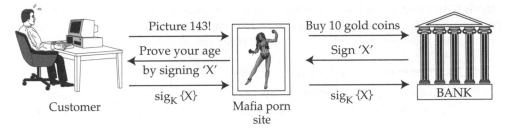

Figure 2.3 The Mafia-in-the-middle attack.

dealer's customer. When the coin dealer sends them the transaction digest for signature, they relay it through their porn site to the waiting customer in the form of a random challenge. The customer signs it, the Mafia gets the gold coins, and when thousands of people suddenly complain about the huge charges to their cards at the end of the month, the porn site has vanished—along with the gold [446].

This is a more extreme variant on the Utrecht scam. There are several lessons: using crypto keys (or other authentication mechanisms) in more than one application can be dangerous; and letting other people bootstrap their own application security off yours can be downright foolish.

2.6 Managing Encryption Keys

The examples of security protocols that we have discussed so far are mostly about authenticating a principal's name, or application data such as the impulses driving a taximeter. There is one further class of authentication protocols that is very important: the protocols used to manage cryptographic keys. Until recently, such protocols were largely used in the background to support other operations; much of the technology was developed to manage the keys used by cash machines and banks to communicate with each other. But now, systems such as pay-TV use key management to control access to the system directly.

Authentication protocols are now also used in distributed computer systems for general key management purposes, and, therefore are going to be very important. Kerberos was the first such system to come into widespread use, and a variant of it is used in Windows 2000. I'll now lay the foundations for an understanding of Kerberos.

2.6.1 Basic Key Management

The basic idea behind key distribution protocols is that where two principals want to communicate, they may use a trusted third party to effect an introduction.

I remarked that in the literature on authentication protocols, it is conventional to give the principals human names to avoid getting lost in too much algebraic notation. So I will call the two communicating principals Alice and Bob, and the trusted third party Sam. But please don't assume that we are talking about human principals. Alice and Bob are likely to be programs, while Sam is a server; Alice might be a program in a taximeter, Bob the program in a gearbox sensor, and Sam the computer at the taxi inspection station. Anyway, a simple authentication protocol could run as follows:

1. Alice first calls Sam and asks for a key for communicating with Bob.

2. Sam responds by sending Alice a pair of certificates. Each contains a copy of a key, the first encrypted so only Alice can read it, and the second encrypted so only Bob can read it.

3. Alice then calls Bob and presents the second certificate as her introduction. Each of them decrypts the appropriate certificate under the key they share with Sam, and thereby gets access to the new key. Alice can now use the key to send encrypted messages to Bob, and to receive messages from him in return.

I mentioned that replay attacks are a known problem with authentication protocols, so in order that both Bob and Alice can check that the certificates are fresh, Sam may include a timestamp in each of them. If certificates never expire, there could well be serious problems dealing with users whose privileges have been revoked.

Using our protocol notation, we could describe this as:

$$A \rightarrow S : A, B$$

$$S \rightarrow A : \{A, B, K_{AB}, T\}_{K_{AS}}, \{A, B, K_{AB}, T\}_{K_{BS}}$$

$$A \rightarrow B : \{A, B, K_{AB}, T\}_{K_{BS}}, \{M\}_{K_{AB}}$$

Expanding the notation, Alice calls Sam and says she'd like to talk to Bob. Sam makes up a session key message consisting of Alice's name, Bob's name, a key for them to use, and a timestamp. Sam encrypts this under the key he shares with Alice, and with the key he shares with Bob. He gives both ciphertexts to Alice. Alice retrieves the key from the ciphertext that was encrypted to her, and passes on to Bob the ciphertext encrypted for him. She now sends him whatever message she wanted to send, encrypted using this key.

2.6.2 The Needham-Schroeder Protocol

Many things can go wrong. We will see plenty of examples later; for now, a famous historical example will suffice. Many existing key distribution protocols are derived from a protocol invented by Roger Needham and Mike Schroeder in 1978 [589]. It is somewhat similar to the one we've just discussed, but uses nonces rather than timestamps. It runs as follows:

$$\text{Message 1} \quad A \rightarrow S : A, B, N_A$$

$$\text{Message 2} \quad S \rightarrow A : \{N_A, B, K_{AB}, \{K_{AB}, A\}_{K_{BS}}\}_{K_{AS}}$$

$$\text{Message 3} \quad A \rightarrow B : \{K_{AB}, A\}_{K_{BS}}$$

$$\text{Message 4} \quad B \rightarrow A : \{N_B\}_{K_{AB}}$$

$$\text{Message 5} \quad A \rightarrow B : \{N_B - 1\}_{K_{AB}}$$

Here, Alice takes the initiative, and tells Sam: "I'm Alice; I want to talk to Bob, and my random nonce is N_A." Sam provides her with a session key, encrypted using the key she shares with him. This ciphertext also contains her nonce so she can confirm it's not a replay. He also gives her a certificate to convey this key to Bob. She passes the certificate to Bob, who then does a challenge-response to check that she is present and alert.

There is a subtle problem with this protocol: Bob has to assume that the key K_{AB} he receives from Sam (via Alice) is fresh. This is not necessarily so: Alice could have waited a year between steps 2 and 3. In many applications this may not be important; it might even help Alice to cache keys against possible server failures. But if an opponent—say Charlie—ever got hold of Alice's key K_{AS} he could use it to set up session keys with many other principals.

Suppose, for example, that Alice had also asked for and received a key to communicate with Dorothy, and after Charlie stole her key he sent messages to Sam pretending to be Alice, and got keys for Freddie and Ginger. He might also have observed message 2 in her protocol exchanges with Dorothy, that is, when Sam sent her a key for communicating with Dorothy, encrypted under the key K_{AS} which is now compromised. So now Charlie could impersonate Alice to Dorothy, and also to Freddie and Ginger. So when Alice finds out that her key has been stolen, perhaps by comparing message logs with Dorothy, she'd have to get Sam contact everyone for whom she'd ever been issued a key, and tell them that her old key was no longer valid. She could not do this herself as she doesn't know anything about Freddie and Ginger. In other words, revocation is a problem: Sam will probably have to keep complete logs of everything he has ever done, and these logs would grow in size forever unless the principals' names expired at some fixed time in the future.

Over 20 years later, this example still generates controversy in the security protocols community. The simplistic view is that Needham and Schroeder just got it wrong; the view argued by Susan Pancho and Dieter Gollmann (for which I have much sympathy) is that this is one more example of a protocol failure brought on by shifting assumptions [345, 600]. 1978 was a kinder, gentler world; computer security then concerned itself with keeping the bad guys out, while nowadays we expect the bad guys to be users of the system. The Needham-Schroeder paper explicitly assumes that all principals behave themselves, and that attacks come only from outsiders [589]. Under these assumptions, the protocol remains sound.

2.6.3 Kerberos

An important practical derivative of the Needham-Schroeder protocol may be found in Kerberos, a distributed access control system that originated at MIT and is now the default authentication option in Windows 2000 [735]. Instead of a single trusted third party, Kerberos has two kinds: an authentication server to which users log on, and a ticket-granting server that gives them tickets allowing access to various resources such as files. This enables more scalable access management. In a university, for example, one might manage students through their halls of residence, but manage file servers by departments; in a company, the personnel people might register users to the payroll system, while departmental administrators manage resources such as servers and printers.

First, Alice logs on to the authentication server using a password. The client software in her PC fetches a ticket from this server, which is encrypted under her password and which contains a session key K_{AS}. Assuming she gets the password right, she now controls K_{AS}; to get access to a resource B, controlled by the ticket-granting server S, the following protocol takes place. Its outcome is a key, K_{AB}, with timestamp T_S and lifetime L, which will be used to authenticate Alice's subsequent traffic with that resource:

$$A \rightarrow S: \ A, B$$

$$S \rightarrow A: \ \{T_S, L, K_{AB}, B, \{T_S, L, K_{AB}, A\}_{K_{BS}}\}_{K_{AS}}$$

$$A \rightarrow B: \ \{T_S, L, K_{AB}, A\}_{K_{BS}}, \{A, T_A\}_{K_{AB}}$$

$$B \rightarrow A: \ \{T_A + 1\}_{K_{AB}}$$

Translating this into English: Alice asks the ticket-granting server for access to B. If this is permissible, the ticket $\{T_S, L, K_{AB}, A\}_{K_{BS}}$ is created containing a suitable key K_{AB} and given to Alice to use. She also gets a copy of the key in a form readable by her, namely encrypted under K_{AS}. She now verifies the ticket by sending a timestamp, T_A, to the resource, which confirms its aliveness by sending back the timestamp incremented by one (this is a convention to indicate that the resource was able to decrypt the ticket correctly and extract the key K_{AB}).

The vulnerability of Needham-Schroeder has been fixed by introducing timestamps rather than random nonces. But, as in most of life, we get little in security for free. There is now a new vulnerability, namely that the clocks on our various clients and servers might get out of synch; they might even be desynchronized deliberately as part of a more complex attack.

2.7 Getting Formal

Subtle difficulties of the kind we have seen with the protocols just discussed, and the many ways in which protection properties depend on quite narrow (and often unobvious) starting assumptions, have led researchers to apply formal methods to key distribution protocols. The goal of this exercise was originally to decide whether a protocol was right or wrong. Either it should be proved correct or an attack should be exhibited. More recently, this has expanded to clarifying the assumptions that underlie a given protocol.

There are a number of different approaches to verifying the correctness of protocols. The best known is a logic of belief, the *BAN logic*, named after its inventors Mike Burrows, Martín Abadi, and Roger Needham [148]. It reasons about what is reasonable for a principal to believe, given sight of certain messages, timestamps, and so on. A second is the *random oracle model*, which I touch on in Chapter 5, and which is favored by many mathematicians working at the theoretical end of the subject; this appears to be less expressive than logics of belief, but can tie protocol properties down to the properties of the underlying encryption algorithms. Finally, a number of researchers have applied mainstream formal methods such as CSP and Lotos.

Some history exists of flaws being found in protocols that had been proved correct using formal methods; the following subsection offers a typical example.

2.7.1 A Typical Smartcard Banking Protocol

This system, currently called COPAC, is an electronic purse system used by VISA in countries with poor telecommunications [35]. It was the first live financial system whose underlying protocol suite was designed and verified using such formal techniques, and in particular a variant of the BAN logic. A very similar protocol is now also used in the "goldbank," an electronic purse issued by banks in Germany to their clients.

Transactions take place from a customer smartcard to a merchant smartcard. The customer gives the merchant an electronic check with two authentication codes on it, one that can be checked by the network and one that can be checked by the customer's bank. A simplified version of the protocol is as follows:

$$C \longrightarrow R : \{C, N_C\}_K$$
$$R \longrightarrow C : \{R, N_R, C, N_C\}_K$$
$$C \longrightarrow R : \{C, N_C, R, N_R, X\}_K$$

In English: the customer and the retailer share a key, K. Using this key, the customer card encrypts a message containing its account number, C, and a customer transaction serial number, N_C. The retailer confirms its name, R, and its transaction serial number, N_R, as well as the information it has just received from the customer. The customer now sends the electronic check, X, along with all the data exchanged so far in the protocol. One can think of the electronic check as being stapled to a payment advice with the customer's and retailer's names, and their respective reference numbers. (The reason for repeating all previous data in each message is to prevent message manipulation attacks using cut-and-paste.)

2.7.2 The BAN Logic

The BAN logic provides a formal method for reasoning about the beliefs of principals in cryptographic protocols. Its underlying idea is that we will believe that a message is authentic if it is encrypted with a relevant key and it is also fresh (that is, generated during the current run of the protocol). Further assumptions include that principals will only assert statements they believe in, and that some principals are authorities for certain kinds of statement. This is formalized using a notation that includes:

- $A \mid\equiv X$: A *believes* X, or, more accurately, that A is entitled to believe X.
- $A \mid\sim X$: A *once said* X (without implying that this utterance was recent or not).
- $A \mid\Rightarrow X$: A *has jurisdiction over* X; in other words, A is the authority on X, and is to be trusted on it.
- $A \triangleleft X$: A *sees* X; that is, someone sent a message to A containing X in such a way that A can read and repeat it.

- $\sharp X$: X *is fresh;* that is, X contains a current timestamp or some information showing that it was uttered by the relevant principal during the current run of the protocol.

- $\{X\}_K$: X *encrypted under the key* K, as in the rest of this chapter.

- $A \leftrightarrow^K B$: *A and B share the key* K; in other words, it is an appropriate key for them to use to communicate.

Other symbols deal, for example, with public key operations and with passwords, but they do not concern us here.

These symbols are manipulated using a set of postulates, which include:

The message-meaning rule. States that if A sees a message encrypted under K, and K is a good key for communicating with B, then A will believe that the message was once said by B. (We assume that each principal can recognize and ignore his or her own messages.) Formally:

$$\frac{A \mid\equiv A \leftrightarrow^K B,\, A \triangleleft \{X\}_K}{A \mid\equiv B \mid\sim X}$$

The nonce-verification rule. States that if a principal once said a message, and the message is fresh, then that principal still believes it. Formally:

$$\frac{A \mid\equiv \sharp X,\, A \mid\equiv B \mid\sim X}{A \mid\equiv B \mid\equiv X}$$

The jurisdiction rule. States that if a principal believes something, and is an authority on the matter, then he or she should be believed. Formally, we write that:

$$\frac{A \mid\equiv B \mid\Rightarrow X,\, A \mid\equiv B \mid\equiv X}{A \mid\equiv X}$$

In this notation, the statements on the top are the conditions; the one on the bottom is the result. A number of further rules cover the more mechanical aspects of manipulation; for example, a principal who sees a statement sees its components provided he or she knows the necessary keys; and if part of a formula is known to be fresh, then the whole formula must be.

2.7.3 Verifying the Payment Protocol

Assuming that the key, K, is available only to principals who can be trusted to execute the protocol faithfully, formal verification is now straightforward. The trick is to start from the desired result and work backward. In this case, we wish to prove that the retailer should trust the check; that is, $R \mid\equiv X$ (the syntax of checks and cryptographic keys is similar for our purposes here; a check is good if and only if it is genuine and fresh).

Now $R \mid\equiv X$ will follow under the jurisdiction rule from $R \mid\equiv C \mid\Rightarrow X$ (R believes C has jurisdiction over X) and $R \mid\equiv C \mid\equiv X$ (R believes C believes X).

The former condition follows from the hardware constraint, that no one except C could have uttered a text of the form $\{C, ...\}_K$.

The latter, that $R \mid\equiv C \mid\equiv X$, must be deduced using the nonce verification rule from $\sharp X$ (X is fresh) and $R \mid\equiv C \mid\sim X$ (R believes C uttered X).

$\sharp X$ follows from its occurrence in $\{C, N_C, R, N_R, X\}_K$ which contains the sequence number N_R, while $R \mid\equiv C \mid\sim X$ follows from the hardware constraint.

This summary of the proof is, of necessity, telegraphic. If you want to understand logics of authentication in detail, you should consult the original papers, and refer to the recommendations for further reading at the end of this chapter.

2.7.4 Limitations of Formal Verification

Formal methods can be an excellent way of finding bugs in security protocol designs, as they force the designer to make everything explicit and thus confront difficult design choices that might otherwise be fudged. However, they have their limitations, too.

One problem is in the external assumptions we make. For example, we assumed that the key wasn't available to anyone who might use it in an unauthorized manner. In practice, this is not always true. Although the COPAC purse protocol is executed in tamper-resistant smartcards, their software can have bugs; and in any case the tamper-resistance they offer is never complete. (I explain this in Chapter 14, "Physical Tamper Resistance.") So the system has various fallback mechanisms for detecting and reacting to card forgery, such as "shadow accounts," which track the amount of money that should be on each card and which are updated as transactions are cleared. It also has lists of hot cards that are distributed to terminals; these are needed anyway for stolen cards, and can be used for forged cards too.

Second, there are often problems with the idealization of the protocol. A well-known example comes from the application of the BAN logic to protocols using public key cryptographing; a version of the message meaning rule which only applies to digital signature was erroneously thought to apply to decryption as well, leading to a positive verification of a flawed protocol. Another example is given by a flaw found in an early version of the COPAC system. There the key, K, actually consisted of two keys; the encryption was done first with a "transaction key," which was diversified (that is, each card had its own variant), then again with a "bank key," which was not diversified. The former was done by the network operator and the latter by the bank that issued the card. The reasons for this included dual control and to ensure that an attacker who managed to drill the keys out of a single card would only be able to forge that card, not make forgeries that would pass as other cards (and thus defeat the hot card mechanism). But since the bank key was not diversified, it would be known to any attacker who has broken a card. This means that the attacker could undo the outer wrapping of encryption; and in some circumstances, message replay was possible. (The bank key was diversified in later versions before any villains discovered and exploited the flaw.)

In this case there was no failure of the formal method, as no attempt was ever made to verify the diversification mechanism. But it does illustrate a common problem in security engineering, that vulnerabilities arise at the boundary between two protection technologies. In this case, there were three technologies: the hardware tamper resistance, the authentication protocol, and the shadow account/hot card list mechanisms. Different protection technologies are often the domain of different experts who don't completely understand the assumptions made by the others. (That's one reason security engineers need a book such as this one: to help subject specialists understand each others' tools and to communicate with each other more effectively.)

For these reasons, people have explored alternative ways of assuring the design of authentication protocols, including the idea of *protocol robustness*. Just as structured programming techniques aim to ensure that software is designed methodically and that nothing of importance is left out, so robust protocol design is largely about explicitness. Robustness principles include that the interpretation of a protocol should depend only on its content, not its context; thus, everything of importance (such as principals' names) should be stated explicitly in the messages. There are other issues concerning the freshness provided by serial numbers, timestamps, and random challenges, and on the way encryption is used. If the protocol uses public key cryptography or digital signature mechanisms, there are further more technical robustness issues.

2.8 Summary

Passwords are not always an adequate means of protection, especially if they have to be used more than once over an open communications channel. Simple authentication protocols, whether one-pass (e.g., using random nonces) or two-pass (challenge-response) are appropriate in many cases, and are fielded in all sorts of systems from remote car-door locks through military IFF systems to authentication in distributed computer systems.

It is difficult to design effective security protocols. They suffer from a number of potential problems, including middleperson attacks, modification attacks, reflection attacks, and replay attacks. These threats can interact with implementation vulnerabilities such as poor random number generators. Using mathematical techniques to verify the correctness of protocols can help, but it won't catch all the bugs. Some of the most pernicious failures are caused by creeping changes in the environment for which a protocol was designed, so that the protection it gives is no longer adequate.

Research Problems

During the past few years, some people have thought that protocols had been "done," and that we should turn to new research topics. These people have been repeatedly proved wrong by the emergence of new protocol applications, with a new crop of errors and attacks to be explored. Key management protocols were a focus of research in the early 1990s; during the mid-1990s, the flood of proposals for electronic commerce mechanisms kept us busy; and in the later 1990s, a whole series of mechanisms proposed for protecting copyright on the Internet provided us with targets.

Will we continue to develop faulty protocols that other people attack, or will we manage to develop a methodology for designing them right first time? What are the exact uses and limitations of formal methods (and other mathematical approaches, such as the random oracle model)?

At the system level, how do we manage the tension between the principle that robust protocols are generally those in which everything is completely specified and checked (principals' names, roles, security policy statement, protocol version, time, date, sequence number, security context, maker of grandmother's kitchen sink) and the system engineering principle that a good specification should not overconstrain the implementer?

Further Reading

Research papers on security protocols are scattered fairly widely throughout the literature. The main introductory papers to read are probably the original Needham-Schroeder paper [589]; the Burrows-Abadi-Needham authentication logic [148]; papers by Martín Abadi and Roger Needham, and by Roger Needham and myself on protocol robustness [2, 47]. There is also a survey paper which Roger and I wrote, and which introduced the phrase 'programming Satan's computer' (discussed by Bruce Schneier in the foreword) as a metaphor for security protocol design [48]. In [449] there is an analysis of a defective security protocol, carried out using three different formal methods. Beyond that, the proceedings of the security protocols workshops [183, 184] provide leads to current research; and many papers appear in a wide range of conferences.

CHAPTER

3

Passwords

Humans are incapable of securely storing high-quality cryptographic keys, and they have unacceptable speed and accuracy when performing cryptographic operations. (They are also large, expensive to maintain, difficult to manage, and they pollute the environment. It is astonishing that these devices continue to be manufactured and deployed. But they are sufficiently pervasive that we must design our protocols around their limitations.)

—KAUFMAN, PERLMAN, AND SPECINER [444]

Taking care of old-fashioned access control tokens such as metal keys is a matter of common sense. But common sense is not always adequate for the measures used to protect computer systems. The human-machine gap causes security problems in a number of contexts, from straightforward system administration to the ways in which users mismanage security products such as encryption software [803]. (I won't use the fashionable euphemism "human computer interface": "chasm" might be better.) However, most of the problems arise in a simple context in which they are relatively easy to analyze and discuss—the management of passwords.

In addition to things that are "obviously" passwords, such as the password you use to log on to your computer and the PIN that activates your bank card, there are many other things (and combinations of things) that have an equivalent effect. The most notorious are the likes of Social Security numbers and your mother's maiden name, which many organizations use to recognize you. For example, AT&T's wireless service contract states that anyone who knows your name, address, phone number and the last four digits of your social security number is authorized to make changes to your account; it also disclaims all liability for lack of privacy [201].

The ease with which such data can be guessed or found out from more or less public sources has given rise to a huge *identity theft* industry [285]. Criminals obtain credit cards, mobile phones, and other assets in your name, loot them, and leave you to sort out the mess. In the United States, about half a million people are the victims of this kind of fraud each year.

Passwords are one of the biggest practical problems facing security engineers today. They are the (often shaky) foundation on which much of information security is built. Remembering a password is contingent on frequent use (so that passwords are imprinted well on memory) and consistent context (so that different passwords do not interfere with each other in memory). Neither of these conditions is met when people are asked to choose passwords for a large number of Web sites that they visit rarely. So as they become principals in more and more electronic systems, the same passwords get used over and over again. Not only may attacks be carried out by outsiders guessing passwords, but by insiders in other systems.

3.1 Basics

In a typical system, human users must authenticate themselves to a client (which may be a PC, a mobile phone, an ATM, or whatever), and the client in turn authenticates itself to one or more servers or services (such as an electronic banking system or a phone company). As explained in Chapter 2, "Protocols," authenticating electronic devices to each other is a more or less manageable problem (at least in theory). Authenticating people to devices is more difficult.

There are basically three ways to do it. The first is that the person retains physical control of the device—as with a remote car-door key, a PDA, or even a laptop computer. The second is that he or she presents something he or she knows, such as a password. The third is to use a biometric, such as a fingerprint or iris pattern. (These options are commonly summed up as "something you have, something you know, or something you are.") For reasons of cost, most systems take the second option. Even where we use a physical token such as a hand-held password generator, it is common to use a password as well to lock it.

So passwords matter, and managing them is a serious real-world problem. We'll look at the human issues first, then at the different kinds of attack model, and finally at technical attacks and defenses. All of these issues are important, so tackling only one of them is likely to lead to a bad design.

3.2 Applied Psychology Issues

There are basically three types of concern:

- Will the user break the system security by disclosing the password to a third party, whether accidentally, on purpose, or as a result of deception?
- Will the user enter the password correctly with a high enough probability?
- Will users remember the password, or will they have to either write it down or choose one that's easy for the attacker to guess?

3.2.1 Social Engineering

One of the most severe practical threats to the confidentiality of information is that the attacker will extract it directly, from people who are authorized to access it, by telling some plausible untruth. This attack, known as *social engineering*, will be discussed at greater length in Chapter 8, which deals with medical systems, as it is the main current threat to medical privacy. The typical perpetrator is an insurance investigator who phones a hospital or doctor's office pretending to be a doctor involved in the emergency care of the target of investigation. This technique, also known as 'blagging' in Britain and 'pretexting' in America, is widely used to extract information from banks, insurance companies, and other firms that hold personal information; some people earn a living at it [261].

Passwords are often extracted by false pretext phone calls. A harrassed system administrator is called once or twice on trivial matters by someone who claims to be a very senior manager's personal assistant; once he has accepted the caller's story, she calls and urgently demands a high-level password on some plausible pretext. Unless an organization has well-thought-out policies, attacks of this kind are very likely to work. In a systematic experimental study, for example, 336 computer science students at the University of Sydney were sent an email message asking them to supply their password on the pretext that it was required to "validate" the password database after a suspected break-in. 138 of them returned a valid password. Some were suspicious: 30 returned a plausible-looking but invalid password, while over 200 changed their passwords without official prompting. But very few of them reported the email to authority [354].

One company controls this vulnerability with a policy that states: "The root password for each machine shall be too long to remember, at least 16 alpha and numeric characters chosen at random by the system; it shall be written on a piece of paper and kept in an envelope in the room where the machine is located; it may never be divulged over the telephone or used over the network; it may only be entered at the console of the machine that it controls." If a rule like this is rigidly enforced throughout an organization, a pretext attack on a root password becomes conspicuous, and is much less likely to succeed.

Another approach, used at the NSA, is to have different-colored internal and external telephones that are not connected to each other, and rules that when the external phone in a room is off-hook, classified material can't even be discussed in the room, let alone on the phone. A somewhat less extreme approach (used at our laboratory) is to have different ring tones for internal and external calls. This works as long as you have alert system administrators. Physical authentication devices, like the password generator discussed in Chapter 2, are even better but are often too expensive, incompatible with legacy systems, or contrary to some policy (whether reasonable or not).

3.2.2 Difficulties with Reliable Password Entry

The second human issue is that if a password is too long or complex, the user might have difficulty entering it correctly. A long random password may confuse the person entering it, and if the operation they are trying to perform is urgent, this might have safety or other implications.

One application in which this is important is encrypted access codes. By quoting a reservation number, we get access to a hotel room or rental car. Airline ticketing is going this way, with many operators giving passengers a number to quote at the departure gate rather than a boarding card. As the numbers get longer, what happens to the error rate?

An interesting study was done in South Africa, in the context of the prepaid electricity meters used to sell electricity in areas where the customers have no credit rating and often not even an address. With one make of meter, the customer hands some money to a sales agent, and in return gets one or more 20-digit numbers printed out on a receipt. He takes this receipt home and enters the numbers at a keypad in his meter. These numbers are encrypted commands, whether to dispense electricity, to change the tariff or whatever; the meter decrypts them and acts on them.

When this meter was introduced, there was concern that since about a third of the population was illiterate, and people might get lost halfway through entering the number, this meter might be unusable in practice. But it turned out that illiteracy was not a problem; even people who could not read had no difficulty with numbers ("Everybody can use a phone," as one of the engineers said). Entry errors were a greater problem, but were solved by printing the 20 digits in two rows, containing, respectively, three and two groups of four digits [39].

A quite different application is the firing codes for U.S. nuclear weapons. These consist of only 12 decimal digits. If they are ever used, it is likely that the operators will be under the most extreme stress, and possibly using improvised or obsolete communications channels. Experiments suggested that 12 digits was the maximum that could be conveyed reliably in such circumstances.

3.2.3 Difficulties with Remembering the Password

The greatest source of complaints about passwords is the fact that most people find them hard to remember [146, 823]. Twelve to twenty digits may be fine when they can be simply copied from a telegram or a meter ticket, but when customers are expected to memorize passwords, they either choose values that are easy for attackers to guess, or write them down, or both.

The problems are not limited to computer access. For example, one chain of hotels in France introduced completely unattended service. You would turn up at the hotel, swipe your credit card in the reception machine, and get a receipt with a numerical access code that would unlock your room door. To keep costs down, the rooms did not have en suite bathrooms, so guests had to use communal facilities. The usual failure mode was that a guest, having gone to the bathroom, would forget his access code. Unless he had taken the receipt with him, he'd end up having to sleep on the bathroom floor until the staff arrived the following morning.

Problems related to password memorability can be discussed under two main headings: design errors, and operational failures.

3.2.3.1 Design Errors

Attempts to design systems so as to make passwords memorable are a frequent source of severe design errors—especially with the many systems being built rapidly by unskilled people for electronic business. An instructive, and important, example of how not to do it is to ask customers for "your mother's maiden name." Many banks, government departments, and other organizations authenticate their customers in this way. There are two rather obvious problems: first, your mother's maiden name is easy for a thief to find out, whether by asking around, chasing birth and marriage records, or using online genealogical databases. Second, even if you decide that from now on your mother's maiden name is going to be, say, Yngstrom (or even yGt5r4ad), rather than Smith, there are problems. You might break your credit card agreement, and perhaps invalidate your insurance cover, by giving false data.

Moreover, asking for a maiden name makes assumptions that don't hold for all cultures (Icelanders have no surnames, and women from many other countries don't change their names on marriage). There might be no provision for changing such a password, so if it ever becomes known to a thief you could have to close and reopen bank accounts. Finally, you will be asked to give it to a lot of organizations, any one of which might have a crooked employee. You could always tell "Yngstrom" to your bank, "Jones" to the phone company, "Geraghty" to the travel agent, and so on; but data are shared extensively between companies, so you could easily end up confusing their systems (not to mention yourself).

Slightly more thoughtfully designed e-commerce sites ask for a password explicitly rather than a maiden name. But the sheer number of applications for which the average person is asked to use a password nowadays exceeds the powers of human memory. So either customers will write passwords down (despite being told not to) or they will use the same password for many different purposes. Thus, the password you use to authenticate the customer of the electronic banking system you've just designed, is quite possibly known to a Mafia-operated porn site as well.

The risk you face as a consumer is not just a direct loss through identity theft or fraud. Badly designed password mechanisms can undermine your credibility and can cause you to lose a genuine legal claim. For example, if a thief manages to forge a copy of your cash machine card, then loots your bank account, the bank will ask whether you have ever shared your personal identification number with any other person or company. If you admit to using the same number for your mobile phone, the bank may well say that either you were grossly negligent by allowing someone to see you using the phone, or somebody at the phone company must be to blame. In either case, it's up to you to find them and sue them.

Some organizations try to find other security information. My bank asks its business customers the value of the last check from their account that was cleared. In theory, this could be a good system: it has the advantage that even if someone compromises my password—such as by overhearing me doing a transaction on the telephone—the security of the system usually recovers more or less automatically. The implementation details bear some attention though. When this system was first introduced, I wondered whether a supplier, to whom I'd just written a check, had a chance of impersonating me. I concluded that asking for the last three checks' values would be safer. But the problem I actually had was different. Having given the checkbook to our accountant for the annual audit, I couldn't authenticate myself to get a balance over the phone and had to visit the branch.

Attempts to find alternative solutions have more often hit the rocks. One bank sent its customers a letter warning them against writing down their PIN, and instead supplied a distinctive piece of cardboard on which they were supposed to conceal their PIN in the following way: suppose your PIN is 2256. Choose a four-letter word, say blue.

1	2	3	4	5	6	7	8	9	0
	b								
	l								
				u					
					e				

Figure 3.1 A bad mnemonic system for bank PINs.

Write these four letters down in the second, second, fifth, and sixth columns of the card, respectively, as shown in Figure 3.1. Then fill up the empty boxes with random letters.

This is clearly a bad idea. Even if the random letters aren't written in a slightly different way, a quick check shows that a 4 by 10 matrix of random letters may yield about two dozen words (unless there's an "s" on the bottom row, when you can get 40 to 50). So the odds that the thief can guess the PIN, given three attempts, have just shortened from 1 in 3000-odd to 1 in 8.

Some banks allow customers to choose their own PINs. It is believed that about a third of customers use a birthdate, in which case the odds against the thief are now a bit over 100 to 1 (and much shorter if the thief knows the victim). Even if this risk is thought acceptable, the PIN might still be set to the same value as the PIN used with a mobile phone that's shared with family members. To analyze this problem, we have to consider a number of different threat models, which we'll come to in the next section.

3.2.3.2 Operational Issues

A failure to think through the sort of rules that organizations should make, and enforce, to support the password mechanisms they have implemented has led to some really spectacular cases. One important case in Britain in the late 1980s was *R v. Gold and Schifreen*. The defendants saw a phone number for the development system for Prestel (an early public email service run by British Telecom) in a note stuck on a terminal at an exhibition. They dialed in later, and found that the welcome screen had an all-powerful maintenance password displayed on it. They tried this on the live system, too, and it worked! They proceeded to take over the Duke of Edinburgh's electronic mail account, and sent mail 'from' him to someone they didn't like, announcing the award of a knighthood. This crime so shocked the establishment that when prosecutors failed to convict the defendants under the laws then in force, Parliament passed Britain's first computer crime law.

Placing an administrator password in an envelope taped to the side of a workstation in an office that is always attended or locked may in some circumstances be reasonable practice. The people who can get at it are those who can physically access the machine anyway. But if you operate a policy like this, then you have to see to it that people understand the reasoning behind it, and don't think that the password can as easily be left on a logon screen. For someone to use the same administrator password for the live system as in the development environment is much less excusable.

A similar and very general error is failing to reset the default passwords supplied with certain system services. For example, one top-selling dial access system in the 1980s had a default software support user name of 999999 and a password of 9999. It also had a default supervisor name of 777777, with a password of 7777. Most sites didn't change these passwords, and many of them were hacked once the practice became widely known. Failure to change default passwords as supplied by the equipment vendor has affected many kinds of computer, some cryptographic equipment, and even mobile phones (where many users never bother to change an installed PIN of 0000).

3.3 System Issues

After gaining an understanding the psychology of the users, the next step is to understand that of the attackers. Just as we can only talk about the soundness of a security protocol in the context of a specific threat model, so we can only judge whether a given password scheme is sound by considering the type of attacks we are trying to defend against. Broadly speaking, these are:

Targeted attack on one account. An intruder tries to guess a particular user's password. He might try to guess the PIN for Bill Gates's bank account, or a rival's logon password at the office, in order to do mischief directly.

Attempt to penetrate any account on a system. The intruder tries to get a logon as any user of the system. This might be to steal service directly (e.g., use a phone card service without paying) or as a stepping stone to a wider attack.

Attempt to penetrate any account on any system. The intruder wants an account on any system in a given domain; it doesn't matter which one. For example, common teenage hacker motives are to get a place to hide pirated software or pornography, or a platform from which attacks can be launched anonymously on other systems. More serious threats come from skilled people attacking a target organization. A spy seeking classified information might initially try to hack any computer in the .mil namespace, while a private eye tasked to get access to Microsoft's intranet might only need a logon to some random machine in microsoft.com.

Service denial attack. The attacker may wish to prevent the legitimate user from using the system. This might be targeted on a particular account (such as cancelling somebody's credit cards in order to annoy them) or systemwide.

This taxonomy is useful because it helps us ask many relevant questions when selecting or designing a password system. However, there are other issues that interact with the type of attacks that are expected and the kind of countermeasures that can be used.

3.3.1 Protecting Oneself or Others?

First, to what extent does the system need to protect users from each other? In some systems—such as mobile phone systems and cash machine systems—no one should be able to use the service at someone else's expense. It is assumed that the attackers are already legitimate users of the system. So systems are (or at least should be) carefully designed so that knowledge of one user's password will not allow another identifiable user's account to be compromised: they provide *multilateral security* (which we discuss at greater length in Chapter 8). A user who chooses a password that is easy to guess harms only himself, and so a wide variation in password strength can perhaps be tolerated. (Bear in mind that the passwords people choose are very often easy for their spouses or partners to guess [146], so some thought needs to be given to issues such as what happens when a cheated partner seeks vengeance. This is a common enough problem.)

But with many systems, it can be bad news if even one enemy gains access. Operating systems such as Unix and Windows may have been designed to protect one user against accidental interference by another, but they are not hardened to protect against capable malicious actions by other users. These systems have many well-publicized vulnerabilities, with more being published constantly on the Web. A competent opponent who can get a single account on a shared computer system can usually become the system administrator fairly quickly; and from there he can do whatever he likes. The typical exploitation path is thus *outsider* to *normal user* to *administrator*, with the first of these steps being the hard one. So it may not be a good idea to let users choose whatever password they like. With military systems in particular, it is common to assign users random passwords in order to guarantee a minimum password strength. (I'll have more to say on this later.)

3.3.2 Intrusion Detection Issues

The second question concerns the manner in which the password system might interact with an intrusion detection system. Organizations such as banks often have a rule that a terminal and user account are frozen after three bad password attempts; it is then necessary to contact an administrator to reactivate them. This could be rather dangerous in a military system, as an enemy who got access to the network could use a flood of false logon attempts to mount a service denial attack; if given a list of all the user names on a machine, it might well be possible to take it out of service completely.

It's not just military systems where you have to pay attention to this. Telephone calling cards are another example; they usually have a prefix, followed by the local number to which they're billed, and a four-digit PIN. One phone company scans calling card numbers and cancels any for which more than one PIN appears. This leaves them wide open to anyone who wants to cancel someone else's card. (It also doesn't stop the crook who wants to guess a valid card number, as he can just try the same PIN with a whole lot of different local phone numbers.)

The design of intrusion detection systems varies greatly by what they are supposed to achieve. They can range from simple threshold alarms, which go off after three bad logon attempts to a particular account, up through much more sophisticated and distributed systems designed to cope with intruders who might try one password on many accounts, or on one account on each of many machines, or whatever. There's more on intrusion detection in Chapter 18; here, I'm just flagging up the fact that password and intrusion detection policies interact.

3.3.3 Can Users Be Trained?

The third question is whether users can be trained and disciplined. In a corporate or military environment—and even to some extent in a university—you can control your user population. You can teach them how to choose good passwords; you can give negative feedback if they choose bad ones; you can issue them with random passwords, and order that if these passwords are written down they must be treated the same as the data they protect (so 'Top Secret' passwords must be sealed in an envelope, in a safe, in a room that's locked when not occupied, in a building patrolled by guards). You can see to it that only cleared people have access to the terminals where the passwords can be used. You can send the guards round at night to check that no-one's left a note of a password lying around. You can operate a *clean desk* policy so that nothing can be overlooked in a pile of papers in plain sight.

Colleagues and I studied the benefits that can be obtained by training users [815]. While writing this book, I could not find any account of experiments on this that would hold water by the standards of applied psychology (i.e., randomized controlled trials with big enough groups for the results to be statistically significant). The closest I found was a study of the recall rates, forgetting rates, and guessing rates of various types of password [146]; this is valuable, but doesn't tell us the actual (as opposed to likely) effects of giving users various kinds of advice. We therefore selected three groups of about a hundred volunteers from our first-year science students.

- The red (control) group was given the usual advice (devise a password of at least six characters long, including one nonletter).

- The green group was told to think of a passphrase and select letters from it to build a password. Thus, "It's 12 noon and I am hungry" would give I'S12&IAH.

- The yellow group was told to select eight characters (alpha or numeric) at random from a table we gave them, write them down, and destroy the note after a week or two once they'd memorized the password.

What we expected to find was that the red group's passwords would be easier to guess than the green group's, which would in turn be easier than the yellow group's; and that the yellow group would have the most difficulty remembering their passwords (or would be forced to reset them more often), followed by green and then red. But that's not what we found.

About 30 percent of the control group chose passwords that could be guessed using cracking software (which I discuss later), versus about 10 percent for the other two groups. So passphrases and random passwords seemed to be about equally effective. When we looked at password reset rates, there was no significant difference between the three groups. When we asked the students whether they'd found their passwords hard to remember (or had written them down), the yellow group had significantly more problems than the other two; but there was no significant difference between red and green.

The conclusions we drew were as follows.

- For those users who follow instructions, the use of passwords based on mnemonic phrases offers the best of both worlds. They are as easy to remember as naively selected passwords, and as hard to guess as random passwords.

- Merely using mnemonic passwords or random passwords does not help much, as the problem then becomes one of *user compliance*. A significant number of users (perhaps a third of them) just don't do what they're told.

So, while centrally assigned, randomly selected passwords may be a good strategy for the military, its value comes from the fact that the passwords are centrally assigned (thus compelling user compliance) rather than from the fact that they're random (mnemonic phrases would do just as well).

However, there are at least two cases where centrally assigned passwords may be inappropriate. The first is where a user controls access to a resource that the organization should not be able to override. Where digital signatures are used to provide evidence, and a user's digital signing key is protected by a password, then assigning this password centrally could enable the system administrator to get at the signing key and forge messages, which would destroy the evidential value of the signature.

The second, and more subtle, case is systems that offer a service to the public. Whether you offer a service through dedicated terminals, such as cash machines or mobile phones, or over the Net to standard PCs, you can't expect to train and discipline your users; and if you try to, there is a real risk that a judge will find your contract terms unreasonable.

Perhaps the ideal solution is instruct users to choose mnemonic passwords, and to have a password cracking program installed as a password filter; users who try to choose a password on its guessing list are told to try again. More empirical psychological research on this topic is needed.

3.3.4 The Growing Famine for Security Data

The fourth question is the really hard one: will your users compromise their passwords by using them on other systems?

People who are allowed to select their own password or PIN will often choose the same one for a number of systems, so it's easy to remember. If you don't let customers change their PINs, some of them will write them down. You can forbid this in their contract, but they'll do it anyway. Some people will just take their business elsewhere (given the option, I prefer to use Web sites that don't ask for a password at all, regardless of whether I choose it or they do).

There is a severe shortage of good security information by which people can be identified and can authorize actions. Attempts to solve the problem by issuing people with "multifunction" smartcards have so far foundered on arguments over whose logo will go on front and who will control the mailing list. It would require less expenditure on infrastructure if we could get people to authorize transactions using existing equipment such as mobile phones. But even if, in a few years' time, everyone in the world has a third-generation mobile phone capable of doing banking transactions and of receiving encrypted text messages containing authorization codes for Web-based e-commerce transactions, there will remain a whole host of technical problems. These include the chosen protocol attack, which we discussed in the previous chapter, and the difficulties of preventing programs from interfering with each other, which we will discuss in the next.

Even more serious problems are likely to arise from business and legal issues, such as what if a single company gets control of everyone's credit card data, or purchase history data, or both. We'll discuss these issues in Chapters 19 through 21.

3.4 Technical Protection of Passwords

A broad range of attacks can be used to recover other people's passwords. Some of them target the password entry mechanism, while others exploit the way that passwords are stored.

3.4.1 Attacks on Password Entry

Password entry is often poorly protected.

3.4.1.1 Interface Design

Sometimes the problem is thoughtless interface design. For example, some very common models of cash machine had a vertical keyboard at head height, making it simple for a pickpocket to watch a customer enter her PIN before lifting her purse from her handbag. The keyboards were at a reasonable height for the men who designed them, but women—and men in many countries are a few inches shorter and were highly exposed. Ironically, one of these machines "protected client privacy" by forcing the customer to gaze at the screen through a narrow slot. Your balance was private, but your PIN was not!

Many pay telephones have a similar problem, and *shoulder surfing* of calling card details (as it's known in the industry) has been endemic at some locations such as major U.S. train stations and airports. For that reason, I usually cover my dialling hand with my body or my other hand when entering a card number or PIN in a public place—but systems shouldn't be designed on the assumption that all customers will do this.

3.4.1.2 Eavesdropping

Taking care with password entry may stop the bad guys looking over your shoulder as you use your calling card at an airport telephone, but it won't stop all the eavesdropping attacks. For example, a hotel manager might abuse his switchboard facilities to log the keystrokes you enter at the phone in your room. That way, he might get the credit card number you used to buy a ticket from an automated service; and if this isn't the card number you use to pay your hotel bill, he can plunder your account with much less risk.

Many networked computer systems still send a password in clear over a local area network for checking at a server; anyone who can program a machine on the network, or attach his own sniffer equipment, can harvest them. This is one reason that Microsoft adopted the Kerberos authentication protocol for Windows 2000—the cleartext password is not transmitted over the network. (NT v 4 used a proprietary authentication protocol.)

3.4.1.3 The Need for Trusted Path

The machine to which you log on may be malicious. A simple attack program may be left running on an unattended machine in a public terminal room; it will look just like the usual logon screen, prompting for a user name and password. When an unsuspecting user does this, it will save the password somewhere in the system, reply "sorry, wrong password" and then vanish, invoking the genuine password program. The user will assume that he made a typing error the first time and think no more of it. This is why Windows NT has a "secure attention sequence," namely `ctrl-alt-del`, which is guaranteed to take you to a genuine password prompt. A facility that assures the user she's talking to a genuine system is called a *trusted path*.

If the whole terminal equipment is bogus, then of course all bets are off. We once caught a student installing modified keyboards in our public terminal room to capture passwords. When the attacker is prepared to take this much trouble, then all the `ctrl-alt-del` sequence achieves is to make his software design task simpler.

There have also been a few cases of criminals setting up false cash machines. In one famous case in Connecticut in 1993, the bad guys even bought genuine cash machines (on credit), installed them in a shopping mall, and proceeded to collect PINs and card details from unsuspecting bank customers who tried to use them [19]. Within a year, crooks in London had copied the idea, then enlarged on it by setting up a whole bogus bank branch [405]. Other cases have involved home-built cash machines, fitting false fronts over the front of genuine cash machines, or even replacing the card-operated door locks at the entrance to ATM facilities. Such attacks are even easier in countries where cards are used with PINs at the point of sale.

3.4.1.4 Technical Defeats of Password Retry Counters

Many kids find out that a bicycle combination lock can usually be broken in a few minutes by solving each ring in order of looseness. The same idea works against a number of computer systems. The PDP-10 TENEX operating system checked passwords one character at a time, and stopped as soon as one of them was wrong. This opened up a *timing attack*, whereby the attacker would repeatedly place a guessed password in memory at a suitable location, have it verified as part of a file access request, and wait to see how long it took to be rejected [493]. An error in the first character would be reported almost at once, an error in the second character would take a little longer to report, and in the third character a little longer still, and so on. So it was possible to guess the characters one after another, and instead of a password of N characters drawn from an alphabet of A characters taking $A^N/2$ guesses on average, it took $A^{N/2}$. (Bear in mind that, in 30 years' time, all that might remain of the system you're building today is the memory of its more newsworthy security failures.)

A similar attack worked on one remote car-locking device: as soon as a wrong byte was transmitted from the key fob, the red telltale light on the receiver came on.

Password retry limits fail in other ways, too. With some smartcards, it has been possible to determine the customer PIN by trying each possible input value and looking at the card's power consumption, then issuing a reset if the input was wrong. The reason was that a wrong PIN caused a PIN retry counter to be decremented, and writing to the EEPROM memory that held this counter caused a current surge of several milliamps, which could be detected in time to reset the card before the write was complete [478].

3.4.2 Attacks on Password Storage

Passwords have often been vulnerable where they are stored. There was a horrendous bug in one operating system update in the 1980s: a user who entered a wrong password, and was told "sorry, wrong password" merely had to hit carriage return to get into the system anyway. This was spotted quickly, and a patch was shipped, but almost a hundred U.S. government systems in Germany were using unlicensed copies of the software and didn't get the patch, with the result that hackers were able to get in and steal information, which they are rumored to have sold to the KGB.

Another horrible programming error struck a U.K. bank, which issued all its customers with the same PIN by mistake. As the procedures for handling PINs were carefully controlled, no one in the bank got access to anyone's PIN other than his or her own, so the mistake wasn't spotted until after thousands of customer cards had been shipped.

3.4.2.1 Attacks via the Audit Trail

In systems that log failed password attempts, the log usually contains a large number of passwords, as users get the "username, password" sequence out of phase. If the logs are not well protected, then attacks become easy. Someone who sees an audit record of a failed login with a nonexistent user name of e5gv,8yp can be 99 percent sure that this string is a password for one of the valid user names on the system.

3.4.2.2 One-Way Encryption

Password storage has also been a problem for some systems. Keeping a plaintext file of passwords can be dangerous. In MIT's Compatible Time Sharing System, ctss (a predecessor of Multics), it once happened that one person was editing the message of the day, while another was editing the password file. Because of a software bug, the two editor temporary files got swapped, with the result that everyone who logged on was greeted with a copy of the password file!

As a result of such incidents, passwords are often protected by encrypting them using a one-way algorithm, an innovation due to Roger Needham and Mike Guy. The password, when entered, is passed through a one-way function, and the user is logged on only if it matches a previously stored value.

Sometimes it isn't possible to protect a file of security information by one-way encryption, however, such as when this information must be processed in some way. The classic example is in GSM mobile phones, where each user has a cryptographic key on the home location register database. As this key is used to compute challenge-response pairs for authenticating users over the air, it is kept in the clear. (We will discuss the reasons for this design decision, and the possible alternatives, in Chapter 17).

3.4.2.3 Password Cracking

However, some systems that do use an encrypted password file make it *world readable* (Unix is the prime example—a design error now too well entrenched to change easily). This means that an opponent who can fetch this file can then try to break passwords offline using a dictionary; he encrypts the values in his dictionary and compares them with those in the file (an activity called a *dictionary attack*, or more colloquially, *password cracking*). NT is slightly better, but the password file can still be accessed by users who know what they're doing, and passwords may be passed to other systems (such as Netware, or earlier versions of NT) in old formats that use old, weak protection mechanisms for compatibility reasons.

Left to their own devices, people will use spouses' names, single letters, or even just hit Enter which gives an empty string as their password. So some systems require minimum password lengths, or even check user-entered passwords against a dictionary of bad choices. Still, designing a password quality enforcement mechanism is harder than one might think. Grampp and Morris's classic paper on Unix security [350] reports that after software became available that forced passwords to be at least six characters long and have at least one nonletter, they made a file of the 20 most common female names, each followed by a single digit. Of these 200 passwords, at least one was in use on each of several dozen machines they examined.

According to one report, when users were compelled to change their passwords, and prevented from using the previous few choices, they changed passwords rapidly to exhaust the history list and get back to their favorite password. A response, of forbidding password changes until after 15 days, meant that users couldn't change compromised passwords without help from the system administrator [603]. In my own experience, insisting on alphanumeric passwords and forcing a password change once a month led people to choose passwords such as julia03 for March, julia04 for April, and so on. So I am not at all convinced that demanding frequent password changes is a good idea.

A well-known study was conducted by Klein who gathered 25,000 Unix passwords in the form of encrypted password files and ran cracking software to guess them [460]. He found that 21 to 25 percent of passwords could be guessed, depending on the amount of effort put in. Dictionary words accounted for 7.4 percent, common names for 4 percent, combinations of user and account name 2.7 percent, and so on down a list of less-probable choices such as words from science fiction (0.4 percent) and sports terms (0.2 percent). Some of these were straighforward dictionary searches; others used patterns. For example, the algorithm for constructing combinations of user and account names would take an account klone belonging to the user Daniel V. Klein and try passwords such as klone,klone1,klone123,dvk,dvkdvk,leinad,neilk,DvkkvD, and so on.

There are publicly available programs (crack for Unix and L0phtcrack for Windows [481]) that implement this kind of search. They can be used by system administrators to find bad passwords on their systems. They can just as easily be used by a bad guy who has got a copy of your password file. So password cracking is something to which you have to pay attention, especially if your system contains any machines running Unix or Linux. One way to use a program like crack is to filter user password choices; another is to use a custom program that understands language statistics and rejects passwords that are too likely to be chosen by others at random [98, 220]; another is to mix the two ideas using a suitable coding scheme [725].

3.4.3 Absolute Limits

Regardless of how well passwords are managed, there are often absolute limits imposed by the design of the operating system or other platform on which the system is built. For example, Unix systems limit the length of the password to eight characters (you can often enter more than this, but the ninth and subsequent characters are ignored). The effort required to try all possible passwords—the *total exhaust time*, in cryptanalytic jargon—is 96^8 or about 2^{52}; the average effort for a search is half of this. A well-financed government agency (or a well-organized hacker group, using PCs distributed across the Internet) could now break any encrypted password in a standard Unix password file.

This motivates more technical defenses against password cracking, including shadow passwords, that is, encrypted passwords hidden in a private file (most modern Unices), using an obscure mechanism to do the encryption (Novell), or using a secret key with the encryption (MVS). The strength of these mechanisms may vary.

For the above reasons, military system administrators often prefer to issue random passwords. This also lets the probability of password-guessing attacks be estimated and managed. For example, if L is the maximum password lifetime, R is login attempt rate, S is the size of the password space, then the probability that a password can be guessed in its lifetime is:

$$P = LR/S$$

This equation is taken from the U.S. Department of Defense password management guideline [242]. There are a couple of problems with this doctrine. First (the niggle) the password space can be completely exhausted, in which case $LR/S > 1$, and P isn't defined as a probability. Second (more serious) is that the attacker is not interested in guessing a password as much as getting acess to an account. So one has to take account of the number of users. If a large defense network has a million possible passwords and a million users, and the alarm goes off after three bad password attempts on any account, then the attack is to try one password for every single account. Thus, the quantity of real interest is the probability that the password space can be exausted in the lifetime of the system at the maximum feasible password guess rate.

To take a concrete example, U.K. government systems tend to issue passwords that have been randomly selected with a fixed template of consonants, vowels, and numbers designed to make them easier to remember, such as CVCNCVCN (e.g., fuR5xEb8). If passwords are not case-sensitive, the guess probability is only $21^4.5^2.10^2$, or about 2^{29}. So if an attacker could guess 100 passwords a second—perhaps distributed across 10,000 accounts on hundreds of machines on a network, so as not to raise the alarm—then he'd need about 5 million seconds, or two months, to get in.

In commercial systems, you can have a policy of simply blocking accounts after a number of false password attempts. If the threshold were three bad guesses in any one month, then with 10,000 accounts the maximum guess rate would be 30,000 passwords per month, and the rate at which guessing could be carried out undetectably would be much lower. But military system designers are reluctant to introduce account blocking, as it leaves them open to service denial attacks. As I mentioned in Section 3.3.2, an enemy who gets access to the network and enters enough wrong password guesses could freeze every account on the whole system.

3.5 Summary

Password management is one of the most important and yet most difficult design problems in many secure systems. As people get accounts on more and more systems, they reuse passwords in ways that expose serious vulnerabilities. But even where users operate in a controlled environment, things are by no means straightforward.

The ability to do offline password guessing more or less guarantees that an attacker will be able to compromise at least some accounts on any system, unless passwords are centrally assigned or filtered when users choose them. Where possible, one should stop offline guessing, for example, by keeping the password file secret. But systems such as Unix are often bought because of their large software base, and the software your customer wants to use may make changing the password mechanism difficult.

Critical questions to ask when designing a password system include not just whether people might reuse passwords, but also whether they need to be protected from each other, whether they can be trained and disciplined, and whether accounts can be frozen after a fixed number of bad guesses. You also have to consider whether attackers will target a particular account, or be happy with breaking any account on a machine or a network; and technical protection issues such as whether passwords can be snooped by malicious software, false terminals, or network eavesdropping.

Research Problems

I mentioned the lack of published empirical research. Although a little has been done, there's a lot more to do. For example, what are the best ways of enforcing user compliance with a password policy? There are some extreme solutions—such as issuing each user with a printed list of random passwords, each of which can be used once only—and these certainly work. But what can be done in applications where such drastic measures aren't justified?

Another problem, which straddles the borderline with security protocol design, is whether we can design interactive password systems that are better. There are various visual schemes and memorization schemes in the literature, and some early products: one system presents users with nine faces, only one of which is of a person they know; they have to pick the right face several times in a row to log on [223]. Other schemes present a table of numbers, and let the user do a secret computation using mental arithmetic. Designing such schemes is fairly easy; evaluating them is harder, as it involves elements of cryptology, psychology, and systems engineering.

An increasingly common mechanism is to ask for several pieces of security information rather than one. A call center might ask not just for your mother's maiden name, a password, and the amount of your last purchase, but also your dog's nickname and your favorite color. The underlying idea is that although an attacker might find out anything you know, it's much harder for him to find out everything you know. Again, such schemes need careful evaluation of their usability and effectiveness using the tools of applied psychology.

Further Reading

There isn't as much literature on passwords as one would like, despite the subject's importance. The papers by Bob Morris and Ken Thompson [561], Fred Grampp and Bob Morris [350], and Dan Klein [460], are the classics. The DoD guidelines are very influential [242].

Access Control

Going all the way back to early time-sharing systems, we systems people regarded the users, and any code they wrote, as the mortal enemies of us and each other. We were like the police force in a violent slum.

—ROGER NEEDHAM

Microsoft could have incorporated effective security measures as standard, but good sense prevailed. Security systems have a nasty habit of backfiring, and there is no doubt they would cause enormous problems.

—RICK MAYBURY

4.1 Introduction

Access control is the traditional center of gravity of computer security. It is where security engineering meets computer science. Its function is to control which principals (persons, processes, machines, ...) have access to which resources in the system—which files they can read, which programs they can execute, how they share data with other principals, and so on.

NOTE This chapter necessarily assumes more computer science background than previous chapters, but I try to keep it to a minimum.

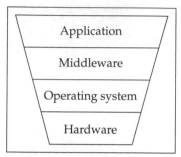

Figure 4.1 Access controls at different levels in a system.

Access control works at a number of levels, as shown in Figure 4.1, and described in the following:

1. *The access control mechanisms, which the user sees at the application level, may express a very rich and complex security policy.* A modern online business could assign staff to one of dozens of different roles, each of which could initiate some subset of several hundred possible transactions in the system. Some of these (such as credit card transactions with customers) might require online authorization from a third party while others (such as refunds) might require dual control.

2. *The applications may be written on top of middleware, such as a database management system or bookkeeping package, which enforces a number of protection properties.* For example, bookkeeping software may ensure that a transaction that debits one ledger for a certain amount must credit another ledger for the same amount.

3. *The middleware will use facilities provided by the underlying operating system.* As this constructs resources such as files and communications ports from lower-level components, it acquires the responsibility for providing ways to control access to them.

4. *Finally, the operating system access controls will usually rely on hardware features provided by the processor or by associated memory management hardware.* These control which memory addresses a given process can access.

As we work up from the hardware through the operating system and middleware to the application layer, the controls become progressively more complex and less reliable. Most actual computer frauds involve staff accidentally discovering features of the application code that they can exploit in an opportunistic way, or just abusing features of the application that they were trusted not to. But in this chapter, we will focus on the fundamentals: access control at the hardware and operating system level. (Application-level controls aren't different in principle, but I leave detailed discussion to Part 2 of this book.)

As with the other building blocks discussed so far, access control makes sense only in the context of a protection goal, typically expressed as a security policy. This puts us at a slight disadvantage when discussing PCs running single-user operating systems such as DOS and Win95/98, which have no overt security policy: any process can modify any data. People do have implicit protection goals, though; you don't expect a shrink-wrap program to trash your hard disk. So an explicit security policy is a good idea, especially when products support some features that appear to provide protection, such as login IDs.

I mention one protection technique—*sandboxing*—later, but leave off a substantial discussion of viruses and the like to Section 18.4. In what follows, the focus will be on protection mechanisms for systems that support the isolation of multiple processes. I discuss operating system mechanisms first, as it is their requirements that usually drive hardware protection system design.

4.2 Operating System Access Controls

The access controls provided with an operating system typically authenticate principals using some mechanism such as passwords or Kerberos, then mediate their access to files, communications ports, and other system resources.

Their effect can often be modelled by a matrix of access permissions, with columns for files and rows for users. We'll write r for permission to read, w for permission to write, x for permission to execute a program, and $(-)$ for no access at all, as shown in Figure 4.2.

In this simplified example, Sam is the system administrator, and has universal access (except to the audit trail, which even he should only be able to read). Alice, the manager, needs to execute the operating system and application, but only through the approved interfaces—she mustn't have the ability to tamper with then. She also needs to read and write the data. Bob, the auditor, can read everything.

This is often enough, but in the specific case of a bookkeeping system, it's not quite what we need. We want to ensure that transactions are well formed—that each debit is matched by a credit somewhere else—so we would not want Alice to have uninhibited write access to the account file. We would also prefer that Sam didn't have this access; so that all write access to the accounting data file was via the accounting program. The access permissions might now look like those shown in Figure 4.3. (There is still an indirect

	Operating System	Accounts Program	Accounting Data	Audit Trail
Sam	rwx	rwx	rw	r
Alice	x	x	rw	–
Bob	rx	r	r	r

Figure 4.2 Naive access control matrix.

User	Operating System	Accounts Program	Accounting Data	Audit Trail
Sam	rwx	rwx	r	r
Alice	rx	x	–	–
Accounts program	rx	r	rw	w
Bob	rx	r	r	r

Figure 4.3 Example access control matrix for bookkeeping.

vulnerability in that Sam could overwrite the accounts program with an unauthorised one of his own devising, but we'll leave off discussing that till Chapter 9.)

Another way of expressing a policy of this type would be with *access triples* of *user, program, file*. In the general case, our concern isn't with a program as much as a *protection domain*, which is a set of processes or threads that share access to the same resources (though at any given time they might have different files open or different scheduling priorities).

Access control matrices (whether in two or three dimensions) can be used to implement protection mechanisms, as well as just model them. But they do not scale well. For instance, a bank with 50,000 staff and 300 applications would have an access control matrix of 15 million entries. This is inconveniently large. It might not only impose a performance problem but also be vulnerable to administrators' mistakes. We will usually need a more compact way of storing and managing this information. The two main ways of doing this are to use groups or roles to manage the privileges of large sets of users simultaneously, or to store the access control matrix either by columns (access control lists) or rows (capabilities, sometimes known as "tickets") or certificates [662, 804].

4.2.1 Groups and Roles

When we look at large organizations, we usually find that most staff fit into one or other of a small number of categories. A bank might have 40 or 50 such categories: teller, chief teller, branch accountant, branch manager, and so on. The remainder (such as the security manager, and chief foreign exchange dealer, . . .), who need to have their access rights defined individually, may amount to only a few dozen people.

So we want a small number of predefined groups, or functional roles, to which staff can be assigned. Some people use the words *group* and *role* interchangeably, and with many systems they are; but the more careful definition is that a group is a list of principals, while a role is a fixed set of access permissions that one or more principals may assume for a period of time using some defined procedure. The classic example of a role is the officer of the watch on a ship. There is exactly one watchkeeper at any one time, and there is a formal procedure whereby one officer relieves another when the watch changes. In fact, in most military applications, it's the role that matters rather than the individual.

Groups and roles can be combined. *The officers of the watch of all ships currently at sea* is a group of roles. In banking, the manager of the Cambridge branch might have his or her privileges expressed by membership of the group *manager* and assumption of the role *acting manager of Cambridge branch*. The group *manager* might express a rank in the organization (and perhaps even a salary scale) while the role *acting manager* might include an assistant accountant standing in while the manager, deputy manager, and branch accountant are all sick.

Whether we need to be careful about this distinction is a matter for the application. In a warship, we want even an able seaman to be allowed to stand watch if all the officers have been killed. In a bank, we might have a policy that "transfers over $10 million must be approved by two staff, one with the rank of manager and one with the rank of assistant accountant." In the event of sickness, the assistant accountant acting as manager would have to get the regional head office to provide the second signature on a large transfer.

Until recently, some support for groups and roles existed but was not very widely used. Developers either implemented this kind of functionality in their application code,

User	Accounting Data
Sam	rw
Alice	rw
Bob	r

Figure 4.4 Access control list (ACL).

or as custom middleware (in the 1980s, I worked on two bank projects where group support was hand-coded as extensions to the mainframe operating system). Recently, Windows 2000 (Win2K) has been launched with very extensive support for groups, while academic researchers have started working on *role-based access control* (RBAC), which I discuss further in Chapter 7. We will have to wait and see whether either of these has a major effect on application development practices.

4.2.2 Access Control Lists

Another way of simplifying access rights management is to store the access control matrix a column at a time, along with the resource to which the column refers. This is called an *access control list*, or ACL. In the first of the examples, the ACL for file 3 (the account file) might look as shown in Figure 4.4.

ACLs have a number of advantages and disadvantages as a means of managing security state. These can be divided into general properties of ACLs and specific properties of particular implementations.

ACLs are widely used in environments where users manage their own file security, such as the Unix systems common in universities and science labs. Where access control policy is set centrally, they are suited to environments where protection is data-oriented; they are less suited where the user population is large and constantly changing, or where users want to be able to delegate their authority to run a particular program to another user for some set period of time. ACLs are simple to implement, but are not efficient as a means of doing security checking at runtime, as the typical operating system knows which user is running a particular program, rather than which files it has been authorized to access since it was invoked. The operating system must either check the ACL at each file access or keep track of the active access rights in some other way.

Finally, distributing the access rules into ACLs can make it tedious to find all the files to which a user has access. Revoking the access of an employee who has just been fired, for example, will usually have to be done by cancelling their password or other authentication mechanism. It may also be tedious to run systemwide checks, such as verifying that no files have been left world-writable. This could involve checking ACLs on millions of user files.

Let's look at two important examples of ACLs: their implementation in Unix and NT.

4.2.3 Unix Operating System Security

In Unix (and its popular variant Linux), files are not allowed to have arbitrary access control lists, but simply rwx attributes for the resource owner, the group, and the world.

These attributes allow the file to be read, written, and executed. The access control list as normally displayed has a flag to show whether the file is a directory; then flags r, w, and x for world, group, and owner respectively; it then has the owner's name and the group name. A directory with all flags set would have the ACL:

```
drwxrwxrwx Alice Accounts
```

In the first example in Figure 4.4, the ACL of file 3 would be:

```
-rw-r----- Alice Accounts
```

This records that the file is not a directory; the file owner can read and write it; group members can read it but not write it; nongroup members have no access at all; the file owner is Alice; and the group is Accounts.

In Unix, the program that gets control when the machine is booted (the operating system kernel) runs as the supervisor, and has unrestricted access to the whole machine. All other programs run as users, and have their access mediated by the supervisor. Access decisions are made on the basis of the userid associated with the program. However if this is zero (root), then the access control decision is "yes." So root can do what it likes—access any file, become any user, or whatever. What's more, there are certain things that only root can do, such as starting certain communication processes. The root userid is typically made available to the system administrator.

This means that (with most flavors of Unix) the system administrator can do anything, so we have difficulty implementing an audit trail as a file that he cannot modify. This not only means that in our example, Sam could tinker with the accounts, and have difficulty defending himself if he were falsely accused of tinkering but that a hacker who managed to become the system administrator could remove all evidence of his intrusion. A common defense is to send the system log to a printer in a locked room or—if the volumes of data are too great—to another machine that is administered by somebody else.

The Berkeley distributions, including FreeBSD, go some way toward fixing the problem. Files can be set to be append-only, immutable or undeletable for user, system or both. When set by a user at a sufficient security level during the boot process, they cannot be overridden or removed later, even by root. Various military variants go to even greater trouble to allow separation of duty. However, the simplest and most common way to protect logs against root compromise is to keep them on a separate server.

Second, ACLs contain only the names of users, not of programs, so there is no straightforward way to implement access triples of (user, program, file). Instead, Unix provides an indirect method: the suid and sgid file attributes.

The owner of a program can mark it as suid. This enables it to run with the privilege of its owner rather than the privilege of the user who has invoked it; sgid does the same for groups. Thus, in order to achieve the functionality needed by Figure 4.3, we could create a user "account-package" to own file 2 (the accounts package), make the file suid, and place it in a directory to which Alice has access. This special user could then be given the access control attributes we want for the accounts program.

One way of looking at this is that an access control problem that is naturally modelled in three dimensions—the triples (user, program, data)—is being implemented using two-dimensional mechanisms. These mechanisms are much less intuitive than triples, and people make many mistakes implementing them. Programmers are often lazy or facing tight deadlines; so they just make the application `suid root`, and it can do anything.

This practice leads to some rather shocking security holes. The responsibility for making access control decisions is moved from the operating system environment to the program, and most programmers are insufficiently experienced and careful to check everything that they should. In particular, the person invoking a `suid root` program controls its environment and can often manipulate this to cause protection failures.

Third, ACLs are not very good at expressing changing state. Managing stateful access rules, such as dual control, becomes difficult; one either has to do it at the application level or use `suid/sgid` again. Also, it's hard to track the files that a user might have open (as you typically want to do when revoking their rights on a system).

Fourth, the Unix ACL names only one user. Older versions allow a process to hold only one group ID at a time and force it to use a privileged program to access other groups; newer Unix systems put a process in all groups that the user is in. This is still much less expressive than one might like. In theory, the ACL and `su` mechanisms can often be used to achieve the desired effect. In practice, programmers are often too lazy to figure out how to do this, and so design their code to require much more privilege than it really ought to.

4.2.4 Windows NT

Another important operating system whose protection is largely based on access control lists is Windows NT. The current version of NT (version 5, or Win2K) is fairly complex, so it's helpful to trace its antecedents. (This can calso be useful if you have to help manage upgrades from NT4 to Win2K).

NT4 protection is very much like Unix, and appears to be inspired by it, so it's simpler to describe the main innovations.

First, rather than just *read*, *write*, and *execute*, there are separate attributes for *take ownership*, *change permissions*, and *delete*, which means that more flexible delegation can be supported. These attributes apply to groups as well as users, and group permissions allow you to achieve much the same effect as `sgid` programs in Unix. Attributes are not simply on or off, as in Unix, but have multiple values: you can set `AccessDenied`, `AccessAllowed`, or `SystemAudit`. These are parsed in that order. If an `AccessDenied` is encountered in an ACL for the relevant user or group, then no access is permitted, regardless of any conflicting `AccessAllowed` flags.

A benefit of the richer syntax is that you can arrange matters so that much less than full administrator privileges are required for everyday configuration tasks, such as installing printers. (This is rarely done, though.)

Second, users and resources can be partitioned into domains with distinct administrators, and trust can be inherited between domains in one direction or both. In a typical large company, you might put all the users into a domain administered by the personnel department, while resources such as servers and printers could be in resource domains under departmental control; individual workstations might even be administered by their users. Things would be arranged so that the departmental resource domains trust the user domain, but not vice versa—so a corrupt or careless departmental administrator couldn't do much damage outside his or her own domain. The individual workstations would in turn trust the department (but not vice versa) so that users could perform tasks that require local privilege (installing many software packages requires this). Administrators are all-powerful (so you can't create truly tamper-resistant audit trails without using write-once storage devices), but the damage they can do can be limited by suitable organization. The data structure used to manage all this, and hide the ACL details from the user interface, is called the *Registry*.

Problems with designing an NT architecture in very large organizations include naming issues (which we'll explore later), the way domains scale as the number of principals increases (badly), and the restriction that a user in another domain can't be an administrator (which can cause complex interactions between local and global groups).

One peculiarity of NT is that `everyone` is a principal, not a default or an absence of control, so `remove everyone` means just prevent a file being generally accessible. A resource can be locked quickly by setting `everyone` to have `no access`. This brings us naturally to the subject of capabilities.

4.2.5 Capabilities

The next way to manage the access control matrix is to store it by rows. These are called *capabilities*. In the example in Figure 4.2, Bob's capabilities would be as shown in Figure 4.5.

The strengths and weaknesses of capabilities are more or less the opposite of ACLs. Runtime security checking is more efficient, and we can do delegation without much difficulty: Bob could create a certificate saying "Here is my capability, and I hereby delegate to David the right to read file 4 from 9 A.M. to 1 P.M.; signed Bob." On the other hand, changing a file's status can suddenly become more tricky, as it can be difficult to find out which users have access. This can be tiresome when investigating an incident or preparing evidence of a crime.

There were a number of experimental implementations in the 1970s, which were rather like file passwords; users would get hard-to-guess bitstrings for the various read, write, and other capabilities to which they were entitled. It was found that such an arrangement could give very comprehensive protection [804]. It was not untypical to find that almost all of an operating system could run in user mode, rather than as supervisor, so operating system bugs were not security critical. (In fact, many operating system bugs caused security violations, which made debugging the operating system much easier.)

The IBM AS/400 series systems employed capability-based protection, and enjoyed some commercial success. Now capabilities are making a comeback in the form of *public key certificates*. We'll discuss the mechanisms of public key cryptography in Chapter 5, and give more concrete details of certificate-based systems, such as SSL/TLS, in Section

User	Operating System	Accounts Program	Accounting Data	Audit Trail
Bob	rx	r	r	r

Figure 4.5   A capability.

19.5. For now, think of a public key certificate as a credential signed by some authority, which declares that the holder of a certain cryptographic key is a certain person, a member of some group, or the holder of some privilege.

As an example of where certificate-based capabilities can be useful, consider a hospital. If we implemented a rule stating "a nurse will have access to all the patients who are on her ward, or who have been there in the last 90 days," naively, each access control decision in the patient record system would require several references to administrative systems, to find out which nurses and which patients were on which ward, when. This means that a failure of the administrative systems can now affect patient safety much more directly than was previously the case, which is a clearly bad thing. Matters can be much simplified by giving nurses certificates that entitle them to access the files associated with their current ward. Such a system is starting to be fielded at our university hospital.

One point to bear in mind is that as public key certificates are often considered to be "crypto" rather than "access control," their implications for access control policies and architectures are not always thought through. The lessons that could have been learned from the capability systems of the 1970s are generally having to be rediscovered (the hard way). In general, the boundary between crypto and access control is a fault line where things can easily go wrong. The experts often come from different backgrounds, and the products from different suppliers.

4.2.6 Added Features in Windows 2000

A number of systems, from mainframe access control products to research systems, have combined ACLs and capabilities in an attempt to get the best of both worlds. But the most important application of capabilities is in Win2K.

Win2K adds capabilities in two ways that can override or complement the ACLs of NT4. First, users or groups can be either whitelisted or blacklisted by means of profiles. (Some limited blacklisting was also possible in NT4.) Security policy is set by groups rather than for the system as a whole. Groups are intended to be the primary method for centralized configuration management and control (group policy overrides individual profiles). Group policy can be associated with sites, domains, or oganizational units, so it can start to tackle some of the real complexity problems with naming. Policies can be created using standard tools or by custom-coding (Microsoft has announced that group policy data will be exposed in a standard schema). Groups are defined in the *Active Directory*, an object-oriented database which organizes users, groups, machines, and organizational units within a domain in a hierarchical namespace, indexing them so they can searched for on any attribute. There are also finer-grained access control lists on individual resources.

As already mentioned, Win2K uses Kerberos as its main means of authenticating users across networks.[1] This is encapsulated behind the *Security Support Provider*

---

[1]In fact, it's a proprietary variant, with changes to the ticket format, which prevent Win2K clients from working with existing Unix Kerberos infrastructures. The documentation for the changes is released on condition that it not be used to make compatible implementations. Microsoft's goal is to get everyone to install Win2K Kerberos servers. This has caused an outcry in the open systems community [76].

Interface (SSPI), which enables administrators to plug in other authentication services. This brings us to the second way in which capabilities insinuate their way into Win2K: in many applications, people are likely to use the public key protocol SSL/TLS, which is widely used on the Web, and which is based on public key certificates. The management of these certificates can provide another, capability-oriented, layer of access control outside the purview of the Active Directory. (I discuss SSL/TLS in Section 19.5.)

There are various backward-compatibility issues. For example, high-security configurations of Win2K with full cryptographic authentication can't interwork with NT4 systems. This is because an active directory can exist alongside the registry of NT4, but the registry can't read it. So the deployment of Win2K's high-security features in large organizations is likely to be delayed until all the important applications have migrated.

Win2K provides a richer and more flexible set of access control tools than any system previously sold in mass markets. It does still have design limitations. Implementing roles whose requirements differ from those of groups could be tricky in some applications; SSL certificates are the obvious way to do this, but would require an external management infrastructure. Second, Windows is still (in most of its incarnations) a single-user operating system, in the sense that only one person can operate a PC at a time. Thus, if I want to run an unprivileged, sacrificial user on my PC for accessing untrustworthy Web sites that might contain malicious code, I have to log off and log on again, or use other techniques that are so inconvenient that few users will bother. So users still do not get the benefit from the operating system's protection properties that they might wish when browsing the Web.

4.2.7 Granularity

A practical problem with all current flavors of access control system is granularity. As the operating system works with files, this will usually be the smallest object with which its access control mechanisms can deal. So it will be application-level mechanisms that, for example, ensure that a bank customer at a cash machine can see his or her own balance but not anybody else's.

But it goes deeper than that. Many applications are built using database tools that give rise to some problems that are much the same whether running DB2 on MVS or Oracle on Unix. All the application data is bundled together in one file, and the operating system must either grant or deny a user access to the lot. So, if you developed your branch accounting system under a database product, then you'll probably have to manage one access mechanism at the operating system level and another at the database or application level. Many real problems result. For example, the administration of the operating system and the database system may be performed by different departments, which do not talk to each other; and often user pressure drives IT departments to put in crude hacks that make the various access control systems seem to work as one, but that open up serious holes.

Another granularity problem is *single sign-on*. Despite the best efforts of computer managers, most large companies accumulate systems of many different architectures, so users get more and more logons to different systems; consequently, the cost of administering them escalates. Many organizations want to give each employee a single logon to all the machines on the network. A crude solution is to endow their PCs with a menu of hosts to which a logon is allowed, and hide the necessary userids and passwords in scripts. More sophisticated solutions may involve a single security server through which all logons must pass, or a smartcard to do multiple authentication protocols for different systems. Such solutions are hard to engineer properly. Whichever route one takes, the security of the best system can easily be reduced to that of the worst.

4.2.8 Sandboxing and Proof-Carrying Code

Another way of implementing access control is a software *sandbox*. Here users want to run some code that they have downloaded from the Web as an applet. Their concern is that the applet might do something nasty, such as taking a list of all their files and mailing it off to a software marketing company.

The designers of Java tackle this problem by providing a "sandbox" for such code—a restricted environment in which it has no access to the local hard disk (or at most only temporary access to a restricted directory), and is only allowed to communicate with the host it came from. These security objectives are met by having the code executed by an interpreter—the Java Virtual Machine (JVM)—which has only limited access rights [346]. Java is also used on smartcards, but (in current implementations at least) the JVM is, in effect, a compiler external to the card, which raises the issue of how the code it outputs can be gotten to the card in a trustworthy manner.

An alternative is proof-carrying code. Here, code to be executed must carry with it a proof that it doesn't do anything that contravenes the local security policy. This way, rather than using an interpreter with the resulting speed penalty, one merely has to trust a short program that checks the proofs supplied by downloaded programs before allowing them to be executed. The huge overhead of a JVM is not necessary [585].

Both of these are less general alternatives to an architecture that supports proper supervisor-level confinement.

4.2.9 Object Request Brokers

There has been much interest of late in object-oriented software development, as it has the potential to cut the cost of software maintenance. An *object* consists of code and data bundled together, accessible only through specified externally visible *methods*. This also gives the potential for much more powerful and flexible access control. Much research is underway with the goal of producing a uniform security interface that is independent of the underlying operating system and hardware.

The idea is to base security functions on the *object request broker*, or ORB, a software component that mediates communications between objects. Many research efforts focus on the *Common Object Request Broker Architecture* (CORBA), which is an attempt at an industry standard for object-oriented systems. The most important aspect of this is that an ORB is a means of controlling calls that are made across protection domains. This approach appears promising but is still under development. (A book on CORBA security is [112].)

4.3 Hardware Protection

Most access control systems set out not just to control what users can do, but to limit what programs can do as well. In most systems, users can either write programs or download and install them. Programs may be buggy or even malicious.

Preventing one process from interfering with another is the *protection problem*. The *confinement problem* is usually defined as that of preventing programs communicating outward other than through authorized channels. This comes in several flavors. The goal may be to prevent active interference, such as memory overwriting, and to stop one process reading another's memory directly. This is what commercial operating systems set out to do. Military systems may also try to protect *metadata*—data about other data, subjects, or processes—so that, for example, a user can't find out which other users are logged on to the system or which processes they are running. In some applications, such as processing census data, confinement means allowing a program to read data but not release anything about it other than the results of certain constrained queries; this is covered further in Chapter 7.

Unless one uses sandboxing techniques (which are too restrictive for general programming environments), solving the confinement problem on a single processor means, at the very least, having a mechanism that will stop one program from overwriting another's code or data. There may be areas of memory that are shared in order to allow interprocess communication; but programs must be protected from accidental or deliberate modification, and they must have access to memory that is similarly protected.

This usually means that hardware access control must be integrated with the processor's memory management functions. A typical mechanism is *segment addressing*. Memory is addressed by two registers, a segment register that points to a segment of memory, and another address register that points to a location within that segment. The segment registers are controlled by the operating system, and often by a special component of it called the *reference monitor*, which links the access control mechanisms with the hardware.

The actual implementation has become more complex as the processors themselves have. Early IBM mainframes had a two-state CPU: the machine was either in authorized state or it was not. In the latter case, the program was restricted to a memory segment allocated by the operating system. In the former, it could alter the segment registers at will. An authorized program was one that was loaded from an authorized library.

Any desired access control policy can be implemented on top of this, given suitable authorized libraries, but this is not always efficient; and system security depends on keeping bad code (whether malicious or buggy) out of the authorized libraries. Later processors have offered more complex hardware mechanisms. Multics, an operating system developed at MIT in the 1960s and that inspired the development of Unix, introduced *rings of protection* which express differing levels of privilege: ring 0 programs had complete access to disk, supervisor states ran in ring 2, and user code at various less privileged levels [687]. Its features have to some extent been adopted in more recent processors, such as the Intel main processor line from the 80286 onward.

There are a number of general problems with interfacing hardware and software security mechanisms. For example, it often happens that a less privileged process such as application code needs to invoke a more privileged process such as a device driver.

The mechanisms for doing this need to be designed with some care, or security bugs can be expected. The IBM mainframe operating system MVS, for example, had a bug in which a program that executed a normal and an authorized task concurrently could make the former authorized too [493]. Also, performance may depend quite drastically on whether routines at different privilege levels are called by reference or by value [687].

4.3.1 Intel 80x86/Pentium Processors

Early Intel processors, such as the 8088/8086 used in early PCs, had no distinction between system and user mode, and thus no protection at all—any running program controlled the whole machine. The 80286 added protected segment addressing and rings, so for the first time it could run proper operating systems. The 80386 had built-in virtual memory and large enough memory segments (4 Gb) that they could be ignored and the machine treated as a 32-bit flat-address machine. The 486 and Pentium series chips added more performance (caches, out-of-order execution and MMX). The Pentium 3 finally added a new security feature—a processor serial number. This caused such a storm of protest, driven by privacy advocates who feared it could be used for all sorts of "big brother" purposes, that it will apparently be discontinued in future Pentium products. (But identifying a PC will remain easy, as there are many other serial numbers in disk controllers and other components that a snooping program can read.)

The rings of protection are supported by a number of mechanisms. The current privilege level can be changed only by a process in ring 0 (the kernel). Procedures cannot access objects in lower-level rings directly; but there are *gates* that allow execution of code at a different privilege level and that manage the supporting infrastructure, such as multiple stack segments for different privilege levels and exception handling. (For more details, see [404].)

The Pentium's successor architecture, the IA-64, was not yet available at the time of writing. According to the advance publicity, its memory management is based on dividing the virtual address space of each process into several *regions* whose identifiers specify the set of translations belonging to a process, and provide a unique intermediate virtual address. This is to help avoid thrashing problems in caches and in translation lookaside buffers. Regions also provide efficient shared areas between processes. Like the Pentium, the IA-64 has four protection rings [382].

4.3.2 ARM Processors

The ARM is the 32-bit processor core most commonly licensed to third-party vendors of embedded systems. The original ARM (which stood for Acorn Risc Machine) was the first commercial RISC design. Its modern day successors are important because they are incorporated in all sorts of security-sensitive applications from mobile phones to the Capstone chips used by the U.S. government to protect secret data. A fast multiply-and-accumulate instruction and low-power consumption make the ARM very attractive for embedded applications doing public key cryptography and/or signal processing. (The standard reference is [325].)

The ARM is licensed as a processor core, which chip designers can include in their products, plus a number of optional add-ons. The basic core contains separate banks of registers for user and system processes, plus a software-interrupt mechanism that puts the processor in supervisor mode and transfers control to a process at a fixed address. The core contains no memory management, so ARM-based designs can have their hardware protection extensively customized. A system control coprocessor is available to help with this. It can support domains of processes that have similar access rights (and thus share the same translation tables) but that retain some protection from each other. This enables fast context switching. Standard product ARM CPU chips, from the model 600 onward, have this memory support built in.

One version, the Amulet, uses self-timed logic. Eliminating the clock saves power and reduces RF interference, but makes it necessary to introduce hardware protection features, such as register locking, into the main processor itself so that contention between different hardware processes can be managed. This is an interesting example of protection techniques typical of an operating system being recycled in mainline processor design.

4.3.3 Security Processors

Some modern smartcards are based on ARM processors, and the preceding remarks apply (though memory limitations mean that only basic hardware protection may be used). But the great majority of the microprocessor smartcards in the field still have 8-bit processors. Some of them have memory management routines that let certain addresses be read only when passwords are entered into a register in the preceding few instructions. The goal is that the various principals with a stake in the card—perhaps a card manufacturer, an OEM, a network, and a bank—can all have their secrets on the card and yet be protected from each other. This may be a matter of software; but some cards have small, hardwired access control matrices to enforce this protection.

There are other kinds of specialized hardware security support for cryptography and access control. Some of the encryption devices used in banking to handle ATM PINs have an *authorized state*, which must be set (by two console passwords or a physical key) when PINs are to be printed. This enables a shift supervisor to control when this job is run. Similar devices are used by the military to distribute keys. We'll discuss cryptoprocessors in more detail in Chapter 14, "Physical Tamper Resistance."

4.3.4 Other Processors

Some research systems in the 1970s implemented very extensive security checking in the hardware, from Multics to various capability systems. Some systems have a *fence address*, a boundary in the hardware below which only the operating system has access. More recent work has looked at quality of service (QoS) issues, and for ways in which one can guarantee that no process will hog the CPU to the extent that other processes are blocked. Such mechanisms are now starting to be introduced commercially ('Quality of Service Technology is promised by Microsoft for 'the Win2K timeframe'.) The interaction of such features with access control and protection generally is one of the things to watch out for in the future.

4.4 What Goes Wrong

Popular operating systems such as Unix / Linux and Windows are very large and complex, so they have many bugs. They are used in a huge range of systems, so their features are tested daily by millions of users under very diverse of circumstances. Consequently, many of the bugs are found and reported. Thanks to the Net, knowledge spreads widely and rapidly. Thus, at any one time, there may be dozens of security flaws that are known and for which attack scripts may be circulating on the Net. Until recently, this problem was limited. The banking industry used mainframes that ran less widely understood operating systems, while the military used custom "multilevel secure" operating systems, which were not available to outsiders at all. Nowadays, both of these industries are being forced by cost pressures to adopt commodity operating systems, so the publication of attack scripts has the potential to undermine a great range of systems.

The usual goal of an attacker is to get a normal account on the system and then become the system administrator, in order to take over the system completely. A surprising number of operating system bugs allow the transition from user to root. Such flaws can be classified in a number of ways, such as by the type of programming error, by the stage in the development process at which it was introduced, or by the level in the system at which things go wrong [493]. The failure might not even be in the technical implementation, but in the higher-level design. The user interface might induce people to mismanage access rights or do other stupid things that cause the access control to be bypassed (see Section 4.4.3 for some examples).

In general, the higher in a system we build the protection mechanisms, the more complex they'll be, the more other software they'll rely on, and the closer they'll be to the error-prone mark 1 human being, thus, the less dependable they are likely to be.

4.4.1 Smashing the Stack

Many, if not most, of the technical attacks on operating systems that are reported in *Computer Emergency Response Team* (CERT) bulletins and security mailing lists involve memory-overwriting attacks, colloquially known as "smashing the stack" (see Figure 4.6).

Programmers are often careless about checking the size of arguments. A classic example was a vulnerability in the Unix `finger` command. A widespread implementation of this would accept an argument of any length, although only 256 bytes had been allocated for this argument by the program. The result was that when an attacker used the command with a longer argument, the trailing bytes of the argument ended up being executed by the CPU.

The usual technique is to arrange for the trailing bytes of the argument to have a *landing pad*, a long space of *no-operation* (NOP) commands or other register commands that don't change the control flow, and whose task is to catch the processor if it executes any of them. The landing pad delivers the processor to the attack code, which will do something like creating a root account with no password or starting a shell with administrative privilege directly.

Many of the vulnerabilities reported routinely by CERT and bugtraq are variants on this theme. There is really no excuse for the problem to continue, as it has been well

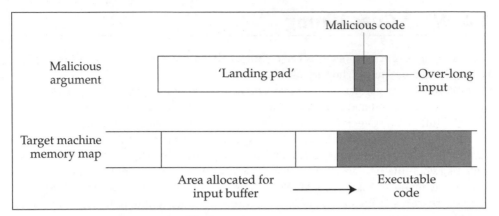

Figure 4.6   Stack Smashing Attack.

known for a generation. Most of the early 1960s time-sharing systems suffered from it, and fixed it [349]. Penetration analysis efforts at the System Development Corporation in the early 1970s showed that the problem of "unexpected parameters" was still one of the most frequently used attack strategies [503]. Intel's 80286 processor introduced explicit parameter-checking instructions—verify read, verify write, and verify length—in 1982, but they were avoided by most software designers to prevent architecture dependencies. In 1988, large numbers of Unix computers were brought down simultaneously by the "Internet worm," which used the `finger` vulnerability just described, and thus brought memory-overwriting attacks to the notice of the mass media [724]. Yet programmers still don't check the size of arguments, and holes continue to be found. The attack isn't even limited to networked computer systems: at least one smartcard could be defeated by passing it a message longer than its programmer had anticipated.

A recent survey paper describes memory-overwriting attacks as the "attack of the decade" [207].

4.4.2 Other Technical Attacks

After memory-overwriting attacks, *race conditions* are probably next. These are where a transaction is carried out in two or more stages, and it is possible for someone to alter it after the stage that involves verifying access rights.

For example, the Unix command to create a directory, `mkdir`, formerly worked in two steps: the storage was allocated, then ownership was transferred to the user. Since these steps were separate, a user could initiate a `mkdir` in background; and if this completed only the first step before being suspended, a second process could be used to replace the newly created directory with a link to the password file. Then the original process would resume, and change ownership of the password file to the user. The `/tmp` directory, used for temporary files, can often be abused in this way; the trick is to wait until an application run by a privileged user writes a file here, then change it to a symbolic link to another file somewhere else—which will be removed when the privileged user's application tries to delete the temporary file.

A wide variety of other bugs have enabled users to assume root status and take over the system. For example, the PDP-10 TENEX operating system had the bug that the program address could overflow into the next bit of the process state word, which was the privilege-mode bit; this meant that a program overflow could put a program in supervisor state. In another example, some Unix implementations had the feature that if a user tried to execute the command su when the maximum number of files were open, then su was unable to open the password file, and responded by giving the user root status.

There have also been a number of bugs that allowed service denial attacks. For example, Multics had a global limit on the number of files that could be open at once, but no local limits. A user could exhaust this limit and lock the system so that not even the administrator could log on [493]. And until the late 1990s, most implementations of the Internet protocols allocated a fixed amount of buffer space to process the SYN packets with which TCP/IP connections are initiated. The result was *SYN flooding attacks*. By sending a large number of SYN packets, an attacker could exhaust the available buffer space and prevent the machine accepting any new connections. This is now fixed using *syncookies*, discussed in Chapter 18, in Part 2.

4.4.3 User Interface Failures

One of the earliest attacks to be devised was the *Trojan Horse*, a program that the administrator is invited to run and that will do some harm if he does so. People would write games that checked occasionally whether the player was the system administrator, and if so would create another administrator account with a known password.

Another trick is to write a program that has the same name as a commonly used system utility, such as the ls command which lists all the files in a Unix directory, and design it to abuse the administrator privilege (if any) before invoking the genuine utility. The next step is to complain to the administrator that something is wrong with this directory. When the administrator enters the directory and types ls to see what's there, the damage is done. The fix is simple: an administrator's PATH variable (the list of directories that will be searched for a suitably named program when a command is invoked) shouldn't contain '.' (the symbol for the current directory). Recent Unix versions are shipped with this as a default; but it's still an unnecessary trap for the unwary.

Perhaps the most serious example of user interface failure, in terms of the number of systems at risk, is in Windows NT. In this operating system, a user must be the system administrator to install anything. This might be useful, as a configuration option, to prevent staff in a bank branch from running games on their PCs at lunchtime, and picking up viruses. However, most environments are much less controlled, and people need to be able to install software to get their work done. In practice, this means that millions of people have administrator privileges who shouldn't need them, and are vulnerable to attacks in which malicious code simply pops up a box telling them to do something. Microsoft's response to this has been the one-way trust mechanism already discussed, which makes it possible to configure systems so that people can administer their own machines without having too much power to damage other IT resources in the company. However, this requires some care to implement properly. It also provides no protection where applications such as Web servers must run as root, are visible to the outside world, and contain software bugs that enable them to be taken over.

Another example, which might be argued is an interface failure, comes from the use of active content of various kinds such as ActiveX controls. These can be a menace because users have no intuitively clear way of controlling them, and they can be used to launch serious attacks. Even Java, for all its supposed security, has suffered a number of attacks that exploited careless implementations [226]. However, many people (and many companies) are unwilling to forgo the bells and whistles that active content can provide.

4.4.4 Why So Many Things Go Wrong

We've already mentioned the basic problems faced by operating system security designers: their products are huge and therefore buggy, and are tested by large numbers of users in parallel, some of whom will publicize their discoveries rather than reporting them to the vendor. There are other structural problems, too.

One of the more serious causes of failure is *kernel bloat*. Under Unix, all device drivers, filesystems, and so on must be in the kernel. The Windows 2000 kernel contains drivers for a large number of smartcards, card readers, and the like, many of which were written by equipment vendors. So large quantities of code are trusted, in that they are put inside the security perimeter. It can't really be a good idea for software companies to enable so many of their suppliers to break their systems, whether on purpose or accidentally. Some other systems, such as MVS, introduced mechanisms that decrease the level of trust needed by many utilities. However, the means to do this in the most common operating systems are few and relatively nonstandard.

Even more seriously, application developers often make their programs run as root. This may be easier, as it avoids permission problems. It also often introduces horrible vulnerabilities where more limited privilege could have been used with only a modicum of thought and a minor redesign. There are many systems—such as lpr/lpd, the Unix lineprinter subsystem—that do not need to run as root but do anyway on most systems. This has also been a source of security failures in the past (e.g., getting the printer to spool to the password file).

Some applications need a certain amount of privilege. For example, mail delivery agents must be able to deal with user mailboxes. But while a prudent designer would restrict this privilege to a small part of the application, most agents are written so that the whole program needs to run as root. The classic example is sendmail, which has a long history of serious security holes; but many other MTAs also have problems. The general effect is that a bug that ought to compromise only one person's mail may end up giving root privilege to an outside attacker.

Sometimes the cure is almost as bad as the disease. Some programmers avoid *root bloat* and the difficulty of getting non-root software installed and working securely by leaving important shared data structures and resources accessible to all users. Many systems store mail in a file per user in a world-writeable directory, which makes mail forgery easy. The Unix file utmp—the list of users logged in—is frequently used for security checking of various kinds, but is also frequently world-writeable! This should have been built as a service rather than a file, but fixing problems like these once the initial design decisions have been made can be difficult.

4.4.5 Remedies

Some classes of vulnerability can be fixed using automatic tools. Stack-overwriting attacks, for example, are largely due to the lack of proper bounds checking in C (the language most commonly used to write operating systems). Various tools are available on the Net for checking C programs for potential problems; there is even a compiler patch called StackGuard, which puts a *canary* next to the return address on the stack. This can be a random 32-bit value chosen when the program is started, and checked when a function is torn down. If the stack has been overwritten meanwhile, then with high probability the canary will change [207].

But, in general, much more effort needs to be put into design, coding, and testing. Rather than overusing powerful tools such as `setuid` in Unix and administrator privilege in NT, designers should create groups with limited powers, and be clear about what the compromise of that group should mean for the rest of the system. Programs should have only as much privilege as necessary: the *principle of least privilege* [662].

Software should also be designed so that the default configuration, and in general, the easiest way of doing something, is safe. But, many systems are shipped with dangerous defaults.

Finally, there's a contrarian view, of which you should be aware, as it's held by some senior Microsoft people: that access control doesn't matter. Computers are becoming single-purpose or single-user devices. Single-purpose devices, such as Web servers that deliver a single service, don't need much in the way of access control as there's nothing for operating system access controls to do; the job of separating users from each other is best left to the application code. As for the PC on your desk, if all the software on it comes from a single source, then again there's no need for the operating system to provide separation [588]. Not everyone agrees with this: the NSA view is at the other extreme, with deep distrust of application-level security and heavy emphasis on using the mechanisms of trusted operating systems [510]. But one way or another, it's remarkable how little effective use is made of the access control mechanisms shipped with modern operating systems.

4.4.6 Environmental Creep

I have pointed out repeatedly that many security failures result from environmental change undermining a security model. Mechanisms that were adequate in a restricted environment often fail in a more general one.

Access control mechanisms are no exception. Unix, for example, was originally designed as a "single-user Multics" (hence the name). It then became an operating system to be used by a number of skilled and trustworthy people in a laboratory who were sharing a single machine. In this environment, the function of the security mechanisms is primarily to contain mistakes, to prevent one user's typing errors or program crashes from deleting or overwriting another user's files. The original security mechanisms were quite adequate for this purpose.

But Unix security became a classic "success disaster." Unix was repeatedly extended without proper consideration being given to how the protection mechanisms also needed to be extended. The Berkeley extensions (`rsh`, `rhosts`, etc.) were based on an extension from a single machine to a network of machines that were all on one LAN and all under one management. Mechanisms such as `rhosts` were based on a tuple *(username,hostname)* rather than just a user name, and saw the beginning of the transfer of trust.

The Internet mechanisms (telnet, ftp, DNS, SMTP), which grew out of Arpanet in the 1970s, were written for mainframes on what was originally a secure WAN. Mainframes were autonomous, the network was outside the security protocols, and there was no transfer of authorization. Remote authentication, which the Berkeley model was starting to make prudent, was simply not supported. The Sun contributions (NFS, NIS, RPC, etc.) were based on a workstation model of the universe, with a multiple LAN environment with distributed management, but still usually in a single organization. (A proper tutorial on topics such as DNS and NFS is beyond the scope of this book, but there is some more detailed background material in Chapter 18, "Network Attack and Defense," Section 18.2.)

Mixing all these different models of computation together has resulted in chaos. Some of their initial assumptions still apply partially, but none of them applies globally any more. The Internet now has hundreds of millions of PCs and workstations, millions of LANs, thousands of interconnected WANs, and managements that are not just independent but may be in conflict (including nation states and substate groups at war with each other). Many workstations have no management at all.

Users, instead of being trustworthy but occasionally incompetent, are now largely incompetent—but some are both competent and hostile. Code used to be simply buggy—but now there is a significant amount of malicious code out there. Attacks on communications networks used to be the purview of national intelligence agencies—now they can be done by *script kiddies*, a term used to refer to relatively unskilled people who have downloaded attack tools from the Net and launched them without any real idea of how they work.

Unix and Internet security gives us yet another example of a system that started out reasonably well designed but that was undermined by a changing environment.

Win2K and its predecessors in the NT product series have more extensive protection mechanisms than Unix, but have been around for much less time. Realistically, all we can say is that the jury is still out.

4.5 Summary

Access control mechanisms operate at a number of levels in a system, from applications down through the operating system to the hardware. Higher-level mechanisms can be more expressive, but also tend to be more vulnerable to attack, for a variety of reasons ranging from intrinsic complexity to implementer skill levels. Most attacks involve the opportunistic exploitation of bugs; and software that is very large, very widely used, or both (as with operating systems) is particularly likely to have security bugs found and publicized. Operating systems are also vulnerable to environmental changes that undermine the assumptions used in their design.

The main function of access control in computer operating systems is to limit the damage that can be done by particular groups, users, and programs whether through error or malice. The most important fielded examples are Unix and NT, which are similar in many respects, though NT is more expressive. Access control is also an important part of the design of special-purpose hardware such as smartcards and other encryption devices. New techniques are being developed to cope with object-oriented systems and mobile code. But implementation remains generally awful.

The general concepts of access control from read, write, and execute permissions to groups and roles will crop up again and again. In some distributed systems, they may not be immediately obvious, as the underlying mechanisms can be quite different. An example comes from public key infrastructures, which are a reimplementation of an old access control concept, the capability.

Research Problems

Most of the issues in access control were identified by the 1960s or early 1970s, and were worked out on experimental systems such as Multics [687] and the CAP [804]. Much of the research in access control systems since has involved reworking the basic themes in new contexts, such as object-oriented systems and mobile code.

A recent thread of research is how to combine access control with the admission control mechanisms used to provide quality of service guaranteed in multimedia operating systems. Another topic is how to implement and manage access control efficiently in large complex systems, using techniques such as roles.

Further Reading

The best textbook to use for a more detailed introduction to access control issues is Dieter Gollmann's *Computer Security* [344]. A technical report from U.S. Navy Labs gives a useful reference to many of the flaws found in operating systems over the last 30 years or so [493]. One of the earliest reports on the subject (and indeed on computer security in general) is by Willis Ware [791]. One of the most influential early papers is by Jerry Saltzer and Mike Schroeder [662]; Butler Lampson's influential paper on the confinement problem is at [488].

The classic description of Unix security is in the paper by Fred Grampp and Bob Morris [350]. The most comprehensive textbook on this subject is Simson Garfinkel and Gene Spafford's *Practical Unix and Internet Security* [331]; the classic on the Internet side of things is Bill Cheswick and Steve Bellovin's *Firewalls and Internet Security* [94], with many examples of network attacks on Unix systems.

The protection mechanisms of Windows NT4 are described briefly in Gollmann, but much more thoroughly in Karanjit Siyan's reference book, *Windows NT Server 4* [711]. For Win2K, I've used the Microsoft online documentation; no doubt a number of textbooks will appear very soon. There is a history of microprocessor architectures at [79], and a reference book for Java security written by its architect Li Gong [346].

All these topics are fast-moving; the attacks that are making the headlines change significantly (at least in their details) from one year to the next. To keep up, you should not just read textbooks, but follow the latest notices from CERT, and mailing lists such as bugtraq.

CHAPTER

5

Cryptography

ZHQM ZMGM ZMFM

—G. JULIUS CAESAR

XYAWO GAOOA GPEMO HPQCW IPNLG RPIXL TXLOA NNYCS YXBOY
MNBIN YOBTY QYNAI

—JOHN F. KENNEDY

5.1 Introduction

Cryptography is where security engineering meets mathematics. It provides us with the tools that underlie most modern security protocols. It is probably the key enabling technology for protecting distributed systems, yet it is surprisingly hard to do right. As we've already seen in Chapter 2, "Protocols," cryptography has often been used to protect the wrong things, or used to protect them in the wrong way. We'll see plenty more examples when we start looking in detail at real applications.

Unfortunately, the computer security and cryptology communities have drifted apart over the last 20 years. Security people don't always understand the available crypto tools, and crypto people don't always understand the real-world problems. There are a number of reasons for this, such as different professional backgrounds (computer science versus mathematics) and different research funding (governments have tried to promote computer security research while suppressing cryptography). It reminds me of a story told by a medical friend. While she was young, she worked for a few years in a country where, for economic reasons, they'd shortened their medical degrees and concentrated on producing specialists as quickly as possible. One day, a patient who'd had both kidneys removed and was awaiting a transplant needed her dialysis shunt redone. The surgeon sent the patient back from the theater on the grounds that there was no urinalysis on file. It just didn't occur to him that a patient with no kidneys couldn't produce any urine.

Just as a doctor needs to understand physiology as well as surgery, so a security engineer needs to be familiar with cryptology as well as computer security (and much else). This chapter is aimed at people without a training in cryptology; cryptologists will find little in it which they don't already know. As I only have a few dozen pages, and a proper exposition of modern cryptography would run into thousands, I won't go into much of the mathematics (there are plenty books that do that; see the end of the chapter for further reading). I'll just explain the basic intuitions and constructions that seem to cause the most confusion. If you have to use cryptography in anything resembling a novel way, then I strongly recommend that you read a lot more about it.

Computer security people often ask for non-mathematical definitions of cryptographic terms. The basic terminology is that *cryptography* refers to the science and art of designing ciphers; *cryptanalysis* to the science and art of breaking them; while *cryptology*, often shortened to just *crypto*, is the study of both. The input to an encryption process is commonly called the *plaintext*, and the output the *ciphertext*. Thereafter, things get somewhat more complicated. There are a number of *cryptographic primitives*—basic building blocks, such as *block ciphers*, *stream ciphers*, and *hash functions*. Block ciphers may either have one key for both encryption and decryption, in which case they're called *shared key* (also *secret key* or *symmetric*), or have separate keys for encryption and decryption, in which case they're called *public key* or *asymmetric*. A *digital signature scheme* is a special type of asymmetric crypto primitive.

In the rest of this chapter, I will first give some simple historical examples to illustrate the basic concepts. I'll then try to fine-tune definitions by introducing the *random oracle model*, which many cryptologists use. Finally, I'll show how some of the more important cryptographic algorithms actually work, and how they can be used to protect data.

5.2 Historical Background

Suetonius tells us that Julius Caesar enciphered his dispatches by writing D for A, E for B and so on [742]. When Augustus Caesar ascended the throne, he changed the imperial cipher system so that C was now written for A, D for B, and so on. In modern terminology, we would say that he changed the key from D to C.

The Arabs generalized this idea to the monoalphabetic substitution, in which a keyword is used to permute the cipher alphabet. We will write the plaintext in lowercase letters, and the ciphertext in uppercase, as shown in Figure 5.1.

OYAN RWSGKFR AN AH RHTFANY MSOYRM OYSH SMSEAC NCMAKO; but breaking ciphers of this kind is a straightforward pencil and paper puzzle, which you may have done in primary school. The trick is that some letters, and combinations of letters, are much more common than others; in English the most common letters are e, t, a, i, o,

```
abcdefghijklmnopqrstuvwxyz
SECURITYABDFGHJKLMNOPQVWXZ
```

Figure 5.1   Monoalphabetic substitution cipher.

n, s, h, r, d, l, u in that order. Artificial intelligence researchers have shown some interest in writing programs to solve monoalphabetic substitutions; using letter and digram (letter-pair) frequencies alone. They typically succeed with about 600 letters of ciphertext, while smarter strategies, such as guessing probable words, can cut this to about 150 letters. A human cryptanalyst will usually require much less.

There are basically two ways to make a stronger cipher: the *stream cipher* and the *block cipher*. In the former, you make the encryption rule depend on a plaintext symbol's position in the stream of plaintext symbols, while in the latter you encrypt several plaintext symbols at once in a block. Let's look at early examples.

5.2.1 An Early Stream Cipher: The Vigenère

An early stream cipher is commonly ascribed to the Frenchman Blaise de Vigenère, a diplomat who served King Charles IX. It works by adding a key repeatedly into the plaintext using the convention that $A = 0$, $B = 1, \ldots, Z = 25$; and addition is carried out modulo 26—that is, if the result is greater than 25, we subtract as many multiples of 26 as are needed to bring us into the range $[0, \ldots, 25]$, that is, $[A, \ldots, Z]$. Mathematicians write this as:

$$C = P + K \bmod 26$$

For example, when we add $P(15)$ to $U(20)$ we get 35, which we reduce to 9 by subtracting 26; 9 corresponds to J, so the encryption of P under the key U (and of U under the key P) is J. In this notation, Julius Caesar's system used a fixed key, $K = D$ (modulo 23, as the alphabet Caesar used wrote U as V, J as I, and had no W), while Augustus Caesar's used $K = C$, and Vigenère used a repeating key, also known as a *running key*. Various means were developed to do this addition quickly, including printed tables and, for field use, cipher wheels. Whatever the implementation technology, the encryption using a repeated keyword for the key would look as shown in Figure 5.2.

A number of people appear to have worked out how to solve polyalphabetic ciphers, from the notorious womanizer Casanova to computing pioneer Charles Babbage. However, the first published solution was in 1863 by Friedrich Kasiski, a Prussian infantry officer [441]. He noticed that given a long enough piece of ciphertext, repeated patterns will appear at multiples of the keyword length.

In Figure 5.2, for example, we see "KIOV" repeated after nine letters, and "NU" after six. Since three divides both six and nine, we might guess a keyword of three letters. It follows that ciphertext letters one, four, seven, and so on all enciphered under the same keyletter; so we can use frequency analysis techniques to guess the most likely values of this letter, then repeat the process for the second and third letters of the key.

Plain:	tobeornottobethatisthequestion
Key:	runrunrunrunrunrunrunrunrunrun
Cipher:	KIOVIEEIGKIOVNURNVJNUVKHVMGZIA

Figure 5.2 A Vigenère polyalphabetic substitution cipher.

5.2.2 The One-Time Pad

One way to make a stream cipher of this type proof against attacks is for the key sequence to be as long as the plaintext, and to never repeat. This was proposed by Gilbert Vernam during World War I [428]; its effect is that given any ciphertext, and any plaintext of the same length, there is a key that decrypts the ciphertext to the plaintext. Regardless of the amount of computation that opponents can do, they are none the wiser, as all possible plaintexts are just as likely. This system is known as the *one-time pad*. Leo Marks' engaging book on cryptography in the Special Operations Executive in World War II [523] relates how one-time key material was printed on silk, which agents could conceal inside their clothing; whenever a key had been used, it was torn off and burned.

An example should explain all this. Suppose you had intercepted a message from a wartime German agent, which you knew started with "Heil Hitler," and that the first 10 letters of ciphertext were DGTYI BWPJA. This means that the first 10 letters of the one-time pad were wclnb tdefj, as shown in Figure 5.3.

Once he had burned the piece of silk with his key material, the spy could claim that he was actually a member of the anti-Nazi underground resistance, and that the message actually said "Hang Hitler." This is quite possible, as the key material could just as easily have been wggsbtdefj, as shown in Figure 5.4.

Now, we rarely get anything for nothing in cryptology, and the price of the perfect secrecy of the one-time pad is that it fails completely to protect message integrity. Suppose that you wanted to get this spy into trouble; you could change the ciphertext to DCYTI BWPJA, as shown in Figure 5.5.

During the World War II, Claude Shannon proved that a cipher has perfect secrecy if and only if there are as many possible keys as possible plaintexts, and if every key is equally likely; therefore, the one-time pad is the only kind of system that offers perfect secrecy [694, 695].

```
Plain:   heilhitler
Key:     wclnbtdefj
Cipher:  DGTYIBWPJA
```

Figure 5.3   A spy's message.

```
Cipher:  DGTYIBWPJA
Key:     wggsbtdefj
Plain:   hanghitler
```

Figure 5.4   What the spy claimed he said.

```
Cipher:  DCYTIBWPJA
Key:     wclnbtdefj
Plain:   hanghitler
```

Figure 5.5   Manipulating the message in Figure 5.3 to entrap the spy.

The one-time pad is still used for high-level diplomatic and intelligence traffic, but it consumes as much key material as there is traffic, hence is too expensive for most applications. It's more common for stream ciphers to use a suitable pseudorandom number generator to expand a short key into a long keystream. The data is then encrypted by exclusive-or'ing the keystream, one bit at a time, with the data. It's not enough for the keystream to appear "random" in the sense of passing the standard series randomness tests; it also must have the property that an opponent who gets their hands on even a number of keystream bits should not be able to predict any more of them. I'll formalize this more tightly in the next section.

Stream ciphers are commonly used nowadays in hardware applications where the number of gates has to be minimized to save power. We'll look at some actual designs in later chapters, including the A5 algorithm used to encipher GSM mobile phone traffic (in Chapter 17, "Telecom System Security"), and the multiplex shift register system used in pay-per-view TV (in Chapter 20, "Copyright and Privacy Protection"). However, block ciphers are more suited for many applications where encryption is done in software, so let's look at them next.

5.2.3 An Early Block Cipher: Playfair

One of the best-known early block ciphers is the Playfair system. It was invented in 1854 by Sir Charles Wheatstone, a telegraph pioneer who also invented the concertina and the Wheatstone bridge. The reason it's not called the Wheatstone cipher is that he demonstrated it to Baron Playfair, a politician; Playfair in turn demonstrated it to Prince Albert and to Lord Palmerston (later Prime Minister) on a napkin after dinner.

This cipher uses a 5 by 5 grid, in which the alphabet is placed, permuted by the keyword, and omitting the letter J (see Figure 5.6).

The plaintext is first conditioned by replacing J with I wherever it occurs, then dividing it into letter pairs, preventing double letters occurring in a pair by separating them with an x, and finally adding a z if necessary to complete the last letter pair. The example Playfair wrote on his napkin was "Lord Granville's letter," which becomes "`lo rd gr an vi lx le sl et te rz.`"

It is then enciphered two letters at a time using the following rules:

- If two letters are in the same row or column, they are replaced by the succeeding letters. For example, "`am`" enciphers to "`LE`."

- Otherwise, the two letters stand at two of the corners of a rectangle in the table, and we replace them with the letters at the other two corners of this rectangle. For example, "`lo`" enciphers to "`MT`."

P	A	L	M	E
R	S	T	O	N
B	C	D	F	G
H	I	K	Q	U
V	W	X	Y	Z

Figure 5.6 The Playfair enciphering tableau.

Plain:	lo rd gr an vi lx le sl et te rz
Cipher:	MT TB BN ES WH TL MP TA LN NL NV

Figure 5.7 Example of Playfair enciphering.

We can now encipher our specimen text as shown in Figure 5.7.

Variants of this cipher were used by the British army as a field cipher in World War I, and by the Americans and Germans in World War II. It's a substantial improvement on Vigenère, as the statistics an analyst can collect are of *digraphs* (letter pairs) rather than single letters, so the distribution is much flatter, and more ciphertext is needed for an attack.

Again, it's not enough for the output of a block cipher to just look intuitively "random." Playfair ciphertexts do look random, but they have the property that if you change a single letter of a plaintext pair, then often only a single letter of the ciphertext will change. Thus, using the key in Figure 5.7, it enciphers to TB while rf enciphers to OB and rg enciphers to NB. One consequence is that, given enough ciphertext or a few probable words, the table (or an equivalent one) can be reconstructed [326]. We will want the effects of small changes in a block cipher's input to diffuse completely through its output: changing one input bit should, on average, cause half of the output bits to change. I'll tighten these ideas up in the next section.

The security of a block cipher can be greatly improved by choosing a longer block length than two characters. For example, the *Data Encryption Standard* (DES), which is widely used in banking, has a block length of 64 bits, which equates to eight ASCII characters and the Advanced Encryption Standard (AES), which is replacing it in many applications, has a block length of twice this. I discuss the internal details of DES and AES below; for the time being, I'll just remark that an eight byte or sixteen byte block size is not enough of itself. For example, if a bank account number always appears at the same place in a transaction format, then it's likely to produce the same ciphertext every time a transaction involving it is encrypted with the same key. This could allow an opponent who can eavesdrop on the line to monitor a customer's transaction pattern; it might also be exploited by an opponent to cut and paste parts of a ciphertext in order to produce a seemingly genuine but unauthorized transaction. Unless the block is as large as the message, the ciphertext will contain more than one block, and we will look later at ways of binding them together.

5.2.4 One-Way Functions

The third classical type of cipher is the *one-way function*. This evolved to protect the integrity and authenticity of messages, which as we've seen is not protected at all by many simple ciphers, where it is often easy to manipulate the ciphertext in such a way as to cause a predictable change in the plaintext.

After the invention of the telegraph in the mid-nineteenth century, banks rapidly became its main users, and developed systems for transferring money electronically. Of course, it isn't the money itself that is "wired," but a payment instruction, such as:

To Lombard Bank, London. Please pay from our account with you no. 1234567890 the sum of £1000 to John Smith of 456 Chesterton Road, who has an account with

HSBC Bank Cambridge no. 301234 4567890123, and notify him that this was for "wedding present from Doreen Smith." From First Cowboy Bank of Santa Barbara, CA, USA. Charges to be paid by us.

Since telegraph messages were relayed from one office to another by human operators, it was possible for an operator to manipulate a payment message.

Banks, telegraph companies, and shipping companies developed *code books*, which not only could protect transactions, but also shorten them—which was very important given the costs of international telegrams at the time. A code book was essentially a block cipher that mapped words or phrases to fixed-length groups of letters or numbers. Thus, "Please pay from our account with you no" might become "AFVCT." A competing technology was *rotor machines*, mechanical cipher devices that produce a very long sequence of pseudorandom numbers, and combine them with plaintext to get ciphertext; these were independently invented by a number of people, many of whom dreamed of making a fortune selling them to the banking industry. Banks weren't in general interested, but rotor machines became the main high-level ciphers used by the combatants in World War II.

The banks realized that neither mechanical stream ciphers nor code books protected message authenticity. If, for example, the codeword for 1000 is mauve and for 1,000,000 is magenta, then the crooked telegraph clerk who can compare the coded traffic with known transactions should be able to figure this out and substitute one for the other.

The critical innovation was to use a code book, but make the coding one-way by adding the code groups together into a number called a *test key*. (Modern cryptographers would describe it as a *hash value* or *message authentication code*, terms I'll define more carefully later.)

Here is a simple example. Suppose that the bank has a code book with a table of numbers corresponding to payment amounts, as in Figure 5.8. In order to authenticate a transaction for $376,514, we add 53 (no millions), 54 (300,000), 29 (70,000) and 71 (6,000). (It's common to ignore the less significant digits of the amount.) This gives us a test key of 217.

Most real systems were more complex than this; they usually had tables for currency codes, dates, and even recipient account numbers. In the better systems, the code groups were four digits long rather than two; and to make it harder for an attacker to reconstruct the tables, the test keys were compressed: a key of 7549 might become 23 by adding the first and second digits, and the third and fourth digits, and ignoring the carry.

Test keys are not strong by the standards of modern cryptography. Given somewhere between a few dozen and a few hundred tested messages, depending on the design details, a patient analyst could reconstruct enough of the tables to forge a transaction. With a few carefully chosen messages inserted into the banking system by an

	0	1	2	3	4	5	6	7	8	9
x 1000	14	22	40	87	69	93	71	35	06	58
x 10,000	73	38	15	46	91	82	00	29	64	57
x 100,000	95	70	09	54	82	63	21	47	36	18
x 1,000,000	53	77	66	29	40	12	31	05	87	94

Figure 5.8 A simple test key system.

accomplice, it's even easier still. But the banks got away with it: test keys worked fine from the late nineteenth century through the 1980s. In several years working as a bank security consultant, and listening to elderly bank auditors' tales over lunch, I only heard of two cases of fraud that exploited it: one external attempt involving cryptanalysis, which failed because the attacker didn't understand bank procedures, and one successful but small fraud involving a crooked staff member. I'll explain the systems that replaced test keys, and cover the whole issue of how to tie cryptographic authentication mechanisms to procedural protection such as dual control, in Chapter 9, "Banking and Bookkeeping." For now, test keys are the classic example of a one-way function used for authentication.

Later examples included functions for applications discussed in the previous chapters, such as storing passwords in a one-way encrypted password file, and computing a response from a challenge in an authentication protocol.

5.2.5 Asymmetric Primitives

Finally, some modern cryptosystems are asymmetric, in that different keys are used for encryption and decryption. For example, I publish on my Web page a *public key* with which people can encrypt messages to send to me; I can then decrypt them using the corresponding *private key*.

There are some precomputer examples of this too; perhaps the best is the postal service. You can send me a private message simply by addressing it to me and dropping it into a post box. Once that's done, I should be the only person who'll be able to read it. There are, of course, many things that can go wrong. You might get my address wrong (whether by error or as a result of deception); the police might get a warrant to open my mail; the letter might be stolen by a dishonest postman; a fraudster might redirect my mail without my knowledge; or a thief might steal the letter from my mailbox. Similar things can go wrong with public key cryptography. False public keys can be inserted into the system; computers can be hacked; people can be coerced; and so on. We'll look at these problems in more detail in later chapters.

Another asymmetric application of cryptography is the *digital signature*. The idea here is that I can sign a message using a *private signature key*, then anybody can check this using my *public signature verification key*. Again, there are precomputer analogues in the form of manuscript signatures and seals; and again, there is a remarkably similar litany of things that can go wrong, both with the old way of doing things and with the new.

5.3 The Random Oracle Model

Before delving into the detailed design of modern ciphers, I want to take a few pages to refine the definitions of the various types of cipher. (Readers who are phobic about theoretical computer science should skip this section at a first pass; I've included it because a basic understanding of random oracles is needed to understand many recent research papers on cryptography.)

The random oracle model seeks to formalize the idea that a cipher is "good" if, when viewed in a suitable way, it is indistinguishable from a random function of a certain type. I will call a cryptographic primitive *pseudorandom* if it passes all the statistical and other tests that a random function of the appropriate type would pass, in whichever model of computation we are using. Of course, the cryptographic primitive will actually be an algorithm, implemented as an array of gates in hardware or a program in software; but the outputs should "look random" by being distinguishable from a suitable random oracle given the type and the number of tests that our computation model permits.

In this way, we can hope to separate the problem of designing ciphers from the problem of using them correctly. Mathematicians who design ciphers can provide evidence that their cipher is pseudorandom. Quite separately, a computer scientist who has designed a cryptographic protocol can try to prove that it is secure on the assumption that the crypto primitives used to implement it are pseudorandom. The process isn't infallible, as we saw with proofs of protocol correctness. Theorems can have bugs, just like programs; the problem could be idealized wrongly; or the mathematicians might be using a different model of computation from the computer scientists. But at least some progress can be made.

You can visualize a random oracle as an elf sitting in a black box with a source of physical randomness and some means of storage (see Figure 5.9)—represented in the figure by the dice and the scroll. The elf will accept inputs of a certain type, then look in the scroll to see whether this query has ever been answered before. If so, it will give the answer it finds there; if not, it will generate an answer at random by throwing the dice. We'll further assume that there is some kind of bandwidth limitation—that the elf will answer only so many queries every second. This ideal will turn out to be useful as a way of refining our notions of a stream cipher, a hash function, a block cipher, a public key encryption algorithm and a digital signature scheme.

Finally, we can get a useful simplification of our conceptual model by noting that encryption can be used to protect data across time as well as across distance. A good example is when we encrypt data before storing it with a third-party backup service, and may decrypt it later if we have to recover from a disk crash. In this case, we need only a single encryption/decryption device, rather than one at each end of a communications

Figure 5.9 The random oracle.

link. This is the sort of application we will be modelling here. The user takes a diskette to the cipher machine, types in a key, issues an instruction, and the data get transformed in the appropriate way.

Let's look at this model in more detail for these different cryptographic primitives.

5.3.1 Random Functions: Hash Functions

The first type of random oracle is the *random function*. A random function accepts an input string of any length, and outputs a random string of fixed length, say n bits long. So the elf just has a simple list of inputs and outputs, which grows steadily as it works. (We'll ignore any effects of the size of the scroll and assume that all queries are answered in constant time.)

Random functions are our model for *one-way functions* or *cryptographic hash functions*, which have many practical uses. They were first used in computer systems for one-way encryption of passwords in the 1960s and—as mentioned in Chapter 2—are used today in a number of authentication systems. They are also used to compute *message digests*; given a message M, we can pass it through a pseudorandom function to get a digest, say $h(M)$, which can stand in for the message in various applications. One example is a digital signature: signature algorithms tend to be slow if the message is long, so it's usually convenient to sign a message digest rather than the message itself.

Another application is timestamping. If we want evidence that we possessed a given electronic document by a certain date, we might submit it to an online timestamping service. However, if the document is still secret—for example an invention that we plan to patent, and for which we merely want to establish a priority date—then we might not send the timestamping service the whole document, but just the message digest.

The output of the hash function is known as the *hash value* or *message digest*; an input corresponding to a given hash value is its *preimage*; the verb *to hash* is used to refer to computation of the hash value. Colloquially, the *hash* is also used as a noun to refer to the hash value.

5.3.1.1 Properties

The first main property of a random function is *one-wayness*. Given knowledge of an input x, we can easily compute the hash value $h(x)$; but it is very difficult given the hash value $h(x)$ to find a corresponding preimage x if one is not already known. (The elf will only pick outputs for given inputs, not the other way round.) As the output is random, the best an attacker who wants to invert a random function can do is to keep on feeding in more inputs until he or she gets lucky. A pseudorandom function will have the same property; or this could be used to distinguish it from a random function, contrary to our definition. It follows that a pseudorandom function will also be a *one-way function*, provided there are enough possible outputs that the opponent can't find a desired target output by chance. This means choosing the output to be an n-bit number where the opponent can't do anything near 2^n computations.

A second property of pseudorandom functions is that the output will not give any information at all about even part of the input. Thus, one-way encryption of the value x

can be accomplished by concatenating it with a secret key k and computing $h(x, k)$. If the hash function isn't random enough though, using it for one-way encryption in this manner is asking for trouble. A topical example comes from the authentication in GSM mobile phones, where a 16-byte challenge from the base station is concatenated with a 16-byte secret key known to the phone into a 32-byte number, and passed through a hash function to give an 11-byte output [138]. The idea is that the phone company also knows k and can check this computation, while someone who eavesdrops on the radio link can only get a number of values of the random challenge x and corresponding output from $h(x, k)$. The eavesdropper must not be able to get any information about k or be able to compute $h(y, k)$ for a new input y. But the one-way function used by most phone companies isn't one-way enough, with the result that an eavesdropper who can pretend to be a base station and send a phone about 150,000 suitable challenges and get the responses can compute the key. I'll discuss this failure in more detail in Chapter 17, Section 17.3.3).

A third property of pseudorandom functions with sufficiently long outputs is that it is hard to find *collisions*, that is, different messages $M_1 \neq M_2$ with $h(M_1) = h(M_2)$. Unless the opponent can find a shortcut attack (which would mean the function wasn't really pseudorandom), then the best way of finding a collision is to collect a large set of messages M_i and their corresponding hashes $h(M_i)$, sort the hashes, and look for a match. If the hash function output is an n-bit number, so that there are 2^n possible hash values, then the number of hashes the enemy will need to compute before he or she can expect to find a match will be about the square root of this, namely $2^{n/2}$ hashes. This fact is of major importance in security engineering, so let's look at it more closely.

5.3.1.2 The Birthday Theorem

The *birthday theorem*, first known as *capture-recapture statistics*, was invented in the 1930s to count fish [679]. Suppose there are N fish in a lake, and you catch m of them, tag them, and throw them back; then when you first catch a fish you've tagged already, m should be "about" the square root of N. The intuitive reason this holds is that once you have $\sqrt{N}$ samples, each could potentially match any of the others, so the number of possible matches is about $\sqrt{N} \times \sqrt{N}$ or N, which is what you need.[1]

The birthday theorem has many applications for the security engineer. For example, if we have a biometric system that can authenticate a person's claim to identity with a probability of only one in a million that two randomly selected subjects will be falsely identified as the same person, this doesn't mean that we can use it as a reliable means of identification in a university with a user population of twenty thousand staff and students. This is because there will be almost two hundred million possible pairs. In fact, you can expect to find the first *collision*—the first pair of people who can be mistaken for each other by the system—once you have somewhat over a thousand people enrolled.

In some applications collision search attacks aren't a problem, such as in challenge response protocols where an attacker would have to be able to find the answer to the challenge just issued, and where you can prevent challenges repeating. (For example, the challenge might not be really random but generated by encrypting a counter.) In

[1]More precisely, the probability that m fish chosen randomly from N fish are different is $\beta = N(N-1)\cdots(N-m+1)/N^m$ which is asymptotically solved by $N \simeq m^2/2 \log(1/\beta)$ [451].

identify-friend-or-foe (IFF) systems, for example, common equipment has a response length of 48 to 80 bits.

However, there are other applications in which collisions are unacceptable. In a digital signature application, if it were possible to find collisions with $h(M_1) = h(M_2)$ but $M_1 \neq M_2$, then a Mafia-owned bookstore's Web site might get you to sign a message M_1 saying something like, "I hereby order a copy of Rubber Fetish volume 7 for \$32.95," and then present the signature together with an M_2, saying something like, "I hereby mortgage my house for \$75,000; and please make the funds payable to Mafia Holdings Inc., Bermuda."

For this reason, hash functions used with digital signature schemes generally have n large enough to make them collision-free, that is, that $2^{n/2}$ computations are impractical for an opponent. The two most common are MD5, which has a 128-bit output and will thus require about 2^{64} computations to break, and SHA1 with a 160-bit output and a work factor for the cryptanalyst of about 2^{80}. MD5, at least, is starting to look vulnerable: already in 1994, a design was published for a \$10 million machine that would find collisions in 24 days, and SHA1 will also be vulnerable in time. So the U.S. National Institute of Standards and Technology (NIST) has recently introduced still wider hash functions—SHA256 with a 256-bit output, and SHA512 with 512 bits. In the absence of cryptanalytic *shortcut attacks*—that is, attacks requiring less computation than brute force search—these should require 2^{128} and 2^{256} effort respectively to find a collision. This should keep Moore's Law at bay for a generation or two. In general, a prudent designer will use a longer hash function where this is possible, and the use of the MD series hash functions in new systems should be avoided (MD5 had a predecessor MD4 which turned out to be cryptanalytically weak, with collisions and preimages being found).

Thus, a pseudorandom function is also often referred to as being *collision-free* or *collision-intractable*. This doesn't mean that collisions don't exist—they must, as the set of possible inputs is larger than the set of possible outputs—just that you will never find any of them. The (usually unstated) assumption is that the output must be long enough.

5.3.2 Random Generators: Stream Ciphers

The second basic cryptographic primitive is the *random generator*, also known as a *keystream generator* or *stream cipher*. This is also a random function, but unlike in the hash function case it has a short input and a long output. (If we had a good pseudorandom function whose input and output were a billion bits long, and we never wanted to handle any objects larger than this, we could turn it into a hash function by throwing away all but a few hundred bits of the output, and a stream cipher by padding all but a few hundred bits of the input with a constant.) At the conceptual level, however, it's common to think of a stream cipher as a random oracle whose input length is fixed while the output is a very long stream of bits, known as the *keystream*. It can be used quite simply to protect the confidentiality of backup data: we go to the keystream generator, enter a key, get a long file of random bits, and exclusive-or it with our plaintext data to get ciphertext, which we then send to our backup contractor. We can think of the elf generating a random tape of the required length each time he is presented with a new key as input, giving it to us and keeping a copy of it on his scroll for reference in case he's given the same input again. If we need to recover the data, we go back to the generator, enter the same key, get the same long file of random data, and exclusive-or it with our ciphertext to get our plaintext data back again. Other people with access to the keystream generator won't be able to generate the same keystream unless they know the key.

I mentioned the one-time pad, and Shannon's result that a cipher has perfect secrecy if and only if there are as many possible keys as possible plaintexts, and every key is equally likely. Such security is called *unconditional* (or *statistical*) security, as it doesn't depend either on the computing power available to the opponent or on there being no future advances in mathematics that provide a shortcut attack on the cipher.

One-time pad systems are a very close fit for our theoretical model, except that they are typically used to secure communications across space rather than time: there are two communicating parties who have shared a copy of the randomly generated keystream in advance. Vernam's original telegraph cipher machine used punched paper tape; of which two copies were made in advance, one for the sender and one for the receiver. A modern diplomatic system might use optical tape, shipped in a tamper-evident container in a diplomatic bag. Various techniques have been used to do the random generation. Marks describes how SOE agents' silken keys were manufactured in Oxford by little old ladies shuffling counters.

One important problem with keystream generators is that we want to prevent the same keystream being used more than once, whether to encrypt more than one backup tape or to encrypt more than one message sent on a communications channel. During World War II, the amount of Russian diplomatic traffic exceeded the quantity of one-time tape they had distributed in advance to their embassies, so it was reused. This was a serious blunder. If $M_1 + K = C_1$, and $M_2 + K = C_2$, then the opponent can combine the two ciphertexts to get a combination of two messages: $C_1 - C_2 = M_1 - M_2$; and if the messages M_i have enough redundancy, then they can be recovered. Text messages do in fact contain enough redundancy for much to be recovered; and in the case of the Russian traffic, this led to the Venona project in which the United States and United Kingdom decrypted large amounts of wartime Russian traffic afterward and broke up a number of Russian spy rings. The saying is: "Avoid the two-time tape!"

Exactly the same consideration holds for any stream cipher, and the normal engineering practice when using an algorithmic keystream generator is to have a *seed* as well as a key. Each time the cipher is used, we want it to generate a different keystream, so the key supplied to the cipher should be different. So, if the long-term key that two users share is K, they may concatenate it with a seed that is a message number N (or some other nonce), then pass it through a hash function to form a working key $h(K, N)$. This working key is the one actually fed to the cipher machine.

5.3.3 Random Permutations: Block Ciphers

The third type of primitive, and the most important in modern commercial cryptography, is the *block cipher*, which we model as a *random permutation*. Here, the function is invertible, and the input plaintext and the output ciphertext are of a fixed size. With Playfair, both input and output are two characters; with DES, they're both bit strings of

64 bits. Whatever the number of symbols and the underlying alphabet, encryption acts on a block of fixed length. (If you want to encrypt a shorter input, you have to pad it, as with the final z in our Playfair example.)

We can visualize block encryption as follows. As before, we have an elf in a box with dice and a scroll. On the left is a column of plaintexts, and on the right is a column of ciphertexts. When we ask the elf to encrypt a message, it checks in the left-hand column to see if has a record of it. If not, it uses the dice to generate a random ciphertext of the appropriate size (and one that doesn't appear yet in the right-hand column of the scroll), and writes down the plaintext/ciphertext pair in the scroll. If it does find a record, it gives us the corresponding ciphertext from the right-hand column.

When asked to decrypt, the elf does the same, but with the function of the columns reversed: he takes the input ciphertext, checks it (this time on the right-hand scroll); and if he finds it, he gives the message with which it was previously associated. If not, he generates a message at random (which does not already appear in the left column) and notes it down.

A block cipher is a keyed family of pseudorandom permutations. For each key, we have a single permutation that is independent of all the others. We can think of each key as corresponding to a different scroll. The intuitive idea is that, given the plaintext and the key, a cipher machine should output the ciphertext; and given the ciphertext and the key, it should output the plaintext; but given only the plaintext and the ciphertext, it should output nothing.

Let's write a block cipher using the notation established for encryption in Chapter 2:

$$C = \{M\}_K$$

The random permutation model also allows us to define different types of attack on block ciphers. In a *known plaintext attack*, the opponent is just given a number of randomly chosen inputs and outputs from the oracle corresponding to a target key. In a *chosen plaintext attack*, the opponent is allowed to put a certain number of plaintext queries and get the corresponding ciphertexts. In a *chosen ciphertext attack*, he gets to make a number of ciphertext queries. In a *chosen plaintext/ciphertext attack*, he is allowed to make queries of either type. Finally, in a *related key attack*, the opponent can make queries that will be answered using keys related to the target key K (such as $K + 1$ and $K + 2$).

In each case, the objective of the attacker may be either to deduce the answer to a query he hasn't already made (a *forgery attack*), or to recover the key (unsurprisingly known as a *key recovery attack*).

This precision about attacks is important. When someone discovers a vulnerability in a cryptographic primitive, it may or may not be relevant to your application. Often, it won't be, but it will be hyped by the media, so you will need to be able to explain clearly to your boss and your customers why it's not a problem. To do this, you have to look carefully at what kind of attack has been found, and what the parameters are. For example, the first major attack announced on the DES algorithm requires 2^{47} chosen plaintexts to recover the key, while the next major attack improved this to 2^{43} known plaintexts. While these attacks were of great scientific importance, their practical engineering effect was zero, as no practical systems make that much known (let alone chosen) text available to an attacker. Such attacks are often referred to as *certificational*. They can have a commercial effect, though: the attacks on DES undermined confidence in it, and started moving people to other ciphers. In some other cases, an attack that started off as certificational has been developed by later ideas into an exploit.

Which sort of attacks you should be worried about depends very much on your application. With a broadcast entertainment system, for example, you can buy a decoder, observe a lot of material, and compare it with the enciphered broadcast signal; so a known-plaintext attack is the main threat to worry about. But there are surprisingly many applications where chosen plaintext attacks are possible. Obvious ones include ATMs, where, if you allow customers to change their PINs at will, they can change them through a range of possible values and observe the enciphered equivalents using a wire-tap on the line from the ATM to the bank. A more traditional example is diplomatic messaging systems, where it has been known for a host government to give an ambassador a message to transmit to her capital that has been specially designed to help the local cryptanalysts fill out the missing gaps in the ambassador's code book [428]. In general, if the opponent can insert any kind of message into your system, it's chosen plaintext attacks you should worry about.

The other attacks are more specialized. Chosen plaintext/ciphertext attacks may be a worry where the threat is a *lunchtime attacker*, someone who gets temporary access to some cryptographic equipment while its authorized user is out. Related key attacks are of concern where the block cipher is used as a building block in the construction of a hash function (which I discuss later).

5.3.4 Public Key Encryption and Trapdoor One-Way Permutations

A *public key encryption* algorithm is a special kind of block cipher in which the elf will perform the encryption corresponding to a particular key for anyone who requests it, but will do the decryption operation only for the key's owner. To continue with our analogy, the user might give a secret name to the scroll, which only she and the elf know, use the elf's public one-way function to compute a hash of this secret name, publish the hash, and instruct the elf to perform the encryption operation for anybody who quotes this hash.

This means that a principal, say Alice, can publish a key; and if Bob wants to, he can now encrypt a message and send it to her, even if they have never met. All that is necessary is that they have access to the oracle. There are some more details that have to be taken care of, such as how Alice's name can be bound to the key, and indeed whether it means anything to Bob. We'll deal with these later.

A common way of implementing public key encryption is the *trapdoor one-way permutation*. This is a computation that anyone can perform, but that can be reversed only by someone who knows a *trapdoor* such as a secret key. This model is like the one-way function model of a cryptographic hash function, but I state it formally nonetheless: a public key encryption primitive consists of a function that, given a random input R, will return two keys, KR (the public encryption key) and KR^{-1} (the private decryption key) with the properties that:

- Given KR, it is infeasible to compute KR^{-1} (so it's not possible to compute R either).

- There is an encryption function $\{\ldots\}$ that, applied to a message M using the encryption key KR, will produce a ciphertext $C = \{M\}_{KR}$.

- There is a decryption function that, applied to a ciphertext C, using the decryption key KR^{-1}, will produce the original message $M = \{C\}_{KR^{-1}}$.

For practical purposes, we will want the oracle to be replicated at both ends of the communications channel, and this means either using tamper-resistant hardware or (more commonly) implementing its functions using mathematics rather than metal. That's why the second of our models, which is somewhat less abstract than the first, can be more useful. Anyway, we'll look at implementation details later.

5.3.5 Digital Signatures

The final cryptographic primitive I'll define here is the *digital signature*. The basic idea is that a signature on a message can be created by only one person, but checked by anyone. It can thus perform the sort of function in the electronic world that ordinary signatures do in the world of paper.

Signature schemes can be *deterministic* or *randomized*: in the first, computing a signature on a message will always give the same result; in the second, it will give a different result each time you compute it. (The latter is more like handwritten signatures; no two are ever alike but the bank has a means of deciding whether a given specimen is genuine or forged). Also, signature schemes may or may not support *message recovery*. If they do, then, given the signature, anyone can recover the message on which it was generated; if they don't, then the verifier needs to know or guess the message before he can perform the verification. (There are further, more specialized, signature schemes, such as blind signatures and threshold signatures, but I'll postpone discussion of them for now.)

Formally, a signature scheme, like public key encryption scheme, has a keypair generation function that, given a random input R will return two keys, σR (the private signing key) and VR (the public signature verification key) with the properties that:

- Given the public signature verification key VR, it is infeasible to compute the private signing key σR.

- There is a digital signature function that, given a message M and a private signature key σR, will produce a signature $Sig_{\sigma R}(M)$.

- There is a signature verification function that, given the signature $Sig_{\sigma R}(M)$ and the public signature verification key VR, will output TRUE if the signature was computed correctly with σR; otherwise, it will output FALSE.

In our random oracle model, we can model a digital signature algorithm as a random function that reduces any input message to a one-way hash value of fixed length, followed by a special kind of block cipher in which the elf will perform the operation in one direction, known as *signature*, for only one principal, while in the other direction, it will perform verification for anybody.

Signature verification can take two forms. In the basic scheme, the elf (or the signature verification algorithm) outputs only TRUE or FALSE, depending on whether the signature is good. But in a scheme with *message recovery*, anyone can input a signature and get back the message corresponding to it. In our elf model, this means that if the elf has seen the signature before, it will give the message corresponding to it on the scroll; otherwise, it will give a random value (and record the input and the random output as a signature and message pair). This is sometimes desirable: when sending short messages over a low-bandwidth channel, it can save space if only the signature has to be sent rather than the signature plus the message. An example is in the machine-printed postage stamps, or *indicia*, being brought into use in the United States and other countries: the stamp consists of a 2-d barcode with a digital signature made by the postal meter and that must contain all sorts of information, such as the value, the date, and the sender's and recipient's post codes. There's more detail about this at the end of Chapter 12, "Security Printing and Seals."

However, in the general case, we do not need message recovery, as the message to be signed may be of arbitrary length; so we will first pass it through a hash function and then sign the hash value. As hash functions are one-way, the resulting compound signature scheme does not have message recovery—although if the underlying signature scheme does, then the hash of the message can be recovered from the signature.

5.4 Symmetric Crypto Primitives

Now that we have defined the basic crypto primitives, we will look under the hood to see how they can be implemented in practice. While most explanations are geared toward graduate mathematics students, the presentation I'll give here is based on one I've developed over several years with computer science students. So I hope it will let the non-mathematician grasp the essentials. In fact, even at the research level, most of cryptography is as much computer science as mathematics. Modern attacks on ciphers are put together from guessing bits, searching for patterns, sorting possible results, and so on, rather than from anything particularly highbrow.

We'll focus in this section on block ciphers, then in the next section move on to how you can make hash functions and stream ciphers from them, and vice versa. (In later chapters, we'll also look at some special-purpose ciphers.)

5.4.1 SP-Networks

Shannon suggested in the 1940s that strong ciphers could be built by combining substitution with transposition repeatedly. For example, one might add some key material to a block of input text, then shuffle subsets of the input, and continue in this way a number of times. He described the properties of a cipher as being *confusion* and *diffusion*—adding unknown key values will confuse an attacker about the value of a plaintext symbol, while diffusion means spreading the plaintext information through the ciphertext. Block ciphers need diffusion as well as confusion.

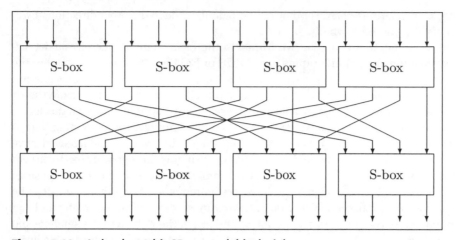

Figure 5.10 A simple 16-bit SP-network block cipher.

The earliest block ciphers were simple networks that combined substitution and permutation circuits, and so were called SP-networks. The diagram in Figure 5.10 shows an SP-network with 16 inputs, which we can imagine as the bits of a 16-bit number, and two layers of 4-bit invertible substitution boxes (or *S-boxes*), each of which can be visualized as a lookup table containing some permutation of the numbers 0 to 15.

The point of this arrangement is that if we were to implement an arbitrary 16-bit to 16-bit function in digital logic, we would need 2^{20} bits of memory—one lookup table of 2^{16} bits for each single output bit. That's hundreds of thousands of gates, while a 4-bit to 4-bit function takes only 64 bits of memory. One might hope that with suitable choices of parameters, the function produced by iterating this simple structure would be indistinguishable from a random 16-bit to 16-bit function to an opponent who didn't know the value of the key. The key might consist of some choice of a number of 4-bit S-boxes, or it might be added at each round to provide confusion, and the resulting text fed through the S-boxes to provide diffusion.

Three things need to be done to make such a design secure:

1. The cipher needs to be "wide" enough.
2. The cipher needs to have enough rounds.
3. The S-boxes need to be suitably chosen.

5.4.1.1 Block Size

First, a block cipher that operated on 16-bit blocks would have rather limited applicability, as an opponent could just build a dictionary of plaintext and ciphertext blocks as he or she observed them. The birthday theorem tells us that even if the input plaintexts were random, the opponent would expect to find a match as soon as she had seen a little over 2^8 blocks. So a practical block cipher will usually deal with plaintexts and ciphertexts of 64 bits, 128 bits, or even more. If we are using 4-bit to 4-but S-boxes, we may have 16 of them (for a 64-bit block size) or 32 of them (for a 128 bit block size).

5.4.1.2 *Number of Rounds*

Second, we must have enough rounds. The two rounds in Figure 5.10 are completely inadequate, as an opponent can deduce the values of the S-boxes by tweaking input bits in suitable patterns. For example, she could hold the rightmost 12 bits constant and try tweaking the leftmost 4 bits, to deduce the values in the top left S-box. (The attack is slightly more complicated than this, as sometimes a tweak in an input bit to an S-box won't produce a change in any output bit, so we have to change one of its other inputs and tweak again. But implementing it is still a simple student exercise.)

The number of rounds we require depends on the speed with which data diffuse through the cipher. In the above simple example, diffusion is very slow because each output bit from one round of S-boxes is connected to only one input bit in the next round. Instead of having a simple permutation of the wires, it is more efficient to have a linear transformation in which each input bit in one round is the exclusive-or of several output bits in the previous round. Of course, if the block cipher is to be used for decryption as well as encryption, this linear transformation will have to be invertible. We'll see some concrete examples below in the sections on AES and Serpent.

5.4.1.3 *Choice of S-Boxes*

The design of the S-boxes also affects the number of rounds required for security, and studying bad choices gives us our entry into the deeper theory of block ciphers. Suppose that the S-box were the permutation that maps the inputs $(0, 1, 2, \ldots, 15)$ to the outputs $(5, 7, 0, 2, 4, 3, 1, 6, 8, 10, 15, 12, 9, 11, 14, 13)$. Then the most significant bit of its input would come through unchanged as the most significant bit of its output. If the same S-box were used in both rounds in the preceding cipher, then the most significant bit of the input block would pass through to become the most significant bit of the output block. So we certainly couldn't pretend that our cipher was pseudorandom.

5.4.1.4 *Linear Cryptanalysis*

Attacks on real block ciphers are usually harder to spot than in this artificial example, but they use the same ideas. It might turn out that the S-box had the property that bit 1 of the input was equal to bit 2, plus bit 4 of the output; more commonly, there will be linear approximations to an S-box, which hold with a certain probability. *Linear cryptanalysis* [526] proceeds by collecting a number of relations such as "bit 2 plus bit 5 of the input to the first S-box is equal to bit 1 plus bit 8 of the output, with probability 13/16," then searching for ways to glue them together into an algebraic relation between input bits, output bits, and keybits that holds with a probability different from one-half. If we can find a linear relationship that holds over the whole cipher with probability $p = 0.5 + 1/M$, then according to probability theory, we can expect to start recovering keybits once we have about M^2 known texts. If the best linear relationship has an M^2 greater than the total possible number of known texts (namely 2^n where the inputs and outputs are n-bits wide), then we consider the cipher to be secure against linear cryptanalysis.

5.4.1.5 Differential Cryptanalysis

Differential cryptanalysis [102] is similar but is based on the probability that a given change in the input to an S-box will give rise to a certain change in the output. A typical observation on an 8-bit S-box might be that "if we flip input bits 2, 3, and 7 at once, then with probability 11/16 the only output bits that will flip are 0 and 1." In fact, with any nonlinear Boolean function, tweaking some combination of input bits will cause some combination of output bits to change with a probability different from one half. The analysis procedure is to look at all possible input difference patterns and look for those values δ_i, δ_o such that an input change of δ_i will produce an output change of δ_o with particularly high (or low) probability.

As in linear cryptanalysis, we then search for ways to join things up so that an input difference that we can feed into the cipher will produce a known output difference with a useful probability over a number of rounds. Given enough chosen inputs, we will see the expected output and be able to make deductions about the key. As in linear cryptanalysis, it's common to consider the cipher to be secure if the number of texts required for an attack is greater than the total possible number of different texts for that key. (We have to be careful of pathological cases, such as if we had a cipher with a 32-bit block and a 128-bit key with a differential attack whose success probability given a single pair was 2^{-40}. Given a lot of text under a number of keys, we'd eventually solve for the current key.)

There are a quite a few variants on these two themes. For example, instead of looking for high-probability differences, we can look for differences that can't happen (or that happen only rarely). This has the charming name of *impossible cryptanalysis*, even though it definitely possible against many systems [101]. There are also various specialized attacks on particular ciphers.

Block cipher design involves a number of trade-offs. For example, we can reduce the per-round information leakage, and thus the required number of rounds, by designing the rounds carefully. However, a complex design might be slow in software, or need a lot of gates in hardware, so using simple rounds but more of them might be better. Simple rounds may also be easier to analyze. A prudent designer will also use more rounds than are strictly necessary to block the attacks known today, in order to give some margin of safety against improved mathematics in the future. We may be able to show that a cipher resists all the attacks we know of, but this says little about whether it will resist the attacks we don't know of yet. (A general security proof for a block cipher would appear to imply a proof about an attacker's computational powers, which might entail a result such as $P \neq NP$ that would revolutionize computer science.)

The point that the security engineer should remember is that block cipher cryptanalysis is a complex subject about which we have a fairly extensive theory, so it is better to use an off-the-shelf design that has been thoroughly scrutinized by experts, rather than rolling your own.

5.4.1.6 Serpent

As a concrete example, the encryption algorithm Serpent is an SP-network with input and output block sizes of 128 bits. These are processed through 32 rounds, in each of which we first add 128 bits of key material, then pass the text through 32 S-boxes of

4-bits width, then perform a linear transformation that takes each output of one round to the inputs of a number of S-boxes in the next round. Rather than each input bit in one round coming from a single output bit in the last, it is the exclusive-or of between two and seven of them. This means that a change in an input bit propagates rapidly through the cipher—a so-called *avalanche* effect that makes both linear and differential attacks harder. After the final round, a further 128 bits of key material are added to give the plaintext. The 33 times 128 bits of key material required are computed from a user-supplied key of up to 256 bits.

This is a real cipher using the structure of Figure 5.10, but modified to be "wide" enough and to have enough rounds. The S-boxes are chosen to make linear and differential analysis hard; they have fairly tight bounds on the maximum linear correlation between input and output bits, and on the maximum effect of toggling patterns of input bits. Each of the 32 S-boxes in a given round is the same; this means that bit-slicing techniques can be used to give a very efficient software implementation on 32-bit processors.

Its simple structure makes Serpent easy to analyze, and it can be shown that it withstands all the currently known attacks. (A full specification of Serpent is given in [40] and can be downloaded, together with implementations in a number of languages, from [41].)

5.4.2 The Advanced Encryption Standard (AES)

This discussion has prepared us to describe the Advanced Encryption Standard, an algorithm also known as Rijndael after its inventors Vincent Rijmen and Joan Daemen.[2] This algorithm acts on 128-bit blocks and can use a key of 128, 192 or 256 bits in length. It is an SP-network; in order to specify it, we need to fix the S-boxes, the linear transformation between the rounds, and the way in which the key is added into the computation.

Rijndael uses a single S-box which acts on a byte input to give a byte output. For implementation purposes it can be regarded simply as a lookup table of 256 bytes; it is actually defined by the equation $S(x) = M(1/x) + b$ over the field $GF(2^8)$ where M is a suitably chosen matrix and b is a constant. This construction gives tight differential and linear bounds.

The linear transformation is based on arranging the 16 bytes of the value being enciphered in a square and then doing bytewise shuffling and mixing operations. (Rijndael is descended from an earlier cipher called Square, which introduced this technique.)

The first step in the linear transformation is the shuffle in which the top row of four bytes is left unchanged, while the second row is shifted one place to the left, the third row by two places and the third row by three places. The second step is a column mixing step in which the four bytes in a column are mixed using a matrix multiplication. This is illustrated in Figure 5.11 which shows, as an example, how a change in the value of the third byte in the first column is propagated. The effect of this combination is that a change in the input to the cipher can potentially affect all of the output after just two rounds.

---

[2]If you're from Holland, Belgium or South Africa, Rijndael is pronounced just as you would expect; if you're not a Dutch speaker, it is something like 'rain-dahl.' The 'J' is not a consonant in Dutch, so Rijndael is not pronounced anything like 'Region Deal,' and Rijmen is pronounced as 'Raymen' not 'Ridgemen.'

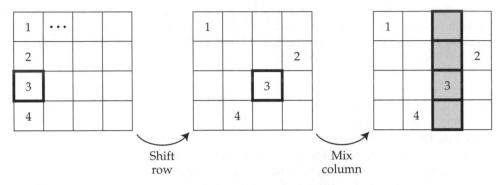

Figure 5.11   The Rijndael linear transformation, illustrated by its effect on byte 3 of the input.

The key material is added byte by byte after the linear transformation. This means that 16 bytes of key material are needed per round; they are derived from the user supplied key material by means of a recurrence relation.

The algorithm uses 10 rounds with 128-bit keys, 12 rounds with 192-bit keys and 14 rounds with 256-bit keys. These give about a 50% margin of safety; the best shortcut attacks known at the time of writing can tackle 6 rounds for 128 bit keys, 7 rounds for 192 bit keys and 9 rounds for 256 bit keys. The general belief in the block cipher community is that even if advances in the state of the art do permit attacks on Rijndael with the full number of rounds, they will be purely certificational attacks in that they will require infeasibly large numbers of texts. (Rijndael's margin of safety against attacks that require only feasible numbers of texts is about 100%.) Although there is no proof of security—whether in the sense of pseudorandomness, or in the weaker sense of an absence of shortcut attacks—there is now a high level of confidence that Rijndael is secure for all practical purposes.

Even although I was an author of Serpent which was an unsuccessful finalist in the AES competition (Rijndael got 86 votes, Serpent 59 votes, Twofish 31 votes, RC6 23 votes and MARS 13 votes at the last AES conference), and although Serpent was designed to have an even larger security margin than Rijndael, I recommend to my clients that they use Rijndael where a general purpose block cipher is required. I recommend the 256-bit-key version, and not because I think that the 10 rounds of the 128-bit-key variant will be broken anytime soon. Longer keys are better because some key bits often leak in real products, as we'll discuss at some length in Chapters 14 and 15. It does not make any sense to implement Serpent as well, 'just in case Rijndael is broken': the risk of a fatal error in the algorithm negotiation protocol is orders of magnitude greater than the risk that anyone will come up with a production attack on Rijndael. (We'll see a number of examples later where using multiple algorithms, or using an algorithm like DES multiple times, caused something to break horribly.)

The definitive specification of Rijndael will be published sometime in 2001 as a Federal Information processing Standard. Meanwhile, the algorithm is described in papers on the Rijndael home page [647]; there are also a number of implementations available both there and elsewhere on the net. The paper describing Rijndael's predecessor, Square, is at [213].

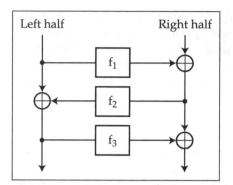

Figure 5.12 The Feistel cipher structure.

5.4.3 Feistel Ciphers

Most block ciphers use a more complex structure, which was invented by Harst Feistel's technicians while they were developing cryptographic protection for IFF in the 1950s and early 1960s. Feistel then moved to IBM and founded a research group that produced the Data Encryption Standard, (DES) algorithm, which is the mainstay of financial transaction processing security.

A Feistel cipher has the ladder structure shown in Figure 5.12. The input is split up into two blocks, the left half and the right half. A *round function* f_1 of the left half is computed and combined with the right half, using exclusive-or (binary addition without carry), though in some Feistel ciphers addition with carry is also used. (We use the notation $\oplus$ for exclusive-or.) Then, a function f_2 of the right half is computed and combined with the left half, and so on. Finally (if the number of rounds is even), the left half and right half are swapped.

A notation you may see for the Feistel cipher is $\psi(f, g, h, \ldots)$ where $f, g, h, \ldots$ are the successive round functions. Under this notation, the preceding cipher is $\psi(f_1, f_2, f_3)$. The basic result that enables us to decrypt a Feistel cipher—and, indeed, the whole point of his design—is that:

$$\psi^{-1}(f_1, f_2, \ldots, f_{2k-1}) = \psi(f_{2k-1}, \ldots, f_2, f_1)$$

In other words, to decrypt, we just use the round functions in the reverse order. Thus, the round functions f_i do not have to be invertible, and the Feistel structure lets us turn any one-way function into a block cipher. This means that we are less constrained in trying to choose a round function with good diffusion and confusion properties; it can more easily satisfy any other design constraints such as code size, table size, software speed, hardware gate count, and so on.

5.4.3.1 The Luby-Rackoff Result

The seminal theoretical result on Feistel ciphers was proved by Mike Luby and Charlie Rackoff in 1988. They showed that if f_i were random functions, then $\psi(f_1, f_2, f_3)$ was indistinguishable from a random permutation under chosen plaintext attack. This result was soon extended to show that $\psi(f_1, f_2, f_3, f_4)$ was indistinguishable under chosen plaintext/ciphertext attack—in other words, it was a pseudorandom permutation.

I am omitting a number of technicalities. In engineering terms, the effect is that, given a really good round function, four rounds of Feistel are enough. So if we have a hash function in which we have confidence, it is straightforward to construct a block cipher from it.

5.4.3.2 DES

The DES algorithm is widely used in banking, government, and embedded applications. For example, it is the standard in automatic teller machine networks.

The DES algorithm is a Feistel cipher, with a 64-bit block and 56-bit key. Its round function operates on 32-bit half-blocks, and consists of four operations:

- First, the block is expanded from 32 bits to 48.
- Next, 48 bits of round key are mixed using exclusive-or.
- The result is passed through a row of eight S-boxes, each of which takes a 6-bit input and provides a 4-bit output.
- Finally, the bits of the output are permuted according to a fixed pattern.

The effect of the expansion, key mixing, and S-boxes is shown in the diagram in Figure 5.13.

The round keys are derived from the user-supplied key by using each user keybit in 12 different rounds according to a slightly irregular pattern. (A full specification of DES is given in [575]; code can be found in [681] or downloaded from many places on the Web.)

DES was introduced in 1974 and caused some controversy. The most telling criticisms was that the key is too short. Someone who wants to find a 56-bit key using brute force—that is by trying all possible keys—will have a *total exhaust time* of 2^{56} encryptions and an *average solution time* of half that, namely 2^{55} encryptions. Diffie and Hellman pointed out that a DES keysearch machine could be built with a million chips, each testing a million keys a second; as a million is about 2^{20}, this would take on average 2^{15} seconds, or just over nine hours, to find the key. They argued that such a machine could be built for $20 million in 1977 [249]. IBM, whose scientists invented DES, retorted that they would charge the U.S. government $200 million to build such a machine. (Perhaps both were right.)

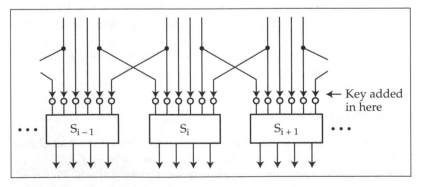

Figure 5.13   The DES round function.

During the 1980s, there were persistent rumors of DES keysearch machines being built by various intelligence agencies, but the first successful public keysearch took place in 1997. In a distributed effort organized over the Net, 14,000 Pentium-level computers took more than four months to find the key to a challenge. In 1998, the Electronic Frontier Foundation (EFF) built a DES keysearch machine for under $250,000; it broke a DES challenge in three days. It contained 1,536 chips run at 40 MHz, each chip containing 24 search units which each took 16 cycles to do a test decrypt. The search rate was thus 2.5 million test decryptions per second per search unit, or 60 million keys per second per chip. (The design of the cracker is public and can be found at [265].) Clearly, the key length of DES is now definitely inadequate for protecting data against a capable motivated opponent, and banks are upgrading their payment systems.

Another criticism of DES was that, since IBM kept its design principles secret at the request of the U.S. government, perhaps there was a trapdoor that would give them easy access. However, the design principles were published in 1992 after differential crypt-analysis was developed and published [205]. Their story was that IBM had discovered these techniques in 1972, and the NSA even earlier. IBM kept the design details secret at the NSA's request. We'll discuss the political aspects of all this in Chapter 21.

We now have a fairly thorough analysis of DES. The best-known *shortcut attack*—is a linear attack using 2^{42} known texts. DES would be secure with more than 20 rounds, but for practical purposes its security appears to be limited by its keylength. I know of no applications where an attacker might get hold of even 2^{40} known texts, so the known shortcut attacks are not an issue in practice. However, its growing vulnerability to keysearch cannot be ignored. If Moore's law continues, then by 2015 or 2020 it will be possible to find a DES key on a single PC in a few months, which means even low-grade systems such as taximeters will be vulnerable to attack using brute-force cryptanalysis. (Your reaction at this point might be "Give me one reason to attack a taximeter!" I will, in Chapter 10, "Monitoring Systems.")

One way of preventing keysearch is *whitening*. In addition to the 56-bit key, say k_0, we choose two 64-bit whitening keys k_1 and k_2, xor'ing the first with the plaintext before encryption and the second with the output of the encryption to get the ciphertext afterward. This composite cipher is known as DESX, and is used in the Win2K encrypting file system. Formally:

$$DESX(k_0, k_1, k_2; M) = DES(k_0; M \oplus k_1) \oplus k_2$$

It can be shown that, on reasonable assumptions, DESX has the properties you'd expect: it inherits the differential strength of DES, but its resistance to keysearch is increased by the amount of the whitening [457].

Another way of dealing with DES keysearch is to use the algorithm multiple times with different keys. This is being introduced in banking networks, and the *triple-DES* algorithm banks use is now a draft U.S. government standard [575]. Triple-DES does an encryption, then a decryption, then a further encryption, all with independent keys. Formally:

$$3\,DES(k_0, k_1, k_2; M) = DES(k_2, DES^{-1}(k_1, DES(k_0; M)))$$

The reason for this design is that, by setting the three keys equal, one gets the same result as a single DES encryption, thus giving a backward-compatibility mode with legacy equipment. (Some systems use *two-key triple-DES*, which sets $k_2 = k_0$; this gives an intermediate step between single- and triple-DES).

5.5 Modes of Operation

In practice, how you use an encryption algorithm is more important than which one you pick. An important factor is the *mode of operation*, which specifies how a block cipher with a fixed block size (8 bytes for DES, 16 for AES) can be extended to process messages of arbitrary length.

There are several modes of operation for using a block cipher on multiple blocks. Understanding them, and choosing the right one for the job, is an important factor in using a block cipher securely.

5.5.1 Electronic Code Book

In *electronic code book* (ECB), we just encrypt each succeeding block of plaintext with our block cipher to get ciphertext, as with the Playfair cipher given as an example earlier. This is adequate for many simple operations, such as challenge-response and some key management tasks; it's also used to encrypt PINs in cash machine systems. However, if we use it to encrypt redundant data, the patterns will show through, letting an opponent deduce information about the plaintext. For example, if a word processing format has lots of strings of nulls, then the ciphertext will have a lot of blocks whose value is the encryption of null characters under the current key.

In one popular corporate email system from the late 1980s, the encryption used was DES ECB with the key derived from an eight-character password. If you looked at a ciphertext generated by this system, you saw that a certain block was far more common than the others—the one that corresponded to a plaintext of nulls. This enabled one of the simplest attacks on a fielded DES encryption system: just encrypt a null block with each password in a dictionary, and sort the answers. You can now break on sight any ciphertext whose password was one of those in your dictionary.

In addition, using ECB mode to encrypt messages of more than one block length and that have an authenticity requirement—such as bank payment messages—would be foolish, as messages could be subject to a *cut-and-splice* attack along the block boundaries. For example, if a bank message said, "Please pay account number X the sum Y, and their reference number is Z," then an attacker might initiate a payment designed so that some of the digits of X could be replaced with some of the digits of Z.

5.5.2 Cipher Block Chaining

Most commercial applications that encrypt more than one block use *cipher block chaining*, or CBC, mode. In it, we exclusive-or the previous block of ciphertext to the current block of plaintext before encryption (see Figure 5.14).

This mode is effective at disguising any patterns in the plaintext: the encryption of each block depends on all the previous blocks. The input IV is an *initialization vector*, a random number that performs the same function as a seed in a stream cipher, and ensures that stereotyped plaintext message headers won't leak information by encrypting to identical ciphertext blocks.

However, an opponent who knows some of the plaintext may be able to cut and splice a message (or parts of several messages encrypted under the same key), so the integrity protection is not total.

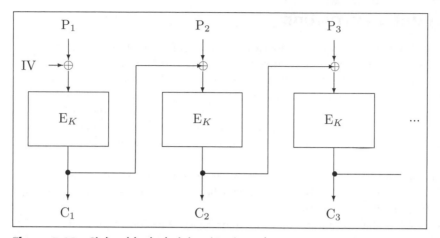

Figure 5.14 Cipher block chaining (CBC) mode.

5.5.3 Output Feedback

Output feedback (OFB) mode consists of repeatedly encrypting an initial value and using this as a keystream in a stream cipher of the kind discussed earlier. Writing "IV" for the initialization vector, or seed, the i-th block of keystream will be given by $K_1 = \{IV\}_K$, $K_i = \{K_{i-1}\}_K$, or:

$$K_i = \{\dots \{\{IV\}_K\}_K \dots total \ of \ i \ times\}$$

This is the standard way of turning a block cipher into a stream cipher. The key K is expanded into a long stream of blocks K_i of *keystream*. Keystream is typically combined with the blocks of a message M_i using exclusive-or to give ciphertext $C_i = M_i \oplus K_i$; this arrangement is sometimes called an *additive stream cipher*, as exclusive-or is just addition modulo 2 (and some old hand systems used addition modulo 26).

Sometimes, a specialist keystream generator is used; for example, the A5 algorithm, which is covered in Chapter 17, has a much lower gate count than DES, and is thus used in mobile applications where battery power is the critical design paramater. However, in the absence of a constraint like this, it is common to use a block cipher in OFB mode to provide the keystream.

All additive stream ciphers have an important vulnerability: they fail to protect message integrity. We mentioned this in the context of the one-time pad in Section 5.2.2, but it's important to realize that this doesn't just affect "perfectly secure" systems but "real life" stream ciphers, too. Suppose, for example, that a stream cipher were used to encipher fund transfer messages. These messages are very highly structured; you might know, for example, that bytes 37–42 contained the amount of money being transferred. You could then carry out the following attack. You cause the data traffic from a local bank to go via your computer (whether by physically splicing into the line, or more simply by using one of the standard routing attacks discussed in Part 2). You go into the bank and send a modest sum (say, $500) to an accomplice. The ciphertext $C_i = M_i \oplus K_i$, duly arrives in your machine. Because you know M_i for bytes 37–42, you know K_i and can easily construct a modified message that instructs the receiving bank to pay not $500 but $500,000! This is an example of an *attack in depth*; it is the price not just of the perfect secrecy we get from the one-time pad, but of much more humble stream ciphers too.

5.5.4 Counter Encryption

One possible drawback of output feedback mode, and in fact of all feedback modes of block cipher encryption, is latency; feedback modes are hard to parallelize. With CBC, a whole block of the cipher must be computed between each block input and each block output; with OFB, we can precompute keystream but storing it requires memory. This can be inconvenient in very high-speed applications, such as protecting traffic on 155 Mbit/s backbone links. There, as silicon is cheap, we would rather pipeline our encryption chip, so that it encrypts a new block (or generates a new block of keystream) in as few clock ticks as possible.

The simplest solution is often is to generate a keystream by just encrypting a counter: $K_i = \{IV + i\}_K$. As before, this is then added to the plaintext to get ciphertext (so it's also vulnerable to attacks in depth).

Another problem that this mode solves when using a 64-bit block cipher such as DES or triple-DES on a very high-speed link is cycle length. An n-bit block cipher in OFB mode will typically have a cycle length of $2^{n/2}$ blocks, after which the birthday theorem will see to it that the keystream will start to repeat. (Once we have a little more than 2^{32} 64-bit values, the odds are that two of them will match.) In CBC mode, too, the birthday theorem ensures that after about $2^{n/2}$ blocks, we will start to see repeats. Counter-mode encryption, however, has a guaranteed cycle length of 2^n rather than $2^{n/2}$.

5.5.5 Cipher Feedback

Cipher feedback, or CFB, mode is another kind of stream cipher. It was designed to be self-synchronizing, in that even if we get a burst error and drop a few bits, the system will recover synchronization after one block length. This is achieved by using our block cipher to encrypt the last n-bits of ciphertext, then adding one of the output bits to the next plaintext bit.

With decryption, the reverse operation is performed, with ciphertext feeding in from the right, as shown in Figure 5.15. Thus, even if we get a burst error and drop a few bits, as soon as we've received enough ciphertext bits to fill up the shift register, the system will resynchronize.

Cipher feedback is not used much any more. It is a specialized mode of operation for applications such as military HF radio links, which are vulnerable to fading, in the days when digital electronics were relatively expensive. Now that silicon is cheap, people use dedicated link-layer protocols for synchronization and error correction rather than trying to combine them with the cryptography.

5.5.6 Message Authentication Code

The next official mode of operation of a block cipher is not used to encipher data, but to protect its integrity and authenticity. This is the *message authentication code*, or MAC. To compute a MAC on a message using a block cipher, we encrypt it using CBC mode and throw away all the output ciphertext blocks except the last one; this last block is the MAC. (The intermediate results are kept secret in order to prevent splicing attacks.)

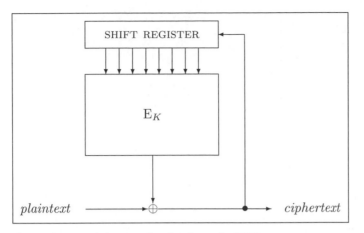

Figure 5.15 Ciphertext feedback mode (CFB).

This construction makes the MAC depend on all the plaintext blocks as well as on the key. It is secure provided the message length is fixed; it can be shown that any attack on a MAC under these circumstances would give an attack on the underlying block cipher [87]. (If the message length is variable, you have to ensure that a MAC computed on one string can't be used as the IV for computing a MAC on a different string, so that an opponent can't cheat by getting a MAC on the composition of the two strings.)

In applications needing both integrity and privacy, the procedure is to first calculate a MAC on the message using one key, then CBC-encrypt it using a different key. If the same key is used for both encryption and authentication, the security of the latter is no longer guaranteed; cut-and-splice attacks are still possible.

There are other possible constructions of MACs: a common one is to use a hash function with a key, which we'll look at in more detail in Section 5.6.2. Before we do that, let's revisit hash functions.

5.6 Hash Functions

Section 5.4.2.1 showed how the Luby-Rackoff theorem enables us to construct a block cipher from a hash function. It's also possible to construct a hash function from a block cipher. (In fact, we can also construct hash functions and block ciphers from stream ciphers—therefore, subject to some caveats described in the next section, given any one of these three primitives, we can construct the other two.)

The trick is to feed the message blocks one at a time to the key input of our block cipher, and use it to update a hash value (which starts off at, say, $H_0 = 0$). In order to make this operation noninvertible, we add feedforward: the $(i-1)$st hash value is exclusive-or'ed with the output of round i. This is our final mode of operation of a block cipher (Figure 5.16).

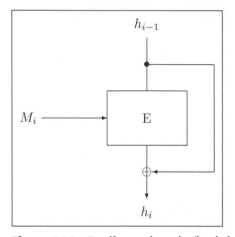

Figure 5.16   Feedforward mode (hash function).

5.6.1 Extra Requirements on the Underlying Cipher

The birthday effect makes another appearance here, in that if a hash function h is built using an n-bit block cipher, it is possible to find two messages $M_1 \neq M_2$ with $h(M_1) = h(M_2)$ (hash about $2^{n/2}$ messages M_i and look for a match). So, a 64-bit block cipher is not adequate, as the cost of forging a message would be of the order of 2^{32} messages, which is quite practical.

This is not the only way in which the hash function mode of operation is more demanding on the underlying block cipher than a mode such as CBC designed for confidentiality. A good illustration comes from a cipher called Treyfer, which was designed to encrypt data using as little memory as possible in the 8051 microcontrollers commonly found in consumer electronics and domestic appliances [819]. (It takes only 30 bytes of ROM.)

Treyfer "scavenges" its S-box by using 256 bytes from the ROM, which may be code, or may even—to make commercial cloning riskier—contain a copyright message. At each round, it acts on eight bytes of text with eight bytes of key by adding a byte of text to a byte of key, passing it through the S-box, adding it to the next byte, then rotating the result by one bit (Figure 5.17). This rotation deals with some of the problems that might arise if the S-box has uneven randomness across its bitplanes (for example, if it contains ascii text such as a copyright message). Finally, the algorithm makes up for its simple round structure and probably less-than-ideal S-box by having a large number of rounds (32 of them, in fact).

No attacks are known on Treyfer that prevent its use for confidentiality and for computing MACs. However, the algorithm does have a weakness that prevents its use in hash functions. It suffers from a *fixed-point attack*. Given any input, there is a fair chance we can find a key that will leave the input unchanged. We just have to look to see, for each byte of input, whether the S-box assumes the output that, when added to the byte on the right, has the effect of rotating it one bit to the left. If such outputs exist for each of the input bytes, then it's easy to choose key values that will leave the data unchanged after

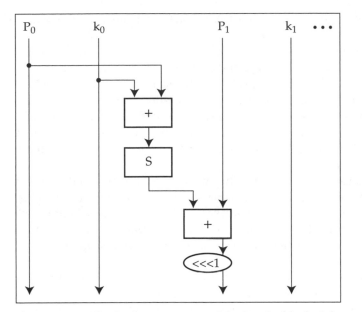

Figure 5.17   The basic component of the Treyfer block cipher.

one round, and thus after 32 rounds. The probability that we can do this depends on the S-box.[3] This means that we can easily find collisions if Treyfer is used as a hash function. (In effect, hash functions have to be based on block ciphers that withstand *chosen key attacks*).

5.6.2 Common Hash Functions and Applications

Algorithms similar to Treyfer have been used in hash functions in key management protocols in some pay-TV systems, but typically they have a modification to prevent fixed-point attacks, such as a procedure to add in the round number at each round, or to mix up the bits of the key in some way (a *key-scheduling* algorithm).

The three hash functions most commonly used in applications are all related, and are based on variants of a block cipher with a 512-bit key and a block size of either 128 or 160 bits. MD4 has three rounds and a 128-bit hash value; and a collision has recently been found for it [255]. MD5 has four rounds and a 128-bit hash value; while the U.S. Secure Hash Standard has five rounds and a 160-bit hash value. The block ciphers underlying these hash functions are similar; their round function is a complicated mixture of the register operations available on 32-bit processors [681]. It seems that SHA1 is a reasonable approximation to a pseudorandom function, as long as our opponents can't perform 2^{80} computations; because this number is coming within range of military

---

[3]Curiously, an S-box that is a permutation is always vulnerable, while a randomly selected one isn't quite so risky. In many cipher designs, S-boxes that are permutations are essential, or at least desirable. Treyfer is an interesting exception.

intelligence agencies and large companies, the 256-bit and 512-bit versions of SHA have been introduced.

Hash functions have many uses. One is to compute MACs. A naive method would be to simply hash the message with a key: $MAC_k(M) = h(k, M)$. However, the accepted way of doing this, called HMAC, uses an extra step in which the result of this computation is hashed again. The two hashing operations are done using variants of the key, derived by exclusive-or'ing them with two different constants. Thus, $HMAC_k(M) = h(k \oplus A, h(k \oplus B, M))$. A is constructed by repeating the byte 0×36 as often as necessary, and B similarly from the byte $0 \times 5C$. The reason for this is that it makes collision finding much harder [474].

Another hash function use is to make commitments that are to be revealed later. For example, I might wish to timestamp a digital document in order to establish intellectual priority, but not be willing to reveal the contents yet. In that case, I can submit a hash of the document to a commercial timestamping service [364]. Later, when I reveal the document, the fact that its hash was timestamped at a given time establishes that I had written it by then.

Finally, before we go on to discuss asymmetric cryptography, there are two particular uses of hash functions that deserve mention: key updating and autokeying.

Key updating means that two or more principals who share a key pass it through a one-way hash function at agreed times: $K_i = h(K_{i-1})$. The point is that if an attacker compromises one of their systems and steals the key, he only gets the current key and is unable to decrypt back traffic. This property is known as *backward security*.

Autokeying means that two or more principals who share a key hash it at agreed times with the messages they have exchanged since the last key change: $K_{i+1} = h(K_i, M_{i1}, M_{i2}, \ldots)$. The point is that if an attacker compromises one of their systems and steals the key, then as soon as they exchange a message which he doesn't observe or guess, security will be recovered in that he can no longer decrypt their traffic. This property is known as *forward security*. It is used, for example, in EFT payment terminals in Australia [83, 85]. The use of asymmetric crypto allows a slightly stronger form of forward security, namely that as soon as a compromised terminal exchanges a message with an uncompromised one that the opponent doesn't control, then security can be recovered even if the message is in plain sight. I'll describe how this trick works next.

5.7 Asymmetric Crypto Primitives

The commonly used building blocks in *asymmetric cryptography*, that is, public key encryption and digital signature, are based on number theory. I'll give only a brief overview here, then in Part 2 where we discuss applications, I'll describe in more detail some of the mechanisms used. (If you find the description assumes too much mathematics, skip the following two sections and read the material from a cryptography textbook.)

The technique of asymmetric cryptography is to make the security of the cipher depend on the difficulty of solving a certain mathematical problem. The two problems used in most fielded systems are factorization (used in most commercial systems) and discrete logarithm (used in many military systems).

5.7.1 Cryptography Based on Factoring

The *prime numbers* are the positive whole numbers with no proper divisors; that is, the only numbers that divide a prime number are 1 and the number itself. By definition, 1 is not prime; so the primes are $\{2, 3, 5, 7, 11, \ldots\}$. The *fundamental theorem of arithmetic* states that each natural number greater than 1 factors into prime numbers in a way that is unique up to the order of the factors. It is easy to find prime numbers and multiply them together to give a composite number, but much harder to resolve a composite number into its factors. The largest composite product of two large random primes to have been factorized to date was 512 bits (155 digits) long; when such a computation was first done, it took several thousand MIPS-years of effort. Recently, however, some Swedish students managed to factor a 512-bit number surreptitiously to solve a challenge cipher, so 512-bit composite numbers are now no more 'secure' than 56-bit DES keys. However, it is believed that a similar number of 1024 bits length could not be factored without an advance in mathematics.

The algorithm commonly used to do public key encryption and digital signatures based on factoring is RSA, named after its inventors Ron Rivest, Adi Shamir, and Len Adleman [649]. It uses *Fermat's (little) theorem*, which states that for all primes p not dividing a, $a^{p-1} \equiv 1$ modulo p. (Proof: take the set $\{1, 2, \ldots, p-1\}$ and multiply each of them modulo p by a, then cancel out $(p-1)!$ each side.) Euler's function $\phi(n)$ is the number of positive integers less than n with which it has no divisor in common; so if n is the product of two primes pq then $\phi(n) = (p-1)(q-1)$ (the proof is similar).

The encryption key is a modulus N which is hard to factor (take $N = pq$ for two large randomly chosen primes p and q), plus a public exponent e that has no common factors with either $p-1$ or $q-1$. The private key is the factors p and q, which are kept secret. Where M is the message and C is the ciphertext, encryption is defined by:

$$C \equiv M^e \text{ modulo } N$$

Decryption is the reverse operation:

$$M \equiv \sqrt[e]{C} \text{ modulo } N$$

Whoever knows the private key—the factors p and q of N—can easily calculate $\sqrt[e]{C}$ (mod N). As $\phi(N) = (p-1)(q-1)$, and e has no common factors with $\phi(N)$, the key's owner can find a number d such that $de \equiv 1$ (modulo $\phi(N)$—she finds the value of d separately, modulo $p-1$ and $q-1$, and combines the answers. Thus, $\sqrt[e]{C}$ (modulo N) is now computed as C^d (modulo N), and decryption works because of Fermat's theorem:

$$C^d \equiv \{M^e\}^d \equiv M^{ed} \equiv M^{1+k\phi(N)} \equiv M.M^{k\phi(N)} \equiv M \times 1 \equiv M \text{ modulo } N$$

Similarly, the owner of the private key can operate on the message with this to produce a digital signature:

$$Sig_d(M) \equiv M^d \text{ modulo } N$$

and this signature can be verified by raising it to the power e mod N (thus, using e and N as the public signature verification key) and checking that the message M is recovered:

$$M \equiv (Sig_d(M))^e \text{ modulo } N$$

Neither RSA encryption nor signature is generally safe to use on its own. The reason is that, encryption being an algebraic process, it preserves certain algebraic properties. For example, if we have a relation such as $M_1 M_2 = M_3$ that holds among plaintexts, then the same relationship will hold among ciphertexts $C_1 C_2 = C_3$ and signatures $Sig_1 Sig_2 = Sig_3$. This property is known as a *multiplicative homomorphism* (mathematicians describe a function that preserves mathematical structure as a *homomorphism*). The homomorphic nature of raw RSA means that it doesn't meet the random oracle model definitions of public key encryption or signature.

There are a number of standards that try to stop attacks based the homomorphic mathematical structure by setting various parts of the input to the algorithm to fixed constants or to random values. Many of them have been broken. The better solutions involve processing the message using hash functions as well as random nonces and padding before the RSA primitive is applied. For example, in *optimal asymmetric encryption padding* (OAEP), we concatenate the message M with a random nonce N, and use a hash function h to combine them:

$$C_1 = M \oplus h(N)$$

$$C_2 = N \oplus h(C_1)$$

In effect, this is a two-round Feistel cipher, which uses h as its round function. The result, the combination C_1, C_2, is then encrypted with RSA and sent. The recipient then computes N as $C_2 \oplus h(C_1)$ and recovers M as $C_1 \oplus h(N)$ [88].

With signatures, things are slightly simpler. In general, it's often enough to just hash the message before applying the private key: $Sig_d = [h(M)]^d \pmod N$. However, in some applications, one might wish to include further data in the signature block, such as a timestamp.

5.7.2 Cryptography Based on Discrete Logarithms

While RSA is used in most Web browsers in the SSL protocol, there are other products (such as PGP) and many government systems that base public key operations on discrete logarithms. These come in a number of flavors, some using "normal" arithmetic, while others use mathematical structures called *elliptic curves*. I'll explain the normal case, as the elliptic variants use essentially the same idea but the implementation is more complex.

A *primitive root* modulo p is a number whose powers generate all the nonzero numbers mod p; for example, when working modulo 7, we find that $5^2 = 25$, which reduces to 4 (modulo 7), then we can compute 5^3 as $5^2 \times 5$ or 4×5, which is 20, which reduces to 6 (modulo 7), and so on, as shown in Figure 5.17.

Thus, 5 is a primitive root modulo 7. This means that given any y, we can always solve the equation $y = 5^x \pmod 7$; x is then called the discrete logarithm of y modulo 7. Small examples like this can be solved by inspection, but for a large random prime number p, we do not know how to do this computation. So the mapping $f : x \rightarrow g^x \pmod p$ is a one-way function, with the additional properties that $f(x + y) = f(x)f(y)$ and

$$
\begin{array}{llll}
5^1 & & = 5 & (\bmod\ 7) \\
5^2 = & 25 & \equiv 4 & (\bmod\ 7) \\
5^3 \equiv & 4 \times 5 & \equiv 6 & (\bmod\ 7) \\
5^4 \equiv & 6 \times 5 & \equiv 2 & (\bmod\ 7) \\
5^5 \equiv & 2 \times 5 & \equiv 3 & (\bmod\ 7) \\
5^6 \equiv & 3 \times 5 & \equiv 1 & (\bmod\ 7)
\end{array}
$$

Figure 5.18 Example of discrete logarithm calculations.

$f(nx) = f(x)^n$. In other words, it is a *one-way homomorphism*. As such, it can be used to construct digital signature and public key encryption algorithms.

5.7.2.1 Public Key Encryption: The Diffie-Hellman Protocol

To understand how discrete logarithms can be used to build a public key encryption algorithm, bear in mind that we want a cryptosystem that does not need the users to start off with a shared secret key. Consider the following "classical" scenario.

Imagine that Anthony wants to send a secret to Brutus, and the only communications channel available is an untrustworthy courier (say, a slave belonging to Caesar). Anthony can take the message, put it in a box, padlock it, and get the courier to take it to Brutus. Brutus could then put his own padlock on it, too, and have it taken back to Anthony. Anthony in turn would remove his padlock, and have it taken back to Brutus, who would now at last open it.

Exactly the same can be done using any encryption function that *commutes*, that is, has the property that $\{\{M\}_{KA}\}_{KB} = \{\{M\}_{KB}\}_{KA}$. Alice can take the message M and encrypt it with her key KA to get $\{M\}_{KA}$ which she sends to Bob. Bob encrypts it again with his key KB getting $\{\{M\}_{KA}\}_{KB}$. But the commutativity property means that this is just $\{\{M\}_{KB}\}_{KA}$, so Alice can decrypt it using her key KA getting $\{M\}_{KB}$. She sends this to Bob and he can decrypt it with KB, finally recovering the message M. The keys KA and KB might be long-term keys if this mechanism were to be used as a conventional public-key encryption system, or they might be transient keys if the goal were to establish a key with forward secrecy.

How can commutative encryption be implemented? If we have found values of g and p such that the discrete log problem to the base g modulo p is hard, then we can use discrete exponentiation as our encryption function. For example, Alice chooses a random number x_A, calculates g^{x_A} modulo p and sends it, together with p, to Bob. Bob likewise chooses a random number x_B and forms $g^{x_A x_B}$ modulo p, which he passes back to Alice. Alice can now remove her exponentiation: using Fermat's theorem, she calculates $g^{x_B} = (g^{x_A x_B})^{p-x_A}$ modulo p and sends it to Bob. Bob can now remove his exponentiation, too, and so finally gets hold of g. The security of this scheme depends on the difficulty of the discrete logarithm problem.

In practice, it is tricky to encode a message to be a primitive root; but there is a much simpler means of achieving the same effect. The first public key encryption scheme to be published, by Whitfield Diffie and Martin Hellman in 1976, uses $g^{x_A x_B}$ modulo p as the key to a shared key encryption system. The values x_A and x_B can be the private keys of the two parties.

Let's see how this might work to provide a public-key encryption system. The prime p and generator g are typically common to all users. Alice chooses a secret random number x_A, calculates $y_A = g^{x_A}$ and publishes it opposite her name in the company phone book. Bob does the same, choosing a random number x_B and publishing $y_B = g^{x_B}$. In order to communicate with Bob, Alice fetches y_B from the phone book, forms $y_B^{x_A}$ which is of course $g^{x_A x_B}$, and uses this to encrypt the message to Bob. On receiving it, Bob looks up Alice's public key y_A and forms $y_A^{x_B}$ which is also equal to $g^{x_A x_B}$, so he can decrypt her message.

Slightly more work is needed to provide a full solution. Some care is needed when choosing the parameters p and g; and there are several other details that depend on whether we want properties such as forward security. Variants on the Diffie-Hellman theme include the U.S. government *key exchange algorithm* (KEA) [577], used in network security products such as the Fortezza card, and the so-called Royal Holloway protocol, which is used by the U.K. government and may be used in third generation mobile phones [50].

The biggest problem with such systems is how to be sure that you've got a genuine copy of the phone book, and that the entry you're interested in isn't out of date. I'll discuss that in Section 5.7.4.

5.7.2.2 *Key Establishment*

Mechanisms for providing forward security in such protocols are of independent interest. As before, let the prime p and generator g be common to all users. Alice chooses a random number R_A, calculates g^{R_A} and sends it to Bob; Bob does the same, choosing a random number R_B and sending g^{R_B} to Alice; they then both form $g^{R_A R_B}$, which they use as a session key.

Alice and Bob can now use the session key $g^{R_A R_B}$ to encrypt a conversation. They have managed to create a shared secret "out of nothing." Even if an opponent had obtained full access to both their machines before this protocol was started, and thus knew all their stored private keys, then, provided some basic conditions were met (e.g., that their random-number generators were not predictable), the opponent still could not eavesdrop on their traffic. This is the strong version of the forward security property referred to in Section 5.6.2. The opponent can't work forward from knowledge of previous keys that he might have obtained. Provided that Alice and Bob both destroy the shared secret after use, they will also have backward security; an opponent who gets access to their equipment subsequently cannot work backward to break their old traffic.

But this protocol has a small problem: although Alice and Bob end up with a session key, neither of them has any idea with whom they share it.

Suppose that in our padlock protocol, Caesar has just ordered his slave to bring the box to him instead; he places his own padlock on it next to Anthony's. The slave takes the box back to Anthony, who removes his padlock, and brings the box back to Caesar who opens it. Caesar can even run two instances of the protocol, pretending to Anthony that he's Brutus and to Brutus that he's Anthony. One fix is for Anthony and Brutus to apply their seals to their locks.

The same idea leads to a middleperson attack on the Diffie-Hellman protocol unless transient keys are authenticated. Charlie intercepts Alice's message to Bob and replies to it; at the same time, he initiates a key exchange with Bob, pretending to be Alice. He ends up with a key $g^{R_A R_C}$, which he shares with Alice, and another key $g^{R_B R_C}$, which he shares with Bob. As long as he continues to sit in the middle of the network and translate the messages between them, they may have a hard time detecting that their communications are being compromised.

In one secure telephone product, the two principals would read out an eight-digit hash of the key they had generated, and check that they had the same value, before starting to discuss classified matters. A more general solution is for Alice and Bob to sign the messages that they send to each other.

Finally, discrete logarithms and their analogues exist in many other mathematical structures; thus, for example, *elliptic curve cryptography* uses discrete logarithms on an elliptic curve—a curve given by an equation such as $y^2 = x^3 + ax + b$. The algebra gets somewhat more complex, but the basic underlying ideas are the same.

5.7.2.3 Digital Signature

Suppose that the base p and the generator g (which may or may not be a primitive root) are public values chosen in some suitable way, and that each user who wishes to sign messages has a private signing key X and a public signature verification key $Y = g^X$. An *ElGamal signature scheme* works as follows: choose a message key k at random, and form $r = g^k$ (modulo p). Now form the signature s using a linear equation in k, r, the message M, and the private key X. There are a number of equations that will do; the particular one that happens to be used in ElGamal signatures is:

$$rX + sk = M \text{ modulo } p - 1$$

So s is computed as $s = (M - rX)/k$; this is done modulo $\phi(p)$. When both sides are passed through our one-way homomorphism $f(x) = g^x$ modulo p we get:

$$g^{rX}g^{sk} \equiv g^M \text{ modulo } p$$

or

$$Y^r r^s \equiv g^M \text{ modulo } p$$

An ElGamal signature on the message M consists of the values r and s, and the recipient can verify it using the above equation.

A few details need to be sorted out to get a functional digital signature scheme. For example, bad choices of p or g can weaken the algorithm; and we will want to hash the message M using a hash function so that we can sign messages of arbitrary length, and so that an opponent can't use the algorithm's algebraic structure to forge signatures on messages that were never signed. Having attended to these details and applied one or two optimisations, we get the *Digital Signature Algorithm* (DSA) which is a U.S. standard and widely used in government applications.

DSA (also known as DSS, for Digital Signature Standard) assumes a prime p of typically 1024 bits, a prime q of 160 bits dividing $(p-1)$, an element g of order q in the integers modulo p, a secret signing key x, and a public verification key $y = g^x$. The signature on a message M, $Sig_x(M)$, is (r, s), where:

$$r \equiv (g^k \text{ (modulo } p\text{)}) \text{ modulo } q$$

$$s \equiv (h(M) - xr)/k \text{ modulo } q$$

The hash function used here is SHA1.

DSA is the classic example of a randomized digital signature scheme without message recovery.

5.7.3 Special-Purpose Primitives

Researchers have discovered a large number of public key and signature primitives with special properties; I'll describe only the two that appear to have been fielded to date: threshold signatures and blind signatures.

Threshold signatures are a mechanism whereby a signing key (or for that matter a decryption key) can be split up among n principals so that any k out of n can sign a message (or decrypt one). For $k = n$, the construction is easy. With RSA, for example, we can split up the private decryption key d as $d = d_1 + d_2 + \cdots + d_n$. For $k < n$ it's slightly more complex (but not much) [246]. Threshold signatures are used in systems where a number of servers process transactions independently and vote independently on the outcome; they may also be used to implement business rules such as "a check may be signed by any two of the seven directors."

With *blind signatures* can be used to make a signature on a message without knowing what the message is. For example, if I am using RSA, I can take a random number R, form $R^e M$ (mod n), and give it to the signer, who computes $(R^e M)^d = R.M^d$ (modulo n). When he or she gives this back to me, I can divide out R to get the signature M^d. The possible application is in *digital cash;* a bank might agree to honor for \$10 any string M with a unique serial number and a specified form of redundancy, bearing a signature that verified as correct using the public key (e, n). Such a string is known as a *digital coin.* The blind signature protocol shows how a customer can get a bank to sign a coin without the banker knowing its serial number. The effect is that the digital cash can be anonymous for the spender. (There are a few more details that need to be sorted out, such as how to detect people who spend the same coin twice; but these are fixable.) Blind signatures and digital cash were invented by Chaum [178], along with much other supporting digital privacy technology covered in Chapter 20 [177].

Researchers continue to suggest new applications for specialist public key mechanisms. A strong candidate is in online elections, where one requires a particular mixture of anonymity and accountability.

5.7.4 Certification

Now that we can do public key encryption and digital signature, we need some mechanism to bind users to keys. The approach proposed by Diffie and Hellman when they invented digital signatures was to have a directory of the public keys of a system's authorized users, such as a phone book. A more common solution, due to Loren Kohn-felder, is for a *certification authority* (CA) to sign the user's public encryption and/or signature verification keys giving certificates that contain the user's name, attributed such as authorizations, and public keys. The CA might be run by the local system administrator; or it might be a third-party service such as Verisign whose business is to sign public keys after checking that they belong to the principals named in them.

A certificate might be described symbolically as:

$$C_A = Sig_{K_S}(T_S, L, A, K_A, V_A)$$

where (using the same notation as with Kerberos) T_S is the certificate's starting date and time, L is the length of time for which it is valid, A is the user's name, K_A is her public encryption key, and V_A is her public signature verification key. In this way, only the administrator's public signature verification key needs to be communicated to all principals in a trustworthy manner.

Distributed system aspects of certification are covered in Chapter 6, "Distributed Systems"; e-commerce applications in Chapter 19, "Protecting E-Commerce Systems"; and the policy aspects in Chapter 21, "E-Policy." At this stage I'll merely point out that the protocol aspects are much harder than they look.

One of the first proposed public key protocols was due to Dorothy Denning and Giovanni Sacco, who in 1981 proposed that two users, say Alice and Bob, set up a shared DES key K_{AB} as follows. When Alice first wants to communicate with Bob, she goes to the certification authority and gets current copies of public key certificates for herself and Bob. She then makes up a key packet containing a timestamp T_A, a session key K_{AB} and a signature, which she computes on these items using her private signing key. She then encrypts this whole bundle under Bob's public encryption key and ships it off to him. Symbolically:

$$A \rightarrow B : C_A, C_B, \{T_A, K_{AB}, Sig_{K_A}(T_A, K_{AB})\}_{K_B}$$

In 1994, Martín Abadi and Roger Needham pointed out that this protocol is fatally flawed [2]. Bob, on receiving this message, can masquerade as Alice for as long as Alice's timestamp T_A remains valid! To see how, suppose that Bob wants to masquerade as Alice to Charlie. He goes to Sam and gets a fresh certificate C_C for Charlie, then strips off the outer encryption $\{\dots\}_{K_B}$ from message 3 in the preceding protocol. He now reencrypts the signed key packet $T_A, K_{AB}, Sig_{K_A}(T_A, K_{AB})$ with Charlie's public key—which he gets from C_C—and makes up a bogus message 3:

$$B \rightarrow C : C_A, C_C, \{T_A, K_{AB}, Sig_{K_A}(T_A, K_{AB})\}_{K_C}$$

It is actually quite alarming that such a simple protocol—essentially, a one-line program—should have such a serious flaw in it and remain undetected for so long. With a normal program of only a few lines of code, you might expect to find a bug in it by looking at it for a minute or two. In fact, public key protocols, if anything, are harder to design than protocols using shared key encryption, as they are prone to subtle and pernicious middleperson attacks. This further motivates the use of formal methods to prove that protocols are correct.

Often, the participants' names aren't the most important things which the authentication mechanism has to establish. In the STU-III secure telephone used by the U.S. government and defense contractors, there is a protocol for establishing transient keys with forward and backward security; to exclude middleperson attacks, users have a *crypto ignition key*, a portable electronic device that they can plug into the phone to identify not just their names, but their security clearance levels. In general, books on the topic tend to talk about identification as the main goal of authentication and key management protocols; but in real life, it's usually authorization that matters. This is more complex, as it starts to introduce assumptions about the application into the protocol design. (In fact, the NSA security manual emphasizes the importance of always knowing whether there is an uncleared person in the room. The STU-III design is a natural way of extending this to electronic communications.)

One serious weakness of relying on public key certificates is the difficulty of getting users to understand all their implications and to manage them properly, expecially where they are not an exact reimplementation of a familiar manual control system [224]. Many other things can go wrong with certification at the level of systems engineering as well, and we'll look at these in the next chapter.

5.7.5 The Strength of Asymmetric Cryptographic Primitives

To provide the same level of protection as a symmetric block cipher, asymmetric cryptographic primitives are believed to require at least twice the block length. Elliptic curve systems appear to achieve this; a 128-bit elliptic scheme could be about as hard to break as a 64-bit block cipher with a 64-bit key. The commoner schemes, based on factoring and discrete log, are less robust because there are shortcut attack algorithms such as the number field sieve, which exploit the fact that some integers are *smooth*, that is, they have a large number of small factors. At the time of writing, the number field sieve has been used to attack keys up to 512 bits, a task comparable in difficulty to performing keysearch on 56-bit DES keys. The current consensus is that private keys for RSA and for standard discrete log systems should be at least 1024 bits long, while 2048 bits gives some useful safety margin against mathematicians making significant improvements in algorithms.

There has been some publicity recently about *quantum computers*. These are devices that perform a large number of computations simultaneously using superposed quantum states. Peter Shor has shown that if a sufficiently large quantum computer can be built, then both factoring and discrete logarithm computations will become easy. So far only very small quantum computers can be built, and many people are sceptical about whether the technology can be made to work well enough to threaten real systems. In the event that it can, asymmetric cryptography may have to be abandoned. So it is fortunate that many of the things that are currently done with asymmetric mechanisms can also be done with symmetric ones; thus many authentication protocols can be redesigned to use variants on Kerberos.

5.8 Summary

Many ciphers fail because they're used improperly, so we need a clear model of what a cipher does. The random oracle model is useful here: we assume that each new value returned by the encryption engine is random in the sense of being statistically independent of all the outputs seen before.

Block ciphers for symmetric key applications can be constructed by the careful combination of substitutions and permutations; for asymmetric applications such as public key encryption and digital signature one uses number theory. In both cases, there is quite a large body of mathematics to guide us. Other kinds of ciphers—stream ciphers and hash functions—can be constructed from block ciphers by using them in suitable modes of operation. These have different error propagation, pattern concealment, and integrity protection properties.

The basic properties the security engineer needs to understand are not too difficult to grasp, though there are some subtle things that can go wrong. In particular, it is surprisingly hard to build systems that are robust even when components fail (or are encouraged to), and where the cryptographic mechanisms are well integrated with other measures such as access control and physical security. We'll return to this repeatedly in later chapters.

Research Problems

There are many active threads in cryptography research. Many of them are where crypto meets a particular branch of mathematics (number theory, algebraic geometry, complexity theory, combinatorics, graph theory, and information theory). The empirical end of the business is concerned with designing primitives for encryption, signature, and composite operations, and that perform reasonably well on available platforms. The two meet in the study of subjects ranging from linear and differential cryptanalysis to attacks on public key protocols. Research is more driven by the existing body of knowledge than by applications, though there are exceptions: copyright protection concerns have been a stimulus, and so has the recent competition to find an Advanced Encryption Standard.

The best way to get a flavor of what's going on is to read the last few years' proceedings of research conferences, such as Crypto, Eurocrypt, Asiacrypt and Fast Software Encryption, all published by Springer-Verlag in the *Lecture Notes on Computer Science* (LNCS) series.

Further Reading

The classic papers by Diffie and Hellman [248] and by Rivest, Shamir, and Adleman [649] are the closest to required reading on this subject. The most popular modern introduction is Bruce Schneier's *Applied Cryptography* [681], which covers a lot of ground at a level a nonmathematician can understand, and which has C source code for a number of algorithms. The *Handbook of Applied Cryptography*, by Alfred Menazes, Paul von Oovschot and Scott Vanstone [544], is the closest to a standard reference book on the mathematical detail.

More specialized texts include a book by Eli Biham and Adi Shamir [102], which is the standard reference on differential cryptanalysis; the best explanation of linear cryptanalysis may be in a textbook by Doug Stinson [738]; the modern theory of block ciphers can be found developing in the papers of the *Fast Software Encryption* conference series during the 1990s (the proceedings are published by Springer-Verlag in the LNCS series). The original book on modes of operation is Carl Meyer and Steve Matyas [548]. Neal Koblitz has a good basic introduction to the mathematics behind public key cryptography [463]; the number field sieve is described in [497]; while quantum factoring is described in [698].

There's a shortage of good books on the random oracle model and on theoretical cryptology in general; all the published texts I've seen are very technical and heavy going. Probably the most well-regarded source is a book being written by Oded Goldreich: the online fragments of this can be found at [342]. If you need something with an ISBN, try his lecture notes on 'Modern Cryptography, Probabilistic Proofs and Pseudorandomness' [343], which are pitched at the level of a postgraduate mathematics student. A less thorough but more readable introduction to randomness and algorithms is in [360]. Current research at the theoretical end of cryptology is found at the FOCS, STOC, Crypto, Eurocrypt, and Asiacrypt conferences.

The history of cryptology is fascinating, and so many old problems keep on recurring in modern guises that the security engineer should be familiar with it. The standard work is by David Kahn [428]; there are also compilations of historical articles from *Cryptologia* [229, 227, 228], as well as several books on the history of cryptology during World War II [188, 429, 523, 800]. The NSA Museum at Fort George Meade, Maryland, is also worth a visit, as is the one at Bletchley Park in England.

Finally, no chapter that introduces public key encryption would be complete without a mention that, under the name of 'non-secret encryption,' it was first discovered by James Ellis in about 1969. However, as Ellis worked for GCHQ—Britain's Government Communications Headquarters, the equivalent of the NSA—his work remained classified. The RSA algorithm was then invented by Clifford Cocks, and also kept secret. This story is told in [267]. One effect of the secrecy was that their work was not used: although it was motivated by the expense of Army key distribution, Britain's Ministry of Defence did not start building electronic key distribution systems for its main networks until 1992. It should also be noted that the classified community did not pre-invent digital signatures; they remain the achievement of Whit Diffie and Martin Hellman.

CHAPTER 6

Distributed Systems

You know you have a distributed system when the crash of a computer you've never heard of stops you from getting any work done.

—LESLIE LAMPORT

We've seen in the last few chapters how people can authenticate themselves to systems (and systems can authenticate themselves to each other) using security protocols; how access controls can be used to manage which principals can perform which operations in a system; and some of the mechanics of how crypto can be used to underpin access control in distributed systems. But there's much more to building a secure distributed system than just implementing access controls, protocols, and crypto. When systems become large, the scale-up problems are not linear; there is often a qualitative change in complexity, and some things that are trivial to deal with in a network of only a few machines and principals (such as naming) suddenly become a big deal.

Over the last 35 years, computer science researchers have built many distributed systems and studied issues such as concurrency, failure recovery, and naming. The theory is also supplemented by a growing body of experience from industry, commerce, and government. These issues are central to the design of effective secure systems, but are often handled rather badly. I've already described attacks on security protocols that can be seen as concurrency failures. If we replicate data to make a system fault-tolerant, then we may increase the risk of a compromise of confidentiality. Finally, naming difficulties are probably the main impediment to the construction of public key infrastructures.

6.1 Concurrency

Processes are said to be *concurrent* if they run at the same time, and concurrency gives rise to a number of well-studied problems. Processes may use old data; they can make inconsistent updates; the order of updates may or may not matter; the system might deadlock; the data in different systems might never converge to consistent values; and when it's important to know the exact time, this can be harder than you might think.

Programming concurrent systems is a hard problem in general; and, unfortunately, most of the textbook examples come from the relatively rarefied world of operating system internals and thread management. But concurrency control is also a security issue; like access control, it exists in order to prevent users interfering with each other, whether accidentally or on purpose. Also, concurrency problems can occur at a number of levels in a system, from the hardware right up to the business environment. In what follows, I provide a number of concrete examples that illustrate the effects of concurrency on security. Of course, these are by no means exhaustive.

6.1.1 Using Old Data versus Paying to Propagate State

I've already described two kinds of concurrency problem. First, there are replay attacks on protocols, where an attacker manages to pass off out-of-date credentials. Second, there are race conditions. I mentioned the mkdir vulnerability from Unix, in which a privileged instruction that is executed in two phases can be attacked halfway through the process by renaming an object on which it acts. These problems have been around for a long time. In one of the first multiuser operating systems, IBM's OS/360, an attempt to open a file caused it to be read and its permissions checked; if the user was authorized to access it, it was read again. The user could arrange things so that the file was altered in between [493].

These are examples of a *time-of-check-to-time-of-use* (TOCTTOU) attack. (A systematic way of finding such attacks is presented in [107].) However, preventing them isn't always economical, as propagating changes in security state can be expensive.

For example, the banking industry manages lists of all *hot* credit cards (whether stolen or abused); but there are millions of them worldwide, so it isn't possible to keep a complete hot-card list in every merchant terminal, and it would be too expensive to verify all transactions with the bank that issued the card. Instead, there are multiple levels of stand-in processing. Terminals are allowed to process transactions up to a certain limit (the *floor limit*) offline; larger transactions need online verification with a local bank, which will know about all the local hot cards, plus foreign cards that are being actively abused; above another limit there might be a reference to an organization such as VISA with a larger international list; while the largest transactions might need a reference to the card issuer. In effect, the only transactions that are checked immediately before use are those that are local or large.

Credit cards are interesting because, as people start to build infrastructures of public key certificates to support Web shopping based on the SSL, and corporate networks based on Win2K, there's a fear that the largest cost will be the revocation of public key certificates belonging to principals whose credentials have changed—because they changed address, changed job, had their private key hacked, or whatever. Credit card networks are the largest existing systems that manage the global propagation of security state—which they do by assuming that most events are local, of low value, or both.

6.1.2 Locking to Prevent Inconsistent Updates

When a number of people are working concurrently on a document, they may use a product such as RCS to ensure that only one person has write access at any one time to any given part of it. This illustrates the importance of *locking* as a way to manage contention for resources, such as filesystems, and to reduce the likelihood of conflicting updates. Another mechanism is *callback;* a server may keep a list of all those clients that rely on it for security state, and notify them when the state changes.

These are also issues in secure distributed systems. Credit cards provide an example. If I own a hotel, and a customer presents a credit card on checkin, I ask the card company for a *preauthorization*, which records the fact that I will want to make a debit in the near future; I might register a claim on "up to $500" of her available credit. If the card is cancelled, the following day, her bank can call me and ask me to contact the police or to get her to pay cash. (My bank might or might not have guaranteed me the money; it all depends on the sort of contract I've managed to negotiate with it.) This is an example of the *publish-register-notify* model of how to do robust authorization in distributed systems (of which there's a more general description in [65]).

Callback mechanisms don't provide a universal solution, though. The credential issuer might not want to run a callback service, and the customer might object on privacy grounds to the issuer being told all her comings and goings. Consider passports, for example. In many countries, government ID is required for many transactions, but governments won't provide any guarantee, and most citizens would object if the government kept a record of every time a government-issue ID was presented.

In general, there is a distinction between those credentials whose use gives rise to some obligation on the issuer, such as credit cards, and the others, such as passports. Among the differences is the importance of the order in which updates are made.

6.1.3 Order of Updates

If two large transactions arrive at the government's bank account—say a credit of $500,000 and a debit of $400,000—then the order in which they are applied may not matter much. But if they're arriving at my bank account, the order will have a huge effect on the outcome! In fact, the problem of deciding the order in which transactions are applied has no clean solution. It's closely related to the problem of how to parallelize a computation, and much of the art of building efficient distributed systems lies in arranging matters so that processes are either simple sequential or completely parallel.

The usual algorithm in retail checking account systems is to batch the transctions overnight and apply all the credits for each account before applying all the debits. The inevitable side effect of this is that payments that bounce have to be reversed out. In practice, chains of failed payments terminate, though in theory this isn't necessarily so. In order to limit the *systemic risk* that a nonterminating payment revocation chain might bring down the world's banking system, some interbank payment mechanisms are moving to *real-time gross settlement* (RTGS), whereby transactions are booked in order of arrival. The downside here is that the outcome can depend on network vagaries.

Credit cards operate a mixture of the two strategies, with credit limits run in real time or near real time (each authorization reduces the available credit limit), while settlement is run just as in a checking account. The downside of this is that by putting through a large preauthorization, a merchant can tie up your card.

The checking account approach has recently been the subject of research in the parallel systems community. The idea is that disconnected applications propose tentative update transactions that are later applied to a master copy. Various techniques can be used to avoid instability; mechanisms for tentative update, such as with bank journals, are particularly important [352].

In other systems, the order in which transactions arrive is much less important. Passports are a good example. Passport issuers only worry about their creation and expiration dates, not the order in which visas are stamped on them.

6.1.4 Deadlock

Deadlock is another problem. Things may foul up because two systems are each waiting for the other to move first. A famous exposition of deadlock is the *dining philosophers' problem*. A number of philosophers are seated round a table; each has a chopstick on his left, and can eat only when he can pick up the two chopsticks on either side. Deadlock can follow if they all try to eat at once, and each picks up, say, the chopstick on his right. (This problem, and the algorithms that can be used to avoid it, are presented in a classic paper by Dijkstra [251].)

This can get horribly complex when you have multiple hierarchies of locks, and they're distributed across systems, some of which fail (especially where failures can mean that the locks aren't reliable). A lot has been written on the problem in the distributed systems literature [64]. But it is not just a technical matter; there are many catch-22 situations in business processes. As long as the process is manual, some fudge may be found to get round the catch, but when it is implemented in software, this option may no longer be available.

Sometimes it isn't possible to remove the fudge. In a well-known problem in business—the *battle of the forms*—one company issues an order with its own terms attached, another company accepts it subject to its own terms, and trading proceeds without any agreement about whose conditions govern the contract. This promises to worsen as trading becomes more electronic.

6.1.5 Non-convergent State

When designing protocols that update the state of a distributed system, the conventional wisdom is ACID—transactions should be *atomic, consistent, isolated, and durable*. A transaction is atomic if you "do it all or not at all"—which makes it easier to recover the system after a failure. It is consistent if some invariant is preserved, such as that the books must still balance. This is common in banking systems, and is achieved by insisting that each credit to one account is matched by an equal and opposite debit to another (I discuss this more in Chapter 9, "Banking and Bookkeeping"). Transactions are isolated if they look the same to each other, that is, are serializable; and they are durable if once done they can't be undone.

These properties can be too much, or not enough, or both. Each of them can fail or be attacked in numerous obscure ways, and it's often sufficient to design the system to be *convergent*. This means that, if the transaction volume were to tail off, then eventually there would be consistent state throughout [565]. Convergence is usually achieved using semantic tricks such as timestamps and version numbers; it can often be enough where transactions get appended to files rather than overwritten.

However, in real life, there must also be ways to survive things that go wrong and that are not completely recoverable. The life of a security or audit manager can be a constant battle against entropy: apparent deficits (and surpluses) are always turning up, and sometimes simply can't be explained. For example, different national systems have different ideas of which fields in bank transaction records are mandatory or optional, so payment gateways often have to guess data in order to make things work. Sometimes they guess wrong; and sometimes people see and exploit vulnerabilities that aren't understood until much later (if ever). In the end, things get fudged by adding a correction factor, called something like "branch differences," and setting a target for keeping it below a certain annual threshold.

The battle of the forms just mentioned gives an example of a distributed nonelectronic system that doesn't converge.

In military systems, there is the further problem of dealing with users who request some data for which they don't have a clearance. For example, someone might ask the destination of a warship that's actually on a secret mission carrying arms to Iran. If the user isn't allowed to know this, the system may conceal the fact that the ship is doing something secret by making up a *cover story*. (The problems this causes will be discussed at greater length in Chapter 7, "Multilevel Security.")

6.1.6 Secure Time

The final kind of concurrency problem with special interest to the security engineer is the provision of accurate time. As authentication protocols such as Kerberos can be attacked by inducing an error in the clock, it's not enough to simply trust a time source on the network. There is a dangerous recursion in relying exclusively on secure time for network authentication, as the master clock signal must itself be authenticated. One of the many bad things that can happen if this isn't done right is a *Cinderella attack*. If a security-critical program such as a firewall has a license with a timelock in it, a bad man (or a virus) could wind your clock forward "and cause your software to turn into a pumpkin."

There are several possible approaches:

■ You could furnish every computer with a radio clock, but that can be expensive, and radio clocks—even GPS—can be jammed if the opponent is serious.

■ There are clock synchronization protocols described in the research literature in which a number of clocks "vote" in a way designed to make clock failures and network delays apparent. Even though these are designed to withstand random (rather than malicious) failure, they can often be hardened by having the messages digitally signed.

■ You can abandon absolute time and instead use *Lamport time*, which means that all you care about is whether event A happened before event B, rather than what date it is [486]. Using challenge-response rather than timestamps in security protocols is an example of this; another is given by timestamping services that continually hash all documents presented to them into a running total that's published, and can thus provide proof that a certain document existed by a certain date [364].

In most applications, you may end up using the *Network Time Protocol* (NTP). This has a moderate amount of protection, with clock voting and authentication of time servers. It is dependable enough for many purposes.

6.2 Fault Tolerance and Failure Recovery

Failure recovery is often the most important aspect of security engineering, yet is one of the most neglected. For many years, most of the research papers on computer security have dealt with confidentiality, and most of the rest with authenticity and integrity; availability has been neglected. Yet the actual expenditures of a typical bank are the other way round. Perhaps a third of all IT costs go to availability and recovery mechanisms, such as hot standby processing sites and multiply redundant networks; a few percent are invested in integrity mechanisms such as internal audit; and an almost insignificant amount gets spent on confidentiality mechanisms such as encryption boxes. As you read through this book, you'll see that many other applications, from burglar alarms through electronic warfare to protecting a company from Internet-based service denial attacks, are fundamentally about availability. Fault tolerance and failure recovery are a huge part of the security engineer's job.

Classical system fault tolerance is usually based on mechanisms such as logs and locking, and is greatly complicated when it must be made resilient in the face of malicious attacks on these mechanisms. It interacts with security in a number of ways: the failure model, the nature of resilience, the location of redundancy used to provide it, and defense against service denial attacks. I'll use the following definitions: a *fault* may cause an *error*, which is an incorrect state; this may lead to a *failure*, which is a deviation from the system's specified behavior. The resilience that we build into a system to tolerate faults and recover from failures will have a number of components, such as fault detection, error recovery, and if necessary, failure recovery. The meaning of *mean-time-before-failure* (MTBF) and *mean-time-to-repair* (MTTR) should be obvious.

6.2.1 Failure Models

To decide what sort of resilience we need, we must know what sort of attacks are expected on our system. Much of this will come from an analysis of threats specific to our operating environment, but there are some general issues that bear mentioning.

6.2.1.1 Byzantine Failure

First, the failures with which we are concerned may be normal or *Byzantine*. The Byzantine fault model is inspired by the idea that there are n generals defending Byzantium,

t of whom have been bribed by the Turks to cause as much confusion as possible in the command structure. The generals can pass oral messages by courier, and the couriers are trustworthy. Each general can exchange confidential and authentic communications with each other general (we can also imagine them encrypting and computing a MAC on each message). What is the maximum number t of traitors that can be tolerated?

The key observation is that, if we have only three generals, say Anthony, Basil, and Charalampos, and Anthony is the traitor, then he can tell Basil, "Let's attack," and Charalampos "Let's retreat." Basil can now say to Charalampos "Anthony says let's attack," but this doesn't let Charalampos conclude that Anthony's the traitor. It could just as easily be Basil; Anthony could have said "Let's retreat" to both of them, but Basil lied when he said "Anthony says let's attack."

This beautiful insight is due to Lamport, Shostack, and Peace, who prove that the problem has a solution if and only if $n \geq 3t + 1$ [487]. Of course, if the generals are able to sign their messages, then no general dare say different things to two different colleagues. This illustrates the power of digital signatures in particular and of end-to-end security mechanisms in general. Relying on third parties to introduce principals to each other or to process transactions between them can give great savings, but if the third parties ever become untrustworthy then it can impose significant costs.

6.2.1.2 Interaction with Fault Tolerance

We can constrain the failure rate in a number of ways. The two most obvious are by using *fail-stop processors* and *redundancy*. Either of these can make the system more *resilient*, but their side effects are rather different. Briefly, while both mechanisms may be effective at protecting the integrity of data, a fail-stop processor is likely to be more vulnerable to service denial attacks, whereas redundancy makes confidentiality harder to achieve. If I have multiple sites with backup data, then confidentiality could be broken if any of them gets compromised; and if I have some data that I have a duty to destroy, perhaps in response to a court order, then purging it from backup tapes can be a nightmare.

It is only a slight simplification to say that while replication provides integrity and availability, tamper resistance provides confidentiality, too. I'll return to this theme later. Indeed, the prevalence of replication in commercial systems, and of tamper resistance in military systems, echoes their differing protection priorities.

Still, there are traps for the unwary. In one case in which I was called on as an expert, my client was arrested while using a credit card in a store, accused of having a forged card, and beaten up by the police. He was adamant that the card was genuine. Much later, we got the card examined by VISA who confirmed that it was indeed genuine. What happened, as well as we can reconstruct it, was this. Credit cards have two types of redundancy on the magnetic strip: a simple checksum obtained by combining all the bytes on the track using exclusive-or, and a cryptographic checksum, which I'll describe in detail later in Section 19.3.2. The former is there to detect errors, the latter to detect forgery. It appears that, in this particular case, the merchant's card reader was out of alignment in such a way as to cause an even number of bit errors, which cancelled each other out by chance in the simple checksum, while causing the crypto checksum to fail. The result was a false alarm, and a major disruption in my client's life.

6.2.2 What Is Resilience For?

When introducing redundancy or other resilience mechanisms into a system, we need to be very clear about what they're for. An important consideration is whether the resilience is contained within a single organization.

In the first case, replication can be an internal feature of the server to make it more trustworthy. AT&T has built a system called Rampart in which a number of geographically distinct servers can perform a computation separately, and combine their results using threshold decryption and signature [639]; the idea is to use it for tasks such as key management [640]. IBM has a variant on this idea called Proactive Security. Here, keys are regularly flushed through the system, regardless of whether an attack has been reported [379]. The idea is to recover even from attackers who break into a server and then simply bide their time until enough other servers have also been compromised. The trick of building a secure "virtual server" on top of a number of cheap off-the-shelf machines has turned out to be attractive to people designing certification authority services, because it's possible to have very robust evidence of attacks on, or mistakes made by, one of the component servers [211]. It also appeals to a number of navies, as critical resources can be spread around a ship in multiple PCs, and survive most kinds of damage that don't actually sink the vessel [309].

But often things are much more complicated. A server may have to protect itself against malicious clients. A prudent bank, for example, will assume that many of its customers would cheat it given the chance. Sometimes, the problem is the other way round, in that we have to rely on a number of services, none of which is completely trustworthy. In countries without national ID card systems, for example, a retailer who wants to extend credit to a customer may ask to see three different items that give evidence of the customer's name and address (say, a gas bill, a phone bill, and a pay slip).

The direction of mistrust has an effect on protocol design. A server faced with multiple untrustworthy clients, and a client relying on multiple servers that may be incompetent, unavailable, or malicious, will both wish to control the flow of messages in a protocol in order to contain the effects of service denial. Thus, a client facing several unreliable servers may wish to use an authentication protocol, such as the Needham-Schroeder protocol discussed above; there, the fact that the client can use old server tickets is no longer a bug but a feature. This idea can be applied to protocol design in general [623]. It provides us with another insight into why protocols may fail if the principal responsible for the design, and the principal who carries the cost of fraud, are different; and why designing systems for the real world, where all principals are unreliable and mutually suspicious, is hard.

At a still higher level, the emphasis might be on *security renewability*. Pay-TV is a good example: secret keys and other subscriber management tools are typically kept in a cheap smartcard rather than in an expensive set-top box, so that even if all the secret keys are compromised, the operator can recover by mailing new cards out to the subscribers. I'll go into this in more detail in Chapter 20, "Copyright and Privacy Protection."

6.2.3 At What Level Is the Redundancy?

Systems may be made resilient against errors, attacks, and equipment failures at a number of levels. As with access control systems, these become progressively more complex and less reliable as we go up to higher layers in the system.

Some computers have been built with redundancy at the hardware level, such as multiple CPUs and mirrored disks, to reduce the probability of failure. From the late 1980s, these machines were widely used in transaction processing tasks. Some more modern systems achieve the same goal using massively parallel server farms; *redundant arrays of inexpensive disks* (RAID disks) are a similar concept. But none of these techniques provides a defense against an intruder, let alone faulty or malicious software.

At the next level up is *process group redundancy*. Here, we may run multiple copies of a system on multiple servers in different locations, and get them to vote on the output. This can stop the kind of attack in which the opponent gets physical access to a machine and subverts it, whether by mechanical destruction or by inserting unauthorized software, and destroys or alters data. It can't defend against attacks by authorized users or damage by bad authorized software.

The next level is *backup*. Here, we typically take a copy of the system (also known as a *checkpoint*) at regular intervals. The backup copies are usually kept on media that can't be overwritten, such as tapes with the write-protect tab set, or CDs. We may also keep *journals* of all the transactions applied between checkpoints. In general, systems are made recoverable by a transaction processing strategy of logging the incoming data, trying to do the transaction, logging it again, and then checking to see whether it worked. Whatever the detail, backup and recovery mechanisms not only enable us to recover from physical asset desctruction, they also ensure that if we do suffer an attack at the logical level—such as a time bomb in our software that deletes our customer database on a specific date—we have some hope of recovering. These mechanisms are not infallible, though. The closest that any bank I know of came to a catastrophic computer failure that would have closed their business was when their mainframe software got progressively more tangled as time progressed, and it just wasn't feasible to roll back processing several weeks and try again.

Backup is not the same as *fallback*. A fallback system is typically a less capable system to which processing reverts when the main system is unavailable. An example is the use of manual "zip-zap" machines to capture credit card transactions when electronic terminals fail.

Fallback systems are an example of redundancy in the application layer—the highest layer where we can put it. We might require that a transaction above a certain limit be authorized by two members of staff, that an audit trail be kept of all transactions, and a number of other things. I'll discuss such arrangements at greater length in Chapter 9.

It is important to realize that hardware redundancy, group redundancy, backup and fallback are different mechanisms, which do different things. Redundant disks won't protect against a malicious programmer who deletes all your account files; and backups won't stop him if, rather than just deleting files, he writes code that slowly inserts more and more errors. Neither will give much protection against attacks on data confidentiality. On the other hand, the best encryption in the world won't help you if your data processing center burns down. Real-world recovery plans and mechanisms can get fiendishly complex, and involve a mixture of all of the above.

6.2.4 Service Denial Attacks

One of the reasons we want security services to be fault-tolerant is to make service denial attacks less attractive, more difficult, or both. These attacks are often used as part of a larger attack plan. For example, one might swamp a host to take it temporarily offline, then get another machine on the same LAN (which had already been subverted) to assume its identity for a while. Another possible attack is to take down a security server to force other servers to use cached copies of credentials.

A very powerful defense against service denial is to prevent the opponent mounting a selective attack. If principals are anonymous—or at least there is no name service that will tell the opponent where to attack—then an attack may be ineffective. I'll discuss this further in the context of burglar alarms and electronic warfare.

Where this isn't possible, and the opponent knows where to attack, some types of service denial attacks can be stopped by redundancy and resilience mechanisms, and others can't. For example, the TCP/IP protocol has few effective mechanisms for hosts to protect themselves against various network flooding attacks. An opponent can send a large number of connection requests, to prevent anyone else establishing a connection. Defense against this kind of attack tends to involve tracing and arresting the perpetrator.

Recently, there has been software on the Net that helps the opponent to hack a number of undefended systems and use these as attack robots to flood the victim. I'll discuss this in Chapter 18, "Network Attack and Defense." For now, I'll just remark that stopping such attacks is hard, and replication isn't a complete solution. If you just switch to a backup machine, and tell the name service, it will happily give the new IP address to the attack software as well as to everybody else. Where such a strategy may be helpful is if the backup machine is substantially more capable and thus can cope better with the load. For example, you might failover to a high-capacity Web hosting service. This is in some sense the opposite concept to "fallback."

Finally, where a more vulnerable fallback system exists, a common technique is to force its use by a service denial attack. The classic example is the use of smartcards for bank payments in countries such as France and Norway. Smartcards are generally harder to forge than magnetic strip cards, but perhaps 1 percent of them fail every year, thanks to environmental insults such as static. Also, foreign tourists still use magnetic strip cards. So smartcard payment systems need a fallback mode that does traditional processing. Many attacks target this fallback mode. One trick is to destroy a smartcard chip by connecting it to the electricity mains; a more common trick is just to use credit cards stolen from foreign tourists, or imported from criminals in countries where magnetic stripes are still the norm. In the same way, burglar alarms that rely on network connections for the primary response and fallback to alarm bells may be very vulnerable if the network can be interrupted by an attacker. Few people pay attention any more to alarm bells.

6.3 Naming

Naming is a minor, if troublesome, aspect of ordinary distributed systems, but it becomes surprisingly hard in security engineering. A topical example (as of 2000) is the problem of what sort of names to put on public key certificates. A certificate that says simply, "The person named Ross Anderson is allowed to administer system X" is of little use. Before the arrival of Internet search engines, I was the only Ross Anderson I knew of; now I know of dozens of us. I am also known by different names to dozens of different systems. Names exist in contexts, and naming the principals in secure systems is becoming ever more important and difficult.

There is some hope. Most (though not all) of the problems encountered so far have come from ignoring the established lessons of naming in ordinary distributed systems.

6.3.1 The Distributed Systems View of Naming

During the last quarter of the twentieth century, the distributed systems research community ran up against many naming problems. The basic algorithm used to bind names to addresses is known as *rendezvous:* the principal exporting a name advertises it somewhere, and the principal seeking to import and use it searches for it. Obvious examples include phone books and directories in file systems.

However, the distributed systems community soon realized that naming can get fiendishly complex, and the lessons learned are set out in a classic article by Needham [587]. I'll summarize the main points, and look at which of them apply to secure systems.

1. *The function of names is to facilitate sharing.* This continues to hold: my bank account number exists in order to provide a convenient way of sharing the information that I deposited money last week with the teller from whom I am trying to withdraw money this week. In general, names are needed when the data to be shared is changeable. If I only ever wished to withdraw exactly the same sum as I'd deposited, a bearer deposit certificate would be fine. Conversely, names need not be shared—or linked—where data will not be; there is no need to link my bank account number to my telephone number unless I am going to pay my phone bill from the account.

2. *The naming information may not all be in one place, so resolving names brings all the general problems of a distributed system.* This holds with a vengeance. A link between a bank account and a phone number assumes both of them will remain stable. When each system relies on the other, an attack on one can affect both. In the days when electronic banking was dial-up rather than Web-based, a bank that identified its customers using calling-line ID was vulnerable to attacks that circumvented the security of the telephone exchange (such as tapping into the distribution frame in an apartment block, hacking a phone company computer, or bribing a phone company employee).

3. *It is bad to assume that only so many names will be needed.* The shortage of IP addresses, which motivated the development of IP version 6 (IPv6), is well enough discussed. What is less well known is that the most expensive upgrade that the credit card industry ever had to make was not Y2K remediation, but the move from 13-digit credit card numbers to 16. Issuers originally assumed that 13 digits would be enough; but the system ended up with tens of thousands of banks (many with dozens of products), so a 6-digit *bank identification number*

(BIN number) was needed. Some card issuers have millions of customers, so a 9-digit account number is the norm. And there's also a *check digit* (a linear combination of the other digits, which is appended to detect errors).

4. *Global names buy you less than you think.* For example, the 128-bit addresses planned for IPv6 can enable every object in the universe to have a unique name. However, for us to do business, a local name at my end must be resolved into this unique name and back into a local name at your end. Invoking a unique name in the middle may not buy us anything; it may even get in the way if the unique naming service takes time, costs money, or occasionally fails (as it surely will). In fact, the name service itself will usually have to be a distributed system, of the same scale (and security level) as the system we're trying to protect. So we can expect no silver bullets from this quarter. One reason the banking industry is wary of initiatives to set up public key infrastructures which would give each citizen the electronic equivalent of an ID card, is that banks already have unique names for their customers (account numbers). Adding an extra number does little good, but it has the potential to add extra costs and failure modes.

5. *Names imply commitments, so keep the scheme flexible enough to cope with organizational changes.* This sound principle was ignored in the design of Cloud Cover, the U.K. government's key management system for secure email [50]. There, principals' private keys are generated by encrypting their names under departmental master keys. So reorganizations mean that the security infrastructure must be rebuilt.

6. *Names may double as access tickets, or capabilities.* We have already seen a number of examples of this in the chapters on protocols and passwords. In general, it's a bad idea to assume that today's name won't be tomorrow's password or capability—remember the Utrecht fraud discussed in Section 2.4. (This is one of the arguments for making all names public keys—"keys speak in cyberspace" in Carl Ellison's phrase—but we've already noted the difficulties of linking keys with names.)

    I've given a number of examples of how things go wrong when a name starts being used as a password. But sometimes the roles of name and password are ambiguous. In order to get entry to the car park I use at the university, I speak my surname and parking badge number into a microphone near the barrier. So if I say, "Anderson, 123" (or whatever), which of these is the password? (In fact it's "Anderson," as anyone can walk through the car park and note down valid badge numbers from the parking permits displayed on the cars.) In this context, a lot deserves to be said about biometrics, which I'll postpone until Chapter 13.

7. *Things are made much simpler if an incorrect name is obvious.* In standard distributed systems, this enables us to take a liberal attitude toward cacheing. In payment systems, credit card numbers may be accepted while a terminal is offline as long as the credit card number appears valid (i.e., the last digit is a proper check digit of the first 15) and is not on the hot-card list. Certificates provide a higher-quality implementation of the same basic concept.

    It's important where the name is checked. The credit card check digit algorithm is deployed at the point of sale, so it is inevitably public. A further check—the *card verification value* (CVV) on the magnetic strip—is computed with secret keys, but can be checked at the issuing bank, the acquiring bank, or even at a network switch (if one trusts these third parties with the keys). This is more expensive, and still vulnerable to network outages.

8. *Consistency is hard, and is often fudged. If directories are replicated, then you may find yourself unable to read, or to write, depending on whether too many or too few directories are available.* Naming consistency causes problems for e-commerce in a number of ways, of which perhaps the most notorious is the barcode system. Although this is simple enough in theory—with a unique numerical code for each product—in practice, it can be a nightmare, as different manufacturers, distributors, and retailers attach quite different descriptions to the barcodes in their databases. Thus, a search for products by "Kellogg's" will throw up quite different results depending on whether or not an apostrophe is inserted, and this can cause great confusion in the supply chain. Proposals to fix this problem can be surprisingly complicated [387].

   There are also the issues of covergence discussed above; data might not be consistent across a system, even in theory. There are also the problems of timeliness, such as the revocation problem for public key certificates.

9. *Don't get too smart. Phone numbers are much more robust than computer addresses.* Amen to that; but it's too often ignored by secure system designers. Bank account numbers are much easier to deal with than the X.509 certificates proposed for protocols such as SET—which was supposed to be the new standard for credit card payments on the Net, but which has so far failed to take off as a result of its complexity and cost. I discuss X.509 and SET in Part 2.

10. *Some names are bound early, others not; and in general it is a bad thing to bind early if you can avoid it.* A prudent programmer will normally avoid coding absolute addresses or filenames, as that would make it hard to upgrade or replace a machine. He will prefer to leave this to a configuration file or an external service such as DNS. (This is another reason not to put addresses in names.) Here, there can be a slight tension with some protection goals: secure systems often want stable and accountable names, as any third-party service used for last-minute resolution could be a point of attack. Knowing them well in advance permits preauthorization of transactions and other such optimizations.

So, of Needham's 10 principles for distributed naming, nine apply directly to distributed secure systems. The (partial) exception is whether names should be bound early or late.

6.3.2 What Else Goes Wrong

Needham's principles, although very useful, are not sufficient. They were designed for a world in which naming systems could be designed and imposed at the system owner's convenience. When we move from distributed systems in the abstract to the reality of modern Internet-based (and otherwise interlinked) service industries, there is quite a lot more to say.

6.3.2.1 Naming and Identity

The most obvious difference is that the principals in security protocols may be known by many different kinds of name—a bank account number, a company registration number, a personal name plus a date of birth or a postal address, a telephone number, a passport number, a health service patient number, or a userid on a computer system.

As I mentioned in the introductory definitions, a common mistake is to confuse naming with identity. *Identity* is when two different names (or instances of the same name) correspond to the same principal (this is known in the distributed systems literature as an *indirect name* or *symbolic link*). The classic example comes from the registration of title to real estate. It is very common that someone who wishes to sell a house uses a different name than they did at the time it was purchased: they might have changed name on marriage, or after a criminal conviction. Changes in name usage are also common. For example, the DE Bell of the Bell-LaPadula system (which I'll discuss in the next chapter) wrote his name "D. Elliot Bell" in 1973 on that paper; but he was always known as David, which is how he now writes his name, too. A land registration system must cope with a lot of identity issues like this.

A more typical example of identity might be a statement such as, "The Jim Smith who owns bank account number 12345678 is the Robert James Smith with passport number 98765432 and date of birth 3/4/56." It may be seen as a symbolic link between two separate systems—the bank's and the passport office's. Note that the latter part of this identity encapsulates a further identity, which might be something like, "The U.S. passport office's file number 98765432 corresponds to the entry in birth register for 3/4/56 of one Robert James Smith." In general, names may involve several steps of recursion.

6.3.2.2 Cultural Assumptions

The assumptions that underlie names often change from one country to another. In the English-speaking world, people may generally use as many names as they please; a name is simply what you are known by. But some countries forbid the use of aliases, and others require them to be registered. This can lead to some interesting scams. In at least one case, a British citizen has evaded pursuit by foreign tax authorities by changing his name. On a less exalted plane, women who pursue academic careers and change their name on marriage may wish to retain their former name for professional use, which means that the name on their scientific papers is different from their name on the payroll. This has caused a huge row at my university, which introduced a unified ID card system keyed to payroll names, without support for aliases.

In general, many of the really intractable problems arise when an attempt is made to unify two local naming systems that turn out to have incompatible assumptions. As electronics invade everyday life more and more, and systems become linked up, conflicts can propagate and have unexpected remote effects. For example, one of the lady professors in dispute over our university card is also a trustee of the British Library, which issues its own admission tickets on the basis of the name on the holder's home university library card.

Even human naming conventions are not uniform. Russians are known by a forename, a patronymic, and a surname; Icelanders have no surname but are known instead by a given name, followed by a patronymic if they are male and a matronymic if they are female. This causes problems when they travel. When U.S. immigration comes across Maria Trosttadóttir and learns that Trosttadóttir isn't a surname or even a patronymic, its standard practice is to compel her to adopt as a surname a patronymic (say, Carlsson if her father was called Carl). This causes unnecessary offense.

The biggest cultural divide is often thought to be that between the English-speaking countries, where identity cards are considered to be unacceptable on privacy grounds (unless they're called drivers' licenses or health service cards), and the countries conquered by Napoleon (or by the Soviets) where identity cards are the norm. Other examples are more subtle. I know Germans who refuse to believe that a country can function at all without a proper system of population registration and ID cards, yet are asked for their ID card only rarely (for example, to open a bank account or get married). Their card number can't be used as a name, because it is a document number and changes every time a new card is issued. A Swiss hotelier may be happy to register a German guest on sight of an ID card rather than a credit card, but if he discovers some damage after a German guest has checked out, he may be out of luck. And the British passport office will issue a citizen with more than one passport at the same time, if he says he needs them to make business trips to (say) Cuba and the USA; so our Swiss hotelier, finding that a British guest has just left without paying, can't rely on the passport number to have him stopped at the airport.

There are many other hidden assumptions about the relationship between governments and people's names, and they vary from one country to another in ways which can cause subtle security failures.

6.3.2.3 Semantic Content of Names

Another hazard arises on changing from one type of name to another without adequate background research. A bank got sued after it moved from storing customer data by account number to storing it by name and address. The bank wanted to target junk mail more accurately, so it had a program written to link all the accounts operated by each of its customers. The effect for one customer was that the bank statement for the account he maintained for his mistress got sent to his wife, who divorced him.

Sometimes naming is simple, but sometimes it merely appears to be. For example, when I got a monthly ticket for the local swimming pool, the cashier simply took the top card off a pile, swiped it through a reader to tell the system it was now live, and gave it to me. I had been assigned a random name—the serial number on the card. Many U.S. road toll systems work in much the same way. Sometimes a random, anonymous name can add commercial value. In Hong Kong, toll tokens for the Aberdeen tunnel could be bought for cash or at a discount in the form of a refillable card. In the run-up to the transfer of power from Britain to Beijing, many people preferred to pay extra for the less traceable version, as they were worried about surveillance by the new police force.

Semantics of names can change. I once got a hardware store loyalty card with a random account number (and no credit checks). I was offered the chance to change this into a bank card after the store was taken over by the supermarket, and the supermarket started a bank. (This appears to have ignored money-laundering regulations that all new bank customers must be identified and have references taken up.)

Assigning bank account numbers to customers might have seemed unproblematic—but as the above examples show, systems may start to construct assumptions about relationships between names that are misleading and dangerous.

6.3.2.4 Uniqueness of Names

Human names evolved when we lived in small communities. They were not designed for the Internet. There are now many more people (and systems) online than we are used to dealing with. As I remarked at the beginning of this section, I used to be the only Ross Anderson I knew of, but thanks to Internet search engines, I now know dozens of namesakes. Some of them work in fields I've also worked in, such as software engineering and electric power distribution; the fact that I'm `www.ross-anderson.com` and `ross.anderson@iee.org` is just luck—I got there first. (Even so, `rjanderson @iee.org` is somebody else.) So even the combination of a relatively rare name and a specialized profession is still ambiguous.

6.3.2.5 Stability of Names and Addresses

Many names include some kind of address, yet addresses change. About a quarter of Cambridge phone book addresses change every year; with email, the turnover is probably higher. A project to develop a directory of people who use encrypted email, together with their keys, found that the main cause of changed entries was changes of email address [42]. (Some people had assumed it would be the loss or theft of keys; the contribution from this source was precisely zero.)

A potentially serious problem could arise with IPv6. The security community assumes that v6 IP addresses will be stable, so that public key infrastructures can be built to bind principals of various kinds to them. All sorts of mechanisms have been proposed to map real-world names, addresses, and even document content indelibly and eternally onto 128-bit strings (see, for example, [365]). The data communications community, on the other hand, assumes that IPv6 addresses will change regularly. The more significant bits will change to accommodate more efficient routing algorithms, while the less significant bits will be used to manage local networks. These assumptions can't both be right.

Distributed systems pioneers considered it a bad thing to put addresses in names [565]. But in general, there can be multiple layers of abstraction, with some of the address information at each layer forming part of the name at the layer above. Also, whether a namespace is better flat depends on the application. Often people end up with different names at the departmental and organizational level (such as `rja14@cam.ac.uk` and `ross.anderson@cl.cam.ac.uk` in my own case). So a clean demarcation between names and addresses is not always possible.

Authorizations have many (but not all) of the properties of addresses. Designers of public key infrastructures are beginning to realize that if a public key certificate contains a list of what it may be used for, then the more things on this list the shorter its period of usefulness. A similar problem besets systems where names are composite. For example, some online businesses recognize me by the combination of email address and credit card number. This is clearly bad practice. Quite apart from the fact that I have several email addresses, I have several credit cards. The one I use will depend on which of them is currently giving the best cashback or the most air miles. (So if the government passes a law making the use of pseudonyms on the Net illegal, does this mean I have to stick to the one ISP and the one credit card?)

6.3.2.6 Restrictions on the Use of Names

This brings us to a further problem. Some names may be used only in restricted circumstances. This may be laid down by law, as with the U.S. *Social Security number* (SSN) and its equivalents in many European countries. Sometimes it is a matter of marketing. I would rather not give out my residential address (or my home phone number) when shopping on the Web, and will avoid businesses that demand them.

Memorable pseudonyms are sometimes required. In a university, one occasionally has to change email addresses, for example, when a student is a victim of cyberstalking. Another example is where a celebrity wants a private mailbox as well as the "obvious" one that goes to her secretary.

Sometimes it's more serious. Pseudonyms are often used as a *privacy-enhancing technology*. They can interact with naming in unexpected ways. For example, it's fairly common for hospitals to use a patient number as an index to medical record databases, as this may allow researchers to use pseudonymous records for some limited purposes without much further processing. This causes problems when a merger of health maintenance organizations, or a new policy directive in a national health service, forces the hospital to introduce uniform names. Patient confidentiality can be completely undermined. (I'll discuss anonymity further in Chapter 20, and its particular application to medical databases in Chapter 8.)

Finally, when we come to law and policy, the definition of a name turns out to be unexpectedly tricky. Regulations that allow police to collect communications data—that is, a record of who called whom and when—are often very much more lax than the regulations governing phone tapping; in many countries, police can get this data just by asking the phone company. An issue that caused a public outcry in the United Kingdom was whether this enables them to harvest the URLs that people use to fetch Web pages. URLs often have embedded in them data such as the parameters passed to search engines. Clearly, there are policemen who would like a list of everyone who hit a URL such as `http://www.google.com/search?q=cannabis+cultivation+UK`; just as clearly, many people would consider such large-scale trawling to be an unacceptable invasion of privacy. On the other hand, if the police are limited to monitoring IP addresses, they could have difficulties tracing criminals who use transient IP addresses provided by free ISP services.

6.3.3 Types of Name

The complexity is organizational and technical, as well as political. I noted in the introduction that names can refer not just to persons and machines acting on their behalf, but also to organizations, roles ("the officer of the watch"), groups, and compound constructions: *principal in role*—Alice as manager; *delegation*—Alice for Bob; *conjunction*—Alice and Bob. Conjunction often expresses implicit access rules: "Alice acting as branch manager plus Bob as a member of the group of branch accountants."

That's only the beginning. Names also apply to services (such as NFS or a public key infrastructure) and channels (which might mean wires, ports, or crypto keys). The same name might refer to different roles: "Alice as a computer game player" ought to have less privilege than "Alice the system administrator." The usual abstraction used in the security literature is to treat them as different principals. This all means that there's no easy mapping between names and principals.

Finally, there are functional tensions that come from the underlying business processes rather from system design. Businesses mainly want to get paid, while governments want to identify people uniquely. In effect, business wants a credit card number while government wants a passport number. Building systems that try to be both—as some governments are trying to encourage—is a tar-pit. There are many semantic differences. You can show your passport to a million people, if you wish, but you had better not try that with a credit card. Banks want to open accounts for anyone who turns up with some money; governments want them to verify people's identity carefully in order to discourage money laundering. The list is a long one.

6.4 Summary

Many secure distributed systems have incurred huge costs or developed serious vulnerabilities, because their designers ignored the basic lessons of how to build (and how not to build) distributed systems. Most of these lessons are still valid, and there are more to add.

A large number of security breaches are concurrency failures of one kind or another; systems use old data, make updates inconsistently or in the wrong order, or assume that data are consistent when they aren't and can't be. Knowing the right time is harder than it seems.

Fault tolerance and failure recovery are critical. Providing the ability to recover from security failures, and random physical disasters, is the main purpose of the protection budget for many organizations. At a more technical level, there are significant interactions between protection and resilience mechanisms. Byzantine failure—where defective processes conspire, rather than failing randomly—is an issue, and interacts with our choice of cryptographic tools. There are many different flavors of redundancy, and we have to use the right combination. We need to protect not just against failures and attempted manipulation, but also against deliberate attempts to deny service, which may often be part of larger attack plans.

Many problems also arise from trying to make a name do too much, or making assumptions about it which don't hold outside of one particular system, or culture, or jurisdiction. For example, it should be possible to revoke a user's access to a system by cancelling their user name without getting sued on account of other functions being revoked. The simplest solution is often to assign each principal a unique identifier used for no other purpose, such as a bank account number or a system logon name. But many problems arise when merging two systems that use naming schemes that are incompatible for some reason. Sometimes this merging can even happen by accident—an example being when two systems use a common combination such as "name plus date of birth" to track individuals.

Research Problems

In the research community, secure distributed systems tend to have been discussed as a side issue by experts on communications protocols and operating systems, rather than as a discipline in its own right. So it is a relatively open field, and one that I feel holds much promise over the next five to ten years.

There are many technical issues which I've touched on in this chapter, such as how we design secure time protocols and the complexities of naming. But perhaps the most important research problem is to work out how to design systems that are resilient in the face of malice, that degrade gracefully, and whose security can be recovered simply once the attack is past. This may mean revisiting the definition of convergent applications. Under what conditions can we recover neatly from corrupt security state? Do we have to rework recovery (which explores how to rebuild databases from backup tapes)? What interactions are there between recovery mechanisms and particular protection technologies? In what respects should protection mechanisms be separated from resilience mechanisms, and in what respects should they be separated? What other pieces are missing from the jigsaw?

Further Reading

There are many books on distributed systems. I've found Sape Mullender's asthology [565] to be helpful and thought-provoking for graduate students, while the textbook we recommend to our undergraduates by Jean Bacon [64] is also worth reading. Geraint Price has a survey of the literature on the interaction between fault tolerance and security [623]. The research literature on concurrency, such as the SIGMOD conferences, has occasional gems. But the most important practical topic for the working security engineer is probably contingency planning. There are many books on this topic; the one I have on my shelf is by Jon Toigo [749].

PART

Two

In the second part of the book, I describe a large number of applications of secure systems, many of which introduce particular protection concepts or technologies.

There are four successive themes. Chapters 7 through 9 look at conventional computer security issues, and by discussing what one is trying to do and how it's done in different environments—the military, banks, and healthcare—I introduce security policy models, which set out the protection concepts that real systems try to implement. I also introduce the first detailed case studies in these chapters. An example is the worldwide network of automatic teller machines, which illustrates many of the problems of transferring familiar protection properties from a bank branch to a global distributed environment using cryptography.

Chapters 10 through 15 look at the hardware engineering aspects of information security. This includes biometrics, the design of various tokens such as smartcards, tamper resistance and tamper evidentness, emission security, and seals. New applications that illustrate the technologies are described, ranging from electronic warfare and nuclear weapons control to taximeters, truck speed limiters, and prepayment gas meters.

The third theme is attacks on networks. I start off in Chapter 16 by covering electronic and information warfare, as these activities give some of the more extreme examples and show how far techniques of denial, deception, and exploitation can be taken by a resourceful opponent under severe operational pressure. This chapter also gives a view of surveillance and intrusion from the point of view of police forces and intelligence agencies, and introduces a number of new concepts, such as anonymity and traffic analysis. We then study the lessons of history by examining frauds on phone systems and on applications that rely on them in Chapter 17. This sets the scene for a discussion in Chapter 18 of attacks on computer networks and defensive technologies such as firewalls and intrusion detection.

The fourth theme is electronic commerce, which I tackle in Chapters 19 and 20. The most high-profile applications are schemes for protecting credit card transactions on the Net, such as SSL/TLS; they are also used for other applications such as medical image distribution. They introduce the debate about public key infrastructures. In addition, I consider mechanisms for copyright protection, specifically, pay-TV, DVD, and copyright watermarking.

One reason for this ordering is to give the chapters a logical progression. Thus, for example, I discuss frauds against magnetic stripe bank cards before going on to describe the smartcards that may replace them and the pay-TV systems that actually use smartcards today. That said, sometimes a neat linear ordering isn't possible, as a particular technology has evolved through a number of iterations involving more than one application. In that case, I try to describe it in a case history.

Finally, to keep the book manageable for readers who will use it primarily as a reference rather than as a textbook, I have put the more technical material toward the end of each chapter or section. That way, if you get lost at a first reading, you can just skip to the next section and carry on.

Multilevel Security

*At times, in the name of national security, secrecy has put that very
security in harm's way.*

—DANIEL PATRICK MOYNIHAN

*I brief;
you leak;
he/she commits a criminal offence
by divulging classified information*

—BRITISH CIVIL SERVICE PROVERB

7.1 Introduction

I mentioned in the introduction that military database systems, which can hold information at a number of different levels of classification (confidential, secret, top secret, . . .)
have to ensure that data can be read only by a principal whose level is at least as high
as the data's classification. These systems are important because:

- A huge amount of research has been done on them, thanks to military funding
  for computer science in the United States. So the military model of protection
  has been worked out in much more detail than any other, and it gives us a lot of
  examples of the second-order and even third-order effects of implementing a
  security policy rigorously.

- Some of the products developed to support military multilevel security may find
  a new lease on life as platforms for firewalls and Web servers. They give some
  assurance that even although a firewall or server software might be hacked, the
  underlying operating system is not likely to be.

- Although multilevel concepts were originally developed to support confidentiality in military systems, there are now many commercial systems that use multilevel integrity policies. For example, phone companies want their billing system to be able to see what's happening in their switching system, but not affect it.

- Multilevel confidentiality ideas are often applied in environments where they're ineffective or even harmful, because of the major vested interests and momentum behind them.

Sir Isaiah Berlin famously described thinkers as either foxes or hedgehogs: a fox knows many little things, while a hedgehog knows one big thing. The multilevel philosophy is the hedgehog approach to security engineering.

7.2 What Is a Security Policy Model?

Where a top-down approach to security engineering is possible, it will typically take the form of *threat model—security policy—security mechanisms*. The critical, and often neglected, part of this process is the security policy.

By a security policy, I mean a document that expresses clearly and concisely what the protection mechanisms are to achieve. It is driven by our understanding of threats, and in turn drives our system design. It will often take the form of statements about which users may access which data. It plays the same role in specifying the system's protection requirements, and evaluating whether they have been met, as the system specification does for general functionality. Indeed, a security policy may be part of a system specification, and like the specification, its primary function is to communicate.

Many organizations use the phrase 'security policy' to mean a collection of vapid statements. Figure 7.1 gives a simple example. This sort of waffle is very common, but is useless to the security engineer.

Its first failing is that it dodges the central issue, namely 'Who determines "need-to-know" and how?' Second, it mixes statements at a number of different levels (organizational approval of a policy logically should not be part of the policy itself). Third, there is a mechanism, but it's implied rather than explicit: "staff shall obey"—but what does this mean they actually have to do? Must the obedience be enforced by the system, or are

---

Megacorp Inc security policy

1. This policy is approved by Management.

2. All staff shall obey this security policy.

3. Data shall be available only to those with a "need-to-know".

4. All breaches of this policy shall be reported at once to Security.

Figure 7.1   A typical corporate information security policy.

users "on their honor?" Fourth, how are breaches to be detected and who has a specific duty to report them?

We must do better than this. In fact, because the term 'security policy' is widely abused to mean a collection of managerialist platitudes, there are three more precise terms that have come into use to describe the specification of protection requirements:

A *security policy model* is a succinct statement of the protection properties that a system, or generic type of system, must have. Its key points can typically be written down in a page or less. It is the document in which the protection goals of the system are agreed to by an entire community, or with the top management of a customer. It may also be the basis of formal mathematical analysis.

A *security target* is a more detailed description of the protection mechanisms that a specific implementation provides, and how they relate to a list of control objectives (some but not all of which are typically derived from the policy model). The security target forms the basis for testing and evaluation of a product.

A *protection profile* is like a security target but expressed in an implementation-independent way to enable comparable evaluations across products and versions. This can involve the use of a semi-formal language or at least of suitable security jargon. A protection profile is a requirement for products that are to be evaluated under the *Common Criteria* [574] (I discuss the Common Criteria in Part 3; they are associated with a scheme used by many governments for mutual recognition of security evaluations of defense information systems).

When I don't have to be so precise, I may use the phrase security policy to refer to any or all of the above. I will never use the term to refer to a collection of platitudes.

Sometimes, we are confronted with a completely new application, and have to design a security policy model from scratch. More commonly, a model already exists; we just have to choose the right one, and develop it into a security target. Neither of these steps is easy. Indeed, one of the purposes of this section is to provide a number of security policy models, describe them in the context of real systems, and examine the engineering mechanisms (and associated constraints) that a security target can use to meet them.

Finally, there is a third usage of the phrase 'security policy,' to mean a list of specific configuration settings for some protection product. I will refer to this as *configuration management* or, occasionally, as *trusted configuration management*, in what follows.

7.3 The Bell-LaPadula Security Policy Model

The best-known example of a security policy model was proposed by David Bell and Len LaPadula in 1973, in response to U.S. Air Force concerns over the security of time-sharing mainframe systems. By the early 1970s, people had realized that the protection offered by many commercial operating systems was poor, and was not getting any better. As soon as one operating system bug was fixed, some other vulnerability would be discovered. (Modern reliability growth models can quantify this and confirm that the pessimism was justified; I discuss them further in Section 23.2.4). There was the constant worry that even unskilled users would discover loopholes, and use them opportunistically; there was also a keen and growing awareness of the threat from malicious code. There was a serious scare when it was discovered that the Pentagon's World Wide Military

Command and Control System was vulnerable to Trojan Horse attacks; this had the effect of restricting its use to people with a 'Top Secret' clearance, which was inconvenient. Finally, academic and industrial researchers were coming up with some interesting new ideas on protection, which we'll discuss below.

A study by James Anderson led the U.S. government to conclude that a secure system should do one or two things well; and that these protection properties should be enforced by mechanisms that were simple enough to verify and that would change only rarely [16]. It introduced the concept of a *reference monitor*, a component of the operating system that would mediate access control decisions and be small enough to be subject to analysis and tests, the completeness of which could be assured. In modern parlance, such components—together with their associated operating procedures—make up the *Trusted Computing Base* (TCB). More formally, the TCB is defined as the set of components (hardware, software, human, etc.) whose correct functioning is sufficient to ensure that the security policy is enforced, or, more vividly, whose failure could cause a breach of the security policy. The Anderson report's goal was to make the security policy simple enough for the TCB to be amenable to careful verification.

But what are these core security properties that should be enforced above all others?

7.3.1 Classifications and Clearances

World War II, and the Cold War that followed, led NATO governments to move to a common protective marking scheme for labelling the sensitivity of documents. *Classifications* are labels, which run upward from *Unclassified* through *Confidential*, *Secret*, and *Top Secret*. The details change from time to time. The original idea was that information whose compromise could cost lives was marked 'Secret' while information whose compromise could cost many lives was 'Top Secret'. Government employees have *clearances* depending on the care with which they've been vetted; in the United States, for example, a 'Secret' clearance involves checking FBI fingerprint files, while 'Top Secret' also involves background checks for the previous 5 to 15 years' employment [244].

The access control policy was simple: an official could read a document only if his clearance was at least as high as the document's classification. So an official cleared to 'Top Secret' could read a 'Secret' document, but not vice versa. The effect is that information may only flow upward, from Confidential to Secret to Top Secret (see Figure 7.2), but it may never flow downward unless an authorized person takes a deliberate decision to declassify it.

There are also document-handling rules; thus, a 'Confidential' document might be kept in a locked filing cabinet in an ordinary government office, while higher levels may require safes of an approved type, guarded rooms with control over photocopiers, and

```
|| TOP SECRET   ||
|| SECRET       ||
|| CONFIDENTIAL ||
|| OPEN         ||
```

Figure 7.2 Multilevel security.

so on. (The NSA security manual [582] gives a summary of the procedures used with 'Top Secret' intelligence data.)

The system rapidly became more complicated. The damage criteria for classifying documents were expanded from possible military consequences to economic harm and even political embarrassment. Britain has an extra level, 'Restricted', between 'Unclassified' and 'Confidential'; the United States had this, too, but abolished it after the Freedom of Information Act was passed. America now has two more specific markings: 'For Official Use only' (FOUO) refers to unclassified data that can't be released under the Freedom of Information Act (FOIA), while 'Unclassified but Sensitive' includes FOUO plus material that might be released in response to a FOIA request. In Britain, restricted information is in practice shared freely, but marking everything 'Restricted' allows journalists and others involved in leaks to be prosecuted under Official Secrets law. (Its other main practical effect is that an unclassified U.S. document sent across the Atlantic automatically becomes 'Restricted' in Britain, and then 'Confidential' when shipped back to the United States. American military system builders complain that the U.K. policy breaks the U.S. classification scheme!)

There is also a system of codewords whereby information, especially at Secret and above, can be further restricted. For example, information that might contain intelligence sources or methods—such as the identities of agents or decrypts of foreign government traffic—is typically classified 'Top Secret Special Compartmented Intelligence,' or TS/SCI, which means that so-called *need-to-know* restrictions are imposed as well, with one or more codewords attached to a file. Some of the codewords relate to a particular military operation or intelligence source, and are available only to a group of named users. To read a document, a user must have all the codewords that are attached to it. A classification label, plus a set of codewords, makes up a *security category* or (if there's at least one codeword) a *compartment*, which is a set of records with the same access control policy. I discuss compartmentation in more detail in the next Chapter 8.

There are also *descriptors*, *caveats*, and *IDO markings*. Descriptors are words such as 'Management', 'Budget', and 'Appointments': they do not invoke any special handling requirements, so we can deal with a file marked 'Confidential—Management' as if it were simply marked 'Confidential'. Caveats are warnings, such as "U.K. Eyes Only," or the U.S. equivalent, 'NOFORN'; there are also *International Defense Organization* (IDO) markings such as 'NATO'. The lack of obvious differences between codewords, descriptors, caveats, and IDO marking is one of the factors that can make the system confusing. (A more detailed explanation can be found in [630].)

The final generic comment about access control doctrine is that allowing upward-only flow of information also models what happens in wiretapping. In the old days, tapping someone's telephone meant adding a physical wire at the exchange; nowadays, it's all done in the telephone exchange software, and the effect is somewhat like making the target calls into conference calls with an extra participant. The usual security requirement is that the target of investigation should not know he is being wiretapped, so the third party should be silent—and its very presence must remain unknown to the target. For example, now that wiretaps are usually implemented as silent conference calls, care has to be taken to ensure that the charge for the conference call facility goes to the wiretapper, not to the target. Wiretapping requires an information flow policy in which the 'High' principal can see 'Low' data, but a 'Low' principal can't tell whether 'High' is reading any data, and if so what.

7.3.2 Information Flow Control

It was in the context of the classification of military and intelligence data that the *Bell-LaPadula* (*BLP*) model of computer security was formulated in 1973 by David Bell and Len LaPadula [86]. It is also known as *multilevel security;* systems that implement it are often called *multilevel secure*, or *MLS*, systems. Their basic property is that information cannot flow downward.

More formally, the Bell-LaPadula model enforces two properties:

- The *simple security property:* no process may read data at a higher level. This is also known as *no read up (NRU);*

- The **-property:* no process may write data to a lower level. This is also known as *no write down (NWD)*.

The *-property was Bell and LaPadula's critical innovation. It was driven by the fear of attacks using malicious code. An uncleared user might write a Trojan and leave it around where a system administrator cleared to 'Secret' might execute it; it could then copy itself into the 'Secret' part of the system, read the data there and try to signal it down somehow. It's also quite possible that an enemy agent could get a job at a commercial software house and embed some code in a product that would look for secret documents to copy. If it could then copy them down to where its creator could read it, the security policy would have been violated. Information might also be leaked as a result of a bug, if applications could write down.

Vulnerabilities such as malicious and buggy code are assumed to be given. It is therefore necessary for the system to enforce the security policy independently of user actions (and, by extension, of the actions taken by programs run by users). So we must prevent programs running at 'Secret' from writing to files at 'Unclassified'; or, more generally, prevent any process at High from signalling to any object (or subject) at Low. In general, when systems are built to enforce a security policy independently of user actions, they are described as having *mandatory access control*, as opposed to the *discretionary access control* in systems such as Unix where users can take their own access decisions about their files. (I won't use these phrases much, as they traditionally refer only to BLP-type policies and don't include many other policies whose rules are just as mandatory).

The Bell-LaPadula model makes it relatively straightforward to verify claims about the protection provided by a design. Given both the simple security property (no read up), and the star property (no write down), various results can be proved about the machine states that can be reached from a given starting state, and this simplifies formal analysis.

There are some elaborations, such as a *trusted subject*, a principal who is allowed to declassify files. To keep things simple, I'll ignore this; I'll also ignore the possibility of incompatible security levels for the time being, and return to them in the next chapter. Finally, in order to simplify matters still further, I will assume from now on that the system has only two levels, High and Low (unless there is some particular reason to name individual compartments).

Multilevel security can be implemented in a number of ways. The textbook mechanism is to implement a reference monitor by beefing up the part of an operating system that supervises all operating system calls and checks access permissions to decide whether the call can be serviced or not. In practice, things get much more complex as it's hard to build systems whose trusted computing base is substantially less than the whole operating system kernel (plus quite a number of its utilities).

Another approach that has been gaining ground as hardware costs have fallen is to replicate systems. One might, for example, have one database at Low and another at High, with a *pump* that constantly copies information from Low up to High. I'll discuss pumps in more detail later.

7.3.3 Standard Criticisms of Bell-LaPadula

The introduction of BLP caused some excitement: here was a straightforward security policy that was clear to the intuitive understanding, yet still allowed people to prove theorems. But John McLean showed that the BLP rules were not in themselves enough. He introduced *System Z*, defined as a BLP system with the added feature that a user can ask the system administrator to temporarily declassify any file from High to Low. In this way, Low users can read any High file without breaking the BLP assumptions.

Bell's argument was that System Z cheats by doing something the model doesn't allow (changing labels isn't a valid operation on the state), and McLean's argument was that it didn't explicitly tell him so. The issue is dealt with by introducing a *tranquility property*. The strong tranquility property says that security labels never change during system operation, while the weak tranquility property says that labels never change in such a way as to violate a defined security policy.

The motivation for the weak property is that in a real system we often want to observe the principle of least privilege, and start a process at the uncleared level, even if the owner of the process were cleared to 'Top Secret'. If she then accesses a confidential email, that session is automatically upgraded to 'Confidential'; and in general, her process is upgraded each time it accesses data at a higher level (this is known as the *high water mark* principle). As subjects are usually an abstraction of the memory management subsystem and file handles, rather than processes, this means that state changes when access rights change, rather than when data actually moves.

The practical implication of this is that a process accumulates the security label or labels of every file that it reads, and these become the default label set of every file that it writes. So a process that has read files at 'Secret' and 'Crypto' will thereafter create files marked (at least) 'Secret Crypto'. This will include temporary copies made of other files. If it then reads a file at 'Top Secret Daffodil', all files it creates after that will be labelled 'Top Secret Crypto Daffodil', and it will not be able to write to any temporary files at 'Secret Crypto.' The effect this has on applications is one of the serious complexities of multilevel security; most application software needs to be rewritten (or at least modified) to run on MLS platforms.

Finally it's worth noting that even with this refinement, BLP still doesn't deal with the creation or destruction of subjects or objects (which is one of the hard problems of building a real MLS system).

7.3.4 Alternative Formulations

Multilevel security properties have been expressed in many other ways. The first multilevel security policy was a version of high water mark written in 1967–8 for the ADEPT-50, a mandatory access control system developed for the IBM S/360 mainframe [798]. This used triples of level, compartment and group, with the groups being files, users, terminals, and jobs. As programs (rather than processes) were subjects, it was vulnerable to Trojan horse compromises, and it was more complex than need be. Nonetheless, it laid the foundation for BLP, and also led to the current IBM S/390 mainframe hardware security architecture [394].

Shortly thereafter, a number of teams produced primitive versions of the lattice model, which I'll discuss in more detail in Chapter 8, Section 8.2.1. These also made a significant contribution to the Bell-LaPadula work, as did Honeywell engineers working on Multics—which led to a system called SCOMP, which I'll discuss in Section 7 below.

Noninterference was introduced by Joseph Goguen and Jose Meseguer in 1982 [339]. In a system with this property, High's actions have no effect on what Low can see. *Nondeducibility* is less restrictive and was introduced by Sutherland in 1986 [743]. Here the idea is to try and prove that Low cannot deduce anything with 100 percent certainty about High's input. Low users can see High actions, just not understand them; a more formal definition is that any legal string of high-level inputs is compatable with every string of low-level events. So for every trace Low can see, there's a similar trace that didn't involve High input. But different low-level event streams may require changes to high-level outputs or reordering of high-level/low-level event sequences.

The motive for nondeducibility is to find a model that can deal with applications such as a LAN on which there are machines at both Low and High, with the High machines encrypting their LAN traffic. (A lot more is needed to do this right, from padding the High traffic with nulls so that Low users can't do traffic analysis, and even ensuring that the packets are the same size—see [659] for an early example of such a system.)

Nondeducibility has historical importance, as it was the first nondeterministic version of Goguen and Meseguer's ideas. But it is hopelessly weak. There's nothing to stop Low making deductions about High input with 99 percent certainty. There are also a whole lot of problems when we are trying to prove results about databases; we have to take into account any information that can be inferred from data structures (such as from partial views of data with redundancy), as well as consider the traces of executing programs. I'll discuss these problems further in Chapter 8, Section 8.3.

Improved models include *generalized noninterference* and *restrictiveness*. The former is the requirement that if one alters a high-level input event in a legal sequence of system events, the resulting sequence can be made legal by, at most, altering one or more subsequent high-level output events. The latter adds a further restriction on the part of the trace, where the alteration of the high-level outputs can take place. This is needed for technical reasons, to ensure that two systems satisfying the restrictiveness property can be composed into a third, which also does. (See [540] which explains these issues.)

The *Harrison-Ruzzo-Ullman* model tackles the problem of how to deal with the creation and deletion of files, an issue on which BLP is silent. It operates on access matrices and verifies whether there is a sequence of instructions that causes an access right to leak to somewhere it was initially not present [373]. This is more expressive than BLP, but more complex and thus less tractable as an aid to verification.

John Woodward proposed a *compartmented mode workstation* (CMW) policy, which attempted to model the classification of information using floating labels, as opposed to the fixed labels associated with BLP [809, 351]. It was ultimately unsuccessful, because labels tend to either float up too far too fast (if done correctly), or they float up more slowly (but don't block all the opportunities for malicious information flow). However, CMW ideas have led to real products—albeit products that provide separation more than information sharing.

The *type enforcement* model, due to Earl Boebert and Richard Kain [122] and later extended by Lee Badger and others [66], assigns each subject to a *domain*, and each object to a *type*. There is a *domain definition table* (DDT), which acts as an access control matrix between domains and types. This is a natural model in the Unix setting, as types can often be mapped to directory structures. It is more general than policies such as BLP, as it starts to deal with integrity as well as confidentiality concerns.

Finally, the policy model getting the most attention at present from researchers is *role-based access control* (RBAC), introduced by David Ferraiolo and Richard Kuhn [291]. This sets out to provide a more general framework for mandatory access control than BLP in which access decisions don't depend on users' names but on the functions they are currently performing within the organization. Transactions that may be performed by holders of a given role are specified, then mechanisms for granting membership of a role (including delegation). Roles, or groups, had for years been the mechanism used in practice in organizations such as banks to manage access control; the RBAC model starts to formalize this. It can deal with integrity issues as well as confidentiality, by allowing role membership (and thus access rights) to be revised when certain programs are invoked. Thus, for example, a process calling untrusted software that had been downloaded from the Net might lose the role membership required to write to sensitive system files.

7.3.5 The Biba Model

Many textbooks mention in passing a model due to Ken Biba [100], which is often referred to as "Bell-LaPadula upside down." It deals with integrity alone and ignores confidentiality entirely. The key observation is that confidentiality and integrity are in some sense dual concepts: confidentiality is a constraint on who can read a message, while integrity is a constraint on who may have written or altered it.

As a concrete application, an electronic medical device such as an ECG may have two separate modes: calibration and use. The calibration data must be protected from being corrupted by normal users, who will therefore be able to read it but not write to it; when a normal user resets the device, it will lose its current user state (i.e., any patient data in memory) but the calibration will remain unchanged.

To model such a system, we can build a multilevel integrity policy with the rules that we must only read up (i.e., a user process can read the calibration data) and write down (i.e., a calibration process can write to a buffer in a user process); but we must never read down or write up, as either could allow High-integrity objects to become contaminated with Low—that is, potentially unreliable—data. The Biba model is often formulated in terms of the *low water mark* principle, which is the dual of the high water mark principle already discussed: the integrity of an object is the lowest level of all the objects that contributed to its creation.

This was the first formal model of integrity. A surprisingly large number of real systems work along Biba lines. For example, the passenger information system in a railroad may get information from the signaling system, but certainly shouldn't be able to affect it (other than through a trusted interface, such as one of the control staff). However, few of the people who build such systems are aware of the Biba model or what it might teach them.

One interesting exception is LOMAC, an extension to Linux that implements a low water mark policy [313]. It is designed to deal with the problem of malicious code arriving somehow over the Net. The system provides two levels—high and low integrity—with system files at High and the network at Low. As soon as a program (such as a demon) receives traffic from the network, it is automatically downgraded to Low. Thus, even if the traffic contains an attack that succeeds in forking a root shell, this shell won't have the capability to write to the password file, for example, as a normal root shell would. As one might expect, a number of system tasks (such as logging) become tricky and require trusted code. Note, though, that this approach merely stops the malware getting root access; it doesn't stop it infecting the Low compartment and using it as a springboard from which to spread elsewhere.

As mentioned above, integrity concerns can also be dealt with by the type enforcement and RBAC models. However, in their usual forms, they revise a principal's privilege when an object is invoked, while low watermark revises it when an object is read. The latter policy is more prudent where we are concerned with attacks exploiting code that is not formally invoked but simply read (as with buffer overflow attacks conducted by "data" read from the Internet).

I will introduce more complex models when I discuss banking and bookkeeping systems in Chapter 9; these are more complex in that they retain security state in the form of dual control mechanisms, audit trails, and so on.

7.4 Examples of Multilevel Secure Systems

Following some research products in the late 1970s (such as KSOS [99], a kernelized secure version of Unix), products that implemented multilevel security policies started arriving in dribs and drabs in the early 1980s. By about 1988, a number of companies had started implementing MLS versions of their operating systems. MLS concepts were extended to all sorts of products.

7.4.1 SCOMP

One of the most important products was the *Secure Communications Processor* (SCOMP), a Honeywell derivative of Multics, launched in 1983 [311]. This was a no-expense-spared implementation of what the U.S. Department of Defense believed it wanted for handling messaging at multiple levels of classification. SCOMP had formally verified hardware and software, with a minimal kernel and four rings of protection (rather than Multics' seven) to keep things simple. Its operating system, STOP, used these rings to maintain up to 32 separate compartments, and to allow appropriate one-way information flows between them.

SCOMP was used in applications such as military *mail guards*, specialized firewalls that typically allow mail to pass from Low to High, but not vice versa [234]. (In general, a device that makes information flow one way only is known as a *data diode*.) SCOMP's successor, XTS-300, supports C2G, the Command and Control Guard. This is used in the *time-phased force deployment data* (TPFDD) system whose function is to plan U.S. troop movements and associated logistics. Overall, military plans are developed as TPFDDs, at a high classification level, then distributed at the appropriate times as commands to lower levels for implementation. The deliberate downgrading of high information raises a number of issues, some of which I'll deal with later. (In the case of TPFDD, the guard examines the content of each record before deciding whether to release it.)

SCOMP's most significant contribution was to serve as a model for the *Orange Book* [240], also known as the *Trusted Computer Systems Evaluation Criteria* (TCSEC). This was the first systematic set of standards for secure computer systems, being introduced in 1985 and finally retired in December 2000. Although it has since been replaced by the Common Criteria, the Orange Book was enormously influential, not just in the United States but among allied powers; countries such as Britain, Germany, and Canada based their own national standards on it, and these national standards were finally subsumed into the Common Criteria [574].

The *Orange Book* allowed systems to be evaluated at a number of levels, with A1 being the highest, and moving down through B3, B2, B1, and C2 to C1. SCOMP was the first system to be rated A1. It was also extensively documented in the open literature. Being first, and being fairly public, it set the standard for the next generation of military systems. This standard has rarely been met since; in fact, the XTS-300 has been evaluated only to B3 (the formal proofs of correctness required for an A1 evaluation were dropped).

7.4.2 Blacker

Blacker was a series of encryption devices designed to incorporate MLS technology. Previously, encryption devices were built with separate processors for the ciphertext, or *Black*, end, and the cleartext, or *Red*, end. Various possible failures can be prevented if one can coordinate the Red and Black processing. One can also make the device simpler, and provide greater operational flexibility: the device isn't limited to separating two logical networks, but can provide encryption and integrity assurance selectively, and interact in useful ways with routers. But a high level of assurance is required that the 'Red' data won't leak out via the 'Black'.

Blacker entered service in 1989, and the main lesson learned from it was the extreme difficulty of accommodating administrative traffic within a model of classification levels [799]. As late as 1994, it was the only communications security device with an A1 evaluation [97]. So it too had an effect on later systems. It was not widely used though, and its successor (the Motorola Network Encryption System), which is still in use, has only a B2 evaluation.

7.4.3 MLS Unix, CMWs, and Trusted Windowing

Most of the available MLS systems are modified versions of Unix, and an example is AT&T's System V/MLS [15]. This added security levels and labels, initially by using some of the bits in the group ID record, and later by using this to point to a more elaborate structure. This enabled MLS properties to be introduced with minimal changes to the system kernel. Other products of this kind included SecureWare (and its derivatives, such as SCO and HP VirtualVault) and Addamax.

Comparted mode workstations (CMWs) allow data at different levels to be viewed and modified at the same time by a human operator, and ensure that labels attached to the information are updated appropriately. The initial demand came from the intelligence community, whose analysts may have access to 'Top Secret' data, such as decrypts and agent reports, and produce reports at the 'Secret' level for users such as political leaders and officers in the field. As these reports are vulnerable to capture, they must not contain any information that would compromise intelligence sources and methods.

CMWs allow an analyst to view the 'Top Secret' data in one window, compose a report in another, and have mechanisms to prevent the accidental copying of the former into the latter (i.e., cut-and-paste works from 'Secret' to 'Top Secret', but not vice versa). CMWs have proved useful in operations, logistics, and drug enforcement as well [396].

For the engineering issues involved in doing mandatory access control in windowing systems, see [273, 274], which describe a prototype for Trusted X, a system implementing MLS but not information labelling. It runs one instance of X Windows per sensitivity level, and has a small amount of trusted code that allows users to cut and paste from a lower level to a higher one. For the specific architectural issues with Sun's CMW product, see [281].

7.4.4 The NRL Pump

It was soon realized that simple mail guards and crypto boxes were too restrictive, as many more networked services were developed besides mail. Traditional MLS mechanisms (such as blind write-ups and periodic read-downs) are inefficient for real-time services.

The US Naval Research Laboratory (NRL) therefore developed the *Pump* (see Figure 7.3), a one-way data transfer device (a data diode) using buffering to allow one-way information flow while limiting the bandwidth of possible backward leakage by a number of mechanisms such as timing randomization of acknowledgment messages [434, 436, 437].

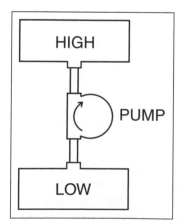

Figure 7.3   The NRL pump.

The attraction of this approach is that it is possible to build MLS systems by using pumps to connect separate systems at different security levels. As these systems don't process data at more than one level, they can be built from cheap commercial-off-the-shelf (COTS) components [438]. As the cost of hardware falls, this becomes the preferred option where it's possible.

The Australian government has developed a product called *Starlight* that uses pump-type technology married to a keyboard switch to provide a nice MLS-type windowing system (albeit without any visible labels), using a bit of trusted hardware that connects the keyboard and mouse with High and Low systems [17]. There is no trusted software. It's been integrated with the NRL Pump. A number of semi-commercial data diode products have also been introduced.

7.4.5 Logistics Systems

Military stores, like government documents, can have different classification levels. Some signals intelligence equipment is 'Top Secret', while things like jet fuel and bootlaces are not; but even such simple commodities may become 'Secret' when their quantities or movements might leak information about tactical intentions. There are also some peculiarities. For example, an inertial navigation system classified 'Confidential' in the peacetime inventory might contain a laser gyro platform classified 'Secret' (thus security levels are *nonmonotonic*).

The systems needed to manage all this seem to be hard to build, as MLS logistics projects in both the United States and Britain have ended up as expensive disasters. The Royal Air Force's Logistics Information Technology System (LITS) was a 10-year (1989–1999), $500 million project to provide a single stores management system for the RAF's 80 bases [571]. It was designed to operate on two levels: 'Restricted' for the jet fuel and boot polish, and 'Secret' for special stores such as nuclear bombs. It was initially implemented as two separate database systems connected by a pump to enforce the MLS property. The project became a classic tale of escalating costs driven by creeping requirements changes. One of these changes was the easing of classification rules at the end of the Cold War. As a result, it was found that almost all the 'Secret' information was now static (e.g., operating manuals for air-drop nuclear bombs, which are now kept in strategic stockpiles rather than at airbases). To save money, the 'Secret' information is now kept on a CD and locked up in a safe.

Logistics systems often have application security features too. The classic example is that ordnance control systems alert users who are about to breach safety rules by putting explosives and detonators in the same truck or magazine [563].

7.4.6 Purple Penelope

In recent years, most governments' information security agencies have been unable to resist user demands to run standard applications (such as MS Office), which are not available for multilevel secure platforms. One response is 'Purple Penelope'. This software, from Britain's Defence Evaluation and Research Agency, puts an MLS wrapper round a Windows NT workstation. It implements the high water mark version of BLP, displaying in the background the current security level of the device, and upgrading it when necessary as more sensitive resources are read. It ensures that the resulting work product is labelled correctly.

Rather than preventing users from downgrading, as a classical BLP system might do, it allows them to assign any security label they like to their output. However, if this involves a downgrade, it requires the user to confirm the release of the data using a trusted path interface, thus ensuring no Trojan or virus can release anything completely unnoticed. Of course, a really clever malicious program can piggyback classified material on stuff that the user does wish to release, so there are other tricks to make that harder. There is also an audit trail to provide a record of all downgrades, so that errors and attacks (whether by users or by malicious code) can be traced after the fact [620].

7.4.7 Future MLS Systems

The MLS industry sees an opportunity in using its products as platforms for firewalls, Web servers, and other systems that are likely to come under attack. Thanks to the considerable effort that has often gone into finding and removing security vulnerabilities, MLS platforms can give more assurance than commodity operating systems that, even if the firewall or Web server software is hacked, the underlying operating system is unlikely to be. The usual idea is to use the MLS platform to separate trusted from untrusted networks, then introduce simple code to bypass the separation in a controlled way. In fact, one of the leading firewall vendors (TIS) was until recently focused on developing MLS operating systems, while Secure Computing Corporation, Cyberguard, and Hewlett-Packard have all offered MLS-based firewall products. The long tradition of using MLS systems as pumps and mail guards means that firewall issues are relatively well understood in the MLS community. (A typical design is described in [162].)

However, the BLP controls do not provide enough of a protection benefit in many commercial environments to justify their high development costs, and widely fielded products are often better because of the evolution that results from large-scale user feedback. We find, for example, two firewall products from the same corporation, doing much the same thing, with one of them MLS (the Standard Mail Guard) and the other based on open source code and aimed at commercial markets (Sidewinder). According to users, the former has "never been able to hold a candle to the latter."

Perhaps the real future of multilevel systems is not in confidentiality, but integrity. Many fielded systems implement some variant of the Biba model (even though their designers may never have heard the word "Biba"). In an electricity utility, for example, the critical operational systems such as power dispatching should not be affected by any others; they can be observed by, but not influenced by, the billing system. Similarly, the billing system and the power dispatching system both feed information into the fraud detection system, and so on, until at the end of the chain we find the executive information systems, which can observe everything (or at least, summaries of everything) while having no direct effect on operations.

Researchers are now starting to build models that accommodate both confidentiality and integrity to observe their interaction and workout how they might apply in environments such as smartcards [440]. Another topic is how mandatory access control models can provide real-time performance guarantees to help prevent service denial attacks [552]. It's already clear that many of the lessons learned in multilevel confidentiality systems also go across. So do a number of the failure modes, which I discuss in the next section.

7.5 What Goes Wrong

As I've frequently pointed out, engineers learn more from the systems that fail than from those that succeed, and MLS systems have certainly been an effective teacher. The large effort expended in building systems to follow a simple policy with a high level of assurance has led to the elucidation of many second- and third-order consequences of information flow controls. I'll start with the more theoretical and work through to the business and engineering end.

7.5.1 Composability

Consider a simple device that accepts two 'High' inputs H_1 and H_2, multiplexes them, encrypts them by xor'ing them with a one-time pad (i.e., a random generator), outputs the other copy of the pad on H_3, and outputs the ciphertext, which being encrypted with a cipher system giving perfect secrecy, is considered to be Low (output L). This is shown in Figure 7.4.

In isolation, this device is provably secure. But if feedback is permitted, then the output from H_3 can be fed back into H_2, with the result that the high input H_1 now appears at the low output L.

Timing inconsistencies can also lead to the composition of two secure systems being insecure (see for example McCullough [534]). Simple information flow doesn't compose; neither does noninterference or nondeducibility. In general, the problem of how to compose two or more secure components into a secure system is hard, even at the relatively uncluttered level of proving results about ideal components. Most of the problems arise when some sort of feedback is introduced into the system; without it, composition can be achieved under a number of formal models [541]. However, in real life, feedback is pervasive, and composition of security properties can be complicated by detailed interface issues, feature interactions, and so on.

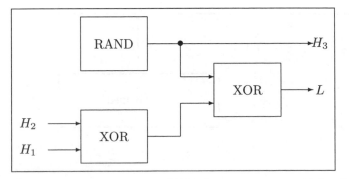

Figure 7.4 Insecure composition of secure systems with feedback.

Finally, the composition of components that have been designed in accordance with two different security policies is harder still. This is bad enough for different variants on the BLP theme but even worse when one of the policies is of a non-BLP type, as we will encounter in the following two chapters.

7.5.2 The Cascade Problem

An example of the difficulty of composing multilevel secure systems is given by the *cascade problem* (Figure 7.5). After the Orange Book introduced a series of graduated evaluation levels, this led to rules about the number of levels a system can span. For example, a system evaluated to B3 is in general allowed to process information for users with a clearance level of Unclassified through Secret, or of Confidential through Top Secret, but not to process Top Secret data with some users restricted to Unclassified only [244].

As the diagram shows, it is straightforward to connect two A1 systems in such a way that this security policy is broken. The first system connects Unclassified and Secret; and its Secret level communicates with the second system, which also processes Top Secret information. (The problem is discussed in more detail in [391].) It illustrates another kind of danger that formal models of security (and practical implementations) must take into account.

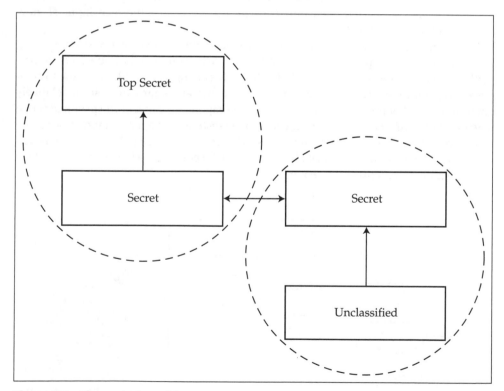

Figure 7.5   The cascade problem.

7.5.3 Covert Channels

One of the reasons these span limits are imposed on multilevel systems emerges from a famous—and extensively studied—problem: the *covert channel*. First pointed out by Butler Lampson in 1973 [488], a covert channel is a mechanism that, though not designed for communication, can nonetheless be abused to allow information to be communicated down from High to Low.

A typical covert channel arises when a High process can signal to a Low process by affecting some shared resource. For example, it could position the disk head at the outside of the drive at time t_i to signal that the i-th bit in a High file was a 1, and position it at the inside to signal that the bit was a 0.

All systems with shared resources must find a balance between covert channel capacity, resource utilization, and fairness. If a machine is shared between High and Low, and resources are not allocated in fixed slices, then the High process can signal by filling up the disk drive, or by using a lot of CPU or bus cycles (some people call the former case a *storage channel* and the latter a *timing channel*, though in practice they can often be converted into each other). There are many others, such as sequential-process IDs, shared file locks, and last access times on files; reimplementing all of these in a multilevel secure way is an enormous task. Various strategies have been adopted to minimize their bandwidth. For example, we can arrange that the scheduler assigns a fixed disk quota to each level, and reads the boot sector each time control is passed downward; we might also allocate a fixed proportion of the available time slices to processes at each level, and change these proportions infrequently. Each change might allow one or more bits to be signalled, but such strategies can significantly reduce the available bandwidth. (A more complex multilevel design, which uses local schedulers at each level, plus a global scheduler to maintain overall consistency, is described in [435].)

It is also possible to limit the covert channel capacity by introducing noise. Some machines have had randomized system clocks for this purpose. But some covert channel capacity almost always remains. (Techniques to analyze the trade-offs between covert channel capacity and system performance are discussed in [353].)

Covert channels also occur at the application layer. A medical example is that, in Britain, personal health information derived from visits to genitourinary meducine (GUM) clinics is High in the sense that it can't be shared with the patient's normal doctor and thus appear in their normal medical record (Low) unless the patient consents. In one case, a woman's visit to a GUM clinic "leaked" when the insurer failed to recall her for a smear test, which her normal doctor knew was due [551]. The insurer knew that a smear test had been done already by the clinic, and didn't want to pay twice. (Some people might say this was a failure of polyinstantiation, which I discuss in 7, or an inference attack, which I'll come to in Chapter 8, Section 8.3.)

The worst case known to me as far as bandwidth is concerned is also a feature of a specific application. It occurs in large early-warning radar systems, where High—the radar processor—controls hundreds of antenna elements that illuminate Low—the target—with high-speed pulse trains that are modulated with pseudorandom noise to make jamming harder. In this case, the radar code must be trusted, as the covert channel bandwidth is many megabits per second.

The case of greatest general interest is multilevel integrity systems, such as banking and utility billing, where a programmer who has inserted Trojan code in a high-integrity bookkeeping system can turn off the billing to an account by a certain pattern of behavior (in a phone system he might call three numbers in succession, for example). Code review is the only real way to block such attacks, though balancing controls can also help (I discuss this in Chapter 9).

The best that developers have been able to do consistently with covert channel bandwidth in time-sharing multilevel operating systems is to limit it to one bit per second or so. (That is now the DoD target [241]; techniques for doing a systematic analysis may be found in [448].) One bit per second may be tolerable in an environment where we wish to prevent large TS/SCI files—such as satellite photographs—leaking down from TS/SCI users to 'Secret' users, and is much less than the rate at which malicious code might hide data in outgoing traffic that would be approved by a guard. However, it is inadequate if we want to prevent the leakage of a cryptographic key. This is one of the reasons for the military doctrine of doing crypto in special-purpose hardware rather than in software. It also explains why span limits are relaxed for *closed security environments*—systems in which application code can be introduced only by suitably cleared personnel (and where "system applications are adequately protected against the insertion of malicious logic"); in such a case, an A1 system is allowed to process both Top Secret and Unclassified data simultaneously [244].

7.5.4 The Threat from Viruses

The vast majority of viruses are found in mass-market products such as PCs and Macs. However, the defense computer community was shocked when Fred Cohen used viruses to penetrate multilevel secure systems easily in 1983. In his first experiment, a file virus which took only eight hours to write-manage to penetrate a system previously believed to be multilevel secure [192].

There are a number of ways in which viruses and other malicious code can be used to perform such attacks. If the reference monitor (or other TCB components) can be corrupted, a virus could deliver the entire system to the attacker, for example by issuing him with an unauthorized clearance. This is why slightly looser rules apply to closed security environments. But even if the TCB remains intact, the virus could still use any available covert channel to signal information down.

In many cases, a TCB will provide some protection against viral attacks, as well as against careless disclosure by users or application software—which is often more important than malicious disclosure. However, the main effect of viruses on military doctrine has been to strengthen the perceived case for multilevel security. The argument goes that, even if personnel can be trusted, one cannot rely on technical measures short of total isolation to prevent viruses moving up the system, so one must do whatever is reasonably possible to stop them signalling back down.

7.5.5 Polyinstantiation

Another problem that has much exercised the research community is *polyinstantiation*. Suppose that our High user has created a file named `agents`, and that our Low user now tries to do the same. If the MLS operating system prohibits this, it will have leaked

Level	Cargo	Destination
Secret	Missiles	Iran
Restricted	–	–
Unclassified	Engine spares	Cyprus

Figure 7.6   How the United States deals with classified data.

Level	Cargo	Destination
Secret	Missiles	Iran
Restricted	Classified	Classified
Unclassified	–	–

Figure 7.7   How Britain deals with classified data.

information—namely, that there is a file called `agents` at High. But if it doesn't, it will now have two files with the same name.

Often, we can solve the problem by a naming convention, which could be as simple as giving Low and High users different directories. But the problem remains a hard one for databases [669]. Suppose that a High user allocates a classified cargo to a ship. The system will not divulge this information to a Low user, who might think the ship is empty, and try to allocate it another cargo or even to change its destination.

The solution favored in the United States for such systems is that the High user allocates a Low cover story at the same time as the real High cargo. Thus, the underlying data will look something like that shown in Figure 7.6.

In the Britain, which does not have a Freedom of Information Act, the theory is simpler: the system will automatically reply 'Classified' to a Low user who tries to see or alter a High record. The two available views would be as shown in Figure 7.7.

This makes the system engineering simpler. It also prevents the mistakes and covert channels which can still arise with cover stories (e.g., a Low user tries to add a container of ammunition for Cyprus). The drawback is that everyone tends to need the highest available clearance to get their work done. (In practice, of course, cover stories may still get used so as not to advertise the existence of a covert mission any more than need be.)

7.5.6 Other Practical Problems

Multilevel secure systems are surprisingly expensive and difficult to build and deploy. There are many sources of cost and confusion.

- MLS systems are built in small volumes, and often to high standards of physical robustness, using elaborate documentation, testing, and other quality control measures driven by military purchasing bureaucracies.

- MLS systems have idiosyncratic administration tools and procedures. A trained Unix administrator can't just take on an MLS installation without significant further training. A USAF survey showed that many MLS systems were installed without their features being used [624].

- Many applications need to be rewritten or at least greatly modified to run under MLS operating systems [655]. For example, CMWs that display information at different levels in different windows, and prevent the user from doing cut-and-paste operations from High to Low, often have problems with code that tries to manipulate the color map. Access to files might be quite different, as might the format of things like access control lists. Another source of conflict with commercial software is the license server; if a High user invokes an application, which goes to a license server for permission to execute, an MLS operating system will promptly reclassify the server High and deny access to Low users. So, in practice, we usually end up (a) running two separate license servers, thus violating the license terms; or (b) having an MLS license server that tracks licenses at all levels and hence must be part of the TCB (this restricts your choice of platforms); or (c) using the licensed software at only one of the levels.

- Because processes are automatically upgraded as they see new labels, the files they use have to be, too. New files default to the highest label belonging to any possible input. The result is a chronic tendency for things to be overclassified.

- It is often inconvenient to deal with "blind write-up"; when a low-level application sends data to a higher-level one, BLP prevents any acknowledgment being sent. The effect is that information vanishes into a "black hole." The answer to this is varied. Some organizations accept the problem as a fact of life; in the words of a former NSA chief scientist, "When you pray to God, you do not expect an individual acknowledgment of each prayer before saying the next one." Others use pumps rather than prayer, and accept a residual covert bandwidth as a fact of life.

- The classification of data is not entirely straightforward:

  - In the run-up to a military operation, the location of "innocuous" stores, such as food, could reveal tactical intentions, and so may be suddenly upgraded. It follows that the tranquility property cannot simply be assumed.

  - Classifications are not necessarily monotone. Equipment classified as 'Confidential' in the peacetime inventory may easily contain components classified 'Secret'.

  - Information may need to be downgraded. An intelligence analyst might need to take a satellite photo classified at TS/SCI, and paste it into an assessment for field commanders at 'Secret'. However, information could have been covertly hidden in the image by a virus, and retrieved later when the file is downgraded. So, downgrading procedures may involve all sorts of special filters, such as lossy compression of images and word processors that scrub and reformat text, in the hope that the only information remaining is that which lies in plain sight. (I discuss information hiding in more detail in the context of copyright marking in Chapter 20.)

  - We may need to worry about the volume of information available to an attacker. For example, we might be happy to declassify any single satellite photo, but declassifying the whole collection would reveal our surveillance capability and the history of our intelligence priorities. Similarly, the government payroll might not be very sensitive per se, but it is well known that journalists can often identify intelligence personnel working under civilian cover from studying the evolution of departmental staff lists over a period of a few years. (I delve into this issue—the "aggregation problem"—in more detail in Chapter 8, Section 8.3.2.)

- A related problem is that the output of an unclassified program acting on unclassified data may be classified. This is related to the aggregation problem just noted.

- There are always system components—such as memory management—that must be able to read and write at all levels. This problem is dealt with by "abstracting it away," and assuming that memory management is part of the trusted computing base that enforces BLP. The practical outcome is that an uncomfortably large part of the operating system (plus utilities, plus windowing system software, plus middleware such as database software) often ends up in the trusted computing base. "TCB bloat" constantly pushes up the cost of evaluation, and reduces assurance.

- Finally, although MLS systems can prevent undesired things (such as information leakage) from happening, they also prevent desired things from happening, too (such as efficient ways of enabling data to be downgraded from High to Low, which are essential if many systems are to be useful). So even in military environments, the benefits MLS systems provide can be very questionable. The associated doctrine also sets all sorts of traps for government systems builders. A recent example comes from the debate over a U.K. law to extend wiretaps to Internet service providers (ISPs). (I discuss this law further in Chapter 21, "E-Policy"). Opponents of the bill forced the government to declare that information on the existence of an interception operation against an identified target would be classified 'Secret'. This would have made wiretaps on Internet traffic impossible without redeveloping all the systems used by ISPs to support an MLS security policy—which would be impractical regardless of the time or budget available. The U.K. government had to declare that it wouldn't apply the laid-down standards in this case because of cost.

7.6 Broader Implications of MLS

The nonmilitary reader's reaction by this point may well be that MLS is clearly impossible to do properly; there are just too many complications. This may be true, but it's also true that Bell-LaPadula is the simplest security policy model we know of; everything else is even harder. We'll look at other models in the next few chapters.

Anyway, although the MLS program has not delivered what was expected, it has spun off a lot of useful ideas and know-how. Worrying about not just the direct ways a secure system can be defeated, but also about the second- and third-order consequences of the protection mechanisms, has been important in developing the underlying science. Practical work on building MLS systems also led people to work through many other aspects of computer security, such as *Trusted Path* (how does a user know he or she is talking to a genuine copy of the operating system?), *Trusted Distribution* (how does a user know he or she is installing a genuine copy of the operating system?) and *Trusted Facility Management* (how can we be sure it's all administered correctly?). In effect, tackling one simplified example of protection in great detail cast light on many things that previously were glossed over. The resulting lessons can be applied to systems with quite different policies. An excellent recent example comes from Cipress, a prototype system built by the Fraunhofer Institute to provide strict copy and usage control of digital media [149]. The security policy amounted to a kind of high water mark; an application which combined a number of protected media streams would produce an output that could only be accessed by a principal with access to all the keys that controlled the input streams. This gave rise to many of the problems we have discussed above, and more: for example, if a media owner revoked access rights to some content, then this could propagate a lock to large numbers of derivative works.

These lessons are set out in the Rainbow Series of books on computer security, which were produced by the NSA following the development of SCOMP and the publication of the Orange Book which it inspired. (These books are so called because of their different-colored covers.) Though the series is notably silent on some topics, such as crypto and emission security, it has done a lot to raise consciousness of operational and evaluation issues which are otherwise easy to ignore (or to dismiss as boring matters best left to the end purchasers). In fact, the integration of technical protection mechanisms with operational and procedural controls is one of the most critical, and neglected, aspects of security engineering. The secure operation of MLS systems is usually much the weakest link in the chain. The main vulnerability of the STU-III secure telephone, for example, is that generals forget to press the 'go secure' button before discussing classified matters. A particularly instructive case history is that of Former CIA Director John Deutch. Deutch was supposed to have separate machines at home for classified and unclassified material, Top Secret communications intelligence files were found on his unclassified machine, which had been used to access high-risk web sites in his absence. Deutch said he was unwilling to use the classified CIA network for some purposes because of the risk that CIA colleagues might get access. A domestic servant, who was an alien, had access to his private machine. Nonetheless, the risk of compromise was held to be less than that of an intruder sneaking into his home to take an image of the disk. The report into this mess by the CIA Office of Inspector General makes instructive reading for anyone concerned with security usability [761]. I will have more to say on this topic in Part 3, and in the context of a number of case studies throughout this book.

All that said, the contribution of the MLS model is not all positive. There is a tactical problem, and a strategic one.

The tactical problem is that the existence of trusted system components, plus a large set of bureaucratic guidelines, has a strong tendency to displace critical thought. Instead of working out a system's security requirements in a methodical way, designers just choose what they think is the appropriate security class of component, then regurgitate the description of this class as the security specification of the overall system [624].

One should never lose sight of the human motivations that drive a system design, and the costs it imposes. Daniel Moynihan [562] provides a critical study of the real purposes and huge costs of obsessive secrecy in U.S. foreign and military affairs. Following a Senate enquiry, He discovered that President Truman was never told of the Venona decrypts because the material was considered 'Army Property'—despite its being the main motivation for the prosecution of Alger Hiss. As he writes in his book: "Departments and agencies hoard information, and the government becomes a kind of market. Secrets become organizational assets, never to be shared save in exchange for another organization's assets." Moynihan reports, for example, that in 1996, the number of original classification authorities decreased by 959 to 4,420 (following post-Cold-War budget cuts), but that the total of all classification actions reported for fiscal year 1996 increased by 62 percent to 5,789,625.

Yet despite the huge increase in secrecy, the quality of intelligence made available to the political leadership appears to have declined over time. Effectiveness is undermined by interagency feuding and refusal to share information, and by the lack of effective external critique.[1] A strong case can be made that MLS systems, by making the classification process easier but controlled data sharing harder, actually impair operational effectiveness.

So the strategic problem is that multilevel security has become so entrenched in government, and in some parts of industry, that it is often used in highly inappropriate ways. Even long-time intelligence insiders have documented this [425]. To solve many problems, we need to be a "fox" rather than a "hedgehog." Even where a simple, mandatory, access control system could be appropriate, we often need to control information flows across, rather than information flows down. Medical systems are a good example of this; and we will look at them in the next chapter.

7.7 Summary

Multilevel secure systems are used in a number of military applications, most notably specialized kinds of firewalls (mail guards and pumps). They may turn out to be excellent platforms for more general kinds of firewall or Web server. Their broader importance comes from two facts: they have been the main subject of computer security research since the mid-1970s, and their assumptions underlie many of the schemes used for security evaluation. It is important for practitioners to understand both the strengths and limitations of MLS systems, so that they can draw on the considerable research literature when it's appropriate, and avoid being dragged into error when it's not.

Research Problems

Multilevel confidentiality appears to have been "done to death" by generations of research students. The opportunities that remain may concern multilevel integrity, and the interaction that multilevel systems have with other security policies: how, for example, should a military hospital combine BLP with the bookkeeping and patient privacy policies discussed in the next two chapters?

---

[1] Although senior people follow the official line when speaking on the record, in private they rail at the penalties imposed by the bureaucracy. My favorite quip is from an exasperated British general: "What's the difference between Jurassic Park and the Ministry of Defence? One's a theme park full of dinosaurs, and the other's a movie!"

Further Reading

One of the better introductions to MLS systems, and especially the problems of databases, is Gollmann's *Computer Security* [344]. Amoroso's *Fundamentals of Computer Security Technology* [15] is the best introduction to the formal mathematics underlying the Bell-LaPadula, noninterference and nondeducibility security models.

The bulk of the published papers on engineering actual multilevel systems can be found in the annual proceedings of three conferences: the IEEE Symposium on Security & Privacy (known as "Oakland," as that's where it's held), the National Computer Security Conference (renamed the National Information Systems Security Conference in 1995), whose proceedings are published by the National Institute of Standards and Technology, and the Computer Security Applications Conference, whose proceedings are (like Oakland's) published by the IEEE. Fred Cohen's experiments on breaking MLS systems using viruses are described in his book, *A Short Course on Computer Viruses* [192]. Many of the classic early papers in the field can be found at the NIST archive [573]. Finally, the classic on the abuse of the classification process to cover up waste, fraud, and mismanagement in the public sector was written by Leslie Chapman [176].

CHAPTER

8

Multilateral Security

Privacy is a transient notion. It started when people stopped believing that God could see everything and stopped when governments realized there was a vacancy to be filled.

—ROGER NEEDHAM

You have zero privacy anyway. Get over it.

—SCOTT MCNEALY

8.1 Introduction

Often, our goal is not to prevent information flowing "down" a hierarchy but to prevent it flowing "across," between departments. Relevant applications range from healthcare to national intelligence, and include most applications where the privacy of individual customers', citizens' or patients' data is at stake. They account for a significant proportion of information processing systems, but their protection is often poorly designed and implemented. This has led to a number of expensive fiascos.

In such systems, instead of the information flow-control boundaries being horizontal, as in the Bell-LaPadula model (Figure 8.1) we instead need the boundaries to be mostly vertical, as shown in Figure 8.2.

TOP SECRET
SECRET
CONFIDENTIAL
OPEN

Figure 8.1 Multilevel security.

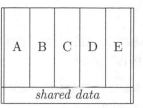

Figure 8.2 Multilateral security.

These lateral information flow controls may be organizational, as in an intelligence organization that wants to keep the names of agents working in one foreign country secret from the department responsible for spying on another. They may be privilege-based, as in a law firm where different clients' affairs, and the clients of different partners, must be kept separate. They may even be a mixture of the two, as in medicine where patient confidentiality is based in law on the rights of the patient, but usually enforced by limiting medical record access to a particular hospital department.

The control of lateral information flows is a very general problem, of which I'll use medical systems as a clear and well-studied example. The problems of these systems are readily understandable by the nonspecialist, and have considerable economic and social importance. Much of what we have to say about them goes across with little or no change to the practice of other professions and to government applications where access to particular kinds of classified data are restricted to particular teams or departments.

One minor problem is that of terminology. Information flow controls of the type we're interested in are known by a number of different names; in the U.S. intelligence community, for example, they are known as *compartmented security* or *compartmentation*. I will use the European term *multilateral security*, as the healthcare application is bigger than intelligence, and the latter term also covers the use of techniques such as anonymity—the classic case being de-identified research databases of medical records. This is an important part of multilateral security. As well as preventing overt information flows, we also have to prevent information leakage through, for example, statistical and billing data that get released.

The use of de-identified data has wider applicability. Another example is the processing of census data. In general, the relevant protection techniques are known as *inference control*. Despite occasional differences in terminology, however, the problems facing the operators of census databases and medical research databases are very much the same.

8.2 Compartmentation, the Chinese Wall, and the BMA Model

There are (at least) three different models of how to implement access controls and information flow controls in a multilateral security model. These are *compartmentation*, used by the intelligence community; the *Chinese Wall* model, which describes the mechanisms used to prevent conflicts of interest in professional practice; and the *BMA model*, developed by the British Medical Association to describe the information flows permitted by medical ethics. Each of these has potential applications outside its field of origin.

8.2.1 Compartmentation and the Lattice Model

For many years, it has been standard practice in the United States and allied governments to restrict access to information by the use of codewords as well as classifications. The best-documented example is the codeword *Ultra* used during World War II, to refer to British and American decrypts of German messages enciphered using the Enigma machine. The fact that the Enigma had been broken was so important that it was worth protecting at almost any cost. So Ultra clearances were given to only a small number of people (in addition to the cryptanalysts and their support staff, the list included the Allied leaders, their senior generals, and handpicked analysts.) No one who had ever held an Ultra clearance could be placed at risk of capture; and the intelligence could never be used in such a way as to let Hitler suspect that his principal cipher had been broken. Thus, when Ultra told of a target, such as an Italian convoy to North Africa, the Allies would send over a plane to "spot" it and report its position by radio an hour or so before the attack. This policy was enforced by special handling rules; for example, Churchill got his Ultra summaries in a special dispatch box, to which he had a key but his staff did not. Because such special rules may apply, access to a codeword is sometimes referred to as an *indoctrination*, rather than simply a clearance. (Ultra security is described by David Kahn [429] and Gordon Welchman [800].)

Much the same precautions are in place today to protect information whose compromise could expose intelligence sources or methods, such as agent names, cryptanalytic successes, the capabilities of equipment used for electronic eavesdropping, and the performance of surveillance satellites. The proliferation of codewords results in a large number of compartments, especially at classification levels above Top Secret.

One reason for this is that classifications are inherited by derived work; so a report written using sources from 'Secret Desert Storm' and 'Top Secret Umbra' can in theory only be read by someone with a clearance of 'Top Secret' and membership of the groups 'Umbra' and 'Desert Storm'. Each combination of codewords gives a compartment, and some intelligence agencies have over a million active compartments. Managing them is a significant problem. Other agencies let people with high-level clearances have relatively wide access. But when the control mechanisms fail, the result can be disastrous; in the Aldrich Ames case, a CIA officer who had accumulated access to a large number of compartments by virtue of long service and seniority, and because he worked in counterintelligence, was able to betray almost the entire U.S. agent network in Russia.

Codewords are, in effect, a pre-computer way of expressing access control groups, and can be dealt with using a variant of Bell-LaPadula, called the *lattice model*. Classifications together with codewords form a lattice, a mathematical structure in which any two objects A and B can be in a dominance relation $A > B$ or $B > A$. They don't have to be: A and B could simply be incomparable (but in this case, for the structure to be a lattice, they will have a least upper bound and a greatest lower bound). As an illustration, suppose we have a codeword, say, 'Crypto'. Someone cleared to 'Top Secret' would be entitled to read files classified 'Top Secret' and 'Secret', but would have no access to files classified 'Secret Crypto' unless he or she also had a crypto clearance. This can be expressed as shown in Figure 8.3.

In order for information systems to support this, we need to distill the essence of classifications, clearances, and labels into a security policy that we can then use to drive security targets, implementation, and evaluation. As it happens, the Bell-LaPadula model appears to go across more or less unchanged. We still have information flows between High and Low as before, where High is a compartment that dominates Low. If two nodes

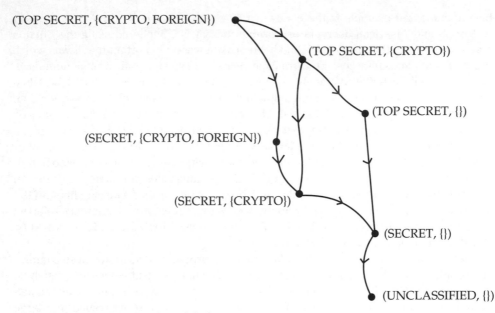

Figure 8.3 A lattice of security labels.

in a lattice are incompatible—as with 'Top Secret' and 'Secret Crypto' in Figure 8.3—then there should be no information flow between them at all.

In fact, the lattice and Bell-LaPadula models are essentially equivalent, and were developed at the same time.

- Roger Schell, Peter Downey, and Gerald Popek of the U.S. Air Force produced an early lattice model in 1972 [675].

- A Cambridge PhD thesis by Jeffrey Fenton included a representation in which labels were managed using a matrix [289].

- About this time, the Pentagon's World Wide Military Command and Control System (WWMCCS) used a primitive lattice model, but without the *-property. As I noted in Chapter 7, the demonstration that a fielded, critical, system handling Top Secret data was vulnerable to attack by Trojan caused some consternation [674]. It meant that all users had to be cleared to the highest level of data in the machine.

- Kenneth Walter, Walter Ogden, William Rounds, Frank Bradshaw, Stan Ames, and David Shumway of Case Western University produced a more advanced lattice model, as well as working out a lot of the problems with file and directory attributes, which they fed to Bell and LaPadula [788, 789].[1]

---

[1] Walter and his colleagues deserve more credit than history has given them. They had the main results first [788], but Bell and LaPadula had their work heavily promoted by the U.S. Air Force. Fenton has also been largely ignored, not being an American.

■ Finally, the lattice model was systematized and popularized by Dorothy Denning [233].

Most products built for the multilevel secure market can be reused in compartmented mode. But, in practice, these products are not as effective as one might like. It is easy to use a multilevel operating system to keep data in different compartments separate—just give them incompatible labels ('Secret Tulip', 'Secret Daffodil', 'Secret Crocus', etc.). But the operating system then becomes an isolation mechanism, rather than a sharing mechanism; the real problem is how to control information sharing.

One solution is to impose least upper bounds in the lattice using some algorithm. An example comes from the system used by the government of Saudi Arabia to manage the Haj, the annual pilgrimage to Mecca [385]. While most compartments are by default Confidential, the combination of data from different compartments is Secret. Thus, 'Haj-visas' and 'Gov-guest' are confidential, but their combination is Secret.

In many intelligence systems, where the users are already operating at the highest level of clearance, data owners don't want a further classification level at which everything is visible. So data derived from two compartments effectively creates a third compartment using the lattice model. The proliferation of millions of compartments is complex to manage and can be intertwined with applications. A more common solution is to use a standard multilevel product, such as a mail guard, to ensure that "untrustworthy" email goes to filters. But now the core of the trusted computing base consists of the filters rather than the guard.

Worse, the guard may lose some of the more important functionality of the underlying operating system. For example, the Standard Mail Guard [715] is built on top of an operating system called LOCK whose basic mechanism is *type enforcement*, which in this context can be thought of as a system of unchangeable access rules for processes and files. Later versions of LOCK support role-based access control, which would be a more appropriate mechanism to manage the relationships between compartments directly [386]. Using it merely as a platform to support BLP is wasteful.

In general, the real problems facing users of intelligence systems have to do with combining data in different compartments, and downgrading it after sanitization. Multilevel and lattice security models offer little help here.

8.2.2 The Chinese Wall

The second model of multilateral security is the Chinese Wall model, developed by Brewer and Nash [137]. Its name comes from the fact that financial services firms such as investment banks have internal rules designed to prevent conflicts of interest, which they call Chinese Walls.

The model's scope is wider than just investment banking. Many professional and services firms have clients who may be in competition with each other: software vendors, advertising agencies, and accountants are other examples. A typical rule is that "a partner who has worked recently for one company in a business sector may not have access to the papers of any other company in that sector." So an advertising copywriter who has worked on, say, the Shell account, will not be allowed to work on any other oil company's account for some fixed period of time.

The Chinese Wall model thus features a mix of free choice and mandatory access control: a partner can choose which oil company to work for, but once that decision is taken their actions in that sector are completely constrained. It also introduces the concept of *separation of duty* into access control; a given user may perform transaction A or transaction B, but not both.

Part of the attraction of the Chinese Wall model to the security research community comes from the fact that it can be expressed in a way that is fairly similar to Bell-LaPadula. If we write, for each client c, $y(c)$ for c's company and $x(c)$ for c's competitors, then, like BLP, it can be expressed in two properties:

The simple security property A subject s has access to c if and only if, for all c' that s can read, either $y(c) \notin x(c')$ or $y(c) = y(c')$.

The *-property A subject s can write to c only if s cannot read any c' with $x(c') \neq \varnothing$ and $y(c) = y(c')$.

The Chinese Wall model made a seminal contribution to the theory of access control. It also sparked a debate about the extent to which it is consistent with the BLP tranquility properties, and some work on the formal semantics of such systems (see, for example, Foley [300] on the relationship with noninterference). There are also some interesting new questions about covert channels. For example, could an oil company find out whether a competitor that used the same investment bank was planning a bid for a third oil company by asking which specialists were available for consultation and noticing that their number had dropped suddenly?

In practice, however, Chinese Walls still are implemented using manual methods. One large software consultancy has each of its staff maintain an "unclassified" curriculum vitae containing entries that have been sanitized and agreed with the customer. A typical entry might be:

September 97–April 98: Consulted on security requirements for a new branch accounting system for a major U.S. retail bank.

This is not the only control. A consultant's manager should be aware of possible conflicts, and not forward the CV to the client if in doubt; if this fails, the client can spot potential conflicts from the CV; and if this also fails, then the consultant is duty-bound to report any potential conflicts as soon as they appear.

8.2.3 The BMA Model

Perhaps the most important, interesting, and instructive example of multilateral security is found in medical information systems. The healthcare sector spends a much larger share of national income than the military in developed countries; and although hospitals are still less automated, they are catching up fast.

Healthcare safety and (especially) privacy have become hot-button issues in many countries. In the United States, the debate over the privacy regulations being introduced by the Department of Health and Human Services under the Health Insurance Portability and Accountability Act is unsetting doctors, patients, privacy advocates, researchers, and marketers; final regulations are due out by the end of 2000. Austrians are arguing about whether to introduce a smartcard to record health insurance data in a portable way, and Germans (who already have such a smartcard) are deliberating the pros and cons of putting emergency medical information (such as current prescriptions and allergies) on the card, too. The main objection here is that if data currently held on a MedAlert bracelet, such as allergies, are moved to a smartcard, there is a significant risk to patients who fall ill in locations where there is no smartcard reader available, such as on an airplane or in a foreign country. Not all privacy-enhancing technologies are without risk!

Everywhere, people are arguing about whether privacy norms will have to be radically revised as genetic data become widely available. In Iceland, for example, a project to build a national medical database that will incorporate not just medical records but also genetic and genealogical data, so that inherited diseases can be tracked across generations, has caused an uproar.

The protection of medical information is also a model for protecting personal information of other kinds, such as that held on individual customers by banks, insurance companies, and government agencies. In all European countries (and in many others, including Canada and Australia) there are *data protection* laws that restrict the dissemination of such data. I'll discuss data protection law in Part 3; for present purposes, it's enough to note that for some classes of data (affecting health, sexual behavior and preferences, political and trade union activity, and religious beliefs) the *data subject* must either give consent to information sharing or have a right of veto. This raises the issue of how one can construct a security policy in which the access control decisions are taken not by a central authority (as in Bell-LaPadula) or by the system's users (as in discretionary access control) but by the data subjects.

We will look first at the access control aspects.

8.2.3.1 The Threat Model

Currently, the main threat to medical privacy is social engineering (which I mentioned briefly in Chapter 3). The typical attack on medical record privacy comes from a private detective who phones a doctor's office or health insurer with a plausible tale:

> Hello, this is Dr. Burnett of the cardiology department at the Conquest Hospital in Hastings. Your patient Sam Simmonds has just been admitted here in a coma, and he has a funny-looking ventricular arrythmia. Can you tell me if there's anything relevant in his record?

This kind of attack is usually so successful that in both the United States and Britain there are people who earn their living doing it [260]. (It's not restricted to health records: in June 2000, millionaire British government minister Lord Levy was acutely embarrassed after someone called the tax office pretending to be him and found out that he'd only paid £5000 in tax the previous year [638]. But the medical context is a good one in which to discuss it.)

In 1996, an experiment was done in England whereby the staff at a health authority (a government-owned insurer that purchases health care for a region or district) were trained to screen out such false pretext telephone calls. The most important element of the advice they were given was that they were to always call back—and not to a number given by the caller, but to the number in the phone book for the hospital or other institution where the caller claimed to work. It turned out that some 30 telephone enquiries a week were bogus. (At that time, there were about 200 health authorities; the advice given is described in [22].)

Training staff in this way is more important than most technical protection measures. But the best staff training in the world won't protect a system in which too many people see too much data. There will always be staff who are careless or even crooked; and the more records they can see, the more harm they can do.

In one high-profile case, a convicted child rapist working as an orthopedic technician at Newton-Wellesley Hospital in Newton, Massachussetts, was caught using a former employee's password to go through the records of 954 patients to get the phone numbers of girls to whom he then made obscene phone calls [136]. He ended up doing jail time. There are many more incidents of a less dramatic nature.

Even where staff behave ethically, a lack of technical understanding can lead to leaks. Old PCs sold on the second-hand market or given to schools often have recoverable data on their hard disks; most people are unaware that the usual delete command does not remove the file, but merely marks the space it occupies as reusable. In a recent headline case, a PC sold on the second-hand market by investment bank Morgan Grenfell Asset Management had recoverable files containing the financial dealings of ex-Beatle Paul McCartney [153]. There have been very similar problems with old health records. Even where staff are honest and conscientious, equipment can still get stolen; some 11 percent of U.K. family doctors have experienced the theft of a practice PC, and in one case two prominent society ladies were blackmailed over terminations of pregnancy following such a theft [23].

The likelihood that a resource will be abused depends on its value and the number of people who have access to it. Aggregating personal information into large databases increases both these risk factors at the same time. Put simply, we can live with a situation in which a doctor's receptionist has access to 2,000 patients' records: there will be abuse from time to time, but at a tolerably low level. However, if the receptionists of the 5,000 family doctors who might work with a large American HMO, or of the 32,000 in Britain's National Health Service, all had access to the records of tens of millions of patients, then abuse would be likely. In a notable recent case, the U.S. Veterans' Administration is being sued in a class action for violating the privacy of its 180,000 employees; their system makes part of their records visible to their colleagues (and to some patients). And privacy issues aren't limited to organizations that treat patients directly; some of the largest collections of personal health information are in the hands of health insurers and research organizations. I discuss their special problems in Section 8.3.

Lateral information flow controls are required even for systems on a much smaller scale. A good illustration comes from a hospital system whose designers believed that for reasons of safety, all staff should have access to all records. This design decision was influenced by lobbying from geriatricians and pediatricians, whose patients are often treated by a number of specialist departments in the hospital; they were frustrated by the incompatibilities between different departmental systems. The system was first fielded in England in Hampshire, where then health minister Gerry Malone had his parliamentary seat. The system made all lab tests performed for local doctors at the hospital's pathology lab visible to most of the hospital's staff. A nurse who had had a test done by her family doctor complained to him after she found the result on the hospital system at Basingstoke where she worked; this caused outrage among local medics, and Malone lost his seat in Parliament at the 1997 election (by two votes) [32].

There are many ad hoc measures that hospitals can take to improve the protection of existing systems. One of the most effective is to keep the records of former patients in a separate archive, and give only a small number of admissions staff the power to move records from there to the main system. Another is to introduce a *honey trap*, a number of bogus records with celebrity names. Reportedly, one Boston hospital uses "medical records" with the names of Kennedy family members for this purpose; staff who browse them can be identified and disciplined. A particularly ingenious proposal, due to Gus Simmons, is to investigate all staff who consult a patient record but do not submit a payment claim to the insurer within 30 days; this aligns the patient's interest in privacy with the hospital's interest in maximizing its income [23].

However, a patchwork of ad hoc measures isn't a good way to secure a system. We need a proper access control policy, thought through from first principles and driven by a realistic model of the threats. Which policy is appropriate for healthcare?

8.2.3.2 *The Security Policy*

This question faced the British Medical Association (BMA) in 1995. The U.K. government had introduced an IT strategy for the National Health Service whose security policy was multilevel. The idea was that AIDS databases would be at a level corresponding to 'Secret'; normal patient records at 'Confidential'; and administrative data, such as drug prescriptions and bills for treatment, at 'Restricted'. It was soon realized that this wasn't going to work. For example, how should a prescription for AZT be classified? It's a drug prescription, so it should be 'Restricted'; it identifies a person as HIV positive, so it must be 'Secret'. So all the 'Secret' AZT prescriptions must be removed from the 'Restricted' file of drug prescriptions. The same goes for most of the other prescriptions, as they identify treatments for named individuals and so should be 'Confidential'. But then what use will the file of prescriptions be to anybody? Pretty well all it will contain will be prescriptions written by doctors for general surgery stocks.

A second problem—and one that's now becoming an issue in the United States—is that the strategy was based on the idea of a single *electronic patient record* (EPR) that would follow the patient around from conception to autopsy, rather than the traditional system of having different records on the same patient at different hospitals and doctors' offices, with information flowing between them in the form of referral and discharge letters. An attempt to devise a security policy for the EPR, which would observe existing ethical norms, became unmanageably complex [355].

In a project for which I was responsible, the BMA developed a security policy to fill the gap. The critical innovation was to define the medical record not as the total of all clinical facts relating to a patient, but as the maximum set of facts relating to a patient and to which the same staff had access. Thus, an individual patient may have more than one record, and this offended the "purist" advocates of the EPR. But multiple records are dictated anyway by law and practice. Depending on the country (and even the state) that you're in, you may have to keep separate medical records for human fertilization, sexually transmitted diseases, prison medical services, and even birth records (as they pertain to the health of the mother as well as the child, and can't simply be released to the child later without violating the mother's confidentiality). This situation is likely to get more complex still as genetic data start being used more widely.

In many countries, including all the members of the European Union, a special status is given to patient consent in law as well as in medical ethics. Records can be shared only with third parties if the patient approves, or in a limited range of statutory exceptions, such as tracing contacts of people with infectious diseases such as TB. Definitions are slightly fluid; in some countries, HIV infection is notifiable, in others it isn't, and in others the data are collected stealthily.

The goals of the BMA security policy were, therefore, to enforce the principle of patient consent, and to prevent too many people getting access to too large databases of identifiable records. It did not try to do anything new, but merely to codify existing best practice. It also sought to express other security features of medical record management such as safety and accountability. For example, it must be possible to reconstruct the contents of the record at any time in the past, so that, for example, if a malpractice suit is brought, the court can determine what information was available to the doctor at the time. (The details of the requirements analysis are in [23].)

The policy consists of nine principles:

1. Access control: each identifiable clinical record shall be marked with an access control list naming the people or groups of people who may read it and append data to it. The system shall prevent anyone not on the access control list from accessing the record in any way

2. Record opening: a clinician may open a record with herself and the patient on the access control list. Where a patient has been referred, she may open a record with herself, the patient and the referring clinician(s) on the access control list

3. Control: One of the clinicians on the access control list must be marked as being responsible. Only she may alter the access control list, and she may only add other health care professionals to it

4. Consent and notification: the responsible clinician must notify the patient of the names on his record's access control list when it is opened, of all subsequent additions, and whenever responsibility is transferred. His consent must also be obtained, except in emergency or in the case of statutory exemptions

5. Persistence: no-one shall have the ability to delete clinical information until the appropriate time period has expired

6. Attribution: all accesses to clinical records shall be marked on the record with the subject's name, as well as the date and time. An audit trail must also be kept of all deletions

7. Information flow: Information derived from record A may be appended to record B if and only if B's access control list is contained in A's

8. Aggregation control: there shall be effective measures to prevent the aggregation of personal health information. In particular, patients must receive special

notification if any person whom it is proposed to add to their access control list already has access to personal health information on a large number of people

9. Trusted computing base: computer systems that handle personal health information shall have a subsystem that enforces the above principles in an effective way. Its effectiveness shall be subject to evaluation by independent experts.

This policy may seem to be just common sense, but it is surprisingly comprehensive and radical in technical terms. For example, it is strictly more expressive than the Bell-LaPadula model; it contains a BLP-type information flow control mechanism in principle 7, but also contains state. (A fuller discussion from the point of view of access control, and for a technical audience, can be found at [24].)

Similar policies were developed by other medical bodies, including the Swedish and German medical associations; the Health Informatics Association of Canada, and an EU project (these are surveyed in [469]). However, the BMA model is the most detailed and has been subjected to the most rigorous review; it was adopted by the Union of European Medical Organisations (UEMO) in 1996. (Feedback from public consultation on the policy can be found in [25].)

8.2.3.3 Pilot Implementations

In a top-down approach to security engineering, one should first determine the threat model, then write the policy, and finally test the policy by observing whether it works in real life.

BMA-compliant systems have now been implemented both in general practice [374], and in a hospital system which enforces access rules such as "a ward nurse can see the records of all patients who have, within the previous 90 days, been on her ward." (The hospital system was initially designed independently of the BMA project. When we learned of each other we were surprised at how much our approaches coincided, and reassured that we had captured the profession's expectations in a reasonably accurate way.)

One of the lessons learned was the difficulty of constructing a small trusted computing base. The hospital records system has to rely on the patient administrative system to tell it which patients and which nurses are on which ward. A different prototype system at a hospital in Cambridge, England, furnishes staff with certificates in smartcards, which they use to log on; combining the two ideas into authorization certificates for access to the records of patients in particular wards may well be the way forward; the support promised in Win2K for both groups and certificates is promising. As for the longer term, people are now researching ways in which medical privacy policy can be expressed using the formalisms and mechanisms of role-based access control. (Other lessons learned are discussed in [231, 232, 374].)

8.2.4 Comparative Analysis

Which of these three models—lattice, Chinese Wall and BMA—should be used in a given application? The lattice model on its own isn't enough, as it shows how to isolate compartments but not how to manage information flows between them. Both BMA and Chinese Wall tackle this problem, but BMA is as decentralized as possible, while in Chinese Wall the assignment of access rights is centralized, and the resulting aggregation risk is managed by a more explicit mechanism to prevent any one user getting their hands on too much data.

There is surprisingly little difference in the protection requirements of medical data and intelligence data, or, for that matter, the files of lawyers, investment bankers, or advertising agents. Some will be the target of more capable motivated opponents, and will need stronger protection mechanisms; but strength of mechanisms should never be confused with functionality. In all these cases, the underlying threat model, of careless or dishonest insiders, is the same.

In fact, the fundamental policy decision is whether or not to centralize. Can you cope better with lots of little traitors or with one big traitor? Medics, lawyers, and other professionals prefer the former, while spies seem to prefer the drama of the latter.

8.3 Inference Control

Access control in medical record systems is hard enough in hospitals and other organizations that care for patients directly. It is much harder to assure patient privacy in secondary applications such as databases for research, cost control, and clinical audit. This is one respect in which doctors have a harder time protecting their data than lawyers; lawyers can lock up their confidential client files and never let any outsider see them at all, while doctors are under all sorts of pressures to share data with third parties.

8.3.1 Basic Problems of Inference Control in Medicine

The standard way of protecting such information is to remove patients' names and addresses from their records, and thus make them anonymous. But this is rarely sufficient. If a database allows detailed enough queries, then individuals can still be identified, and this is especially so if information about different clinical episodes can be linked. For example, if I am trying to find out whether a politician born on the June 2, 1946, and treated for a broken collar bone after a college football game on the May 8, 1967, had since been treated for drug or alcohol problems, and I could make an enquiry on those two dates, then I could very probably pull out a single medical record from a national database. Even if the date of birth is replaced by a year of birth, I am still likely to be able to compromise patient privacy if the records are detailed or if records of different individuals can be linked. For example, a query such as "show me the records of all women aged 36 with daughters aged 14 and 16, such that the mother and exactly one daughter have psoriasis" is also likely to narrow down the search to one family out of millions. And, complex queries with lots of conditions are precisely the kind that researchers want to make.

For this reason, the U.S. Healthcare Financing Administration (HCFA), which is responsible for paying doctors and hospitals for treatments provided under the Medicare program, maintains three sets of records. There are complete records, used for billing. There are *beneficiary-encrypted* records, with only patients' names and social security numbers obscured. These records are still considered personal data (as they still have dates of birth, postal codes and so on) and so are only usable by trusted researchers. Finally there are *public-access* records which have been stripped of identifiers down to the level at which patients are identified only in general terms such as 'a white female aged 70–74 living in Vermont.' Nonetheless, researchers have found that many patients can still be identified by cross-correlating the public access records with commercial databases, and following complaints by privacy advocates, a recent report from the General Accounting Office criticized HCFA for lax security [333].

Many other countries have healthcare monitoring systems that use similar technologies. New Zealand has a national database of encrypted-beneficiary medical records, with access restricted to a small number of specially cleared medical statisticians. No query is answered with respect to fewer than six records [584]. Germany has very strict privacy laws, and the fall of the Berlin Wall forced the former East German cancer registries to install protection mechanisms rapidly [118]. In other countries, protection has been less adequate. Britain's National Health Service started out with strict guidelines but then built a number of centralized databases that make personal health information widely available within government, and that have led to confrontation with doctors [32]. Similar systems in Switzerland were replaced at the insistence of local privacy regulators [685]. The most controversial of all has been a genetic database in Iceland, which I'll discuss shortly.

De-identifying personal information is important in many other fields. Under the rubric of *privacy enhancing technology* (PET), it is being promoted actively by regulators in Europe and Canada as a general privacy mechanism (along with smartcards, encryption, and a few other tools). But, as the medical examples show, there can be serious tension between the desire of researchers for detailed data, and the right of patients (or other data subjects) to privacy. It is important to understand what can, and what cannot, be achieved with this technology.

8.3.2 Other Applications of Inference Control

The inference control problem was first seriously studied in the context of census information. A census collects a vast amount of sensitive data about individuals, then makes statistical summaries of it available by geographical (and governmental) units such as regions, districts, and wards. This information is used not just in the general formulation of policy, but also in determining electoral districts and the levels of government funding for public services for many years. The census problem is somewhat simpler than the medical record problem, as the data are rather restricted and in a standard format (age, sex, race, income, number of children, highest educational attainment, and so on).

There are two broad approaches, depending on whether the data are de-identified before or during processing—or equivalently whether the software that will process the data is untrusted or trusted.

An example of the first kind of processing comes from the treatment of U.S. census data until the 1960s. The procedure was that one record in a thousand was made available on tape—minus names, exact addresses, and other sensitive data. Noise was also added to the data to prevent people with some broader knowledge (such as of the salaries paid by the employer in a company town) from tracing individuals. In addition to the sample records, local averages were given for people selected by various attributes; and records with extreme values (such as very high incomes) were suppressed.

The reason for this might not be immediately obvious. But consider a wealthy family living in a small village. Their income might make a significant difference to the per capita village income, and thus be deduced on the assumption that the per capita income of the other villagers is no different from that in nearby villages. Hence the policy of excluding extreme values before averaging.

In the second type of processing, identifiable data are retained in a database, and privacy protection comes from controls on the kind of queries that may be made. Early attempts at this were not very successful, and various attacks were proposed on the processing used at that time by the U.S. census. The question was whether it was possible to construct a number of inquiries about samples containing a target individual, and work back to obtain supposedly confidential information about that individual.

If our census system allows a wide range of statistical queries, such as "tell me the number of households headed by a man earning between $50,000 and $55,000," "tell me the proportion of households headed by a man aged 40–45 years earning between $50,000 and $55,000," "tell me the proportion of households headed by a man earning between $50,000 and $55,000 whose children have grown up and left home," and so on, then an attacker can quickly home in on an individual. Such queries, in which we add additional circumstantial information to defeat averaging and other controls, are known as *trackers*. They are usually easy to construct.

A problem related to inference is that an opponent who gets hold of a number of unclassified files might deduce sensitive information from them. For example, a New Zealand journalist deduced the identities of many officers in GCSB (that country's equivalent of the NSA) by examining lists of service personnel and looking for patterns of postings over time [368]. Intelligence officers' cover postings might also be blown if an opponent gets hold of the internal phone book for the unit where the officer is supposed to be posted, and doesn't find his name there. The army list might be public, and the phone book 'Restricted', but the fact that a given officer is involved in intelligence work might be 'Secret'. Combining low-level sources to draw a high-level conclusion is known as an *aggregation attack*. It is clearly related to (but not the same as) the increased risk to personal information that arises when databases are aggregated together, thus making more context available to the attacker, and making tracker and other attacks easier. The techniques that can be used to counter aggregation threats are similar to those used for general inference attacks on databases, although there are some particularly difficult problems where we have a multilevel security policy, and the inference or aggregation threats have the potential to subvert it.

8.3.3 The Theory of Inference Control

A theory of inference control was developed by Dorothy Denning and others in late 1970s and early 1980s, largely in response to problems of census bureaux [234]. The developers of many modern privacy systems are unaware of this work, and repeat many of the mistakes of the 1960s. (Inference control is not the only problem in computer security where this happens.) The following is an overview of the most important ideas.

A *characteristic formula* is the expression (in some database query language) that selects a set, known as the *query set*, of records. An example might be "all female employees of the computer laboratory at the grade of professor." The smallest query sets, obtained by the logical AND of all the attributes (or their negations), are known as *elementary sets* or *cells*. The statistics corresponding to query sets may be *sensitive statistics* if they meet criteria which I will discuss below (such as the set size being too small). The objective of inference control is to prevent the disclosure of sensitive statistics.

If we let D be the set of statistics that are disclosed, and P the set of sensitive statistics that must be protected, then we need $D \subseteq P'$ for privacy, where P' is the complement of P. If $D = P$, then the protection is said to be *precise*. Protection that is not precise will usually carry some cost in terms of the range of queries that the database can answer, and thus its usefulness to its owner.

8.3.3.1 Query Set Size Control

The obvious protection mechanism is simply to specify a minimum query size. As mentioned, New Zealand's National Health Information System databases will reject statistical queries whose answers would be based on fewer than six patients' records. But this is not enough in itself. An obvious tracker attack is to make an enquiry on six patients' records, then on those records plus the target's. Rather than reduce the effectiveness of the database by building in more restrictive query controls, the designers opted to restrict access to a small number of specially cleared medical statisticians.

Even so, one extra control is needed, and is often forgotten. We must prevent the attacker from querying all but one of the records in the database. In general, if there are N records, query set size control with a threshold of t means that between t and $N - t$ of them must be the subject of a query for it to be allowed.

8.3.3.2 Trackers

Probably the most important attacks on statistical databases come from trackers. There are many simple examples. In our laboratory, only one of the full professors is female, so we can find out her salary with only two queries: "average salary professors?" and "average salary male professors?"

This is an example of an *individual tracker*. There are also *general trackers*, sets of formulae that will enable any sensitive statistic to be revealed. A surprising discovery made about trackers in the late 1970s was that, provided the minimum query set size n is less than a quarter of the total number of statistics N, and there are no further restrictions on the type of queries that are allowed, we can find formulae specifying sets with more than $2n$ and fewer than $N - 2n$ statistics, and these provide general trackers. Thus, tracker attacks are easy, unless we place severe restrictions on the query set size or control the allowed queries in some other way.

8.3.3.3 More Sophisticated Query Controls

There are a number of alternatives to simple query set size control. The U.S. census, for example, uses the "n-respondent, $k\%$-dominance rule": it will not release a statistic of which $k\%$ or more is contributed by n or fewer values. Other techniques include, as mentioned, suppressing data with extreme values. A census bureau may deal with high-net-worth individuals in national statistics, but not in the local figures, while some medical databases do the same for less common diseases. For example, a U.K. prescribing statistics system suppresses sales of the AIDS drug AZT from local statistics.

8.3.3.4 Cell Suppression

The next question is how to deal with the side effects of suppressing certain statistics. Suppose, for example, that a university wants to release average grades for various combinations of courses, so that people can check that the grading is fair across courses. Suppose now that the table in Figure 8.4, contains the number of students studying two science subjects, one as their major subject and one as their minor subject.

Next suppose that our minimum query set size is 3 (if we set it at 2, then either of the two students who studied geology with chemistry could trivially work out the other's grade); then we cannot release the average for geology with chemistry. But if the average for chemistry is known, then this can easily be reconstructed from the averages for biology with chemistry and physics with chemistry. Therefore, we have to suppress at least one other average in the chemistry row; and for similar reasons we need to suppress one in the geology column. But if we suppress geology with biology and physics with chemistry, then we'd also better suppress physics with biology to prevent these values being worked out in turn. The remaining table is shown in Figure 8.5.

This process is called *complementary cell suppression*. If there are further attributes in the database schema—for example, if figures are also broken down by race and sex, to show compliance with anti-discrimination laws—then even more information may be lost. Where a database scheme contains m-tuples, blanking a single cell generally means suppressing $2^m - 1$ other cells, arranged in a hypercube with the sensitive statistic at

Major:	Biology	Physics	Chemistry	Geology
Minor:				
Biology	-	16	17	11
Physics	7	-	32	18
Chemistry	33	41	-	2
Geology	9	13	6	-

Figure 8.4 Table containing data before cell suppression.

Major:	Biology	Physics	Chemistry	Geology
Minor:				
Biology	-	blanked	17	blanked
Physics	7	-	32	18
Chemistry	33	blanked	-	blanked
Geology	9	13	6	-

Figure 8.5 Table after cell suppression.

one vertex. Clearly, even precise protection can rapidly make the database unusable. (where a database is not homogeneous, things are even worse: there can be many *pivot points*—cells that prevent large numbers of queries having answers.)

Sometimes complementary cell suppression can be avoided, as when large incomes (or rare diseases) are tabulated nationally and excluded from local figures, but it is often necessary when we are publishing microstatistics, as in the preceding tables of exam grades. Where the database is open for online queries, we can get much the same effect by *implied queries control*, whereby we allow a query on m attribute values only if all of the 2^m-implied query sets, given by setting the m attributes to true or false, have at least k records.

8.3.3.5 Maximum Order Control and the Lattice Model

The next thing we might try to make it harder to construct trackers is to limit the type of inquiries that can be made. *Maximum order control* limits the number of attributes that any query can have. However, to be effective, the limit may have to be severe. One study found that of 1,000 medical records, three attributes were safe; with four attributes, one individual record could be found; and with 10 attributes, most records could be isolated. A more thorough approach (where it is feasible) is to reject queries that would partition the sample population into too many sets.

We saw how lattices can be used in compartmented security to define a partial order to control permitted information flows between compartments with combinations of codewords. They can also be used in a slightly different way to systematize query controls in some databases. If we have, for example, three attributes A, B, and C (say, area of residence, birth year, and medical condition), we may find that, while inquiries on any one of these attributes are nonsensitive, as are inquiries on A and B and on B and C, the combination of A and C might be sensitive. It follows, that an inquiry on all three would not be permissible either. Thus, the lattice divides naturally into a top half of prohibited queries and a bottom half of allowable queries, as shown in Figure 8.6.

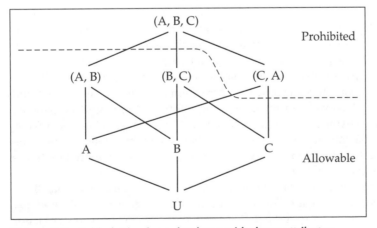

Figure 8.6   Table lattice for a database with three attributes.

8.3.3.6 Audit-Based Control

As mentioned, some people try to get round the limits imposed by static query control by keeping track of who accessed what. Known as *query overlap control*, this involves rejecting any query from a user that, combined with what the user knows already, would disclose a sensitive statistic. This may sound perfect in theory, but in practice it suffers from two usually unsurmountable drawbacks. First, the complexity of the processing increases over time, and often exponentially. Second, it's extremely hard to be sure that your users aren't in collusion, or that one user hasn't registered under two different names. Even if your users are all honest and distinct persons today, it's always possible that one of them will take over another, or that two of them get taken over by a predator, tomorrow.

8.3.3.7 Randomization

The cell suppression example shows that if various kinds of query control are the only protection mechanism used in a statistical database, they can often have an unacceptable performance penalty. So query control is often used in conjunction with various kinds of randomization, which are designed to degrade the signal-to-noise ratio from the attacker's point of view while impairing that of the legitimate user as little as possible.

The simplest such technique is *perturbation*, or adding noise with zero mean and a known variance to the data. One way of doing this is to round, or truncate, the data by some deterministic rule; another is to swap some records. Perturbation is often not as effective as one would like, as it tends to damage the legitimate user's results precisely when the sample set sizes are small, and leave them intact when the sample sets are large (where we might have been able to use simple query controls anyway). There is also the worry that suitable averaging techniques might be used to eliminate some of the added noise.

Often, a better randomization technique is to use *random sample queries*. This is another of the methods used by census bureaux. The idea is to make all the query sets the same size, selecting them at random from the available relevant statistics. Thus all the released data are computed from small samples rather than from the whole database. If this random selection is done using a pseudorandom number generator keyed to the input query, then the results will have the virtue of repeatability. Random sample queries are a natural protection mechanism for large medical databases, where the correlations being investigated are often such that a sample of a few hundred is sufficient. For example, when investigating the correlation between a given disease and some aspect of lifestyle, the correlation must be strong before doctors will advise patients to make radical changes to their way of life, which might have undesirable side effects. If a teaching hospital has records on five million patients, and five thousand have the disease being investigated, then a randomly selected sample of two hundred sufferers might be all the researcher could use.

This doesn't work so well where the disease is rare, or where for other reasons there is only a small number of relevant statistics. A possible strategy here is *randomized response*, where we randomly restrict the data we collect (the subjects' responses). For example, if the three variables under investigation are obesity, smoking, and AIDS, we

Week:	1	2	3	4
Doctor A	17	26	19	22
Doctor B	25	31	9	29
Doctor C	32	30	39	27
Doctor D	16	19	18	13

Figure 8.7   Sample of deidentified drug-prescribing data.

might ask each subject with HIV infection to record whether they smoke or whether they are overweight, but not both. Of course, this can limit the value of the data.

8.3.4 Limitations of Generic Approaches

As with any protection technology, statistical security can only be evaluated in a particular environment and against a particular threat model. Whether it is adequate or not depends to an even greater extent than usual on the details of the application.

An instructive example is a system used for analyzing trends in drug prescribing. Here, prescriptions are collected (minus patient names) from pharmacies. A further stage of de-identification removes the doctors' identities; the information is then sold to drug company marketing departments. The system has to protect the privacy of doctors as well as of patients (the last thing a busy family doctor wants is to be pestered by a drug rep for prescribing a competitor's brands).

One problem with an early prototype of this system was that it merely replaced the names of doctors in a cell of four or five practices with Doctor A, Doctor B, and so on, as in Figure 8.7. We realized that an alert drug rep could identify doctors from prescribing patterns, by noticing, for example, "Well, Doctor B must be Susan Jones because she went skiing in the third week in January, and look at the fall-off in prescriptions here. And Doctor C is probably her partner Mervyn Smith who would have been covering for her." The fix was to replace absolute numbers of prescriptions with the percentage of each doctor's prescribing that went to each particular drug, and to randomly perturb the timing by shifting the figures backward or forward a few weeks [530].

In general, contextual knowledge is extremely hard to quantify, and is quite likely to grow over time. Latarya Sweeney has shown that even the HCFA's "public-use" files can often be reidentified by cross-correlating them with commercial databases [744]. (Such *data detective* work is an important part of assessing the level of protection that an actual statistical database gives, just as we only have confidence in cryptographic algorithms that have withstood extensive analysis by capable motivated opponents.) And even without cross-correlation, there may be contextual information available internally. Users of medical research databases are often doctors who have normal access to parts of the patient record databases from which the statistical data are drawn.

8.3.4.1 Active Attacks

Active attacks are particularly powerful. These are where users have the ability to insert or delete records into the database. A user might add records to create a group that contains the target's record, plus those of a number of nonexistent subjects created by himself. One (imperfect) countermeasure is to add or delete new records in batches. Taking this to an extreme gives *partitioning*, whereby records are added in groups and any query must be answered with respect to all of them or none. However, this is once more equivalent to publishing tables of microstatistics.

Active attacks are not limited to data, but can also target metadata. A nice example, due to Whit Diffie, is the *chosen drug attack*. Suppose a drug company has access through a statistical system to the amounts of money spent on behalf of various groups of patients, and wants to find out which patients are receiving which drug, in order to direct its marketing better (there was a scandal in Quebec about just such an inference attack). A powerful trick is to set the drug prices in such a way as to make the resulting equations easy to solve.

A prominent case at the moment involves a new medical research database in Iceland, which comprises three linked databases: one with the nation's medical records, one with the genealogy of the whole population, and one with genetic data acquired from sequencing. The rationale is that since Iceland's population is largely descended from a few founding families that settled there about a thousand years ago, there is much less genic variance than in the general human population, and so genes for hereditary illnesses should be much easier to find.

The privacy problem in the Icelandic database is much more acute than in the general case. For example, by linking medical records to genealogies, which are in any case public (genealogy is a common Icelandic hobby), patients can be identified by such factors as the number of their uncles, aunts, great-uncles, great-aunts and so on—in effect, by the shape of their family trees. There was much debate about whether the design could even theoretically meet legal privacy requirements [33], and European privacy officials expressed grave concern about the possible consequences for Europe's system of privacy laws [217]. However, the Icelandic government pressed ahead with it anyway over the strong objections of local doctors. The result was that 11% of the population opted out of the system, including a majority of medical practitioners.

8.3.5 The Value of Imperfect Protection

So doing de-identification right is hard, and the issues can be politically fraught. But it is often worthwhile to make some attempt, even if the protection you can provide is imperfect.

Some kinds of security mechanism may be worse than useless if they can be compromised. Weak encryption is a good example. The main problem facing the world's signals intelligence agencies is how to filter out interesting nuggets from the mass of international phone, fax, email, and other traffic. A principal who helpfully encrypts his important traffic makes this part of his an opponent's job easier. If the encryption used is breakable (or one of the end systems can be hacked), then the net result is worse than if the traffic had been sent in clear.

Statistical security is not generally like this. The main threat to databases of personal information is often *mission creep*. Once an organization has access to data that are potentially valuable, then all sorts of ways of exploiting that value will be developed.

Some of these are likely to be highly objectionable; a topical U.S. example is the resale of medical records to banks for use in filtering loan applications. However, even an imperfect de-identification system may destroy the value of medical data to a bank's loan department. If only five percent of the patients can be identified, and then only with effort, the bank may decide that it's simpler to tell loan applicants to take out their own insurance, and let the insurance companies send out medical questionnaires if they wish. So de-identification can help, even if the main effect is prophylaxis against future harm rather than treatment of existing defects.

As well as harming privacy, mission creep can have safety implications. In at least one European country, diabetic registers—databases designed to monitor the quality of diabetes care—are abused to provide a rudimentary means of electronic communication between family doctors and hospital diabetologists, who are frustrated at not having email. But as the diabetes registers were never designed as communications systems, they lack the safety and other mechanisms that they should have if they are to be used for this purpose. Even the most rudimentary form of de-identification would have prevented this abuse.

So in statistical security, the question of whether one should let the best be the enemy of the good can require a finer judgment call than elsewhere.

8.4 The Residual Problem

The two previous sections may have convinced you that the problem of managing medical record privacy in the context of immediate care (such as in a hospital) is reasonably straightforward, while in the context of secondary databases (such as for research, audit, and cost control) there are statistical security techniques that, with care, can solve much of the problem. Somewhat similar techniques are used to manage intelligence information in military organizations and for highly sensitive commercial data such as details of forthcoming mergers and acquisitions in an investment bank. In all cases, the underlying concept is that the really secret material is restricted to a compartment of a small number of identified individuals, and less secret versions of the data are manufactured for wider use. This involves not just suppressing the names of the patients, spies, or target companies, but also controlling any contextual and other information by which they might be re-identified.

But making such systems work well in real life is much harder than it looks. First, determining the sensitivity level of information is fiendishly difficult, and many initial expectations turn out to be wrong. You might expect, for example, that HIV status would be the most sensitive medical data there is; yet many HIV sufferers are quite open about their status. You might also expect that people would rather entrust sensitive personal health information to a healthcare professional such as a doctor or pharmacist rather than to a marketing database; yet many women are so sensitive about purchasing feminine hygiene products that, rather than going into a pharmacy and buying them for cash, they prefer to use an automatic check-out facility in a supermarket, even if this means they have to use their store card and credit card, so that the purchase is linked to their name and stays on the marketing database forever. The actual embarrassment of being seen with a packet of tampons is immediate, and outweighs the potential future embarrassment of being sent discount coupons for baby wear six months after the menopause.

Second, it is extraordinarily difficult to exclude single points of failure, no matter how hard you try to build watertight compartments. The CIA's Soviet assets were compromised by Rick Ames, who, as a senior man in counterintelligence, had access to too many compartments. The KGB's overseas operations were similarly compromised by Vassily Mitrokhin, an officer who had become disillusioned with communism after 1968, yet was sent to work in the archives while waiting for his pension [51].

In medicine, many of the really hard problems lie in the systems that process medical claims for payment. When a patient is treated, and a request for payment is sent to the insurer, it has not just full details of the illness, the treatment, and the cost, but also the patient's name, insurance number, and other details such as date of birth. There have been proposals for payment to be effected using anonymous credit cards [117], but as far as I am aware, none of them has been fielded. Insurers want to know which patients, and which doctors, are the most expensive. This holds whether the insurer is a private insurance company (or employer) or a government-owned health authority, such as HCFA or Britain's National Health Service. And once an insurer possesses large quantities of personal health information, it becomes very reluctant to delete it in case it might be useful or valuable in the future.

In the United States, the retention of copies of medical records by insurers, employers, and others is now widely seen as a serious problem. Writers from such widely different political viewpoints as the communitarian Amitai Etzioni [277] and the libertarian Simson Garfinkel [330] agree on this point, if on little else. Public concern spurred Congress to pass the Health Insurance Portability and Accountability Act (HIPAA), which empowered the Department of Health and Human Services (DHHS) to regulate the security of health data. The debate now is over how the regulations are to be implemented. If the private medical insurance sector were brought up to the standards of HCFA, this would probably be a good thing for most patients. But given the sums involved, one can anticipate a lot of foot-dragging and litigation. Even so, the act only enables the DHHS to regulate health plans, healthcare clearinghouses, and healthcare providers, leaving many organizations that process medical information (such as lawyers, employers, and universities) outside its scope.

What lessons can be drawn from other countries?

As we noted above, Britain's system has been a source of conflict with doctors and with patients' associations. The Swiss system, which was initially similar to Britain's, has now been de-identified much more thoroughly at the insistence of privacy regulators. In Germany, the richer people use private insurers (who are bound by tight data protection laws), while the poor use state health insurers, which are run by doctors, so non-doctors don't have access to records. The most radical solution is in Japan, where cost control is done by regulating fees: doctors are discouraged from performing expensive procedures, such as heart transplants, by pricing them below cost. This mechanism doesn't involve large-scale access to personal health information, and is much more effective than the case-by-case cost control practiced in most other countries. Healthcare takes up some 3 percent of GNP in Japan, versus 7 to 8 percent for the typical developed country, and 15 percent for America. Oh, and Japanese live longer than Europeans, who live longer than Americans. A variant of the Japanese solution was adopted in Oregon in February

1994 and proved popular with Oregonians, but was resisted fiercely by health industry lobbyists as "rationing."

To sum up, the problem of health record privacy is fundamentally a political one. Whether large quantities of medical records ever accumulate in one database depends on how the health care system is organized, and whether these are destroyed—or at least properly de-identified—after payment has been processed is a matter of regulation, not primarily of technology. In such debates, one role of the security engineer is to see to it that policymakers understand the likely consequences of their actions.

Other privacy problems also tend to have a serious political entanglement. Bank customer privacy can be tied up with the bank's internal politics; often the best privacy protection comes from branch managers' reluctance to let other branches learn about their customers. Access to criminal records and intelligence depends on how law enforcement agencies decide to share data with each other, and the choices they make internally about whether access to highly sensitive information about sources and methods should be decentralized (risking occasional losses), or centralized (bringing lower-probability but higher-cost exposure to a traitor at head office).

8.5 Summary

In this chapter, we looked at the problem of assuring the privacy of medical records. This is representative of a number of information security problems, ranging from the protection of national intelligence data through professional practice in general to the protection of census data.

It turns out that with medical records there is an easy problem, a harder problem, and a really hard problem.

The easy problem is setting up systems of access controls so that access to a particular record is limited to a sensible number of staff. Such systems can be designed largely by automating existing working practices. The harder problem is statistical security: how one designs databases of medical records (or census returns) so as to allow researchers to make statistical enquiries without compromising individuals' privacy. The hardest problem is how to manage the interface between the two, and in the specific case of medicine, how to prevent the spread of payment information. The only realistic solution for this lies in regulation.

Research Problems

In the near future, a lot of medical treatment may involve genetic information. Your medical records may involve personal health information about your parents, siblings, cousins, and so on. How can the BMA model be extended to deal with medical records that relate to multiple individuals?

Are there any ways of linking access control policies for privacy with statistical security with (perhaps) digital cash for payment? Can there be such a thing as seamless privacy where everything fits neatly together?

What other ways of writing privacy policies are there? For example, are there useful ways to combine BMA and Chinese Wall? Are there any technical or semi-technical ways of aligning the data subject's interest with others?

Further Reading

The literature on compartmented mode security is somewhat scattered: most of the public domain papers are in the proceedings of the NCSC/NISSC and ACSAC conferences cited in detail at the end of Chapter 8. Standard textbooks such as Amoroso [15] and Gollmann [344] cover the basics of the lattice and Chinese Wall models.

For the BMA model, see the policy document itself—the Blue Book [23], the shorter version at [24], and the proceedings of the conference on the policy [29]. See also the papers on the pilot system at Hastings [231, 232]. For more on Japanese healthcare, see [159]. For a National Research Council study of medical privacy issues in the United States, see [581]; there is also an HHS report on the use of de-identified data in research at [511].

For inference control, Denning's book [234] is the classic reference, and there's an update at [238]. A more modern textbook on database security is the one by Castano, et al. [172] whose chapter on statistical security is a useful update on Denning and whose other chapters also cover some related multilevel security and intrusion detection issues.

CHAPTER 9

Banking and Bookkeeping

Computers are not (yet?) capable of being reasonable any more than is a Second Lieutenant.

—CASEY SCHAUFLER

Against stupidity, the Gods themselves contend in vain.

—J.C. FRIEDRICH VON SCHILLER

9.1 Introduction

Banking systems include the back-end bookkeeping systems that record customers' account details and transaction processing systems such as cash machine networks and high-value interbank money transfer systems that feed them with data. They are important for a number of reasons.

First, bookkeeping was for many years the main business of the computer industry, and banking was its most intensive area of application. Personal applications such as Netscape and Powerpoint might now run on more machines, but accounting is still the critical application for the average business. So the protection of bookkeeping systems is of great practical importance. It also gives us a well-understood model of protection in which confidentiality plays almost no role, but where the integrity of records (and their immutability once made) is of paramount importance.

Second, transaction processing systems—whether for small debits such as $50 cash machine withdrawals or multimillion-dollar wire transfers—were the applications that launched commercial cryptography. Banking applications drove the development not just of encryption algorithms and protocols, but also of the supporting technologies, such as tamper-resistant cryptographic processors. These processors provide an important and interesting example of a trusted computing base that is quite different from the hardened operating systems discussed in the context of multilevel security. Many instructive mistakes were first made (or at least publicly documented) in the area of commercial cryptography. The problem of how to interface crypto with access control was studied by financial cryptographers before any others in the open research community.

Third, an understanding of basic electronic banking technology is a prerequisite for tackling the more advanced problems of electronic commerce in an intelligent way. In fact, many dot-coms fall down badly on basic bookkeeping, which is easy to overlook in the rush to raise money and build a Web site.

Finally, banking systems provide another example of multilateral security, but aimed at authenticity rather than confidentiality. A banking system should prevent customers from cheating each other or the bank; it should prevent bank employees from cheating the bank or its customers; and the evidence it provides should be sufficiently strong that none of these principals can get away with falsely accusing another principal of cheating.

9.1.1 The Origins of Bookkeeping

Bookkeeping appears to have started in the Neolithic Middle East in about 8500 BC, just after the invention of agriculture [678]. When people started to store and trade the food they had produced, they needed a way to keep track of which village member had put how much in the communal warehouse. To start with, each unit of food (sheep, wheat, oil, . . .) was represented by a clay token, or *bulla*, which was placed inside a clay envelope and sealed by rolling it with the pattern of the warehouse keeper (see Figure 9.1). When the farmer wanted to get his food back, the seal was broken by the keeper in the presence of a witness. (This is may be the oldest known security protocol.)

Figure 9.1   Clay envelope and its content of tokens from Susa, Iran, ca. 3300 BC (courtesy Denise Schmandt-Besserat and The Louvre Museum).

By about 3000 BC, this had led to the invention of writing [609]; after another thousand years, we find equivalents of promissory notes, bills of lading, and so on. At about the same time, metal ingots started to be used as an intermediate commodity, often sealed inside a bulla by an assayer. In 700 BC, Lydia's King Croesus started stamping the metal directly, and thus invented coins [625]; by the Athens of Pericles, there were a number of wealthy individuals in business as bankers [338].

The next significant innovation dates to the time of the Crusades. As the Dark Ages came to a close and trade started to spread, some businesses became too large for a single family to manage. The earliest of the recognizably modern banks date to this period; by having branches in a number of cities, they could finance trade efficiently. But as the economy grew, it was necessary to hire managers from outside, and the owner's family could not supervise them closely. This brought with it an increased risk of fraud, and the mechanism that evolved to control it was double-entry bookkeeping. This appears to have been invented sometime in the 1300s, though the first book on it did not appear until 1494, after the invention of the printing press [222].

9.1.2 Double-entry Bookkeeping

The idea behind double-entry bookkeeping is, like most hugely influential ideas, extremely simple. Each transaction is posted to two separate books, as a credit in one and a debit in the other. For example, when a firm is paid $100 by a debtor, the amount is entered as a debit in the accounts receivable book (the firm is now owed $100 less) and as a credit in the cash account book (the firm now has $100 more cash). At the end of the day, the books should *balance*, that is, add up to zero; the assets and the liabilities should be equal. (Any profit the firm has made is a liability to the shareholders.) In all but the smallest firms, the books will be kept by different clerks, and have to balance at the end of every month (at banks, every day). By suitable design of the ledger system, we can see to it that each shop, or branch, can be balanced separately. Thus most frauds will need the collusion of two or more members of staff; and this principle of *split responsibility*, also known as *dual control*, is complemented by audit.

Many computer systems are used for bookkeeping tasks, and implement variations on the double-entry theme. However, the control is often illusory. The double-entry features may be implemented only in the user interface, while the underlying file formats have no integrity controls. And even if the ledgers are kept on the same system, someone with root access—or with physical access and a debugging tool—may be able to change two or more records so that the balancing controls are bypassed. It may also be possible to evade the balancing controls in various ways; staff may notice bugs in the software and take advantage of them.

So how can we organize and formalize our protection goals?

9.2 How Bank Computer Systems Work

Banks were among the first large organizations to use computers for bookkeeping. They began to do so in the late 1950s and early 1960s, with applications such as check processing, and once they found that even the slow and expensive computers of that era were much cheaper than armies of clerks, they proceeded to automate most of the rest of their operations during the 1960s and 1970s.

A typical banking system has a number of data structures. There is an *account master file*, which contains each customer's current balance together with previous transactions for a period of perhaps 90 days; a number of *ledgers*, which track cash and other assets on their way through the system; various *journals*, which hold transactions that have been received from teller stations, cash machines, check sorters, and so on, but not yet entered in the ledgers; and an *audit trail* that records which staff member did what and when.

The processing software that acts on these data structures will include a suite of overnight batch-processing programs, which apply the transactions from the journals to the various ledgers and the account master file. The online processing will include a number of modules that post transactions to the relevant combinations of ledgers. For example, when a customer pays $100 into as savings account, the teller will make a transaction that records a debit to the savings account ledger of $100 (the bank now has an increased liability to the customer), while crediting the same amount to the ledger recording the amount of cash in the drawer. The fact that all the ledgers should always add up to zero provides an important check; if the bank (or one of its branches) is ever out of balance, an alarm will go off and people will start looking for the cause.

The invariant provided by the ledger system is checked daily during the overnight batch run; this means that a programmer who wants to add to his own account balance will have to take the money from some other account, rather than just create it out of thin air by tweaking the account master file. Just as in a traditional business one has different ledgers managed by different clerks, so in a banking data processing shop there are different programmers in charge of them. In addition, all code is subjected to scrutiny by an internal auditor and to testing by a separate test department. Once the code has been approved, it will be run on a production machine that does not have a development environment, but only approved object code and data.

9.2.1 The Clark-Wilson Security Policy Model

Although such systems have been in the field since the 1960s, a formal model of their security policy was only introduced in 1987, by David Clark and David Wilson (the former was a computer scientist, and the latter an accountant) [187]. In their model, some data items are constrained so that they can be acted on only by a certain set of transformation procedures.

More formally, there are special procedures whereby data can be input—turned from an *unconstrained data item*, or UDI, into a *constrained data item*, or CDI; *integrity verification procedures* (IVPs) to check the validity of any CDI (e.g., that the books balance); and *transformation procedures* (TPs), which may be thought of in the banking case as transactions that preserve balance. In the general formulation, they maintain the integrity of CDIs; they also write enough information to an append-only CDI (the audit trail) for transactions to be reconstructed. Access control is by means of triples *(subject, TP, CDI)*, which are so structured that a shared control policy is enforced. In the formulation in Amoroso [15]:

1. The system will have an IVP for validating the integrity of any CDI.

2. The application of a TP to any CDI must maintain its integrity.

3. A CDI can only be changed by a TP.

4. Subjects can only initiate certain TPs on certain CDIs.

5. Triples must enforce an appropriate separation of duty policy on subjects.

6. Certain special TPs on UDIs can produce CDIs as output.

7. Each application of a TP must cause enough information to reconstruct it to be written to a special append-only CDI.

8. The system must authenticate subjects attempting to initiate a TP.

9. The system must let only special subjects (i.e., security officers) make changes to authorization-related lists.

A number of things bear saying about Clark-Wilson.

First, unlike Bell-LaPadula, Clark-Wilson involves maintaining state. Quite apart from the audit trail, this is usually necessary for dual control as you have to keep track of which transactions have been partially approved—such as those approved by only one manager when two are needed. If dual control is implemented using access control mechanisms, it typically means holding partially approved transactions in a special journal file. This then means that some of the user state is actually security state, which in turn makes the trusted computing base harder to define. If it is implemented using crypto instead, such as by having managers attach digital signatures to transactions of which they approve, there can be problems managing all the partially approved transactions so that they get to a second approver in time.

Second, the model doesn't do everything. It captures the idea that state transitions should preserve an invariant, such as balance, but not that state transitions should be correct. Incorrect transitions, such as paying into the wrong bank account, are still allowed.

Third, Clark-Wilson ducks the hardest question, namely: how do we control the risks from dishonest staff? Rule 5 says that "an appropriate separation of duty policy" must be supported, but nothing about what this means.

9.2.2 Separation of Duties

There are basically two kinds of separation of duty policy: dual control and functional separation.

In dual control, two or more different staff members must act together to authorize a transaction. The classic military example is in nuclear command systems, which may require two or three officers to turn their keys simultaneously in consoles that are too far apart for a single person to operate. (I discuss nuclear matters further in Chapter 11, "Nuclear Command and Control.") The classic civilian example is when a bank issues a letter of guarantee, which will typically undertake to carry the losses should a loan made by another bank go sour. If a single manager could issue such an instrument, then an accomplice could plunder the guaranteed loan account at the other bank, and the alarm might not be raised for months. I discuss this further in Section 9.3.2.

With functional separation of duties, two or more different staff members act on a transaction at different points in its path. The classic example is corporate purchasing. A manager makes a purchase decision and tells the purchasing department; a clerk there writes a purchase order; the store clerk records the arrival of goods; an invoice arrives at accounts; the accounts clerk correlates it with the purchase order and the stores receipt, and cuts a check; the accounts manager signs the check.

However, it doesn't stop there. The manager now gets a debit on her monthly statement for that internal account; her boss reviews the accounts to make sure the division's profit targets are likely to be met; the internal audit department can descend at any time to audit the division's books; and when the external auditors come in once a year, they will check the books of a randomly selected sample of departments. Finally, when frauds are discovered, the company's lawyers may make vigorous efforts to get the money back.

The model can be described as *prevent-detect-recover*. The level of reliance placed on each of these three legs will depend on the application. Where detection may be delayed for months or years, and recovery may therefore be very difficult—as with bogus bank guarantees—it is prudent to put extra effort into prevention, using techniques such as dual control. Where prevention is difficult to enforce, it is essential that detection be fast enough, and recovery vigorous enough, to provide a deterrent effect. The classic example here is that bank tellers can quite easily take cash, so you need to count the money every day and catch any shortfall by close of business.

Bookkeeping and management control systems are not only one of the earliest security systems, they also have given rise to much of management science and civil law. They are entwined with a company's business processes, and exist in its cultural context. In Swiss banks, two managers' signatures appear on almost everything, while Americans are much more relaxed. In most countries' banks, staff get background checks, can be moved randomly from one task to another, and are required to take holidays at least once a year. But this would be excessive in the typical university department where the opportunities for fraud are much less.

Designing a good bookkeeping system is hard because it's such an interdisciplinary problem. The financial controllers, the personnel department, the lawyers, the auditors, and the systems people all come at the problem from different directions, offer partial solutions, fail to understand each other's control objectives, and things fall down the hole in the middle. Human factors are very often neglected, and systems end up being vulnerable to helpful subordinates or authoritarian managers who can cause dual control to fail. It's important not just to match the controls to the culture, but also to motivate people to use them. For example, in the better-run banks, management controls are marketed to staff as a means of protecting them against blackmail and kidnapping.

Security researchers have so far focused on the small part of the problem, which pertains to creating dual control (or in general, where there are more than two principals, *shared control*) systems. Even this is not at all easy. For example, rule 9 in Clark-Wilson says that security officers can change access rights, so what's to stop a security officer creating logons for two managers and using them to send all the bank's money to Switzerland?

One possible answer is to use cryptography, and split the relevant signing key between two or more principals. In an NT network, the obvious way to manage things is to put users in separately administered domains. With a traditional banking system, using the mainframe operating system MVS, we can separate duties between the system administrator (sysadmin) and the auditor; the former can do anything he wishes, except find out which of his activities the latter is monitoring [95]. But in real life, dual control is hard to do end to end because there are many system interfaces that provide single points of failure; and, in any case, split-responsibility systems administration is tedious.

The practical answer, then, is that most bank sysadmins could do just this type of fraud. Some have tried—where they fall down is that the back-office balancing controls set off the alarm after a day or two, and money laundering controls stop them from getting away with very much. I discuss this further in Section 9.3.2. The point to bear in mind here is that serial controls in the prevent-detect-recover model are usually more important than shared control. They depend ultimately on some persistent state in the system, and are in tension with programmers' desire to keep things simple by making transactions atomic.

There are also tranquility issues. For example, could an accountant, knowing that he was due to be promoted to manager tomorrow, end up doing both authorizations on a large transfer? A technical fix for this might involve a Chinese Wall mechanism supporting a primitive "X may do Y but not Z" ("a manager can confirm a payment only if her name doesn't appear on it as the creator"). In this way, we would end up with a number of exclusion rules involving individuals, groups, and object labels; once the number of rules became large (as it will in a real bank) we would need a systematic way of examining this rule set and verifying that it didn't have any loopholes.

In the medium term, banking security policy—just like medical security policy—may end up finding its most convenient expression using role-based access control; platforms such as Win2K may be heading in this direction. This offers the potential for managing separation of duty policies that involve both parallel elements, such as dual control, and serial elements, such as functional separation along a transaction's path.

A final remark on dual control is that it's often inadequate for transactions involving more than one organization, because of the difficulties of dispute resolution: "My two managers say the money was sent!" "But my two say it wasn't!"

9.2.3 What Goes Wrong

Theft can take a variety of forms, from the purely opportunist to clever insider frauds; but regardless of size most thefts from the average company are due to insiders. There are many surveys. A recent one, by accountants Ernst and Young, reports that 82 percent of the worst frauds in 1999–2000 were committed by employees; nearly half of the perpetrators had been there over five years, and a third of them were managers [697].

Typical computer crime cases include:

- A bank had a system of suspense accounts, which would be used temporarily if one of the parties to a transaction could not be identified (such as when an account number was entered wrongly on a funds transfer). This was a workaround added to the dual control system to deal with transactions that got lost or otherwise couldn't be balanced immediately. As it was a potential vulnerability, the bank had a rule that suspense accounts would be investigated if they were not cleared within three days. One of the clerks exploited this by setting up a scheme whereby she would post a debit to a suspense account and an equal credit to her boyfriend's account; after three days, she would raise another debit to pay off the first. In almost two years, she netted hundreds of thousands of dollars. (The bank negligently ignored a regulatory requirement that all staff take at least 10 consecutive days' vacation no more than 15 months from the last such vacation.) In the end, she was caught when she could no longer keep track of the growing mountain of bogus transactions.

■ A clerk at the Inner London Education Authority wanted to visit relatives in Australia, and to get some money, she created a fictitious school, complete with staff whose salaries were paid into her own bank account. It was discovered only by accident when someone noticed that different records gave the authority different numbers of schools.

■ A bank clerk in Hastings, England, noticed that the branch computer system did not audit address changes. He picked a customer who had a lot of money in her account and got a statement only once a year; he then changed her address to his, issued a new ATM card and personal identification number (PIN), and changed her address back to its original value. In total, he stole £8,600 from her account. When she complained, she was not believed: the bank maintained that its computer systems were infallible, and so the withdrawals must have been her fault. The matter was cleared up only when the clerk got an attack of conscience and started stuffing the cash in brown envelopes through the branch's letter box at night. The branch manager finally realized that something was seriously wrong.

All the really large frauds—the cases over a billion dollars—have involved lax internal controls. The collapse of Barings Bank is a good example; there, managers failed to control rogue trader Nick Leeson, as they were blinded by greed for the bonuses his apparent trading profits earned them. The same holds true for other big financial sector frauds, such as the Equity Funding scandal, in which an insurance company's management created thousands of fake people on their computer system, insured them, and sold the policies on to reinsurers; and frauds in other sectors such as Robert Maxwell's looting of the *Daily Mirror* newspaper pension funds in Britain. (For a collection of computer crime case histories, see Parker [602].) Either the victim's top managers were grossly negligent, as in the case of Barings, or were the perpetrators, as with Equity Funding and Maxwell. As a result, a number of standards have been put forward by the accountancy profession, by stock markets, and by banking regulators, about how bookkeeping and internal control systems should be designed. In the United States, for example, there is the *Committee of Sponsoring Organizations* (COSO), a group of U.S. accounting and auditing bodies [196]. I'll return to COSO and explore how to go about designing an internal control system in Chapter 22, "Management Issues," Section 22.4.1.2.

But changing technology also has a habit of eroding controls, which therefore need constant attention and maintenance. For example, thanks to new systems for high-speed processing of bank checks, banks in California will no longer honor requests by depositors that checks have two signatures. Even when a check has printed on it "Two Signatures Required," banks will honor that check with only one signature [651]. This might seem to be a problem for the customer's security rather than the bank's, but bank checks can also be at risk and if something goes wrong even with a merchant transaction, the bank might still get sued. The vulnerability of shared control to technical attacks continues to grow. Most major accounting packages do not use double-entry bookkeeping internally, but rather create an appearance of it at the presentation layer; and the current trend appears to be toward event databases in which all transactions in an accounting period are accumulated, with reports being generated directly as required. New control strategies may be needed. One possible technical approach is to maintain separate logs of all original events (purchase orders, invoices, payments, etc.) and have programs that constantly cross-check. People-based measures are also highly advisable. Accounts software should empower line managers so that they can monitor their departments' income, expenditure and commitments. Making the technical and managerial controls overlap, so that they cover each others' weaknesses, is the goal; unfortunately, the common outcome is that the technical controls merely duplicate the managerial ones, resulting in common failure modes that fraudsters can exploit.

The lessons to be learned include the following.

- It's not always obvious which transactions are security-sensitive.
- It's hard to maintain a working security system in a changing environment.
- If you rely on customer complaints to alert you to fraud, you had better listen to them.
- There will always be people in positions of relative trust who can get away with a scam—for a while.
- No security policy will ever be completely rigid; there will always have to be workarounds for people to cope with real life, and some of these workarounds will create vulnerabilities.
- It's often hard to tell at first sight whether an exception is due to fraud or to error. So the lower the transaction error rate, the better.

There will always be residual risks. Managing these remains one of the hardest and most neglected of jobs. It requires not just technical measures, such as involving knowledgeable industry experts, auditors, and insurance people in the detailed design, and iterating the design once some loss history is available. It also means training managers, auditors, and others to detect problems and react to them appropriately. I'll revisit this topic in Chapter 22.

The banking industry has gone a long way along this learning curve. The general experience of banks in the English-speaking world is that some 1 percent of staff are fired each year. The typical offense is minor embezzlement, incurring a loss of a few thousand dollars. No one has found an effective way of predicting which staff will go bad; previously loyal staff can be thrown off the rails by shocks such as divorce, or may over time develop a gambling or alcohol habit.

9.3 Wholesale Payment Systems

Systems for transferring money electronically were one of the first applications of the telegraph when it was introduced in the middle of the nineteenth century; and I explained in Chapter 5, "Cryptography," Section 5.2.4 how the system of test keys was developed to compute authentication codes on the messages manually. By the early 1970s, bankers started to realize that a better system was needed:

- The cryptographic vulnerability of the system became apparent.

- Although the test key tables were kept in the safe, it was at least theoretically possible for a bank employee to memorize one of the simpler schemes. With the more complex schemes, even an employee working under close supervision could mentally compute the test on an unauthorized message, while overtly computing the test on an authorized one.

- The schemes didn't support dual control. Although tests were computed by one staff member and checked by another, this doubled the risk rather than halving it. (There are ways to do dual control with manual authenticators, and these had been developed extensively for use in the control of nuclear weapons—I discuss them in Chapter 11, Section 11.4—but this technology was still classified at the time.)

- The major concern was cost and efficiency. There seemed little point in having the bank's computer print out a transaction in the telex room, having a test computed manually, composing a telex to the other bank, checking the test, and then entering it into the other bank's computer. Surely the payments could flow directly from one bank's computer to another?

Clearly, a fresh design was needed.

9.3.1 SWIFT

The Society for Worldwide International Financial Telecommunications (SWIFT) was set up in the 1970s by a consortium of banks to provide a more secure and efficient means of sending payment instructions between member banks. It can be thought of as an email system with built-in encryption, authentication, and nonrepudiation services.

The SWIFT design constraints are interesting. The banks did not wish to trust SWIFT, in the sense of enabling some combination of dishonest employees there to forge transactions. The authenticity mechanisms had to be independent of the confidentiality mechanisms, since at the time a number of countries (such as France) forbade the civilian use of cryptography for confidentiality. The nonrepudiation functions had to be provided without the use of digital signatures, as these hadn't been invented yet. Finally, the banks had to be able to enforce Clark-Wilson type controls over interbank transactions. (Clark-Wilson also hadn't been invented yet, but its components—dual control, balancing, audit, and so on—were well enough established.)

The SWIFT design is summarized in Figure 9.2. Authenticity of messages was assured by computing a message authentication code (MAC) at the sending bank and checking it at the receiving bank. Formerly, the keys for this MAC were managed end-to-end:

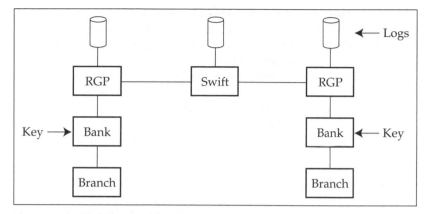

Figure 9.2   Architecture of SWIFT.

whenever a bank set up a relationship overseas, the senior manager who negotiated it would exchange keys with her opposite number, whether in a face-to-face meeting or afterward by post to each other's private addresses. There would typically be two key components to minimize the risk of compromise, with one sent in each direction (on the grounds that even if a bank manager's mail is stolen from her mailbox by a criminal at one end, it's not likely to happen at the other end as well). The key would not be enabled until both banks confirmed that it had been safely received and installed.

This way, SWIFT had no part in the message authentication. As long as the authentication algorithm SWIFT chose was sound, none of their staff could forge a transaction. (The authentication algorithm used is supposed to be a trade secret; but because banks like their security mechanisms to be international standards, a natural place to look might be the algorithm described in ISO 8731 [657].) In this way, they got the worst of all possible worlds: the algorithm was fielded without the benefit of public analysis but got it later once it was expensive to change. (An attack was found on the ISO 8731 message authentication algorithm and published in [621], but the number of messages required to break it is too large for a practical attack on a typical system that is used prudently.)

Although SWIFT itself was largely outside the trust perimeter for message authentication, it did provide a nonrepudiation service. Banks in each country sent their messages to a *regional general processor* (RGP), which logged them and forwarded them to SWIFT, which also logged them and sent them on to the recipient bank via the RGP in its country, which also logged them. The RGPs were generally run by different facilities management firms. Thus, a bank (or a crooked bank employee) wishing to dishonestly repudiate a done transaction—or claim that one had been done when it hadn't—would have to subvert not just SWIFT itself, but also two independent local contractors (in order to alter their log entries). Logs can be a powerful evidential resource, and are much easier for judges to understand than cryptography.

Confidentiality depended on line encryption devices between the banks and the RGP node, and between these nodes and the main SWIFT processing sites. Key management was straightforward. Keys were hand-carried in EEPROM cartridges between the devices at either end of a leased line. In countries where confidentiality was illegal, these devices could be omitted without impairing the authenticity and nonrepudiation mechanisms.

Dual control was provided either by the use of specialized terminals (in small banks) or by mainframe software packages that could be integrated with a bank's main production system. The usual method of operation is to have three separate staff to do a SWIFT transaction: one to enter it, one to check it, and one to authorize it. (As the checker can modify any aspect of the message, this really gives only dual control, not triple control; and the programmers who maintain the interface can always attack the system there). Reconciliation was provided by checking transactions against daily statements received electronically from correspondent banks. This meant that someone who managed to get a bogus message into the system would sound an alarm within two or three days.

9.3.2 What Goes Wrong

SWIFT I ran for 20 years without a single report of external fraud. In the mid-1990s, it was enhanced by the addition of public key mechanisms. MAC keys are now shared between correspondent banks using public key cryptography, and the MACs themselves may be further protected by a digital signature. The key management mechanisms have been ensconced as ISO standard 11166, which in turn has been used in other systems (such as CREST, which is used by banks and stockbrokers to register and transfer U.K. stocks and shares). There has been some debate over the security of this architecture [47, 657]: Quite apart from the centralization of trust brought about by the adoption of public key cryptography—in that the central certification authority can falsely certify a key as belonging to a bank when it doesn't—CREST (at least) adopted public keys that are too short (512 bits). At least one RSA public key of this length has been factored surreptitiously by a group of students.

However, the main practical attacks on such systems have not involved the payment system mechanisms themselves. The typical attack comes from a bank programmer inserting a bogus message into the processing queue. It usually fails because he does not understand the other controls in the system or the procedural controls surrounding large transfers. For example, banks typically keep mutual overdraft limits of perhaps a million dollars, so transfers of larger amounts need the prior involvement of the foreign exchange dealers; there's the daily back-office reconciliation; money-laundering laws require staff to report large cash withdrawals; and anyone who opens a bank account, receives a large incoming wire transfer, then starts frantically moving money out again will need a very convincing excuse. Consequently, the programmer who inserts a bogus transaction into the system usually gets arrested when he turns up to collect the cash.

Other possible technical attacks—such as inserting Trojan software into the PCs used by bank managers to initiate transactions, wiretapping the link from the branch to the bank mainframe, subverting the authentication protocol used by bank managers to log on, and even inserting a bogus transaction in the branch LAN to appear on the relevant printer—would also run up against these controls.

In fact, most large-scale bank frauds that "worked" have not used technical attacks but exploited procedural vulnerabilities, such as the following:

■ The classic example is a letter of guarantee. It is common enough for a company in one country to guarantee a loan to a company in another. This can be set up as a SWIFT message or even a paper letter. But as no cash changes hands at the time, the balancing controls are inoperative. If a forged guarantee is accepted as genuine, the "beneficiary" can take his time borrowing money from the accepting bank, laundering it, and disappearing. Only when the victim bank realizes that the loan has gone sour, and tries to call in the guarantee, is the forgery discovered.

- An interesting fraud of a slightly different type took place in 1986 between London and Johannesburg. At that time, the South African government operated two exchange rates, and in one bank the manager responsible for deciding which rate applied to each transaction conspired with a rich man in London. They sent money out to Johannesburg at an exchange rate of seven Rand to the Pound, and back again the following day at four. After two weeks of this, the authorities became suspicious, and the police came round. On seeing them in the dealing room, the manager fled without stopping to collect his jacket, drove over the border to Swaziland, and flew via Nairobi to London. There, he boasted to the press about how he had defrauded the wicked apartheid system. As Britain has no exchange control, exchange control fraud isn't an offense, so he couldn't be extradited. The conspirators got away with millions, and the bank couldn't even sue them.

- Perhaps the best-known funds transfer fraud occurred in 1979 when Stanley Rifkin, a computer consultant, embezzled over $10 million from Security Pacific National Bank. He circumvented the money-laundering controls by agreeing to buy a large shipment of diamonds from a Russian government agency in Switzerland. He got the transfer into the system by observing an authorization code used internally when dictating transfers to the wire transfer department, and simply used it over the telephone (a classic example of dual control breakdown at a system interface). He even gave himself extra time to escape by doing the deal just before a U.S. bank holiday. Where he went wrong was in not planning what to do after he collected the stones. If he had hidden them in Europe, gone back to the United States, and helped investigate the fraud, he might well have got away with it; as it was, he ended up on the run and got caught.

The moral is that we must always be alert to things which defeat separation-of-duty controls by introducing a single point of failure. Even if we can solve the technical problems of systems administration, interfaces, and so on, there's still the business system analysis problem of what we control—quite often, critical transactions aren't obvious to a casual inspection.

9.4 Automatic Teller Machines

Another reason that dual control—although necessary—is not sufficient, emerges from the study of "phantom withdrawals"—complaints of unauthorized cash withdrawals from *automatic teller machines* (ATMs).

ATMs, also known as cash machines, have been one of the most influential technological innovations of the twentieth century. Quite apart from their social and economic impact, they are just as important to the security engineer both as a source of technology and as a case study.

ATMs were the first large-scale retail transaction processing systems. They have been around since 1968; the world installed base is now about 500,000 machines. The technology developed for them is now also used in terminals for *electronic funds transfer at the point of sale* (EFTPOS, or just POS) in shops. Modern block ciphers were first used on a large scale in ATM networks, to generate and verify PINs in secure hardware devices located within the ATMs and at bank computer centers. This technology, including block ciphers, tamper-resistant hardware, and the supporting protocols, ended up being used in many other applications, from postal franking machines to lottery ticket terminals. ATMs were the "killer app" that got modern commercial cryptology off the ground.

9.4.1 ATM Basics

Many ATMs operate using some variant of a system developed by IBM for its 3614 series cash machines in the mid-1970s. This uses a secret key, called the *PIN key*, to encrypt the account number, then decimalize it and truncate it. The result of this operation is called the *natural PIN;* an offset can be added to it to give the PIN the customer must enter. The offset has no real cryptographic function; it just enables customers to choose their own PIN. An example of the process is shown in Figure 9.3.

Dual control is implemented in this system using tamper-resistant hardware. A cryptographic processor, often called a *security module*, is kept in the bank's central computer room. It will perform a number of defined operations on customer PINs and on related keys in such a way that:

- Operations on the clear values of customer PINs, and on the keys or other material needed to compute them or used to protect them, are all done in tamper-resistant hardware and the clear values are never made available to any single member of the bank's staff.

- Thus, for example, the cards and PINs are sent to the customer via separate channels. The cards are personalized in a facility with embossing and mag-strip printing machinery; the PIN mailers are printed in a separate facility containing a printer attached to a security module.

- A *terminal master key* is supplied to each ATM in the form of two printed components, which are carried to the branch by two separate officials, input at the ATM keyboard, and combined to form the key. Similar procedures are used to set up keys between banks and network switches such as VISA.

- If ATMs are to perform PIN verification, the PIN key is encrypted under the terminal master key, then sent to the ATM.

Account number N (on the mag stripe):	8807012345691715
PIN key KP:	FEFEFEFEFEFEFEFE
Result of DES $\{N\}_{KP}$:	A2CE126C69AEC82D
$\{N\}_{KP}$ decimalized:	0224126269042823
Natural PIN:	0224
Offset:	6565
Customer PIN:	6789

Figure 9.3 IBM method for generating bank card PINs.

- If the PIN verification is to be done centrally over the network, the PIN is encrypted under a key that is set up using the terminal master key, and sent from the ATM to the security module for checking.

- If the bank's ATMs are to be networked with other banks', then one uses transactions that will take an encrypted PIN from one source (such as encrypted under an ATM key), decrypt it, and re-encrypt it for its destination (such as using a key shared with VISA). This *PIN translation* function is done entirely within the hardware security module, so that clear values of PINs are never available to the bank's programmers.

During the 1980s and 1990s, the hardware security modules became more and more complex, as ever more functionality got added. An example of a leading product in 2000 is the IBM 4758, this also has the virtue of having its documentation available publicly online for study (see [397] for the command set, and [718] for the architecture and hardware design). I'll discuss this in Chapter 14, "Physical Tamper Resistance."

But extending the dual control security policy from a single bank to tens of thousands of banks worldwide, as modern ATM networks do, proved not to be completely straightforward:

- When people started building ATM networks in the mid-1980s, many banks used software encryption rather than hardware security modules to support the machines. So in theory, any bank's programmers might get access to the PINs of any other bank's customers. The remedy was to push through standards for security module use. In many countries (such as the United States), these standards were largely ignored; but even where they were respected, some banks continued using software for transactions involving their own customers. So some keys (such as those used to communicate with ATMs) had to be available in software, too, and knowledge of these keys could be used to compromise the PINs of other banks' customers. Consequently, the protection given by the hardware TCB was rarely complete.

- It is not feasible for 10,000 banks to share keys in pairs, so each bank connects to a switch provided by an organization such as VISA or Cirrus, and the security modules in these switches translate the traffic. The switches also do accounting, and enable banks to settle their accounts for each day's transactions with all the other banks in the system, by means of a single electronic debit or credit. The switch is highly trusted; if something goes wrong, the consequences could be severe. In one case, there turned out to be not just security problems but also dishonest staff. The switch manager ended up a fugitive from justice, and the bill for remediation was in the millions.

- Corners are cut to reduce the cost of dealing with huge transaction volumes. For example, it is common for authentication of authorization responses to be turned off. The effect is that anyone with access to the network can cause a given ATM to accept any card presented to it, simply by replaying a positive authorization response. Network managers claim that should a fraud ever start, the authentication can always be turned back on. This might seem reasonable; attacks involving manipulated authorization responses are very rare. But such shortcuts—even when reasonable on grounds of risk and cost—mean that a bank that claims, in response to a customer dispute, that its ATM network cannot possibly be attacked, and so the transaction must be the customer's fault, is not telling the truth. What's more, turning on the message authentication codes suddenly in response to a fraud could be difficult. Some banks' implementations might not support them properly or at all, and performance degradation might result unless more encryption devices are installed rapidly. One is reminded of the saying that 'optimization is the process of taking something which works, and replacing it by something which doesn't quite but is cheaper'.

There are many other ways in which ATM networks can be attacked in theory. For example, they mostly use single-key DES encryption, even for top-level keys, and DES can now be broken by exhaustive keysearch. However, one of the interesting things about these systems is that they have now been around long enough, and have been attacked enough by both insiders and outsiders, to give us a lot of data points on how such systems fail in practice.

9.4.2 What Goes Wrong

ATM fraud is an interesting study, as the ATM system is mature, with huge volumes and a wide diversity of operators. An extensive survey can be found in [19], and further material in [20]. Here, I'll summarize the more important and interesting points.

The engineers who designed ATM security systems in the 1970s and 1980s (of whom I was one) assumed that criminals would be relatively sophisticated, fairly well informed about the system design, and rational in their choice of attack methods. In addition to worrying about the many banks that were slow to buy security modules, and about the implementation loopholes such as omitting authentication codes on authorization responses, we agonized over whether the encryption algorithms were strong enough, and whether the tamper-resistant boxes were resistant enough. We were afraid that a maintenance engineer could disable the tamper sensing circuitry on one visit, and extract the keys on the next. We worried whether the random-number generators used to manufacture keys were random enough. And a very serious concern was that we just couldn't enforce dual control properly. Bank managers considered it beneath their dignity to touch a keyboard, so rather than entering the ATM master key components themselves after a maintenance visit, most of them would just give both key components to the ATM engineer. We believed that sooner or later a repairman would get his hands on a bank's PIN key, forge cards in industrial quantities, close down the whole system, and wreck public confidence in electronic banking.

The bulk of the actual phantom withdrawals, however, have one of the following three simple causes:

- *Simple processing errors account for a lot of disputes*. With U.S. customers making something like 5 billion ATM withdrawals a year, even a system that makes only one error per 100,000 transactions will give rise to 50,000 disputes a year. In practice, the error rate seems to lie somewhere between 1 in 10,000 and 1 in 100,000. One source of errors we tracked down was that a large bank's ATMs would send a transaction again if the network went down before a confirmation message was received from the mainframe; periodically, the mainframe itself crashed, and "forgot" about open transactions. We also found customers whose accounts were debited with other customers' transactions, and other customers who were never debited at all for their card transactions. (We used to call these cards "directors' cards," and joked that they were issued to bank directors.)

- *Thefts from the mail are also huge.* They are reckoned to account for 30 percent of all U.K. payment card losses, but most banks' postal control procedures are dismal. For example, in February 1992, I asked my bank for an increased card limit: the bank sent not one, but two, cards and PINs through the post. These cards arrived only a few days after intruders had got hold of our apartment block's mail and torn it up looking for valuables. It turned out that this bank did not have the systems to deliver a card by registered post. (I'd asked them to send the card to the branch for me to pick up, but someone at the branch had simply readdressed the envelope to me.) Since then, many banks have found that better postal controls are the one way they can make enough of a dent in their fraud rates to affect their bottom line.

- *Frauds by bank staff appear to be the third major cause of phantoms.* I mentioned the Hastings case in Section 9.2.3; there are many others. For example, in Paisley, Scotland, an ATM repairman installed a portable computer inside an ATM to record customer card and PIN data, then went on a spending spree with forged cards. In London, England, a bank stupidly used the same cryptographic keys in its live and test systems; maintenance staff found out that they could work out customer PINs using their test equipment, and started offering this as a service to local criminals at £50 a card. Such frauds are particularly common in countries such as Britain, where banks had for many years a policy of denying that their cash machines could possibly make an error. Bank staff knew that customer complaints would be stonewalled rather than investigated.

These failures are all very much simpler and more straightforward than the ones we engineers had worried about. In fact, the only fraud we had anticipated, and that happened to any great extent, came from the practice (common in the 1980s) of letting ATMs process transactions while the network was down or the central mainframe was offline. Though this was convenient—it meant 24-hour service—criminals, especially in Italy and England, learned to open bank accounts, duplicate the cards, then use them to withdraw money simultaneously from a large number of ATMs overnight when the network was down [494]. Such frauds led most banks to make ATM operation online-only by the mid-1990s.

However, there were numerous frauds that happened in quite unexpected ways. We already mentioned the Utrecht case in Section 2.8, where a tap on a garage point-of-sale terminal was used to harvest card and PIN data; and the "encryption replacement" trick by which banks that just encrypted the customer PIN and wrote it on the customer card enabled crooks to change the account number on their own card to somebody else's. There were many more.

- A favorite modus operandi was for villains to stand in ATM queues, observe customers' PINs, pick up the discarded ATM tickets, copy the account numbers from the tickets to blank cards, and use these to loot the customers' accounts. This trick was first reported in New York in the mid-1980s; it was still working in the San Francisco Bay Area in the mid-1990s. Yet there are many simple countermeasures, such as incorporating extra data on the mag strip, or just not printing the full account number on the ticket.

■ One bank's systems had this feature: when a telephone card was entered at an ATM, it believed that the previous card had been inserted again. Crooks stood in line, observed customers' PINs, and helped themselves. This seems to have been an obscure programming error involving the card reader's error handler; one can't expect all such errors to be found during testing.

■ One make of ATM would output 10 banknotes from the lowest-denomination nonempty cash drawer whenever a certain 14-digit sequence was entered at the keyboard. One bank printed this sequence in its branch manual, and three years later there was a sudden spate of losses. These went on until all the banks using the machine put in a software patch to disable the transaction.

■ One small institution issued the same PIN to all its customers, as a result of a simple programming error.

■ Several banks thought up check-digit schemes to enable PINs to be checked by offline ATMs and point-of-sale devices without these devices having a full encryption capability. For example, customers of one British bank would get a credit card PIN with digit 1 plus digit 4 equal to digit 2 plus digit 3, and a debit card PIN with 1 plus 3 equals 2 plus 4. This meant that crooks could use stolen cards in offline devices by entering a PIN such as 4455.

■ Some banks show a complete disregard for prudent procedure. In August 1993, my wife went into a branch of our bank with a witness and said that she'd forgotten her PIN. The teller helpfully printed her a new PIN mailer from a printer attached to a PC behind the counter. There were no visible dual controls. Worse, this was not the branch where our account is kept. Nobody knew her and the only identification she offered was our bank card and her checkbook. When procedural controls are so lax that anyone can walk in off the street and get a PIN for a random customer account, no amount of encryption technology will do much good. (The bank in question has since fallen victim to a takeover.)

■ A rapidly growing modus operandi is to use false terminals to collect customer card and PIN data. Attacks of this kind were first reported from the United States in 1988; there, crooks built a vending machine that would accept any card and PIN, and dispense a packet of cigarettes. They put their invention in a shopping mall, and harvested PINs and magnetic strip data by modem. In 1993, two villains installed a bogus ATM in the Buckland Hills Mall in Connecticut [421, 590]. They had managed to get a proper ATM and a software development kit for it—all bought on credit. Unfortunately for them, they decided to use the forged cards in New York, where cash machines have hidden video cameras; they ended up getting long stretches in Club Fed. The largest and most recent case to date took place in 1999 in Canada. This involved doctored point-of-sale terminals, and led to the arrest of dozens of alleged Eastern European organized-crime figures in the Toronto area and elsewhere [54, 91].

In conclusion, the main thing we did wrong when designing ATM security systems in the early to mid-1980s was to worry about criminals being clever; we should rather have worried about our customers—the banks' system designers, implementers, and testers—being stupid.

Crypto is usually only part of a very much larger system. It gets a lot of attention because it is mathematically interesting; but as correspondingly little attention is paid to the "boring" bits such as training, usability, standards, and audit, it's rare that the bad guys have to break the crypto to compromise a system. It's also worth bearing in mind that there are so many users for large systems, such as ATM networks, that we must expect the chance discovery and exploitation of accidental vulnerabilities that were simply too obscure to be caught in testing.

9.4.3 Practical Implications

In some countries (including the United States), the banks have to carry the risks associated with new technology. Following a legal precedent, in which a bank customer's word that she had not made a withdrawal was found to outweigh the banks' experts' word that she must have done so [427], the U.S. Federal Reserve passed Regulation E, which requires banks to refund all disputed transactions unless they can prove fraud by the customer [276]. This has led to some minor abuse—misrepresentations by customers are estimated to cost the average U.S. bank about $15,000 a year—but this is an acceptable cost (especially as losses from vandalism are typically three times as much) [813].

In other countries—such as Britain and Norway—the banks got away for many years with claiming that their ATM systems were infallible. Phantom withdrawals, they maintained, could not possibly occur, and a customer who complained of one must be mistaken or lying. This position was finally demolished (in the Britain at least) when significant numbers of criminals were jailed for ATM fraud, and the problem couldn't plausibly be denied any more. (A number of these cases are described in [19, 20].) Until that happened, however, there were some rather unpleasant incidents that got banks a lot of bad publicity. Perhaps the worst was the Munden case.

John Munden was one of our local police constables, based in Bottisham, Cambridgeshire; his beat included the village of Lode where I lived at the time. He came home from holiday in September 1992 to find his bank account empty. He asked for a statement, found six unexpected withdrawals for a total of £460 (then about $700), and complained. His bank responded by having him prosecuted for attempting to obtain money by deception. It came out during the trial that the bank's system had been implemented and managed in a ramshackle way; the disputed transactions had not been properly investigated; and all sorts of wild claims were made by the bank, such as that its ATM system couldn't suffer from bugs as its software was written in Assembler. Nonetheless, it was basically the constable's word against the bank's. He was convicted in February 1994 and fired from the police force.

This miscarriage of justice was overturned on appeal, and in an interesting way. Just before the appeal was due to be heard, the prosecution served up a fat report from the bank's auditors claiming that the system was secure. The defense demanded equal access to the bank's systems for its own expert. The bank refused, and the court therefore disallowed all the bank's computer evidence—including its bank statements. The appeal succeeded, and Munden got reinstated. But this was only in July 1996—he'd spent the better part of four years in limbo, and his family had suffered terrible stress. Had the incident happened in California, he could have won enormous punitive damages, a point bankers should ponder as their systems become global and their customers can be anywhere.

The lesson to be drawn from such cases is that dual control is not enough. If a system is to provide evidence, it must be able to withstand examination by hostile experts. In effect, the bank in the Munden case had used the wrong security policy. What it really needed wasn't dual control, but *nonrepudiation:* the ability for the principals in a transaction to prove afterward what happened. This could have been provided by installing ATM cameras; although these were available (and are used in some U.S. states), they were not being used in Britain.

The issue of nonrepudiation arises in a number of other applications. Often, the right question to ask is not about the mechanism (cameras, biometrics, digital signatures, . . .) but about the motive. Why should a U.K. bank have spent money on ATM cameras that would have undermined its infallibility policy? (One English bank did install ATM cameras during the spate of phantom withdrawals, but took them out again under pressure from the other banks.) And why for that matter should people shopping on the Net use digital signatures, if these will just make it harder to deny a transaction when things go wrong? We will revisit this issue again and again in later chapters.

9.5 Summary

Banking systems are interesting in a number of ways.

Bookkeeping applications give us a mature example of systems whose security is oriented toward authenticity and accountability rather than confidentiality. Their protection goal is to prevent and detect frauds being committed by dishonest insiders. The Clark-Wilson security policy provides a model of how they operate. It can be summarized as:

> All transactions must preserve an invariant of the system, namely that the books must balance (so a negative entry in one ledger must be balanced by a positive entry in another one); some transactions must be performed by two or more staff members; and records of transactions must not be destroyed after they are committed.

This was based on time-honored bookkeeping procedures, and led the research community to consider systems other than variants of Bell-LaPadula.

But manual bookkeeping systems use more than just dual control. Although some systems do need transactions to be authorized in parallel by two or more staff, a separation of duty policy more often works in series, in that different people do different things to each transaction as it passes through the system. Designing bookkeeping systems that do this effectively is a major problem which is often neglected and which involves input from many disciplines. Another common requirement is nonrepudiation—that principals should be able to generate, retain, and use evidence about the relevant actions of other principals.

The other major banking application, remote payment, is increasingly critical to e-commerce. In fact, wire transfers of money go back to the middle of the Victorian era. Because there is an obvious motive to attack these systems, and villains who steal large amounts and get caught are generally prosecuted, payment systems are a valuable source of information about what goes wrong. Their loss history teaches us the importance of minimizing the background error rate, preventing procedural attacks that defeat technical controls (such as thefts of ATM cards from the mail), and having adequate controls to deter and detect internal fraud.

Payment systems have also played a significant role in the development and application of cryptology. One innovation was the idea that cryptography could be used to confine a critical part of the application to a trusted computing base consisting of tamper-resistant processors—an approach since used in many other applications.

Research Problems

Designing transaction sets for bookkeeping applications is still pre-scientific; we could do with tools to help us do it in a more systematic, less error-prone way. Accountants, lawyers, financial market regulators, and system engineers all seem to feel that this is someone else's responsibility. This is a striking opportunity to do multidisciplinary research that might actually be useful.

At an even more basic level, we don't even fully understand stateful access control systems, such as Clark-Wilson and Chinese Wall. To what extent does one do more than the other on the separation-of-duty front? How should dual control systems be designed anyway? How much of the authorization logic can we abstract out of application code into middleware? Can we separate policy and implementation to make enterprise-wide policies easier to administer?

There are some useful distinctions, such as policy versus mechanism versus management, push versus pull, and specification versus runtime controls. There are some prototype engines for enforcing an arbitrary policy—such HP's authorization server product [772] and AT&T's Policymaker [115]. Developing such engines to deal with the full generality of possible security policies is still an open problem.

As for robustness of cryptographic systems, the usability of security mechanisms, and assurance generally, these are huge topics that are still only partially mapped. Robustness and assurance are partially understood, but usability is still a very gray area. There are many more mathematicians active in security research than applied psychologists, and it shows.

Further Reading

I don't know of a comprehensive book on banking computer systems, although there are many papers on specific payment systems available from the Bank for International Settlements [72]. When it comes to developing robust management controls and business processes that limit the amount of damage that any one staff member can do, there is a striking lack of hard material (especially given the need that new e-businesses have for such systems). There was one academic conference in 1997 [416]; but the business books that touch on these issues all seem to focus on financial management and on the soft aspects of management control such as "tone at the top." I'll revisit this in Chapter 22.

For the specifics of financial transaction processing systems, the cited articles [19, 20] provide a basic introduction. More comprehensive, if somewhat dated, is [221], while [336] describes the CIRRUS network as of the mid-'80s. The most informative public domain source—though somewhat heavy going—is probably the huge online manuals for the equipment in question, such as the IBM 4758 and CCA [397].

CHAPTER 10

Monitoring Systems

For if a man watch too long, it is odds he will fall asleepe.
—FRANCIS BACON

10.1 Introduction

A significant number of secure systems are concerned with monitoring the environment. The most obvious example is the burglar alarm. Then there are meters for measuring consumption of utilities such as gas and electricity. At the top end of the scale, there are systems used to verify nuclear nonproliferation treaties, where a number of sensors (seismometers, closed-circuit TV, and so on) are emplaced in a state's nuclear facilities by the International Atomic Energy Authority (IAEA) to create an immediate, indelible, and remote log of all movements of fissile substances. There are also vehicle systems, such as missile telemetry, taximeters, and tachographs (devices used in Europe to record the speed and working hours of truck and bus drivers).

These have a number of interesting features in common. For example, to defeat a burglar alarm it is sufficient to make it stop working, or—in many cases—to persuade its operators that it has become unreliable. This raises the spectre of *denial of service attacks*, which are increasingly important yet often difficult to deal with.

Just as we have seen military messaging systems designed to enforce confidentiality, and bookkeeping systems whose goal is to preserve record authenticity, monitoring applications give us the classic example of systems designed to be dependably available. If there is a burglar in my bank vault, then I do not care very much who else finds out (so I'm not worried about confidentiality) or who it was who told me (so authenticity isn't a major concern); but I do care very much that an attempt to tell me is not thwarted.

An alarm in a bank vault is very well protected from tampering (at least by outsiders), so it provides the simplest case study. We are largely concerned with attacks on communications (though sensor defeats are also a worry). But many other monitoring systems are very exposed physically. Utility meters are usually on the premises of the consumer, who has a motive to cause them to make incorrect readings. Much the same goes with taximeters: the taxi driver (or owner) may want the meter to read more miles or more minutes than were actually worked. With tachographs, it's the reverse. The truck driver usually wants to drive above the speed limit, or work dangerously long hours, so both types of attack are found. The driver can either cause the tachograph to fail, or to make false readings of time and distance. These devices, too, are very exposed to tampering. In both metering and monitoring systems (and especially with nuclear verification) we are also concerned with evidence. An opponent could get an advantage not just by manipulating communications (such as by replaying old messages) but by falsely claiming that someone else had done so.

Monitoring systems are also important because they have quite a lot in common with systems designed to enforce the copyright of software and other digital media, which I will discuss in a later chapter. They also provide a gentle introduction to the wider problem of service denial attacks, which dominate the business of electronic warfare, and are starting to be of grave concern to electronic commerce.

10.2 Alarms

Alarms are used to deal with much more than burglary. Their applications range from monitoring freezer temperatures in supermarkets (to stop staff "accidentally" switching off freezer cabinets in the hope of being given spoiling food to take home) right through to improvised explosive devices that are booby-trapped to deter the bomb disposal squad. However, it's convenient to discuss them in the context of burglary and of protecting rooms where computer equipment is kept.

Standards and requirements for alarms vary between countries and between different types of risk. Normally, you will use a local specialist firm for this kind of work; but as a security engineer, you must be aware of the issues. Alarms often affect larger system designs in my own professional practice, this has ranged from the alarms built into automatic teller machines through the evaluation of the security of the communications used by an alarm system for large risks such as wholesale jewelers, to continually staffed systems such as those used to protect bank computer rooms.

It's easier to teach someone with an electrical engineering/computer science background the basics of physical security than the other way round. Therefore, interactions between physical and logical protection will be up to the systems person to deal with. You are also likely to be asked for your opinion on your client's installations—which will often have been designed and installed by local contractors who may have established links with your clients but rather narrow horizons as far as system issues are concerned.

10.2.1 Threat Model

An important design consideration is the level of skill, equipment, and determination that the attacker might have. Movies such as *Entrapment* might be good entertainment, but they don't give a realistic view of the world of theft. In the absence of an "international standard burglar," the nearest I know to a working classification is one developed by a U.S. Army expert [74].

- Derek is a 19-year-old addict. He's looking for a low-risk opportunity to steal something such as a video recorder to fund his next fix.

- Charlie is a 40-year-old inadequate with seven convictions for burglary. He has spent seventeen of the last twenty-five years in prison. Although not very intelligent, he is cunning and experienced; he has picked up a lot of "lore" during his spells "inside." He steals from small shops and prosperous-looking suburban houses, taking whatever he thinks he can sell to local fences.

- Bruno is a "gentleman criminal." His business is mostly stealing art. As a cover, he runs a small art gallery. He has a (forged) university degree in art history on the wall, and one conviction for robbery eighteen years ago. After two years in jail, he changed his name and moved to a different part of the country. He has done occasional "black bag" jobs for intelligence agencies, who know his past. He'd like to get into computer crime, but the most he has done so far is to strip $100,000 worth of memory chips from a university's PCs back in the mid-1990s, when there was a memory famine.

- Abdurrahman heads a cell of a dozen militants, most with military training. They have infantry weapons and explosives, with PhD-grade technical support provided by a disreputable country. Abdurrahman was third in a class of 280 at the military academy of that country, but was not promoted because he's from the wrong ethnic group. He thinks of himself as a good man rather than a bad man. His mission is to steal plutonium.

So Derek is unskilled; Charlie is skilled; Bruno is highly skilled, and may have the help of an unskilled insider such as a cleaner; while Abdurrahman is not only highly skilled but has substantial resources. He may even have the help of a technician or other skilled insider who has been suborned.

The sociologists are interested in Derek, the criminologists in Charlie, and the military in Abdurrahman; our concern is mainly with Bruno. He isn't the highest available grade of "civilian criminal" (that distinction probably goes to the bent bankers and lawyers who launder money for drug gangs, whom I'll get to later). But in countries without a terrorism problem, the physical defenses of computer rooms tend to be designed with someone like Bruno in mind. (Whether this is rational, or an overplay, will depend on the kind of business your client is in.)

The common view of Bruno is that he organizes cunning attacks on alarm systems, having spent days poring over the building plans in the local town hall. You probably read about this kind of crime several times a year in the papers.

HOW TO STEAL A PAINTING (1)

A Picasso is stolen from a gallery, with supposedly state-of-the-art alarm systems, by a thief who removed a dozen roofing tiles and lowered himself down a rope so as not to activate the pressure mats under the carpet. He grabbed the painting, climbed back out without touching the floor, and probably sold the thing for a quarter of a million dollars to a wealthy cocaine dealer.

The press loves this kind of stuff, and it does happen from time to time. Reality is both simpler and stranger.

10.2.2 How Not to Protect a Painting

A common mistake when designing alarm systems is to be captivated by the latest sensor technology. There's a lot of impressive stuff on the market, such as a fiber optic cable that you can loop around protected objects and that will sense if the cable is stretched or relaxed by less than a thousandth of a millimeter. The naive art gallery owner will buy a few feet of this magic cable, glue it to the back of the Picasso and connect it to an alarm company.

HOW TO STEAL A PAINTING (2)

Bruno's attack is to visit as a tourist and hide in a broom cupboard. At one in the morning, he emerges, snatches the painting and heads for the fire exit. Off goes the alarm, but so what! In less than a minute, Bruno is on his motorcycle. By the time the cops arrive 12 minutes later, he has vanished.

This sort of theft is much more likely than a bosun's chair through the roof. It's often easy because alarms are rarely integrated well with building entry controls. Many designers don't realize that where they can't positively account for all the people who enter the premises during the day, it may be prudent to take some precautions against the "stay-behind" villain—even if this means only an inspection tour after the gallery has closed. Serious physical security means serious controls on people. In fact, the first recorded use of the RSA cryptosystem—in 1978—was not to encrypt communications but to provide digital signatures on credentials used by staff to get past the entry barrier to a plutonium reactor at Idaho Falls. The credentials contained data such as body weight and hand geometry [701, 705]. But I continue to be amazed by the ease with which building entry controls are defeated at most secure sites I visit—whether by mildly technical means, such as sitting on somebody else's shoulders to go through an entry booth, or by helpful people holding the door open.

Moreover, the alarm response process often hasn't been thought through carefully. (The *Titanic effect* of over-reliance on the latest gee-whiz technology often blinds people to common sense.) As we'll see shortly, this leads to still simpler attacks on most systems.

So we mustn't think of the alarm mechanism in isolation. A physical security system has a number of elements:

Deter – detect – alarm – delay – respond

The emphasis will vary from one application to another. If our opponent is Derek or Charlie, we will be concerned primarily with deterrence. At the sort of targets Abdurrahman is interested in, an attack will almost certainly be detected; the main problem is to delay him long enough for the Marines to arrive. Bruno is the most interesting case as we won't have the military budget to spend on keeping him out, and there are many more premises whose defenders worry about Bruno than about Abdurrahman. Depending on the circumstances, they might have a problem with detection, and also with the response.

10.2.3 Sensor Defeats

Burglar alarms use a wide range of *sensors*, including

- Vibration detectors, to sense fence disturbance, footsteps, breaking glass, or other attacks on buildings or perimeters
- Switches on doors and windows
- Passive infrared devices to detect body heat
- Motion detectors that use ultrasonics or microwave
- Invisible barriers of microwave or infrared beams
- Pressure pads under the carpet, which in extreme cases may extend to instrumenting the entire floor with pressure transducers under each tile
- Video cameras, perhaps with movement detectors, to alarm automatically or to provide a live video feed to a monitoring center
- Movement sensors on equipment, ranging from simple tie-down cables through seismometers to loops of optical fiber.

Most of these sensors can be circumvented one way or another. Fence-disturbance sensors can be defeated by vaulting the fence; motion sensors by moving very slowly; door and window switches by breaking through a wall. Designing a good combination of sensors comes down to skill and experience (with the latter not always guaranteeing the former).

The main problem is limiting the number of false alarms. Ultrasonics don't perform well near moving air such as central heating inlets, while vibration detectors can be rendered useless by traffic. Severe weather, such as lightning, will trigger most systems, and a hurricane can increase the number of calls per day on a town's police force from dozens to thousands. In some places, even normal weather can make protection difficult. Protecting a site where the intruder might be able to ski over your sensors (and even over your fence) is an interesting challenge for the security engineer. (For an instructive worked example of the design of intruder detection systems for a nuclear power station in a snow zone see [74]).

But regardless of whether you're in Alaska or Arizona, the principal dilemma is that the closer you get to the object being protected, the more tightly you can control the environment, and so the lower the achievable false alarm rate. Conversely, at the perimeter, it's hard to keep the false alarm rate down. But to delay an intruder long enough for the guards to get there, the outer perimeter is exactly where you need reliable sensors.

HOW TO STEAL A PAINTING (3)

Bruno's next attack is to wait for a dark and stormy night. He sets off the alarm somehow, taking care not to get caught on CCTV or otherwise leave any hard evidence that the alarm was a real one. He retreats few hundred yards and hides in the bushes. The guards come out and find nothing. He waits half an hour and sets off the alarm again. This time the guards don't bother, and in he goes.

False alarms—whether induced deliberately or not—are the bane of the industry. They provide a direct denial-of-service attack on the alarm response force. Experience from the world of electronic warfare is that a false alarm rate of greater than about 15% degrades the performance of radar operators; and most intruder alarm response forces are operating well above this threshold. Deliberately induced false alarms are especially effective against sites that don't have round-the-clock guards. Many police forces have a policy that, after a certain number of false alarms from a given site (typically two to five in a year), they will no longer send a squad car there until the alarm company, or another keyholder, has been there to check.

In addition to service denial issues, false alarms degrade systems in other ways. The rate at which they are caused by environmental stimuli, such as weather conditions and traffic noise, limits the sensitivity of the sensors that can usefully be deployed. Also, the very success of the alarm industry has greatly increased the total number of alarms, and thus decreased police tolerance of false alarms. So many people install remote video surveillance, so the customer's premises can be inspected by the alarm company's dispatcher. Many police forces prioritize alarms confirmed by such means [417].

But even online video links are not a panacea. The attacker can disable the lighting, start a fire, or set off alarms in other buildings nearby. The failure of a telephone exchange, as a result of a flood or hurricane, may well lead to opportunistic looting.

After environmental constraints such as traffic and weather, Bruno's next ally is time. Vegetation grows into the path of sensor beams; fences become slack, and the vibration sensors don't work so well; and the criminal community learns new tricks. Meanwhile, the sentries become complacent.

For this reason, sites with a serious physical protection requirement typically have several concentric perimeters. The outer fence keeps out drunks, wildlife, and other low-grade intruders; next there may be level grass with buried sensors, then an inner fence with an infrared barrier, and finally a building of sufficiently massive construction to delay the bad guys until the cavalry gets there. (The international regulations laid down by the IAEA for sites that hold more than 15g of plutonium are an instructive read [409].)

At most sites, this kind of protection isn't possible; it is too expensive. And even if you have loads of money, you may be in a city such as Hong Kong where real estate's in really short supply, and like it or not, your bank computer room will just be a floor of an office building that you'll have to protect as best you can.

In any case, the combination of sensors and physical barriers you select and install are still less than half the story.

10.2.4 Feature Interactions

Intruder alarms and barriers interact in a number of ways with other services. The most obvious of these is electricity. A power cut will leave many sites dark and unprotected, so a serious alarm installation needs batteries or other backup power supplies. A less obvious interaction is with fire alarms and firefighting.

HOW TO STEAL A PAINTING (4)

Bruno again visits the gallery as a tourist and leaves a smoke grenade on a timer. This goes off at one in the morning and sets off the fire alarm, which in turn causes the burglar alarm to ignore signals from its passive infrared sensors. (If it doesn't, the alarm dispatcher will probably ignore them anyway as he concentrates on getting the fire trucks to the scene). Bruno smashes his way in through a fire exit and grabs the Picasso. He'll probably manage to escape in the general chaos, but if he doesn't, he has a cunning plan: to claim he was a public-spirited bystander who saw the fire and risked his life to save the town's priceless cultural heritage. The police might not believe him, but they'll have a hard time prosecuting him.

The interaction between fire and intrusion works in a number of ways. Some fire precautions can be used only if there are effective barriers to keep out innocent intruders. Many computer rooms have automatic fire extinguishers, and since fears over global warming made Halon unavailable, this means carbon dioxide flooding. A CO_2 dump is lethal to untrained personnel. Getting out of a room on the air you have in your lungs is much harder than it looks when visiblity drops to a few inches and you are disoriented by the terrible shrieking noise of the dump. A malfunctioning intruder alarm that let a drunk into your computer room, where he lit up a cigarette and was promptly executed by your fire extinguisher, might raise a few chuckles among the anti-smoking militants but is unlikely to make your lawyers very happy.

In any case, the most severe feature interactions are between alarm and communication systems.

10.2.5 Attacks on Communications

A sophisticated attacker is at least as likely to attack the communications as the sensors. Sometimes, this will mean the cabling between the sensors and the alarm controller.

HOW TO STEAL A PAINTING (5)

Bruno goes into an art gallery and, while the staff are distracted, he cuts the wire from a window switch. He goes back that evening and helps himself.

It's also quite possible that one of your staff, or a cleaner, will be bribed, seduced, or otherwise coerced into creating a vulnerability (especially if you're dealing with Abdurrahman rather than Bruno). So frequent operational testing is a good idea, along with sensor overlap, means to detect equipment substitution (such as scals), strict configuration management, and tamper-resistant cabling. (Serious sites insist that alarm maintenance and testing be done by two people rather than one.)

The old-fashioned way of protecting the communications between the alarm sensors and the controller was physical: lay multiple wires to each sensor and bury them in concrete, or use armored gas-pressurized cables. The more modern way is to encrypt the communications. An example is Argus, a system originally developed for nuclear labs, which uses DES encryption to protect sensor links [303].

But the more typical attack on communications is to go for the link between the alarm controller and the security company that provides or organizes the response force.

HOW TO STEAL A PAINTING (6)

Bruno calls his rival gallery claiming to be from the security company that handles its alarms. He says that he's updating his computers and he needs the serial number on their alarm controller unit. An office junior helpfully gives it to him, not realizing that the serial number on the box is also the cryptographic key that secures the communications. Bruno buys an identical controller for $200 and, after spending half an hour learning how to use an EEPROM programmer, he has a functionally identical unit, which he splices into his rival's phone line. This continues to report "all's well" even when it isn't.

Substituting bogus alarm equipment, or using a computer that mimics it, is known as *spoofing*. There have been many reports of 'black boxes' that spoof the older or less well-designed alarm controllers. In one case, thieves made off with $1.5 million in jade statuary and gold jewelry imported from China, a theft which drove the importer into bankruptcy. The alarm system protecting its warehouse in Hackensack, New Jersey, was cut off. Normally, that would have triggered an alarm at a security company, but the burglars had attached a homemade electronic device to an external cable to ensure a continuous "all's well" signal [371].

With modern systems, either the alarm controller in the vault sends a cryptographic pseudorandom sequence to the alarm company, which will assume the worst if it's interrupted, or the alarm company sends the controller periodic random challenges, which are encrypted and returned, just as with IFF.

However, the design is often faulty, having been done by engineers with no training in security protocols. The cryptographic algorithm may be primitive, or its key may be too short (whether because of incompetence or export regulations). It may well be possible for Bruno to record the pseudorandom sequence and replay it slightly more slowly, so that by early Monday morning he might have accumulated five minutes of "slack" to cover a lightning raid.

An even more frequent cause of failure is the gross design blunder. One typical example is having a dial-up modem port that allows remote maintenance, with a default password that many users never change; another is making the crypto key equal to the device serial number. Besides being vulnerable to social engineering, the serial number often appears in the purchase order, invoice, and other paperwork, which lots of people get to see. (In general, it's a good idea to buy your alarm controller for cash. This also makes it less likely that you'll get one that's been "spiked." But big firms often have difficulty doing this.)

By now you've probably decided not to go into the art gallery business. But I've saved the best for last. Here is the most powerful attack on burglar alarm systems. It's a variant on 3, but rather than targeting the sensors, it goes for the communications.

HOW TO STEAL A PAINTING (7)

Bruno cuts the telephone line to his rival's gallery, then hides a few hundred yards away in the bushes. He counts the number of blue uniforms that arrive, and the number that depart. If the two numbers are equal, then it's a fair guess the custodian has said, 'Oh bother, we'll fix it in the morning,' or words to that effect. Bruno now knows he has several hours to work.

This is more or less the standard way to attack a bank vault, and it has also been used on computer installations. The modus operandi can vary, from simply reversing a truck into the phone company's curbside junction box to more sophisticated attempts to cause multiple simultaneous alarms in different premises and thus swamp the local police force. (This is why it's so much more powerful than just rattling the fence.)

In one case, thieves in New Jersey cut three main telephone cables, knocking out phones and alarm apparatus in three police stations and thousands of homes and businesses in the Hackensack Meadowlands. They used this opportunity to steal Lucien Piccard wristwatches from the American distributor, with a value of $2.1 million wholesale and perhaps $8 million retail [371]. In another, an Oklahoma deputy sherriff cut the phone lines to 50,000 homes in Tulsa before burgling a narcotics warehouse [762]. In a third, a villain set off a bomb at the telephone exchange in Holborn, London, interrupting service to dozens of shops in the Hatton Garden jewelry quarter. Blanket service denial attacks of this kind, which saturate the response force's capacity, are the burglarious equivalent of a nuclear strike.

In the future as computers and communications converge these attacks might not involve explosives but a software-based distributed denial-of-service attack on network facilities. Rather than causing all the alarms to go off in a neighborhood (which could be protected to some extent by swamping it with police), it might be possible to set off several thousand random alarms all over New York, creating an effect similar to that of a hurricane or a power outage, but at a time convenient for the crooks.

An angle that seriously concerns insurers is that phone company staff might be bribed to create false alarms. Insurance companies would prefer it if alarm communications consisted of anonymous packets, which most of the phone company's staff could not relate to any particular alarm. This would make targeted service denial attacks harder. But phone companies—which carry most of the alarm signal traffic—prefer to concentrate it in exchanges, which makes targeted service denial attacks easier. (These tensions are discussed in [586].)

For these reasons, the rule in the London insurance market (which does most of the world's major reinsurance business) is that alarm controllers in places insured for over £20 million must have two independent means of communication. One option is a leased line and a packet radio service. Another is a radio system with two antennas, each of which will send an alarm if the other is tampered with.[1] In the

---

[1] I used to wonder, back in the days when I was a banker, whether two bad men who practiced a bit could cut both cables simultaneously. I concluded that the threat wasn't worth worrying about for bank branches with a mere $100,000 or so in the vault. Our large cash processing centers were staffed 24/7, so the threat model there focused on dishonest insiders, hostage taking, and so on.

nuclear world, IAEA regulations stipulate that sites containing more than 500 g of plutonium or 2 Kg of U-235 must have their alarm control center and response force on the premises [409].

Finally, although physical security isn't a main topic of this book, it's worth noting that many physical security incidents arise from angry people coming into the workplace—whether spouses, former employees, or customers. Alarm systems should be able to cope with incidents that occur during the day as well as at night.

10.2.6 Lessons Learned

You might be wondering why a book that's essentially about security in computer systems should spend several pages describing burglar alarm systems. There are many reasons.

- Dealing with service denial attacks is the hardest part of many secure system designs. And, as the bad guys come to understand system-level vulnerabilities, it's also often the most important. Intruder alarms give us one of the largest available bodies of applicable knowledge and experience.

- The lesson that one must look at the overall system—from intrusion through detection, alarm, delay and response—is widely applicable, yet increasingly hard to follow in general-purpose distributed systems.

- The observation that the outermost perimeter defenses are the ones that we'd most like to rely on, but also those on which the least reliance can be placed, is also quite general.

- The trade-off between the missed alarm rate and the false alarm rate is a pervasive problem in security engineering.

- There are some subtleties though where we can learn from the alarm business. For example, some U.S. airport X-ray machines use *false alarm insertion* to ensure that alarm systems and personnel stay effective: they insert an image of a gun or bomb about once per shift. Staff are graded continually on their error rates.

- Failure to understand the threat model—designing for Charlie and hoping to keep out Bruno—causes many real-life failures. It's necessary to know what actually goes wrong, not just what crime writers think goes wrong.

- And, finally, we can't just leave the technical aspects of a security engineering project to specialist subcontractors, as critical stuff will always fall between the cracks.

In addition to these system-level lessons, there are a number of other applications where the experience of the burglar alarm industry is relevant. I already mentioned improvised explosive devices; in a later chapter, I'll discuss tamper-resistant processors that are designed to detect attempts to dismantle them and destroy all their cryptographic key material by way of an alarm response.

10.3 Prepayment Meters

Our next case study comes from prepayment metering. In many systems, the user pays in one place for a token—whether a magic number, or a cardboard ticket with a magnetic strip, or even a rechargeable token such as a smartcard—and uses this stored value in some other place.

Examples include postal franking machines, the stored value cards that operate photocopiers in libraries, lift passes at ski resorts, and washing machine tokens in university residence halls. Many transport tickets are similar—especially if the terminals that validate the tickets are mounted on buses or trains, and so are not usually online.

The main protection goal in these systems is to prevent the stored value tokens being duplicated or forged en masse. Duplicating a single subway ticket is not too hard, and repeating a magic number a second time is trivial. This can be made irrelevant if we make all the tokens unique and log their use at both ends. But things get more complicated when the device that accepts the token does not have a channel of communication back to the ticket issuer; in this case, all the replay and forgery detection must be done offline, on a terminal that is often vulnerable to physical attack. So if we simply enciphered all our tokens using a universal master key, we might expect that a villain would extract this key from a stolen terminal, then set up as a token vendor in competition with us.

There are also attacks on the server end of things. One neat attack on a vending card system used in the staff cafeteria of one of our local supermarkets exploited the fact that when a card was recharged, the vending machine first read the old amount, then asked for money, and then wrote the amended amount. The attack was to insert a card with some money in it, say, £49, on top of a blank card. The top card would then be removed and a £1 coin inserted in the machine, which would duly write £50 to the blank card. This left the perpetrator with two cards, with a total value of £99. This kind of attack was supposed to be prevented by two levers that extended to grip the card in the machine. However, by cutting the corners off the top card, this precaution could easily be defeated (see Figure 10.1) [479]. This attack is interesting because no amount of encryption of the card contents would make any difference. Although it could, in theory, be stopped by keeping logs at both ends, the design would not be trivial.

But we mustn't get carried away with neat tricks like this, or we risk getting so involved with even more clever countermeasures that we fall prey to the Titanic effect again by ignoring the system-level issues. In most ticketing systems, petty fraud is easy. A free rider can jump the barrier at a subway station; an electricity meter can have a bypass switch wired across it; while barcoded ski lift passes, parking lot tickets, and the like can be forged with a scanner and printer. The goal is to prevent fraud becoming systematic. Petty fraud should be at least slightly inconvenient and—more importantly—there should be more serious mechanisms to prevent anyone forging tickets on a large enough scale to develop a black market that could affect your client's business.

The example I'll discuss in detail is the prepayment electricity meter. I chose this because I was lucky enough to consult on a project to electrify more than 2.5 million households in South Africa (a central election pledge made by Nelson Mandela when he took power). (This work is described in some detail in [39].) Most of the lessons learned apply directly to other ticketing systems.

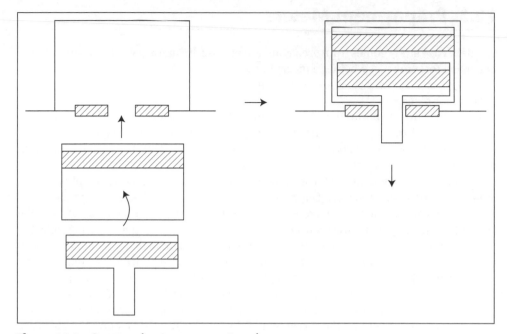

Figure 10.1   Superposing two payment cards.

10.3.1 Utility Metering

In a number of European countries, householders who can't get credit (because they are on welfare, have court judgments against them, or whatever) buy gas and electricity services using prepayment meters. In the old days, they were coin-operated, but the costs of coin collection led vendors to develop token-based meters instead. The customer goes to a shop and buys a token, which may be a smartcard, a disposable cardboard ticket with a magnetic strip, or even just a magic number. A magic number is often the most convenient, as no special vending apparatus is required: a ticket can be dispensed at a supermarket checkout, or even over the phone. U.S. readers may be used to replenishing a postal meter by phoning a call center and buying a magic number with a credit card: the magic number replenishes the meter. This is exactly the same kind of system as a prepayment utility meter.

The token should be thought of as a string of bits containing one or more instructions, encrypted using a key unique to the meter, which decodes them and acts on them. Most tokens read something like, "meter 12345, dispense 50 kWh of electricity!" but some have maintenance functions, too (see Figure 10.2). The idea is that the meter will dispense the purchased amount and then interrupt the supply.

The manufacture of these meters has become big business. Britain has about a million electricity meters using two proprietary schemes, and some six hundred thousand gas meters using smartcards. Prepaid electricity meters have been installed in a number of other countries, including Brazil, India, Namibia, and the Ivory Coast. Growth in the Third World is strong because the customers may not even have addresses, let alone credit ratings. This was the case in South Africa: prepayment metering was the only way

Figure 10.2 A prepayment electricity meter (courtesy of Schlumberger).

the government could meet its election pledge to electrify millions of homes quickly. In the developed world, the main impetus for metering is reducing administrative costs. Electric utilities find that billing systems can devour 20 percent of retail customer revenue in urban areas, while prepayment systems typically cost under 10 percent.

10.3.2 How the System Works

The security requirements for a prepayment meter system seem fairly straightforward. Tokens should not be easy to forge, and genuine tokens should not work in the wrong meter, or in the right meter twice. Tokens should either be tamper-resistant (which is expensive) or unique (which can be done fairly easily using serial numbers and cryptography). But it has taken a surprising amount of field experience to develop the idea into a robust system.

The meter needs a cryptographic key to authenticate its instructions from the vending station. The typical system has a vend key, K_V, which acts as the master key for a neighborhood, and derives the device key when needed by encrypting the meter ID under the vend key:

$$K_{ID} = \{ID\}_{K_V}$$

This is the same key diversification technique described for parking lot access devices in Chapter 2. Diversifying the vend key K_V to a group of meter keys K_{ID}, provides a very simple solution where all the tokens are bought locally. It's often less straightforward than this. In South Africa, many people commute long distances from townships or homelands to their places of work, so are never at home during business hours and prefer to buy tickets where they work. So they can register at an out-of-area vending station, where there is a security protocol to send their meter key to this vending station from the vending station that "owns" the meter. Sales data then get passed in the opposite direction for balancing and settlement. These mechanisms are very much like those developed for ATM networks.

Statistical balancing is used to detect what are euphemistically known as *non-technical losses*, that is, theft of power through meter tampering or unauthorized direct connections to mains cables. The mechanism is to compare the readings on a feeder meter, which might supply 30 houses, with token sales to those houses. This turns out to be harder than it looks. Customers hoard tickets, meter readers lie about the date when they read the meter, and many other things go wrong. Vending statistics are also used in conventional balancing systems, like those discussed in Chapter 9.

The vending machines themselves maintain a credit balance. They rely on tamper-resistant security processors to keep the vendor from extracting vend keys and foreign meter keys, or interfering with the credit balance. The balance is decremented with each sale, and only credited again when cash is banked with the local operating company. This company in turn has to account to the next level up in the distribution network, and so on. Here we have an example of an accounting system partially enforced by a value counter at the point of sale, rather than just by ledger data kept on servers in a vault. Subversion of value counters can, in theory, be picked up by statistical and balancing checks at higher layers. This distribution of security state is something we may see a lot more of; for example, it's the model used by the Mondex electronic purse scheme promoted by Mastercard.

So what can go wrong?

10.3.3 What Goes Wrong

Service denial remains an important issue. As there is no return channel from the meter to the vending station, the only evidence of how much electricity has been sold resides in the vending equipment itself. The agents who operate the vending machines are typically small shopkeepers or other township entrepreneurs who have little capital and so are allowed to sell electricity on credit. In some cases, agents just dumped their equipment, then claimed that it got stolen. This is manageable with small agents, but when an organization such as a local government is allowed to sell large amounts of electricity through multiple outlets, there is definitely an exposure. A lot of the complexity was needed to deal with untrustworthy (and mutually mistrustful) principals.

As with burglar alarms, environmental robustness is critical. Apart from the huge range of temperatures (as variable in South Africa as in the continental United States) many areas have severe thunderstorms—the meter is in effect a microprocessor with a 3-kilometer lightning conductor attached.

When meters were destroyed by lightning, the customers complained and got credit for the value they said was still unused. So their next step was to poke live mains wires into the meter to emulate the effects of the lightning. It turned out that one make of meter would give unlimited credit if a particular part of the circuitry (which lay under the token slot) was destroyed. Thus, service denial attacks worked well enough to become popular. (They could become a serious problem if banks field offline electronic purse smartcards that don't do full balancing, but rely instead on value counters plus statistical balancing. When a customer complains that a card has stopped working, all the bank can do is either refund the amount the customer claims was on the card, or tell him or her to get lost.)

It was to get worse. The most expensive security failure in the program came when kids in Soweto observed that when there was a brown-out—a fall in voltage from 220 to 180 volts—a particular make of meter went to maximum credit. Soon kids were throwing steel chains over the 11 KV feeders and crediting all the meters in the neighborhood. This was the fault of a simple bug in the meter ROM, which wasn't picked up because brown-out testing hadn't been specified. In fact, developed country environmental standards were inadequate and had to be rewritten. The effect on the business was that 100,000 meters had to be pulled out and re-ROMmed; the responsible company almost went bust.

There were numerous other bugs. One make of meter didn't vend a specified quantity of electricity, rather so much worth of electricity at such-and-such a rate. It turned out that the tariff could be set to a tiny amount by vending staff, so that it would operate almost forever. Another make allowed refunds, but a copy of the refunded token could still be used (blacklisting the serial numbers of refunded tokens in subsequent token commands is hard, as tokens are hoarded and used out of order). Another meter remembered the last token serial number entered, and by alternately entering duplicates of two tokens, it could be charged up indefinitely.

As with cash machines, the real security breaches resulted from bugs and blunders, which could be quite obscure, but were discovered by accident and exploited in quite opportunistic ways. These exploits were sometimes on a large scale, costing millions to fix.

Other lessons learned were the following.

- Prepayment may be cheap as long as you control the marketing channel, but when you try to make it even cheaper by selling prepayment tokens through third parties (such as banks and supermarkets) it can rapidly become expensive, complicated, and risky. This is largely because of the security engineering problems created by mutual mistrust between the various organizations involved.

- Changes to a business process can be very expensive if they affect the security infrastructure. For example, the requirement to sell meter tokens other than at local shops, to support commuters, was not anticipated and was costly to implement.

- Recycle technology if possible, as it's likely to have fewer bugs than something designed on a blank sheet of paper. Much of what we needed for prepayment metering was borrowed from the world of cash machines.

- Use multiple experts. One expert alone can not usually span all the issues, and even the best will miss things.

■ No matter what is done, small mistakes with large consequences will still creep in. So you absolutely need prolonged field testing. This is where many errors and impracticalities will first make themselves known.

Meters are a good case study for ticketing. Transport ticketing, theater ticketing, and even sports ticketing may be larger applications, but I don't know of any publicly available studies of their failure modes. In many cases, the end systems—such as the meters or turnstiles—are fairly soft, so our main concern is to prevent large-scale fraud. This means paying a lot of attention to the intermediate servers such as vending machines, and hardening them to ensure they will resist manipulation and tampering. One still does what one economically can to prevent people developing efficient systematic attacks on the end systems that are too hard to detect.

We'll now look at a class of applications where there are severe and prolonged attacks on end systems, which must therefore be made much more tamper-resistant than electricity meters. The threat model includes sensor manipulation, service denial, accounting fiddles, procedural defeats, and the corruption of operating staff. This exemplary field of study is vehicle monitoring systems.

10.4 Taximeters, Tachographs, and Truck Speed Limiters

A number of systems are used to monitor and control vehicles. The most familiar is probably the odometer in your car. When buying a used car you'll be worried whether the car has been *clocked*, that is, had its indicated mileage reduced. As odometers become digital, clocking is becoming a type of computer fraud; a conviction has already been reported [170].

The next most familiar may be the taximeter. A taxi driver has an incentive to manipulate the meter to show more miles travelled (or minutes waited), if he can get away with it. There are various other kinds of "black box" used to record the movement of vehicles, from aircraft through fishing vessels to armored bank trucks, and their operators have differing levels of motive for tampering with them. Starting in 1990, for example, General Motors equipped 6 million vehicles with black boxes to record crash data. This could be a bonanza for trial lawyers; there are also privacy aspects, as the existence of the boxes only became public in 1999 [768]. (I'll discuss these issues in Chapter 21.)

The case study we're going to use here is the tachograph. A driver falling asleep at the wheel is the cause of several times more accidents than drunkenness (20 percent versus 3 percent of accidents in Britain, for example). An accidents involving a truck is more likely to lead to fatal injuries because of the truck's mass. So most countries regulate truck drivers' working hours. While these laws are enforced in the United States using weigh stations, countries in Europe use devices called *tachographs*, which record a 24-hour history of the vehicle's speed on a circular waxed paper chart (see Figure 10.3).

The chart is loaded into the tachograph, which is part of the vehicle's speedometer/odometer unit. It turns slowly on a turntable inside the instrument; there are three style which record, the speed (the outside trace), whether the driver was working or resting (the middle trace), and the distance travelled (the inner trace—each tick being 10 km). With some exceptions, which needn't concern us here, it is an offense to drive a truck

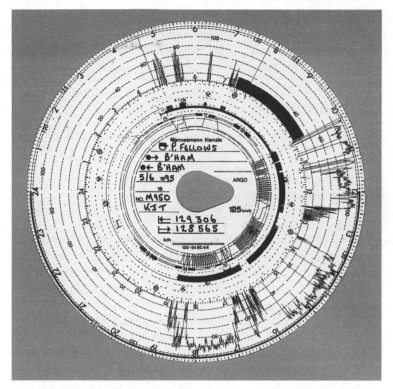

Figure 10.3   A tachograph chart.

in Europe unless you have a tachograph chart installed, and have written on it your starting time and location. You must also keep several days' charts with you to establish that you've complied with the relevant driving hours regulations (typically 8.5 hours per day, with rules for rest breaks per day and rest days per week). Some tachographs have extra needles to record some environmental variable: examples include the flashing lights of emergency vehicles, the temperature of refrigerated trucks, and whether the doors of armored trucks are open or closed. (It is for such applications that tachographs are most widely used in North America.)

European law also restricts trucks to 100 km/h (62 mph) on freeways and less on other roads. This is enforced not just by police speed traps and the tachograph record, but directly by a speed limiter which is also driven by the tachograph. Tachograph charts are also used to investigate other offenses, such as unlicensed toxic waste dumping, and by fleet operators to detect fuel theft. Clearly, there are plenty reasons why a truck driver might want to fiddle his tachograph.[2]

The EU is in the process of moving from paper-based to smartcard-based systems, which makes the issue highly topical. As with any security engineering task, we first

[2]It's a general principle in security engineering that one shouldn't aggregate targets. Thus, NATO rules prohibit money or other valuables being carried in a container for classified information—you don't want someone who set out to steal your regiment's payroll also getting away with your spy satellite photographs. Forcing a truck driver to defeat his or her tachograph to circumvent the speed limiter, and vice versa, was a serious design error—but one that's now too entrenched to change easily.

need to know what actually goes wrong. Most of what I have to say applies equally well to taximeters and other monitoring devices. While the truck driver wants his vehicle to appear to have gone less distance, the taxi driver wants the opposite. This has little effect on the actual tampering techniques.

10.4.1 What Goes Wrong

According to a 1998 survey of 1,060 convictions of drivers and operators [31], the offenses were distributed as follows.

10.4.1.1 How Most Tachograh Manipulation Is Done

About 70% of offenses that result in conviction do not involve tampering but exploit procedural weaknesses. For example, a company with premises in Dundee and Southampton should have four drivers to operate one vehicle per day in each direction, as the distance is about 500 miles and the journey takes about 10 hours—which is illegal for a single driver to do every day. The standard fiddle is to have two drivers who meet at an intermediate point such as Penrith, change trucks, and insert new paper charts into the tachographs. The driver who had come from Southampton now returns home with the vehicle from Dundee. When stopped and asked for his charts, he shows the current chart from Penrith to Southampton, the previous day's for Southampton to Penrith, the day before's for Penrith to Southampton, and so on. In this way the driver can give the false impression that he spent every other night in Penrith, and was thus legal. This (widespread) practice, of swapping vehicles halfway through the working day, is called *ghosting*. It's even harder to detect in mainland Europe, where a driver might be operating out of a depot in France on Monday, in Belgium on Tuesday, and in Holland on Wednesday.

Simpler frauds include setting the clock wrongly; pretending that a hitchhiker is a relief driver; and recording the start point as a village with a very common name—such as Milton in England or La Hoya in Spain. If stopped, the driver can claim he started from a nearby Milton or La Hoya. (The chart in Figure 10.3 shows several violations of this type. For example, the start point is listed as "B'HAM" which could be Birmingham or Buckingham, and the clock was wound back from 14.30 to 14.00, as can be seen from the overlapping traces.)

Such tricks often involve collusion between the driver and the operator. When the operator is ordered to produce charts and supporting documents such as pay records, weigh station slips and ferry tickets, his office may well conveniently burn down. (It's remarkable how many truck companies operate out of small cheap wooden sheds that are located at a safe distance from the trucks in their yard.)

10.4.1.2 Tampering with the Supply

The next largest category of fraud, amounting to about 20% of the total, involves tampering with the supply to the tachograph instrument, including interference with the power and impulse supply, cables, and seals.

When old-fashioned tachographs used a rotating wire cable—as did the speedometers in cars up until the early 1980s—it was hard to fiddle with. For example, if you jammed the truck's odometer it was quite likely that you'd shear off the cable. Electronic tachographs have made fiddling much easier. They get their input from a sensor in the gearbox, which sends electrical impulses as the prop shaft rotates. A common attack is to unscrew the sensor about a tenth of an inch. This causes the impulses to cease, as if the vehicle were stationary. To prevent this, sensors are fixed in place with a wire and lead seal. Fitters are bribed to wrap the wire anticlockwise rather than clockwise, which causes it to loosen rather than break when the sensor is unscrewed. The fact that seals are issued to workshops rather than to individual fitters complicates prosecution.

Most of the fiddles are much simpler still. Drivers short out the cable or replace the tachograph fuse with a blown one. (One manufacturer tried to stop this trick by putting the truck's antilock braking system on the same fuse. Many drivers preferred to get home sooner than to drive a safe vehicle.) Again, there is evidence of a power supply interruption on the chart in Figure 10.3: around 11 A.M., there are several places where the speed indicated in the outside trace goes suddenly from zero to over 100 km/h. These indicate power interruptions, except where there's also a discontinuity in the distance trace. There, the unit was open.

10.4.1.3 Tampering with the Instrument

The third category of fraud is tampering with the tachograph unit itself. This amounts for some 6% of offenses, but is in decline with modern equipment, because tampering with digital communications is so much easier than tampering with a rotating wire cable used to be. The typical offense in this category is miscalibration, usually done in cahoots with the fitter, but sometimes by the driver defeating the seal on the device.

10.4.1.4 High-Tech Attacks

The state of the tampering art is the equipment in Figure 10.4. The plastic cylinder on the left of the photo is marked "Voltage Regulator—Made in Japan," and is certainly not a voltage regulator. (It actually appears to be made in Italy.) It is spliced into the tachograph cable and controlled by the driver using the remote control key fob. A first press causes the indicated speed to drop by 10%, a second press causes a drop of 20%, a third press causes it to fall to 0, and a fourth causes the device to return to proper operation.

This kind of device amounts for under 1% of convictions, but its use is believed to be much more widespread. It's extremely hard to find as it can be hidden at many different places in the truck's cable harness. Police officers who stop a speeding truck equipped with such a device, and can't find it, have difficulty getting a conviction: the sealed and apparently correctly calibrated tachograph contradicts the evidence from their radar or camera. The next step in the arms race is the use by the police of electronic warfare techniques to detect and neutralize these "interruptors"—after that, no doubt, the bad guys will start using cryptography to secure the communications from the key fob.

10.4.2 Countermeasures

The countermeasures taken against tachograph manipulation vary by country. In Britain, trucks are stopped at the roadside for random checks by vehicle inspectors;

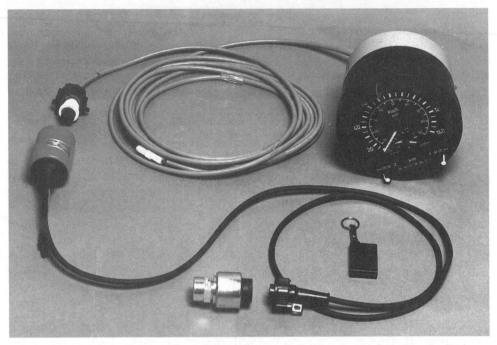

Figure 10.4 A tachograph with an interruptor controlled by the driver using a radio key fob (courtesy of Hampshire Constabulary, England).

particularly suspect trucks may be shadowed across the country. In the Netherlands, enforcement focuses on inspectors descending on a trucking company and going through their delivery documents, drivers' timesheets, fuel records, and the like. In Italy, data from the toll booths on the freeways are used to prosecute drivers who've averaged more than the speed limit (this is why you can often see trucks parked just in front of Italian toll booths). But such measures are only partially effective, and drivers can arbitrage between the differing control regimes. For example, a truck driver operating between France and Holland can keep his documents at a depot in France where the Dutch inspectors can't get at them.

10.4.2.1 Tachosmart

So the European Union is taking an initiative to design a unified electronic tachograph system, called Tachosmart, which will replace the existing paper-based charts with smartcards. Each driver will have a "driver card" that will, in effect, be the truck driver's license and contain a record of his driving hours over the last 28 days. Each vehicle will have a vehicle unit with a year's history. Special types of smartcard will used by mechanics to calibrate devices, and by law enforcement officers to read them out at the roadside.

The most substantial objection to the move to smartcards is that it's not clear how it will help combat the procedural frauds that make up 70% of the current total. Indeed, our pair of drivers ghosting between Dundee and Southampton will have their lives made even easier. It will take maybe ten years—the lifetime of a truck—to change over to the new system; in the meantime, they can run one truck with an old chart system and the other with the new card system. Each driver will now have one chart and one card, with five hours a day on each, rather than two charts which they might accidentally mix up when stopped.

10.4.2.2 System Level Problems

The response to this problem varies by country. Germany wants an infrastructure of fleet management systems that will accept digital tachograph data, digitized versions of the analogue data from the existing paper charts, fuel data, delivery data, and even payroll—and reconcile them all to provide not just management information for the trucking company but surveillance data for the police. The idea, as with some mid-1990s proposals for the regulation of cryptography, is that large companies would be trusted to run their own fleet management systems, while small ones would have to use a licensed bureau.

Britain doesn't have as large a share of the existing bureau business as Germany does, so British proposals have included integrating tachograph systems either with GPS location sensors in the trucks or with an existing system of automatic number plate readers. (This was first deployed around London to make IRA bombing attacks harder and has now been extended nationwide to detect car tax evaders.)

However, disagreements about privacy issues and about national economic interests have prevented any EU-wide standardization. It's going to be up to individual countries whether they require truck companies to download and analyze the data from their trucks.

Even if everyone does this, it won't be a panacea, because of arbitrage. At present, the German police are much more vigorous at enforcing drivers' hours regulations than their Italian counterparts. So an Italian driver who normally doesn't bother to put a chart in his machine will do so while driving over the Alps. Meanwhile, the driver of the German truck going the other way takes his chart out. The net effect is that all drivers in a given country are subject to the same level of law enforcement. But if the driving data get regularly uploaded from the Italian driver's card and kept on a PC at a truck company in Rome, then they'll be subject to Italian levels of enforcement (or even less if the Italian police decide they don't care about accidents in Germany). It's easy to see that this will cause downward pressure on enforcement.

10.4.2.3 Other Problems

The move from analogue devices to digital isn't always an improvement. In addition to the lower tamper-resistance of electronic versus mechanical signalling, and the system-level problem that the location of the security state can't be tackled in a uniform way, there are several other interesting problems with tachographs being digital.

First, the loss of detailed, redundant data on the tachograph chart will make enforcement harder. At present, experienced vehicle inspectors have a "feel" for when a chart isn't right; but once the analogue trace is replaced by a binary signal, which says either that the driver complied with the regulations or that he didn't, they have little else to go on (especially if the truck company's HQ with the supporting paperwork is in another jurisdiction). The new digital system is less likely to degrade gracefully under attack than its analogue predecessor.

Second, there will be new kinds of service denial attacks (as well as the traditional ones involving gearbox sensors, fuses, and so on). A truck driver can easily destroy his smartcard by feeding it with mains electricity; and under the regulations, he will be allowed to drive for 15 days while waiting for a replacement. As static electricity destroys maybe 1 percent of cards a year anyway, it would be hard to prosecute drivers for doing this. Similar card-destruction attacks have been perpetrated on bank smartcard systems in France and elsewhere, to force systems back into less robust fallback modes of operation.

Third, some of the cards in the system (notably the workshop and calibration cards used to set up the instruments) are very powerful. They can be used to erase evidence of wrongdoing and to restore a tachograph to a virgin state. A black market in them is likely, and they may become valuable enough for it to be worth someone's while to forge them. As a result of this problem, plus some other technical concerns, the Tachosmart system is being redesigned to use public key cryptography rather than universal master secrets in the cards and vehicle units.

A particularly difficult problem turns out to be key management. This is a general problem with security systems involving vehicles—not just tachographs and similar devices such as taximeters, but even such simple devices as car-door locks and the PIN codes used to protect car radios against theft. If the garage must always be able to override the security mechanisms, and a third of garage mechanics have criminal records, then what sort of secure system do you think you can build?

10.4.2.4 *The Resurrecting Duckling*

A recent EU directive stated that, in order to frustrate the use of interruptors of the kind shown in Figure 10.4, all digital tachographs had to encrypt the pulse train from the gearbox sensor to the vehicle unit. As both of these devices contain a microcontroller, and the data rate is fairly low, this shouldn't in theory have been a problem. But how on earth could we distribute the keys? If we just set up a hotline that garages could call, it is likely to be abused. There's a long history of fitters conspiring with truck drivers to defeat the system, and of garage staff abusing helplines to get unlocking data for stolen cars, and PIN codes for stolen car radios.

One solution is given by the *resurrecting duckling* security policy model. This is named after the fact that a duckling emerging from its egg will recognize as its mother the first moving object it sees that makes a sound; this is called *imprinting*. Similarly, a "newborn" vehicle unit, just removed from the shrink wrap, will recognize as its owner the first gearbox sensor that sends it a secret key. The sensor does this on power-up. As soon as this key is received, the vehicle unit is no longer a newborn, and will stay faithful to the gearbox sensor for the rest of its 'life'. If the sensor fails, and has to be replaced, there is a procedure whereby the vehicle unit can be 'killed' and resurrected as a newborn, whereupon it can imprint on the new sensor. Each act of resurrection is indelibly logged in the vehicle unit to make abuse harder.

The resurrecting duckling model of key management was originally developed to deal with the secure imprinting of a digital thermometer or other piece of medical equipment to a doctor's PDA or a bedside monitor. It can also be used to imprint consumer electronics to a remote control in such a way as to make it more difficult for a thief who steals the device, but not the controller, to make use of it [731].

Another possible application is weapons security. Many of the police officers who are shot dead on duty are killed with their own guns, so there is now a lot of interest in safety mechanisms. One approach is to design the gun to fire only when within a foot or so of a signet ring that the officer wears. The problem is managing the relationship between rings and guns, and a possible solution is to let the gun imprint on any ring, but after a delay of a minute or so. This is not a big deal for police officers signing the gun out of the armory, but is a problem for the crook who snatches it. (One may assume that if a policeman can't either overpower the crook or run for it within a minute, then he's a goner in any case.) Such mechanisms might also mitigate the effects of battlefield capture of military weapons, for which passwords are often unacceptable [106].

10.5 Summary

Many security systems are concerned one way or another with monitoring some aspect of the environment. They range from ordinary domestic burglar alarms through utility meters to taximeters, tachographs, and even a number of systems critically concerned with nuclear safety.

The protection of these systems is most often more concerned with preventing attacks that involve denial of service, such as swamping communications, overwhelming sensors with noise, or doing other things which, directly or indirectly, decrease the amount of trust that the system owners place in it. Service denial attacks may be augmented, or complemented, with various kinds of data manipulation. Key management can be an issue, especially in low-cost widely distributed systems where a central key management facility can't be justified or trustworthy field personnel doesn't exist. Systems may have to deal with numerous mutually suspicious parties, and must often be implemented on the cheapest possible microcontrollers. Finally, many of them are routinely in the hands of the enemy.

I've illustrated the problems of this exacting environment with three case studies—burglar alarms, utility meters, and vehicle tachographs—which may be instructive now that denial of service attacks on the Internet such as SYN floods and DDoS have become a major issue.

Research Problems

We don't yet have a really general set of tools to manage keys in embedded systems. Although the mechanisms (and products) developed for automatic teller machine networks can be (and are) adapted, much of the design work has to be redone; the result often has security vulnerabilities (I'll discuss this in Chapter 14, which deals with the special processors used for this purpose).

Although we have some industry standards (such as CANBUS, which is used for communications between vehicle systems), we don't have any top-level standards for ways in which cryptography and other mechanisms, such as anonymity and balancing, can be built into a range of monitoring and ticketing systems. Such standards could save a lot of engineers a lot of effort.

Further Reading

The best all-round reference I know of on alarm systems is [74]; the system issues are discussed succinctly in [586]. Resources for specific countries are often available through trade societies, such as the American Society for Industrial Security [14], and through the local insurance industry; many countries have a not-for-profit body such as Underwriters' Laboratories [756] in the United States, and schemes to certify products, installations, or both. Research papers on the latest sensor technologies appear at the IEEE Carnahan conferences [399].

Prepayment electricity meters are described in [39], and a rather similar application—postal metering machines—in [753]. Tachographs, including the Tachosmart project, are written up in [31]. Finally, the systems used to monitor compliance with nuclear arms control treaties are discussed in [702].

Nuclear Command and Control

In Germany and Turkey they viewed scenes that were particularly distressing. On the runway stood a German (or Turkish) quick-reaction alert airplane loaded with nuclear weapons and with a foreign pilot in the cockpit. The airplane was ready to take off at the earliest warning, and the nuclear weapons were fully operational. The only evidence of U.S. control was a lonely 18-year-old sentry armed with a carbine and standing on the tarmac. When the sentry at the German airfield was asked how he intended to maintain control of the nuclear weapons should the pilot suddenly decide to scramble (either through personal caprice or through an order from the German command circumventing U.S. command), the sentry replied that he would shoot the pilot; Agnew directed him to shoot the bomb.

—JEROME WIESNER, PRESIDENTIAL SCIENCE ADVISOR, REPORTING TO PRESIDENT KENNEDY ON NUCLEAR COMMAND AND CONTROL AFTER THE CUBAN CRISIS

11.1 Introduction

The uniquely catastrophic harm that could result from the unauthorized use of a nuclear weapon, or from the proliferation of nuclear technology to unsuitable states or substate groups, has led the United States (and other nuclear states) to spend colossal amounts of money protecting not just nuclear warheads but also the supporting infrastructure, industry, and materials.

Quite a lot of nuclear security know-how has been published. In fact, there are severe limits on how much could be kept secret, even if this was thought desirable. Many countries are capable of producing nuclear weapons, but have decided not to (Japan,

Australia, Switzerland, . . .) and so maintain controls on nuclear materials in a civilian context. There are also international nonproliferation agreements, such as the Convention on the Physical Protection of Nuclear Material [409], enforced by the International Atomic Energy Authority (IAEA).

Eleven tons of plutonium are produced annually by civil reactors. So ways have to be found to guard the stuff, and these have to inspire international confidence—not just between governments but from an increasingly sceptical public.

A vast range of security technology has spun off from the nuclear program. The U.S. Department of Energy weapons laboratories—Sandia, Lawrence Livermore, and Los Alamos—have worked, with almost unlimited budgets, for two generations to make nuclear weapons and materials as safe as can be achieved. We've already seen some of their more pedestrian spin-offs, from the discovery that passwords of more than twelve digits were not usable under battlefield conditions to high-end burglar alarm systems. The trick of wrapping an optical fiber around the devices to be protected and using interference effects to detect a change in length of less than a micron is another of theirs. It was designed to loop around the warheads in an armory and alarm without fail if any of them are moved.

In later chapters, we'll see still more technology of nuclear origin. For example, iris recognition—the most accurate system known for biometric identification of individuals—was developed using U.S. Department of Energy funds with a view to controlling entry to the plutonium store; and much of the expertise in tamper-resistance and tamper-sensing technology originally evolved to prevent the abuse of stolen weapons or control devices.

In this chapter, I describe the environment in which these technologies were developed, and some of the tricks that might find applications—or pose threats—elsewhere. As I'm not an insider, I've assembled this chapter from public sources, and so may have missed important points (a proofreader with the relevant clearance and experience assures me that the material is indeed "accurate but incomplete"). Nevertheless, even from the available material, there are useful lessons to be learned.

11.2 The Kennedy Memorandum

Following the Cuban missile crisis, the U.S. government became concerned that a world war could start by accident. Hundreds of U.S. nuclear weapons were kept in allied countries such as Greece and Turkey, which were not particularly stable and occasionally fought with each other. These weapons were protected only by token U.S. custodial forces; there was no physical reason why the weapons couldn't be seized in time of crisis. There was also some concern about possible unauthorized use of nuclear weapons by U.S. commanders; for example, if a local commander under pressure felt that, "If only they knew in Washington how bad things were here, they would let us use the bomb." These worries were confirmed by three emergency studies carried out by presidential science adviser Jerome Wiesner. (The passage quoted at the beginning of this chapter can be found in [734].)

President Kennedy's response was National Security Action Memo number 160. This ordered that America's 7,000 nuclear weapons then in other countries should be got under positive control, or got out [705].

The Department of Energy was already working on safety devices for nuclear weapons. The basic principle was that one or more unique aspects of the environment had to be sensed before the weapon would arm. For example, missile warheads and some free-fall bombs had to experience zero gravity, while artillery shells had to experience an acceleration of thousands of G. There was one exception: atomic demolition munitions. These are designed to be taken to their targets by ground troops and detonated using time fuses. There appears to be no scope for a unique environmental sensor to prevent their accidental or malicious detonation.

The solution then under development was a secret arming code, which activated a solenoid safe lock buried deep in the plutonium pit at the heart of the weapon. The main engineering problem was maintenance. When the lock was exposed—for example, to replace the power supply—the code might become known. Clearly, it was not acceptable to have the same code in every weapon. Group codes had to be used—firing codes shared by only a small batch of warheads.

Following the Kennedy memo, it was proposed that all nuclear bombs should be protected using code locks, and that there should be a "universal unlock" action message that only the president or his legal successors could send. The problem was to find a way to translate this code securely to a large number of individual firing codes, each of which enabled a small batch of weapons. The problem became worse in the 1960s and 1970s, when the doctrine changed from massive retaliation to "measured response." Instead of arming all nuclear weapons or none, the president now had to be able to arm selected batches (such as "all nuclear artillery in Germany").

11.3 Unconditionally Secure Authentication Codes

This requirement led to the development of a theory of one-time authentication codes. These are similar in concept to the test keys invented to protect telegraphic money transfers, in that a keyed transformation is applied to the message to yield a short authentication code, also known as an *authenticator* or *tag*. As the keys are only used once, authentication codes can be made unconditionally secure. They do for authentication what the one-time pad does for confidentiality.

Recall from Chapter 5, "Cryptography," that while the perfect security provided by the one-time pad is independent of the computational resources available to the attacker, a computationally secure system could be broken by some known computation, and depends on this being infeasible.

There are differences, though, between authentication codes and the one-time pad. As the authentication code is of finite length, it's always possible for the opponent to guess it; and the probability of a successful guess might be different depending on whether the opponent is trying to guess a valid message from scratch (*impersonation*) or to modify an existing valid message to get another one (*substitution*).

An example should make this clear. Let's assume that a commander has agreed to an authentication scheme with a subordinate under which an instruction is to be encoded as a three-digit number from 000 to 999. The instruction may have two values: "Attack Russia" and "Attack China." One of these will be encoded as an even number, and the other by an odd number; which is which will be part of the secret key. The authenticity of the message will be vouched for by making its remainder, when divided by 337, equal to a secret number that is the second part of the key.

Now suppose the key is that:

- "Attack Russia" codes to even numbers, and "Attack China" to odd.

- An authentic message is one that has the remainder 12 when divided by 337.

Therefore, "Attack Russia" is 686 (or 12) and "Attack China" is 349.

An enemy who has taken over the communications channel between the commander and the subordinate, and who knows the scheme but not the key, has a probability of only 1 in 337 of successfully impersonating the commander. However, once he sees a valid message (say, 12 for "Attack Russia"), then he can easily change it to the other by adding 337. Then (provided he understood what it meant), he can send the missiles to the other country. Thus, the probability of a successful substitution attack in this case is 1.

As with computationally secure authentication, the unconditional variety can provide message secrecy or not: it might work like a block cipher, or like a MAC on a plaintext message. Similarly, it can use an arbitrator or not. One might even want multiple arbitrators, so that they don't have to be trusted individually. If the first arbitrator wrongfully finds in favor of the cheated party, then his victim should be able to denounce him.

Schemes may combine unconditional with computational security. For example, an unconditional code without secrecy could have computationally secure secrecy added simply by enciphering the message and the authenticator using a conventional cipher system.

Authentication is, in some sense, the dual of coding. In the latter, given an incorrect message, we want to find the nearest correct message efficiently; in the former, we want finding a correct message to be impossible unless you've seen it already or are authorized to construct it. And just as the designer of an error-correcting code wants the shortest length of code for a given error recovery capability, so the designer of an authentication code wants to minimize the key length required to achieve a given bound on the deception probabilities.

The authentication terminology used in civil and military applications is slightly different [703]. More importantly, the threat models are different. Soldiers are, in general, more concerned about enemies than traitors and are not so worried about nonrepudiation (except when enforcing treaties with other countries, which might later repudiate a message claiming that the key had been leaked by a "defector"). In business, the majority of frauds are carried out by insiders, so shared control systems are the main issue when designing authentication mechanisms.

11.4 Shared Control Schemes

The nuclear command and control business became even more complex with the concern, from the late 1970s, that a Soviet decapitation strike against the U.S. *national command authority* (i.e., the President and his lawful successors in office) might leave the arsenal intact but useless. There was also concern that, past a certain threshold of readiness, it wasn't sensible to assume that communications between authority and field commanders could be maintained, because of the possible effects of electromagnetic pulse and other attacks on communications. The solution was found in another branch of cryptomathematics known as *secret sharing*, whose development it helped to inspire. The idea is that, in time of tension, a backup control system will be activated, whereby combinations of office holders or field commanders can jointly allow a weapon to be armed. Otherwise, the problems of maintaining detailed central control of a large number of weapons would likely become insoluble.

There is a simple and obvious way to do shared control: just give half of the authentication key to each of two people. This has the drawback that we need twice the length of key, assuming that the original security parameter must apply even if one of them is suborned. A better approach is to give each of them a number and have the two numbers add up to the key. This is how keys for automatic teller machines are managed.

However, this still may not be enough in command applications, as no one can be sure that the personnel operating the equipment will consent, without discussion or query, to unleash Armageddon.

A more general approach was invented independently by Blakley and Shamir in 1979 [111, 692]. Their basic idea is illustrated in Figure 11.1. Suppose the rule Britain wants to enforce, if the Prime Minister is assassinated, is that a weapon can be armed by any two cabinet ministers, or by any three generals, or by a cabinet minister and two generals. Let the point C on the z axis be the unlock code that has to be supplied to the weapon. We now draw a line at random through C, and give each cabinet minister a random point on the line. Now any two of them can together work out the coordinates of the line and find the point C where it meets the z axis. Similarly, we embed the line in a random plane and give each general a random point on the plane. Now any three

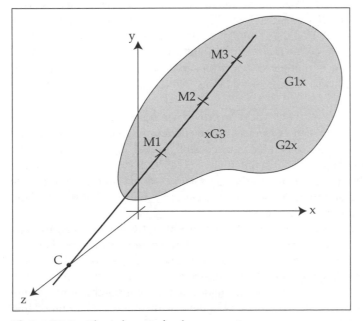

Figure 11.1   Shared control using geometry.

generals, or two generals plus a minister, can reconstruct the plane and thence the firing code C.

By generalizing this simple construction to geometries of n dimensions, or to general algebraic structures rather than lines and planes, this technique enables weapons, commanders, and options to be linked with a complexity limited only by the available bandwidth. (An introduction to secret sharing can be found in [738], and a more detailed exposition in [704].) Secret sharing also inspired the development of threshold signature schemes, which I described in Chapter 5, and can be used in products that enforce a rule such as, "Any two vice presidents of the company may sign a check."

As with authentication codes, there is a difference between civil and military views of shared secrets. In the typical military application, two-out-of-n control is used; n must be large enough that at least two of the keyholders will be ready and able to do the job, despite combat losses. Many details need attention. For example, the death of a commander shouldn't enable his deputy to use both halves of the key. So they typically have to be used simultaneously at consoles several yards apart.

In many civilian applications, however, many insiders may conspire to break a system. The classic example is pay-TV, where a pirate may buy several dozen subscriber cards and reverse engineer them for their secrets. Obviously, the pay-TV operator wants a system that's robust against multiple compromised subscribers.

11.5 Tamper Resistance and PALs

In modern weapons, the solenoid safe locks have been superseded by *prescribed action links* (PALs), which are used to protect most U.S. nuclear devices. (A summary of the open source information about PALs can be found in [92].) PAL development started in about 1961, but deployment was slow. Even 20 years later, about half the U.S. nuclear warheads in Europe still used the four-digit code locks. As more complex arming options were introduced, the codes increased in length from 4 to 6 and finally to 12 digits. Devices started to have multiple codes, with separate "enable" and "authorize" commands, and the capability to change codes in the field (presumably to recover from false alarms).

The PAL system is supplemented by various coded switch systems and operational procedures; and in the case of weapons such as atomic demolition munitions, which are not complex enough for the PAL to be made inaccessible in the core of the device, the weapon is also stored in tamper-sensing containers called PAPS (for *prescribed action protective system*). Other mechanisms used to prevent accidental detonation include the deliberate weakening of critical parts of the detonator system, so that they will fail if exposed to certain abnormal environments.

Whatever combination of systems is used, there are penalty mechanisms to deny a thief the ability to obtain a nuclear yield from a stolen weapon. These mechanisms vary from one weapon type to another, but include gas bottles to deform the pit and hydride the plutonium in it; shaped charges to destroy components, such as neutron generators and the tritium boost; and asymmetric detonation that results in plutonium dispersal rather than yield. It is always a priority to destroy the code. It is assumed that a renegade government prepared to deploy "terrorists" to steal a shipment of bombs would be prepared to sacrifice some of the bombs (and some technical personnel) to obtain a single serviceable weapon.

To perform authorized maintenance, the tamper protection must be disabled, and this requires a separate unlock code. The devices that hold the various unlock codes—for servicing and firing—are themselves protected in similar ways to the weapons.

The protection goal is summarized in [734]:

> It is currently believed that even someone who gained possession of such a weapon, had a set of drawings, and enjoyed the technical capability of one of the national laboratories would be unable to successfully cause a detonation without knowing the code.

Meeting such an ambitious goal requires a very substantial effort. There are several examples of the level of care needed:

- after tests showed that 1 mm chip fragments survived the protective detonation of a control device carried aboard airborne command posts, the software was rewritten so that all key material was stored as two separate components, which were kept at addresses more than 1 mm apart on the chip surface;

- the "football," the command device carried around behind the president, is said to be as thick as it is out of fear that shaped charges might be used to disable its protective mechanisms. (This may or may not be an urban myth.) Shaped charges can generate a plasma jet with a velocity of 8000 m/s, which could, in theory, be used to disable tamper-sensing circuitry. So some distance may be needed to give the alarm circuit enough time to zeroize the code memory.

This care must extend to many details of implementation and operation. The weapons-testing process includes not just independent verification and validation, but hostile "black hat" penetration attempts by competing laboratories or agencies. Even then, all practical measures are taken to prevent access by possible opponents. The devices (both munition and control) are defended in depth by armed forces; there are frequent zero-notice challenge inspections; and staff may be made to retake the relevant examinations at any time of the day or night.

I discuss tamper resistance in much more detail in a later chapter, as it's becoming rather widely used in applications from pay-TV to bank cards. However, tamper resistance, secret sharing, and one-time authenticators aren't the only technologies to have benefitted from the nuclear industry's interest. There are more subtle system lessons too.

11.6 Treaty Verification

A variety of verification systems are used to monitor compliance with nonproliferation treaties. For example, the IAEA and the U.S. Nuclear Regulatory Commission (NRC) monitor fissile materials in licensed civilian power reactors and other facilities.

An interesting example comes from the tamper-resistant seismic sensor devices designed to monitor the Comprehensive Test Ban Treaty [701]. The goal was to emplace sufficiently sensitive sensors in each signatory's test sites so that any violation of the treaty (such as by testing too large a device) could be detected with high probability. The tamper sensing here is fairly straightforward: the seismic sensors are fitted in a steel tube and inserted into a drill hole that is backfilled with concrete. The whole assembly is so solid that the seismometers themselves can be relied upon to detect tampering events with a fairly high probability. This physical protection is reinforced by random challenge inspections.

The authentication process becomes somewhat more complex because one has to make an assumption of pervasive deceit. Because of the lack of a third party trusted by both sides, and because the quantity of seismic data being transmitted is of the order of 10^8 bits per day, a digital signature scheme (RSA) was used instead of one-time authentication tags. But this is only part of the answer. One party might, for example, disavow a signed message by saying that the official responsible for generating the key had defected, and so the signature was forged. So keys must be generated within the seismic package itself once it has been sealed by both sides. Also, if one side builds the equipment, the other will suspect it of having hidden functionality. Several protocols were proposed of the *cut-and-choose* variety, whereby one party would produce several devices of which the other party would dismantle a sample for inspection. A number of these issues have since resurfaced in electronic commerce. (Many e-commerce system builders should have paid more attention to the lessons in [701].)

11.7 What Goes Wrong

Despite the huge amounts of money invested in developing high-tech protection mechanisms, nuclear control and safety systems appear to suffer from the same kind of design bugs, implementation blunders, and careless operations as any others.

Recently, Britain's main waste reprocessing plant at Sellafield, which handles plutonium in multiple-ton quantities, has been plagued with a series of scandals. Waste documentation has been forged; radiation leaks have been covered up; workers altered entry passes so they could bring their cars into restricted areas; and there have been reports of sabotage. The nuclear police force only managed to clear up 17 out of 158 thefts, and 3 out of 20 cases of criminal damage [495]. It now looks as if the facility will be closed following loss of confidence by customers. The situation in the former Soviet Union appears to be very much worse. A recent survey of nuclear safekeeping describes how dilapidated security mechanisms have become in the decade following the collapse of the USSR, with fissile materials occasionally appearing on the black market and whistleblowers being prosecuted [401].

There are also a number of problems relating to the reliability of communications and other systems under attack. How can communication between the president and many sites around the world be assured? I'll discuss these problems in Chapter 16, "Electronic and Information Warfare."

There have also been a number of interesting high-tech security failures. One example is a possible attack, which led to the development of a new branch of crypto-mathematics—the study of subliminal channels—which is relevant to later discussions on copyright marking and steganography.

The story of the invention of subliminal channels is told in [707]. During the Carter administration, the United States proposed a deal with the Soviet Union under which each side would cooperate with the other to verify the number of intercontinental ballistic missiles. At the same time, in order to protect U.S. Minuteman missiles against a possible Soviet first strike, it was proposed that 100 missiles be moved randomly around a field of 1,000 silos by giant trucks, which were designed so that observers couldn't determine whether they were moving a missile or not. The Soviets would have had to destroy all 1,000 silos to make a successful first strike; and in the context of the proposed arms controls this was thought impractical.

This raised the interesting problem of how to assure the Soviets that there were at most 100 missiles in the silo field, but without letting them find out which silos were occupied. The proposed solution was that the silos would have a Russian sensor package that would detect the presence or absence of a missile, sign this single bit of information, and send it via a U.S. monitoring facility to Moscow. The sensors would be packaged and randomly shuffled by the Americans before emplacement, so that the Russians could not correlate "full" or "empty" signals with particular silos. The catch was that only this single bit of information could be sent; if the Russians could smuggle any more information into the message, they could quickly locate the full silos—as it would take only 10 bits of address information to specify a single silo in the field. (There were many other security requirements to prevent either side cheating, or falsely accusing the other of cheating: for more details, see [706].)

To understand how subliminal channels work, consider the Digital Signature Algorithm described in Chapter 5. The systemwide values are a prime number p, a 160-bit prime number q dividing $p-1$, and a generator g of a subgroup of F_p^* of order q. The signature on the message M is r, s where $r = (g^k \text{ (modulo } p)) \text{ (modulo } q)$, and k is a random session key. The mapping from k to r is fairly random, so a signer who wishes to hide 10 bits of information in this signature for covert transmission to an accomplice can first agree how the bits will be hidden (such as "bits 72–81") and, second, try out one value of k after another until the resulting value r has the desired value in the agreed place.

This could have caused a disastrous failure of the security protocol, as there had been an agreement that the monitoring messages would be authenticated first with a Russian scheme, using Russian equipment, then by an American scheme using American equipment. Had the Russians specified a signature scheme like DSA, they could have leaked the location of the occupied silos and acquired the capability to make a first strike against the Minuteman force.

In the end, the "missile shell game," as it had become known in the popular press, wasn't used. The cooling of relations following the 1980 election put things on hold. Eventually, with the Medium Range Ballistic Missile Treaty, statistical methods were used. The Russians could say, "We'd like to look at the following 20 silos," and they would be uncapped for their satellites to take a look. Since the end of the Cold War, inspections have become much more intimate with inspection flights in manned aircraft carrying observers from both sides, rather than satellites.

Still, the discovery of subliminal channels was significant. Ways in which they might be abused include putting HIV status, or the fact of a felony conviction, into a next-generation digital identity card. Where this is unacceptable, and the card issuer isn't sufficiently trusted not to do it, the remedy is to use a completely deterministic signature scheme such as RSA instead of one that uses a random session key like DSA.

11.8 Secrecy or Openness?

Finally, the nuclear industry provides a nice case history of secrecy. In the 1930s, physicists from many countries had freely shared the scientific ideas that led to the development of the bomb; but after the "atomic spies" (Fuchs, the Rosenbergs, and others) had leaked the designs of the Hiroshima and Nagasaki devices to the Soviet Union, things swung to the other extreme. The United States adopted a policy that atomic knowledge was *born classified*. That meant that if you were within U.S. jurisdiction and had an idea relevant to nuclear weapons, you had to keep it secret regardless of whether you held a security clearance or even worked in the nuclear industry. This was clearly in tension with the Constitution. Things have greatly relaxed since then, as the protection issues were thought through in detail.

"We've a database in New Mexico that records the physical and chemical properties of plutonium at very high temperatures and pressures," a former head of U.S. nuclear security once told me. "At what level should I classify that? Who's going to steal it, and will it do them any good? The Russians, they've got that data for themselves. The Israelis can figure it out. Gaddafi? What the hell will he do with it?"

As issues like this got worked though, a surprising amount of the technology has been declassified and sometimes published, at least in outline. Starting from early publication at scientific conferences of results on authentication codes and subliminal channels in the early 1980s, the benefits of public design review have been found to outweigh the possible advantage to an opponent of knowing broadly the system in use.

Many implementation details are kept secret, though; information that could facilitate sabotage, such as which of a facility's 50 buildings contains the alarm response force, gets marked *unclassified controlled nuclear information* (UCNI), adding yet another layer of complexity to the security policy model. There are also numerous nitty-gritty issues, such as who is authorized to shoot whom (on the same side) and under what circumstances.

Still, the big picture is open (or so we're assured); and even before the recent classification reviews, command and control technologies were explicitly offered to other states, including hostile ones like the former Soviet Union. Again, the benefits of reducing the likelihood of an accidental war were considered to outweigh the possible benefits of secrecy. This is a modern reincarnation of Kerckhoffs' doctrine, first put forward in the nineteenth century, that the security of a system should depend on its key, not on its design remaining obscure [454].

11.9 Summary

The command and control of nuclear weapons, and subsidiary activities—from protecting the integrity of the national command system through physical security of nuclear facilities to monitoring international arms control treaties—has made a disproportionate contribution to the development of security technology.

The quite rational decision that the relevant assets had to be protected almost regardless of the cost drove the development of a lot of mathematics and science that has found application elsewhere. The particular examples given in this chapter are authentication codes, shared control schemes, and subliminal channels. We also started to discuss tamper-resistant devices, about which I'll have more to say later.

Research Problem

Find interesting applications for technologies developed in this area, such as authentication codes.

Further Reading

Simmons was a pioneer of authentication codes, shared control schemes, and subliminal channels. His book [703] remains the best reference for most of the technical material discussed in this chapter. A more concise introduction to both authentication and secret sharing can be found in [738].

One of the best open sources for public information on nuclear weapons is the Federation of American Scientists [286]. The rationale for the recent declassification of many nuclear arms technologies is presented in detail on their website [286]. Declassification issues are discussed in [812], and the publicly available material on PALs has been assembled by Steve Bellovin [92].

Control failures in nuclear installations are documented in a range of places. The problems with Russian installations are discussed in [401]; U.S. nuclear safety is overseen by the Nuclear Regulatory Commission [593]; and shortcomings with U.K. installations are documented in the quarterly reports posted by the Health and Safety Executive [375].

CHAPTER 12

Security Printing and Seals

A seal is only as good as the man in whose briefcase it's carried.

—KAREN SPÄRCK JONES

12.1 Introduction

Many computer systems rely to some extent on secure printing, packaging, and seals to guarantee important aspects of their protection.

- Many software products get some protection against forgery, using tricks such as holographic stickers that are supposed to tear when removed from the package. They can raise the costs of large-scale forgery; on the individual scale, a careful implementation can help with *trusted distribution*, that is, assuring the user that the product hasn't been tampered with since leaving the factory.

- We discussed how monitoring systems, such as taximeters, often use seals to make it harder for users to tamper with input. No matter how sophisticated the cryptography, a defeat for the seals can be a defeat for the system.

- Many security tokens, such as smartcards, are difficult to make truly tamper-proof. It's often feasible for the opponent to dismantle the device and probe out the content. The realistic goal for such a system may be *tamper evidence*, rather than tamper proofness: if someone dismantles their smartcard and gets the keys out, that person should not be able to reassemble it into something that will pass close examination. Security printing can be the key technology here. If a bank smartcard really is tamper-evident, then the bank might tell its customers that disputes will be entertained only if they can produce the card intact. (Banks might not get away with this, though, because consumer protection lawyers will demand that they deal fairly with honest customers who lose their cards or have them stolen).

Quite apart from these direct applications of printing and sealing technology in computer systems, the ease with which modern color scanners and printers can be used to make passable forgeries has opened up another front. Banknote printers are now promoting digital protection techniques [109]. These include invisible copyright marks that enable forgeries to be detected or even set off alarms in image-processing software [357]. The digital world and the world of "funny inks" are growing rapidly closer together.

12.2 History

Seals have a long and interesting history. In the chapter on banking systems, I explained that bookkeeping systems had their origin in the clay tablets, or bullae, used by neolithic warehouse keepers in Mesopotamia as receipts for produce. Over 5000 years ago, the bulla system was adapted to resolve disputes by having the warehouse keeper bake the bulla in a clay envelope with his mark on it.

In classical times and in ancient China, seals were commonly used to authenticate documents. They were used in Europe until a few hundred years ago for letters. Even after signatures had taken over as the principal authentication mechanism, seals lingered on as a secondary mechanism until the nineteenth century. Letters were not placed in envelopes, but folded over several times and sealed using hot wax and a signet ring.

Seals are still the preferred authentication mechanism for important documents in China, Japan, and Korea. Elsewhere, traces of their former importance survive in company seals and notaries' seals, which are affixed to important documents, and the national seals that some countries' heads of state apply to archival copies of legislation.

However, by the middle of the last century, their use with documents had become less important in the West than their use to authenticate packaging. The move from loose goods to packaged goods, and the growing importance of brands, created not just the potential for greater quality control but also the vulnerability that bad people might tamper with products. The United States suffered an epidemic of tampering incidents, particularly of soft drinks and medical products, leading to a peak of 235 reported cases in 1993 [445]. This helped push many manufacturers towards making products tamper-evident.

The ease with which software can be copied, coupled with consumer resistance to technical copy-protection mechanisms from the mid-1980s, drove software companies to rely increasingly on packaging to deter counterfeiters. That was just part of a much larger market in preventing the forgery of high-value, branded goods, ranging from perfume and cigarettes through aircraft spares to pharmaceuticals.

In short, huge amounts of money have been poured into seals and other kinds of secure packaging. Unfortunately, most seals are still fairly easy to defeat.

The typical seal consists of a substrate with security printing, which is then glued or tied around the object being sealed, so we must look first at security printing. If the whole seal can be forged easily, then no amount of glue or string is going to help.

12.3 Security Printing

The introduction of paper money into Europe by Napoleon in the early 1800s, and of other valuable documents such as bearer securities and passports, kicked off a battle between security printers and counterfeiters that exhibits many of the characteristics of a coevolution of predators and prey. Photography (1839) helped the attackers, then color printing and steel etching (1850s) the defenders. In recent years, the color copier and the cheap scanner have been countered by holograms and other optically variable devices. Sometimes, the same people are involved on both sides, as when a government's intelligence services try to forge another government's passports (and in some cases, even its currency, as both sides did in World War II).

On occasion, the banknote designers succumb to the Titanic effect, of believing too much in the latest technology, and place too much faith in some particular trick. An example comes from the forgery of British banknotes in the 1990s. These notes have a *window thread*—a metal strip through the paper about 1 mm wide that comes to the paper surface every 8 mm. When you look at the note in reflected light, it appears to have a dotted metallic line running across it, but when you hold it up and view it through transmitted light, the metal strip is dark and solid. Duplicating this was thought to be hard, but a criminal gang came up with a beautiful hack. They used a cheap hot-stamping process to lay down a metal strip on the surface of the paper, then printed a pattern of solid bars over it using white ink to leave the expected metal pattern visible. At their trial, they were found to have forged tens of millions of pounds' worth of notes over a period of several years [299]. (There may also have been a complacency issue here, as European banks tend to believe that forgers will go for the U.S. notes, which have only three colors.)

12.3.1 Threat Model

As always, we have to evaluate a protection technology in the context of a model of the threats. Broadly speaking, the threat can be from a properly funded organization (such as a government trying to forge another nation's banknotes), from a medium-sized organization (such as a criminal gang forging several million dollars a month, or a distributor forging labels on vintage wines) to amateurs using equipment they have at home or in the office.

In the banknote business, the big growth area in the last years of the twentieth century was in amateur forgery. Knowledge had spread in the printing trade of how to manufacture high-quality forgeries of many banknotes, which one might have thought would increase the level of professional forgery. But the spread of high-quality color scanners and printers has put temptation in the way of many people who would never have dreamed of getting into forgery in the days when it required messy wet inks. In the past, amateurs were thought a minor nuisance, but since about 1997 or 1998, they have accounted for most of the forgeries detected in the United States (it varies from one country to another; most U.K. forgers use traditional litho printing, while in Spain, as in the United States, the inkjet printer has taken over [393]). Amateur forgers are hard to combat as there are many of them; they mostly work on such a small scale that their product takes a long time to come to the attention of authority, and they are less likely to have criminal records. The notes they produce are often not good enough to pass a bank teller, but are uttered in places such as dark and noisy nightclubs.

The industry distinguishes three different levels of inspection that a forged banknote or document may or may not pass [765].

A *primary* or *first-level* inspection is one performed by an untrained, inexperienced person, such as a member of the public or a new cashier at a store. Very often, the primary inspector has no motivation, or even a negative motivation. If he gets a banknote that feels slightly dodgy, he may try to pass it on without looking at it closely enough to have to decide between becoming an accomplice or going to the hassle of reporting it.

A *secondary* or *second-level* inspection is one performed in the field by a competent and motivated person, such as an experienced bank teller in the case of banknotes or a trained manufacturer's inspector in the case of product labels. This person may have some special equipment such as an ultraviolet lamp, a pen with a chemical reagent, or even a scanner and a PC. However, the equipment will be limited in both cost and bulk, and will be completely understood by serious counterfeiters.

A *tertiary* or *third-level* inspection is one performed at the laboratory of the manufacturer or the note-issuing bank. The experts who designed the security printing (and perhaps even the underlying industrial processes) will be on hand, with substantial equipment and support.

The executive summary of the state of the security printing art is that getting a counterfeit past a primary inspection is usually easy, whereas getting it past tertiary inspection is usually impossible if the product and the inspection process have been competently designed. Thus, secondary inspection is the battleground (except in a few applications such as banknote printing, where attention is now being paid to the primary level); and the main limits on what sort of counterfeits can be detected by the inspector in the field have to do with the bulk and the cost of the equipment needed.

12.3.2 Security Printing Techniques

Traditional security documents utilize a number of printing processes, including:

- *Intaglio*, a process where an engraved pattern is used to press the ink on to the paper with great force, leaving a raised ink impression with high definition. This is often used for scroll work on banknotes and passports.

- *Letterpress* in which the ink is rolled on raised type which is then pressed on to the page, leaving a depression. The numbers on banknotes are usually printed this way, often with numbers of different sizes and using different inks to prevent off-the-shelf numbering equipment being used.

- Special printing presses, called *Simultan presses*, which transfer all the inks, for both front and back, to the paper simultaneously. This means that the printing on front and back can be accurately aligned; patterns can be printed partly on the front and partly on the back so that they match up perfectly when the note is held up to the light (*see-through register*). Reproducing this is believed too hard for cheap color printing equipment. The Simultan presses also have special ducting to make ink colors vary along the line (*rainbowing*).

- Rubber stamps which are used to endorse documents, or to seal photographs to them.

- Embossing and laminates which are also used to seal photographs, and on bank cards to push up the cost of forgery. Embossing can be physical, or require laser engraving techniques to burn a photo into an ID card.

- *Watermarks* which are an example of putting protection features in the paper. They are more translucent areas inserted into the paper by varying its thickness when it is manufactured. There are many other special properties in use, such as fluorescent threads. An extreme example is the Australian $10 note, which is printed on plastic and has a see-through window.

More modern techniques include:

- Optically variable inks, such as the patches on Canadian $20 bills that change color from green to gold depending on the viewing angle.

- Inks with magnetic or photoacoustic properties.

- Printing features visible only with special equipment, such as the microprinting on U.S. bills, which requires a magnifying glass to see, and printing in ultraviolet, infrared, or magnetic inks (the last of these being used in the black printing on U.S. bills).

- Metal threads and foils, from simple iridescent features to foil color copying to foils with optically variable effects such as *holograms* and *kinegrams*, as found on British £20 and £50 notes. Holograms are typically produced optically, and look like a solid object behind the film, while kinegrams are produced by computer and may show a number of startlingly different views from slightly different angles.

- *Screen traps* such as details too faint to scan properly, and *alias band structures* which contain detail at the correct size to form interference effects with the dot separation of common scanners and copiers.

- *Digital copyright marks* which may vary from images hidden by microprinting their Fourier transforms directly, to spread spectrum signals that will be recognized by a color copier, scanner, or printer, and cause it to stop.

- Unique stock, such as paper that has had magnetic fibers randomly spread through it during manufacture so that each sheet has a characteristic pattern that can be digitally signed and printed on the document using some kind of barcode.

For the design of the new U.S. $100 bill, see [566]; and for a study of counterfeit banknotes, with an analysis of which features provide what evidence, see [766]. In general, banknotes' genuineness cannot readily be confirmed by the inspection of a single security feature. Many of the older techniques, and some of the newer, can be mimicked in ways that will pass primary inspection. The tactile effects of intaglio and letterpress printing wear off, so crumpling and dirtying the forged note is standard practice, and skilled banknote forgers mimic watermarks with faint gray printing (though watermarks remain surprisingly effective against amateurs). Holograms and kinegrams can be vulnerable to people using electrochemical techniques to make mechanical copies; or villains may originate their own master copies from scratch.

When a hologram of Shakespeare was introduced on U.K. check guarantee cards in 1988, I visited the factory as the representative of a bank and was told proudly that, as the industry had demanded a second source of supply, they had given a spare set of plates to a large security printing firm—and this competitor of theirs had been quite unable to manufacture acceptable foils. (The Shakespeare foil was the first commercially used diffraction hologram to be in full color and to move as the viewing angle changed). Surely a device that couldn't be forged, even by a major security printing company with access to genuine printing plates, must give total protection? But when I visited Singapore seven years later, I bought a similar (but larger) hologram of Shakespeare in the flea market. This was clearly a boast by the maker that he could forge U.K. bank cards if he wished to. By then, a police expert estimated that there were more than 100 forgers in China with the skill to produce passable holograms [591].

The technology constantly moves on; and the kind of progress that aids the villain can come from such unexpected directions that technology controls have little effect. For example, ion beam workstations—machines that can be used to create the masters for kinegrams—cost many millions of dollars in the mid-1990s, but have turned out to be so useful in metallurgical lab work that sales have shot up, prices have plummeted, and there are now many bureaus that rent out machine time for a few hundred dollars an hour. So it is imprudent to rely on a single protection technology. Even if one defense is completely defeated (such as if it becomes easy to make mechanical copies of metal foils), you have at least one completely different trick to fall back on (such as optically variable ink).

But designing a security document is much harder than this. There are complex trade-offs between protection, aesthetics and robustness, and it is coming to be realized that, for many years, designers had their focus on preventing forgeries passing secondary or tertiary inspection (the technological focus), rather than on the more common primary inspection (the business focus). Much time was spent handwringing about the difficulty of training people to examine documents properly, while not enough attention was paid to studying how the typical user of a product such as a banknote actually decides subconsciously whether it's acceptable. This defect is now receiving serious attention.

The lessons drawn so far are [765]:

- Security features should convey a message relevant to the product. So it's better to use iridescent ink to print the denomination of a banknote than some obscure feature of it.
- They should obviously belong where they are, so that they become embedded in the user's cognitive model of the object.
- Their effects should be obvious, distinct and intelligible.
- They should not have existing competitors that can provide a basis for imitations.
- They should be standardized.

This work deserves much wider attention, as the banknote community is one of the few subdisciplines of the trade to have devoted a lot of thought to security usability. (We'll see later in Chapter 23 that one of the main failings of current evaluation schemes for security products is that usability gets ignored.) When it comes to documents other than banknotes, such as passports, there are also issues relating to political environment of the country and the mores of the society in which they will be used [546].

Usability also matters during second-line inspection, but here the issues are more subtle, focusing on the process that the inspector has to follow to distinguish genuine from fake.

With banknotes, the theory is that you design a note with perhaps 20 features that are not advertised to the public. A number of features are made known to secondary inspectors such as bank staff. In due course, these become known to the forgers. As time goes on, more and more features are revealed. Eventually, when they are all exposed, the note is withdrawn from circulation and replaced. This may become harder as the emphasis switches from manual to automatic verification. A thief who steals a vending machine, dismantles it, and reads out the software, gains a complete description of the checks currently in use. Having once spent several weeks or months doing this, he will find it much easier the second time around. So when the central bank tells manufacturers the secret polynomial for the second-level digital watermark (or whatever), and this gets fielded, he can steal another machine and get the new data within days. So failures can be more sudden and complete than with manual systems, and the cycle of discovery could turn more quickly than in the past.

With product packaging, the typical business model is that samples of forgeries are found and taken to the laboratory, where the scientists find some way in which they are different—such as because the hologram is not quite right. Kits are then produced for field inspectors to go out and track down the source. If these kits are bulky and expensive, fewer of them can be fielded. If there are many different forgery detection devices from different companies, then it is hard to persuade customs officers to use any of them. Ideas such as printing individual microscopic ultraviolet barcodes on plastic product shrinkwrap often fail because of the cost of the microscope, laptop, and online connection needed to do the verification. As with banknotes, you can get a much more robust system with multiple features, but this pushes the cost and bulk of the reading device up still further. There is now a substantial research effort aimed at developing unique marks, such as special chemical coatings containing proteins or even DNA molecules, which encode hidden serial numbers and which might enable one type of verification equipment to check many different products.

With financial instruments, and especially checks, alteration is a much bigger problem than copying or forgery from scratch. In numerous scams, villains got genuine checks from businesses by tricks such as by prepaying deposits or making reservations in cash, then cancelling the order. The victim duly sends out a check, which is altered to a much larger amount, often using readily available domestic solvents. The standard countermeasure is background printing using inks that discolor and run in the presence of solvents. But the protection isn't complete because of tricks for removing laser printer toner (and even simple things like typewriter correction ribbon). One enterprising villain even presented his victims with pens that had been specially selected to have easily removable ink [5].

While the security literature says a lot about debit card fraud (as the encryption systems that ATMs use are interesting to techies), and a little about credit card fraud (as there's a lot of talk about credit card fraud on the Net), very little has been written about check fraud. Yet check fraud is many times greater in value than credit card fraud, and debit cards are almost insignificant by comparison with either. Although check fraud is critically important, the research community considers it to be boring.

The practical problem for the banks is the huge volume of checks processed daily. This makes scrutiny impossible except for very large amounts—and the sums stolen by small-time check fiddlers may be low by the standards of the victim organization (say, in the thousands to tens of thousands of dollars). In the Far East, where people use a personal *chop* or signature stamp to sign checks instead of a manuscript signature, low-cost automatic checking is possible [395]. However, with handwritten signatures, automated verification with acceptable error rates is still beyond the state of the art; I'll discuss this in Section 13.2. In some countries, such as Germany, check frauds have been largely suppressed by businesses making most payments using bank transfers rather than checks (even for small customer refunds). Making such a change involves overcoming huge cultural inertia, but perhaps the lower costs of online payments (cents rather than tens of cents) will persuade business in most countries to make the switch eventually.

Alterations are also a big problem for the typical bank's credit card department. It is much simpler to alter the magnetic strip on a card than to re-originate the hologram. In fact, during the early 1980s, the system was to verify a card's magnetic strip data using an online terminal, then collect the actual transaction using a zip-zap machine. The effect was that the authorization was done against the card number on the strip, while the transaction was booked against the card number on the embossing. So villains would take stolen cards and reencode them with the account details of cardholders with high credit limits—captured, for example, from waste carbons in the bins outside fancy restaurants—and use these to authorize transactions which would then be billed to the stolen card's account. The bank would then repudiate the transaction, as the authorization code didn't match the recorded account number. So banks started fighting with their corporate customers over liability, and the system was changed so that drafts were captured electronically from the magnetic strip.

Of course, alterations aren't just a banking problem. Most fake travel documents are altered rather than counterfeited from scratch: names are changed, photographs are replaced, or pages are added and removed.

Finally, one promising technology is the use of optically readable digital signatures instead of traditional serial numbers. These can bind printed matter either to the underlying substrate or to information about enclosed materials. When I introduced digital signatures in Section 5.3.5, I mentioned that the United States and some other countries were introducing a new postal meter system that prints out stamps, known as *indicia*, with contain 2-D barcodes. These contain the amount of postage, the sender, and recipient post codes, the serial number of the postal meter, and the date. Although, in theory, a stamp could be pulled off one envelope and put on another—or just photocopied—this arrangement is enough to stop the kind of frauds of greatest concern to the U.S. Postal Service, which involve junk mailers bribing postal employees to introduce large sacks of mail into the system [753]. A sample of the indicia being introduced is reproduced in Figure 12.1.

Figure 12.1   The new format for U.S. postal meters (courtesy of Symbol Technologies).

12.4 Packaging and Seals

This brings us to the added problems of packaging and seals.

Not all seals work by gluing a substrate with security printing to the object being sealed. I mentioned the wire and lead seals used to prevent tampering with truck speed sensors, and there are many products following the same general philosophy but using different materials, such as plastic straps, which are supposed to be easy to tighten but hard to loosen without cutting. I also mentioned the special chemical coatings, microscopic barcodes, and other tricks used to make products or product batches traceable. However, most of the seals in use work by applying some kind of security printing to a substrate, then gluing this to the material to be protected.

12.4.1 Substrate Properties

Some systems add random variability to the substrate material. Recall the trick of loading paper with magnetic fibers; there are also *watermark magnetics*, in which a random high-coercivity signal is embedded in a card strip that can subsequently be read and written using standard low-coercivity equipment without the unique random pattern being disturbed. Watermark magnetics are used in bank cards in Sweden, in telephone cards in Korea, and in entry control cards in some of the buildings in my university.

A similar idea is used in arms control. Many materials have surfaces that are unique, or that can be made so by eroding them with a small explosive charge. This makes it easy to identify capital equipment such as heavy artillery, where identifying each gun barrel is enough to prevent either side from cheating. The surface pattern of the gun barrel is measured using laser speckle techniques, and either recorded in a log or attached to the device as a machine-readable digital signature [703].

Similar techniques are being developed for postal systems. An alignment grid is printed on an envelope, and a small microscope is used to observe the paper fibers there. A paper fibre pattern is extracted and recorded in the postal franking mark, which is digitally signed. This has the potential to enable sheets of ordinary paper to become recognizably unique, like the special fiber-loaded papers just mentioned, only much more cheaply.

12.4.2 The Problems of Glue

However, many seals do work by gluing security-printed matter on to the target object. This raises the question of how the beautiful piece of iridescent printed art can be attached to a crude physical object in a way that is difficult to remove. The usual answer is to use a glue that is stronger than the seal substrate itself, so that the seal will tear or at least deform noticeably if pulled away.

However, in most products, the implementation is rather poor. Many seals are vulnerable to direct removal using only hand tools and a little patience. You can experiment with this by taking a sharp knife to the next few letters that arrive in self-seal envelopes. Many of these envelopes are supposed to tear, rather than peel open; the flap may have a few vertical slots cut into it for this purpose. But this hoped-for tamper evidence usually assumes that people will open them by pulling the envelope flap back carelessly from the body. By raising the flap slightly and working the knife back and forth, it is often possible to cut the glue without damaging the flap, and thus open the envelope without leaving suspicious marks. (Some glues should be softened first using a hairdryer, or made more fragile by freezing.) The result may be an envelope that looks slightly crumpled on careful examination, but crumples can be ironed out. This attack usually works against a primary inspection, probably fails a tertiary inspection, and may well pass secondary inspection: crumples happen in the post anyway.

Many of the seals on the market can be defeated using similarly simple techniques. For example, there is a colored adhesive tape that, when ripped off, leaves behind a warning such as "Danger" or "Do not use." The colored layer is sandwiched between two layers of glue, and the bottom of these is stronger where the color is supposed to remain behind if the seal is tampered with. But the tape behaves in this way only if it is pulled from above. By cutting from the side, one can remove it intact and reuse it [479].

12.5 Systemic Vulnerabilities

We turn now from the specific threats against particular printing tricks, glues, and markets to the system-level threats, of which there are many.

A possibly useful example is in Figure 12.2. At our local swimming pool, congestion is managed by issuing swimmers with wristbands during busy periods. A different color is issued every twenty minutes or so, and from time to time all people with bands of a certain color are asked to leave. The band is made of waxed paper. At the end it has a printed pattern and serial number on one side and glue on the other; the paper is cross-cut with the result that it is destroyed if you tear it off carelessly. (It's very similar to the luggage seals used at some airports.)

The simplest attack is to phone up the supplier; boxes of 100 wristbands cost about $8. If you don't want to spend money, you can use each band once, then ease it off

Figure 12.2 A wristband seal from our local swimming pool.

gently by pulling it alternately from different directions, giving the result shown in the photo. The printing is crumpled, though intact; the damage isn't such as to be visible by a poolside attendant, and could have been caused by careless application. The point is that the damage done to the seal by fixing it twice, carefully, is not easily distinguishable from the effects of a naive user fixing it once. (An even more powerful attack is to not remove the backing tape from the seal at all, but use some other means—a safety pin, or your own glue—to fix it.)

Despite this, the wristband seal is perfectly fit for purpose. There is little incentive to cheat: people in such intensive training that they swim for two hours at a stretch use the pool when it's not congested. They also buy a season ticket, so they can go out at any time to get a band of the current color. But it illustrates many of the things that can go wrong. The customer is the enemy; it's the customer who applies the seal; the effects of seal re-use are indistinguishable from those of random failure; unused seals can be bought in the marketplace; counterfeit seals could also be manufactured at little cost; and effective inspection is infeasible. (And yet this swimming pool seal is still harder to defeat than many sealing products sold for high-value industrial applications.)

12.5.1 Peculiarities of the Threat Model

We've seen systems where your customer is your enemy, as in banking. In military systems, the enemy could be a single disloyal soldier, or the other side's special forces trying to sabotage your equipment. In nuclear monitoring systems it can be the host government trying to divert fissile materials from a licensed civilian reactor.

But some of the most difficult sealing tasks arise in commerce. Their difficulty arises from the fact that it is the enemy who will apply the seal. A typical application is where a company subcontracts the manufacture of some of its products, and is afraid that the contractor will produce more of the goods than agreed. Overproduction is the main source by value of counterfeit goods worldwide; the perpetrators have access to the authorized manufacturing process and raw materials, and gray markets provide natural distribution channels. Even detecting such frauds—let alone proving them in court—can be hard.

A typical solution for high-value goods, such as cosmetics, may involve buying packaging materials from a number of different companies, whose identities are kept secret from the firm operating the final assembly plant. Some of these materials may have serial numbers embedded in various ways (such as by laser engraving in bottle glass or by printing on cellophane using inks visible only under UV light). There may be an online service whereby the manufacturer's field agents can verify the serial numbers of samples purchased randomly in shops; or there might be a digital signature on the packaging that links all the various serial numbers together for offline checking.

There are limits on what seals can achieve in isolation. Sometimes the brand owner himself is the villain, as when a vineyard falsely labels as vintage an extra thousand cases of wine that were actually made from bought-in blended grapes. So bottles of South African wine all carry a government-regulated seal with a unique serial number; here, the seal doesn't prove the fraud, but makes it harder for a dishonest vintner to evade the other controls such as inspection and audit. So sealing mechanisms usually must be designed with the audit, testing, and inspection process in mind.

Inspection can be trickier than one would think. The distributor who has bought counterfeit goods on the gray market, believing them to be genuine, may set out to deceive the inspectors without any criminal intent. Where gray markets are an issue, inspectors should expect to see only authorized products in distributors' stockrooms, while products bought from "Fred" will be pushed out rapidly to the customers. Also, the distributor may be completely in the dark; it could be his staff who are peddling the counterfeits. In a recent high-profile case, staff at a major airline bought counterfeit perfumes, watches, and the like in the Far East, sold them in-flight to customers, and trousered the proceeds. The stocks in the airline's warehouses (and in the duty-free carts after the planes had landed) were all completely genuine. So it is usually essential to have agents go out and make sample purchases, and the sealing mechanisms must support this.

12.5.2 Staff Diligence

Whether the seal adheres properly to the object being sealed may also depend on the honesty of low-level staff. I mentioned in Section 10.4.1.2 how in truck speed limiter systems, the gearbox sensor is secured in place using a piece of wire on which the calibrating garage crimps a lead disc in place with sealing tongs. The defeat is to bribe the garage mechanic to wrap the wire the wrong way, so that when the sensor is unscrewed the wire will loosen, instead of tightening and breaking the seal. There is absolutely no need to go to amateur sculptor classes to learn to take a cast of the seal and forge a pair of sealing tongs out of bronze (unless you want to save on bribes, or to frame the garage).

The people who apply seals may be careless as well as corrupt. In the last few years, some airports have taken to applying tape seals to passengers' checked bags after X-raying them using a machine near check-in queue. On about half of the occasions this has been done to my baggage, the tape has been poorly fixed: it didn't cross the fastener between the suitcase and the lid, or it came off at one end, or the case had several compartments big enough to hold a bomb but only one of their fasteners was sealed. Carelessness and corruption interact. If enough of the staff applying a seal are careless, then if I bribe one of them the defect doesn't of itself prove dishonesty.

12.5.3 The Effect of Random Failure

There are similar effects when seals break for completely innocent reasons. For example, speed limiter seals often break when a truck engine is steam-cleaned, so a driver will not be prosecuted for tampering if a broken seal is all the evidence the traffic policeman can find. (Truck drivers know this.)

There are other consequences, too. For example, after opening a too-well-sealed envelope, a villain can close it again with a sticker saying 'Opened by customs' or 'Burst in transit—sealed by the Post Office'. He could even just tape it shut and scrawl 'delivered to wrong address try again' on the front.

The consequences of such failures and attacks have to be thought through carefully. If the goal is to prevent large-scale forgery of a product, occasional breakages may not matter; but if it is to support prosecutions, spontaneous seal failure can be a serious problem. In extreme cases, placing too much trust in the robustness of a seal might lead to a miscarriage of justice, and completely undermine the sealing product's evidential (and thus commercial) value.

12.5.4 Materials Control

Another common vulnerability is that supplies of sealing materials are uncontrolled. Corporate seals are a nice example. In Britain, these typically consist of two metal embossing plates that are inserted into special pliers. There are several suppliers who manufacture the plates, and a lawyer who has ordered hundreds of them tells me that no check was ever made. Although it might be slightly risky to order a seal for "Microsoft Corporation," it should be easy to have a seal made for almost any less-well-known target—just write a letter that looks like it came from a law firm.

Or consider the plastic envelopes used by some courier companies, which are designed to stretch and tear when opened. This is a promising technology, but as long as the company's regular customers have supplies of envelopes lying around (and they can also be obtained at the depot) it may not deter an attacker from tampering with a package either before, or after, its trip through the courier's network.

It has for some time been an "urban myth" that the police and security services cannot open envelopes tracelessly if the flaps have been reinforced with sticky tape that has been burnished down by rubbing it with a thumbnail (I recently received some paperwork from a bank that had been sealed in just this way). This is not entirely believable—even if no police lab has invented a magic solvent for sellotape glue, the nineteenth century Tsarist police already used forked sticks to wind up letters inside a sealed envelope so that they could be pulled out, read, and then put back [428].

Even if sellotape were guaranteed to leave a visible mark on an envelope, one would have to assume that the police's envelope-steaming department have no stock of comparable envelopes, and that the recipient would be observant enough to spot a forged envelope. Given the ease with which an envelope with a company logo can be scanned and then duplicated using desktop publishing equipment, these assumptions are fairly ambitious. In any case, the arrival of high-quality desktop color printers has caused a lot of organizations to stop using preprinted stationery for all their letters. This makes the forger's job much easier.

12.5.5 Not Protecting the Right Things

I mentioned how credit cards were vulnerable in the late 1980s: the authorization terminals read the magnetic strip, while the payment draft capture equipment used the embossing; Crooks who changed the mag strip but not the embossing defeated the system.

There are also attacks involving partial alterations. For example, as the hologram on a credit card covers only the last four digits, the attacker could always change the other twelve. When the algorithm the bank used to generate credit card numbers was known, this involved only flattening, reprinting, and re-embossing the rest of the card, which could be done with cheap equipment.

Such attacks are now rare, because villains now realize that very few shop staff check that the account number printed on the slip is the same as that embossed on the card. So the account number on the strip need bear no resemblance at all to the numbers embossed on the face. In effect, all the hologram says is, "This was once a valid card."

Finally, food and drug producers often protect products against tampering by using shrinkwrap or blister packaging, which (if well designed) can be moderately difficult to forge well enough to withstand close inspection. However when selecting protective measures one has to be very clear about the threat model—is it counterfeiting, alteration, duplication, simulation, diversion, dilution, substitution, or something else [615]? If the threat model is a psychotic with a syringe full of poison, then simple blister or shrink-wrap packaging is not quite enough. What's really needed is a tamper-sensing membrane, which will react visibly and irreversibly to even a tiny penetration. (Such membranes exist but are still too expensive for consumer products. I'll discuss one of them in the chapter on tamper resistance.)

12.5.6 The Cost and Nature of Inspection

There are many stories in the industry of villains replacing the hologram on a bank card with something else—say a rabbit instead of a dove—whereupon the response of shopkeepers is just to say: "Oh, look, they changed the hologram!" This isn't a criticism of holograms; the issue is much deeper, involving applied psychology and public education. Bankers worry when new notes are being introduced—the few weeks before everyone is familiar with the new notes can be a bonanza for forgers. (This is one of the big worries with the planned introduction of the new Euro currency notes.)

A related problem is the huge variety of passports, driver's licenses, letterheads, corporate seals, and variations in packaging. Without samples of genuine articles for comparison, inspection is more or less limited to the primary level, so forgery is easy. Even though bank clerks have books with pictures of foreign banknotes, and immigration officers similarly have pictures of foreign passports, there is often only a small amount of information on security features; and in any case the absence of real physical samples means that the tactile aspects of the product go unexamined.

As already mentioned, the limiting factor with many technologies is the cost of second-line inspection in the field. If detecting a forged bottle of perfume requires equipment costing $5,000 (e.g., a laptop with a scanner, a UV lamp, and a special microscope), then this may be viable for an exclusive perfume sold only through a few upmarket stores, but is less likely to be viable for medium-value products and is very unlikely to be distributed to all customs posts and market inspectors worldwide.

The ideal remains a seal that can be checked by the public or by staff with minimal training. Firms that take forgery seriously, such as large software companies, are starting to adopt many of the techniques pioneered by banknote printers. But high-value product packages are harder to protect than banknotes. Familiarity is important: people get a "feel" for things they handle frequently, such as local money, but are much less likely to notice something wrong with a package they see only rarely, such as a car part or a medicine bottle. Humans are very vulnerable when they see something for the first or only time—such as the packaging on the latest version of a computer operating system.

12.6 Evaluation Methodology

This section offers a systematic way to evaluate a seal product for a given application. Rather than just asking, "Can you remove the seal in ways other than the obvious one?" we need to follow it from design and field test through manufacture, application, use, checking, destruction, and finally retirement from service. Here are some of the questions that should be asked:

- Has anybody who really knows what they're doing tried hard to defeat the system? And what's a defeat anyway—tampering, forgery, alteration, destruction of evidential value, or a "PR" attack on your commercial credibility?

- What is the reputation of the team that designed it—did they have a history of successfully defeating opponents' products?

- How long has the system been in the field, and how likely is it that technological progress will make a defeat significantly easier?

- How widely available are the sealing materials—who else can buy, forge, or steal supplies?

- Will the person who applies the seal be careless or corrupt?

- Does the way the seal will be used protect the right part (or enough) of the product?

- What are the quality issues? What about the effects of dirt, noise, vibration, cleaning, and manufacturing defects? Will the product have to survive weather, fuel splashes, being carried next to the skin, or being dropped in a glass of beer? Is it supposed to respond visibly if such a thing happens? How often will there be random seal failures, and what effect will they have?

- If a seal is forged, who's supposed to spot this? If it's the public, then how often will they see genuine seals? Has the vendor done experiments, that pass muster by the standards of applied psychology, to establish the likely false accept and false reject rates? If it's your inspectors in the field, how much will their equipment and training cost?

- Are there any evidential issues? If you're going to end up in court, are there experts other than your own (or the vendor's) on whom the other side can rely? If the answer is no, then is this a good thing or a bad thing? Why should the jury believe you, the system's inventor, rather than the sweet little old lady in the dock? Will the judge let her off on fair trial grounds—because rebutting your technical claims would be an impossible burden of proof for her to discharge? (This is exactly what happened in *Judd vs. Citibank*, the case that settled U.S. law on phantom withdrawals from cash machines [427].)

- Once the product is used, how will the seals be disposed of? Are you worried that someone might recover a few old seals from the trash?

When considering whether the people who apply and check the seals will perform their tasks faithfully and effectively, it is important to analyze motive, opportunity, skills, audit, and accountability. Be particularly cautious where the seal is applied by the enemy (as in the case of contract manufacture) or by someone open to corruption (such as the garage mechanic eager to win the truck company's business). Finally, think through the likely consequences of seal failure and inspection error rates, not just from the point of view of the client company and its opponents, but also from the points of view of innocent system users and of legal evidence.

Of course, this whole-lifecycle assurance process should also be applied to computer systems in general. I'll talk about that some more in Part 3.

12.7 Summary

Most commercially available sealing products are relatively easy to defeat, particularly where seal inspection is performed casually by untrained personnel. Sealing has to be evaluated over the lifetime of the product, from manufacture through materials control, application, verification, and eventual destruction; hostile testing is highly advisable in critical applications. Seals often depend on security printing, about which broadly similar comments may be made.

Research Problems

A lot of money is currently being spent on research and product development in this area. The problem appears to be that much of it isn't being spent effectively, or that third-rate products continue to dominate the market because of low cost and user ignorance. An important contribution could be a better evaluation methodology for seals, and for security printing in general. More results on how specific techniques and products can be defeated might also be useful in undermining suppliers' complacency.

Further Reading

The definitive textbook on security printing is van Renesse [765], which goes into not just the technical tricks, such as holograms and kinegrams, but how they work in a variety of applications from banknote printing through passports to packaging. This is very important background reading.

I don't know of a definitive textbook on seals. Most products are proprietary, and depend for their success on criminals' ignorance—which is one of the shakiest foundations I know of. One of the most systematic efforts to overcome this ignorance can be found in a series of publications by the seal vulnerability assessment team at Los Alamos National Laboratory (e.g., [422]).

Biometrics

And the Gileadites took the passages of Jordan before the Ephraimites: and it was so, that when those Ephraimites which were escaped said, Let me go over; that the men of Gilead said unto him, Art thou an Ephraimite? If he said, Nay; Then said they unto him, Say now Shibboleth: and he said Sibboleth: for he could not frame to pronounce it right. Then they took him, and slew him at the passages of the Jordan: and there fell at that time of the Ephraimites forty and two thousand.

—JUDGES 12:5–6

13.1 Introduction

The above quotation may be the first recorded military use of a security protocol in which the authentication relies on a property of the human being—in this case his accent. (There had been less formal uses before this, as when Isaac tried to identify Esau by his bodily hair, but got deceived by Jacob; or indeed when people recognized each other by their faces, which I'll discuss later.)

Biometrics identify people by measuring some aspect of individual anatomy or physiology (such as your hand geometry or fingerprint), some deeply ingrained skill, or other behavioral characteristic (such as your handwritten signature), or something that is a combination of the two (such as your voice).

Over the last quarter century or so, people have developed a large number of biometric devices; this rapidly growing market is now worth about $50 million a year [414]. Earlier I mentioned the use of hand geometry to identify staff at a nuclear reactor in the late 1970s. But the best established biometric techniques predate the computer age altogether—namely the use of handwritten signatures, facial features, and fingerprints. We will look at these first, then go on to the fancier, more high-tech techniques.

13.2 Handwritten Signatures

Handwritten signatures had been used in classical China, but carved personal seals were considered to be higher status, and are still used for serious transactions in China, Japan, and Korea to this day. Europe was the other way around: seals had been used in medieval times, but as writing spread after the Renaissance, people increasingly just wrote their names to signify assent to business and other documents. Over time, the signature became accepted as the standard way of doing this in the West. Every day, billions of dollars' worth of contracts are concluded by handwritten signatures on documents, and how these can be replaced by electronic signatures is a hot policy and technology issue.

How secure are handwritten signatures?

The probability that a forged signature will be accepted as genuine mainly depends on the amount of care taken when examining it. Many bank card transactions in stores are accepted without even a glance at the specimen signature on the card—so much so that many Americans do not even bother to sign their credit cards. (This can cause problems when traveling in more punctilious countries such as Germany or Switzerland.) But even diligent signature checking doesn't reduce the risk of fraud to zero. An experiment showed that 105 professional document examiners, who each did 144 pairwise comparisons, misattributed 6.5% of documents. Meanwhile, a control group of 34 untrained people of the same educational level got it wrong 38.3% of the time [431], and the nonprofessionals' performance couldn't be improved by giving them monetary incentives [432]. Errors made by professionals are a subject of continuing discussion in the industry, but are thought to reflect the examiner's assumptions and preconceptions [81]. As the participants in these tests were given reasonable handwriting samples rather than just a signature, it seems fair to assume that the results for verifying signatures on checks or credit card vouchers would be significantly worse.

So handwritten signatures are surrounded by a number of conventions and special rules which vary from one country to another. For example, to buy a house in England using money borrowed from a bank of which you're not an established customer, the procedure is to go to a lawyer's office with a document such as a passport, sign the property transfer and loan contract, and get the contract countersigned by the lawyer. The requirement for government-issued photo-ID is imposed by the mortgage lender to keep its insurers happy, while the requirement that a purchase of real estate be in writing was imposed by the government some centuries ago in order to collect stamp duty on property transactions. Other types of document (such as expert testimony) may have to be notarized in particular ways. Many curious anomalies go back to the nineteenth century, and the invention of the typewriter. Some countries require that machine-written contracts be initialed on each page, while some don't; and these differences have sometimes persisted for over a century. Clashes in conventions still cause serious problems. In one case, a real estate transaction in Spain was held to be invalid because the deal had been concluded by fax, and a U.K. company went bust as a result.

In most of the English-speaking world, however, most documents do not need to be authenticated by special measures. The essence of a signature is the intent of the signer, so an illiterate's "X" on a document is just as valid as a monarch's flourish. In fact, a plaintext name at the bottom of an email message also has just as much legal force [810], except where there are specific regulations requiring the transaction to be in writing. There may be thousands of such in each jurisdiction. Meanwhile, it's actually very rare for signatures to be disputed in court cases, as the context generally makes it clear who did what. So we have a very weak biometric mechanism that works quite well in practice—except that it's choked by procedural rules that vary by country and by application.

Sorting out this mess, and imposing reasonably uniform rules for electronic documents, is a subject of much international activity. A summary of the issues can be found in [811], with an analysis by country in [68]; and I'll discuss some of the issues further in Part 3. For now, note that the form of a signature, the ease with which it can be forged, and whether it has legal validity in a given context, are largely independent questions.

There is one application, though, where effective automatic recognition of handwritten signatures could be very valuable. This is check clearing.

In a bank's check processing center, it is typical practice that you only verify signatures on checks over a certain amount—perhaps $1,000, perhaps $10,000, perhaps a percentage of the last three months' movement on the account. The signature verification is done by an operator who sees, simultaneously presented on-screen the check image and the customer's reference signature.

Verifying checks for small amounts is not economic unless it can be automated, so a number of researchers have worked on systems to compare handwritten signatures automatically. This turns out to be a very difficult image-processing task because of the variability between one genuine signature and another. A much easier option is to use a *signature tablet*. This is a sensor surface on which the user does a signature; it records not just the shape of the curve but also its dynamics (the velocity of the hand, where the pen was lifted off the paper, and so on). Tablets are used to identify users in some high-value applications, including securities dealing.

Like alarm systems, most biometric systems have a trade-off between false accept and false reject rates, often referred to in the banking industry as the *fraud* and *insult* rates, and in the biometric literature as *type 1* and *type 2* errors. Many systems can be tuned to favor one over the other. The *equal error rate* is when the system is tuned so that the probabilities of false accept and false reject are equal. For common signature recognition systems, the equal error rate is about 1%. This is not fatal in an operation such as a bank dealing room. If one of the dealers tries to log on one morning and his PC rejects his signature, he can just try again. If there is a persistent failure, he can call the system administrator and have the machine reset. However, it is a show-stopper in a retail store. If one transaction in a hundred fails, the aggravation to customers would be unacceptable. So U.K. banks set a target for biometrics of a fraud rate of 1% and an insult rate of 0.01%, which is beyond the current state of the art in signature verification [317].

What can be done to bridge the gap? An interesting experiment was conducted by the University of Kent, England, to cut fraud by welfare claimants who were drawing their benefits at a post office near Southampton. The novel feature of this system is that it was used to screen signatures and to support human decisions, rather than to take decisions itself. So instead of being tuned for a low insult rate, with a correspondingly high fraud rate, it had fraud and insult rates approximately equal. When a signature was rejected, this merely told the staff to look more closely, and to ask for a driver's license or other photo ID. With 8,500 samples taken from 343 customers, 98.2% were verified correctly at the first attempt, rising to 99.15% after three attempts. The experiment was judged to be a success [282]. However, this rate was achieved by excluding *goats*—a term used by the biometric community for people whose templates don't classify well. With them included, the false reject rate was 6.9% [283].

In general, biometric mechanisms tend to be much more robust in attended operations, where they assist a guard rather than replacing him. The false alarm rate may then actually help by keeping the guard alert.

13.3 Face Recognition

Recognizing people by their facial features is the oldest identification mechanism of all, going back at least to our early primate ancestors. Biologists believe that a significant part of our cognitive function evolved to provide efficient ways of recognizing other people's facial features and expressions [646]. For example, we are extremely good at detecting whether another person is looking at us or not. In theory, humans' ability to identify people by their faces appears to be very much better than any automatic system produced to date.

The human ability to recognize faces is also important to the security engineer because of the widespread reliance placed on photo IDs. Drivers' licenses, passports, and other kinds of identity card are not only used directly to control entry to computer rooms, but also bootstrap most other systems. The issue of a password, or a smartcard, or the registration of a user for a biometric system using some other technique such as iris recognition, is often the end point of a process which was started by that person presenting photo ID when applying for a job, opening a bank account, or whatever.

But even if people are good at recognizing friends in the flesh, how good are they at identifying strangers by photo ID?

The simple answer is that they're not. Psychologists at the University of Westminster conducted a fascinating experiment with the help of a supermarket chain and a bank [450]. They recruited 44 students and issued each of them with four credit cards each with a different photograph on it, as follows.

- One of the photos was a "good, good" one. It was genuine and recent.

- The second was a "bad, good one." It was genuine but a bit old; the student now had different clothing, hairstyle, or whatever. In other words, it was typical of the photo that most people have on their photo ID.

- The third was a "good, bad one." From a pile of a hundred or so random photographs of different people, investigators chose the one that most looked like the subject. In other words, it was typical of the match that criminals could get if they had a stack of stolen cards.

- The fourth was a "bad, bad" one. It was chosen at random except that it had the same sex and race as the subject. In other words, it was typical of the match that really lazy, careless criminals would get.

The experiment was conducted in a supermarket after normal business hours, but with experienced cashiers on duty who were aware of the purpose of the experiment. Each student made several trips past the checkout using different cards. It transpired that none of the checkout staff could tell the difference between "good, bad" photos and "bad, good" photos. In fact, some of them could not even tell the difference between "good, good" and "bad, bad." As this experiment was done under optimum conditions—with experienced staff, plenty of time, and no threat of embarrassment or violence if a card was rejected—real-life performance can be expected to be worse. (In fact, many stores do not pass on to their checkout staff the reward offered by credit card companies for capturing stolen cards, so even the basic motivation may be absent.)

The response of the banking industry to this experiment was ambivalent. At least two banks that had experimented with photos on credit cards had experienced a substantial drop in fraud—to less than one percent of the expected amount in the case of one Scottish bank [67]. The overall conclusion was that the benefit to be had from photo ID is essentially its deterrent effect [293].

The extreme difficulty of getting people to use their facial recognition skills effectively is one of the reasons for trying to automate the process. Attempts go back to the nineteenth century, when Galton devised a series of spring-loaded "mechanical selectors" for facial measurements [328]. But automated face recognition actually subsumes a number of separate problems. In identity verification, the subject looks straight at the camera under controlled lighting conditions, and their face is compared with the one on file. A related but harder problem is found in forensics, where we may be trying to establish whether a suspect's face fits a low-quality recording on a security video. The hardest of all is surveillance, where the goal may be to scan a moving crowd of people at an airport and try to pick out anyone who is on a list of perhaps a few hundred known suspects.

Even picking out faces from an image of a crowd is a nontrivial computational task [502]. A recent empirical study of the robustness of different facial feature extraction methods found that, given reasonable variations in lighting, viewpoint, and expression, no method was sufficient by itself, and error rates were up to 20% [10]. Systems that use a combination of techniques can get the error rate down, but not to the 1% or less which is possible with many other biometrics [556, 818].

In short, the technology still does not work very well, when viewed solely in terms of error rates. However, from the system viewpoint, it can work very well indeed. In 1998, the London borough of Newham placed video cameras prominently in the high street and ran a PR campaign about how their new computer system constantly scanned the faces in the crowd for several hundred known local criminals. They managed to get a significant reduction in burglary, shoplifting, and street crime. The system even worries civil libertarians—despite the fact that it appears to work primarily by deterrence [739]. Of course, as time passes and technology improves, both the potential and the worries may increase.

13.4 Fingerprints

Fingerprints are important. By 1998, fingerprint recognition products accounted for 78% of the total sales of biometric technology. These products look at the friction ridges that cover the fingertips and classify patterns of *minutiae*, such as branches and end points of the ridges. Some also look at the pores in the skin of the ridges. A technical description of the leading automatic fingerprint identification systems can be found in [496].

The use of fingerprints to identify people was discovered independently a number of times. Mark Twain mentioned thumbprints in 1883, in *Life on the Mississippi*, where he claims to have learned about them from an old Frenchman who had been a prison-keeper. Long before that, they were accepted in a seventh-century Chinese legal code as an alternative to a seal or a signature; and they were required by an eighth-century Japanese code when an illiterate man wished to divorce his wife. They were mentioned in work by Malpighi in Italy in the seventeenth century; and used in 1691 by 225 citizens of Londonderry in Ireland to sign a petition asking for reparations following the siege of the city by King William.

The first modern systematic use appears to have been in India during the mid-nineteenth century, when William Herschel (grandson of the astronomer) was a colonial official in Hooghly. He used fingerprints to stop impersonation of pensioners who had died, and to prevent rich criminals paying poor people to serve their jail sentences for them. Henry Faulds, a medical missionary in Japan, discovered them independently in the 1870s and brought them to the attention of Darwin, who in turn motivated Galton to work out a scheme for classifying their patterns. His classification, of *loops*, *whorls*, *arches*, and *tents*, is still in use today.

According to the English-language version of history, fingerprints passed into main-stream police use in 1900, when a former police chief from Bengal, Edward Henry, became Commissioner of the Metropolitan Police in London.[1] Henry's contribution was to develop Galton's classification into an indexing system known as *binning*. By assigning one bit to whether or not each of a suspect's 10 fingers had a whorl—a type of circular pattern—he divided the fingerprint files into 1,024 bins. In this way, it was possible to reduce the number of records that have to be searched by orders of magnitude.

Fingerprints are now used by the world's police forces for essentially two different purposes. In the United States, their main use is in identification. FBI files are used to check out arrested suspects to determine whether they're currently wanted by other law enforcement agencies. They are also used to screen job applicants; for example, anyone wanting a U.S. government clearance at Secret or above must have an FBI fingerprint check. They are also used in crime scene forensics. In Europe, where people carry identity cards and identity is thus more readily established, forensics provide the main application.

Fingerprints found at a crime scene are matched against database records. Prints that match to more than a certain level are taken as hard evidence that a suspect visited the crime scene, and are often enough to secure a conviction on their own. In some countries, fingerprints are required from all citizens and all resident foreigners.

To cut the costs of manual fingerprint matching, a number of automated systems have been developed. Algorithms suitable for the image-processing step are surveyed in [522],

---

[1] In the Spanish version, they were first used in Argentina where they secured a murder conviction in 1892; while Cuba, which set up its fingerprint bureau in 1907, beat the United States, whose first conviction was in Illinois in 1911. The Croation version notes that the Argentinian system was developed by one Juan Vucetich, who had emigrated from Dalmatia. The German version refers to Professor Purkinje of Breslau, who wrote about fingerprints in 1828. Indians point to the bureau established in Calcutta in 1898. Success truly has many fathers!

and there is a tutorial plus a description of an IBM system in [415]. While some of these systems simply replace the previous manual classification and matching process, or aim to improve on it [779], others use fingerprint reading devices to authenticate people in real time for applications such as building entry control and benefit payment [258]. They are also used in banking systems in countries such as India and Saudi Arabia, where the use of ink fingerprints was already common thanks to the large proportion of people who are without formal education.

They have not really taken off in banking systems in North America or Europe because of the association with crime, though a few U.S. banks do ask for fingerprints if you cash a check there and are not a customer. They find this cuts check fraud by about a half. Some have gone as far as fingerprinting new customers, and found that customer resistance is less than expected, especially if they use scanners rather than ink and paper [314]. Again, the effect is largely deterrent: matching a single print against the whole FBI database is much harder than typical crime scene work, where the suspects are the hundred or so locally active burglars. Nonetheless, there have been moves to ban the use of fingerprints in U.S. banking as a violation of privacy.

So how good is fingerprint recognition? The error rate in forensic applications can be very low, the limitation being the size and quality of the image taken from the crime scene. It varies from one country to another, depending on police procedures. Britain traditionally required that fingerprints match in 16 *points* (corresponding minutiae), and a U.K. police expert estimated that this will only happen by chance somewhere between one in four billion and one in ten billion matches [485]. Greece accepts 10 matching minutiae, Turkey 8; the United States has no set limit (it certifies examiners instead). This means that in the United States, matches can be found with poorer quality prints, but they can be open to doubt. In Britain, fingerprint evidence went for almost a century without a successful challenge; in the United States, challenges do succeed from time to time, and disputes between rival experts are not unknown.

A recent case has upset the traditional U.K. complacency [538]. Shirley McKie, a Scottish policewoman, was prosecuted on the basis of a fingerprint match on the required 16 points, verified by four examiners of the Scottish Criminal Records Office. The defense called two American examiners who presented testimony that it is not an identification.

McKie was acquitted and, as no indication was made as to whether the jury concurred with the foreign experts or merely considered their testimony as negating the Scottish experts, the Scottish Criminal Records Office asserted for over a year that this was a valid identification. But by June 2000, the matter had gone as far as the Scottish Parliament, and the justice minister himself had to climb down. The problem appears to have been that if they accepted that the fingerprint was not Shirley's, they might also have to release one David Asbury who had been convicted of murder in that case. His fingerprint identification is now also being questioned by experts and an appeal on his behalf is underway [334].

Four comments are in order here.

- Even if the probability of a false match on 16 points is one in ten billion (10^{-10}) as claimed by the police, once many prints are compared against each other, probability theory starts to bite. A system that worked well in the old days, whereby a crime scene print would be compared manually with the records of 57 known local burglars, breaks down once thousands of prints are compared every

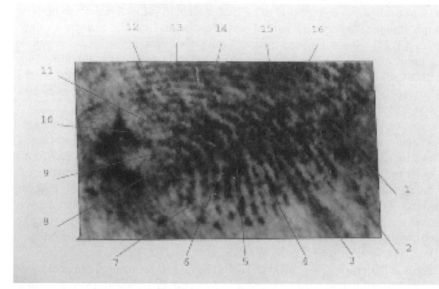

Figure 13.1   Crime scene print.

year with an online database of millions. It was inevitable that, sooner or later, enough matches would have been done to find a 16-point mismatch. Indeed, as most people on the fingerprint database are petty criminals who will not be able to muster the kind of resolute defense that McKie did, I wouldn't be surprised if there had already been other wrongful convictions.

 As Figure 13.1 should make clear, fingerprint impressions are often very "noisy," being obscured by dirt, so mistakes are quite possible. The skill (and prejudices) of the examiner enter into the equation in a much more significant way than a naive jury might think. The errors caused by noise can manifest themselves at more than one level. For example, binning error rates are believed to cause a false reject rate of several percent [154].

■ The belief that any security mechanism is infallible generates the complacency and carelessness needed to undermine its proper use. No consideration appears to have been given to increasing the number of points required from 16 to, say, 20, with the introduction of computer matching. Sixteen was tradition, the system was infallible, and there was certainly no reason to make public funds available for defendants to hire their own experts. In fact, as all the U.K. experts are policemen or former policemen, there are no independent experts available for hire.

■ A belief of infallibility ensures that the consequences of the eventual failure will be severe. As with the Munden case described in Section 9.4.3, which helped torpedo claims about cash machine security, an assumption that a security mechanism is infallible causes procedures, cultural assumptions, and even laws to spring up which ensure that its eventual failure will be denied for as long as possible, and may have disastrous effects for the individuals involved.

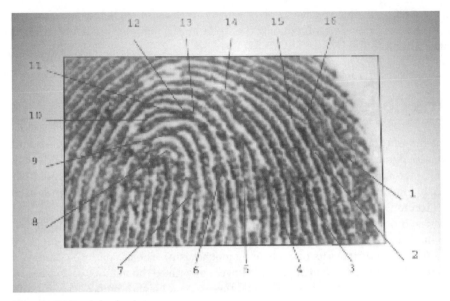

Figure 13.2 Inked print.

However, even when we do have a correct match (with 20, or 24, or however many points), its implications are not entirely obvious. It is possible for fingerprints to be transferred using adhesive tape, or for molds to be made—even without the knowledge of the target—using techniques originally devised for police use. So it is possible that the suspect whose print is found at the crime scene was framed by another criminal (or by the police—most fingerprint fabrication cases involve law enforcement personnel rather than other suspects [110]). Of course, even if the villain wasn't framed, he can always claim that he was and the jury might believe him.

Moving now to automated identification, the better systems have an equal error rate which seems to be somewhat below 1%. Although in theory the false accept probability can be made arbitrarily small, in practice false accepts happen because of features incorporated to reduce the false reject rate—such as allowance for distortion and flexibility in feature selection [650].

Fingerprint damage can also impair recognition. When I was a kid, I slashed my finger while cutting an apple, and this left a scar about half an inch long on my left middle finger. When I presented this finger to the system used in 1989 by the FBI for building entry control, my scar crashed the scanner. (It was registered and worked OK with the successor system from the same company when I tried again 10 years later.) But even where scars don't cause gross system malfunctions, they still increase the error rate. A number of people, such as manual workers and pipe smokers, damage their fingerprints frequently; and both the young and the old have faint prints [171]. Automated systems also have problems with amputees, people with birth defects such as extra fingers, and the (rare) people born without conventional fingerprint patterns at all [485].

Perhaps the most important aspect of fingerprint systems is not their error rate, as measured under laboratory conditions, but their deterrent effect. This is particularly pronounced in welfare payment systems. Even though the fingerprint readers used to authenticate welfare claimants have an error rate as much as 5% [163], they have turned out to be such an effective way of reducing the welfare rolls that they are being adopted in one place after another [553].

13.5 Iris Codes

We turn now from the very traditional ways of identifying people to the modern and innovative. Recognizing people by the patterns in the irises of their eyes is far and away the technique with the best error rates of automated systems when measured under lab conditions. It appears to be the most secure possible way of controlling entry to premises such as plutonium stores.

As far as is known, every human iris is measurably unique. It is fairly easy to detect in a video picture, does not wear out, and is isolated from the external environment by the cornea (which in turn has its own cleaning mechanism). The iris pattern contains a large amount of randomness, and appears to have many times the number of degrees of freedom of a fingerprint. It is formed between the third and eighth month of gestation, and (like the fingerprint pattern) is *phenotypic* in that there appears to be limited genetic influence; the mechanisms that form it appear to be chaotic. So the patterns are different even for identical twins (and for the two eyes of a single individual), and they appear to be stable throughout life.

A signal processing technique (Gabor filters) has been found which extracts the information from an image of the iris into a 256-byte *iris code*. This involves a circular wavelet transform taken at a number of concentric rings between the pupil and the outside of the iris (Figure 13.3), and has the beautiful property that two codes computed from the same iris will typically match in 90% of their bits [218]. This is much simpler than in fingerprint scanners where orienting and classifying the minutiae is a hard task. The speed and accuracy of iris coding has led to a number of commercial iris recognition products [794]. Iris codes provide the lowest false accept rates of any known verification system—zero, in tests conducted by the U.S. Department of Energy. The equal error rate has been shown to be better than one in a million, and if one is prepared to tolerate a false reject rate of one in ten thousand, then the theoretical false accept rate would be less than one in a trillion.

The main practical problem facing deployment of iris scanning in the field is getting the picture without being too intrusive. The iris is small (less than half an inch) and an image including several hundred pixels of iris is needed. A cooperative subject can place his eye within a few inches of a video camera, and the best standard equipment will work up to a distance of two or three feet. Cooperation can be assumed with entry control to computer rooms, but it is less acceptable in general retail applications, as some people find being so close to a camera uncomfortable. There's no technical reason why a camera could not acquire the iris from a distance of several feet given automatic facial feature recognition, pan and zoom—it would just cost a bit more—but that brings Orwellian overtones of automatic recognition of individuals passing in a crowd. (In Europe, data protection law would be a potential show-stopper.) Secondary problems include blinking, eyelashes obscuring the eye, and sunglasses.

Possible attacks on iris recognition systems include—in unattended operation at least—a simple photograph of the target's iris. This may not be a problem in entry control

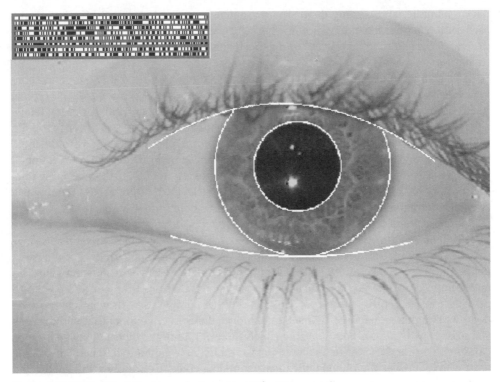

Figure 13.3   An iris with iris code (courtesy John Daugman).

to supervised premises, but if everyone starts to use iris codes to authenticate bank card transactions, then your code will become known to many organizations. As iris codes can be compared rapidly (just exclusive-or them together and count the number of zero bits), they may start to assume the properties of names, rather than being passwords (as in current systems). So it might be possible to use your iris code to link together your dealings with different organizations.

A possible solution to the impersonation problem is to design terminals that measure *hippus*—a natural fluctuation in the diameter of the pupil which happens at about 0.5 Hz. But even this isn't infallible. One might try, for example, to print the target's iris patterns on contact lenses (though existing vanity contact lens printing techniques are so coarse-grained that they are detectable).

Despite the difficulties, iris codes remain a very strong contender as they can, in the correct circumstances, provide much greater certainty than any other method that the individual in question is the same as the one who was initially registered on the system. They can meet the goal of automatic recognition with zero false acceptances.

13.6 Voice Recognition

Voice recognition—also known as *speaker recognition*—is the problem of identifying a speaker from a short utterance. While *speech recognition* systems are concerned with transcribing speech and need to ignore speech idiosyncrasies, voice recognition systems need to amplify and classify them. There are many subproblems, such as whether the recognition is text-dependent or not, whether the environment is noisy, whether operation must be real time, and whether one needs only to verify speakers or to recognize them from a large set.

In *forensic phonology*, the objective is, usually, to match a recorded telephone conversation, such as a bomb threat, to speech samples from a number of suspects. Typical techniques involve filtering and extracting features from the spectrum; for more details see [461]. A more straightforward biometric authentication objective is to verify a claim to identity in some telephone systems. These range from telephone banking to the identification of military personnel, with over a dozen systems on the market. Campbell describes a system that can be used with the U.S. government STU-III encrypting telephone, and that achieves an equal error rate of about 1% [161]; and the NSA maintains a standard corpus of test data for evaluating speaker recognition systems [414].

There are some interesting attacks on these systems, quite apart from the possibility that a villain might somehow manage to train himself to imitate your voice in a manner that the equipment finds acceptable. In [324] there is a brief description of a system fielded in US EP-3 aircraft which breaks up intercepted messages from enemy aircraft and ground controllers into quarter second segments that are then cut and pasted to provide new, deceptive messages. This is primitive compared with what can now be done with digital signal processing. Some informed observers expect that within a few years, there will be products available which support real-time voice and image forgery. Crude voice morphing systems already exist, and enable female victims of telephone sex pests to answer the phone with a male sounding voice. Better ones will enable call centers to have the same 'person' always greet you when you phone. With that sort of commercial pressure driving the technology, it's only a matter of time before remote biometrics become very much harder.

13.7 Other Systems

A number of other biometric technologies have been proposed. For a survey of the market, see [553]. Some, such as those based on *facial thermograms* (maps of the surface temperature of the face, derived from infrared images), the shape of the ear, gait, lip prints, and the patterns of veins in the hand, don't seem to have been marketed as products. Other technologies may provide interesting biometrics in the future. For example, the huge investment in developing digital noses for quality control in the food and drink industries may lead to a "digital doggie," which recognizes its master by scent.

Others biometric techniques, such as typing patterns, were used in products in the 1980s but don't appear to have been successful (typing patterns, also known as keystroke dynamics, had a famous precursor in the wartime technique of identifying wireless telegraphy operators by their *fist*, the way in which they used a Morse key).

Still others, such as hand geometry, have useful niche markets. In addition to its use since the 1970s in nuclear premises entry control, hand geometry is now used at airports by the U.S. Immigration and Naturalization Service to provide a "fast track" for frequent flyers. It is fairly robust, with an equal error rate under lab conditions of 0.1–0.2%.

(In fact, hand geometry derives from *anthropometrics*, a system of identifying criminals by skeletal measurements, which was introduced in Paris in 1882 by Alphonse Bertillon, but replaced by fingerprints a generation later.)

One other biometric deserves passing mention—the use of DNA typing. This has become a valuable tool for crime-scene forensics and for determining parenthood in child support cases, but is too slow for applications such as building entry control. Being genotypic rather than phenotypic, its accuracy is also limited by the incidence of monozygotic twins—about one white person in 120 has an identical twin. There's also a privacy problem, in that it should soon be possible to reconstruct a large amount of information about an individual from their DNA sample. For a survey of forensic DNA analysis techniques, and suggestions of how to make national DNA databases consistent with European data protection law, see [680].

13.8 What Goes Wrong

As with other aspects of security, we find the usual crop of failures due to bugs, blunders, and complacency. The main problem faced by DNA typing, for example, was an initially high rate of false positives, due to careless laboratory procedure. This not only scared off some police forces, which had sent in samples from different volunteers and got back false matches, but also led to disputed court cases and alleged miscarriages of justice.

Biometrics are like many other protection mechanisms (alarms, seals, tamper-sensing enclosures, ...) in that environmental conditions can cause havoc. Noise, dirt, vibration, and unreliable lighting conditions all take their toll. Some systems, like speaker recognition, are vulnerable to alcohol intake and stress. Changes in environmental assumptions, such as from closed to open systems, from small systems to large ones, from attended to standalone, from cooperative to recalcitrant subjects, and from verification to identification—can all undermine a system's viability.

There are a number of more specific and interesting attacks on various biometric systems.

- There have been some attacks on the methods used to index biometric data. The classic one is the helpful villain who gives an inexperienced policeman his fingerprints in the wrong order, so that instead of the hand being indexed under the Henry system as '01101' it becomes perhaps '01011', so his record isn't found and he gets the lighter sentence due a first offender [485].

- Forensic biometrics often don't tell as much as one might assume. Apart from the possibility that a fingerprint or DNA sample might have been planted by the police, it may just be old. The age of a fingerprint can't be determined directly, and prints on areas with public access say little. A print on a bank door says much less than a print in a robbed vault. So in premises vulnerable to robbery, cleaning procedures may be critical for evidence. If a suspect's prints are found on a bank counter, and she claims to have gone there three days previously, she may be convicted by evidence that the branch counter is polished every evening. Putting this in system terms, freshness is often a critical issue, and some quite unexpected things can find themselves inside the "trusted computing base."

- Another aspect of freshness is that most biometric systems can, at least in theory, be attacked using suitable recordings. We mentioned direct attacks on voice recognition, attacks on iris scanners by photos on a contact lens, and molds of fingerprints. Even simpler still, in countries where fingerprints are used to pay pensions, there are persistent tales of "Granny's finger in the pickle jar" being the most valuable property she bequeathed to her family. This reinforces the lesson that unattended operation of biometric authentication devices is tricky.

- Certain systems—notably handwriting systems—are vulnerable to collusion. Villains can voluntarily degrade handwriting ability. By giving several slightly different childish sample signatures, they can force the machine to accept a lower threshold than usual. The kind of attack to expect is that Alice opens a bank account and her accomplice Betty withdraws money from it; Alice then complains of theft and produces a watertight alibi. As with alarm and shared control systems, commercial users have to worry about colluding employees or customers, while the military threat model is usually just the single disloyal soldier.

- Commercial system builders must also worry about false repudiation—such as whether a user who practices enough can generate two signatures that pass for identical on the signature tablet, even if they are visually quite different.

- The statistics are often not understood by system designers, and the birthday theorem is particularly poorly appreciated. With 10,000 biometrics in a database, for example, there are about 50,000,000 pairs. So even with a false accept rate of only one in a million, the likelihood of there being at least one false match will rise above one-half as soon as there are somewhat over a thousand people (in fact, 1,609 people) enrolled. So identification is a tougher task than verification [219]. The practical consequence is that a system designed for authentication may fail when you try to rely on it for evidence. A good way to explain to judges, and other non-technical people, why the system error rate differs from the single sample error rate is that there is "one chance to get it right, but N chances to get it wrong." For a good discussion of error rates see [154].

- Another aspect of statistics comes into play when designers assume that by combining biometrics they can get a lower error rate. The curious and perhaps counter-intuitive result is that a combination will typically result in improving either the false accept or the false reject rate, while making the other worse. One way to look at this is that if you install two different burglar alarm systems at your home, then the probability that they will be simultaneously defeated goes down while the number of false alarms goes up. In some cases, such as when a very good biometric is combined with a very imprecise one, the effect can be worse overall [219].

- Most biometrics are not as accurate for all people, and some of the population can't be identified as reliably as the rest (or even at all). The elderly, and manual workers, often have damaged or abraded fingerprints. People with dark-colored eyes and large pupils give poorer iris codes. Disabled people, with no fingers or no eyes, risk exclusion if such systems become widespread. Illiterates who make an "X" are more at risk from signature forgery.

Biometric engineers sometimes refer to such subjects dismissively as goats, but this is blind to political reality. A biometric system that is (or is seen to be) socially regressive—in that it puts the disabled, the poor, the old, and ethnic minorities at greater risk of impersonation—may meet with principled resistance. In fact, a biometric system might be defeated by legal challenges on a number of grounds [626]. It may also be vulnerable to villains who are (or pretend to be) disabled. Fallback modes of operation will have to be provided; if these are less secure, then forcing their use may yield an attack, and if they are at least as secure, then why use biometrics at all?

■ Finally, Christian fundamentalists are uneasy about biometric technology. They find written of the Antichrist in Revelation 13:16-18: "And he causes all, both small and great, rich and poor, free and slave, to receive a mark on their right hand or on their foreheads, and that no one may buy or sell except one who has the mark or the name of the beast, or the number of his name." So biometrics can arouse political opposition on the right as well as the left.

So there are some non-trivial problems to be overcome before biometrics will be ready for mass-market use, in the way that magnetic strip cards are used at present. But despite the cost and the error rates, they have proved their worth in a number of applications, most notably where their deterrent effect is useful.

13.9 Summary

Biometric measures of one kind or another have been used to identify people since ancient times, with handwritten signatures, facial features, and fingerprints being the traditional methods. Systems have been built that automate the task of recognition, using these methods and newer ones, such as hand geometry, voiceprints, and iris patterns. These systems have different strengths and weaknesses. In automatic operation, most have error rates of the order of 1% (though iris recognition is better, hand geometry slightly better, and face recognition worse). There is always a trade-off between the false accept rate (the fraud rate) and the false reject rate (the insult rate). The statistics of error rates are deceptively difficult.

If any biometric becomes very widely used, there is increased risk of forgery in unattended operation: voice synthesizers, photographs of irises, fingerprint molds, and even good old-fashioned forged signatures must all be thought of in system design. These do not rule out the use of biometrics, as traditional methods such as handwritten signatures are usable in practice despite very high error rates. Biometrics are usually more powerful in attended operation, where, with good system design, the relative strengths and weaknesses of the human guard and the machine recognition system may complement one another. Finally, many biometric systems achieve most or all of their result by deterring criminals rather than being effective at identifying them.

Research Problems

Potentially profitable research problems relate to the design, or improvement, of biometric systems. Is it possible to build a system—other than iris scanning—that will meet the banks' goal of a 1% fraud rate and a 0.01% insult rate? Is it possible to build a static signature verification system that has a good enough error rate (say 1%) for it to be used for screening images of checks? Are there any completely new biometrics that might be useful in some circumstances?

One I thought up while writing this chapter, in a conversation with William Clocksin and Alan Blackwell, was instrumenting a car so as to identify a driver by the way in which he or she operated the gears and the clutch. This might be hooked in to a high-end car alarm system of the kind that, if your car appears to be stolen, phones a GPS fix to a control center which then calls you to check. We haven't patented this; if you can make it work, all we ask is an acknowledgment—and some thought about how to prevent insurance companies (and governments) demanding access to the data!

Further Reading

The history of fingerprints is good reading. The standard reference is Lambourne [485], while Block has a good collection of U.S. case histories [120]. In addition to the references cited for facial and handwriting recognition in the text, there's an IBM experimental system described at [433] and a survey of the literature at [181]. The standard work on iris codes is Daugman [218]. For voice recognition, there is a tutorial in [161] which focuses on speaker identification while for the forensic aspects, see Klevans and Rodman [461]. A special issue of the *Proceedings of the IEEE* on biometric systems—volume 85 no 9 (September 1997) provides a very useful snapshot of the state of the technical art. Finally, for technical detail on a range of systems, there is a book by Anil Jain, Ruud Bolle, and Sharath Pankanti which contains chapters on a number of biometric system written by their designers [414].

CHAPTER 14

Physical Tamper Resistance

It is relatively easy to build an encryption system that is secure if it is working as intended and is used correctly but it is still very hard to build a system that does not compromise its security in situations in which it is either misused or one or more of its sub-components fails (or is 'encouraged' to misbehave) ... this is now the only area where the closed world is still a long way ahead of the open world and the many failures we see in commercial cryptographic systems provide some evidence for this.

—BRIAN GLADMAN

14.1 Introduction

The techniques discussed in the previous few chapters—physical protection involving barriers, sensors, and alarms—are often used to protect critical information processing resources:

- A bank's main servers will typically be kept in a guarded computer room.
- The seismic sensor packages used to detect unlawful nuclear tests may be at the bottom of a borehole several hundred feet deep which is backfilled with concrete.
- A hole-in-the-wall automatic teller machine is in effect a PC in a one-ton safe with a number of fancy peripherals. These include not just banknote dispensers but also temperature sensors to detect attempts to cut into the device, and accelerometers to detect if it's moved. An alarm should cause the immediate erasure of all crypto key material in the device.

But often it's inconvenient to use a massive construction, and this has spawned a market for portable tamper-resistant processors. These range from smartcards, which typically perform a limited set of operations in support of an application such as pay-TV; through tamper-resistant cryptoprocessors, which are fitted into the servers that manage PINs in cash machine networks; to elaborate high-end devices used in military command and control.

I should note that there is some similarity between tamper-resistant devices and replicated devices. If a service is implemented as a number of different servers in different sites that perform transactions simultaneously and vote on the result, then it may be possible to provide a high level of integrity protection against many types of attack. The secret sharing schemes I discussed in Section 11.4 can also provide confidentiality for key material. But tamper-resistant devices can at least in theory provide confidentiality for the data too. This is one respect in which the principle that many things can be done either with mathematics or with metal, breaks down.

14.2 History

The use of tamper resistance in cryptography goes back for centuries [428]. Naval codebooks have been weighted so they could be thrown overboard and sink in the event of imminent capture; to this day, the dispatch boxes used by British government ministers' aides to carry state papers are lead-lined so they will sink. Codes and, more recently, the keys for wartime cipher machines have been printed in water-soluble ink; Russian one-time pads were printed on cellulose nitrate, so that they would burn furiously if lit; and one U.S. wartime cipher machine came with self-destruct thermite charges so it could be destroyed quickly if need be.

But such mechanisms depended on the vigilance of the operator, and key material was often captured in surprise attacks. So attempts were made to automate the process. Early electronic devices, as well as some mechanical ciphers, were built so that opening the case erased the key settings.

Following a number of cases in which cipher staff sold key material to the other side—such as the notorious Walker family in the United States—engineers paid more attention to the question of how to protect keys in transit as well as in the terminal equipment itself. The goal was 'to reduce the street value of key material to zero', and this can be achieved either by *tamper resistant* devices from which the key cannot be extracted, or *tamper evident* ones from which key extraction would be obvious.

Paper keys were once carried in "tattle-tale containers," designed to show evidence of tampering. When electronic key distribution came along, a typical solution was the "fill gun," a portable device that would dispense crypto keys in a controlled way. Nowadays, this function is usually performed using a small security processor such as a smartcard. Control protocols range from a limit on the number of times a key can be dispensed, to mechanisms that use public key cryptography to ensure that keys are loaded only into authorized equipment. The control of key material also acquired broader purposes. In both the United States and Britain, it was centralized and used to enforce the use of properly approved computer and communications products. Live key material would only be supplied to a system once it had been properly accredited.

Once initial keys have been loaded, further keys may be distributed using various kinds of authentication and key agreement protocols. I already talked about many of the basic tools, such as key diversification, in Chapter 2, "Protocols," and I'll have more to say on protocols later in this chapter. Let's first look at the physical defenses against tampering.

14.3 High-End Physically Secure Processors

An example worth studying is the IBM 4758 (Figure 14.1). This is important for two reasons. First, it is the only commercially available processor to have been successfully evaluated (at the time of writing) to the highest level of tamper resistance (FIPS 140-1 level 4) [576] set by the U.S. government. Second, there is extensive literature about it available in the public domain, including the history of its design evolution, its protection mechanisms, and the transaction set it supports [718, 795, 796].

The evolution that led to this product is briefly as follows. From the earliest days of computing, computers were protected physically because of their high value. However, the spread of multi-user operating systems in the 1960s, and the regularity with which bugs were found in their protection mechanisms, meant that large numbers of people might potentially have access to the data being processed. With particularly sensitive data—such as long-term cryptographic keys and the personal identification numbers (PINs) used by bank customers to identify themselves to cash machines—it was realized that the level of protection available from commercial operating systems was likely to remain insufficient.

Figure 14.1   The IBM 4758 cryptoprocessor (courtesy of Steve Weingart).

Figure 14.2 The 4758 partially opened, showing (from top left downward) the circuitry, aluminium electromagnetic shielding, tamper-sensing mesh and potting material (courtesy of Frank Stajano).

This led to the development of standalone *security modules* of which the first to be commercially successful were the IBM 3848 and the VISA security module. Both of these were microcomputers encased in robust metal enclosures, with encryption hardware and special *key memory*, which was static RAM designed to be zeroized when the enclosure was opened (Figure 14.2). This was accomplished by wiring the power supply to the key memory through a number of lid switches. The device operator would then have to reload the key material.

How to Hack a Cryptoprocessor (1)

The obvious attack on such a device is for the operator to steal the keys. In early banking security modules, the master keys were kept in PROMs which were loaded into a special socket in the device, to be read during initialization, or as strings of numbers that were typed in at a console. The PROMs could easily be pocketed, taken home and read out using hobbyist equipment. Cleartext paper keys were even easier to steal.

The fix was shared control—to have two or three PROMs with master keys, and make the device master keys the exclusive-or of all the components. These devices can then be kept in different safes. (With the virtue of hindsight, the use of exclusive-or for this purpose was an error, and a hash function should have been used instead. I'll explain why shortly.)

However, this procedure is somewhat tedious, and may well degrade as it becomes routine. In theory, when a device is maintained, its custodians should open the lid to erase the live keys, let the maintenance engineer load test keys, and then re-load live keys afterwards. But the managers with custodial responsibility will often give the PROMs to the engineer rather than bothering with them. I've even come across cases of the master keys for an automatic teller machine being kept in the correspondence file in a bank branch, where any of the staff could look them up. Thus, the goal was to minimize the number of times that a reload would be necessary, such as for maintenance or following a power failure. So security modules typically have batteries to back up the mains power supply (at least to the key memory). This meant that in practice, the custodians had to load the keys only when the device was first installed, and after occasional maintenance visits subsequently.

It has been debated whether frequent or infrequent key loading is best. If key loading is very infrequent, the responsible personnel will likely never have performed the task before, and may either delegate it out of ignorance or be hoodwinked by a more technically astute member of staff into doing it in an insecure way (see [19] for a case history of this). The modern trend is toward devices that generate keys (or have them loaded) in a secure facility after manufacture but before distribution. Such keys may be kept on smartcards and used to bootstrap the keying of more substantial devices.

How to Hack a Cryptoprocessor (2)

Early devices were vulnerable to attackers cutting through the casing, and to maintenance engineers who could disable the lid switches on one visit and extract the keys on the next. Second-generation devices dealt with the easier of these problems, namely physical attack, by adding more sensors such as photocells and tilt switches. These may be enough for a device kept in a secure area to which access is controlled. But the hard problem is to prevent attacks by the maintenance staff.

The strategy adopted by many of the better products is to separate all the components that can be serviced (such as batteries) from the core of the device (such as the tamper sensors, crypto, processor, key memory, and alarm circuitry). The core is then "potted" in a solid block of a hard, opaque substance such as epoxy. The idea is that any physical attack will be "obvious" in that it involves an action such as cutting or drilling, which can be detected by the guard who accompanies the maintenance technician into the bank computer room.

How to Hack a Cryptoprocessor (3)

However, if a competent person can get unsupervised access to the device for even a short period of time (or if the guard has not been properly trained), then potting the device core is inadequate. For example, it is often possible to scrape away the potting with a knife, and drop the probe from a logic analyzer on to one of the bus lines in the core. Most common cryptographic algorithms, such as RSA and DES, have the property that an attacker who can monitor any bitplane during the computation can recover the key [370]. So an attacker who can get a probe anywhere into the device while it is operating can likely extract secret key material.

So the high-end products have a tamper-sensing barrier whose penetration triggers destruction of the secrets inside. An early example appeared in IBM's μABYSS system in the mid-1980s. This used loops of 40-gauge nichrome wire, which were wound loosely around the device as it was embedded in epoxy, then connected to a sensing circuit [795]. Bulk removal techniques such as milling, etching, and laser ablation break the wire, which erases the keys. But the wire-in-epoxy technique can be vulnerable to slow erosion using sand blasting; when the sensing wires become visible at the surface of the potting, shunts can be connected around them. So the next major product from IBM, the 4753, used a metal shield combined with a membrane printed with a pattern of conductive ink and surrounded by a more durable material of similar chemistry. The idea was that any attack would break the membrane with high probability.

How to Hack a Cryptoprocessor (4)

The next class of methods an attacker can try involve the exploitation of *memory remanence*, the fact that many kinds of computer memory retain some trace of data that have been stored there. Sometimes, all that is necessary is that the same data were stored for a long time. An attacker might bribe the garbage truck operator to obtain a bank's discarded security modules: as reported in [44], once a certain security module had been operated for some years using the same master keys, the values of these keys were *burned in* to the device's static RAM. On power-up, about 90% of the relevant bits would assume the values of the corresponding keybits, which was more than enough to recover the keys.

Memory remanence affects not just static and dynamic RAM, but other storage media as well. For example, the heads of a disk drive change alignment over time, so that it may be impossible to completely overwrite data that were first written some time ago. The relevant engineering and physics issues are discussed in [362]. The NSA has published guidelines (the *Forest Green Book*) on preventing remanence attacks [243].

The better third-generation devices have *RAM savers*, which function in much the same way as screen savers; they move data around the RAM to prevent it being burned in anywhere.

How to Hack a Cryptoprocessor (5)

A further problem is that computer memory can be frozen by low temperatures. By the 1980s it was realized that below about $-20°$C, static RAM contents can persist for some time—seconds to minutes—after power is removed. Data remanence gets steadily longer at lower temperatures. So an attacker might freeze a device, remove the power, cut through the tamper sensing barrier, extract the RAM chips containing the keys and power them up again in a test rig. RAM contents can also be *burned in* by ionizing radiation. (For the memory chips of the 1980s, this required a fairly serious industrial X-ray machine; but as far as I'm aware, no-one has tested the current, much smaller, memory chip designs.)

So the better devices have temperature and radiation alarms. These can be difficult to implement properly, as modern RAM chips exhibit a wide variety of memory remanence behaviors, with the worst of them keeping data for several seconds even at room temperature [712]. (This shows the dangers of relying on a property of some component to whose manufacturer the control of this property is unimportant.) Some military devices use protective detonation; there are memory chips potted in steel cans with a thermite charge precisely calculated to destroy the chip without causing gas release from the can.

How to Hack a Cryptoprocessor (6)

The next set of attacks on cryptographic hardware involve either monitoring the RF and other electromagnetic signals emitted by the device, or even injecting signals into it and measuring their externally visible effects. This technique, which is variously known as *Tempest* or *power analysis*, is such a large subject that I devote the next chapter to it. As far as the 4758 is concerned, the strategy is to have solid aluminium shielding, and to low-pass-filter the power supply to block the egress of any signals at the frequencies used internally for computation.

The 4758 also has an improved tamper-sensing membrane, in which four overlapping zig-zag conducting patterns are doped into a urethane sheet, which in turn is potted in a chemically similar substance so that an attacker cutting into the device has difficulty even detecting the conductive path, let alone connecting to it. This potting surrounds the metal shielding which in turn contains the cryptographic core (see Figure 14.2). The design is described more detail in [718].

I don't know how to attack the hardware of the 4758. IBM declined to sell us samples for attack, but we did come up with a number of ideas after scrutinizing one, such as:

How to Hack a Cryptoprocessor (7)

Here are some speculative ideas about how to break into a 4758.

- The straightforward approach would be to devise some way to erode the protective potting, detect mesh lines, and connect shunts around them. Probably the first thing I'd try is a magnetic force microscope.

- One could invent a means of drilling holes eight millimeters long and only 0.1 millimeters wide (that is, much less than the mesh line diameter). This isn't feasible with current mechanical drills, which are limited to an aspect ratio of 15 or so, and the same holds for laser ablation and ion milling. However I speculate that some combination of nanotechnology and ideas from the oil industry might make such a drill possible eventually. Then one could drill right through the protective mesh with a fair probability of not breaking the circuit.

- Having dismantled a few instances of the device and understood the operation of its hardware, the attacker might use shaped explosive charges to send plasma jets of the kind discussed in Section 11.5 into the device to destroy the tamper-sensing and memory zeroization circuitry before they have time to react.

The success of such attacks is uncertain, and they are likely to remain beyond the resources of the average villain for some time.

When I shipped the first draft of this book in September 2000, I wrote at this point: "So by far the most likely attacks on 4758 based systems involve the exploitation of logical rather than physical flaws." By the time I edited this paragraph at the proof stage, this had come true in spades. Most users of the 4758 use an application called CCA which is described in [388] and contains many features that make it difficult to use properly. Having been suspicious of the complexity of this instruction set, I passed the manual to a new research student, Mike Bond, and asked him if he could find any vulnerabilities. By the middle of November, he had found a number of problems, including a protocol-level attack that enables a capable opponent to extract all the interesting keys from the device. We'll discuss this attack below.

Finally, it should be mentioned that the main constraints on the design and manufacture of security processors are remarkably similar to those encountered with more general alarms. There is a trade-off between the false alarm rate and the missed alarm rate, and thus between security and robustness. Security processors often need to be handled with care; if they self-destruct at temperatures of −20°C, they cannot be distributed through normal computer industry channels, where goods are often subjected to −40°C in winter. Vibration, power transients, and electromagnetic interference can also be a problem with some designs. Military equipment makers have a particularly tough problem. For example, if exposing the crypto processor of a military tactical radio to radiation causes it to self-destruct, then hardening the device sufficiently might make it too heavy to carry.

14.4 Evaluation

A few comments about the evaluation of tamper-resistant devices are in order before we go on to discuss cheaper devices.

The IBM paper that describes the design of the 4758's predecessor, the 4753 [4], proposed the following classification scheme for attackers:

1. Class 1 attackers—'clever outsiders'—are often very intelligent but may have insufficient knowledge of the system. They may have access to only moderately sophisticated equipment. They often try to take advantage of an existing weakness in the system, rather than try to create one.

2. Class 2 attackers—'knowledgeable insiders'—have substantial specialized technical education and experience. They have varying degrees of understanding of parts of the system but potential access to most of it. They often have highly sophisticated tools and instruments for analysis.

3. Class 3 attackers—'funded organizations'—are able to assemble teams of specialists with related and complementary skills backed by great funding resources. They are capable of in-depth analysis of the system, designing sophisticated attacks, and using the most advanced analysis tools. They may use class 2 adversaries as part of the attack team.

Within this scheme, the 4753 was aimed at blocking knowledgeable insiders, while its successor, the 4758, is aimed at (and certified for) blocking funded organizations.

The FIPS certification scheme is operated by laboratories licensed by the U.S. government and set out in the FIPS 140-1 standard. This sets out four levels of protection, with level 4 being the highest (currently, the 4758 is the only device certified at this level). There is a large gap between level 4 and the next one down, level 3, where only potting is required; this means that attacks which exploiting electromagnetic leakage, memory remanence, drilling, sandblasting, and so on may still be possible. I have handled a level 3 certified device from which I could scrape off the potting with my Swiss army knife! So while FIPS 140-1 level 3 devices can be (and have been) defeated by class 1 attackers in the IBM sense, the next step up—FIPS 140-1 level 4—is expected to keep out an IBM class 3 opponent. There is no FIPS level corresponding to a defense against IBM's class 2.

The original paper on levels of evaluation, written by IBM engineers, had proposed six levels [796]; the FIPS standard adopted the first three of these as its levels 1–3, and the proposed level 6 as its level 4. The gap, commonly referred to as "level 3.5," is where many of the better commercial systems are aimed. Such equipment certainly attempts to keep out the class 1 attack community, while making life hard for class 2, and expensive for class 3.

That said, I am not convinced that the IBM classification is correct. I know of one large funded organization that bought chip-testing equipment, tried to break into a smartcard, and failed; they concluded that smartcards were completely tamper-proof. However, as we shall see shortly, many smartcards have been broken by level 1 attackers. The persistence and cunning of the attacker is far more important than the number of people on his employer's payroll.

14.5 Medium-Security Processors

Good examples of level 3.5 products are the iButton and 5002 security processors from Dallas Semiconductor, and the Capstone chip used to protect U.S. military communications up to Secret. While the 4758 costs $2000, these products cost of the order of $10–20. Yet mounting an attack on them is far from trivial.

14.5.1 The iButton

The iButton from Dallas Semiconductor is designed to be a minimal, self-contained cryptographic processor. It has an 8051 microcontroller with a modular exponentiation circuit, static RAM for keys and software, a clock, and tamper sensors. These are encased in a steel can with a lithium battery, which can maintain keys in the RAM for a design life of 10 years (see Figure 14.3). It is small enough to be worn in a signet ring or

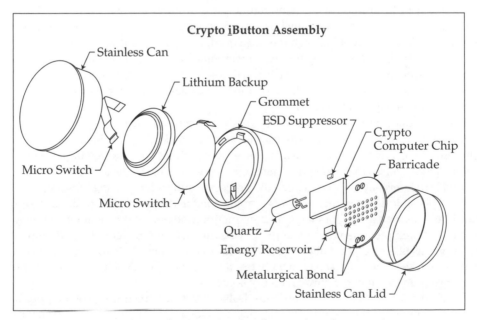

Figure 14.3   iButton internals (courtesy of Dallas Semiconductor Inc.).

carried as a key fob. An early application was as an access token for the "Electronic Red Box", a secure laptop system designed for use by U.K. government ministers. To access secret documents, the minister had to press his signet ring into a reader at the side of the laptop. (One of the design criteria had been: "Ministers shall not have to use passwords.") Other applications include the İstanbul mass transit system, parking meters in Argentina, and the electronic stamps for the U.S. Postal Service that I mentioned in the previous chapter [753]. The device is now being equipped with a Java interpreter, and marketed as the Java ring, a tamper-resistant device that users can program for their own applications.

How might an iButton be attacked? The most obvious difference from the 4758 is the lack of a tamper-sensing barrier. So one might try drilling in through the side, then either probe the device in operation or disable the tamper-sensing circuitry. Because the iButton has lid switches to detect the can being opened, and its processor is mounted upside-down on the circuit board (with a mesh in the top metal layer of the chip), this is unlikely to be a trivial exercise. It might well involve building custom jigs and tools. In short, it's a tempting target for the next bright graduate student who wants to win their spurs as a hardware hacker.

14.5.2 The Dallas 5002

Another medium-grade security device from Dallas is the DS5002 microcontroller, which is widely used in devices such as point-of-sale terminals, where it holds the keys used to encrypt customer PINs.

The ingenious idea behind this device is *bus encryption*. The chip has added hardware that encrypts memory addresses and contents on the fly as data are loaded and stored. This means that the device can operate with external memory, and is not limited to the small amount of RAM that can be fitted into a low-cost tamper-sensing package. Each device has a unique master key, which is generated at random when it is powered up. The software is then loaded through the serial port, encrypted, and written to external memory. The device is then ready for use. Power must be maintained constantly, or the internal register that holds the master key will lose it; this also happens if a physical tampering event is sensed (like the iButton, the DS5002 has a tamper-sensing mesh built into the top metal layer of the chip).

An early version of this processor (1995) fell victim to an ingenious protocol level attack by Markus Kuhn, the *cipher instruction search attack* [477]. The idea is that some of the processor's instructions have a visible external effect such as I/O. In particular, one instruction causes the next byte in memory to be output to the device's parallel port. The trick is to intercept the bus between the processor and memory using a test clip, and feed in all possible 8-bit instruction bytes at some point in the instruction stream. One of them should decrypt to the parallel output instruction, and output the plaintext versions of the next "encrypted memory" byte. By varying this byte, a table could be built up of corresponding plaintext and ciphertext. After using this technique to learn the encryption function for a sequence of seven or eight bytes, the attacker could encipher and execute a short program to dump the entire memory contents.

The full details are a bit more intricate. Dallas has since fixed the problem, but it is a good example of the completely unexpected things that go wrong when trying to implement a clever new security concept for the first time.

14.5.3 The Capstone/Clipper Chip

In 1993, the security world was convulsed when the U.S. government introduced the
Clipper chip as the replacement for DES. Clipper, also known as the Escrowed Encryption Standard (EES), was a tamper-resistant chip that implemented the Skipjack block
cipher in a protocol designed to allow the U.S. government to decrypt any traffic encrypted using Clipper. The idea was that when a user supplied Clipper with a string of
data and a key with which to encrypt it, the chip returned not just the ciphertext but
also a Law Enforcement Access Field, or LEAF, which contained the user-supplied key
encrypted under a key embedded in the device and known to the government. To prevent people cheating and sending along the wrong LEAF with a message, the LEAF had
a cryptographic checksum computed with a "family key," shared by all interoperable
Clipper chips. This functionality was continued into the next-generation chips, called
Capstone, which incorporate ARM processors to do public key encryption and digital
signature operations.

Almost as soon as Capstone chips hit the market, a vulnerability was found in the
LEAF mechanism [113]. The cryptographic checksum used to bind the LEAF to the
message was only 16 bits long, making it possible to feed random message keys into
the device until one with a given LEAF was found, thus enabling a message to be sent
with a LEAF that would remain impenetrable to the government. The Clipper initiative
was abandoned and replaced with other policies aimed at controlling the "proliferation"
of cryptography. Nevertheless, Capstone quietly entered government service and is now
widely used in the Fortezza card, a PCMCIA card used in PCs to encrypt data at levels
up to Secret. The Skipjack block cipher, which was initially classified, has since been
placed in the public domain [577].

Of greater interest here are the tamper protection mechanisms used, as they are
perhaps the most sophisticated in any single-chip tamper resistant device, and were
claimed at the time to be sufficient to withstand a "very sophisticated, well-funded adversary" [578]. Although the NSA claimed that the Clipper chip would be unclassified
and exportable, I've not been able to get hold of one for dismantling, despite repeated
attempts.

Its successor is the QuickLogic military FPGA, designed to enable its users to conceal proprietary algorithms from their customers; it is advertised as being "virtually
impossible to reverse-engineer." Like Clipper, it uses *vialink read-only memory* (VROM),
in which bits are set by blowing antifuses between the metal 1 and metal 2 layers on the
chip. A programming pulse at a sufficiently high voltage is used to melt a conducting
path through the polysilicon that separates the two metal layers. Further details and
micrographs can be found in the data book [347].

There are basically three approaches to reverse engineering an antifuse FPGA.

- The first is to determine the presence of blown antifuses using optical or
electron microscopy, having first removed the top metal layer of the chip. This
can be extremely tedious; even if the bits are read out correctly, a lot more work
remains to figure out what they mean.

- A smarter approach is to abuse the programming circuit. This sends a pulse to
the fuse and stops it once the resistance drops, which means that the metal has
melted and established contact; if the pulse isn't stopped, the metal might

vaporize and go open-circuit again. Thus, the circuits for detecting whether a circuit is open or short must be provided; and if they aren't sufficiently disabled after programming, they can be used to read the device out.

- The fastest approach, which is particularly easy when the cryptographic algorithm being executed is known, is to drop microprobes directly on to the gate array and look at the signals. Suitable analysis techniques, such as those described in Section 15.4, should quickly yield the key. Signals can also be collected using electromagnetic or electro-optic sensors, voltage contrast microscopy and a growing number of other chip-testing techniques. Even where the algorithm isn't known initially, it may be faster to reconstruct it from observing on-chip signals than from doing a full circuit reconstruction.

This technology isn't infallible, but used intelligently it certainly appears to have some potential.

14.6 Smartcards and Microcontrollers

The most common secure processors nowadays are smartcards and similar self-contained security processors. These cost maybe a dollar each in bulk, and are being deployed in environments such as telephone cards, pay-TV subscriber cards, hotel door locks, and even (in some countries) bank cards.

In such applications, opponent can often obtain many sample devices and take them away to probe at their leisure. As a result, many attacks on them have been developed.

Although they are now being marketed as the "new" security solution, smartcards actually go back a long way, with the early patents (which date from the late 1960s through mid-1970s) having long since expired [247]. For a history of the development of smartcards, see [358]. For many years, they were mostly used in France, where much of the original development work was done with government support. In the late 1980s and early 1990s, they started to be used on a large scale outside France, principally as the *subscriber identity modules* (SIMs) in GSM mobile phones and as subscriber cards for pay-TV stations.

A smartcard is a self-contained microcontroller, with a microprocessor, memory and a serial interface integrated on to a single chip that is packaged in a plastic card. Smartcards used in banking and in the older mobile phones use a standard-size bank card, while in the newer, smaller mobile phones, a much smaller size is used. Smartcard chips are also packaged in other ways. For example, most U.K. prepayment electricity meters use them packaged in a plastic key, as do Nagravision pay-TV set-top boxes. In the STU-III secure telephones used in the U.S. government, each user has a *crypto ignition key*, which is also packaged to look and feel like a physical key.

The single most widespread application that uses smartcards is the GSM mobile phone system, a digital standard used in some U.S. networks and in almost all countries outside the United States. The telephone handsets are commodity items, and are personalized for each user by means of a SIM, a smartcard which contains not just your personal phone book, call history and so on, but also a cryptographic key with which you authenticate yourself to the network.

The strategy of using a cheap smartcard to provide the authentication and other security functions of a more expensive consumer electronic device has a number of advantages. The expensive device can be manufactured in bulk, with each unit being exactly the same; while the smartcard, which provides subscriber-level control, can be replaced relatively quickly and cheaply in the event of a successful attack. This has led many pay-TV operators to adopt smartcards. The satellite TV dish and decoder become commodity consumer durables, while each subscriber gets a personalized smartcard containing the key material needed to decrypt the channels to which they have subscribed.

Chipcards are also used in a range of other applications, from hotel keys to public payphones—though in such applications it's common for the card to contain no microprocessor but just some EEPROM memory to store a counter or certificate, and some logic to perform a simple authentication protocol.

Devices such as prepayment electricity meters are typically built around a microcontroller that performs the same kind of functions as a smartcard but has less sophisticated protection. Typically, this consists of setting a single "memory protection" bit that prevents the EEPROM contents being read out easily by an attacker. There have been many design defects in particular products; for example, a computer authentication token called iKey had a master password that was hashed using MD5 and stored on an EEPROM external to the processor, enabling a user to overwrite it with the hash of a known password and assume complete control of the device [459].

Many other low-cost security products are based on some kind of microcontroller (or dedicated logic that performs an authentication protocol of some kind). An increasing number are *contactless*, and function as *radio frequency identifiers* that provide theft protection or just "smart labels" for a wide range of products. As for more systemic vulnerabilities, the attacks on smartcards also tend to work on microcontroller-based devices, so I won't treat them separately from this point on. For more details of attacks specific to microcontrollers, see [43].

14.6.1 Architecture

The typical smartcard consists of a single die of up to 25 square millimeters of silicon, containing an 8-bit microprocessor (such as an 8051 or 6805), although some of the newer devices are starting to appear with a 32-bit processor such as the ARM. It also has serial I/O circuitry and a hierarchy of three classes of memory: ROM to hold the program and immutable data; EEPROM to hold customer-specific data, such as the registered user's name and account number as well as crypto keys, value counters and the like; and RAM registers to hold transient data during computation.

The memory is very limited by the standards of normal computers. A typical card on sale in 2000 might have 16 Kbytes of ROM, 16 Kbytes of EEPROM and 256 bytes of RAM. The bus is not available outside the device; the only connections supplied are for power, reset, a clock, and a serial port. The physical, electrical, and low-level logical connections, together with a file-system-like access protocol, are specified in ISO 7816.

14.6.2 Security Evolution

When I first heard a sales pitch from a smartcard vendor—in 1986, when I was working as a banker—I asked how come the device was secure. I was assured that because the machinery needed to make the card cost $20 million, just as for making banknotes, the system must be secure. I didn't believe this, but didn't then have the time or the tools to prove the claim wrong. I later learned from industry executives that none of their customers were prepared to pay for serious security until about 1995, so until then they relied on the small size of the devices, the obscurity of their design, and the relative unavailability of chip-testing tools.

The application that changed all this was satellite TV. Operators broadcast their signals over a large footprint—such as all of Europe—and gave subscribers smartcards that would compute the keys needed to decipher the channels they'd paid for. Since the operators had usually only purchased the rights to the movies for one or two countries, they couldn't sell the subscriber cards elsewhere. This created a black market in pay-TV cards, into which forged cards could be sold. Another major factor was that *Star Trek*, which people in Europe had been picking up from U.K. satellite broadcasts for years, was suddenly encrypted in 1993. This motivated a lot of keen young computer science and engineering students to look for vulnerabilities.

Since then, major financial frauds have been carried out with cloned cards. The first to be reported involved a smartcard used to give Portuguese farmers rebates on fuel. The villain conspired with petrol stations that registered other fuel sales to the bogus cards in return for a share of the proceeds. The fraud, which took place in February–March 1995, is reported to have netted about thirty million dollars [557].

How to Hack a Smartcard (1)

The earliest hacks targeted the protocols in which the cards were used. For example, some early pay-TV systems gave each customer a card with access to all channels, then sent messages over the air to cancel those channels to which the customer hadn't subscribed after an introductory period. This allowed an attack whereby a device was inserted between the smartcard and the decoder to intercept and discard any messages addressed to the card. Subscribers could then cancel their subscription without the vendor being able to cancel their service.

The same kind of attack was launched on the German phone card system. A hacker called Urmel tipped off Deutsche Telekom that it was possible to make phone cards that gave unlimited free calls. He had discovered this by putting a laptop between a card and a phone to analyze the traffic. Telekom's experts refused to believe him, so he exploited his knowledge by selling handmade chipcards in brothels and in hostels for asylum seekers [726]. Such low-cost attacks were particularly distressing to the phone companies, as the main reason for moving to smartcards was to cut the cost of having to validate cheaper tokens online [78]. I'll discuss these protocol failures further in the chapter on copyright enforcement systems. There has also been a fairly full range of standard computer attacks, such as stack overwriting by sending too long a string of parameters. In the following, I concentrate on the attacks that are peculiar to smartcards.

How to Hack a Smartcard (2)

Smartcards use an external power supply, and store security state such as crypto keys and value counters in EEPROM, so an attacker could freeze the EEPROM contents by removing the programming voltage, V_{PP}. Early smartcards received V_{PP} on a dedicated connection from the host interface. This led to very simple attacks: by covering the V_{PP} contact with sticky tape, cardholders could prevent cancellation signals from affecting their card. The same trick could be used with some payphone chipcards; a card with tape over the appropriate contact had "infinite units."

The fix was to generate V_{PP} internally from the supply voltage V_{CC} using a voltage multipler circuit. However, this isn't entirely foolproof as this circuit can be destroyed by an attacker. So a prudent programmer, having (for example) decremented the retry counter after a user enters an incorrect PIN, will read it back and check it. She will also check that memory writing actually works each time the card is reset, as otherwise the bad guy who has shot away the voltage multiplier can just repeatedly reset the card and try every possible PIN, one after another.

How to Hack a Smartcard (3)

Another early attack was to slow down the card's execution, or even single-step it through a transaction by repeatedly resetting it and clocking it n times, then $n + 1$ times, and so on. In one card, it was possible to read out RAM contents with a suitable transaction after reset, as working memory wasn't zeroized. With many cards, it was possible to read the voltages on the chip surface using an electron microscope. (The low-cost scanning electron microscopes generally available in universities can't do voltage contrast microscopy at more than a few tens of kilohertz, hence the need to slow down the execution.)

Now many smartcard processors have a circuit to detect low clock frequency, which will either freeze or reset the card. But, as with burglar alarms, there is a trade-off between the false alarm rate and the missed alarm rate. This leads to many of the alarm features provided by smartcard chip makers simply not being used by the OEMs or application developers. For example, with cheap card readers, there can be wild fluctuations in clock frequency when a card is powered up, causing so many false alarms that some developers do not use the feature. Clearly, low clock frequency detectors need careful design.

How to Hack a Smartcard (4)

Once pay-TV operators had fixed most of the simple attacks, pirates turned to attacks using physical probing (see Figure 14.4). Most smartcards have no protection against physical tampering beyond the microscopic scale of the circuit, a thin glass *passivation layer* on the surface of the chip, and potting, which is typically some kind of epoxy. Techniques for depackaging chips are well known, and discussed in detail in standard works on semiconductor testing, such as [80]. In most cases, a few milliliters of fuming nitric acid are all that's required to dissolve the epoxy; the passivation layer is then removed where required for probing.

Probing stations consist of microscopes with micromanipulators attached for landing fine probes on the surface of the chip. They are widely used in the semiconductor manufacturing industry for manual testing of production-line samples, and can be obtained

Figure 14.4 Low-cost probing station.

second-hand for under $10,000. They may have specialized accessories, such as a laser to shoot holes in the chip's passivation layer (see Figure 14.5).

The usual target of a probing attack is the processor's bus. If the bus traffic can be recorded, this gives a trace of the program's operation with both code and data. If the attacker is lucky, the card designer will have computed a checksum on memory immediately after reset (a recommended defense industry practice), and this operation will immediately give him a complete listing of the card memory contents. So the attacker will identify the bus, and expose the bus lines for probing.

The first defense used by the pay-TV card industry against attacks of this kind was to endow each card with multiple keys and/or algorithms, and arrange things so that only those in current use would appear on the processor bus. Whenever pirate cards appeared on the market, a command would be issued over the air to cause the legitimate card population to activate new keys or algorithms from a previously unused area of memory. In this way, the pirates' customers would suffer a loss of service until the probing attack could be repeated and either new pirate cards, or updates to the existing ones, could somehow be distributed.

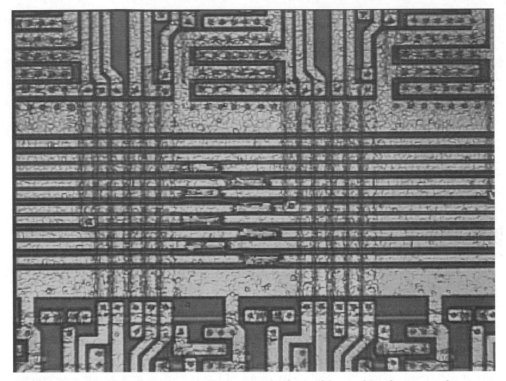

Figure 14.5 The data bus of an ST16 smartcard prepared for probing by excavating eight trenches through the passivation layer with laser shots (photo courtesy Oliver Kömmerling).

How to Hack a Smartcard (5)

The defeat for this strategy was Oliver Kömmerling's *memory linearization attack*, whereby the analyst damages the chip's instruction decoder in such a way that instructions which change the program address other than by incrementing it—such as jumps and calls—become inoperable [470]. One way to do this is to drop a grounded micro-probe needle on the control line to the instruction latch, so that whatever instruction happens to be there on power-up is executed repeatedly. The memory contents can now be read off the bus. In fact, once some of the device's ROM and EEPROM are understood, the attacker can skip over unwanted instructions and cause the device to execute only instructions of his choice. So with a single probing needle, he can get the card to execute arbitrary code, and in theory could get it to output its secret key material on the serial port. But probing the memory contents off the bus is usually more convenient.

In practice, there are often several places in the instruction decoder where a grounded needle will have the effect of preventing programmed changes in the control flow. So even if the processor isn't fully understood, memory linearization can often be achieved by trial and error. Some of the more modern processors have traps that prevent memory linearization, such as hardware access control matrices which prevent particular areas of memory being read unless some specific sequence of commands is presented. But such circuits can often be defeated by shooting away carefully chosen gates using a laser or an ion beam.

Some cards could be attacked through their test circuitry. A typical smartcard chip has a self-test routine in ROM that is executed in the factory and allows all the memory contents to be read and verified. After this has been done, a polysilicon fuse is blown in the chip to stop an attacker using the same facility. All that the attacker had to do was to find the fuse and repair it—which could involve as little as bridging it with two probing needles [130]. Then, in some cases, the entire memory contents could be read out over the serial port. A more careful design might put the test circuitry on the part of the silicon that is sawn away when the wafer is diced into individual chips.

How to Hack a Smartcard (6)

The next thing the pay-TV card industry tried was to incorporate hardware cryptographic processors, to force attackers to reconstruct hardware circuits rather than simply clone software, and to force them to use more expensive processors in their pirate cards. In the first such implementation, the crypto processor was a separate chip packaged into the card. This design had an interesting protocol failure: it would always work out the key needed to decrypt the current video stream, then pass it to the CPU, which would decide whether or not to release it to the outside world. Hackers broke this system by developing a way to tap into the wiring between the two chips.

More modern implementations have the crypto hardware built into the CPU itself. Where this consists of just a few thousand gates, it is feasible for an attacker to reconstruct the circuit manually from micrographs of the chip. But with larger gate counts and deep submicron processes, a successful attack may require automatic layout reconstruction: successively etching away the layers of the chip, taking electron micrographs, and using image processing software to reconstruct a 3-D map of the chip, or at least identify its component cells [121]. However, assembling all the equipment, writing the software, and integrating the systems involves significant effort and expense.

A much simpler, and common, attack is for pirates to ask one of the dozen or so existing commercial reverse-engineering labs to reconstruct the relevant area of the chip. Such labs get much of their business from analyzing commercial integrated circuits on behalf of the chip maker's competitors, looking for possible patent infringements. They are used to operating in conditions of some secrecy, and it doesn't seem to be too difficult for a pirate to sneak in a sample that is targeted for piracy rather than litigation.

How to Hack a Smartcard (7)

The next defense that the card industry thought up was to furnish the chip with protective surface mesh, implemented in a top metal layer as a serpentine pattern of ground, power and sensor lines. The idea was that any break or short in the pattern would be sensed as soon as the chip was powered up, thereby triggering a self-destruct mechanism.

I mentioned such meshes in connection with the Dallas processors; after the usual initial crop of implementation blunders, they have proved to be an effective way of pushing up the cost of an attack. The appropriate tool to defeat them is the *Focused Ion Beam Workstation* (FIB). This is a device similar to a scanning electron microscope, but it uses a beam of ions instead of electrons. By varying the beam current, it is possible to use it as a microscope or as a milling machine. By introducing a suitable gas, which is broken down by the ion beam, it is possible to lay down either conductors or insulators with a precision of a few tens of nanometers.

FIBs are such extremely useful devices in all sorts of applications—from semiconductor testing through metallurgy and forensics to nanotechnology—that they are rapidly becoming widely available, and their prices are tumbling. Many universities and industrial labs now have one. FIB time can also be rented from a number of agencies for a few hundred dollars an hour.

Given a FIB, it is straightforward to attack a sensor mesh that is not powered up. One simply drills a hole through the mesh to the metal line that carries the desired signal, fills it up with insulator, drills another hole through the center of the insulator, fills it with metal, and plates a contact on top—typically, a platinum L or X a few microns wide, which is easy to contact with a needle from the probing station (see Figure 14.6).

Defeating a sensor mesh that is continually powered up is much harder, but the necessary tools are starting to emerge from the labs of the chip-testing industry. For example, there are techniques to mill through the back side of a chip with a suitably equipped FIB, and make contact directly to the electronics without disturbing the sensor mesh at all.

Many other defensive techniques can force the attacker to do more work. Some chips are said to be packaged in much thicker glass than in a normal passivation layer. The idea is that the obvious ways of removing this (such as applying hydrofluoric acid) are likely to damage the chip. However, optoelectronic techniques developed in the past few

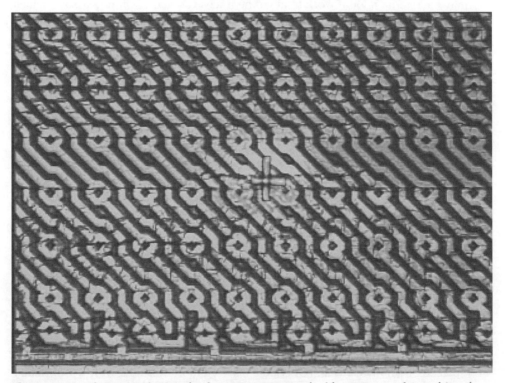

Figure 14.6 The protective mesh of an ST16 smartcard with a FIB cross for probing the bus line visible underneath (photo courtesy Oliver Kömmerling).

years enable an attacker to read out a voltage directly using a laser [11]. Other chips have protective coatings of substances such as silicon carbide or boron nitride. (Chips with protective coatings are on display at the NSA Museum at Fort Meade, Maryland). Such coatings can force the FIB operator to go slowly, rather than damage the chip through a build-up of electrical charge. However, protective layers in smartcard chip packaging are, like much else in the security industry, often a matter of marketing rather than engineering. The one chip that our team has dismantled recently and whose vendors claimed to have such a layer, turned out to have no special protection at all.

14.6.3 The State of the Art

At the time of writing, I know of no technology, or combination of technologies, that can make a smartcard resistant to penetration by a skilled and determined attacker. Some industry experts even believe that absolute protection in chip-sized packages will remain infeasible, because it's not economic to fabricate devices that you can't test.

Despite this, smartcards are certainly a lot harder to copy than magnetic stripe cards, and there is room for them to be made harder still. The latest cards have up to three layers of defensive mesh; registers that use dynamic logic, making it impossible to just shoot away a low clock frequency detector, then single-step the chip; circuits that insert dummy instructions from time to time so that if you probe the bus lines one after another, you may have to do a lot of work to align the traces you get; 32-bit processors, which make trace alignment even harder; proprietary instruction sets; and a whole host of other tricks. But as industry insiders say, 'the man with the ion beam will always get in'.

So what sort of strategies are available to you if you are designing a system that depends on smartcards?

14.6.3.1 Defense in Depth

The first, used by pay-TV companies, is *defense in depth*. Smartcards may combine a whole menagerie of the tricks described above, and even obscure proprietary encryption algorithms. Normally, using home-brewed encryption schemes is a bad thing: Kerckhoffs' principle almost always wins in the end, and a bad scheme, once published, can be fatal. Defense in depth of pay-TV provides an interesting exception. The goal is to minimize, insofar as possible, the likelihood of a shortcut probing attack, and to force the attacker to go to the trouble of reverse engineering substantially the whole system.

It's prudent to assume that even an amateur will be able to drop a probe on to a number of signal lines in the device. If it is performing a known cryptographic protocol with well-understood algorithms, then unless there's an effective mechanism to introduce lots of dummy instructions, a trace from a single bus line is likely to give away the key [370]. Using a proprietary (and complicated) encryption algorithm can force the attacker to do a more complete analysis and delay him for a few weeks or months. This can make a huge difference to the economics of piracy in an industry such as pay-TV where cards are replaced about once a year. (Of course it's even more essential with a proprietary design to have it evaluated thoroughly by competent experts—and for the experts to analyze not just the abstract cryptographic strength of the algorithm, but how easily it can be reconstructed from observable signals.)

Technical measures on their own are not enough, though. Over the last few years of the twentieth century, the pay-TV industry managed to reduce piracy losses from over 5% of revenue to an almost negligible proportion. More complex smartcards played a role, but much of the improvement came from legal action against pirates, and from making technical and legal measures work together efficiently. I'll discuss this further in Chapter 20, when we explore the world of copyright.

14.6.3.2 Tamper Resistance versus Tamper Evidence

It can often be very useful to draw a careful distinction between devices that are tamper-resistant and those that are merely tamper-evident. Even if the former can't yet be produced for mass markets, it is more or less within our grasp to make smartcards against which the only attacks are invasive, such as probing, and therefore leave physical evidence behind. (This is still harder than it looks—in the next chapter we'll discuss noninvasive attacks.)

For example, in a banking application where smartcards are used to manufacture and verify electronic checks, the bank might have a rule that disputes will be considered only if customers can produce their smartcard undamaged. This is not quite as simple as it seems, as smartcards can always be damaged by accident. Maybe 1% of smartcards issued to the public will be destroyed every year by material failures or static electricity; consumer laws in many countries may prevent banks from disregarding claims when that happens. Once again, the legal and engineering aspects of the problem interact. Nonetheless, cards that are tamper-evident (as well as being fairly difficult to probe) can be a useful part of a risk management strategy.

14.6.3.3 Stop Loss

Whether one goes for the defense-in-depth approach or the tamper-evident approach will depend on the extent to which one can limit the losses that result from a single card being successfully probed.

In early pay-TV systems, the system architecture forced all customer cards to contain the same master secret. Once this secret became known, pirate cards could be manufactured at will, and the card base had to be replaced. The pay-TV systems currently being deployed for digital broadcasting use crypto protocols in which cards have different keys, so that cloned cards can be revoked. I'll describe these protocols in Section 20.2.4.5.

In other systems, such as the banking card application described in Section 2.7.1, there are limits on the amount that can be spent using a stolen or forged card, set by a system of merchant floor limits, random online authorizations, lists of hot cards and so on. Here, a tamper-evident card may be a perfectly adequate solution. Even a card that's relatively easy to forge may be viable, as it's still harder to forge than the magnetic stripe card it replaces.

14.7 What Goes Wrong

There are failure modes of systems involving tamper-resistant processors that are more or less independent of whether the device is low or high end. Many failures occurred because the device was exposed to more capable attackers than its designers anticipated: it just never seems to have occurred to the designers of early chip cards that bad people might have access to semiconductor test equipment. Many more occur because people protect the wrong things, or protect the right things in the wrong way; a survey of flaws found by a commercial evaluation laboratory showed that most of them were at the interfaces between physical, logical, and organizational measures [131].

14.7.1 Protecting the Wrong Things: Architectural Errors

A good example of misuse of the technology is the drive to have smartcards adopted as the preferred device for digital signatures. Some government initiatives give enhanced legal validity to signatures made using an approved smartcard. While this may be a Full Employment Act for the card industry, it makes little sense technically.

None of the devices described in the preceding sections has a really trustworthy user interface. Some of the bank security modules have a physical lock (or two) on the front to ensure that only the person with the metal key can perform certain privileged transactions. But whether you use a $2,000 4758 or a $2 smartcard to do digital signatures, you still trust the PC that drives them. If it shows you a text reading "Please pay amazon.com $37.99 for a copy of Anderson's *Security Engineering*," while the message it actually sends for signature is "Please remortgage my house at 13 Acacia Avenue and pay the proceeds to Mafia Real Estate Inc.," then the tamper resistance has not bought you much.

It may even make your situation worse, as you will have a harder time repudiating the transaction. Information policy experts have pointed out that the proposed approach to digital signatures is likely to undermine the very consumer protection laws that give people confidence when conducting business electronically over the Net [124]. What customers really need is a secure PC—or at least a firewall to shield their PC from the worst of the external threats, such as malicious code. That is a separate engineering problem, and has little to do with hardware security. In fact, researchers are coming to realize that a palmtop computer may be a much better platform for digital signature applications; whatever its vulnerability to probing, customers can at least see what they're signing and protect the device using common sense [69].

An example of more appropriate use of hardware protection technology comes from the prepayment electricity metering system, discussed in Chapter 11. There, the function of tamper resistance was to limit the loss if one of the vending machines that sold meter tokens was stolen. By keeping the keys needed to encrypt the tokens in a secure processor, which also contained a value counter, it was possible to enforce a credit limit on each vendor. Had someone managed to drill into the device, he would have been able to defeat the value counter, extract the crypto keys for the individual meters, and thus sell unlimited numbers of tokens to the meters in the vending area. But this would not have destroyed the whole metering system, just forced the rekeying of a few thousand meters.

14.7.2 Protecting the Wrong Things: Security-by-Obscurity and Evaluation Errors

Many of the smartcard systems that have been broken, in ways that resulted in real frauds, appear to have become vulnerable because their operators did not fully understand the technology and its limitations. This is hardly surprising; until recently, no published information was readily available on how smartcards could be attacked. The industry also sought to keep all serious technical information about its products secret. To this day, one has to sign a nondisclosure agreement to get proper software development tools for smartcards. (There are Java cards, Basic cards, and so on, but these use interpreted languages to shield the developer from the hardware and don't support users who want to run their own machine code on the device).

In fact, the security target used for evaluating smartcards under the Common Critera focuses on maintaining obscurity of the design. Chip masks must be secret, staff must be vetted, developers must sign nondisclosure agreements—there are many requirements that push up industry's costs. Obscurity is also a common requirement for export approval, and there remains a suspicion that it covers up deliberately inserted vulnerabilities. For example, a card my colleagues tested would always produce the same value when instructed to generate a private/public keypair, and output the public part.

Obscurity certainly does little for the customer in most smartcard applications. Almost none of the actual attacks on fielded smartcard systems used inside information. Most of them started out with a probing attack on a card bought at retail.

Better protection targets were published by VISA, which specify extensive penetration testing [777]. However, as no existing products can pass such a test, the industry took the route of protecting what it could rather than what it should. I'll return to this subject to discuss the underlying economics and politics in Section 23.3.3.1.

14.7.3 Protecting Things Wrongly: Protocol Failure

As elsewhere in security engineering, one of the most pervasive kinds of failure at the technical level is the use of inappropriate protocols. A device such as the 4758 comes with a transaction set of several hundred "verbs," or combinations of cryptographic operations that can be carried out on data passed to the device. Further verbs can be defined by the application developer. How can one be sure that some combination of these verbs won't enable a user to do something that breaks the security policy?

From about 1981 until 1991, there was a protocol attack that worked against many of the security modules used by banks to manage ATM networks. As the working life of a security module is about seven years, the defective devices should all have retired by the time this book appears (but they completely destroy the claim made by many banks in the course of phantom withdrawal litigation in the early 1990s that "nothing could possibly go wrong").

The security modules provided by VISA and VISA-compatible vendors such as Racal had a transaction to generate a key component and print out its clear value on an attached security printer. They also returned its value to the calling program, encrypted under a master key KM which was kept in the tamper-resistant hardware:

$$\text{VSM} \longrightarrow \text{printer: } KMT_i$$

$$\text{VSM} \longrightarrow \text{host: } \{KMT_i\}_{KM}$$

and another that combined two of the components to produce a terminal key:

$$\text{Host} \longrightarrow \text{VSM: } \{KMT_1\}_{KM}, \{KMT_2\}_{KM}$$

$$\text{VSM} \longrightarrow \text{host: } \{KMT_1 \oplus KMT_2\}_{KM}$$

The idea was that, to generate a terminal key for the first time, you'd use the first of these transactions twice, followed by the second. Then you'd have $KMT = KMT_1 \oplus KMT_2$. However, there is nothing to stop the programmer taking any old encrypted key and supplying it twice in the second transaction, resulting in a known terminal key (the key of all zeroes, as the key is exclusive-or'ed with itself):

$$\text{Host} \longrightarrow \text{VSM: } \{KMT_1\}_{KM}, \{KMT_1\}_{KM}$$

$$\text{VSM} \longrightarrow \text{host: } \{KMT_1 \oplus KMT_1\}_{KM}$$

The module also has a transaction that will take two keys, encrypted under the master key, and return one encrypted with the other:

$$\text{Host} \longrightarrow \text{VSM: } \{KMT_1\}_{KM}, \{KMT_2\}_{KM}$$

$$\text{VSM} \longrightarrow \text{host: } \{KMT_1\}_{KMT_2}$$

(This is intended to allow the terminal master key in a cash machine to be replaced, or a PIN key to be sent to a cash machine encrypted under the terminal master key, to support offline PIN verification.)

The attack is now simple, and devastating. Having a zero key, encrypted under KM, we can translate the PIN key (and everything else of interest) from being encrypted under KM to being encrypted under the zero key. Thus, the physical protection that was promised to customers was a phantasm: a programmer could extract any key of interest with only two unprivileged instructions.

This is interesting from the scientific point of view, because the security policy enforced by the VSM is a kind of kludge between a multilevel policy ("PINs are Secret and must not leak to any process with a lower classification") and a shared control policy ("no single member of bank staff should be able to work out a customer PIN"). It's also interesting from the public policy viewpoint, as it was known to the equipment vendors at the time of the Munden case described in Section 9.4.3. But the vendors didn't own up to it, despite the fact that its existence would have directly undermined the prosecution testimony in a highly publicized miscarriage-of-justice case. This should be remembered whenever one of the parties in a court case relies on vendor assurances about a system's capabilities.

The fix adopted was to remove the offending instruction. This means that dual control key management now involves a trusted process at the host, which will have access to key material. (This has always been the case with the ATM support application, CCA, supplied for the 4758.) A better fix would have been to compute terminal keys using a hash function, such as $KMT = SHA1(KMT_1, KMT_2)$, but this would not have been backward-compatible. With hindsight, the choice of a combining function with arithmetic properties meant that all the protocols subsequently developed on this foundation should have been checked for ways in which these properties could misbehave. In other words, the choice of combining function raised the complexity of transaction set verification.

This brings us to the attack found on the 4758 by Mike Bond. This enables any key to be extracted from the device with only a modest keysearch. The vulnerability is that the two-key, triple-DES encryption used internally by the 4758 can have its key pairs cut and spliced. Given a known pair of keys, KA and KB, and a target pair of keys KC and KD, one can compare the results of encryption under the spliced keys (KC,KB) and (KA,KD) with a brute-force search of all possibilities, thus breaking the target keys one component at a time. This reduces the cost of an attack from the 2^{112} of a standard triple-DES keysearch to the more tractable 2^{56} of single-DES. There is also a time-memory tradeoff available; for example, with 2^{16} trial keys it is possible to break the 4758 with an effort of about 2^{40} test encryptions. For full details, see [125].

Let's step back for a minute and consider the implications. IBM spent over a decade evolving a highly strategic product, that is used by many banks to protect zillions of dollars' worth of transactions. The US government certified it as the most secure crypto processor available to civilian purchasers, and kept it export-controlled. IBM further protected it by refusing to sell us a sample. Yet a typical Cambridge graduate student broke it within six weeks by studying the manuals available from IBM's Web site.

Verifying the correctness of the transaction set of a cryptographic processor is a hard, and as yet unsolved, problem. Verifying an individual protocol is difficult enough, and the research community spent much the 1990s learning how to do it. Yet a protocol might consist of perhaps two to five messages, while a cryptoprocessor might have from dozens to hundreds of verbs. Many protocols fail because their goals are not made sufficiently explicit; yet cryptoprocessors are sold as general-purpose machines, and may be used to enforce a very wide range of security policies. We don't yet really know how to formalize security policies, let alone track them back to crypto primitives. Checking that there isn't some obscure sequence of transactions that breaks your security policy is hard enough; when your policy isn't even precisely stated, it looks impossible.

14.7.4 Function Creep

I've given numerous examples of how function creep, and changes in environmental conditions in general, have broken many secure systems by undermining their design assumptions. The flexibility of some modern cryptographic processors makes this a particular problem.

Function creep can also interact with physical tamper-resistance directly, and is particularly pernicious in smartcard applications. It is easy to move subtly from a system in which smartcards act much like magnetic strip cards and perform transactions on underlying bank accounts that are cleared every night, to a system in which they act like wallets and can transfer value to each other. In the former, cards can have different keys shared only with the bank, and so the compromise of a single card need mean no more than the cloning of a credit card does in the magnetic strip world. In the latter, each card has a key that enables it to transfer money to any other card, and the constraints of centralized accounting are relaxed. A relatively low-risk environment suddenly becomes a relatively high-risk one.

Another way a low-risk environment can become a high-risk one is when multiple applications are put on the same card. If a device that was previously just a health insurance card or a welfare claimants' card suddenly starts to double as a national identity card, then it may attract a much higher grade of attacker. If large numbers of different organizations can run their own applications on the card—which is the stated purpose of Java cards—then the *chosen protocol attack* described in Chapter 2 becomes a particularly dangerous threat. A bad man may design an application specifically to attack yours.

14.8 What Should Be Protected?

With many technologies—including the steam engine, telephone, and computer—the original proposed use of the device was not that which eventually took off in the market. (Consider the size of the market today for pumping water out of coal mines; reading text to telegraph operators rather than sending it through a pneumatic tube; and working out artillery range tables.)

The currently fashionable sales pitch for smartcards is that they will be the *advanced electronic signature devices* envisaged in EU electronic commerce regulations—that is, devices that people will use to sign legal documents and that will be sufficiently dependable that the existence of such a signature can be taken as proof that the owner of the device signed it. Quite apart from the obvious legal objections (that it shifts the burden of proof from the party relying on the signature to the device owner, and that devices can always be stolen), there is, as I mentioned earlier, the technical problem that the user doesn't know what the smartcard is signing; and if the PC software, that supplies the matter to be signed, is guaranteed to be bug-free and free from viruses, then what value does the smartcard add?

The industry has been trying for much of the 1990s to sell the idea of a multifunction card, which would replace many of the plastic cards and metal keys that the average person carries with them. The application that makes this finally happen may be putting bank transaction processing into mobile phones. As mobile phones have slots for precisely one smartcard, a bank would have to rent space on the card from the phone network operator. We shall see.

So what value can tamper-resistant devices actually add?

First, they can control information processing by linking it to a single physical token. A pay-TV subscriber card can be bought and sold in a gray market, but as long as it isn't copied, the station operator isn't too concerned. Another example comes from a Dallas product used in quality control in the food industry: it is physically sealed into a food shipment to provide a reliable log of temperature history. Yet another is the use of crypto to enforce evaluation standards in government networks: if you only get key material once your system has been inspected and accredited, then it's inconvenient to connect an unlicensed system of any size to the classified government network.

Second, tamper-resistant devices can give assurance that data are destroyed at a definite and verifiable time. The anti-trust case against Microsoft has highlighted the damage that can be done by the seizure under subpoena of email archives; many corporations would like to enforce a policy that every email be destroyed after a fixed time, unless either the sender or the recipient takes positive action to preserve it. At my university, for example, we destroy exam scripts and examiners' working notes after four months. If we held on to them for too long, we would have to give the students access under data protection law, but if we destroyed them too soon, we could prejudice an appeal. Once everything is electronic, implementing such a policy will be complicated by all the system backups we keep. A solution is to encrypt archives with keys kept in a device that is programmed to erase them at the right time.

Third, these devices can reduce the need to trust human operators. As I remarked, their main purpose in some government systems was "reducing the street value of key material to zero". A crypto ignition key for a STU-III should allow a thief only to masquerade as the rightful owner, and only if he has access to an actual STU-III telephone, and only as long as neither the key nor the phone have been reported stolen. The same general considerations applied in ATM networks: no bank wanted to make its own customers' security depend on the trustworthiness of the staff of another bank.

Fourth, tamper-resistant devices can be used to control value counters, as with the prepayment electricity discussed in Section 14.7.1. These typically use devices such as the DS5002 or the iButton to hold both the vend keys for local meters and a credit counter. Even if the device is stolen, the total value of electricity tokens it can vend is limited.

This seems to be a special case of a more general application, in which some part of a central server's processing is delegated to a device in the field. But the most compelling examples I can think of concern value. Note that a guarded corporate data-processing center is also a tamper-resistant processor; applications of this type can often be spotted by the fact that they could also be implemented centrally if a completely reliable network existed. For example, if all electricity meters and vend stations were online, then prepayment metering could be done using straightforward authenticated messaging. Note, too, that delegation also occurs between corporate data processing centers, as when banks use hot-card lists to authenticate card transactions on other banks. Here, tamper-resistant devices may be used to provide extra assurance (though often logging mechanisms are sufficient where the continued solvency of the principals can be relied on).

This is an incomplete list. But what these applications have in common is that a security property can be provided independently of the trustworthiness of the surrounding computer environment. In other words, be careful when using tamper-resistant devices to try to offset the lack of a trustworthy user interface. This doesn't mean that no value at all can be added where the interface is problematic. For example, the tamper-resistant crypto modules used in ATM networks cannot prevent small-scale theft using bogus ATMs; but they can prevent large-scale PIN compromise if used properly. In general, tamper-resistant devices are often a useful component, but only very rarely provide a fully engineered solution.

Finally, it is worth noting that tamper-resistance provides little protection against legal attack. If you rely on it to keep algorithms proprietary, your competitors can bring a patent infringement suit (however frivolous) simply to force disclosure of your design. This actually happens!

14.9 Summary

Tamper-resistant devices and systems have a long history, and predate the development of electronic computing. Computers can be protected against physical tampering in a number of ways, such as by keeping them locked up in a guarded room. There are also several cheaper and more portable options.

This chapter looked at a number of them, from devices costing thousands of dollars that are certified by the U.S. government to resist all currently known attacks, down to smartcards that can be penetrated by an attacker with a few thousand dollars' worth of equipment with a few weeks' work. I discussed a number of applications, and a number of failures. Very often, the failures are not the fault of the hardware barriers or alarms themselves, but a result of using the technology in an inappropriate way.

Research Problems

There are basically three strands of research in tamper-resistant processor design. The first concerns itself with making faster, better, cheaper processors: how can the protection offered by a high-end device be brought to products with midrange prices and sizes, and how can midrange protection can be brought to smartcards? The second concerns itself with pushing forward the state of the attack art. How can the latest chip-testing technologies be used to make faster, better, cheaper attacks?

The third strand concerns itself with the logical aspects of protection. Even assuming that you can put a perfectly impenetrable barrier around a processor—imagine, for example, a processor in orbit around Mars—how do you design the transaction set (and the surrounding application) so that it can do useful work, with a high level of assurance that some simple attack won't be found?

Further Reading

For the early history of crypto, including things like weighted code books and water-soluble inks, the source is, of course, Kahn [428]. The IBM and Dallas products mentioned have extensive documentation available online [397]; the U.S. FIPS documents are also online [576]. For an introduction to chip card technology, see [632]; and for the gory details of tampering attacks on chip cards, see [43, 44, 470]. Noninvasive attacks on security processors, such as power analysis, are discussed in the next chapter.

CHAPTER 15

Emission Security

The hum of either army stilly sounds,
That the fixed sentinels almost receive
The secret whispers of each other's watch;
Fire answers fire, and through their paly flames
Each battle sees the other's umbered face.

—WILLIAM SHAKESPEARE, KING HENRY V, ACT IV

15.1 Introduction

Emission security, or *Emsec*, refers to preventing a system being attacked using *compromising emanations*, namely conducted or radiated electromagnetic signals. It has many aspects. Military organizations are greatly concerned with *Tempest* defenses, which prevent the stray RF emitted by computers and other electronic equipment from being picked up by an opponent and used to reconstruct the data being processed. The smartcard industry has been greatly exercised by *power analysis*, in which a computation being performed by a smartcard—such as a digital signature—is observed by measuring the current drawn by the CPU and the measurements used to reconstruct the key. These threats are closely related, and have a number of common countermeasures.

People often underestimate the importance of Emsec. However, it seems that the world's military organizations spent as much on it as on cryptography during the last quarter of the twentieth century. In the commercial world, the uptake of smartcards was materially set back in the last few years of that century by the realization that all the smartcards then on the market were extremely vulnerable to simple attacks, which required the attacker only to trick the customer into using a specially adapted terminal that would analyze the current it drew during a small number of transactions. These attacks did not involve penetrating the card (at least, once the research needed to design the attack had been carried out), and thus might leave no trace. Once fielded, they were very much cheaper than probing attacks, and potentially allowed large-scale card-cloning attacks against an unsuspecting cardholder population.

Electromagnetic eavesdropping attacks have been demonstrated against other commercial systems, including automatic teller machines. There has also been much speculation about disruptive electromagnetic attacks, whereby, for example, a terrorist group uses a high-energy microwave source to destroy the computers in a target organization without killing people. (I'll discuss these in more detail in the chapter on electronic warfare.)

Both active and passive Emsec measures are closely related to preventing random system disruption happening as a result of problems with *electromagnetic compatibility* (EMC) and *radio frequency interference* (RFI). If you fly regularly, you've no doubt heard the captain say something like, "All electronic devices must be switched off now, and not switched on again until I turn off the seat belt sign 10 minutes after takeoff." This problem is worsening as everything becomes electronic and clock frequencies go up. And how do you do as the captain says when more and more devices are designed to be "always on,"—so that the off switch only turns off the green tell-tale light?

As more and more everyday devices get hooked up to wireless networks, and as processor speeds head into the gigahertz range, all these problems—RFI/EMC, Emsec and various electronic warfare threats—are set to get worse.

15.2 History

"Crosstalk" between telephone wires was a problem known to the pioneers of telephony in the nineteenth century, with their two-wire circuits stacked on tiers of crosstrees on supporting poles. One way of dealing with it was to use "transpositions," whereby the wires were crossed over at intervals to make the circuit a twisted pair. This problem appears to have first come to the attention of the military during the British Army expedition to the Nile and Suakin in 1884–1885 [569].

The first appearance of compromising emanations in warfare seems to date to 1914. Field telephone wires were laid to connect the troops with their headquarters, and these often ran for miles, parallel to enemy trenches that were only a few hundred yards away. These wires used a single-core insulated cable and earth return in order to halve the weight and bulk of the cable. It was soon discovered that earth leakage caused a lot of crosstalk, including messages from the enemy side. Listening posts were quickly established and protective measures were introduced, including the use of twisted-pair cable. By 1915, valve amplifiers had extended the earth-leakage listening range to 100 yards for telephony and 300 yards for Morse code. It was found that the tangle of abandoned telegraph wire in no-man's land provided such a good communications channel, and leaked so much traffic to the Germans, that clearing it away become a task for which lives were spent. By 1916, earth-return circuits had been abolished within 3,000 yards of the front. When the Unied States joined the war, the techniques were passed on. More information can be found in [542, 569].

During the World War II, radio engineering saw advances in radar, passive direction finding, and low-probability-of-intercept techniques, which I'll discuss in the next chapter. By the 1960s, the stray RF leaking from the local oscillator signals in domestic television sets was being targeted by direction-finding equipment in "TV detector vans," in Britain, where TV owners must pay an annual license fee that is supposed to support public broadcast services. Its use has since expanded to satellite and cable TV operators, who use detector vans to find pirate decoders. Some people in the computer security community were also aware that information could leak from cross-coupling and stray RF (see, for example, [259, 791]).

The intelligence community also started to exploit RF effects. In 1960, the British prime minister ordered surveillance on the French embassy in the course of negotiations about joining the European Economic Community. Scientists from his domestic intelligence agency, MI5, noticed that the enciphered traffic from the embassy carried a faint secondary signal, and constructed equipment to recover it. It turned out to be the plaintext, which somehow leaked through the cipher machine [814]. This is more common than one might suppose; there has been more than one case of a cipher machine broadcasting in clear on radio frequencies, though often there is reason to suspect that the vendor's government was aware of this.

During the 1970s, emission security became a highly classified topic and vanished from the open literature. It came back to public attention in 1985 when Wim van Eck, a Dutch researcher, published an article describing how he had managed to reconstruct the picture on a VDU at a distance [259]. The revelation that Tempest attacks were not just feasible, but could be mounted with simple equipment that could be built at home, sent a shudder through the computer security industry.

Published research in emission security and related topics took off in the second half of the 1990s. In 1996, Markus Kuhn and I observed in [43] that many smartcards could be broken by inserting transients, or *glitches*, in their power or clock lines (this attack wasn't discovered by us, but by pay-TV hackers). Paul Kocher also showed that many common implementations of cryptosystems could be broken by making precise measurements of the time taken [466]. In 1998, Kuhn and I published a paper showing that many of the compromising emanations from a PC could be made better, or worse, by appropriate software measures [478]. In 1998–9, Kocher showed that crypto keys used in smartcards could be recovered by appropriate processing of precise measurements of the current drawn by the card—which we'll discuss in detail in Section 15.4.1.2 below [467]. In 2000, David Samyde and Jean-Jacques Quisquater demonstrated that similar attacks could be carried out by bringing small electromagnetic field sensors close to the card's surface [668].

15.3 Technical Surveillance and Countermeasures

Before getting carried away with high-tech toys such as Tempest monitoring receivers, we need to stop and think about bugs. The simplest and most widespread attacks that use the electromagnetic spectrum are not those that exploit some unintended design feature of innocuous equipment, but those in which a custom-designed device is introduced by the attacker.

No matter how well it is protected by encryption and access controls while in transit or storage, most highly confidential information originally comes into being either as speech or as keystrokes on a PC. If it can be captured by the opponent at this stage, then no subsequent protective measures are likely to help very much.

An extraordinary range of bugs is available on the market:

- At the low end, a few tens of dollars will buy a simple radio microphone, which you can stick under a table when visiting the target. Battery life is the main constraint on these devices. They typically have a range of only a few hundred yards, and a lifetime of a few days or weeks.

- At the next step up are devices that draw their power from the mains, a telephone cable or some other external electricity supply. This means that they can last indefinitely once positioned. Some are simple microphones, which can be installed quickly in cable ducting by an adversary who can get a few minutes alone in a room. Others are inserted from a neighboring building or apartment by drilling most of the way through a wall or floor. Still others, used by the U.K. police in recent gangland surveillance cases, look like electrical adaptors, but actually contain a microphone, a radio transmitter, and a TV camera. Others monitor data—for example, there is a Trojan computer keyboard with bugging hardware contained in the cable connector.

- Many modern bugs use off-the-shelf mobile radio technology. They can be seen as slightly modified cellphone handsets which go off-hook silently when called.

- One exotic device, on show at the NSA Museum in Fort Meade, was presented to the U.S. ambassador in Moscow in 1946 by a class of schoolchildren. It was a wooden replica of the Great Seal of the United States, and the ambassador hung it on the wall of the office in his residence. In 1952, it was discovered to contain a resonant cavity that acted as a microphone when illuminated by microwaves from outside the building, and retransmitted the conversations that took place in the office. Right up to the end of the Cold War, embassies in Moscow were regularly irradiated with microwaves, so presumably variants of the technique continued to be used.

- Laser microphones work by shining a laser beam at a reflective or partially reflective surface, such as a window pane, in the room where the target conversation is taking place. The sound waves modulate the reflected light, which can be picked up and decoded at a distance.

- High-end devices used today by governments, which can cost upward of $10,000, use low-probability-of-intercept radio techniques such as frequency hopping and burst transmission. They can also be turned on and off remotely. These features can make them much harder to find.

A number of countermeasures can give a fair amount of protection against such attacks.

- The *nonlinear junction detector* is a device that can find hidden electronic equipment at close range. It works because the transistors, diodes, and other nonlinear junctions in electronic equipment have the effect of rectifying incident radio frequency signals. The device broadcasts a weak radio signal, and listens for harmonics of this signal. It can detect unshielded electronics at a range of a few feet. However, if the bug has been planted in or near existing electronic equipment, then the nonlinear junction detector is not much help. There are also expensive bugs designed not to re-radiate at all. An interesting variant was invented by the investigative journalist Duncan Campbell in the early 1970s, to detect telephone taps: the amplifier used at that time by the security services re-radiated harmonics down the line. Following a raid on his house, the plans for this device were seized; it was then "invented" in a government laboratory, and credited to a government scientist.

- A number of *surveillance receivers* are on the market. The better ones sweep the radio spectrum from about 10 KHz to 3 GHz every few tens of seconds, and look for signals that can't be explained as broadcast, police, air traffic control and so on. (Above 3 GHz, signals are so attenuated by building materials, and device antennas can be so directional, that general spectrum search is no longer as effective as nonlinear junction detectors and physical searching.) Contrary to popular belief, some low-probability-of-intercept techniques do not give complete protection. Direct sequence spread spectrum can be spotted from its power spectrum, and frequency hoppers will typically be observed at different frequencies on successive sweeps. Burst transmission does better. But the effectiveness of surveillance receivers is increasingly limited by the availability of bugs that use the same frequencies and protocols as legitimate mobile or cordless phones. Security-conscious organizations can always try to forbid the use of mobiles, but this tends not to last long outside the military. For example, Britain's parliament forbade mobiles until 1997, but the rule was overturned when the government changed.

- Breaking the line of sight, such as by planting trees around your laboratory, can be effective against laser microphones. But is often impractical. It can be cheaper to have a shielded internal room for particularly sensitive meetings; and there are vendors who sell prefabricated rooms with acoustic and electromagnetic shielding for just this purpose.

- Some facilities at military organizations are placed in completely shielded buildings, or underground, so that even if bugs are introduced their signals can't be heard outside [55]. This is very expensive, and in many cases impractical. A second-best option is to ensure that devices such as wire-line microphones aren't installed in the building when it's constructed, that there are frequent sweeps, and that untrusted visitors (and contractors such as cleaning staff) are kept out of the most sensitive areas. But this is harder than it looks. A new U.S. embassy building in Moscow had to be abandoned after large numbers of microphones were found in the structure; and it was recently reported that Britain's counterintelligence service had to tear down and rebuild a large part of a new headquarters building, at a cost of about $50 million, after an employee of one of the building contractors was found to have past associations with the Provisional IRA.

The traditional tension here is between technological defenses, which can be very effective but very expensive, and procedural controls, which are cheap but tedious.

All that said, technological developments are steadily making life easier for the bugger and harder for the defense. As more and more devices acquire intelligence and short-range radio or infrared communications—as "things that think" become "things that chatter"—there is greater scope for attacks involving equipment that's already in place rather than stuff that has to emplaced for the purpose. For example:

- The risks associated with telephones are much higher than many people would like to believe. More and more people use cordless phones for convenience, and forget that they're easy to eavesdrop. Phones can be doctored so that they'll go off-hook under remote control; some digital (ISDN) phones have a facility built into them that allows this (it's said that some repressive countries make this feature a condition of import licensing). Also, some makes of PBX can be reprogrammed to support this kind of surveillance.

- The typical laptop computer has a microphone that can be switched on under software control, and is increasingly likely to have a radio LAN connection. An attacker might infect the device with a virus that listens to conversations in the room, compresses them, encrypts them, and emails them back to its creator.

- The NSA banned Furby toys in its buildings, as the Furby remembers (and randomly repeats) things said in its presence.

But there are many more ways in which existing electronic equipment can be exploited by an adversary.

15.4 Passive Attacks

We'll first consider passive attacks, that is, attacks in which the opponent makes use of whatever electromagnetic signals are presented to him without any effort on her part to create. Broadly speaking, there are two categories. The signal can either be conducted over some kind of circuit (such as a power line or phone line) or it may be radiated as radio frequency energy. These two types of threat are referred to by the military as *Hijack* and *Tempest*, respectively. They are not mutually exclusive; RF threats often have a conducted component. For example, radio signals emitted by a computer can be picked up by the mains power circuits and conducted into neighboring buildings. Still, it's a reasonable working classification most of the time.

15.4.1 Leakage through Power and Signal Cables

Since the nineteenth century, engineers have been aware that high-frequency signals leak everywhere, and that careful measures are needed to stop them causing problems; as noted, the leakage has been exploited for military purposes since in 1914. Conducted leakage of information can be largely suppressed by careful design, with power supplies and signal cables suitably filtered and suppressed. This makes up a significant part of the cost difference between otherwise comparable military and civilian electronics.

15.4.1.1 Red/Black Separation

Red equipment (carrying confidential data such as plaintext) has to be isolated by filters and shields from *black* equipment (which can send signals directly to the outside world). Equipment with both red and black connections, such as cipher machines, is particularly difficult to get right. It's made more expensive by the fact that the standards for emission security, such as the NACSIM 5100A that specifies the test requirements for Tempest-protected equipment, and its NATO equivalent AMSG 720B, are classified [660].

So properly shielded equipment tends to be available only in small quantities, and made specifically for defense markets. This makes it extremely expensive. And the costs don't stop there. The operations room at an air base can have thousands of cables leading from it; filtering them all, and imposing strict enough configuration management to preserve red/black separation, can cost millions.

15.4.1.2 Power Analysis

Often, people aren't aware of the need to filter signals until an exploit is found. A recent, and very important, example comes from the discovery of power attacks on smartcards. As a smartcard is usually a single silicon chip in a very thin carrier, there is little scope for filtering the power supply using chokes, capacitors and so on. The power supply may also be under the control of the enemy. If you use your bank smartcard to make a purchase in a Mafia-owned store, then the terminal might have extra electronics built into it to cheat you.

By the early 1990s, it appears to have been known to pay-TV hackers and to some government agencies that a lot of information could be gathered about the computations being performed in a smartcard simply by measuring the current it drew from its power supply. This attack, known as *power analysis* or *rail noise analysis*, may involve as little as inserting a $10\,\Omega$ resistor in the ground line and connecting a digital storage oscilloscope across it to observe fluctuations in the current drawn by the device. An example of the resulting power trace can be seen in Figure 15.1.

Different instructions have quite different power-consumption profiles, and, as you can see in the figure, the power consumption also depends on the data being processed. The main data-dependent contribution in many circumstances is from the bus driver transistors, which are quite large (see the top of Figure 14.5). Depending on the design, the current may vary by several hundred microamps over a period of several hundred nanoseconds for each bit of the bus whose state is changed [547]. Thus, the Hamming weight of the difference between each data byte and the preceding byte on the bus (the *transition count*) is available to an attacker. In some devices, the Hamming weight of each data byte is available, too [549]. EEPROM reads and writes can give even more substantial signals.

The effect of this leakage is that an attacker who understands how a cipher is implemented (for example, as a result of probing out the card software and disassembling it) can obtain significant information about the card's secrets and, in many cases, deduce the value of the key in use. It is particularly significant because it is a noninvasive attack, and can be carried out by suitably modified terminal equipment on a smartcard carried by an unsuspecting customer. This means that once the attacker has taken the trouble

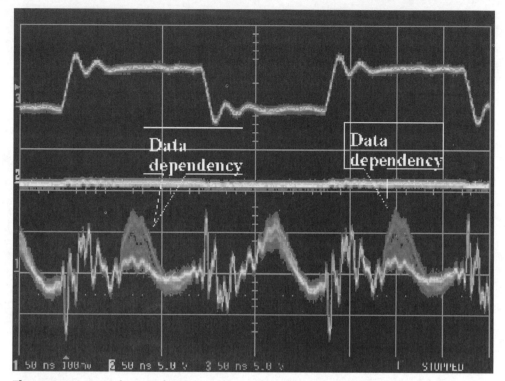

Figure 15.1 Superimposed power consumption traces of a Siemens SLE44 smartcard, showing data dependency (courtesy of Andy Santoso). The upper half of the screen shows the clock signal; the lower shows the power consumption.

to dismantle a card, understand its contents, and design the attack, a very large number of cards may be compromised at little marginal cost.

The threat posed to smartcards by power analysis was brought forcefully to the industry's attention in 1998 with the development by Paul Kocher of a specific signal-processing technique to extract the key bits used in a block cipher, such as DES, from a collection of power curves, without knowing the implementation details of the card software. This technique, *differential power analysis*, works as follows [467].

The attacker first collects a number of curves (typically several hundred) by performing known transactions with the target card—transactions for which the encryption algorithm and either the plaintext or the ciphertext is known. She then guesses some of the internal state of the cipher. In the case of DES, each round of the cipher has eight table look-ups in which six bits of the current input is exclusive-or'ed with six bits of key material, and then used to look up a four-bit output from an S-box. So if it's the ciphertext to which the attacker has access, she will guess the six input bits to an S-box in the last round. The power curves are then sorted into two sets based on this guess and synchronized. Average curves are then computed and compared. The difference between the two average curves is called a *differential trace*.

The process is repeated for each of the 64 possible six-bit inputs to the target S-box. It is generally found that the correct input value—which separates the power curves into two sets each with a different S-box output value—will result in a differential trace with a noticeable peak. Wrong guesses of input values, however, generally result in randomly sorted curves and thus in a differential trace that looks like random noise. In this way, the six keybits which go to the S-box in question can be found, followed by the others used in the last round of the cipher. In the case of DES, this gives 48 of the 56 keybits, and the remainder can be found trivially by exhaustive search. If the cipher has many more keybits, then the attacker can unroll it a round at a time.

The effect is that, even if a card could be constructed that resisted probing attacks, it is likely to be vulnerable unless specific power analysis defenses are built in. (In fact, all smartcards on the market in 1998 were claimed to be vulnerable [467].) Furthermore, even attackers without access to probing equipment could mount attacks cheaply and quickly.

This discovery was widely publicized, and held up the deployment of smartcards while people worked on defenses. In some cases, protocol-level defenses are possible; one can design protocols that update the key with every few encryptions, and thus prevent the attacker getting enough data (some point-of-sale terminals are designed this way). But most existing protocols are too well entrenched to be changed radically. Another idea was to insert randomness into the way the cryptography was done. For example, at each round of DES, one might look up the eight S-boxes in a random order. However, all this achieves is that instead of one large spike in the differential trace, one gets eight spikes each with an eighth the amplitude; the attacker only has to collect some more power curves.

The defenses now being fielded against power analysis are hardware-based. One of the common cards has hardware that inserts a dummy operation about every 64 machine instructions; another has an internal clock that is only loosely coupled to the external one and that changes frequency about every 64 cycles. Neither of these is foolproof, as an attacker might use signal-processing techniques to realign the power curves for averaging. The next generation of cards may use more robust defenses, such as potting capacitors with the smartcard chip to enable the supply voltage to be properly decoupled, or using silicon design techniques such as dual-rail encoding where the current drawn is independent of the data being processed. Yet another approach is to use self-timed logic, which uses no clock. At the time of writing, this is an area of active research.

15.4.2 Leakage through RF Signals

When I first learned to program in 1972 at the Glasgow Schools' Computer Centre, we had an early IBM machine with a 1.5 MHz clock. A radio tuned to this frequency in the machine room would emit a loud whistle, which varied depending on the data being processed. Similar phenomena were noted by many people, some of whom used the noise as a debugging aid. A school colleague of mine had a better idea: he wrote a set of subroutines of different lengths such that by calling them in sequence, the computer could be made to play a tune. We didn't think of the security implications at the time.

Moving now to more modern equipment, all VDUs emit a weak TV signal—a VHF or UHF radio signal, modulated with a distorted version of the image currently being displayed—unless they have been carefully designed not to. The video signal is available at a number of places in the equipment, notably in the beam current that is modulated with it. This signal contains many harmonics of the dot rate, some of which radiate better than others because cables and other components resonate at their wavelength. Given a suitable broadband receiver, these emissions can be picked up and reconstituted as video. The design of suitable equipment is discussed in [259, 478]. Contrary to popular belief, LCD displays are also generally easy for the eavesdropper.

Other researchers quickly established the possibility of remote snooping on everything from fax machines through shielded RS-232 cables to Ethernet [719, 230]. A few companies sprang up to sell "jammers," but these are hard to implement properly [60], as they can interfere with TV and other services. Military Tempest-shielded equipment remained unavailable to the commercial sector. In any case, it is usually a generation out of date and five times as expensive as off-the-shelf PCs. The view taken in the banking industry was, "Well, we don't do it to our competitors, so they probably don't do it to us; and we don't know where to get effective countermeasures anyway, so put it in the 'too hard' file." This view got shaken somewhat in the late 1990s when Hans-Georg Wolf demonstrated a Tempest attack that could recover card and PIN data from a cash machine at a distance of eight meters [239]. However, Tempest precautions remain a rarity in commerce and in nondefense-sector industry.[1]

Meanwhile, with the end of the Cold War, military budgets were cut, and often there was no alternative to using commercial off-the-shelf equipment; there was no longer the money to develop systems exclusively for government use. Government organizations in NATO countries have switched to a *zone* model of Emsec protection, whereby the most sensitive equipment is kept in the rooms furthest from the facility perimeter, and shielding is reserved for the most sensitive systems (such as national intelligence) or where the threat is highest (such as in overseas embassies). Nonetheless, the bill for Tempest protection in NATO government agencies comes to over a billion dollars a year.

A lower-cost protection technology, called Soft Tempest, has emerged and been deployed in some commercial products (such as the email encryption package PGP) [478]. Soft Tempest uses software techniques to filter, mask, or render incomprehensible the information bearing electromagnetic emanations from a computer system.

Markus Kuhn and I discovered that most of the information bearing RF energy from a VDU was concentrated in the top of the spectrum, so filtering out this component is a logical first step. We removed the top 30% of the Fourier transform of a standard font by convolving it with a suitable low-pass filter (see Figures 15.2 and 15.3).

This turns out to have an almost imperceptible effect on the screen contents as seen by the user. Figures 15.4 and 15.5 display photographs of the screen with the two video signals from Figures 15.2 and 15.3.

The difference in the emitted RF is dramatic, as illustrated in the photographs in Figures 15.6 and 15.7. These show the potentially compromising emanations, as seen by a Tempest monitoring receiver.

The level of protection that Soft Tempest techniques can provide for VDUs is only on the order of 10–20dB, but this translates to a difference of a zone—which, in an organization the size of a government, can give a considerable cost saving [45].

There are other attacks that software tricks can block completely. For example, computer keyboards can be snooped on while the microcontroller goes through a loop that

[1]Just as I got the copyedited manuscript of this book back from Wiley for checking. I heard, for the first time, a believable report of a commercial Tempest attack. Apparently, one financial institution was spied on by a private investigator retained by a rival. But the big picture remains military.

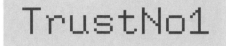

Figure 15.2   Normal text.

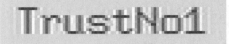

Figure 15.3   Same text, low-pass filtered.

Figure 15.4   Screenshot, normal text.

Figure 15.5   Screenshot, filtered text.

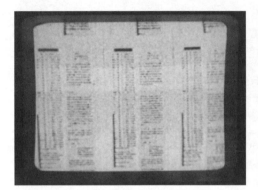

Figure 15.6   Page of normal text.

Figure 15.7   Page of filtered text.

scans all the keys until it encounters one that is pressed. The currently pressed key is modulated on to the RF emissions from the keyboard. By encrypting the order in which the keys are scanned, this kind of attack can be completely blocked.

15.5 Active Attacks

But it's not enough to simply encrypt a keyboard scan pattern to protect it, as the attacker can use active as well as passive techniques. Against a keyboard, the technique is to irradiate the cable with a radio wave at its resonant frequency. Thanks to the non-linear junction effect, the keypress codes are modulated into the return signal, which is reradiated by the cable. This can be picked up at a distance of 50 to 100 yards. To prevent it, one must also encrypt the signal from the keyboard to the PC [478].

15.5.1 Tempest Viruses

There are quite a few other active attacks possible on various systems. The phenomenon observed with our school computer in 1972—that a suitable program would cause a computer to play a tune on the radio, in effect turning it into a low-grade radio transmitter—is

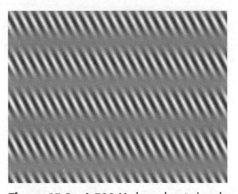

Figure 15.8   A 300 Hz broadcast signal.

Figure 15.9   A 1200 Hz broadcast signal.

easy enough to reimplement on a modern PC. Figures 15.8 and 15.9 show what the screen on a typical PC looks like when the video signal is an RF carrier at 2 MHz, modulated with pure tones of 300 and 1200 Hz.

Using phenomena like this, it is possible to write a *Tempest virus*, which will infect a target computer and transmit the secret data it steals to a radio receiver hidden nearby. This can happen even if the machine is not connected to the Net. The receiver need not be expensive; a short wave radio with a cassette recorder will do, and exploit code has already been published on the Net. With more sophisticated techniques, such as spread-spectrum modulation, it's possible for the attacker with more expensive equipment to get much better ranges [478].

Some of these methods may already have been known to the intelligence community. There have been reports of the CIA using software-based RF exploits in economic espionage against certain European countries (for example, in a TV documentary accompanying the release of [464]). Material recently declassified by the NSA in response to a FOIA request [542, 420] reveals the use of the codeword *Teapot* to refer to "the investigation, study, and control of intentional compromising emanations (i.e., those that are hostilely induced or provoked) from telecommunications and automated information systems equipment." A further example is to attack equipment that has been shielded and Tempest-certified up to a certain frequency (say, 1 GHz) by irradiating it through the ventilation slots using microwaves of a much higher frequency (say 10 GHz), at which these slots become transparent [478].

The possibility of attacks using malicious code is one reason why Tempest testing may involve not just listening passively to the emanations from the device under test, but injecting into it signals such as long linear feedback shift register sequences. These create a spread spectrum signal which will likely be detectable outside the equipment and thus simulate the worst case attack in which the opponent has used a software exploit to take over the device [108].

15.5.2 Nonstop

Another class of active methods, called *Nonstop* by the U.S. military [55], is the exploitation of RF emanations that are accidentally induced by nearby radio transmitters and other RF sources. If equipment that is processing sensitive data is used near a mobile phone, the phone's transmitter may induce in it currents that get modulated with sensitive data by the nonlinear junction effect and reradiated.

For this reason, it used to be forbidden to use a mobile phone within 5 meters of classified equipment. Nonstop attacks are also the main Emsec concern for ships and aircraft. Here, an attacker who can get close enough to do a passive Tempest attack can probably do much more serious harm than eavesdropping; but because military ships and aircraft often carry very powerful radios and radars, one must be careful that their signals don't get modulated accidentally with something useful to the enemy.

15.5.3 Glitching

Active Emsec threats are also significant in the smartcard world, where perhaps the best known is the *glitch attack* [43]. Here, as I mentioned above, the opponent inserts transients into the power or clock supply to the card in the hope of inducing a useful error.

For example, one smartcard used in early banking applications had the feature that an unacceptably high clock frequency triggered a reset only after a number of cycles, so that transients would be less likely to cause false alarms. So it was possible to replace a single clock pulse with two much narrower pulses without causing an alarm that would reset the card. This reliably caused the processor to execute a NOP, regardless of what instruction it was supposed to execute. By introducing glitches at suitable times, the attacker could step over jump instructions, and thus bypass access controls.

15.5.4 Differential Fault Analysis

Even where the attacker does not know the card's software in detail, glitch attacks can still be a threat. It had been noticed that a number of public key cryptographic algorithms would break if a random error could be induced [126]. For example, when doing an RSA signature, the secret computation $S = h(m)^d \pmod{pq}$ is typically carried out mod p, then mod q; the results are then combined. However, if the card returns a defective signature S_p which is correct modulo p but incorrect modulo q, then we will have:

$$p = \gcd\big(pq, S_p^e - h(m)\big)$$

which breaks the system at once. These attacks can be implemented easily if the card isn't protected against glitches; they can also be extended to many symmetric algorithms and protocols [103].

15.5.5 Combination Attacks

Other attacks use a combination of active and passive methods. I mentioned in passing in Part 1 a trick that could be used to find the PIN in a stolen smartcard. Early card systems would ask the customer for a PIN, and if it was incorrect, they would decrement a retry counter. This involved writing a byte to EEPROM, so the current consumed by the card rose measurably as the capacitors in the EEPROM voltage multiplier circuit were charged up. On noticing this, the attacker could simply reset the card and try the next candidate PIN.

15.5.6 Commercial Exploitation

Not all Emsec attacks are conducted in the context of covert military surveillance or laboratory attacks on tamper-resistant devices. I already mentioned the TV detector vans used in Britain to catch TV license defaulters and the customers of pay-TV pirates. There are also marketing applications. U.S. venue operator SFX Entertainment monitors what customers are playing on their car radios as they drive into venue parking lots by picking up the stray RF from the radio's local oscillator. Although legal, this alarms privacy advocates [728]. The same equipment has been sold to car dealers, mall operators, and radio stations.

15.5.7 Defenses

The techniques that can be used to defend smartcards against active Emsec threats are similar, though not quite the same, to those used in the passive case.

Timing randomness—jitter—is still useful, as a naive opponent might no longer know precisely when to insert the glitch. However, a clever opponent may well be able to analyze the power curve from the processor in real time, and compare it against the code so as to spot the critical target instructions. In addition, fault attacks are hard to stop with jitter, as the precise location of the fault in the code is not usually critical.

In some cases, defensive programming is enough. For example, the PIN search described in Section 15.5.5 is prevented in more modern implementations by decrementing the counter, soliciting the PIN, then increasing the counter again if it's correct. Differential fault attacks on public key protocols can be made a lot harder if you just check the result.

Other systems use specific protective hardware, such as a circuit that integrates the card reset with the circuit that detects clock frequencies that are too high or too low. Normal resets involve halving the clock frequency for a few cycles, so an attacker who found some means of disabling the monitoring function would quite likely find himself unable to reset the card at all on power-up [470].

Current defenses against glitch attacks are not entirely foolproof, and extensive device testing is highly advisable. New technologies, such as the use of self-timed logic, may improve things by providing a high level of protection against both active and passive threats. In the meantime, if you have to write a smartcard application, attacks based on glitching merit careful consideration.

15.6 How Serious Are Emsec Attacks?

Technical surveillance and its countermeasures are the most important aspect of Emsec, in both government and industry; they are likely to remain so. The range of bugs and other surveillance devices that can be bought easily is large and growing. The motivation for people to spy on their rivals, employees, and others will continue. If anything, the move to a wired world will make electronic surveillance more important, and countermeasures will take up more of security budgets.

Those aspects of Emsec that concern equipment not designed for surveillance— Tempest, Teapot, Hijack, Nonstop, and the various types of power and glitch attack—are set to become another of the many technologies that were initially developed in the government sector but then start being important in the design of commercial products.

15.6.1 Governments

The Emsec threats to embassies in hostile countries are real. If your country is forced by the president of Lower Slobovia to place its embassy in the second floor of an office block whose first and third floors are occupied by the local secret police, then security is an extremely hard problem. Shielding all electronic equipment (except that used for deception) will be part of the solution. In less threatening environments, the use of hardware Tempest shielding is more doubtful.

Despite the hype with which the Tempest industry maintained itself during the Cold War, there is growing scepticism about whether any actual Tempest attacks had ever been mounted by foreign agents, though anecdotes abound. It's said, for example, that the only known use of such surveillance techniques against U.S. interests in the whole of North America was by Canadian intelligence personnel, who overheard U.S. diplomats discussing the U.S. bottom line in grain sales to China; and that the East German Stasi were found to have maps of suitable parking places for Tempest vans in West German towns. But I've not found anything that can be nailed down to a reliable source, and having been driven around an English town looking for Tempest signals, I can testify that launching such attacks is much harder in practice than it might seem in theory. Governments now tend to be much more relaxed about Tempest risks than 10 years ago.

15.6.2 Businesses

In the private sector, the reverse is the case. The discovery of fault attacks, and then power attacks, was a big deal for the smartcard industry, and held up for probably two years the deployment of smartcards in banking applications in those countries that hadn't already committed to them. Blocking these attacks turns out to be difficult, and doing it properly will involve a further generation of hardware design.

And what about the future?

The "nonsecurity" aspects of emission management, namely RFI/EMC, are becoming steadily more important. Ever higher clock speeds, plus the introduction of all sorts of wireless devices and networks, and the proliferation of digital electronics into many devices that were previously analogue or mechanical, are making electromagnetic compatibility a steadily harder and yet more pressing problem. Different industry groups, manage a host of incompatible standards many of which are rapidly becoming obsolete— for example, by not requiring testing above 1 GHz, or by assuming protection distances that are no longer reasonable [455].

On the security side, attacks are likely to become easier. The advent of *software radios*—radios that digitize a signal at the intermediate frequency stage and do all the demodulation and subsequent processing in software—were, until recently, an expensive military curiosity [482], but are now finding applications in places like cellular radio base stations. The next generation may be consumer devices, designed to function as GPS receivers, GSM phones, radio LAN basestations, and to support whatever other radio-based services have been licensed locally—all with only a change in software. Once people learn how to program them, they might just as easily use them for Tempest attacks.

Finally, Emsec issues are not entirely divorced from electronic warfare. As society becomes more dependent on devices that are vulnerable to strong radio frequency signals—such as the high-power microwaves generated by military radars—the temptation to mount attacks will increase. I'll discuss high-energy radio frequency attacks in the next chapter.

15.7 Summary

Emission security covers a whole range of threats in which the security of systems can be subverted by compromising emanations, whether from implanted bugs, from unintentional radio frequency or conducted electromagnetic leakage, or from emanations that are induced in some way. Although originally a concern in the national intelligence community, Emsec is now a real issue for companies that build security products such as smartcards and cash machines. Many of these products can be defeated by observing stray RF or conducted signals. Protecting against such threats isn't as straightforward as it might seem.

Research Problems

The security industry badly needs a comprehensive set of emission security standards for commercial use. Military standards are classified, and the RFI/EMC standards are fragmented and contradictory, so a new and unified approach is overdue.

Further Reading

There is a shortage of open literature on Emsec. The classic van Eck article [259] is still worth a read; and the only book on computer security (until this one) to have a chapter on the subject is by Deborah Russell and G.T. Gangemi [660]. Our recent work on Soft Tempest, Teapot, and related topics can be found in [478]. For power analysis, see the papers by Paul Kocher [467], and by Tom Messergues, Ezzy Dabish and Robert Sloan [547]; more papers are appearing regularly. Finally, Joel McNamara runs a comprehensive unofficial Tempest Web site at [542].

CHAPTER 16

Electronic and Information Warfare

All warfare is based on deception ... hold out baits to entice the enemy. Feign disorder, and crush him.

—SUN TZU, *THE ART OF WAR*, 1.18–20

Force, and Fraud, are in warre the two Cardinal Virtues.

—THOMAS HOBBES

16.1 Introduction

For decades, electronic warfare has been a separate subject from computer security, even though they have some common technologies (such as cryptography). This is starting to change as elements of the two disciplines fuse to form the new subject of information warfare. The military's embrace of information warfare as a slogan over the last years of the twentieth century has established its importance—even if its concepts, theory, and doctrine are still underdeveloped.

There are other reasons why a knowledge of electronic warfare is important to the security professional. Many technologies originally developed for the warrior have been adapted for commercial use, and there are many instructive parallels. In addition, the struggle for control of the electromagnetic spectrum has consumed so many clever people and so many tens of billions of dollars that we find deception strategies and tactics of a unique depth and subtlety. It is the one area of electronic security to have experienced a lengthy period of coevolution of attack and defense involving capable motivated opponents.

Electronic warfare is also our main teacher when it comes to service denial attacks, a topic that computer security people have largely ignored, but that is now center stage thanks to distributed denial-of-service attacks on commercial Web sites. As I develop this discussion I'll try to draw out the parallels. In general, while people say that computer security is about confidentiality, integrity and availability, electronic warfare has this reversed and back-to-front. The priorities are:

1. Denial of service, which includes jamming, mimicry and physical attack.

2. Deception, which may be targeted at automated systems or at people.

3. Exploitation, which includes not just eavesdropping but obtaining any operationally valuable information from the enemy's use of his electronic systems.

16.2 Basics

The goal of electronic warfare is to control the electromagnetic spectrum. It is generally considered to consist of:

- *Electronic attack*, such as jamming enemy communications or radar, and disrupting enemy equipment using high-power microwaves.

- *Electronic protection*, which ranges from designing systems resistant to jamming, through hardening equipment to resist high-power microwave attack, to the destruction of enemy jammers using anti-radiation missiles.

- *Electronic support* which supplies the necessary intelligence and threat recognition to allow effective attack and protection. It allows commanders to search for, identify and locate sources of intentional and unintentional electromagnetic energy.

These definitions are taken from Schleher [677]. The traditional topic of cryptography, namely *communications security* (Comsec), is only a small part of electronic protection, just as it is becoming only a small part of information protection in more general systems. Electronic support includes *signals intelligence* (Sigint), which consists of *communications intelligence* (Comint) and *electronic intelligence* (Elint). The former collects enemy communications, including both message content and traffic data about which units are communicating, while the latter concerns itself with recognizing hostile radars and other non-communicating sources of electromagnetic energy.

Deception is central to electronic attack. The goal is to mislead the enemy by manipulating his perceptions in order to degrade the accuracy of his intelligence and target acquisition. Its effective use depends on clarity about who (or what) is to be deceived, about what and how long, and—where the targets of deception are human—the exploitation of pride, greed, laziness, and other vices. Deception can be extremely cost-effective and is also relevant to commercial systems.

Physical destruction is an important part of the mix; while some enemy sensors and communications links may be neutralized by jamming (*soft kill*), others will often be destroyed (*hard kill*). Successful electronic warfare depends on using the available tools in a coordinated way.

Electronic weapon systems are like other weapons in that there are *sensors*, such as radar, infrared and sonar; *communications* links, which take sensor data to the command and control center; and *output devices* such as jammers, lasers, and so on. I'll discuss the communications system issues first, as they are the most self-contained, then the sensors and associated jammers, and finally other devices such as electromagnetic pulse generators. Once we're done with e-war, we'll look at the lessons we might take over to i-war.

16.3 Communications Systems

Military communications were dominated by physical dispatch until about 1860, then by the telegraph until 1915, and then by the telephone until recently [569]. Nowadays, a typical command and control structure is made up of various tactical and strategic radio networks, that support data, voice, and images, and operate over point-to-point links and broadcast. Without situational awareness and the means to direct forces, the commander is likely to be ineffective. But the need to secure communications is much more pervasive than one might at first realize, and the threats are much more diverse.

- One obvious type of traffic is the communications between fixed sites such as army headquarters and the political leadership. The main threat here is that the cipher security might be penetrated, and the orders, situation reports and so on compromised. This might result from cryptanalysis or—more likely—equipment sabotage, subversion of personnel, or theft of key material. The insertion of deceptive messages may also be a threat in some circumstances. But cipher security will often include protection against traffic analysis (such as by link encryption) as well as of the transmitted message confidentiality and authenticity. The secondary threat is that the link might be disrupted, such as by destruction of cables or relay stations.

- There are more stringent requirements for communications with covert assets such as agents in the field. Here, in addition to cipher security issues, location security is important. The agent will have to take steps to minimize the risk of being caught as a result of communications monitoring. If she sends messages using a medium that the enemy can monitor, such as the public telephone network or radio, then much of her effort may go into frustrating traffic analysis and radio direction finding.

- Tactical communications, such as between HQ and a platoon in the field, also have more stringent (but slightly different) needs. Radio direction finding is still an issue, but jamming may be at least as important; and deliberately deceptive messages may also be a problem. For example, there is equipment that enables an enemy air controller's voice commands to be captured, cut into phonemes and spliced back together into deceptive commands, in order to gain a tactical advantage in air combat [324]. As voice-morphing techniques are developed for commercial use, the risk of spoofing attacks on unprotected communications will increase. Therefore, cipher security may include authenticity as well as confidentiality and/or covertness.

- Control and telemetry communications, such as signals sent from an aircraft to a missile it has just launched, must be protected against jamming and modification. It would also be desirable if they could be covert (so as not to trigger a target aircraft's warning receiver), but that is in tension with the power levels needed to defeat defensive jamming systems.

The protection of communications will require some mix, depending on the circumstances, of content secrecy, authenticity, resistance to traffic analysis and radio direction finding, and resistance to various kinds of jamming. These interact in some rather unobvious ways. For example, one radio designed for use by dissident organizations in Eastern Europe in the early 1980s operated in the radio bands normally occupied by the Voice of America and the BBC World Service—and routinely jammed by the Russians. The idea was that unless the Russians were prepared to turn off their jammers, they would have great difficulty doing direction finding.

Attack also generally requires a combination of techniques, even where the objective is not analysis or direction finding but simply denial of service. Owen Lewis summed it up succinctly: according to Soviet doctrine, a comprehensive and successful attack on a military communications infrastructure would involve destroying one third of it physically, denying effective use of a second third through techniques such as jamming, trojans or deception, and then allowing one's adversary to disable the remaining third in attempting to pass all his traffic over a third of the installed capacity [500]. This applies even in guerilla wars: in Malaya, Kenya, and Cyprus, the rebels managed to degrade the telephone system enough to force the police to set up radio nets [569].

In the 1980s, NATO developed a comparable doctrine, called *Counter-Command, Control and Communications* operations (C-C3, pronounced C cubed). It achieved its first flowering in the Gulf War; the command and control systems used there are described in [643]. (Of course, attacking an army's command structures is much older than that; it's a basic principle to shoot at an officer before shooting at his men.)

16.3.1 Signals Intelligence Techniques

Before communications can be attacked, the enemy's network must be mapped. The most expensive and critical task in signals intelligence is identifying and extracting the interesting material from the cacophony of radio signals and the huge mass of traffic on systems such as the telephone network and the Internet. The technologies in use are extensive and largely classified, but some aspects are public.

In the case of radio signals, communications intelligence agencies use receiving equipment, that can recognize a huge variety of signal types, to maintain extensive databases of signals—which stations or services use which frequencies. In many cases, it is possible to identify individual equipment by signal analysis. The clues can include any unintentional frequency modulation, the shape of the transmitter turn-on transient, the precise center frequency, and the final-stage amplifier harmonics. This *RF fingerprinting* technology was declassified in the mid-1990s for use in identifying cloned cellular telephones, where its makers claim a 95% success rate [341, 677]. It is the direct descendant of the World War II technique of recognizing a wireless operator by his *fist*—the way he sent Morse code [523].

Radio direction finding (RDF) is also critical. In the old days, this involved triangulating the signal of interest using directional antennas at two monitoring stations. Spies might have at most a few minutes to send a message home before having to move. Modern monitoring stations use *time difference of arrival* (TDOA) to locate a suspect signal rapidly, accurately, and automatically by comparing the phase of the signals received at two sites. Nowadays, anything more than a second or so of transmission can be a giveaway.

Traffic analysis—looking at the number of messages by source and destination—can also give very valuable information, not just about imminent attacks (which were signalled in World War I by a greatly increased volume of radio messages) but also about unit movements and other routine matters. However, traffic analysis really comes into its own when sifting through traffic on public networks, where its importance (both for national intelligence and police purposes) is difficult to overstate.

If you suspect Alice of espionage (or drug dealing, or whatever), you note everyone she calls and everyone who calls her. This gives you a list of dozens of suspects. You eliminate the likes of banks and doctors, who receive calls from too many people to analyze (your *whitelist*), and repeat the procedure on each remaining number. Having done this procedure recursively several times, you have a mass of thousands of contacts, which you sift for telephone numbers that appear more than once. If (say) Bob, Camilla, and Donald are Alice's contacts, with Bob and Camilla in contact with Eve, and Donald and Eve in touch with Farquhar, then all of these people are considered to be suspects. You now draw a *friendship tree*, which gives a first approximation to Alice's network, and refine it by collating it with other intelligence sources.

This is not as easy as it sounds. People can have several numbers; Bob might get a call from Alice at his work number, then call Eve from a phone booth. (In fact, if you're running an IRA cell, your signals officer should get a job at a dentist's or a doctor's or some other place that will be called by so many different people that they will probably be whitelisted. But that's another story.) Also, you will need some means of correlating telephone numbers to people. Even if you have access to the phone company's database of unlisted numbers, prepaid mobile phones can be a serious headache, as can cloned phones and hacked PBXs. I'll discuss these in the chapter on telecomms security; for now, I'll just remark that anonymous phones aren't new. There have been public phone booths for generations. But they are not a universal answer for the crook, as the discipline needed to use them properly is beyond most criminals, and in any case causes severe disruption.

Signals collection is not restricted to agreements with phone companies for access to the content of phone calls and the communications data. It also involves a wide range of specialized facilities ranging from expensive fixed installations, which copy international satellite links, through temporary tactical arrangements. A book by Nicky Hager [368] describes the main fixed collection network operated by the United States, Canada, Britain, Australia, and New Zealand. Known as *Echelon*, this consists of a number of collection stations that monitor international phone, fax, and data traffic using computers called *dictionaries*. These search the passing traffic for interesting phone numbers, network addresses, and machine-readable content; this is driven by search strings entered by intelligence analysts. The fixed network is supplemented by tactical collection facilities as needed; Hager describes, for example, the dispatch of Australian and New Zealand navy frigates to monitor domestic communications in Fiji during military coups in the 1980s. Egmont Koch and Jochen Sperber discuss U.S. and German installations in Germany in [464]; David Fulghum describes airborne signals collection in [324]; satellites are also used to collect signals, and there are covert collection facilities that are not known to the host country.

Despite this huge capital investment, the most difficult and expensive part of the whole operation is traffic selection, not collection [490]. Thus, contrary to naïve expectations, cryptography can make communications more vulnerable rather than less (if used incompetently, as it usually is). If you just encipher all the traffic you consider to be important, you have thereby marked it for collection by the enemy. On the other hand, if everyone encrypted all their traffic, then hiding traffic could be much easier (hence the push by signals intelligence agencies to prevent the widespread use of cryptography, even if it's freely available to individuals). This brings us to the topic of attacks.

16.3.2 Attacks on Communications

Once you have mapped the enemy network, you may wish to attack it. People often talk in terms of "codebreaking," but this is a gross oversimplification.

First, although some systems have been broken by pure cryptanalysis, this is fairly rare. Most production attacks have involved theft of key material as when the U.S. State Department code book was stolen during World War II by the valet of the U.S. ambassador to Rome or errors in the manufacture and distribution of key material as in the U.S. "Venona" attacks on Soviet diplomatic traffic [428]. Even where attacks based on cryptanalysis have been possible, they have often been made much easier by errors such as these, an example being the U.K./U.S. attacks on the German Enigma traffic during World War II [429]. The pattern continues to this day. A recent history of Soviet intelligence during the Cold War reveals that the technological advantage of the United States was largely nullified by Soviet skills in "using Humint in Sigint support"— which largely consisted of recruiting traitors who sold key material, such as the Walker family [51].

Second, access to content is often not the desired result. In tactical situations, the goal is often to detect and destroy nodes, or to jam the traffic. Jamming can involve not just noise insertion but active deception. In World War II, the Allies used German speakers as bogus controllers to send German nightfighters confusing instructions, and there was a battle of wits as authentication techniques were invented and defeated. More recently, as I noted in the chapter on biometrics, the U.S. Air Force has deployed more sophisticated systems based on voice morphing. I mentioned in an earlier chapter the tension between intelligence and operational units: the former want to listen to the other side's traffic, and the latter to deny them its use [63]. Compromises between these goals can be hard to find. It's not enough to jam the traffic you can't read, as that tells the enemy what you can read!

Matters can, in fact, be simplified if the opponent uses cryptography—even in a competent way. This removes the ops/intel tension, and you switch to RDF or link destruction as appropriate. This can involve the hard-kill approach of digging up cables or bombing telephone exchanges (both of which the allies did during the Gulf War), the soft-kill approach of jamming, or whatever combination of the two is economic. Jamming is a useful expedient where a link is to be disrupted for a short period, but is often expensive; not only does it tie up facilities, but the jammer itself becomes a target. (There are cases where it is more effective, such as against some satellite links where the uplink can be jammed using a tight beam from a hidden location using only a modest amount of power.)

The increasing use of civilian infrastructure, and in particular the Internet, raises the question of whether systematic denial-of-service attacks might be used to jam traffic. (There are anecdotes of Serbian information warfare cells attempting such attacks on NATO Web sites.) This threat is still considered real enough that many Western countries have separate intranets for government and military use.

16.3.3 Protection Techniques

As should be clear from the above, communications security techniques involve not just protecting the authenticity and confidentiality of the content—which can be achieved in a relatively straightforward way by encryption and authentication protocols—but also preventing traffic analysis, direction finding, jamming and physical destruction. Encryption can stretch to the first of these if applied at the link layer, so that all links appear to have a pseudorandom bitstream on them at all times, regardless of whether there is any message traffic. But link-layer encryption alone is not in general enough, as enemy capture of a single node might put the whole network at risk.

Encryption alone cannot protect against interception, RDF, jamming, and the destruction of links or nodes. For this, different technologies are needed. The obvious solutions are:

- Dedicated lines or optical fibers.

- Highly directional transmission links, such as optical links using infrared lasers or microwave links using highly directional antennas and extremely high frequencies, 20 GHz and up.

- *Low-probability-of-intercept* (LPI), *low-probability-of-position-fix* (LPPF), and antijam radio techniques.

The first two of these options are fairly straightforward to understand, and where feasible, they are usually the best. Cabled networks are very hard to destroy completely, unless the enemy knows where the cables are and has physical access to cut them. Even with massive artillery bombardment, the telephone network in Stalingrad remained in use (by both sides) all through the siege.

The third option is a substantial subject in itself, which I will now describe (albeit only briefly).

There are a number of LPI/LPPF/antijam techniques that go under the generic name of *spread spectrum* communications. They include *frequency hoppers, direct sequence spread spectrum* (DSSS), and *burst transmission*. From beginnings around World War II, spread-spectrum has spawned a substantial industry, and the technology (especially DSSS) has been applied to numerous other problems, ranging from high-resolution ranging (in the GPS system) through copyright marks in digital images (which I'll discuss later). Let's look at each of these three approaches in turn.

16.3.3.1 Frequency Hopping

Frequency hoppers are the simplest spread-spectrum systems to understand and to implement. They do exactly as their name suggests: they hop rapidly from one frequency to another, with the sequence of frequencies determined by a pseudorandom sequence known to the authorized principals. Hoppers were invented, famously, over dinner in 1940 by actress Hedy Lamarr and screenwriter George Antheil, who devised the technique as a means of controlling torpedos without the enemy detecting them or jamming their transmissions [484]. A frequency-hopping radar was independently developed at about the same time by the Germans [686]; in response to steady improvements in British jamming, German technicians adapted their equipment to change frequency daily, then hourly, and finally, every few seconds [627].

Hoppers are resistant to jamming by an opponent who doesn't know the hop sequence. Such an opponent may have to jam much of the band, and thus needs much more power than would otherwise be necessary. The ratio of the input signal's bandwidth to that of the transmitted signal is called the *process gain* of the system; thus, a 100 bit/sec signal spread over 10 MHz has a process gain of $10^7/10^2 = 10^5 = 50$ dB. The *jamming margin*, which is defined as the maximum tolerable ratio of jamming power to signal power, is essentially the process gain modulo implementation and other losses (strictly speaking, process gain divided by the minimum bit energy-to-noise density ratio). The optimal jamming strategy, for an opponent who can't predict the hop sequence, is *partial band jamming*—to jam enough of the band to introduce an unacceptable error rate in the signal.

Although hoppers can give a large jamming margin, they give little protection against an opponent who merely wants to detect their existence. A signal analysis receiver that sweeps across the frequency band of interest will often intercept them. (Depending on the relevant bandwidths, sweep rate, and dwell time, it might intercept a hopping signal several times).

However, because frequency hoppers are simple to implement, they are often used in combat networks, such as man-pack radios, with slow hop rates of 50–500 per second. To disrupt their communications, the enemy will need a fast or powerful jammer, which is inconvenient for the battlefield. Fast hoppers (defined in theory as having hop rates exceeding the bit rate; in practice, with hop rates of 10,000 per second or more) can pass the limit of even large jammers.

16.3.3.2 DSSS

In direct sequence spread spectrum, we multiply the information-bearing sequence by a much higher-rate pseudorandom sequence, usually generated by some kind of stream cipher. This spreads the spectrum by increasing the bandwidth (Figure 16.1). The technique was first described by a Swiss engineer, Gustav Guanella, in a 1938 patent application [686], and developed extensively in the United States in the 1950s. Its first deployment in anger was in Berlin in 1959.

Like hopping, DSSS can give substantial jamming margin (the two systems have the same theoretical performance). But it can also make the signal significantly harder to intercept. The trick is to arrange things so that at the intercept location, the signal strength is so low that it is lost in the noise floor unless you know the spreading sequence with

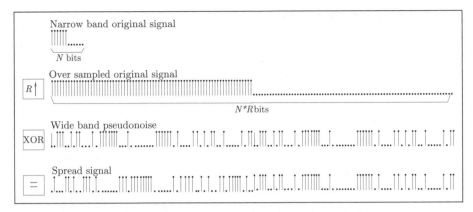

Figure 16.1   Spreading in DSSS (courtesy of Roche and Dugelay).

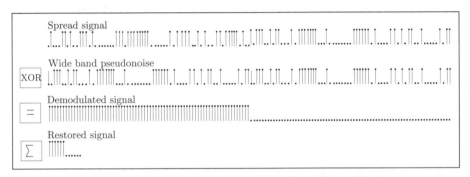

Figure 16.2   Unspreading in DSSS (courtesy of Roche and Dugelay).

which to recover it. Of course, it's harder to do both at the same time, since an antijam signal should be high power and an LPI/LPPF signal low power; the usual modus operandi is to work in LPI mode until detected by the enemy (for example, when coming within radar range), then boost transmitter power into antijam mode.

There is a large literature on DSSS; and the techniques have now been taken up by the commercial world as *code division multiple access* (CDMA) in various mobile radio and phone systems. DSSS is sometimes referred to as "encrypting the RF," and it comes in a number of variants. For example, when the underlying modulation scheme is FM rather than AM, it's called *chirp*. (The classic introduction to the underlying mathematics and technology is [616].) The engineering complexity is higher than with frequency hop, for various reasons. For example, synchronization is particularly critical. Users with access to a reference time signal (such as GPS or an atomic clock) can do this much more easily; of course, if you don't control GPS, you may be open to synchronization attacks; and even if you do, the GPS signal might be jammed. (It has recently been reported that the French jammed GPS in Greece in an attempt to sabotage a British bid to sell 250 tanks to the Greek government, a deal in which France was a competitor. This caused the British tanks to get lost during trials. When the ruse was discovered, the Greeks found it all rather amusing [757].) Another strategy is to have your users take turns at providing a reference signal.

16.3.3.3 Burst Communications

Burst communications, as their name suggests, involve compressing the data and transmitting it in short bursts at times unpredictable by the enemy. They are also known as *time-hop*. Usually, they are not so jam-resistant (except insofar as the higher data rate spreads the spectrum), but they can be difficult to intercept; if the duty cycle is low, a sweep receiver can easily miss them. They are often used in radios for special forces and intelligence agents.

An interesting variant is *meteor burst* transmission (also known as *meteor scatter*). This relies on the billions of micrometeorites that strike the Earth's atmosphere each day, each leaving a long ionization trail that persists for about a third of a second, and providing a temporary transmission path between a "mother station" and an area that might be a hundred miles long and a few miles wide. The mother station transmits continuously, and whenever one of the "daughters" hears mother, it starts to send packets of data at high speed, to which mother replies. With the low power levels used in covert operations, it is possible to achieve an average data rate of about 50 bps, with an average latency of about 5 minutes and a range of 500–1,500 miles. With higher power levels, and in higher latitudes, average data rates can rise into the tens of kilobits per second.

As well as special forces, the U.S. Air Force in Alaska uses meteor scatter as backup communications for early warning radars. It's also used in civilian applications such as monitoring rainfall in Lesotho, Africa. In niche markets, where low bit rates and high latency can be tolerated, but where equipment size and cost are important, meteor scatter can be hard to beat. (The technology is described in [676].)

16.3.3.4 Combining Covertness and Jam Resistance

There are some rather complex trade-offs between different LPI, LPPF, and jam resistance technologies, and other aspects of performance such as their resistance to fading and multipath, and the number of users that can by accommodated simultaneously. They also behave differently in the face of specialized jamming techniques such as *swept-frequency jamming* (where the jammer sweeps repeatedly through the target frequency band) and *repeater jamming* (where the jammer follows a hopper as closely as it can). Some types of jamming translate; for example, an opponent with insufficient power to block a signal completely can do *partial time jamming* on DSSS by emitting pulses that cover most of its utilized spectrum, and on frequency hop by partial band jamming.

There are also engineering trade-offs. For example, DSSS tends to be about twice as efficient as frequency hop in power terms, but frequency hop gives much more jamming margin for a given complexity of equipment. On the other hand, DSSS signals are much harder to locate using direction-finding techniques [287].

System survivability requirements can impose further constraints. It may be essential to prevent an opponent who has captured one radio and extracted its current key material from using this to jam a whole network.

A typical modern military system will use some combination of tight beams, DSSS, hopping and burst.

- The Jaguar tactical radio used by U.K. armed forces hops over one of nine 6.4 MHz bands, and has an antenna with a steerable null that can be pointed at a jammer or at a hostile intercept station.

- Both DSSS and hopping are used with *Time Division Multiple Access* (TDMA) in the *Joint Tactical Information Distribution System* (JTIDS), a U.S. data link system used by AWACS—the Airborne Warning and Control System—to communicate with fighters [677]. TDMA separates transmission from reception, and lets users know when to expect their slot. The DSSS signal has a 57.6 KHz data rate and a 10 MHz chip rate (and so a jamming margin of 36.5 dB), which hops around in a 255 MHz band with a minimum jump of 30 MHz. The hopping code is available to all users, while the spreading code is limited to individual circuits. The rationale is that if an equipment capture leads to the compromise of the spreading code, this would allow jamming of only a single 10 MHz band, not the full 255 MHz.

- MILSTAR is a U.S. satellite communications system with 1-degree beams from a geostationary orbit (20 GHz down, 44 GHz up). The effect of the narrow beam is that users can operate within three miles of the enemy without being detected. Jam protection is from hopping; its channels hop several thousand times a second in bands of 2 GHz.

- A system designed to control MX missiles (but not in the end deployed) is described in [337] and gives an example of extreme survivability engineering. To be able to withstand a nuclear first strike, the system had to withstand significant levels of node destruction, jamming, and atmospheric noise. The design adopted was a frequency hopper at 450 KHz with a dynamically reconfigurable network.

- French tactical radios have remote controls. The soldier can use the handset a hundred meters from the radio. This means that attacks on the high-power emitter don't endanger the troops so much [216].

There are also some system-level tricks, such as *interference cancellation*, where the idea is to communicate in a band you are jamming and whose jamming waveform is known to your own radios, so they can cancel it out or hop around it. This can make jamming harder for the enemy by forcing him to spread his available power over a larger bandwidth, and can make signals intelligence harder, too [644].

16.3.4 Interaction Between Civil and Military Uses

Civil and military uses of communications are increasingly intertwined. Operation Desert Storm (the Gulf War against Iraq) made extensive use of the Gulf States' civilian infrastructure: a huge tactical communications network was created in a short space of time using satellites, radio links, and leased lines. Experts from various U.S. armed services claim that the effect of communications capability on the war was absolutely decisive [398]. It appears inevitable that both military and substate groups will attack civilian infrastructure to deny it to their opponents. Already, satellite links are particularly vulnerable to uplink jamming. Satellite-based systems such as GPS have been jammed as an exercise; and there is some discussion of the systemic vulnerabilities that result from overreliance on it [310].

Another example of growing interdependency is given by the Global Positioning System, GPS. This started as a U.S. military navigation system, and had a *selective availability* feature that limited the accuracy to about a hundred yards unless the user had the relevant cryptographic key. This had to be turned off during Desert Storm as there weren't enough military GPS sets to go around, and civilian equipment had to be used instead. As time went on, GPS turned out to be so useful, particularly in civil aviation, that the FAA helped find ways to defeat selective availability that give an accuracy of about three yards, compared with a claimed eight yards for the standard military receiver [270]. Finally, in May 2000, President Clinton announced the cessation of selective availability. (Presumably, this preserves its usability in wartime.)

The civilian infrastructure also provides some defensive systems of which government organizations (especially in the intelligence field) can make use. I mentioned the prepaid mobile phone, which provides a fair degree of anonymity; secure Web servers offer some possibilities; and another example is the *anonymous remailer*, a device that accepts encrypted email, decrypts it, and sends it on to a destination contained within the outer encrypted envelope. I'll discuss this technology in more detail in Section 20.4.3; one of the pioneers of anonymous networking was the U.S. Navy [637]. Conspiracy theorists suspect that public use of the system provides cover traffic for classified messages.

Although communications security on the Net has, until now, been interpreted largely in terms of message confidentiality and authentication, it looks likely that the future will become much more like military communications, in that various kinds of service denial attacks, anonymity, and deception plays will become increasingly important. I'll return to this theme later. For now, let's look at the aspects of electronic warfare that have to do with target acquisition and weapon guidance, as these are where the arts of jamming and deception have been most highly developed. (In fact, although there is much more in the open literature on the application of electronic attack and defense to radar than to communications, much of the same material clearly applies to both.)

16.4 Surveillance and Target Acquisition

Although some sensor systems use passive direction finding, the main methods used to detect hostile targets and guide weapons to them are sonar, radar, and infrared. The first of these to be developed was sonar, which was invented and deployed in World War I (under the name of Asdic) [366]. Except in submarine warfare, the key sensor is radar. Although radar was invented by Christian Hülsmeyer in 1904 as a maritime anti-collision device, its serious development only occurred in the 1930s, and it was used by all major participants in World War II [369, 424]. The electronic attack and protection techniques developed for it tend to be better developed than, and often go over to, systems using other sensors. In the context of radar, "electronic attack" usually means jamming (though in theory it also includes stealth technology), and "electronic protection" refers to the techniques used to preserve at least some radar capability.

16.4.1 Types of Radar

A very wide range of systems are in use, including search radars, fire-control radars, terrain-following radars, counterbombardment radars, and weather radars. They have a wide variety of signal characteristics. For example, radars with a low RF and a low *pulse repetition frequency* (PRF) are better for search, while high-frequency, high PRF devices are better for tracking. A good textbook on the technology is by Schleher [677].

Simple radar designs for search applications may have a rotating antenna that emits a sequence of pulses and detects echos. This was an easy way to implement radar in the days before digital electronics; the sweep in the display tube could be mechanically rotated in synch with the antenna. Fire-control radars often used *conical scan;* the beam would be tracked in a circle around the target's position, and the amplitude of the returns could drive positioning servos (and weapon controls) directly. Now the beams are often generated electronically using multiple antenna elements, but tracking loops remain central. Many radars have a *range gate*, circuitry that focuses on targets within a certain range of distances from the antenna; if the radar had to track all objects between, say, 0 and 100 miles, then its pulse repetition frequency would be limited by the time it takes radio waves to travel 200 miles. This would have consequences for angular resolution and for tracking performance generally.

Doppler radar measures the velocity of the target by the change in frequency in the return signal. It is very important in distinguishing moving targets from *clutter*, the returns reflected from the ground. Doppler radars may have *velocity gates* that restrict attention to targets whose radial speed with respect to the antenna is within certain limits.

16.4.2 Jamming Techniques

Electronic attack techniques can be passive or active.

The earliest countermeasure to be widely used was *chaff*—thin strips of conducting foil cut to a half the wavelength of the target signal, then dispersed to provide a false return. Toward the end of World War II, allied aircraft were dropping 2,000 tons of chaff a day to degrade German air defenses. Chaff can be dropped directly by the aircraft attempting to penetrate the defenses (which isn't ideal, as they will then be at the apex of an elongated signal) or by support aircraft, or fired forward into a suitable pattern using rockets or shells. The main counter-countermeasure against chaff is the use of Doppler radars; the chaff is very light, so it comes to rest almost at once and can be distinguished fairly easily from moving targets.

Other techniques include small decoys with active repeaters that retransmit radar signals, and larger decoys that simply reflect them; sometimes one vehicle (such as a helicopter) acts as a decoy for another more valuable one (such as an aircraft carrier). The principles are quite general. Weapons that home using RDF are decoyed by special drones that emit seduction RF signals, while infrared guided missiles are diverted using flares.

The passive countermeasure in which the most money has been invested is *stealth*, reducing the *radar cross-section* (RCS) of a vehicle so that it can be detected only at very much shorter range. This means, for example, that the enemy has to place his air defense radars closer together, so he has to buy a lot more of them. Stealth includes a wide range of techniques, and a proper discussion is well beyond the scope of this book. Some people think of it as "extremely expensive black paint," but there's more to it than that. Because an aircraft's RCS is typically a function of its aspect, it may have a fly-by-wire system that continually exhibits an aspect with a low RCS to identified hostile emitters.

Active countermeasures are much more diverse. Early jammers simply generated a lot of noise in the range of frequencies used by the target radar; this technique is known as *noise jamming* or *barrage jamming*. Some systems used systematic frequency patterns, such as pulse jammers, or swept jammers which traversed the frequency range of interest (also known as *squidging oscillators*). But such a signal is fairly easy to block—one trick is to use a *guard band* receiver, a receiver on a frequency adjacent to the one in use, and to blank the signal when this receiver shows a jamming signal. It should also be noted that jamming isn't restricted to one side. As well as being used by the radar's opponent, the radar itself can also send suitable spurious signals from an auxiliary antenna to mask the real signal or simply to overload the defenses.

At the other end of the scale lie hard-kill techniques such as *anti-radiation missiles* (ARMs), often fired by support aircraft, which home in on the sources of hostile signals. Defenses against such weapons include the use of decoy transmitters, and blinking transmitters on and off.

In the middle lies a large toolkit of *deception jamming* techniques. Most jammers used for self-protection are deception jammers of one kind or another; barrage and ARM techniques tend to be more suited to use by support vehicles.

The usual goal with a self-protection jammer is to deny range and bearing information to attackers. The basic trick is *inverse gain jamming* or *inverse gain amplitude modulation*. This is based on the observation that the directionality of the attacker's antenna is usually not perfect; in addition to the main beam, it has *sidelobes* through which energy is also transmitted and received, albeit much less efficiently. The sidelobe response can be mapped by observing the transmitted signal, and a jamming signal can be generated so that the net emission is the inverse of the antenna's directional response. The effect, as far as the attacker's radar is concerned, is that the signal seems to come from everywhere; instead of a "blip" on the radar screen you see a circle centered on your own antenna. Inverse gain jamming is very effective against the older conical-scan fire-control systems.

More generally, the technique is to retransmit the radar signal with a systematic change in delay and/or frequency. This can be either noncoherent, in which case the jammer is called a *transponder*, or coherent—that is, with the right waveform—when it's a *repeater*. (It is now common to store received waveforms in *digital radio frequency memory* (DRFM) and manipulate them using signal processing chips.)

An elementary countermeasure is *burn-through*. By lowering the pulse repetition frequency, the dwell time is increased, so the return signal is stronger—at the cost of less precision. A more sophisticated countermeasure is *range gate pull-off* (RGPO). Here, the radar transmits a number of fake pulses that are stronger than the real ones, thus capturing the receiver, and then moving them out of phase so that the target is no longer in the receiver's range gate. Similarly, with Doppler radars the basic trick is *velocity gate pull-off* (VGPO). With older radars, successful RGPO would cause the radar to break lock and the target to disappear from the screen. Modern radars can reacquire lock very quickly, so RGPO must either be performed repeatedly or combined with another technique—commonly, with inverse gain jamming to break angle tracking at the same time.

An elementary counter-countermeasure is to jitter the pulse repetition frequency. Each outgoing pulse is either delayed or not, depending on a *lag sequence* generated by a stream cipher or random number generator. This means that the jammer cannot anticipate when the next pulse will arrive, and so has to follow it. Such *follower jamming* can only make false targets that appear to be further away. The (counter)[3]-measure is for the radar to have a *leading-edge tracker*, which responds only to the first return pulse; and the (counter)[4]-measures can include jamming at such a high power that the receiver's automatic gain control circuit is captured, or *cover jamming* in which the jamming pulse is long enough to cover the maximum jitter period.

The next twist of the screw may involve tactics. Chaff is often used to force a radar into Doppler mode, which makes PRF jitter difficult (as continuous waveforms are better than pulsed for Doppler), while leading-edge trackers may be combined with frequency agility and smart signal processing. For example, true target returns fluctuate, and have realistic accelerations, while simple transponders and repeaters give out a more or less steady signal. Of course, it's always possible for designers to be too clever; the Mig-29 could decelerate more rapidly in level flight by a rapid pull-up than some radar designers had anticipated, and so pilots could use this maneuver to break radar lock. And now, of course, enough MIPS are available to manufacture realistic false returns.

16.4.3 Advanced Radars and Countermeasures

A number of advanced techniques are used to give an edge on the jammer.

Pulse compression, first developed in Germany in World War II, uses a kind of direct sequence spread-spectrum pulse, filtered on return by a matched filter to compress it again. This can give processing gains of 10–1,000. Pulse compression radars are resistant to transponder jammers, but are vulnerable to repeater jammers, especially those with digital radio frequency memory. However, the use of LPI waveforms is important if you do not wish the target to detect you first.

Pulsed Doppler is much the same as Doppler, and sends a series of phase stable pulses. It has come to dominate many high-end markets, and is widely used, for example, in *look-down shoot-down* systems for air defense against low-flying intruders. As with elementary pulsed tracking radars, different RF and pulse repetition frequencies have different characteristics: we want low-frequency/PRF for unambiguous range/velocity and also to reduce clutter—but this can leave many blind spots. Airborne radars that have to deal with many threats use high PRF and look only for velocities above some threshold, say 100 knots—but are weak in tail chases. The usual compromise is medium PRF—but this suffers from severe range ambiguities in airborne operations. Also, search radar requires long, diverse bursts, whereas tracking needs only short, tuned ones. An advantage is that pulsed Doppler can discriminate some very specific signals, such as modulation provided by turbine blades in jet engines. The main deception strategy used against pulsed Doppler is velocity gate pull-off, although a new variant is to excite multiple velocity gates with deceptive returns.

Monopulse is becoming one of the most popular techniques. It is used, for example, in the Exocet missiles that proved so difficult to jam in the Falklands war. The idea is to have four linked antennas so that azimuth and elevation data can be computed from each return pulse using interferometric techniques. Monopulse radars are difficult and expensive to jam, unless a design defect can be exploited; the usual techniques involve tricks such as formation jamming and terrain bounce. Often the preferred defensive strategy is just to use towed decoys.

One of the more recent tricks is *passive coherent location*. Lockheed's Silent Sentry system has no emitters at all, but rather utilizes reflections of commercial radio and television broadcast signals to detect and track airborne objects [508]. The receivers, being passive, are hard to locate and attack; and knocking out the system entails destroying major civilian infrastructures, which opponents will often prefer not to do for various propaganda reasons. This strategy is moderately effective against some kinds of stealth technology.

The emergence of digital radio frequency memory and other software radio techniques holds out the prospect of much more complex attack and defense. Both radar and jammer waveforms may be adapted to the tactical situation with much greater flexibility than before. But fancy combinations of spectral, temporal, and spatial characteristics will not be the whole story. Effective electronic attack is likely to continue to require the effective coordination of different passive and active tools with weapons and tactics. The importance of intelligence, and of careful deception planning, is likely to increase.

16.4.4 Other Sensors and Multisensor Issues

Much of what I've said about radar applies to sonar as well, and a fair amount applies to infrared. Passive decoys—flares—worked very well against early heat-seeking missiles that used a mechanically spun detector, but are less effective against modern detectors that incorporate signal processing. Flares are like chaff in that they decelerate rapidly with respect to the target, so the attacker can filter on velocity or acceleration. Flares are also like repeater jammers in that their signals are relatively stable and strong compared with real targets.

Active infrared jamming is harder, and thus less widespread, than radar jamming. It tends to exploit features of the hostile sensor by pulsing at a rate or in a pattern that causes confusion. Some infrared defense systems are starting to employ lasers to disable the sensors of incoming weapons; and it has recently been admitted that a number of UFO sightings were actually due to various kinds of jamming (both radar and infrared) [75].

One growth area is *multisensor data fusion*, whereby inputs from radars, infrared sensors, video cameras, and even humans are combined to give better target identification and tracking than any could individually. The Rapier air defense missile, for example, uses radar to acquire azimuth while tracking is carried out optically in visual conditions. Data fusion can be harder than it seems. As discussed in Section 13.8, combining two alarm systems will generally result in improving either the false alarm or the missed alarm rate, while making the other worse. If you scramble your fighters when you see a blip on either the radar or the infrared, there will be more false alarms; but if you scramble only when you see both, it will be easier for the enemy to jam you or to sneak through.

System issues become more complex where the attacker himself is on a platform that's vulnerable to counterattack, such as a fighter bomber. He will have systems for threat recognition, direction finding, and missile approach warning; and the receivers in these will be deafened by his jammer. The usual trick is to turn the jammer off for a short "look-through" period at random times.

With multiple friendly and hostile platforms, things get much more complex still. Each side might have specialist support vehicles with high-power dedicated equipment, which makes it to some extent an energy battle—"he with the most watts wins." A SAM belt may have multiple radars at different frequencies to make jamming harder. The overall effect of jamming (as of stealth) is to reduce the effective range of radar. But the jamming margin also matters, and who has the most vehicles, and the tactics employed.

With multiple vehicles engaged, it's also necessary to have a reliable way of distinguishing friend from foe.

16.5 IFF Systems

The technological innovations of World War II—and especially jet aircraft, radar, and missiles—made it impractical to identify targets visually, and imperative to have an automatic way to *identify friend or foe* (IFF). Early IFF systems emerged during that war, using a vehicle serial number or "code of the day"; but this is open to spoofing. Since the 1960s, U.S. aircraft have used the Mark XII system, which has cryptographic protection as discussed in Section 2.3. Here, it isn't the cryptography that's the hard part, but rather the protocol and operational problems.

The Mark XII has four modes, of which the secure mode uses a 32-bit challenge and a 4-bit response. This is a precedent set by its predecessor, the Mark X; if challenges or responses were too long, the radar's pulse repetition frequency (and thus it accuracy) would be degraded. The Mark XII sends a series of 12–20 challenges at a rate of one every four milliseconds. In the original implementation, the responses were displayed on a screen at a position offset by the arithmetic difference between the actual response and the expected one. The effect was that while a foe had a null or random response, a friend would have responses at or near the center screen, which would light up. Reflection attacks are prevented, and MIG-in-the-middle attacks made much harder, because the challenge uses a focused antenna, while the receiver is omnidirectional. (In fact, the antenna used for the challenge is typically the fire control radar, which in older systems was conically scanned).

I mentioned in Section 2.3 that cryptographic protection alone isn't bulletproof: the enemy might record and replay valid challenges, with a view to using your IFF signal for direction finding purposes. This can be a real problem in dense operational areas with many vehicles and emitters, such as on the border between East and West Germany during the Cold War, and parts of the Middle East to this day. There, the return signal can be degraded by overlapping signals from nearby aircraft—an effect known as *garbling*. In the other direction, aircraft transponders subjected to many challenges may be unable to decode them properly—an effect known as *fruiting*. Controlling these phenomena means minimizing the length of challenge and response signals, which limits the usefulness of cryptographic protection. As a result, the Royal Air Force resisted American demands to make the Mark XII a NATO requirement and continues using the World-War-II-vintage Mark X, changing the codes every 30 minutes. (The details of Mark X and Mark XII, and the R.A.F.-U.S.A.F. debate, can be found in [348].) This is yet another example of the surprising difficulty of getting cryptography to add value to a system design.

The system-level issues are even less tractable. The requirement is to identify enemy forces, but an IFF system reliant on cooperation from the target can only identify friends positively. Neither neutrals, nor friends with defective or incorrectly set transponders, can be distinguished from enemies. So while IFF may be used as a primary mechanism in areas where neutrals are excluded (such as in the vicinity of naval task forces at sea in wartime), its more usual use is as an adjunct to more traditional methods, such as correlation with flight plans. In this role it can still be very valuable.

Since the Gulf war, in which 25% of Allied troop casualties were caused by "friendly fire", a number of experimental systems have been developed that extend IFF to ground troops. One U.S. system combines laser and RF components. Shooters have lasers, and soldiers have transponders; when the soldier is illuminated with a suitable challenge, his equipment broadcasts a "don't shoot me" message using frequency-hopping radio [820]. An extension allows aircraft to broadcast targeting intentions on millimeter wave radio. This system was due to be fielded in the year 2000. Britain is developing a cheaper system called MAGPIE, in which friendly vehicles carry a low-probability-of-intercept millimeter wave transmitter, and shooters carry a directional receiver [381]. (Dismounted British foot soldiers, unlike their American counterparts, have no protection.) Other countries are developing yet other systems.

16.6 Directed Energy Weapons

In the late 1930s, there was panic in Britain and America on rumors that the Nazis had developed a high-power radio beam that would burn out vehicle ignition systems. British scientists studied the problem and concluded that this was infeasible [424]. They were correct—given the relatively low-powered radio transmitters, and the simple but robust vehicle electronics, of the 1930s.

Things started to change with the arrival of the atomic bomb. The detonation of a nuclear device creates a large pulse of gamma-ray photons, which in turn displace electrons from air molecules by *Compton scattering*. The large induced currents give rise to an *electromagnetic pulse* (EMP), which may be thought of as a very high amplitude pulse of radio waves with a very short rise time.

Where a nuclear explosion occurs within the earth's atmosphere, the EMP energy is predominantly in the VHF and UHF bands, though there is enough energy at lower frequencies for a *radio flash* to be observable thousands of miles away. Within a few tens of miles of the explosion, the radio frequency energy may induce currents large enough to damage most electronic equipment that has not been hardened. The effects of a blast outside the earth's atmosphere are believed to be much worse (although there has never been a test). The gamma photons can travel thousands of miles before they strike the earth's atmosphere, which could ionize to form an antenna on a continental scale. It is reckoned that most electronic equipment in Northern Europe could be burned out by a one megaton blast at a height of 250 miles above the North Sea. For this reason, critical military systems are carefully shielded.

Western concern about EMP grew after the Soviet Union started a research program on non-nuclear EMP weapons in the mid-80s. At the time, the United States was deploying "neutron bombs" in Europe—enhanced radiation weapons that could kill people without demolishing buildings. The Soviets portrayed this as a "capitalist bomb" which would destroy people while leaving property intact, and responded by threatening a "socialist bomb" to destroy property (in the form of electronics) while leaving the surrounding people intact.

By the end of World War II, the invention of the cavity magnetron had made it possible to build radars powerful enough to damage unprotected electronic circuitry for a range of several hundred yards. The move from valves to transistors and integrated circuits has increased the vulnerability of most commercial electronic equipment. A terrorist group could in theory mount a radar in a truck and drive around a city's financial sector wiping out the banks. For battlefield use, a more compact form factor is preferred, and so the Soviets are said to have built high-energy RF (HERF) devices from capacitors, magnetohydrodynamic generators and the like.

By the mid 1990s, the concern that terrorists might get hold of these weapons from the former Soviet Union led the agencies to try to sell commerce and industry on the idea of electromagnetic shielding. These efforts were dismissed as hype. Personally, I tend to agree. The details of the Soviet HERF bombs haven't been released, but physics suggests that EMP is limited by the dielectric strength of air and the cross-section of the antenna. In nuclear EMP, the effective antenna size could be a few hundred meters for an endoatmospheric blast, up to several thousand kilometers for an exoatmospheric one. But in "ordinary" EMP/HERF, it seems that the antenna will be at most a few meters. NATO planners concluded that military command and control systems that were already hardened for nuclear EMP should be unaffected.

As for the civilian infrastructure, I suspect that a terrorist can do a lot more damage with an old-fashioned truck bomb made with a ton of fertilizer and fuel oil, and he doesn't need a PhD in physics to design one! Anyway, the standard reference on EMP is [645].

Concern remains however, that the EMP from a single nuclear explosion 250 miles above the central United States could do colossal economic damage, while killing few people directly [53]. This potentially gives a blackmail weapon to countries such as Iran and North Korea, both of which have nuclear ambitions but primitive infrastructures. In general, a massive attack on electronic communications is more of a threat to countries such as the United States that depend heavily on them than on countries such as North Korea, or even China, that don't. This observation goes across to attacks on the Internet as well, so let's now turn to information warfare.

16.7 Information Warfare

Since about 1995, the phrase *information warfare* has come into wide use. Its popularity appears to have been catalyzed by operational experience in Desert Storm. There, air power was used to degrade the Iraqi defenses before the land attack was launched; and one goal of NSA personnel supporting the allies was to enable the initial attack to be made without casualties—even though the Iraqi air defenses were at that time intact and alert. The attack involved a mixture of standard e-war techniques, such as jammers and antiradiation missiles; cruise missile attacks on command centers; attacks by special forces, who sneaked into Iraq and dug up lengths of communications cabling from the desert; and, allegedly, the use of hacking tricks to disable computers and telephone exchanges. (By 1990, the U.S. Army was already calling for bids for virus production [518].) The operation successfully achieved its mission of ensuring zero Allied casualties on the first night of the aerial bombardment. Military planners and think tanks started to consider how the success could be extended.

There is little agreement about definitions. The conventional view, arising out of Desert Storm, was expressed by Major YuLin Whitehead ([790, p 9]):

> The strategist ... should employ [the information weapon] as a precursor weapon to blind the enemy prior to conventional attacks and operations.

The more aggressive view is that properly conducted information operations should encompass everything from signals intelligence to propaganda; and, given the reliance that modern societies place on information, it should suffice to break the enemy's will without fighting.

16.7.1 Definitions

In fact, there are roughly three views on what information warfare means:

- It is just a remarketing of the stuff that the agencies have been doing for decades anyway, in an attempt to maintain the agencies' budgets post-Cold-War.

- It consists of the use of hacking in a broad sense—network attack tools, computer viruses, and so on—in conflict between states or substate groups, in order to deny critical military and other services, whether for operational or propaganda purposes. It has been observed, for example, that the Internet, though designed to withstand thermonuclear bombardment, was knocked out by the Morris worm.

- It extends the electronic warfare doctrine of controlling the electromagnetic spectrum to control of all information relevant to the conflict. It thus extends traditional e-war techniques, such as radar jammers, by adding assorted hacking techniques, but also incorporates propaganda and news management.

The first of these views was the one taken by some cynical defense insiders to whom I've spoken. The second is the popular view found in newspaper articles, and also Whitehead's. It's the one I'll use as a guide in this section, but without taking a position on whether it actually contains anything really new, either technically or doctrinally.

The third finds expression in a book by Dorothy Denning [235], whose definition of information warfare is, "operations that target or exploit information media in order to win some advantage over an adversary." Its interpretation is so broad that it includes not just hacking but all of electronic warfare and all existing intelligence-gathering techniques (from sigint through satellite imagery to spies), and propaganda, too. In a later article, she's discussed the role of the Net in the propaganda and activism surrounding the Kosovo war [236]. However the bulk of her book is given over to computer security and related topics.

A similar view of information warfare, and from a writer whose background is defense planning rather than computer security, is by Edward Waltz [790]. He defines *information superiority* as "the capability to collect, process and disseminate an uninterrupted flow of information while exploiting or denying an adversary's ability to do the same". The theory is that such superiority will allow the conduct of operations without effective opposition. The book has less technical detail on computer security matters than Denning's, but sets forth a first attempt to formulate a military doctrine of information operations.

16.7.2 Doctrine

When writers such as Denning and Waltz include propaganda operations in information warfare, the cynical defense insider may remark that nothing has changed. From Roman and Mongol efforts to promote a myth of invincibility, through the use of propaganda radio stations by both sides in World War II and the Cold War, to the bombing of Serbian TV during the Kosovo campaign and denial-of-service attacks on Chechen Web sites by Russian agencies [198]—the tools may change but the game remains the same.

But there is a twist, perhaps thanks to government and military leaders' lack of familiarity with the Internet. When teenage kids deface a U.S. government department Web site, an experienced computer security professional is likely to see it as the equivalent of graffiti scrawled on the wall of a public building. After all, it's easy enough to do, and easy enough to remove. But the information warfare community can paint it as undermining the posture of information dominance that a country must project in order to deter aggression.

So there is a fair amount of debunking to be done before the political and military leadership can start to think clearly about the issues. For example, it's often stated that information warfare provides casualty-free way to win wars: "just hack the Iranian power grid and watch them sue for peace." The three obvious comments are as follows.

- The denial-of-service attacks that have so far been conducted on information systems without the use of physical force have mostly had a transient effect. A computer goes down; the operators find out what happened; they restore the system from backup and restart it. An outage of a few hours may be enough to let a wave of bombers get through unscathed, but it appears unlikely to bring a country to its knees. In this context, the failure of the Millennium Bug to cause the expected damage may be a useful warning.

- Insofar as there is a vulnerability, developed countries are more exposed. The power grid in the United States or Britain is much more computerized than that in the average developing country.

- Finally, if such an attack causes the deaths of several dozen people in Iranian hospitals, the Iranians aren't likely to see the matter much differently from a conventional military attack that killed the same number of people. Indeed, if information war targets civilians to greater extent than the alternatives, then the attackers' leaders are likely to be portrayed as war criminals. The Pinochet case, in which a former head of government only escaped extradition on health grounds, should give pause for thought.

Having made these points, I will restrict discussion in the rest of this section to technical matters.

16.7.3 Potentially Useful Lessons from Electronic Warfare

Perhaps the most important policy lesson from the world of electronic warfare is that conducting operations that involve more than one service is very much harder than it looks. Things are bad enough when army, navy, and air force units have to be coordinated—during the U.S. invasion of Grenada, a ground commander had to go to a pay phone and call home using his credit card in order to call down an air strike, as the different services' radios were incompatible. (Indeed, this was the spur for the development of software radios [482]). Things are even worse when intelligence services are involved, as they don't train with warfighters in peacetime, and so take a long time to become productive once the fighting starts. Turf fights also get in the way: under current U.S. rules, the air force can decide to bomb an enemy telephone exchange but has to get permission from the NSA and/or CIA to hack it [63]. The U.S. Army's communications strategy is now taking account of the need to communicate across the traditional command hierarchy, and to make extensive use of the existing civilian infrastructure [672].

At the technical level, many concepts may go across from electronic warfare to information protection in general.

- The electronic warfare community uses guard band receivers to detect jamming, so it can be filtered out (for example, by blanking receivers at the precise time a sweep jammer passes through their frequency). Using bait addresses to detect spam is essentially the same concept.

- There is also an analogy between virus recognition and radar signal recognition. Virus writers may make their code *polymorphic*, in that it changes its form as it propagates, to make life harder for the virus scanner vendors. Similarly, radar designers use very diverse waveforms to make it harder to store enough of the waveform in digital radio frequency memory to do coherent jamming effectively.

- Our old friends, the false accept and false reject rate, will continue to dominate tactics and strategy. As with burglar alarms or radar jamming, the ability to cause many false alarms (however crudely) will always be worth something: as soon as the false alarm rate exceeds about 15%, operator performance is degraded. As for filtering, it can usually be cheated.

- The limiting economic factor in both attack and defense will increasingly be the software cost, and the speed at which new tools can be created and deployed.

- It is useful, when subjected to jamming, not to let the jammer know whether, or how, his attack is succeeding. In military communications, it's usually better to respond to jamming by dropping the bit rate rather than by boosting power; similarly, when a nonexistent credit card number is presented at your Web site, you might say, "Sorry, bad card number, try again," but the second time it happens you should take a different line (or the attacker will keep on trying).

Something such as, "Sorry, the items you have requested are temporarily out of stock and should be mailed within five working days" may do the trick.

- Although defense in depth is in general a good idea, you have to be careful of interactions between the different defenses. The classic case in e-war is when chaff dispensed by a warship to defend against an incoming cruise missile knocks out its anti-aircraft guns. The side effects of defenses can also be exploited. The most common case on the Net is the mail bomb: an attacker forges offensive newsgroup messages, which appear to come from the victim, who then gets subjected to a barrage of abuse and attacks.

- Finally, some perspective can be drawn from the differing roles of hard kill and soft kill in electronic warfare. Jamming and other soft-kill attacks can be cheaper in the short term; they can be used against multiple threats; and they have reduced political consequences. But damage assessment is hard, and you may just divert the weapon to another target. As most i-war is soft kill, these comments can be expected to go across, too.

16.7.4 Differences Between E-War and I-War

There are differences as well as similarities between traditional electronic warfare and the kinds of attack that can potentially be run over the Net.

- There are roughly two kinds of war: open war and guerilla war. Electronic warfare comes into its own in the former case, such as in air combat, most naval engagements, and the desert. In forests and mountains, the man with the AK-47 can still get a result against mechanized forces. Guerilla war has largely been ignored by the e-war community, except insofar as they make and sell radars to detect snipers and concealed mortar batteries.

    In cyberspace, the "forests and the mountains" are likely to be the large numbers of insecure hosts belonging to friendly or neutral civilians and organizations. The distributed denial-of-service (DDoS) attack, in which hundreds of innocent machines are subverted and used to bombard a target Web site with traffic, has no real analogue in the world of electronic warfare. Nevertheless, it is the likely platform for launching attacks even on "open" targets such as large commercial Web sites. So it's unclear where the open countryside in cyberspace actually is.

- Another possible source of asymmetric advantage for the guerilla is complexity. Large countries have many incompatible systems; this makes little difference when fighting another large country with similarly incompatible systems, but can leave them at a disadvantage to a small group that has built simple, coherent systems.

- Anyone trying to attack the United States is unlikely to repeat Saddam Hussein's mistake of trying to fight a tank battle. Guerilla warfare will be the norm, and cyberspace appears to be fairly well suited for this.

- There is no electronic warfare analogue of "script kiddies," people who download attack scripts and launch them without really understanding how they work. That such powerful weapons are available universally, and for free, has few analogues in meatspace. Perhaps the closest is in the lawless areas of countries such as Afghanistan, where all men go about with military weapons.

16.8 Summary

Electronic warfare is much more developed than most other areas of information security. There are many lessons to be learned, from the technical level up through the tactical level to matters of planning and strategy. We can expect that, as information warfare evolves from a fashionable concept to established doctrine, these lessons will become important for practitioners.

Research Problems

An interesting research problem is how to port techniques and experience from the world of electronic warfare to the Internet. This chapter is only a sketchy first attempt at setting down the possible parallels and differences.

Further Reading

A good (although nontechnical) introduction to radar is by P. S. Hall [369]. The best all-round reference for the technical aspects of electronic warfare, from radar through stealth to EMP weapons, is by Curtis Schleher [677]; a good summary was written by Doug Richardson [644]. The classic introduction to the anti-jam properties of spread-spectrum sequences is by Andrew Viterbi [778]; the history of spread-spectrum is ably told by Robert Scholtz [686]; the classic introduction to the mathematics of spread-spectrum is by Raymond Pickholtz, Donald Schilling, and Lawrence Milstein [616]; while the standard textbook is by Robert Dixon [254]. An overall history of British electronic warfare and scientific intelligence, which was written by a true insider, that gives a lot of insight not just into how the technology developed but also into strategic and tactical deception, is by R. V. Jones [424, 425].

Finally, the history of the technical aspects of radar, jammers, and IFF systems is available from three different and complementary viewpoints: the German by David Pritchard [627], the British by Jack Gough [348], and the American by Robert Buderi [142].

Telecom System Security

I rarely had to resort to a technical attack. Companies can spend millions of dollars toward technological protections and that's wasted if somebody can basically call someone on the telephone and either convince them to do something on the computer that lowers the computer's defenses or reveals the information they were seeking.

—KEVIN MITNICK

17.1 Introduction

The protection of telecommunications systems is an important case study for a number of reasons. First, many distributed systems rely on the underlying fixed or mobile phone network in ways that are often not obvious. Second, the history of security failures in telecoms is instructive. Early attacks were carried out on phone companies by enthusiasts ("phone phreaks") to get free calls; next the phone system's vulnerabilities began to be exploited by crooks to evade police wiretapping; then premium rate calls were introduced, which created the motive for large-scale fraud; then, when telecoms markets were liberalized, some phone companies started conducting attacks on each other's customers, and some phone companies have even attacked each other. At each stage, the defensive measures undertaken were not only very expensive but also tended to be inadequate for various reasons. It appears that the same pattern is repeating with the Internet—only that history will be much speeded up.

17.2 Phone Phreaking

The abuse of communication services goes back centuries. In the days before postage stamps were invented, postage was paid by the recipient. Unsolicited mail became a huge problem (especially for famous people), so recipients were allowed to inspect a letter and reject it if they wished rather than paying for it. People soon worked out schemes to send short messages on the covers of letters which their correspondents rejected, and the regulations brought in to stop this were never really effective [594]. The early optical telegraphs, which worked using semaphores or heliographs, were abused by people to place foreknowledge bets on races; here, too, attempts to legislate the problem away were a failure [729].

The telephone was to be no different.

17.2.1 Attacks on Metering

Early metering systems were wide open to abuse.

- In the 1950's, the operator in some systems had to listen for the sound of coins dropping on a metal plate to tell that a callbox customer had paid, so some people acquired the knack of hitting the coinbox with a piece of metal that struck the right note.

- Initially, the operator had no way of knowing which phone a call had come from, so she had to ask the caller his number. The caller could give the number of someone else, who would be charged. This was risky to do from your own phone, but people did it from callboxes. When operators started calling back to verify the number for international calls, people worked out social engineering attacks ("This is IBM here; we'd like to book a call to San Francisco, and because of the time difference, we'd like our managing director take it at home tonight. His number is xxx-yyyy"). Therefore, callbox lines had a feature added to alert the operator. But in the U.K. implementation, there was a bug: a customer who had called the operator from a callbox could depress the rest for a quarter-second or so, whereupon he'd be disconnected and reconnected (often to a different operator), with no signal this time that the call was from a callbox. He could then place a call to anywhere and bill it to any local number.

- This system also signalled the entry of a coin by one or more pulses, each of which consisted of the insertion of a resistance in the line followed by a brief open circuit. At a number of colleges, enterprising students installed "magic buttons" that could simulate this in a callbox in the student union so people could phone for free. (The bill in this case went to the student union, for which the magic button was not quite so amusing.)

Attacks on metering mechanisms continue. Many countries have changed their payphones to use chip cards in order to cut the costs of coin collection and vandalism. Some of the implementations have been poor (as I remarked in the chapter on tamper resistance) and villains have manufactured large quantities of bogus phone cards. Other attacks involve what's called *clip-on:* physically attaching a phone to someone else's line to steal their service.

In the 1970s, when international phone calls were very expensive, foreign students would clip their own phone on to a residential line in order to call home; an unsuspecting home owner could get a huge bill. Despite the fact that, in most countries, the cable was the phone company's legal responsibility up to the service socket in the house, phone companies were mostly adamant that householders should pay, and could threaten to blacklist them if they didn't. Now that long distance calls are cheap, the financial incentive for clip-on fraud has largely disappeared. But it's still enough of a problem that the Norwegian phone company designed a system whereby a challenge and response are exchanged between a wall-socket-mounted authentication device and the exchange software before a dial tone is given [426].

Clip-on fraud had a catastrophic effect on a family in Cramlington, a town in the Northeast of England. The first sign they had of trouble was hearing a conversation on their line. The next was a visit from the police, who said there'd been complaints of nuisance phone calls. The complainants were three ladies, all of whom had a number that was one digit different from a number to which this family had supposedly made a huge number of calls. When the family's bill was examined, there were also calls to clusters of numbers that turned out to be payphones; these had started quite suddenly at the same time as the nuisance calls. Later, when the family had complained to the phone company about a fault, their connection was rerouted and this had solved the problem.

The phone company denied the possibility of a tap, despite the report from its maintenance person, who noted that the family's line had been tampered with at the distribution box. (The phone company later claimed this report was in error.) It turned out that a drug dealer had lived close by, and it seemed a reasonable inference that he had tapped their line in order to call his couriers at the payphones using the victim's calling line ID. But both the police and the local phone company refused to go into the house where the dealer had lived, claiming it was too dangerous—even though the dealer had by now got six years in jail. The Norwegian phone company declined an invitation to testify about clip-on for the defense. The upshot was that the subscriber was convicted of making harrassing phone calls, in a case widely believed to have been a miscarriage of justice. Discussion continues about whether the closing of ranks between the phone company and the police was a policy of denying that clip-on was possible, a reflex to cover a surveillance operation—or something more sinister.

Stealing dial tone from cordless phones is another variant on the same theme. In the early 1990s, this became so widespread in Paris that France Telecom broke with phone company tradition and announced that it was happening, claiming that the victims were using illegally imported cordless phones that were easy to spoof [475]. Yet to this day I am unaware of any cordless phones—authorized or not—with decent air link authentication. The new digital cordless phones use the DECT standard, which allows for challenge-response mechanisms [769]; but the terminals fielded so far seem to simply send their names to the base station.

Social engineering is another widespread trick. A crook calls you pretending to be from AT&T security, and asks whether you made a large number of calls to Peru on your calling card. When you deny this, she says that the calls were obviously fake, but, in order to reverse the charges, can she confirm that your card number is 123-456-7890-6543? No, you say (if you're not really alert), it's 123-456-7890-5678. Because 123-456-7890 is your phone number, and 5678 your password, you've just given that caller the ability to bill calls to you.

The advent of premium rate phone services has also led to scamsters developing all sorts of tricks to get people to call them: pager messages, job ads, fake emergency messages about relatives, "low-cost" calling cards with 900-access numbers—you name it. The 809 area code for the Caribbean used to be a favorite cover for crooks targeting U.S. subscribers; recently, the introduction of new area codes there, such as 345 for the

Cayman Islands, makes it even harder to spot the numbers of premium rate operators. Phone companies' advice is "Do not return calls to unfamiliar telephone numbers" and "Beware of faxes, email, voice mail, and pages requesting a return call to an unfamiliar number" [13]. But just how practical is that?

17.2.2 Attacks on Signalling

The term phone phreaking refers to attacks on signalling, as well as to pure toll fraud. Until the 1980s, phone companies used signalling systems that worked *in-band* by sending tone pulses in the same circuit that carried the speech. The first attack I've heard of dates back to 1952; and by the mid-to-late 1960s, many enthusiasts in both America and Britain had worked out ways of rerouting calls. They typically used homemade tone generators, of which the most common were called *blue boxes*. The trick was to call an 800 number, then send a tone that would *clear down* the line at the far end—that is, disconnect the called party while leaving the caller with a trunk line connected to the exchange. The caller could now enter the number he really wanted and be connected without paying. Notoriously, Steve Jobs and Steve Wozniak first built blue boxes before they diversified into computers [319].

Phone phreaking started out with a strong ideological element. In those days, most phone companies had monopolies. They were large, faceless, and unresponsive. People whose domestic phone lines had been tapped in a service theft found they were stuck with the charges. If the young man who had courted your daughter was (unknown to you) a phone phreak who hadn't paid for the calls he made to her, you would suddenly find the company trying to extort either his name or a payment. Phone companies were also aligned with the state. In many countries, it turned out that there were signalling codes or switch features that would enable the police to tap your phone from the comfort of the police station, without having to send out a lineman to install a wiretap. Back in the days of Vietnam and student protests, this was inflammatory stuff. Phone phreaks were counterculture heroes, while phone companies aligned themselves firmly with the Forces of Darkness.

As there was no way to stop blue-box type attacks as long as telephone signalling was carried in-band, the phone companies spent years and many billions of dollars upgrading exchanges so that the signalling was carried out-of-band, in separate channels to which the subscribers had no easy access. Gradually, region by region, the world was closed off to blue-box attacks, though there are still a few places left. For example, the first time that USAF operations were disrupted by an information warfare attack by noncombatants was in 1994, when two British hackers broke into the Rome Air Force Base via an analog link through an ancient phone system in Argentina. This cut-out was used effectively to hold up investigators [722]. But to defeat a modern telephone network, different techniques are needed.

17.2.3 Attacks on Switching and Configuration

The second wave of attacks targeted the computers that did the switching. Typically, these were Unix machines on a LAN in an exchange, which also had machines with administrative functions such as maintenance scheduling. By hacking one of these less well-guarded machines, a phreak could go across the LAN and break into the switching equipment—or into secondary systems such as subscriber databases. For a survey of PacBell's experience of this, see [167]; for Bellcore's, see [462].

Using these techniques, unlisted phone numbers could be found, calls could be forwarded without a subscriber's knowledge, and all sorts of mischief became possible. A Californian phone phreak called Kevin Poulsen got root access to many of PacBel's switches and other systems in 1985–1988; this apparently involved burglary as much as hacking (he was eventually convicted of conspiring to possess 15 or more counterfeit, unauthorized, and stolen access devices.) He did petty things like obtaining unlisted phone numbers for celebrities, and winning a Porsche from Los Angeles radio station KIIS-FM. (Each week, KIIS would give a Porsche to the 102nd caller, so Kevin and his accomplices blocked out all calls to the radio station's 25 phone lines save their own, made the 102nd call, and collected the Porsche.) Poulsen was also accused of unlawful wiretapping and espionage; these charges were dismissed. In fact, the FBI came down on him so heavily that there were allegations of an improper relationship between the agency and the phone companies, along the lines of "you scratch our backs with wiretaps when needed, and we'll investigate your hacker problems" [294].

Although the unauthorized wiretapping charges against Poulsen were dismissed, the FBI's sensitivity does highlight the possibility that attacks on phone company computers can be used by foreign intelligence agencies to conduct remote wiretaps. Some of the attacks mentioned in [167] were from overseas, and the possibility that such tricks might be used to crash the whole phone system in the context of an information warfare attack has for some years been a concern of the NSA [321, 480]. Also, prudent nations assume that their telephone switchgear has vulnerabilities known to the government of the country in which it was made.

But although high-tech attacks do happen—and newspaper articles on phone phreaking tend to play up the "evil hacker" aspects—most real attacks are much simpler. Many involve insiders, who deliberately misconfigure systems to provide free calls from (or through) favored numbers. This didn't matter all that much when the phone company's marginal cost of servicing an extra phone call was near zero, but with the modern proliferation of value-added services, people with access to the systems can be tempted to place (or forge) large numbers of calls to accomplices' sex lines. Deregulation, and the advent of mobile phones, have also made fraud serious, as they give rise to cash payments between phone companies [200]. Insiders also get up to mischief with services that depend on the security of the phone network. In a hack reminiscent of Poulsen, two staff at British Telecom were dismissed after they each won 10 tickets for Concorde from a phone-in offer at which only one randomly selected call in a thousand was supposed to get through [754].

As for outsiders, consider the "arch-hacker," Kevin Mitnick. He got extensive press coverage when he was arrested and convicted following a series of break-ins, many of which involved phone systems, and which made him the target of an FBI manhunt. But he testified after his release from prison that almost all of his exploits had involved social engineering. His congressional testimony, quoted at the head of this chapter, sums up the problem neatly [555]. Phone company systems are vulnerable to careless insiders as well as to malicious insiders—just like hospital systems and many others I've discussed.

17.2.4 Insecure End Systems

After direct attacks on the systems kept on phone company premises, the next major vulnerabilities of modern phone systems are insecure terminal equipment and feature interaction.

There have been a number of cases where villains exploited people's answering machines by tricking them into dialing premium rate numbers. The problem arises from phone company switches that give you dial tone 12 seconds after the other party hangs up. So I can record 13 blank seconds on your answering machine, followed by the tones of the number to which I'd like a message delivered, with the message; I then call again, get the machine to play back its messages and hang up on it. Recently, a similar trick has been done with computers—that three-hour call to a sex line in Sierra Leone that appears on your phone bill may well have been dialed by a virus on your PC.

But the really big frauds using insecure end systems are directed against companies. Fraud against corporate *private branch exchange* systems (PBXes) had become big business by the mid-1990s, and costs business billions of dollars a year [202]. PBXes are usually supplied with facilities for *refiling* calls, also known as *direct inward system access* (DISA). The typical application is that the company's sales force can call in to an 800-number, enter a PIN or password, then call out again, taking advantage of the low rates a large company can get for long distance calls. As you'd expect, these PINs become known and get traded by villains [564]. The result is known as *dial-through* fraud.

In many cases, the PINs are set to a default by the manufacturer, and never changed by the customer. In other cases, PINs are captured by crooks who monitor telephone traffic in hotels to steal credit card numbers; phone card numbers and PBX PINs are a useful sideline. Many PBX designs have fixed engineering passwords that allow remote maintenance access, and prudent people reckon that any PBX will have at least one back door installed by the manufacturer to give easy access to law enforcement and intelligence agencies (it's said, as a condition of export licensing). Of course such features get discovered and abused. In one case, the PBX at Scotland Yard was compromised, and used by villains to refile calls, costing the Yard a million pounds, for which they sued their telephone installer. The crooks were never caught [745]. This case was particularly poignant, as one of the criminals' motivations in such cases is to get access to communications that will not be tapped.

Dial-through fraud is mostly driven by premium rate services; the main culprits are crooks who are in cahoots with premium line owners. Secondary culprits are organized criminals who use the calling line ID of respectable companies to hide calls, such as from the United States to Colombia, or from England to Pakistan and China—often via a compromised PBX in a third country to mask the traffic. (This appears to be what happened in the Scotland Yard case, as the crooks made their calls out of America.) Most companies don't understand the need to guard their dial tone, and wouldn't know how to even if they wanted to. PBXes are typically run by company telecoms managers who know little about security, while the security manager often knows little about phones.

Exploits of insecure end-systems sometimes affect domestic subscribers too, now that many people have computers attached to their phones. A notorious case was the Moldova scam. In 1997, customers of a porn site were told to download a "viewer" program, which dropped their phone line and connected them to a phone number in Moldova (having turned off their modem speakers so they wouldn't notice). The new connection stayed up until they turned off their computers. The result was that thousands of subscribers incurred hundreds of thousands of dollars in international long distance charges at over $2 per minute. Their phone companies tried to collect this money, but there was an outcry; eventually, the subscribers got their money back and the Federal Trade Commission enjoined and prosecuted the perpetrators [284]. Since then, there have been a number of copycat scams; most recently, AT&T has been getting complaints about calls to Chad, routed there by a Web company that appears to be in Ireland [543].

Premium rate scams and anonymous calling are not the only motives. As phones start to be used for tasks such as voting, securing entry into apartment buildings, checking that offenders are observing their parole terms, and authenticating financial transactions, more motives are created for ever more creative kinds of mischief, especially for hacks that defeat caller line ID. One of the more extreme cases occurred in London. A crook turned up to buy gold bullion with a bank check; the bullion dealer phoned the bank to verify it; and having got assurances from the voice at the other end, he handed over the gold. The check turned out to be forged; an accomplice had tapped the bank's phone line at the distribution box in the street.

Sometimes, attacks are conducted by upstanding citizens for perfectly honorable motives. A neat example, due to Udi Manber, is as follows. Suppose you have bought something that breaks, and the manufacturer's helpline has only an answering machine. To get service, you have to take the answering machine out of service. This can often be done by recording its message, and playing it back so that it appears as the customer message. With luck, the machine's owner will think it's broken and it'll be sent off for maintenance.

17.2.5 Feature Interaction

More and more cases of telephone manipulation involve feature interaction.

- Inmates at the Clallam Bay Correctional Center in Washington state, who were only allowed to make collect calls, found an interesting exploit of a system that the phone company (Fone America) introduced to handle collect calls automatically. The system would call the dialed number, after which a synthesized voice would say: "If you will accept a collect call from (name of caller), please press the number 3 on your telephone twice." Prisoners were supposed to state their name for the machine to record and insert. The system had, as an additional feature, the capability to have the greeting delivered in Spanish. Inmates did so; and when asked to identify themselves, said, "If you want to hear this message in English, press 33." This worked often enough that they could get through to corporate PBXes and talk the operator into giving them an outside line. The University of Washington was hit several times by this scam [298].

- In November 1996, British Telecom launched a feature called Ringback. If you dialed an engaged number, you could then enter a short code; as soon as the called number was free, both your phone and theirs would ring. The resulting call would be billed to you. However, when it was used from a payphone, it was the phone's owner who ended up with the bill, rather than the caller. People with private payphones, such as pub landlords and shopkeepers, lost a lot of money, which the phone company was eventually obliged to refund [412].

■ Call forwarding is a source of many scams. There have been cases in which hackers have persuaded a phone company operator to forward calls for someone they didn't like to a sex line. The victim then gets billed for the premium rate charges.

■ Conference calls also cause a lot of trouble. For example, football hooligans in some countries are placed under a curfew that requires them to be at home during a match, and to prove this by calling the probation service, which verifies their number using caller ID. The trick is to get one of your kids to set up a conference call with the probation service, and the mobile you've taken to the match. If the probation officer asks about the crowd noise, you tell him it's the TV and you can't turn it down or your mates will kill you. (And if he wants to call you back, you get your kids to forward the call.)

This brings us to the many problems caused by mobile phones.

17.3 Mobile Phones

Since the early 1980s, mobile phones have ceased to be an expensive luxury and have become one of the big technological success stories, with 30–50 percent annual sales growth worldwide. In some countries, notably Scandinavia, most people have at least one mobile, and many new electronic services are built on top of them. For example, there are machines that dispense a can of soda when you call a number displayed on the front; the drink gets added to your phone bill. Growth is particularly rapid in developing countries, where the wireline network is often dilapidated and people used to wait years for phone service to be installed.

Also, although most people use their mobiles sparingly because of the call charges (most phone calls by duration are made from and to wireline phones), criminals make heavy use of mobiles. In Britain, for example, over half of the police wiretaps are now on mobile numbers.

So mobile phones are very important to the security engineer, both as part of the underlying infrastructure and as a channel for service delivery. They can also teach us a lot about fraud techniques and countermeasures.

17.3.1 Mobile Phone Cloning

The first generation of mobile phones used analogue signals and no real authentication. The handset simply sent its serial numbers in clear over the air link. (In the U.S. system, there are two of them: one for the equipment, and one for the subscriber.) So villains built devices that would capture these numbers from calls in the neighborhood. (I've even seen a phone that was reprogrammed to do this by a simple software hack.) One of the main customers was the *call-sell operation*, which would steal phone service and resell it cheaply, often to immigrants or students who wanted to call home. The call-sell operators would hang out at known pitches with cloned mobiles, and their customers would line up to phone home for a few dollars.

A black market developed in phone serial numbers, and enterprising engineers built *tumblers*—mobile phones that used a different identity for each call. Tumblers are designed to be hard for the police to track [406]. The demand for serial numbers got so large that satisfying it was increasingly difficult, even by snooping at places like airports where lots of mobiles were turned on. So as well as passive listening, active methods started to get used.

Modern mobile phones are cellular, in that the operator divides the service area up into cells, each covered by a base station. The mobile uses whichever base station has the strongest signal, and there are protocols for "handing off" calls from one cell to another as the customer roams. (For a survey of mobile phone technology, see [636].) The active attack consists of a fake base station, typically at a place with a lot of passing traffic such as a freeway bridge. As phones pass by, they hear a stronger base station signal and attempt to register by sending their serial numbers.

A number of mechanisms have been tried to cut the volume of fraud. Most operators have intrusion detection systems that watch out for suspicious patterns of activity, such as calls being made from New York and Los Angeles within an hour of each other, or a rapid increase in the volume of calls. A number of heuristics have been developed. For example, genuine mobiles that roam and that call home regularly, but then stop calling home, have usually been stolen.

In the chapter on electronic warfare, I mentioned RF fingerprinting, a formerly classified military technology in which signal characteristics that vary from one handset to another are used to identify individual devices and tie them to the claimed serial numbers [341]. Although this technique works—it was used by Vodafone in Britain to nearly eliminate cloning fraud from analogue mobiles—it is expensive, as it involves modifying the base stations. (Vodafone also used an intrusion detection system, which tracked customer call patterns and mobility, described in [769]; its competitor, Cellnet, simply blocked international calls from analogue mobiles—which helped move its high-value customers to its more modern digital network.) Another proposed solution was to adopt a cryptographic authentication protocol, but there are limits on how much can be done without changing the whole network. For example, one can use a challenge-response protocol to modify the serial number [305]. But many of the mechanisms people have proposed to fortify the security of analogue cellular phones have turned out to be weak [780].

Eventually, the industry decided that it made sense to redesign the entire system, not just to make it more secure but to support a host of new features such as the ability to roam from one country to another without requiring a new handset (important in Europe where lots of small countries are jammed close together), and the ability to send and receive short text messages.

17.3.2 GSM System Architecture

The second generation of mobile phones uses digital technology. By the year 2000, most handsets worldwide used the *Global System for Mobile Communications*, or GSM, which was designed from the start to facilitate international roaming, and launched in 1992. The United States, Japan, and Israel have different digital standards (although there is a competing GSM service in parts of America).

GSM's designers set out to secure the system against cloning and other attacks; the goal was that it should be at least as secure as the wireline system it was to replace. What they did, how they succeeded, and where they failed, make an interesting case history.

17.3.3 Communications Security Mechanisms

The authentication protocols used in GSM are described in a number of places, such as [141] (which also describes the mechanisms in an incompatible U.S. system). But the industry tried to keep secret the cryptographic and other protection mechanisms that form the core of the GSM security system. This didn't work; some eventually leaked, and the rest were discovered by reverse-engineering. I'll describe them briefly here; more can be found on sites such as [713].

Each network has two databases, a *home location register* (HLR), which contains the location of its own mobiles, and a *visitor location register* (VLR), for the location of mobiles that have roamed in from other networks. These databases enable incoming calls to be forwarded to the correct cell; see Figure 17.1 for an overview.

The handsets are commodity items. They are personalized using a *subscriber identity module* (SIM), a smartcard you get when you sign up for a network service, and which you load into your handset. The SIM can be thought of as containing three numbers:

1. There's a *personal identification number*, which you use to unlock the card. In theory, this stops stolen mobiles being used. In practice, many networks set an initial PIN of 0000, and most users never change it.

2. There's an *international mobile subscriber identification* (IMSI), a unique number that maps on to your mobile phone number.

3. Finally there is a *subscriber authentication key K_i*, a 128-bit number that serves to authenticate that IMSI and is known to your home network.

Unlike the banks, which used master keys to generate PINs, the phone companies decided that master keys were too dangerous. Instead of diversifying a master key, KM, to manufacture the authentication keys as $K_i = \{IMSI\}_{KM}$, the keys are generated randomly and kept in an authentication database attached to the HLR.

The protocol used to authenticate the handset to the network runs as follows. On power-up, the SIM requests the customer's PIN; once this is entered correctly, it emits the IMSI, which the handset sends to the nearest base station. This is sent to the subscriber's HLR, which generates five *triplets*. Each triplet consists of:

- RAND, a random challenge
- SRES, a response
- K_c, a ciphering key

The relationship between these values is that RAND, encrypted under the SIM's authentication key K_i, gives an output that is SRES concatenated with K_c:

$$\{RAND\}_{K_i} = (SRES \mid K_c)$$

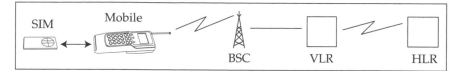

Figure 17.1 GSM authentication system components.

The standard way to do this encryption is using a one-way function called Comp128, or A3/A8 (A3 refers to the SRES output, and A8 to the K_c output). (This is a hash function with 40 rounds, described in detail in [138].) The basic idea is much like in Figure 5.9: each round consists of table look-ups followed by mixing. There are five tables, with 512, 256, 128, 64, and 32 byte entries each, and the hash function uses them successively in each block of five rounds; there are eight of these blocks.

On the face of it, this looks like such a complex hash function that it should be impossible to find preimages of output hash values. Yet once its design finally leaked, a vulnerability was noticed. Four of the bytes—i, $i + 8$, $i + 16$, and $i + 24$, at the output of the second round depend only on the value of the same bytes of the input. Two of these input bytes (i and $i + 8$) are bytes of the key, and thus are fixed for any given SIM card, while the other two bytes of the input come from the challenge input.

This four-byte-to-four-byte channel is called a *narrow pipe*, and it's possible to probe it by varying the two input bytes that come from the challenge. Since the rounds are nonbijective, you can hope for a collision to occur after two rounds; and the birthday paradox guarantees that collisions will occur pretty rapidly (since the pipe is only four bytes wide). Once all the details have been worked out, it turns out that you need about 150,000 suitably chosen challenges to extract the key [781, 783]. The effect is that, given access to a SIM issued by a network that uses Comp128, the authentication key can be extracted in several hours using software that is now available on the Net. Almost all networks do use Comp128. So someone who rents a car with a mobile phone could clone its SIM overnight using his laptop and a suitable adaptor; and someone who sells you a GSM mobile phone might have made a "spare copy" of the authentication key, which he can use later to bill calls to your account.

This attack is yet another example of the dangers of using a secret cryptographic primitive that has been evaluated by only a small group of people. The cryptanalytic techniques necessary to find the flaw were well known [773], and it's likely that if Comp128 had been open to public scrutiny, the flaw would have been found.

Anyway, the triplets are sent to the base station, which now presents the first RAND to the mobile. It passes this to the SIM, which computes SRES. The mobile returns this to the base station; if it's correct, the mobile and the base station can now communicate using the ciphering key K_c. The whole authentication protocol looks like that shown in Figure 17.2.

There's a vulnerability in this protocol. In most countries, the communications between base stations and the VLR pass unencrypted on microwave links. (They tend to be preferred to the local wireline network because the local phone company is often a competitor, and, even if not, microwave makes installation simpler and quicker.) So an attacker could send out an IMSI of his choice, then intercept the triplet on the microwave link back to the local base station. A German mobile operator, which offered a reward

SIM → HLR	IMSI
HLR → BSC	(RAND, SRES, K_c), ...
BSC → SIM	RAND
SIM → BSC	SRES
BSC → mobile	{traffic}$_{K_c}$

Figure 17.2 GSM authentication protocol.

of 100,000 Deutschmarks to anyone who could bill a call to a mobile number whose SIM card was held in its lawyer's office, backed down when we asked for the IMSI [30].

Triples can also be replayed. An unscrupulous foreign network can get five triples while you are roaming on it, then keep on reusing them to allow you to phone as much as you want. This means that the network doesn't have to refer back to your network for further authorization (and even if they do, it doesn't protect you, as the visited network might not send in its bills for a week or more). So your home network can be prevented from shutting you off while you roam, and (depending on the terms of the contract between the phone companies) it may still be liable to pay the roamed network the money. This means that even if you thought you'd limited your liability by using a prepaid SIM, you might still end up with your network trying to collect money from you. This is why, to enable roaming with a prepaid SIM, you're normally asked for a credit card number. You can end up being billed for more than you expected.

I have no reliable report of any frauds being carried out by outsiders (that is, attackers other than phone company staff) using these techniques. When GSM was introduced, the villains simply switched their modus operandi to buying phones using stolen credit cards, using stolen identities, or bribing insiders [807]. Robbery is also getting big; in the London borough of Lewisham, theft of mobile phones accounts for 30–35% of street robberies, with 35% of victims being male and under 18 [501].

From about 1997, prepaid mobile phones were introduced, and many criminals promptly started using them. In most European countries, prepaids can be bought for well under $100, including enough airtime for three months' worth of moderate use. Prepaids have turned out to be very good not just for evading police wiretapping but for stalking, extortion, and other kinds of harrassment. Prepaid phones are also liable to all sorts of simple frauds. For example, if your identity isn't checked when you buy it, there's little risk to you if you recharge it, or enable roaming, with a stolen credit card number [214].

In addition to authentication, the GSM system is supposed to provide two additional kinds of protection: location security and call content confidentiality.

The location security mechanism is that once a mobile is registered to a network, it is issued with a *temporary mobile subscriber identification* (TMSI), which acts as its address as it roams through the network. The attack on this mechanism uses a device called an *IMSI-catcher*, which is sold to police forces [308]. The IMSI-catcher, which can be operated in a police car tailing a suspect, acts as a GSM base station. Because it is closer than the genuine article, its signal is stronger, so the mobile tries to register with it. The IMSI-catcher claims not to understand the TMSI, and so the handset helpfully sends it the cleartext IMSI. (This feature is needed if mobiles are to be able to roam from one network to another without the call being dropped, and to recover from failures at the VLR [769].) The police can now get a warrant to intercept the traffic to that mobile or—if they're in a hurry—just do a middleperson attack, in which they pretend to be the network to the mobile and the mobile to the network.

The GSM system is supposed to provide call content confidentiality by encrypting the traffic between the handset and the base station once the authentication and registration are completed. The speech is digitized, compressed, and chopped into packets; each packet is encrypted by xor-ing it with a pseudorandom sequence generated from the ciphering key K_c and the packet number. The algorithm commonly used in Europe is A5.

A5, like Comp128, was originally secret; like Comp128, it was leaked and attacks were found on it. The algorithm is shown in Figure 17.3. It has three linear feedback shift registers of lengths 19, 22, and 23; their outputs are combined using exclusive-or to form the output keystream. The nonlinearity in this generator comes from a majority-clocking arrangement, whereby the middle bits c_i of the three shift registers are compared and the two or three shift registers whose middle bits agree are clocked.

The obvious attack on this arrangement is to guess the two shorter registers, then work out the value of the third. As there are 41 bits to guess, one might think that about 2^{40} computations would be needed on average. But it's slightly more complex than this, as the generator loses state; many states have more than one possible precursor, so more guesses are needed. That said, Alex Biryukov and Adi Shamir found that by putting together a number of suitable optimizations, A5 could be broken without an unreasonable amount of effort. Their basic idea was to compute a large file of special points to which the state of the algorithm converges, then look for a match with the

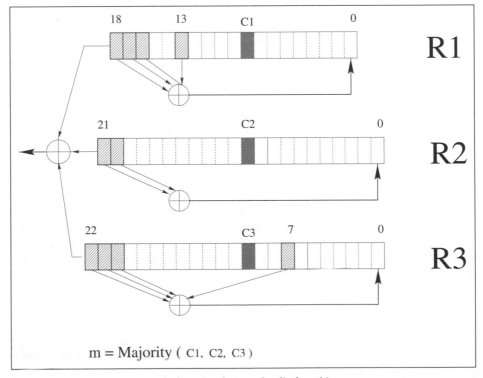

Figure 17.3   A5 (courtesy of Alex Biryukov and Adi Shamir).

observed traffic. Given this precomputed file, the attack could use several seconds of traffic and several minutes' work on a PC, or several minutes of traffic and several seconds' work [104].

Reverse-engineering actual systems also showed that the keying of A5 was deliberately weakened. Although, in theory, A5 has a 64-bit key (the initial loads for the shift registers) the actual implementations set the ten least significant key bits to zero. What's more, phones sold to phone companies in many countries have a further weakened version of A5, called A5/2. (There was a political row in Australia when it was realized that A5/2 was being used there.)

The conspiracy theorists had a field day with all this—security mechanisms being deliberately weakened at the behest of intelligence agencies to make mobile phones easy to tap. The truth is, as always, more subtle.

Intelligence agencies gain access to cleartext from their own countries' networks and from countries where an outstation (such as in an embassy) can intercept a suitable microwave link. Even in the home country, interception can occur with or without the cooperation of the phone company; equipment to grab traffic from the microwave links is fairly widely available. But in most countries, police are getting laws passed that give them direct access to phone company systems, as this gives them even more—such as location register data which enables them to track the past movements of suspects. There was a storm in Switzerland in 1997 when the press found that the phone company was giving location data to the police [618]. In the United States, the FCC ordered mobile phone companies to be able to locate people "so that 911 calls could be dispatched to the right place." This was imposed on every user of mobile phone service, rather than letting users decide whether to buy mobile location services or not. U.S. privacy activists are currently in litigation with the FCC over this.

Undoubtedly, there has been agency interference in the design of GSM, but the benefits from having weak authentication and confidentiality mechanisms appear limited to tactical sigint situations. Consider the case mentioned in the chapter on electronic warfare, where the New Zealand navy sent a frigate to monitor a coup in Fiji. Even if the Fijian phone company had been allowed to use A5 rather than A5/2, this would not have frustrated the mission, because signals intelligence officers could snatch the triplets off the microwave links, hack the location register, or whatever. If all else failed, a key could be found by brute force. But being able to break the traffic quickly is convenient— especially when you are dispatched on a peacekeeping mission in a country to which your intelligence people have never paid enough attention to emplace a hack (or a human asset) in the local phone company.

The net effect is that the initial GSM security mechanisms provided slightly better protection than the wireline network in countries allowed to use A5, and slightly worse protection elsewhere. The vulnerabilities in the communications security mechanisms neither expose subscribers in developed countries to much additional wiretapping, nor prevent the frauds that cause them the most grief.

17.3.4 The Next Generation: 3gpp

The third generation of digital mobile phones was initially known as the *Universal Mobile Telecommunications System* (UMTS) but now as the *Third-Generation Partnership*

Project (3gpp). The security is much the same as GSM, but upgraded to deal with a number of GSM's known vulnerabilities. The system is supposed to enter service in 2003–2004; some of the design details are still being worked on, so this section is necessarily somewhat tentative. However, the overall security strategy is described in [786], and the current draft of the security architecture is at [775].

The crypto algorithms A5 and Comp128 are replaced by a block cipher called Kasumi [442]. This is public and is based on a design by Mitsuru Matsui, called Misty, which has withstood public scrutiny for some years [527]. All keys are now 128 bits. Cryptography will be used to protect the integrity and confidentiality of both message content and signalling data, rather than just content confidentiality—although in the first phase of 3gpp the protection will not be end-to-end. The practice of transferring triples in the clear between base stations will cease, as will the vulnerability to rogue base stations; so IMSI-catchers will not work against third-generation mobiles. Instead, there will be a properly engineered interface for lawful interception [776]. Originally, this was supposed to supply plaintext only; now, the provision of key material will also be available as a national option.

In the basic 3gpp protocol, the authentication is pushed back from the base station controller to the visitor location register. The home location register is now known as the *home environment* (HE), and the SIM as the *UMTS SIM* (USIM). The home environment chooses a random challenge *RAND* as before, and enciphers it with the USIM authentication key K to generate a response *RES*, a confidentiality key *CK*, an integrity key *IK*, and an anonymity key *AK*.

$$\{RAND\}_K = (RES \mid CK \mid IK \mid AK)$$

There is also a sequence number *SEQ* known to the HE and the USIM. A MAC is computed on *RAND* and *SEQ*, then the sequence number is masked by exclusive-or'ing it with the anonymity key. The challenge, the expected response, the confidentiality key, the integrity key, and the masked sequence number are made up into an *authentication vector AV*, which is sent from the HE to the VLR. The VLR then sends the USIM the challenge, the masked sequence number, and the MAC; the USIM computes the response and the keys, unmasks the sequence number, verifies the MAC, and, if it's correct, returns the response to the VLR (see Figure 17.4).

3gpp has many other features, including details of sequence number generation, identity and location privacy mechanisms, backward compatability with GSM, mechanisms for public key encryption of authentication vectors in transit from HEs to VLRs, and negotiation of various optional cryptographic mechanisms. Many of these still were not defined at the time of writing.

In first phase of 3gpp, confidentiality will be, in effect, a higher-quality implementation of what's already available in GSM: eavesdropping on the air link will be prevented as

USIM → HE	IMSI (this can optionally be encrypted)
HE → VLR	RAND, XRES, CK, IK, $SEQ \oplus AK$, MAC
VLR → USIM	RAND, $SEQ \oplus AK$, MAC
USIM → VLR	RES

Figure 17.4 The 3gpp authentication protocol.

before, and the currently possible attacks on the backbone network, or by bogus base stations, will be excluded. Police wiretaps will still be possible at the VLR. In the second phase, 3gpp is proposed to have end-to-end encryption, so that the call content and some of the associated signalling will be protected from one handset to another. This has led to government demands for the use of a *key escrow protocol*—a protocol that would make keys available to police and intelligence services on demand. The catch is that, if a mobile phone call takes place from a British phone company's subscriber using a U.S. handset, roaming in France, to a German company's subscriber roaming in Switzerland using a Finnish handset, and the call goes via a long-distance service based in Canada and using Swedish exchange equipment, then which of these countries' intelligence agencies will have access to the keys? (Traditionally, most of them would have had access to the call content one way or another.)

The solution favored by the agencies in Britain and France (at least) is the so-called Royal Holloway protocol [418], designed largely by Vodafone. It gives access to the countries where the subscribers are based (in this case, Britain and Germany). This is achieved by using a variant of Diffie-Hellman key exchange, in which the users' private keys are obtained by encrypting their names under a super-secret master key known to the local phone company and/or intelligence agency. Although this protocol has been adopted in the British civil service and the French health service, it is at odds with the phone company security philosophy that master keys are a bad thing. Quite apart from this, and from the unease which many people feel with built-in eavesdropping facilities, the protocol is clunky and inefficient [50]. There is also tension with local law enforcement requirements: in the above example, the police forces of the two countries in which the targets are roaming (France and Switzerland) will also want access to the traffic [776]. The debate continues; one possible resolution is *tromboning*, an established wiretap technique in which traffic is routed from the switch to the monitoring service and back, before going on its way. However, internetwork tromboning can introduce noticeable delays that could alert the target of investigation.

Consequently, 3gpp won't provide a revolution in confidentiality. As with GSM, its design goal is that security should be comparable with that of the wired network [390]. This looks like being doable.

The security of the billing mechanisms is a thornier issue. The GSM billing mechanism is inadequate for 3gpp, for a number of reasons:

- A *call detail record* (CDR) is generated only after the calling phone goes on-hook. This is an established feature of wireline networks, but when the environment changed to mobile, it became a serious problem. The attack is that someone running a call-sell operation sets up a long conference call using a mobile that was stolen, or a prepaid for which roaming was enabled using a stolen credit card (as discussed in Section 17.3.3). His clients join and leave this call one after the other, and the advice-of-charge facility lets him know how much to bill them. The phone stays off-hook continuously for several days. As soon as it goes on-hook, a CDR for several thousand dollars is generated, and the alarm goes off. So he throws the phone in the river and starts using the next one. By 1996, this had become so serious that Vodafone introduced a six-hour limit on all mobile calls.

- However, it won't be acceptable to just drop all 3gpp calls after six hours. Many users are expected to have always-on internet connections (such as from their laptops) with relatively light packet traffic most of the time.

- The phone companies also want to be able to charge for relatively high-value product and service delivery, ranging from the current premium services through services based on location ("give me a map showing me how to drive to the nearest McDonald's") to multimedia services.[1] Customers will be charged not just by the phone company but by other service providers; in addition to call duration and data volume, they will be billed according to the quality of service they receive, such as the effective bandwidth.

- Finally, the European Commission intends to require that all 3gpp operators retain location information on mobile phones for at least a year, for law enforcement purposes. Having a location history in the subscriber billing records may be the cheapest way to do this.

It is clear that the existing GSM mechanisms are inadequate—even adding such features as real-time international settlement would be extremely expensive. A redesign is needed. The proposed solution is to redesign the CDR to contain the required data quantity, location and quality-of-service information, and to build an online cost-control mechanism to limit the charges incurred for each user [558]. The cost-control mechanisms are not being standardized, but can involve forwarding charging data from either the local network or the gateway to the home environment, which will be able to have the call terminated if the available credit is exhausted (as with a prepaid SIM card) or if the use appears to be fraudulent.

One proposed way of implementing this is to incorporate a micropayment mechanism [56]. The idea is that the phone will send regular *tick payments* to each of the networks or service providers that are due to be paid for the call. The tick payments can be thought of as electronic coins and are cryptographically protected against forgery.

At the start of the call, the handset will compute a number of phone ticks by repeated hashing: $t_1 = h(t_0)$, $t_2 = h(t_1)$, and so on, with t_k (for some credit limit k, typically 2^{10} units) being signed by the phone company. The phone will then release ticks regularly in order to pay for the services as the call progresses. It will start by releasing t_k, then t_{k-1}, then t_{k-2}, and so on. If a charge is subsequently disputed—whether by a subscriber or a network operator—the party claiming an amount of, say, j ticks must exhibit the ticks t_{k-j} and t_k, the latter with a certificate. As the hash function h is one-way, this should be hard to do unless the handset actually released that many ticks. The tick t_{k-j} can now be checked by applying the hash function to it j times and verifying that the result is t_k. (This protocol is an example of multiple simultaneous discovery, having been invented by our group at Cambridge, by Pedersen, and by Rivest and Shamir, independently in 1995 [26, 605, 648].)

---

[1]Presumably, given that many new communications services are used first for porn, this will mean live strip shows to order on the screen of your mobile, beamed to you from a country with relaxed indecency laws. So more prudish governments will demand ways to get round the 3gpp privacy mechanisms so they can censor content—just as the music industry will want ways to prevent user-to-user copying. We'll discuss this more in Chapter 20.

One advantage of using a tick payment mechanism is that, as well as protecting the phone companies from conference call frauds, it could protect the subscriber from many more. Phone users will at least in principle be able to spot the kind of 900 numbers that charge $24 per call or that masquerade as ordinary numbers or both.

17.3.5 GSM Security: A Success or Failure?

Whether GSM security was a success or a failure depends on whom you ask.

From the point of view of cryptography, it was a failure. Both the Comp128 hash function and the A5 encryption algorithm were broken once they became public. In fact, GSM is often cited as an object lesson in Kerckhoff's Principle—that cryptographic security should reside in the choice of the key, rather than in the obscurity of the mechanism. The mechanism will leak sooner or later, and it's better to subject it to public review before, rather than after, a hundred million units have been manufactured. (GSM security wasn't a disaster for most cryptographers, of course, as it provided plenty of opportunities to write research papers.)

From the phone companies' point of view, GSM was a success. The shareholders of GSM operators, such as Vodafone, have made vast amounts of money, and a (small) part of this is due to the challenge-response mechanism in GSM stopping cloning. The crypto weaknesses were irrelevant, as they were never exploited (at least not in ways that did significant harm to call revenue). One or two frauds persist, such as the long conference call trick; but, on balance, the GSM design has been good to the phone companies.

From the criminals' point of view, GSM was also fine. It did not stop them stealing phone service; their modus operandi merely changed, with the cost falling on credit card companies or on individual victims of identity theft or street robbery. It did not stop calls from anonymous phones; the rise of the prepaid phone industry made them even easier. (The phone companies were happy with both of these changes.) And, of course, GSM did nothing about dial-through fraud.

From the point of view of the large-country intelligence agencies, GSM was fine. They have access to local and international traffic in the clear anyway, and the weakened version of A5 facilitates tactical sigint against developing countries. And the second wave of GSM equipment is bringing some juicy features, such as remote control of handsets by the operator [636]. If you can subvert (or masquerade as) the operator, then there seems to be nothing to stop you quietly turning on a target's mobile phone without his knowledge and listening to the conversation in the room.

From the point of view of the police and low-resource intelligence agencies, things are not quite so bright. The problem isn't the added technical complexity of GSM networks: court-ordered wiretaps can be left to the phone company (although finding the number to tap can be a hassle if the suspect is mobile). The problem is the introduction of prepaid mobile phones. This not only decreases the signal to noise ratio of traffic analysis algorithms and makes it harder to target wiretaps, but also encourages crimes such as extortion and stalking.

From the customer's point of view, GSM was originally sold as being completely secure. Was this accurate? The encryption of the air link certainly did stop casual eavesdropping, which was an occasional nuisance with analogue phones. (There had been some high-profile cases of celebrities being embarrassed, including one case in Britain where Prince Charles was overheard talking to his mistress before his divorce, and one in the United States involving Newt Gingrich.) But almost all the phone tapping in the world is done by large intelligence agencies, to whom the encryption doesn't make much difference.

Things are even less positive for the subscriber when we look at billing. Cryptographic authentication of handsets can't stop the many frauds perpetrated by premium rate operators and phone companies. If anything it makes it harder to wriggle out of bogus charges, as the phone company can say in court that your smartcard and your PIN must have been used in the handset that made the call. The same will apply to 3gpp if micropayments aren't used. The one minor compensation is that GSM facilitated the spread of prepaid phones, which can limit the exposure.

So the security features designed into GSM don't help the subscriber much. They were designed to provide "security" from the phone company's point of view: they dump much of the toll fraud risk, while not interrupting the flow of premium rate business—whether genuine or fraudulent.

In the medium term, the one ray of comfort for the poor subscriber is that one real vulnerability in GSM—the long conference call—may drive the introduction of micropayment schemes, which may, as a side effect, make premium rate scams harder. I say "may" rather than "will," as it will be interesting to see whether the phone companies implement them properly. There is a business incentive to provide a user interface that enables subscribers to monitor their expenditure (so they can be blamed for frauds they don't spot), while discouraging most of them from actually monitoring it (so the phone companies continue to make hundreds of millions from their share of the premium rate scam revenue). We shall have to wait and see.

17.4 Corporate Fraud

The question of corporate fraud is particularly relevant, as one of the fastest growing scams in the United States is the unscrupulous phone company that bills lots of small sums to unwitting users. It collects phone numbers in various ways. (For example, if you call an 800 number, then your own number will be passed to the far end regardless of whether you tried to block caller line ID.) It then bills you a few dollars. Your own phone company passes on this charge, and you find there's no effective way to dispute it. Sometimes, the scam uses a legal loophole: if you call an 800 number in the United States, the company may say, "Can we call you right back?" If you agree, you're deemed to have accepted the charges, which are likely to be at a high premium rate. The same can happen if you respond to voice prompts as the call progresses. These practices are known as *cramming.*

Another problem is *slamming*—the unauthorized change of a subscriber's long distance telephone service provider without their consent. The slammers tell your local phone company that you have opted for their services; your phone company routes your long distance calls through their service; they hope you don't notice the change and dispute the bill; and the telephone charges can then be jacked up. Some local phone

companies, such as Bell Atlantic, allow their customers to freeze their chosen long distance carrier [13].

It would be a mistake to assume that cramming and slamming are done only by small
fly-by-night operators. AT&T is one of the worst offenders, having been fined $300,000
not only for slamming, but for actually using forged signatures of subscribers to make it
look as if they had agreed to switch to their service. They got caught when they forged
a signature of the deceased spouse of a subscriber in Texas [252].

Another problem *is* the fly-by-night phone company. Anyone in the United States is
legally entitled to set up a phone company; it is fairly straightforward to set one up,
collect some cash from subscribers, then vanish once the invoices for interconnect fees
come in from the established players. In Britain, there is a company that advertises
sex lines with normal phone numbers to trap the unwary; it then sends them huge
bills at their residential addresses and tries to intimidate them into paying. In a case
currently before the courts, they justify this in terms of non-discrimination rules: if British
Telecom can make huge charges for phone sex, why can't they?

It's not just the small operators that indulge in dubious business practices. An example
that affects even some large phone companies is the short termination of international
calls.

Although premium rate numbers are used for a number of more or less legitimate purposes, such as software support, many of them exploit minors or people with compulsive
behavior disorders. So regulators have forced phone companies in many countries to
offer premium rate number blocking to subscribers. Phone companies get around this
by disguising premium rate numbers as international ones. I mentioned the scams with
Caribbean numbers in Section 17.2.1. Now, many other phone companies from small
countries with lax regulators have got into the act, offering sex line operators a range of
numbers on which they share the revenue.

Often, a call made to a small-country phone company doesn't go anywhere near its
ostensible destination. One of the hacks used to do this is called *short termination*,
and works as follows. Normally, calls for the small Pacific country of Tuvalu go via
Telstra in Perth, Australia, where they are forwarded by satellite. However, the sex line
numbers are marked as invalid in Telstra's system, so they are automatically sent via the
second-choice operator—a company in New Zealand. (The girls—or to be more precise,
the elderly retired hookers who pretend to be young girls—are actually in Manchester,
England.) Technically, this is an interesting case of a fallback mechanism being used as an
attack vehicle. Legally, it is hard to challenge, as there is an international agreement (the
Nairobi Convention) that prevents phone companies selectively blocking international
destinations. Thus, if you want to stop your kids phoning the sex line in Tuvalu, you have
to block all international calls, which makes it harder for you to phone that important
client in Germany.

Problems like these are ultimately regulatory failures, and they are increasingly common. (For example, in the Moldova scam mentioned above, the calls didn't go to Moldova
but to Canada [151].) These problems may well get worse as technology makes many
new, complex services possible and the regulators fail to keep up.

Even the phone companies themselves sometimes fall foul of the growing complexity.
There are two cases before the courts as I write this, in which phone companies are
chasing people who noticed that calling an international premium number at their best

discount rate actually cost less than the amount they could get paid by operating the premium service. The profits they're alleged to have made have two commas rather than the usual one. The phone companies claim this was fraud; the defendants that it was honest arbitrage. We shall have to wait and see what the juries think.

17.5 Summary

Phone fraud is a fascinating case study. People have been cheating phone companies for decades, and recently the phone companies have been vigorously returning the compliment. To start off with, systems were not really protected at all, and it was easy to evade charges and redirect calls. The mechanism adopted to prevent this—out-of-band signalling—has proved inadequate as the rapidly growing complexity of the system opened up many more vulnerabilities. These range from social engineering attacks on users through poor design and management of terminal equipment such as PBXes to the exploitation of various hard-to-predict feature interactions.

Overall, the security problems in telecoms have been the result of environmental changes. These have included deregulation, which brought in many new phone companies. However, the main change has been the introduction of premium rate numbers. While previously phone companies sold a service with a negligible marginal cost of provision, suddenly real money was involved; and while previously about the only serious benefit to be had from manipulating the system was calls that were hard for the police to tap, suddenly serious money could be earned. The existing protection mechanisms were unable to cope with this evolution.

The growing complexity nullified even the fairly serious effort made to secure the GSM digital mobile system. Their engineers concentrated on communications security threats rather than computer security threats; they also concentrated on the phone companies' interests at the expense of the customers'. The next-generation mobile service, 3gpp, looks capable of doing slightly better; but we shall have to wait and see how it gets implemented in practice.

Research Problems

Relatively little research has been done outside phone company and intelligence agency labs on issues related specifically to phone fraud and wiretapping. However, there is growing interest in protocols and other mechanisms for use with novel telecommunications services. The recently published 3gpp protocol suite is sufficiently large and complex that it may take some time for the formal methods and security protocol people to analyze fully. Next-generation value-added services are bound to introduce new vulnerabilities. The interaction between all these communications and security protocols, and the mechanisms used for distributed systems security, is fertile ground for both interesting research and horrendously expensive engineering errors: there are already regular workshops on how to use system engineering techniques to manage feature interactions in telecommunications.

Further Reading

There are a lot of scattered articles about phone fraud, but nothing I know of which brings everything together. A useful site for the fraud techniques currently being used in the United States is the Alliance to Outfox Phone Fraud, an industry consortium [13]. The underlying technologies are described in a number of reference books, such as [636] on GSM, and more can be found on Web sites such as [713]. An overview of UMTS can be found in [400], and the 'full Monty' in [56]. To keep up with phone fraud, a useful resource is the *Discount Long Distance Digest* [252].

CHAPTER 18

Network Attack and Defense

Whoever thinks his problem can be solved using cryptography, doesn't understand his problem and doesn't understand cryptography.

—ATTRIBUTED BY ROGER NEEDHAM AND BUTLER LAMPSON TO EACH OTHER

18.1 Introduction

Internet security is a fashionable and fast-moving field; the attacks that are catching the headlines can change significantly from one year to the next. Regardless of whether they're directly relevant to the work you do, network-based attacks are so high-profile that they are likely to have some impact, even if you only use hacker stories to get your client to allocate increased budgets to counter the more serious threats. The point is, some knowledge of the subject is essential for the working security engineer.

There are several fashionable ideas, such as that networks can be secured by encryption and that networks can be secured by firewalls. The best place to start debunking these notions may be to look at the most common attacks. (Of course, many attacks are presented in the media as network hacking when they are actually done in more traditional ways. A topical example is the leak of embarrassing emails that appeared to come from the office of the U.K. prime minister, and were initially blamed on hackers. As it turned out, the emails had been fished out of the trash at the home of his personal pollster by a private detective called Benji the Binman, who achieved instant celebrity status [520].)

18.1.1 The Most Common Attacks

Many actual attacks involve combinations of vulnerabilities. Examples of vulnerabilities we've seen in earlier chapters include stack overflow attacks (where you pass an over-long parameter to a program that carelessly executes part of it) and password guessing, both of which were used by the Internet worm. A common strategy is to get an account on any machine on a target network, then install a password sniffer to get an account on the target machine, then use a stack overflow to upgrade to a root account.

The exact vulnerabilities in use change from one year to the next, as bugs in old software get fixed and new software releases a new crop of them. Still, there are some patterns, and some old favorites that keep coming back in new guises. Here's a list of the top 10 vulnerabilities, as of June 2000 [670].

1. *A stack overflow attack on the BIND program*, used by many Unix and Linux hosts for DNS, giving immediate account access.

2. *Vulnerable CGI programs on Web servers*, often supplied by the vendor as sample programs and not removed. CGI program flaws are the common means of taking over and defacing Web servers.

3. *A stack overflow attack on the remote procedure call (RPC) mechanism*, used by many Unix and Linux hosts to support local networking, and which allows intruders immediate account access (this was used by most of the distributed denial of service attacks launched during 1999 and early 2000).

4. *A bug in Microsoft's Internet Information Server (IIS) Web server software*, which allowed immediate access to an administrator account on the server.

5. *A bug in* `sendmail`, *the most common mail program on Unix and Linux computers*. Many bugs have been found in `sendmail` over the years, going back to the very first advisory issued by CERT in 1988. One of the recent flaws can be used to instruct the victim machine to mail its password file to the attacker, who can then try to crack it.

6. *A stack overflow attack on Sun's Solaris operating system*, which allows intruders immediate root access.

7. *Attacks on NFS (which I'll describe shortly) and their equivalents on Windows NT and Macintosh operating systems*. These mechanisms are used to share files on a local network.

8. *Guesses of usernames and passwords*, especially where the root or administrator password is weak, or where a system is shipped with default passwords that people don't bother to change.

9. *The IMAP and POP protocols*, which allow remote access to email but are often misconfigured to allow intruder access.

10. *Weak authentication in the SNMP protocol*, used by network administrators to manage all types of network-connected devices. SNMP uses a default password of "public" (which a few "clever" vendors have changed to "private").

Observe that none of these attacks is stopped by encryption, and not all of them by firewalls. For example, vulnerable Web servers can be kept away from back-end business systems by putting them outside the firewall, but they will still be open to vandalism;

and if the firewall runs on top of an operating system with a vulnerability, then the bad guy may simply take it over.

Although some of these attacks may have been fixed by the time this book is published, the underlying pattern is fairly constant. Most of the exploits make use of program bugs, of which the majority are stack overflow vulnerabilities. The exploitation of protocol vulnerabilities (such as NFS) vies with weak passwords for second place.

In effect, there is a race between the attackers, who try to find loopholes, and the vendors, who develop patches for them. Capable motivated attackers may find exploits for themselves and keep quiet about them, but most reported attacks involve exploits that are not only well known but for which tools are available on the Net.

18.1.2 Skill Issues: Script Kiddies and Packaged Defense

One of the main culture changes brought by the Net is that, until recently, sophisticated attacks on communications (such as middleperson attacks) were essentially the preserve of national governments. Today, we find not just password-snooping attacks but also more subtle routing attacks being done by kids, for fun. The critical change here is that people write the necessary exploit software, then post it on sites such as www.rootshell.com, from which *script kiddies* can download it and use it. This term refers primarily to young pranksters who use attack scripts prepared by others, but it also refers to any unskilled people who download and launch tools they don't fully understand. As systems become ever more complicated, even sophisticated attackers are heading this way; no individual can keep up with all the vulnerabilities that are discovered in operating systems and network protocols. In effect, hacking is being progressively deskilled, while defence is becoming unmanageably complex.

As discussed in Chapter 4, the Internet protocol suite was designed for a world in which trusted hosts at universities and research labs cooperated to manage networking in a cooperative way. That world has passed away. Instead of users being mostly honest and competent, we have a huge user population that's completely incompetent (many of whom have high-speed always-on connections), a (small) minority that's competent and honest, a (smaller) minority that's competent and malicious, and a (less small) minority that's malicious but uses available tools opportunistically.

Deskilling is also a critical factor in defense. There are a few organizations, such as computer companies, major universities, and military intelligence agencies, that have people who know how to track what's going on and tune the defenses appropriately. But most companies rely on a combination of standard products and services. The products include firewalls, virus scanners, and intrusion detection systems; the services are often delivered in the form of new configuration files for these products. In these ways, vulnerabilities become concentrated. An attacker who can work out a defeat of a widely sold system has a wide range of targets to aim at.

We'll now look at a number of specific attack and defense mechanisms. Keep in mind here that the most important attack is the stack overwriting attack, and the second most important is password guessing; but because I already covered the first in Chapter 4 and the second in Chapters 2–3, we'll move down to number three: vulnerabilities in network protocols.

18.2 Vulnerabilities in Network Protocols

Commodity operating systems such as Unix and NT are shipped with a very large range of network services, many of which are enabled by default, and/or shipped with configurations that make "plug and play" easy—for the attacker as well as the legitimate user. We will look at both local area and Internet issues; a common theme is that mapping methods (between addresses, filenames, etc.) provide many of the weak points.

This book isn't an appropriate place to explain network protocols, so I offer a telegraphic summary, as follows: the *Internet Protocol* (IP) is a stateless protocol that transfers packet data from one machine to another; it uses 32-bit *IP addresses*, often written as four decimal numbers in the range 0–255, such as 172.16.8.93. Most Internet services use a protocol called *Transmission Control Protocol* (TCP), which is layered on top of IP, and provides virtual circuits by splitting up the data stream into IP packets and reassembling it at the far end, asking for repeats of any lost packets. IP addresses are translated into the familiar Internet host addresses using the *Domain Name System* (DNS), a worldwide distributed service in which higher-level name servers point to local name servers for particular domains. Local networks mostly use Ethernet, in which devices have unique Ethernet addresses, which are mapped to IP addresses using the *Address Resolution Protocol* (ARP).

There are many other components in the protocol suite for managing communications and providing higher-level services. Most of them were developed in the days when the Net had only trusted hosts, and security wasn't a concern. So there is little authentication built in; and attempts to remedy this defect with the introduction of the next generation of IP (IPv6) are likely to take many years.

18.2.1 Attacks on Local Networks

Let's suppose that the attacker is one of your employees; he has a machine attached to your LAN, and he wants to take over an account in someone else's name to commit a fraud. Given physical access to the network, he can install packet sniffer software to harvest passwords, get the root password, and create a suitable account. However, if your staff use challenge-response password generators, or are careful enough to only use a root password at the keyboard of the machine it applies to, then he has to be more subtle.

One approach is to try to masquerade as a machine where the target user has already logged on. ARP is one possible target; by running suitable code, the attacker can give wrong answers to ARP messages and claim to be the victim. The victim machine might notice if alert, but the attacker can always wait until it is down—or take it down by using another attack. One possibility is to use *subnet masks*.

Originally, IP addresses used the first 3 bits to specify the split between the network address and the host address. Now they are interpreted as addressing network, subnetwork, and host, with a variable *network mask*. Diskless workstations, when booting, broadcast a request for a subnet mask; many of them will apply any subnet mask they receive at any time. So by sending a suitable subnet mask, a workstation can be made to vanish.

Another approach, if the company uses Unix systems, is to target Sun's *Network File System* (NFS), the de facto standard for Unix file sharing. This allows a number of workstations to use a network disk drive as if it were a local disk; it has a number of well-known vulnerabilities to attackers who're on the same LAN. When a volume is first mounted, the client requests from the server a *root filehandle*, which refers to the root directory of the mounted filesystem. This doesn't depend on the time, or the server generation number, and it can't be revoked. There is no mechanism for per-user authentication; the server must trust a client completely or not at all. Also, NFS servers often reply to requests from a different network interface to the one on which the request arrived. So it's possible to wait until an administrator is logged in at a file server, then masquerade as her to overwrite the password file. For this reason, many sites use alternative file systems, such as ANFS.

18.2.2 Attacks Using Internet Protocols and Mechanisms

Moving up to the Internet protocol suite, the fundamental problem is similar: there is no real authenticity or confidentiality protection in most mechanisms. This is particularly manifest at the lower-level TCP/IP protocols.

Consider, for example, the three-way handshake used by Alice to initiate a TCP connection to Bob and to set up sequence numbers, shown in Figure 18.1.

This protocol can be exploited in a surprising number of different ways. Now that service denial is becoming really important, let's start off with the simplest service denial attack: the *SYN flood*.

18.2.2.1 SYN Flooding

The SYN flood attack is, simply, to send a large number of SYN packets and never acknowledge any of the replies. This leads the recipient (Bob, in Figure 18.1) to accumulate more records of SYN packets than his software can handle. This attack had been known to be theoretically possible since the 1980s, but came to public attention when it was used to bring down Panix, a New York ISP, for several days in 1996.

A technical fix, the so-called SYNcookie, has been found and incorporated in Linux and some other systems. Rather than keeping a copy of the incoming SYN packet, B simply sends out as Y an encrypted version of X. That way, it's not necessary to retain state about sessions that are half-open.

$$
\begin{array}{ll}
A \rightarrow B: & \text{SYN; my number is X} \\
B \rightarrow A: & \text{ACK; now X+1} \\
& \text{SYN; my number is Y} \\
A \rightarrow B: & \text{ACK; now Y+1} \\
& \text{(start talking)}
\end{array}
$$

Figure 18.1   TCP/IP handshake.

18.2.2.2 Smurfing

Another common way of bringing down a host is known as *smurfing*. This exploits the *Internet Control Message Protocol* (ICMP), which enables users to send an echo packet to a remote host to check whether it's alive. The problem arises with broadcast addresses that are shared by a number of hosts. Some implementations of the Internet protocols respond to pings to both the broadcast address and their local address (the idea was to test a LAN to see what's alive). So the protocol allowed both sorts of behavior in routers. A collection of hosts at a broadcast address that responds in this way is called a *smurf amplifier*.

The attack is to construct a packet with the source address forged to be that of the victim, and send it to a number of smurf amplifiers. The machines there will each respond (if alive) by sending a packet to the target, and this can swamp the target with more packets than it can cope with. Smurfing is typically used by someone who wants to take over an *Internet relay chat* (IRC) server, so they can assume control of the chatroom. The innovation was to automatically harness a large number of "innocent" machines on the network to attack the victim.

Part of the countermeasure is technical: a change to the protocol standards in August 1999 so that ping packets sent to a broadcast address are no longer answered [691]. As this gets implemented, the number of smurf amplifiers on the Net is steadily going down. The other part is socioeconomic: sites such as www.netscan.org produce lists of smurf amplifiers. Diligent administrators will spot their networks on there and fix them; the lazy ones will find that the bad guys utilize their bandwidth more and more; and thus will be pressured into fixing the problem.

18.2.2.3 Distributed Denial-of-service Attacks

A more recent development along the same lines made its appearance in October 1999. This is the *distributed denial of service* (DDoS) attack. Rather than just exploiting a common misconfiguration as in smurfing, an attacker subverts a large number of machines over a period of time, and installs custom attack software in them. At a predetermined time, or on a given signal, these machines all start to bombard the target site with messages [253]. The subversion may be automated using methods similar to those in the Morris worm.

So far, DDoS attacks have been launched at a number of high-profile Web sites, including Amazon and Yahoo. They could be even more disruptive, as they could target services such as DNS and thus take down the entire Internet. Such an attack might be expected in the event of information warfare; it might also be an act of vandalism by an individual. Curiously, the machines most commonly used as hosts for attack software in early 2000 were U.S. medical sites. They were particularly vulnerable because the FDA insisted that medical Unix machines, when certified for certain purposes, had a known configuration. Once bugs had been discovered in this, there was a guaranteed supply of automatically hackable machines to host the attack software (another example of the dangers of software monoculture).

At the time of writing, the initiative being taken against DDoS attacks is to add *ICMP traceback messages* to the infrastructure. The idea is that whenever a router forwards an IP packet, it will also send an ICMP packet to the destination with a probability of about 1 in 20,000. The packet will contain details of the previous hop, the next hop, and as much of the packet as will fit. System administrators will then be able to trace large-scale flooding attacks back to the responsible machines, even when the attackers use forged source IP addresses to cover their tracks [93]. It may also help catch large-scale spammers who abuse *open relays*, relays that do not add audit information to email message headers.

18.2.2.4 Spam and Address Forgery

Services such as email and the Web (SMTP and HTTP) assume that the lower levels are secure. The most that's commonly done is a look-up of the hostname against an IP address using DNS. So someone who can forge IP addresses can abuse the facilities. The most common example is mail forgery by spammers; there are many others. For example, if an attacker can give DNS incorrect information about the whereabouts of your company's Web page, the page can be redirected to another site—regardless of anything you do, or don't do, at your end. As this often involves feeding false information to locally cached DNS tables, it's called *DNS cache poisoning*.

18.2.2.5 Spoofing Attacks

We can combine some of the preceding ideas into spoofing attacks that work at long range (that is, from outside the local network or domain).

Say that Charlie knows that Alice and Bob are hosts on the target LAN, and wants to masquerade as Alice to Bob. He can take Alice down with a service denial attack of some kind, then initiate a new connection with Bob [559, 90]. This entails guessing the sequence number Y, which Bob will assign to the session, under the protocol shown in Figure 18.1. A simple way of guessing Y, which worked for a long time, was for Charlie to make a real connection to Alice shortly beforehand and use the fact that the value of Y changed in a predictable way between one connection and the next. Modern stacks use random number generators and other techniques to avoid this predictability, but random number generators are often less random than expected—a source of large numbers of security failures [774].

If sequence number guessing is feasible, then Charlie will be able to send messages to Bob, which Bob will believe come from Alice (though Charlie won't be able to read Bob's replies to her). In some cases, Charlie won't even have to attack Alice, just arrange things so that she discards Bob's replies to her as unexpected junk. This is quite a complex attack, but no matter; there are scripts available on the Web that do it.

18.2.2.6 Routing Attacks

Routing attacks come in a variety of flavors. The basic attack involves Charlie telling Alice and Bob that a convenient route between their sites passes through his. Source-level routing was originally introduced into TCP to help get around bad routers. The under-lying assumptions—that "hosts are honest" and that the best return path is the best source route—no longer hold, and the only short-term solution is to block source routing. However, it continues to be used for network diagnosis.

Another approach involves redirect messages, which are based on the same false assumption. These effectively say, "You should have sent this message to the other gateway instead," and are generally applied without checking. They can be used to do the same subversion as source-level routing.

Spammers have taught almost everyone that mail forgery is often trivial. Rerouting is harder, since mail routing is based on DNS; but it is getting easier as the number of service providers goes up and their competence goes down. DNS cache poisoning is only one of the tricks that can be used.

18.3 Defense against Network Attack

It might seen reasonable to hope that most attacks—at least those launched by script kiddies—can be thwarted by a system administrator who diligently monitors the security bulletins and applies all the vendors' patches promptly to his software. This is part of the broader topic of configuration management.

18.3.1 Configuration Management

Tight configuration management is the most critical aspect of a secure network. If you can be sure that all the machines in your organization are running up-to-date copies of the operating system, that all patches are applied as they're shipped, that the service and configuration files don't have any serious holes (such as world-writeable password files), that known default passwords are removed from products as they're installed, and that all this is backed up by suitable organizational discipline, then you can deal with nine and a half of the top ten attacks. (You will still have to take care with application code vulnerabilities such as CGI scripts, but by not running them with administrator privileges you can greatly limit the harm that they might do.)

Configuration management is at least as important as having a reasonable firewall; in fact, given the choice of one of the two, you should forget the firewall. However, it's the harder option for many companies, because it takes real effort as opposed to buying and installing an off-the-shelf product. Doing configuration management by numbers can even make things worse. As noted in Section 18, U.S. hospitals had to use a known configuration, which gave the bad guys a large supply of identically mismanaged targets.

Several tools are available to help the systems administrator keep things tight. Some enable you to do centralized version control, so that patches can be applied overnight, and everything can be kept in synch; others, such as Satan, will try to break into the machines on your network by using a set of common vulnerabilities [320]. Some familiarity with these penetration tools is a very good idea, as they can also be used by the opposition to try to hack you.

The details of the products that are available and what they do change from one year to the next, so it is not appropriate to go into details here. What is appropriate is to say that adhering to a philosophy of having system administrators stop all vulnerabilities at the source requires skill and care; even diligent organizations may find that it is just too expensive to fix all the security holes that were tolerable on a local network but not with an Internet connection. Another problem is that, often, an organisation's most critical applications run on the least secure machines, as administrators have not dared to apply operating system upgrades and patches for fear of losing service.

This leads us to the use of firewalls.

18.3.2 Firewalls

The most widely sold solution to the problems of Internet security is the *firewall*. This is a machine that stands between a local network and the Internet, and filters out traffic that might be harmful. The idea of a "solution in a box" has great appeal to many organizations, and is now so widely accepted that it's seen as an essential part of corporate due diligence. (Many purchasers prefer expensive firewalls to good ones.)

Firewalls come in basically three flavors, depending on whether they filter at the IP packet level, at the TCP session level, or at the application level.

18.3.2.1 Packet Filtering

The simplest kind of firewall merely filters packet addresses and port numbers. This functionality is also available in routers and in Linux. It can block the kind of IP spoofing attack discussed earlier by ensuring that no packet that appears to come from a host on the local network is allowed to enter from outside. It can also stop denial-of-service attacks in which malformed packets are sent to a host, or the host is persuaded to connect to itself (both of which can be a problem for people still running Windows 95).

Basic packet filtering is available as standard in Linux, but, as far as incoming attacks are concerned, it can be defeated by a number of tricks. For example, a packet can be fragmented in such a way that the initial fragment (which passes the firewall's inspection) is overwritten by a subsequent fragment, thereby replacing an address with one that violates the firewall's security policy.

18.3.2.2 Circuit Gateways

More complex firewalls, called *circuit gateways*, reassemble and examine all the packets in each TCP circuit. This is more expensive than simple packet filtering, and can also provide added functionality, such as providing a virtual private network over the Internet by doing encryption from firewall to firewall, and screening out black-listed Web sites or newsgroups (there have been reports of Asian governments building national firewalls for this purpose).

However, circuit-level protection can't prevent attacks at the application level, such as malicious code.

18.3.2.3 Application Relays

The third type of firewall is the *application relay*, which acts as a proxy for one or more services, such as mail, telnet, and Web. It's at this level that you can enforce rules such as stripping out macros from incoming Word documents, and removing active content from Web pages. These can provide very comprehensive protection against a wide range of threats.

The downside is that application relays can turn out to be serious bottlenecks. They can also get in the way of users who want to run the latest applications.

18.3.2.4 Ingress versus Egress Filtering

At present, almost all firewalls point outwards and try to keep bad things out, though there are a few military systems that monitor outgoing traffic to ensure that nothing classified goes out in the clear.

That said, some commercial organizations are starting to monitor outgoing traffic, too. If companies whose machines get used in service denial attacks start getting sued (as has been proposed in [771]), egress packet filtering might at least in principle be used to detect and stop such attacks. Also, as there is a growing trend toward *snitchware*, technology that collects and forwards information about an online subscriber without their authorization. Software that "phones home," ostensibly for copyright enforcement and marketing purposes, can disclose highly sensitive material such as local hard disk directories. I expect that prudent organizations will increasingly want to monitor and control this kind of traffic, too.

18.3.2.5 Combinations

At really paranoid sites, multiple firewalls may be used. There may be a *choke*, or packet filter, connecting the outside world to a screened subnet, also known as a *demilitarized zone* (DMZ), which contains a number of application servers or proxies to filter mail and other services. The DMZ may then be connected to the internal network via a further filter that does network address translation. Within the organization, there may be further boundary control devices, including pumps to separate departments, or networks operating at different clearance levels to ensure that classified information doesn't escape either outward or downward (Figure 18.2).

Such elaborate installations can impose significant operational costs, as many routine messages need to be inspected and passed by hand. This can get in the way so much that people install unauthorized back doors, such as dial-up standalone machines, to get their work done. And if your main controls are aimed at preventing information leaking outward, there may be little to stop a virus getting in. Once in a place it wasn't expected, it can cause serious havoc. I'll discuss this sort of problem in Section 18.4.6 later.

18.3.3 Strengths and Limitations of Firewalls

Since firewalls do only a small number of things, it's possible to make them very simple, and to remove many of the complex components from the underlying operating system (such as the RPC and sendmail facilities in Unix). This eliminates a lot of vulnerabilities

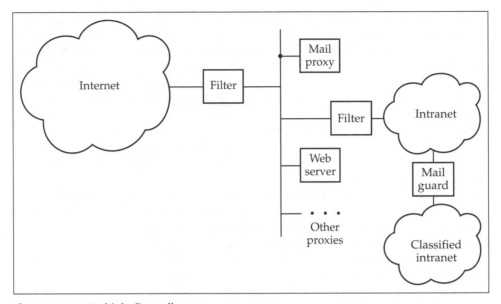

Figure 18.2 Multiple firewalls.

and sources of error. Organizations are also attracted by the idea of having only a small number of boxes to manage, rather than having to do proper system administration for a large, heterogeneous population of machines.

Conversely, the appeal of simplicity can be seductive and treacherous. A firewall can only be as good as its configuration, and many organizations don't learn enough to do this properly. They hope that by getting the thing out of the box and plugged it in, the problem will be solved. It won't be. It may not require as much effort to manage a firewall as to configure every machine on your network properly in the first place, but it still needs some. In [203], there is a case study of how a firewall was deployed at Hanscom Air Force Base. The work involved the following: surveying the user community to find which network services were needed; devising a network security policy; using network monitors to discover unexpected services that were in use; and lab testing prior to installation. Once it was up and running, the problems included ongoing maintenance (due to personnel turnover), the presence of (unmonitored) communications to other military bases, and the presence of modem pools. Few nonmilitary organizations are likely to take this much care.

A secondary concern, at least during the late 1990s, was that many of the products crowding into the market simply weren't much good. The business had grown so quickly, and so many vendors had climbed in, that the available expertise was spread too thinly.

The big trade-off remains security versus performance. Do you install a simple filtering router, which won't need much maintenance, or do you go for a full-fledged set of application relays on a DMZ, which not only will need constant reconfiguration—as your users demand lots of new services that must pass through it—but will also act as a bottleneck?

An example in Britain was the NHS Network, a private intranet intended for all health service users (family doctors, hospitals, and clinics—a total of 11,000 organizations employing about a million staff in total). Initially, this had a single firewall to the outside world. The designers thought this would be enough, as they expected most traffic to be local (as most of the previous data flows in the health service had been). What they didn't anticipate was that, as the Internet took off in the mid-1990's, 40% of traffic at every level became international. Doctors and nurses found it very convenient to consult medical reference sites, most of which were in America. Trying to squeeze all this traffic through a single orifice was unrealistic. Also, since almost all attacks on healthcare systems come from people who're already inside the system, it was unclear what this central firewall was ever likely to achieve.

Another issue with firewalls (and boundary control devices in general) is that they get in the way of what people want to do, and so ways are found round them. As most firewalls will pass traffic that appears to be Web pages and requests (typically because it's for port 80), more and more applications use port 80, as it's the way to get things to work through the firewall. Where this isn't possible, the solution is for whole services to be reimplemented as Web services (webmail being a good example). These pressures continually erode the effectiveness of firewalls, and bring to mind John Gilmore's famous saying that 'the Internet interprets censorship as damage, and routes around it.'

Finally, it's worth going back down the list of top ten attacks and asking how many of them a firewall can stop. Depending on how it's configured, the realistic answer might be about four.

18.3.4 Encryption

In the context of preventing network attacks, many people have been conditioned to think of encryption. Certainly, it can sometimes be useful. For example, on the network at the lab I work in, we use a product called *secure shell* (SSH), which provides encrypted links between Unix and Windows hosts [817, 1, 597]. When I dial in from home, my traffic is protected; and when I log on from the PC at my desk to another machine in the lab, the password I use doesn't go across the LAN in the clear.

Let's stop and analyze what protection this gives me. Novices and policymakers think in terms of wiretaps, but tapping a dial-up modem line is hard now that modems use adaptive echo cancellation. It essentially involves the attacker inserting two back-to-back modems into the link from my house to the lab. So this is a low-probability threat. The risk of password sniffing on our LAN is much higher; it has happened in the past to other departments. Thus, our network encryption is really providing a lower-cost alternative to the use of handheld password generators.

Another approach is to do encryption and/or authentication at the IP layer, which is to be provided in IPv6, and is available as a retrofit for the current IP protocol as IPsec. An assessment of the protocol can be found in [290]; an implementation is described in [782]. IPsec has the potential to stop some network attacks, and to be a useful component in designing robust distributed systems, but it won't be a panacea. Many machines will have to connect to all comers, and if I can become the administrator of your Web server by smashing the stack, then no amount of encryption or authentication is likely to help you very much. Many other machines will be vulnerable to attacks from inside the network, where computers have been suborned somehow or are operated by dishonest insiders. There will still be problems such as service denial attacks. Also, deployment is likely to take some years.

A third idea is the *virtual private network* (VPN). The idea here is that a number of branches of a company, or a number of companies that trade with each other, arrange for traffic between their sites to be encrypted at their firewalls. This way the Internet can link up their local networks, but without their traffic being exposed to eavesdropping. VPNs also don't stop the bad guys trying to smash the stack of your Web server or sniff passwords from your LAN, but for companies that might be the target of adversarial interest by developed-country governments, it can reduce the exposure to interception of international network traffic. (It must be said, though, that intercepting bulk packet traffic is much harder than many encryption companies claim; and less well-funded adversaries are likely to use different attacks.)

Encryption can also have a downside. One of the more obvious problems is that if encrypted mail and Web pages can get through your firewall, then they can bring all sorts of unpleasant things with them. This brings us to the problem of malicious code.

18.4 Trojans, Viruses, and Worms

If this book had been written even five years earlier, malicious code would have merited its own chapter.

Computer security experts have long been aware of the threat from malicious code, or *malware*. The first such programs were *Trojan horses*, named after the horse the Greeks ostensibly left as a gift for the Trojans but that hid soldiers who subsequently opened the gates of Troy to the Greek army. The use of the term for malicious code goes back many years (see the discussion in [493, p. 7].)

There are also *viruses* and *worms*, which are self-propagating malicious programs, and to which I have referred repeatedly in earlier chapters. There is debate about the precise definitions of these three terms: the common usage is that a Trojan horse is a program that does something malicious (such as capturing passwords) when run by an unsuspecting user; a worm is something that replicates; and a virus is a worm that replicates by attaching itself to other programs.

18.4.1 Early History of Malicious Code

Malware seems likely to appear whenever a large enough number of users share a computing platform. It goes back at least to the early 1960s. The machines of that era were slow, and their CPU cycles were carefully rationed among different groups of users. Because students were often at the tail of the queue—they invented tricks such as writing computer games with a Trojan horse inside to check whether the program was running as root, and if so to create an additional privileged account with a known password. By the 1970s, large time-sharing systems at universities were the target of more and more pranks involving Trojans. All sorts of tricks were developed.

In 1984, there appeared a classic paper by Thompson in which he showed that even if the source code for a system were carefully inspected, and known to be free of vulnerabilities, a trapdoor could still be inserted. His trick was to build the trapdoor into the compiler. If this recognized that it was compiling the login program, it would insert a trapdoor such as a master password that would work on any account. Of course, someone might try to stop this by examining the source code for the compiler, and then compiling it again from scratch. So the next step is to see to it that, if the compiler recognizes that it's compiling itself, it inserts the vulnerability even if it's not present in the source. So even if you can buy a system with verifiably secure software for the operating system, applications and tools, the compiler binary can still contain a Trojan. The moral is that you can't trust a system you didn't build completely yourself; vulnerabilities can be inserted at any point in the tool chain [746].

Computer viruses also burst on the scene in 1984, thanks to the thesis work of Fred Cohen. He performed a series of experiments with different operating systems that showed how code could propagate itself from one machine to another, and (as mentioned in Chapter 7) from one compartment of a multilevel system to another. This caused alarm and consternation; and within about three years, the first real, live viruses began to appear "in the wild." Almost all of them were PC viruses, as DOS was the predominant operating system. They spread from one user to another when users shared programs on diskettes or via bulletin boards.

One of the more newsworthy exceptions was the Christmas Card virus, which spread through IBM mainframes in 1987. Like the more recent Love Bug virus, it spread by email, but that was ahead of its time. The next year brought the Internet worm, which alerted the press and the general public to the problem.

18.4.2 The Internet Worm

The most famous case of a service denial attack was the Internet worm of November 1988 [263]. This was a program written by Robert Morris Jr which exploited a number of vulnerabilities to spread from one machine to another. Some of these were general (e.g., 432 common passwords were used in a guessing attack, and opportunistic use was made of .rhosts files), and others were system specific (problems with sendmail, and the fingerd bug mentioned in Section 4.4.1). The worm took steps to camouflage itself; it was called sh and it encrypted its data strings (albeit with a Caesar cipher).

Morris claimed that this code was not a deliberate attack on the Internet, merely an experiment to see whether his code could replicate from one machine to another. It could. It also had a bug. It should have recognized already infected machines, and not infected them again, but this feature didn't work. The result was a huge volume of communications traffic that completely clogged up the Internet.

Given that the Internet (or, more accurately, its predecessor the ARPANET) had been designed to provide a very high degree of resilience against attacks—up to and including a strategic nuclear strike—it was remarkable that a program written by a student could disable it completely.

What's less often remarked on is that the mess was cleaned up, and normal service was restored within a day or two; that it only affected Berkeley Unix and its derivatives (which may say something about the dangers of the creeping Microsoft monoculture today); and that people who stayed calm and didn't pull their network connection recovered more quickly, because they could find out what was happening and get the fixes.

18.4.3 How Viruses and Worms Work

A virus or worm will typically have two components: a replication mechanism and a payload. A worm simply makes a copy of itself somewhere else when it's run, perhaps by breaking into another system (as the Internet worm did) or by mailing itself as an attachment to the addresses on the infected system's address list (as a number of more recent worms have done). In the days of DOS viruses, the most common way for a virus to replicate was to append itself to an executable file, then patch itself in, so that the execution path jumped to the virus code, then back to the original program.

Among the simplest common viruses were those that infected `.com` type executables under DOS. This file format always had code starting at address 0x100, so it was simple for the virus to attach itself to the end of the file and replace the instruction at 0x100 with a jump to its start address. Thus, the viral code would execute whenever the file was run; it would typically look for other, uninfected, `.com` files and infect them. After the virus had done its work, the missing instruction would be executed and control would be returned to the host program.

Given a specific platform, such as DOS, there are usually additional tricks available to the virus writer. For example, if the target system has a file called accounts.exe, it is possible to introduce a file called accounts.com, which DOS will execute first. This is called a *companion virus*. DOS viruses may also attack the boot sector or the partition table; there are even printable viruses, all of whose opcodes are printable ASCII characters, meaning they can even propagate on paper. A number of DOS viruses are examined in detail in [512].

The second component of a virus is the payload. This will usually be activated by a trigger, such as a date, and may then do one or more of a number of bad things:

- Make selective or random changes to the machine's protection state (this is what we worried about with multilevel secure systems).
- Make selective or random changes to user data (e.g., trash the disk).
- Lock the network (e.g., start replicating at maximum speed).
- Steal resources for some nefarious task (e.g., use the CPU for DES keysearch).
- Get your modem to phone a premium-rate number in order to make money from you for a telephone scamster.
- Steal or even publish your data, including your crypto keys.
- Create a backdoor through which its creator can take over your system later, perhaps to launch a distributed denial of service attack.

Until recently, the most damaging payloads were those that leave backdoors for later use, and those that do their damage slowly and imperceptibly. An example of the second are viruses that occasionally swap words in documents or blocks in files; by the time this kind of damage comes to the administrator's attention, all extant generations of backup may be corrupted. Finally, on September 21st 2000 came a report of a virus with a payload that had long been awaited. Swiss bank UBS warned its customers of a virus that, if it infected their machines, would try to steal the passwords used to access its electronic home banking system.

Various writers have also proposed "benevolent" payloads, such as to perform software upgrades in a company, to enforce licensing terms, or even to roam the world looking for cheap airline tickets (so-called intelligent agents)—though the idea that a commercial Web site owner would enable alien code to execute on their Web server with a view to driving down their prices was always somewhat of a pious hope.

18.4.4 The Arms Race

Once viruses and antivirus software companies had both appeared, there was an arms race in which each tried to outwit the other.

As a virus will usually have some means of recognizing itself, so that it does not infect the same file twice, some early antivirus software *immunized* files, by patching in enough of the virus to fool it into thinking that the file was already infected. However, this is not efficient, and won't work at all against a large virus population. The next generation were *scanners*, programs that searched through the early part of each executable file's execution path for a string of bytes known to be from an identified virus.

Virus writers responded in various ways, such as by delaying the entry point of the virus in the host file code, thereby forcing scanners to check the entire filespace for infection; and by specific counterattacks on popular antivirus programs. The most recent evolution was polymorphic viruses. These change their code each time they replicate, to make it harder to write effective scanners. Typically, they are encrypted, but have a small header that contains code to decrypt them. With each replication, the virus re-encrypts itself under a different key; it may also insert a few irrelevant operations into the decryption code, or change the order of instructions where this doesn't matter. The encryption algorithm is often simple and easy to break, but even so is enough to greatly slow down the scanner.

The other main technical approach to virus prevention is the *checksummer*. This is a piece of software that keeps a list of all the authorized executables on the system, together with checksums of the original versions of these files. However, one leading commercial product merely calculates cyclic redundancy checks using two different polynomials—a technique that could easily be defeated by a smart virus writer. Where the checksummer does use a decent algorithm, the main countermeasure is *stealth*, which in this context means that the virus watches out for operating system calls of the kind used by the checksummer and hides itself whenever a check is being done.

18.4.5 Recent History

By the late 1980s and early 1990s, PC viruses had become such a problem that they gave rise to a whole industry of antivirus software writers and consultants. Many people thought that this wouldn't last, as the move from DOS to "proper" operating systems like Windows would solve the problem. Some of the antivirus pioneers even sold their companies: one of them tells his story in [720].

But the spread of interpreted languages has provided even more fertile soil for mischief. There was a brief flurry of publicity about bad Java applets in the late 1990s, as people found ways of penetrating Java implementations in browsers; this raised security awareness considerably [537]. But the main sources of infection at the start of the twenty-first century are the macro languages in Microsoft products such as Word, and the main transmission mechanism is the Internet. An industry analysis claims that the Net "saved" the antivirus industry [423]. Another view is that it was never really under threat, that users will always want to share code and data, and that, in the absence of trustworthy computing platforms, we can expect malware to exploit whichever sharing mechanisms they use. Still another view is that Microsoft is responsible, as it was reckless in incorporating such powerful scripting capabilities in applications such as word processing. As they say, your mileage may vary.

In any case, Word viruses took over as the main source of infection in the United States in 1996, and in other countries shortly afterward [57]. By 2000, macro viruses accounted for almost all incidents of mobile malicious code. A typical macro virus is a macro that copies itself into uninfected word processing documents on the victim's hard disk, and waits to be propagated as users share documents. Some variants also take more active steps to replicate, such as by causing the infected document to be mailed to people in the victim's address book. (There's a discussion of macro viruses in [128], which also points out that stopping them is harder than was the case for DOS viruses, as the Microsoft programming environment is now much less open, less well documented, and complex.)

In passing, it's worth noting that malicious data can also be a problem. An interesting example is related by David Mazières and Frans Kaashoek, who operate an anonymous remailer at MIT. This device decrypts incoming messages from anywhere on the Net, uncompresses them, and acts on them. Someone sent them a series of 25 Mb messages consisting of a single line of text repeated over and over; these compressed very well and so were only small ciphertexts when input; but when uncompressed, they quickly filled up the spool file and crashed the system [531]. There are also attacks on other programs that do decompression such as MPEG decoders. However, the most egregious cases involve not malicious data but malicious code.

18.4.6 Antivirus Measures

In theory, defense has become simple: if you filter out Microsoft executables at your firewall, you can stop most of the bad things out there. In practice, life isn't so simple. A large Canadian company with 85,000 staff did just that, but many of their staff had personal accounts at Web-based email services, so when the Love Bug virus came along it got into the company as Web pages, without going through the mail filter at the firewall. The company had configured its mail clients so that each of them had the entire corporate directory in their personal address book. The result was meltdown as 85,000 mail clients all tried to send an email to each of 85,000 addresses.

For a virus infestation to be self-sustaining, it needs to pass an *epidemic threshold*, at which its rate of replication exceeds the rate at which it's removed [452]. This depends not just on the infectivity of the virus itself, but on the number (and proportion) of connected machines that are vulnerable. Epidemic models from medicine can be applied to some extent, though they are limited by the different topology of software intercourse (sharing of software is highly localized), and so predict higher infection rates than are actually observed. One medical lesson that does seem to apply is that the most effective organizational countermeasures are centralized reporting, and response using selective vaccination [453].

In the practical world, this comes down to managerial discipline. In the days of DOS-based file viruses, this meant controlling all software loaded on the organization's machines, and providing a central reporting point for all incidents. Now that viruses arrive primarily in email attachments or as active content in Web pages, it may involve filtering these things out at the firewall, and, seeing to it that users have prudent default settings on their systems—such as disabling active content on browsers and macros in word processing documents.

The nature of the things that users need to be trained to do, or to not do, will change over time as systems and threats evolve. For example, in the mid-1990s, the main tasks were to stop infections coming in via PCs used at home, both for work and for other things (such as kids playing games), and to get staff to "sweep" all incoming email and diskettes for viruses, using standalone scanning software. (An effective way of doing the latter, adopted at a London law firm, was to reward whoever found a virus with a box of chocolates—which would then be invoiced to the company that had sent the infected file). Now that typical antivirus software includes automatic screening and central reporting, the issues are more diffuse, such as training people not to open suspicious email attachments, and having procedures to deal with infected backups. But as with the organic kind of disease, prevention is better than cure; and software hygiene can be integrated with controls on illegal software copying and unauthorized private use of equipment.

18.5 Intrusion Detection

The typical antivirus software product is an example of an *intrusion detection system*. In general, it's a good idea to assume that attacks will happen, and it's often cheaper to prevent some attacks and detect the rest than it is to try to prevent everything. The systems used to detect bad things happening are referred to generically as intrusion detection systems. Other examples from earlier chapters are the application-specific mechanisms for detecting mobile phone cloning and fraud by bank tellers. Certain stock markets have installed systems to try to detect insider trading by looking for suspicious patterns of activity. Although they are all performing very similar tasks, their developers don't talk to each other much, and we see the same old wheels being reinvented again and again.

Intrusion detection in corporate and government networks is a fast-growing field of security research; for example, U.S. military funding grew from almost nothing to millions in the last few years of the twentieth century. This growth has been prompted by the realization that many systems make no effective use of log and audit data. In the case of Sun's operating system Solaris, for example, we found in 1996 that the audit formats were not documented, and tools to read them were not available. The audit facility seemed to have been installed to satisfy the formal checklist requirements of government systems buyers, rather than to perform any useful function. There was the hope that improving this would help system administrators detect attacks, whether after the fact or even when they were still in progress.

18.5.1 Types of Intrusion Detection

The simplest intrusion detection methods involve sounding an alarm when a threshold is passed. Three or more failed logons, a credit card expenditure of more than twice the moving average of the last three months, or a mobile phone call lasting more than six hours, might all flag the account in question for attention. More sophisticated systems generally fall into two categories.

The first, *misuse detection systems*, use a model of the likely behavior of an intruder. An example would be a banking system that alarms if a user draws the maximum permitted amount from a cash machine on three successive days. Another would be a Unix intrusion detection system that looked for a user's account being taken over by someone who used the system in a much more sophisticated way; thus an account whose user previously used only simple commands would alarm if the log showed use of a compiler. An alarm might also be triggered by specific actions such as an attempt to download the password file. In general, most misuse detection systems, like antivirus scanners, look for a *signature*, a known characteristic of some particular attack. One of the most general misuse detection signatures is interest in a *honey trap*—something enticing left to attract attention. I mentioned, for example, that some hospitals maintain dummy records with celebrities' names to entrap staff who don't respect medical confidentiality.

The second type of intrusion detection strategy is *anomaly detection*. Such systems attempt the much harder job of looking for anomalous patterns of behavior in the absence of a clear model of the attacker's modus operandi. The hope is to detect attacks that have not been previously recognized and catalogued. Systems of this type often use artificial intelligence techniques—neural networks are particularly fashionable.

The dividing line between misuse and anomaly detection is somewhat blurred. A particularly good borderline case is given by Benford's law, which describes the distribution of digits in random numbers. One might expect that numbers beginning with the digits 1, 2, ... 9 would be equally common. But, in fact, numbers that come from random natural sources, so that their distribution is independent of the number system in which they're expressed, have a logarithmic distribution: about 30% of decimal numbers start with 1. (In fact, all binary numbers start with 1, if initial zeroes are suppressed.) Crooked clerks who think up numbers to cook the books, or even use random number generators without knowing Benford's law, are often caught using it [529].

18.5.2 General Limitations of Intrusion Detection

Some intrusions are really obvious. If what you're worried about is a script kiddie vandalizing your corporate Web site, then the obvious thing to do is to have a machine in your operations room that fetches the page once a second, displays it, and rings a really loud alarm when it changes. (Make sure you do this via an outside proxy; and don't forget that it's not just your own systems at risk. The kiddie could replace your advertisers' pictures with porn, for example, in which case you'd want to pull the links to them pretty fast.)

In general however, intrusion detection is a difficult problem. Fred Cohen proved that detecting viruses (in the sense of deciding whether a program is going to do something bad) is as hard as the halting problem, meaning we can't ever expect a complete solution [192].

Another fundamental limitation comes from the fact that there are basically two different types of security failure: those that cause an error (which I defined in Section 6.2 to be an incorrect state) and those that don't. An example of the former is a theft from a bank that leaves traces on the audit trail. An example of the latter is an undetected confidentiality failure caused by a radio microphone placed by a foreign intelligence service in your room. The former can be detected (at least in principle, and forgetting for now about the halting problem) by suitable processing of the data available to you. But the latter can't be. It's a good idea to design systems so that as many failures as possible fall into the former category, but it's not always practicable [182].

There's also the matter of definitions. Some intrusion detection systems are configured to block any instances of suspicious behavior, and, in extreme cases, to take down the affected systems. Apart from opening the door to service denial attacks, this turns the intrusion detection system into an access control mechanism. As we've already seen, access control is in general a hard problem, that incorporates all sorts of issues of security policy which people often disagree on or simply get wrong. (The common misconceptions that you can do access control with intrusion detection mechanisms and that all intrusion detection can be done with neural networks together would imply that some neural network bolted on to a LAN could be trained to enforce something like Bell-LaPadula. This seems fatuous.)

I prefer to define an intrusion detection system as one that monitors the logs and draws the attention of authority to suspicious occurrences. This is closer to the way mobile phone operators work. It's also critical in financial investigations; see [658] for a discussion, by a special agent with the U.S. Internal Revenue Service, of what he looks for when trying to trace hidden assets and income streams. A lot hangs on educated suspicion, based on long experience. For example, a $25 utility bill may lead to a $250,000 second house hidden behind a nominee. Building an effective system means having the people, and the machines, each do the part of the job they're best at; and this means getting the machine to do the preliminary filtering.

Then there's the cost of false alarms. For example, I used to go to San Francisco every May, and I got used to the fact that after I'd used my U.K. debit card in an ATM five days in a row, it would stop working. Not only does this upset the customer, but villains quickly learn to exploit it (as do the customers—I just started making sure I got enough dollars out in the first five days to last me the whole trip). As in so many security engineering problems, the trade-off between the fraud rate and the insult rate is the critical one; And, as I noted in Chapter 13, "Biometrics," Section 13.8, we can't expect to improve this trade-off simply by looking at lots of different indicators. In general, we must expect that an opponent will always get past the threshold if he or she is patient enough, and either does the attack very slowly or does a large number of small attacks.

A particularly intractable problem with commercial intrusion detection systems is *redlining*. When insurance companies used claim statistics on postcodes to decide the level of premiums to charge, it was found that many poor and minority areas suffered high premiums or were excluded altogether from coverage. In a number of jurisdictions, this is now illegal. But the problem is much broader. For example, Washington is pushing airlines to bring in systems to profile passengers for terrorism risk, so they can be subjected to more stringent security checks. The American-Arab Anti-Discrimination Committee has reported many incidents where innocent passengers have been harassed by airlines that have implemented some of these recommendations [516].

In general, if you build an intrusion detection system based on data-mining techniques, you are at serious risk of discriminating. If you use neural network techniques, you'll have no way of explaining to a court what the rules underlying your decisions are, so defending yourself could be hard. Opaque rules can also contravene European data protection law, which entitles citizens to know the algorithms used to process their personal data.

In general, most fielded intrusion detection systems use a number of different techniques [661]. They tend to draw heavily on knowledge of the application, and to be developed by slow evolution.

18.5.3 Specific Problems Detecting Network Attacks

Turning now to the specific problem of detecting network intrusion, the problem is much harder than, say, detecting mobile phone cloning, for a number of reasons. For starters, the available products still don't work very well, with success rates of perhaps 60–80% in laboratory tests and a high false alarm rate. For example, at the time of writing, the U.S. Air Force has so far not detected an intrusion using the systems it has deployed on local networks—although once one is detected by other means, the traces can be found on the logs.

The reasons for the poor performance include the following, in no particular order.

- *The Internet is a very "noisy" environment, not just at the level of content but also at the packet level.* A large amount of random crud arrives at any substantial site, and enough of it can be interpreted as hostile to generate a significant false alarm rate. A survey by Bellovin [89] reports that many bad packets result from software bugs; others are the fault of out-of-date or corrupt DNS data; and some are local packets that escaped, travelled the world, and returned.

- *There are too few attacks.* If there are ten real attacks per million sessions—which is almost certainly an overestimate—then even if the system has a false alarm rate as low as 0.1%, the ratio of false to real alarms will be 100. I talked about similar problems with burglar alarms in Chapter 10; it's also a well known issue for medics running screening programs for diseases such as HIV where the test error exceeds the organism's prevalence in the population. In general, where the signal is so far below the noise, an alarm system is likely to so fatigue the guards that even the genuine alarms get missed.

- *Many network attacks are specific to particular versions of software, so most of them concern vulnerabilities in old versions.* Thus, a general misuse detection tool must have a large, and constantly changing, library of attack signatures.

- *In many cases, commercial organizations appear to buy intrusion detection systems simply to tick a "due diligence" box.* This is done to satisfy insurers or consultants.

- *Encrypted traffic, such as SSL-encrypted Web sessions, can't easily be subjected to content analysis or filtered for malicious code.* It's theoretically possible to stop the encryption at your firewall, or install a monitoring device with which your users share their confidentiality keys. However, in practice, this can be an absolute tar-pit [3].

- *The issues raised in the context of firewalls largely apply to intrusion detection, too.* You can filter at the packet layer, which is fast but can be defeated by packet fragmentation; you can reconstruct each session, which takes more computation and so is not really suitable for network backbones; or you can examine application data, which is more expensive still, and needs to be constantly updated to cope with the arrival of new applications.

Although the USAF has so far not found an attack using local intrusion detection systems, attacks have been found using network statistics. Histograms are kept of packets by source and destination address and by port. This is a powerful means of detecting *stealthy* attacks, in which the opponent sends one or two packets per day to each of maybe 100,000 hosts. Such attacks would probably never be found using local statistics, and they'd be lost in the noise floor. But when data collection is done over a large network, the suspect source addresses stick out like the proverbial sore thumb.

For all these reasons, it appears unlikely that a single-product solution will do the trick. Future intrusion detection systems are likely to involve the coordination of a number of monitoring mechanisms at different levels, both in the network (backbone, LAN, individual machine) and in the protocol stack (packet, session, and application). This doesn't mean a clean partition in which packet filtering is done in the backbone and application level stuff at proxies; bulk keyword searching might be done on the backbone (as long as IPsec doesn't cause all the traffic to vanish behind a fog of crypto).

18.6 Summary

Preventing and detecting attacks that are launched over networks, and particularly over the Internet, is probably the most newsworthy aspect of security engineering. The problem is unlikely to be solved any time soon, as so many different kinds of vulnerability contribute to the attacker's toolkit. Ideally, people would run carefully written code on secure platforms; in real life, this won't always happen. But there is some hope that firewalls can keep out the worst of the attacks, that careful configuration management can block most of the rest, and that intrusion detection can catch most of the residue that make it through.

Because hacking techniques depend so heavily on the opportunistic exploitation of vulnerabilities introduced accidentally by the major software vendors, they are constantly changing. In this chapter, I concentrated on explaining the basic underlying science (of which there's surprisingly little). Although the Internet has connected hundreds of millions of machines that are running insecure software, and often with no administration to speak of, and scripts to attack common software products have started to be widely distributed, most of the bad things that happen are the same as those that happened a generation ago. The one new thing to have emerged is the distributed denial-of-service attack, which is made possible by the target system's being connected to many hackable machines. Despite all this, the Internet is not a disaster.

Perhaps a suitable analogy for the millions of insecure computers is given by the herds of millions of gnu which once roamed the plains of Africa. The lions could make life hard for any one gnu, but most of them survived for years by taking shelter in numbers. Things were a bit more tense for the very young, the very old, and those who went for the lusher grazing ahead of the herd. The Internet's much the same. There are analogues of the White Hunter, who'll carefully stalk a prime trophy animal; so you need to take special care if anyone might see you in these terms. (If you think that the alarms in the press about 'Evil Hackers Bringing Down the Internet' are somehow equivalent to the hungry peasant with a Kalashnikov, then it may well be worth bearing in mind the even greater destruction done by colonial ranching companies with the capital to fence off the veld in 100,000-acre lots.)

Of course, if you are going for the lusher grazing, or will have to protect high-profile business-critical systems against network attack, then you should read all the hacker Web pages, examine all the hacker software worth looking at, subscribe to the mailing lists, read the advisories, and install the patches. Although hacking has, to a great extent, been deskilled, a similar approach to defense cannot be expected to work more than some of the time, and box-ticking driven by due-diligence concerns isn't likely to achieve more than a modest amount of operational risk reduction.

Research Problems

In the academic world, research is starting to center on intrusion detection. One interesting theme is to make smarter antivirus products by exploiting analogies with biology. IBM is automating its techniques for identifying and culturing viruses, with a view to shipping its corporate clients a complete "path lab" [452]; Stephanie Forrest and colleagues at the University of New Mexico mimic the immune system by generating a lot of random "antibodies," then removing those that try to "kill" the system's own tissue [302]. How appropriate are such biological analogies? How far can we take them?

Further Reading

The classic on Internet security was written by Steve Bellovin and Bill Cheswick [94]. Another solid book is by Simson Garfinkel and Eugene Spafford [331], which is a good reference for the detail of many of the network attacks and system administration issues. An update on firewalls, and a survey of intrusion detection technology, has been written recently by Terry Escamilla [275]. The seminal work on viruses is by Fred Cohen [192], though it was written before macro viruses became the main problem. Java security is discussed by Gary McGraw and Ed Felten [537] and by Li Gong (its quondam architect) [346]. A survey of security incidents on the Internet appears in a thesis by John Howard [392]. Advisories from CERT [199] and bugtraq [144] are also essential reading if you want to keep up with events; and hacker sites such as www.phrack.com and (especially) www.rootshell.com bear watching.

Protecting E-Commerce Systems

If you try to buck the markets, then the markets will buck you.

—MARGARET THATCHER

19.1 Introduction

The protection of electronic commerce systems pulls together a lot of the topics discussed in previous chapters. Failures come from misconfigured access control, implementation blunders, theft of network services, inappropriate use of crypotology—you name it. In this chapter, I'll cover some protection issues specific to e-commerce, such as how online credit card payments are handled, and what goes wrong.

If you are a programmer building e-commerce systems for a dot-com startup, much of the material in this chapter should be fairly familiar to you. You are much more likely to get value from the chapters on access control, network security, and (particularly) on banking. The most likely attacks on your business don't involve the vulnerabilities in the Internet protocol suite or the payment infrastructure—and you can't do anything about those anyway.

The typical e-business startup appears to be most at risk from internal fraud. This is where most frauds in normal businesses come from, despite things like double-entry bookkeeping, which have evolved over centuries to control them. Many startups have none of these internal controls. They begin as a few people who all know each other and, if successful at raising capital, rapidly hire a lot of new staff who're focused on money and not very carefully screened. A survey found in October 2000, for example, that 37% of dot-com executives have shady pasts, compared with 10% found in due diligence checks on normal companies [257].

19.2 A Telegraphic History of E-Commerce

Many of the problems afflicting e-businesses stem from the popular notion that e-commerce is something completely new, invented in the mid-1990s. This is simply untrue.

Various kinds of visual signalling were deployed from classical times. Systems included heliographs (which used mirrors to flash sunlight at the receiver), semaphones (which used the positions of moving arms to signal letters and numbers), and flags. Land-based systems sent messages along chains of beacon towers, and naval systems between ships. To begin with, their use was military, but after the Napoleonic War, the French government opened its heliograph network to commercial use. Very soon, the first frauds were carried out. For two years, until they were discovered in 1836, two bankers bribed an operator to signal the movements of the stock market to them covertly by making errors in transmissions, which they could observe from a safe distance. Other techniques were devised to signal the results of horseraces. Various laws were passed to criminalize this kind of activity, but they were ineffective. The only solution for the bookies was to "call time" by a clock, rather than waiting for the result and hoping that they were the first to hear it.

From the 1760s to the 1840s, the electric telegraph was developed by a number of pioneers, of whom the most influential was Samuel Morse. He persuaded Congress in 1842 to fund an experimental line from Washington to Baltimore; this so impressed people that serious commercial investment started, and by the end of that decade, there were 12,000 miles of line being operated by 20 companies. This was remarkably like the Internet boom of the late 1990s [729].

Banks were the first big users of the telegraph, and they decided that they needed technical protection mechanisms to prevent transactions being altered by crooked operators en route. (I discussed the *test key* systems they developed for the purpose in the chapter on banking systems.) Telegrams were also used to create national markets. For the first time, commodity traders in New York could find out within minutes the prices that had been set in auctions in Chicago; likewise, fishing skippers arriving in Boston could find out the price of cod in Gloucester. A recent history of the period shows that most of the concepts and problems of electronic commerce were familiar to the Victorians [729]. How do you know who you're speaking to? How do you know if they're trustworthy? How do you know whether the goods will be delivered, and whether payments will arrive? The answers found in the nineteenth century involved intermediaries—principally banks that helped businesses manage risk using instruments such as references, guarantees, and letters of credit.

In the 1960s, banks in many countries computerized their bookkeeping, and introduced national interbank systems for handling direct payments to customer accounts, enabling banks to offer services such as payroll to corporate customers. In the early 1970s, this was extended to international payments, as described in the banking systems chapter. The next large expansion of electronic commerce took place in the late 1970s to mid-1980s with the spread of *electronic data interchange* (EDI). Companies ranging from General Motors to Marks and Spencer built systems that enabled them to link up their computers to their suppliers', so that goods could be ordered automatically. Travel agents built similar systems to order tickets in real time from airlines.

In 1985, the first retail electronic banking system was offered by the Bank of Scotland, whose customers could use Prestel, a proprietary email system operated by British Telecom, to make payments. When Steve Gold and Robert Schifreen hacked Prestel—as described in the chapter on passwords—it initially terrified the press and the bankers. They realized that the hackers could easily have captured and altered transactions. But once the dust settled and people thought through the detail, it became clear there was little real risk. The system allowed only payments between your own accounts and to accounts which you'd previously notified to the bank, such as you gas and electricity suppliers.

This pattern, of high-profile hacks—which caused great consternation but which, on sober reflection, turned out to be not really a big deal—has continued ever since.

To resume this brief history, the late 1980s and early 1990s saw the rapid growth of call centers, which—despite all the hoopla about the Web—remain in 2000 by far the largest delivery channel for business-to-consumer electronic commerce. As for the Internet, it was not something that suddenly sprung into existence in 1995, as a Martian monitoring our TV channels might believe. The first time I used an online service to sell software I'd written was in 1984 or 1985; and I first helped the police investigate an online credit card fraud in 1987. In the latter case, the bad guy got a list of hot credit card numbers from his girlfriend, who worked in a supermarket; he used them to buy software from companies in California, which he downloaded to order for his customers. This worked because hot card lists at the time carried only those cards that were being used fraudulently in that country; it also guaranteed that the bank would not be able to debit an innocent customer. As it happens, the criminal quit before there was enough evidence to nail him. A rainstorm washed away the riverbank opposite his house and exposed a hide which the police had built to stake him out.

The use of credit cards to buy stuff electronically "suddenly" became mainstream in about 1994 or 1995, when the public started to go online in large numbers. Suddenly there was a clamor that the Internet was insecure, that credit card numbers could be harvested on a huge scale, and that encryption would be needed.

19.3 An Introduction to Credit Cards

For many years after their invention in the 1950s, credit cards were treated by most banks as a loss leader used to attract high-value customers. Eventually, in most countries, the number of merchants and cardholders reached critical mass, and the transaction volume took off. In Britain, it took almost 20 years before most banks found the business profitable; then all of a sudden it became extremely profitable. The credit card system is now extremely well entrenched as the payment mechanism used on the Net.

Because of the huge investment involved in rolling out a competitor to tens of thousands of banks, millions of merchants, and billions of customers worldwide, any new payment mechanism is likely to take some time to get established—with a possible exception, which I'll discuss shortly. When you use a credit card to pay for a purchase in a store, the transaction flows from the merchant to her bank (the acquiring bank), which pays her after deducting a *merchant discount* of, typically, 4–5%. If the card was issued by a different bank, the transaction next flows to a switching center run by the brand (such as VISA), which takes a commission and passes it to the issuing bank for payment. Daily payments between the banks and the brands settle the net cash flows. The issuer also gets a slice of the merchant discount, but makes most of its money from extending credit to cardholders at rates usually much higher than the interbank rate.

19.3.1 Fraud

The risk of fraud from stolen cards was traditionally managed by a system of *hot card lists* and *merchant floor limits*. Each merchant get a local hot card list—formerly on paper, now stored in her terminal—plus a limit set by their acquiring bank, above which they have to call for authorization. The call center, or online service, which she uses for this has access to a national hot card list; above a higher limit, they will contact the brand which has a complete list of all hot cards being used internationally; above a still higher limit, the transaction will be checked all the way back to the card issuer.

The introduction of *mail order and telephone order* (MOTO) transactions in the 1970s meant that the merchant did not have the customer present, and was not able to inspect the card. What was to stop a crook ordering goods using a credit card numbers he'd picked up from a discarded receipt?

Banks managed the risk by using the expiry date as a password, lowering the floor limits, increasing the merchant discount, and insisting on delivery to a cardholder address, which is supposed to be checked during authorization. But the main change was to shift liability so that the merchant bore the full risk of disputes. If you challenge an online credit card transaction (or in fact any transaction made under MOTO rules), the full amount is immediately debited back to the merchant, together with a significant handling fee. The same procedure applies whether the debit is a fraud, a dispute, or a return.

Of course, having the cardholder present doesn't guarantee that fraud will be rare. For many years, most fraud was done in person with stolen cards, and the stores that got badly hit tended to be those selling goods that can be easily fenced, such as jewelry and consumer electronics. Banks responded by lowering their floor limits. More recently, as technical protection mechanisms have improved, there has been an increase in scams involving cards that were never received by genuine customers. This *pre-issue fraud* can involve thefts from the mail of the many "pre-approved" cards that arrive in junk mail, or even applications made in the names of people who exist and are creditworthy, but are not aware of the application (*identity theft*). These attacks on the system are intrinsically hard to tackle using purely technical means.

19.3.2 Forgery

In the early 1980s, electronic terminals were introduced through which a sales clerk could swipe a card and get an authorization automatically. But the sales draft was still captured from the embossing, so crooks figured out how to re-encode the magnetic strip of a stolen card with the account number and expiry date of a valid card, which they often got by fishing out discarded receipts from the trash cans of expensive restaurants. A re-encoded card would authorize perfectly, but when the merchant submitted the draft for payment, the account number didn't match the authorization code (a six-digit number typically generated by encrypting the account number, date, and amount). The merchants didn't get paid, and raised hell.

Banks responded in the mid-1980s by introducing *terminal draft capture*, where a sales draft is printed automatically using the data on the card strip. The crooks' response was a flood of forged cards, many produced by Triad gangs: between 1989 and 1992, magnetic strip counterfeiting grew from an occasional nuisance into half the total fraud losses [6]. VISA's response was *card verification values* (CVVs), three-digit MACs computed on the card strip contents (account number, version number, expiry date) and written at the end of the strip. They worked well at first; in the first quarter of 1994, VISA International's fraud losses dropped by 15.5%, while Mastercard's rose 67% [165]. Subsequently, Mastercard adopted similar checksums, too.

The crooks' response was *skimming*—operating businesses where genuine customer cards were swiped through an extra, unauthorized, terminal to grab a copy of the magnetic strip, which would then be re-encoded on a genuine card. The banks' response was intrusion detection systems, which in the first instance tried to identify criminal businesses by correlating the previous purchase histories of customers who complained.

In the late 1990s, credit card fraud rose sharply due to another simple innovation in criminal technology: the crooked businesses that skim card data absorb the cost of the customer's transaction rather than billing it. You have a meal at a Mafia-owned restaurant, offer a card, sign the voucher, and fail to notice when the charge doesn't appear on your bill. Perhaps a year later, there is suddenly a huge bill for jewelry, electronic goods, or even casino chips. By then you've completely forgotten about the meal, and the bank never had a record of it [318].

19.3.3 Automatic Fraud Detection

Consequently, a lot of work was done in the 1990s on beefing up intrusion detection. There are a number of generic systems that do anomaly detection, using techniques such as neural networks, but it's unclear how effective they are. When fraud is down one year, it's hailed as a success for the latest fraud-spotting system [61]; when the figures go up a few years later, the vendors let the matter pass quietly [714].

More convincing are projects undertaken by specific store chains that look for known patterns of misuse. For example, an electrical goods chain in the New York area observed that offender profiling (by age, sex, race, and so on) was ineffective, and used purchase profiling instead to cut fraud by 82% in a year. Its technique involved not just being suspicious of high-value purchases, but training staff to be careful when customers were careless about purchases and spent less than the usual amount of time discussing options and features. These factors can be monitored online, too, but one important aspect of the New York success is harder for a Web site: employee rewarding. Banks give a $50 reward per bad card captured, which many stores just keep, so their employees don't make an effort to spot cards or risk embarrassment by confronting a customer. In New York, some store staff were regularly earning a weekly bonus of $150 or more [525].

With the human out of the loop at the sales end, the only psychology from which a site designer can leverage is that of the villain. It has been suggested that an e-commerce site should have an unreasonably expensive "platinum" option, which few genuine customers will want to buy [721]. This performs two functions. First, it allows you to do rudimentary purchase profiling. Second, it fits with the model of *Goldilocks pricing*, developed by online economists Shapiro and Varian, who point out that the real effect of airlines offering first-class fares is to boost sales of business class seats to travelers who can now convince their bosses (or themselves) that they are being "economical" [696]. Another idea is to have a carefully engineered response to suspect transactions: if you just say "bad card, try another one," then the fraudster probably will. You may even end up being "used" by the crooks as an online service that tells them which of their stolen cards are on the hot list, and this can upset your bank (even though the banks are to blame for the system design). A better approach is claim that you're out of stock, so the bad guy will go elsewhere [721].

19.3.4 Economics

There's a lot of misinformation about credit card fraud, with statistics quoted selectively to make points. In one beautiful example, VISA was reported to have claimed that card fraud was up *and* that card fraud was down, on the same day [380].

However, a consistent pattern of figures can be dug out of the trade publications. The actual cost of credit card fraud, before the recent rise, was about 0.15% of all international transactions processed by VISA amd MasterCard [652], while national rates varied from 1% in America to 0.2% in the U.K. to under 0.1% in France and Spain. The prevailing business culture has a large effect on the rate. U.S. banks, for example, are much more willing to send out huge junk mailings of pre-approved cards to increase their customer base, and write off the inevitable pre-issue fraud as a cost of doing business. In other countries, banks are more risk-averse.

France is interesting, as it seems, at first sight, to be an exceptional case, in which a particular technology has brought real benefits. French banks introduced chip cards for all domestic transactions in the late 1980s, and this reduced losses from 0.269% of turnover in 1987 to 0.04% in 1993 and 0.028% in 1995. However, there is now an increasing amount of cross-border fraud. French villains use foreign magnetic stripe cards—particularly from Britain [315, 652]—while French chip cards are used at merchants in non-chip countries [166]. But the biggest reduction in Europe was not in France but in Spain, where the policy was to reduce all merchant floor limits to zero and make all transactions online. This cut their losses from 0.21% of turnover in 1988 to 0.008% in 1991 [73].

The lessons appear to be that, first, card fraud is cyclical, as new defenses are introduced and the villains learn to defeat them; and second, that the most complicated and expensive technological solution doesn't necessarily work best in the field.

19.4 Online Credit Card Fraud: The Hype and the Reality

We turn now from traditional credit card fraud to the online variety. There was great anxiety in the mid-1990s that the use of credit cards on the Internet would lead to an avalanche of fraud, as "Evil Hackers" intercepted emails and Web forms, and harvested credit card numbers by the million. These fears drove banks and software vendors to devise two protocols to protect Web-based credit card transactions: SSL and SET, which I'll explain in the next section.

The hype surrounding this type of fraud has been grossly overdone. Intercepting email is indeed possible, but it's surprisingly difficult in practice—so much so that governments are bullying ISPs to install snooping devices on their networks to make court-authorized wiretaps easier [114]. But the cost of such devices is so high that the ISPs are resisting this pressure as forcefully as they can. I'll go into this further in Chapter 21. And although it is possible to redirect a popular Web page to your own site using tricks such as DNS cache poisoning, it's a lot simpler to tap the plain old telephone system—and no one worries much about the few credit card numbers that get harvested from hotel guests this way.

Credit card numbers are indeed available on the Net, but usually because someone hacked the computer of a merchant who disobeyed the standard bank prohibition against retaining customer credit card numbers after being paid. (As this book was going to press, VISA announced that, starting in 2001, all its merchants will have to obey 10 new security rules; for example, they must install a firewall, keep security patches up to date, encrypt stored and transmitted data, and regularly update antivirus software [752].) Likewise, fraudulent Web-based transactions do occur, but mainly because of poor implementation of the system whereby cardholder addresses are checked during authorization. The real problem facing dot-coms is disputes.

It is easy to repudiate a transaction. Basically, all the customer has to do is call the credit card company and say, "I didn't authorize that," and the merchant will be saddled with the bill. This was workable in the days when almost all credit card transactions took place locally, and most were for significant amounts. If a customer fraudulently repudiated a transaction, the merchant would pursue them through the courts and harrass them using local credit reference agencies. In addition, the banks' systems are often quite capable of verifying local cardholder addresses.

But the Internet differs from the old mail order/telephone order regime, in that many transactions are international, amounts often are small, and verifying overseas addresses via the credit card system is problematic. Often, all the call center operator can do is check that the merchant seems confident when reading an address in the right country. Thus, the opportunity for repudiating transactions—and getting away with it—is hugely increased. There are particularly high rates of repudiation of payment to porn sites. No doubt some of these disputes happen when a transaction made under the influence of a flush of hormones turns up on the family credit card bill, and the cardholder has to repudiate it to save his marriage; but many are the result of blatant fraud by operators.

At the time of writing, the press was reporting that the Federal Trade Commission was prosecuting the operators of scores of adult Web sites, including playboy.com, for billing thousands of users for supposedly free services. The scam was to offer a "free tour" of the site, demand a credit card number, supposedly to verify that the user was over 18, and then bill him anyway. Some sites billed other consumers who have never visited them at all [389]. (Of course, none of this should have surprised the student of more traditional telecomms fraud, as it's just cramming in a new disguise.) If even apparently large and "respectable" Web sites such as playboy.com indulge in such practices, it's much easier for consumers to get away with fraudulently repudiating transactions.

The critical importance of this for online businesses is that, if more than a small percentage of your transactions are challenged by customers, your margins will be eroded; and in extreme cases your bank may withdraw your card acquisition service. It has been reported that the collapse of sportswear merchant boo.com was because it had too many returns: its business model assumed a no-quibble exchange or refund policy. But too many of its shipments were the wrong size, or the wrong color, or just didn't appeal to the customers. In the end, the credit card penalties were the straw that broke the camel's back [721].

This history suggests that technological fixes may not be as easy as many vendors claim, and that the main resources will be essentially procedural. American Express has announced that it will offer its customers credit card numbers that can be used once only; this will protect customers from some of the scams. In order not to run out of numbers, they will issue them one at a time to customers via their Web site (which will drive lots of traffic to them) [204]. Many other bankers are already coming to the conclusion that the way forward lies with better address verification, rather than with cryptography [62].

However, if you're working as a security engineer, then a lot of your clients will want to talk about technical matters, such as encrypting credit card numbers, so we'll look at the available crypto mechanisms anyway.

19.5 Cryptographic Protection Mechanisms

The existing cryptographic protection mechanisms used by the bank card industry—the PINs used at ATMs and some point-of-sale terminals, and the CVVs described in Section 19.3.2, which make card forgery more difficult—are largely ineffective online, so new mechanisms were developed. The most widely used is the Secure Sockets Layer protocol (SSL), an encryption system bundled with most Web browsers.

19.5.1 SSL

Recall that in public key encryption, a server can publish a public key KS and any Web browser can then send a message M containing a credit card number to it, encrypted using $KS: \{M\}_{KS}$. This is, in essence, what SSL does, although in practice it is more complicated. SSL was developed to support encryption and authentication in both directions, so that both http requests and responses could be protected against both eavesdropping and manipulation.

Here is a simplified description of the SSL version used to protect Web pages that solicit credit card numbers.

1. The client sends a *client hello* message to the server, which contains its name C, a transaction serial number $C\#$, and a random nonce N_C.

2. The server sends a *server hello* message, which contains its name S, a transaction serial number $S\#$, a random nonce N_S, and a certificate CS containing its public key KS. The client now checks the certificate CS back to a root certificate issued by a company such as Verisign and stored in the browser.

3. The client sends a *key exchange* message containing a *pre-master-secret* key K_0, encrypted under the server public key KS. It also sends a *finished* message with a message authentication code (MAC) computed on all the messages to date. The key for this MAC is the *master-secret* K_1. This key is computed by hashing the pre-master-secret key with the nonces sent by the client and server: $K_1 = h(K_{CS}, N_C, N_S)$. From this point onward, all the traffic is encrypted; we'll write this as $\{\ldots\}_{KCS}$ in the client-server direction and $\{\ldots\}_{KSC}$ from the server to the client. These keys are generated in turn by hashing the nonces with K_1.

4. The server also sends a *finished* message with a MAC computed on all the messages to date. It then finally starts sending the data.

$$C \rightarrow S\colon C,\ C\#,\ N_C$$

$$S \rightarrow C\colon S,\ S\#,\ N_S,\ CS$$

$$C \rightarrow S\colon \{K_0\}_{KS}$$

$$C \rightarrow S\colon \{finished,\ MAC(K_1,\ everything\_to\_date)\}_{KCS}$$

$$S \rightarrow C\colon \{finished,\ MAC(K_1,\ everything\_to\_date)\}_{KSC},\ \{data\}_{KSC}$$

The SSL design goals included minimizing the load on the browser, and then minimizing the load on the server. Thus, the public key encryption operation is done by the client, and the decryption by the server; the standard encryption method (*ciphersuite*) uses RSA, for which encryption can be arranged to be much faster than decryption. (This was a wrong design decision, as browsers generally have a lot more compute cycles to spare than servers; the use of RSA has created a brisk aftermarket for crypto accelerator boards for Web servers.) Also, once a client and server have established a pre-master-secret, no more public key operations are needed, as further master-secrets can be obtained by hashing it with new nonces.

The full SSL protocol is more complex than this, and has gone through a number of versions. It supports a number of different ciphersuites; for example, export versions of browsers can be limited to 40-bit keys—a condition of export licensing that was imposed for many years by the U.S. government. Other ciphersuites support signed Diffie-Hellman key exchanges for transient keys, to provide forward and backward secrecy. SSL also has options for bidirectional authentication, so that if the client also has a certificate, this can be checked by the server. In addition, the working keys KCS and KSC can contain separate subkeys for encryption and authentication. For example, the most commonly used ciphersuite uses the stream cipher RC4 for the former and HMAC for the latter, and these need separate keys.

Although early versions of SSL had a number of bugs [784], the latest version (called TLS by Microsoft) appears to be sound (but it has to be implemented carefully [116]). It is being used for much more than electronic commerce—an example being medical privacy, where it's likely to replace proprietary networks and allow confidential patient data to be sent over the Internet [175]. SSL is also spreading from Web applications, and is now incorporated as an option in Win2K, where it can be used to set up secure sessions between machines in different domains. There are problems, though, and some of the most glaring have to do with the nature and management of certificates. We'll talk about them in Section 19.5.3.

19.5.2 SET

Early experience with credit cards and the Internet showed that the real risk of compromise of credit card numbers did not come from eavesdropping on IP traffic—of which no case has ever been confirmed—but from hacking merchant Web servers and other end systems, which often retain credit card numbers, and are frequently attacked. So, in 1995–1996, there was an effort to develop a better payment protocol, which would use digital signatures rather than credit card numbers.

Eventually, a consortium which included Microsoft, Netscape, VISA, and MasterCard, came up with the *Secure Electronic Transaction* (SET) protocol. The ideas behind SET were:

- Customers will have public key certificates too, not just merchants. So customers can sign transactions, which include payment orders to their banks.

- The customer signs and enciphers two separate messages, one to the merchant, which contains a description of the goods and the price but not the credit card number; and another to the bank, which contains the price and the credit card number but not the description of the goods. The signatures are linked.

- The back-end transaction processing from the acquiring bank to the brand to the card-issuing bank uses the existing legacy systems.

SET was supposed to reassure customers that online transactions would be secure, and to reduce the cost of fraud (mainly by denying credit card numbers to merchants). The business model was that SET transactions would be treated as if the cardholder were present; that is, the bank would assume the fraud risk, and the merchant discount would be lower.

Because of the number of different legacy systems that had to be supported, and the range of features demanded by various industry players, SET is even more complex than SSL. Again, I'll give a simplified account of it.

First, the customer sends the merchant server her certificate CC for her public key KC, and a nonce, N_C. The server replies with certificated public keys for the merchant (CS, KS) and its bank (CB, KB), plus a transaction sequence number $S\#$. Then the customer sends a message containing an order, encrypted under the merchant's public key, and a payment instruction, encrypted under the bank's public key. Hashes of both of these are signed with the customer's private signing key. Next is an authorization step, which can be performed online or deferred, as appropriate: the server sends the payment instruction to the acquiring bank, together with a summary of the order, which includes the amount payable but not the exact description of the goods. The bank checks all this and refers to the card-issuing bank, if necessary. If everything's in order, it sends the server an authorization response similar to the traditional one (with an amount and an authorization code), fortified with a signature.

$C \rightarrow S$: C, N_C, CC

$S \rightarrow C$: $S, S\#, CS, CB$

$C \rightarrow S$: $\{Order\}_{KC}, \{Payment\}_{KB}, sig_{KC} \{h(Order), h(Payment)\}$

$S \rightarrow B$: $\{Summary\}_{KB}$, $\{Payment\}_{KB}$

$B \rightarrow S$: $sig_{KB}\ \{Auth\_response\}$

SET appears to have met its specifications, but failed to succeed in the marketplace. The reasons are instructive.

- *First, the benefits turned out to be less than expected.* Many large merchants were breaking their cardholder agreements by retaining customer credit card numbers—principally for use as indexes in marketing databases—and were not prepared to stop using them. So a feature was added whereby merchants could get the credit card number from the acquiring bank. This was thought to negate much of the hoped-for security improvement. (In fact, it wasn't that bad as banks could have issued credit card numbers that were valid only for SET transactions, so stealing them wouldn't have mattered.)

- *Second, the costs were too high.* Building a public key infrastructure to issue all credit cardholders with public key certificates would have been enormously expensive. Performance was also an issue.

- *Third, there was nothing in it for the customers.* Customers trading on the Web under MOTO rules could reverse the transaction if they were unhappy—not just about the payment, but about the service, the product, or anything else. Using SET transferred them to cardholder-present rules, and in many countries removed this protection. Thus, customers were much worse off and would have been insane to use SET. Also, installing SET usually involved downloading megabytes of SET wallet and going through a laborious certification procedure.

In the end, SET cost too much and delivered too little; and as far as the customers were concerned, it was a disaster. It is being allowed to expire quietly. The main lesson is, perhaps, that when designing systems for e-business, you should deal with issues as they are in practice, rather than in theory, and think about how your design will affect the interests of principals other than your client.

19.5.3 PKI

Public key infrastructures (PKIs) are still an issue; there is frequent semantic confusion between "public (key infrastructure)" and "(public key) infrastructure." In the first, the infrastructure can be used by whatever new applications come along; I call this an *open PKI*; in the second, it can't; I call this a *closed PKI*.

Examples of open PKIs are:

- Merchants using SSL are supposed to have certificates for their public keys, and several companies such as Verisign will certify a public key as belonging to a particular company after doing appropriate due diligence.

- There are many proposals to base new online services, and particularly business-to-business services, on certified digital signatures.

- Many governments are thinking of issuing their citizens with public key certificates, probably in smartcards, as next-generation identity cards. Although most businesses are really only interested in whether they will be paid, governments offer a range of services (such as tax and welfare) that can be cheated by people who can masquerade as more than one person. So there is much government interest in promoting the use of PKI technology, and this has led to legislation, which I'll discuss in Chapter 21.

The classic examples of closed PKIs are to be found in the networks operated by military agencies and by banking service providers such as SWIFT, which use asymmetric cryptography but do not publish any keys. Now that Win2K includes SSL as an authentication mechanism, it can be used to set up secure wide area networking across a number of scattered sites in a company; and if the number of sites is at all large, this may involve the company operating its own PKI to manage the keys. So closed PKIs may become much more common; and even where a service using asymmetric cryptography is offered to the public, there may be no keys published. An example is the Mondex electronic purse, which uses RSA cryptography and further protects the keys in tamper-resistant smartcards.

At the time of writing, PKI was one of the most heavily promoted protection technologies. However, it has a number of intrinsic limitations, many of which have to do with the first interpretation—namely that the infrastructure is provided as a public service that anyone can use. I discussed many of the underlying problems in Chapter 6. Naming is difficult; and a certificate saying, "Ross Anderson has the right to administer the machine foo.com" means little in a world with dozens of people of that name.

One way to solve the naming problem is for each business to run its own closed PKI, which might be thought of at the system level as giving customers a unique account number which isn't shared with anyone else. This leads to the "one key or many" debate. Should I expect to have a single signing key to replace each of the metal keys, credit cards, swipe access cards, and other tokens that I currently carry around? Or should each of these be replaced by a different signing key? The second option is more convenient for business, as sharing access tokens can lead to huge administrative costs and liability issues. It also protects the customer: I don't want to have to use a key with which I can remortgage my house to make calls from a payphone. It's just too easy to dupe me into signing a message by having the equipment display another, innocuous, one. (I don't know how to be confident even of a digital signature I make on my own PC, and I've worked in security for over fifteen years. Checking all the software in the critical path between the display and the signature software is way beyond my patience.) But the existing PKI machinery was largely developed to provide an electronic replacement for the telephone book, and tends to assume that everyone will have a unique name and a unique key. This in turn means an open PKI architecture.

This leads to political issues, such as, which CAs do we trust, and why? Various attempts have been made by governments to license certification authorities and to impose a condition that there be "back doors" for law enforcement access. Governments overwhelmingly favor the one-key-fits-all model of the world. It's also possible that open PKIs will be favored by network economics, which I discuss in Section 19.6: once a single PKI becomes dominant, the pressure on everyone to use it could lead to its being entrenched as a monopoly. (This is the reason for the high stock market valuation of VeriSign.)

There are numerous issues of implementation detail. For example, the dominant certificate format (X.509) does not have the kind of flexible and globally scalable 'hot card' system that the credit card industry has developed over the years. It rather assumes that anyone relying on a certificate can download a *certificate revocation list* from the issuing authority. This is tiresome and inefficient. Better ways of managing certificate revocation have been proposed; the question is whether they'll get implemented. Also, X.509 is designed to certify names, when for most purposes people want to certify an authorization.

There are many other limitations of certificates:

- *Most users disable the security features on their browsers*, even if these weren't disabled by default when the software shipped. Recall that the third step of the SSL protocol was for the client browser to check the certificate against its stored root certificates. If the check fails, the browser may ask the client for permission to proceed; but the way most browsers are configured, it will just proceed anyway. This lets many e-commerce sites save themselves money by using expired certificates or even self-signed certificates; most users don't see the warnings (and wouldn't know how to respond if they did).

- *The main vendors' certificates bind a company name to a DNS name*, but are not authorities on either; and they go out of their way to deny all liability.

- *Competition in the certificate markets is blocked* by the need to get a new root certificate into Microsoft Internet Explorer (VeriSign stockholders will consider this to be not a bug but a feature).

- *Even when you do get a valid certificate, it may be for a company and/or DNS name different from that of the site you thought you were shopping at*, because the Web site hosting or the credit card acquisition was outsourced.

- *U.S. export regulations have meant that large numbers of sites use weak encryption.* A recent survey of SSL security showed that of 8,081 different secure Web servers, 32% weren't, for various reasons—too-short keys, weak ciphersuites, and expired certificates being the main causes [567].

There is also a serious problem with consumer protection law. Introducing a presumption that digital signatures are valid undermines the signer's rights; in paper systems the risk of fraud is borne by the party who relies on the signature. In the absence of such a presumption, it makes no difference to the cardholder's liability whether the sites at which he shopped had valid certificates with appropriate names; and in any case, there's no convenient way for him to record his transactions to show that he exercised due diligence. I go into some of these issues at greater length in Chapter 21.

In short, while public key infrastructures can be useful in some applications, they are unlikely to be the universal solution to security problems as their advocates seem to believe. They don't tackle most of the really important issues at all.

19.5.4 EDI and Business-to-Business Systems

The early examples of electronic commerce given in Section 19.2, such as the telegraph and EDI, were largely business-to-business systems. These systems provide many of the examples of working PKIs. We looked at an example in detail in Section 9.3.1—the SWIFT network used since the mid-1970s to send secure payment messages between banks in different countries, and upgraded in the 1990s to use public key techniques. Essentially, the same architecture has been adopted for a number of other systems, including the CREST system used to register ownership of all U.K.-listed equities and to support share dealing between banks and brokers.

A more modern example of a business-to-business system is Bolero, an EU system that handles electronic bills of lading [262, 458, 492]. These are the legal documents that confer ownership of shipping cargoes. Their average value is about $25,000, but, depending on the price of oil, an oil tanker's cargo can be worth $100,000,000. Cargoes are often traded many times while the ship is at sea, and many of the traders are rather dubious shell companies. In addition, the enforcement of sanctions against rogue states means that their national intelligence agencies are often involved in using such shell companies to buy things like oil when they shouldn't. So this is a high-value, high-threat environment. Quite some care has to be taken to ensure that bills of lading cannot be duplicated, and that their ownership history can be established.

Bolero uses two main protection mechanisms. First, there is tamper resistance. IBM 4753 or 4758 cryptoprocessor cards are used to hold the bills; and there is a protocol involving digital signatures that is used to transfer them. Second, a central registry is used to ensure that the name of the unique holder can be determined at all times. There is also a registration authority (which vets the credentials of organizations) and a certification authority (which signs the public keys of individuals authorized by registered organizations).

Another example is healthcare EDI systems, which typically send test results, such as radiology and cytology from large hospitals and laboratories, to family doctors and local clinics. Here the requirement isn't non-duplicability, but authenticity plus confidentiality. Early systems provided this using closed, proprietary messaging networks; more modern systems have encryption and authentication mechanisms that work at message gateways. The dozens of messages sent each day from a hospital laboratory to a general medical practice are batched up, signed with the hospital's signing key, encrypted with the practice's public key, and shipped by email. In an ideal world, messages would be signed individually by the consultant writing the opinion, and addressed to the physician treating the patient; in practice, this is hard, as both labs and physicians use proprietary systems that can communicate only using EDIFACT gateways. These are specialized system that do format conversion; they are too expensive for everyone to have them running on their PC. This design causes a number of problems. For example, if a record of the digital signatures of lab reports is to be kept in case of malpractice litigation, then the whole batch must be kept, which conflicts with privacy rules about the destruction of records pertaining to patients who have died or moved away.

This kind of problem isn't limited to healthcare. Many systems have message processing functions that cause subsets of transaction data to go to different destinations in an organization. Protecting the integrity of structured data can be much harder than it looks.

So, for a number of reasons, implementing business-to-business secure communications isn't at all straightforward. As innovative business models proliferate, there are bound to be expensive design errors. I'll discuss how to reduce the probability of these in Part 3.

19.5.5 E-Purses and Micropayments

In the first half of the 1990s, a large number of *electronic purse* systems were developed. The idea was to replace debit cards with something that would work offline without being more vulnerable to forgery. The typical implementation involved both customers and merchants having chip cards, each with a value counter, plus a card-to-card payment protocol whereby two cards would authenticate each other—one would be debited and the other would be credited. I described the design of a typical protocol in Section 2.7.1.

The promoters of these schemes had huge hopes. Europay Austria, for example, was confident that its product would displace 20% of cash transactions within three years. But by the end of the decade, the outcome was disappointing. Even where an e-purse chip has been built into standard bank cards and issued to the entire customer base, as with Proton in Belgium and the Geldkarte in Germany, usage remains disappointing. (The business is surveyed in [763].) The slow take-off might have been expected, given the history of credit cards; like them, e-purses suffer from what economists call *network externalities*, meaning that the more the cards are used, the more merchants accept them, and the more useful they become—not just to their existing customers but to potential adopters. But when few people use them, merchants don't have a motive to buy terminals; and with few terminals, they attract few users. At best, such schemes have some way to go before they reach critical mass; they may get there eventually, driven by applications such as payphones, and then they could grow very quickly indeed. I discuss the underlying economics further in Section 19.6.

The one exception to the slow start imposed on new payment mechanisms by network externalities may be the micropayment mechanism that might be shipped with the second phase of third-generation mobile phones, which I described in Section 17.3.4. As all purchasers of next-generation phones will be using this system to pay for calls, as well as for value-added services, the extra cost involved in adding a new service should be low, while the customer base should be substantial within a few years. There is a risk that, as with Geldkarte, this will end up as a system that's widely deployed but has few active users; but there's also the possibility that it might fly. (Phone-based payments could also become a serious problem if, as seems likely, third-generation phones get the capability to run Java applets—with all the potential for malicious code, feature interaction, and general confusion that this would bring.)

It's also conceivable that third-generation phones could provide a close thing to a universal open PKI, if certification authorities are used to sign users' public key certificates in a way that's usable by other services. On the other hand, if the top-level public key protocol is the Royal Holloway one, and (as in its established government uses), this escrows signing keys as well as confidentiality keys [50], then it will be much less useful, because the evidential value of signatures produced by the system will be undermined.

19.6 Network Economics

The network externalities mentioned above don't just apply to people trying to launch new payment systems, but are of very much wider importance. Many communications systems, and the downstream applications they support, suffer from them. They dictate not just e-commerce business models, but also many of the problems that the security engineer must wrestle with.

The key observation is that the more users there are on a system, the more people there are to talk to, and so the more useful it is to each user. (This is sometimes referred to as *Metcalfe's law*.) There are many documented examples of how the resulting positive feedback can give a large advantage to the early players in a market, and lead toward a monopoly. For example, in the early years of the twentieth century, AT&T's dominance of long-distance telephone communication enabled it to crush local competition and to establish itself as the near-monopoly provider in the United States until its break-up in 1984. Compatability is also crucial. In the 1950s, there was a battle between CBS and RCA over whose standard for color television would prevail; although the FCC endorsed CBS, its standard wasn't backward-compatible with the millions of installed black-and-white TV sets. RCA's standard was, so it won.

The most obvious effect of this positive feedback is that once a network passes a certain critical size, it grows rapidly. The telegraph, the telephone, the fax machine and, most recently, the Internet, have all followed this model. Another effect is that there are enormous rewards for being first. This happens to some extent in traditional businesses such as cars where supplyside economies of scale help big firms to grow bigger. But there are limits: once they became too large, companies such as General Motors couldn't react quickly enough to compete against upstarts such as Toyota. With networks, the economies of scale occur on the demand side, and so there is no upper limit on growth.

Network effects aren't limited to the kind of networks that involve shipping electrical or optical signals, which economists refer to as *real networks*. They also apply to *virtual networks*, of which the classic example is software. Recall the battle for supremacy between the PC and the Mac in the mid-1980s: once it was clear that there were going to be more users of PCs than Macs, software houses concentrated on shipping their products for the PC first and the Mac only afterward, if at all. This meant that there was more software for the PC, so people were more likely to buy PCs, and the positive feedback continued.

This isn't limited to PC architecures, but works at all sorts of levels including application software and file formats. Once most people started using Microsoft Word for documents, that was even more reason for everybody else to (regardless of the risk from Word macro viruses). And such a network effect can be enhanced by arranging that your file formats are difficult for other companies' programs to read, and change them often; I'll discuss this in the next section.

One of the features of markets exposed to network effects is lock-in. This can be either technology lock-in or vendor lock-in. Technology lock-in often involves complementary suppliers, as with the software vendors whose bandwagon effect carried Microsoft to victory over Apple. A side effect of this is that successful networks appeal to complementary suppliers rather than to users—the potential creators of "killer apps" need to be courted. Once the customers have a substantial investment in complementary assets, they will be locked in. Andrew Odlyzko observes that much of the lack of user-friendliness of both Microsoft software and the Internet is due to the fact that both Microsoft and the Internet achieved success by appealing to developers. The support costs that Microsoft dumps on users—and, in fact, even the cost of the time wasted waiting for PCs to boot up and shut down—greatly exceed its turnover [595].

So there are three particularly important features of information technology markets.

■ *First, technology often has high fixed costs and low marginal costs.* The first copy of a chip or a software package may cost millions to produce, but subsequent copies may cost very little. This isn't unique to information markets; it's also seen in business sectors such as airlines and hotels. In all such sectors, pricing at marginal cost will tend to drive revenues steadily down toward the cost of production (which in the case of information is zero).

■ *Second, there are often high costs to users from switching technologies, which leads to lock-in.* Such markets may remain very profitable, despite the low marginal costs.

■ *Third, there are often network externalities of the sort discussed earlier.* The value of a product to a user depends on how many other users adopt it.

All three of these effects tend to lead to winner-take-all market structures with dominant firms. Indeed, firms will attempt to manipulate these effects to gain competitive advantage in various ways.

One common strategy, for example, is differentiated pricing. This means pricing the product or service not to its cost but to its value to the customer. This is familiar from the world of air travel: you can spend $200 to fly the Atlantic in coach class, $2,000 in business class, or $5,000 in first. (As noted in Section 19.3.3, this is also a classic case of Goldilocks pricing: the main function of the first-class fare is to enable people who fly business class to claim they are being economical.) This business model is spreading widely in the software and online services sectors. A basic program or service may be available free; a much better one for a subscription; and a "gold" service at a ridiculous price. In many cases, the program is the same except that some features are disabled for the budget user while the "gold" user gets a high-quality helpline. Many of the protection mechanisms you will come across have as their real function the maintenance of this differential.

Another strategy is to manipulate *switching costs*. The long-term value to your ISP of your account, in the sense of the discounted future earnings, should be equal to the total amount of money (and hassle) involved in the customers' switching to a competitor. So the ISP will do its utmost to make it easy for you to switch to them, but difficult to switch from them. This applies with particular force to dominant-firm markets where the incumbent tries to build a monopoly which its competitors try to attack. Incumbents try to increase the cost of switching, whether by indirect methods, such as controlling marketing channels and building industries of complementary suppliers, or by direct methods, such as making systems incompatible and hard to reverse-engineer. Meanwhile, market entrants try to do the reverse: they look for ways to reuse the base of complementary products and services, and to reverse-engineer whatever protection the incumbent builds in. They may use penetration pricing—selling cheaply to subsidize switching—and the incumbent may respond with vaporware, designed to increase users' perception of the opportunity cost of switching.

As technology advances, even seemingly impregnable monopolies can be replaced, so the competition can be vicious. Extensive use is made of protection mechanisms, from tamper-resistant devices to proprietary encryption algorithms.

19.7 Competitive Applications and Corporate Warfare

This leads us to the applications of information security mechanisms whose goal isn't to protect the customers or their data, but to either entrench or attack a monopoly.

Sometimes the mechanisms in use are obvious. For example, manufacturers of game consoles try to keep their platforms closed so that they can monopolize sales of accessories and impose conditions on games software vendors—which may involve not just royalties but also exclusivity agreements. Legal solutions such as copyrighted interfaces aren't enough, as in many countries there is an exemption from copyright law for firms doing reverse-engineering in order to build a compatible product. So cryptographic challenge-response protocols are used to authenticate genuine accessories and game cartridges; competitors hire reverse-engineering labs to dig out the keys. I mentioned other applications of accessory control in Section 2.2.

Another example comes from Microsoft Passport. This is a system whose ostensible purpose is single sign-on: a Passport user doesn't have to think up separate passwords for each participating Web site, with all the attendant hassle and risk. Instead, some sites use Passport, a central authentication server run by Microsoft, to which users log on. Servers use Web redirection to connect their Passport-carrying visitors to this server; authentication requests and responses are passed between them by the user's browser in encrypted cookies. So far, so good.

But the real functions of Passport are somewhat more subtle [727]. First, by patching itself into all the Web transactions of participating sites, Microsoft can collect a huge amount of data about online shopping habits, and enable participants to swap it. The redirection and cookie mechanisms mean that, in effect, all the browsing sessions you have at participating sites become one single session, managed by Microsoft. If every site can exchange data with every other site, then the value of a network of Web sites is the square of the number of sites, and there is a strong network externality. So one such network may come to dominate, and Microsoft hopes to own it. Second, the authentication protocols used between the merchant servers and the Passport server are proprietary variants of Kerberos, meaning the Web server must use Microsoft software rather than Apache or Netscape. In short, Passport isn't as much a security product as a play for control of both the Web server and purchasing information markets. It comes bundled with services such as Hotmail, is already used by 40 million people, and does 400 authentications per second on average. Its known flaws include that Microsoft keeps all the users' credit card details, creating a huge target; various possible middleperson attacks; and that a user can be impersonated by someone who steals their cookie file. Passport has a "logout" facility that's supposed to delete the cookies for a particular merchant, so users can use a shared PC with less risk, but this feature doesn't work properly for Netscape users [473].

The constant struggles to entrench or undermine monopolies, and to segment and control markets, determine many of the environmental conditions that make the security engineer's work harder. The markup language XML enables document content to be processed easily, and has the potential to build in a rich syntax of protection attributes [46]. However, it's not taking off as many people had hoped, because if Web pages become easily machine-readable, then comparison shopping bots are easier to build. In addition, many online merchants guage demand by discounting perhaps every hundredth transaction by a random amount. This wouldn't work if shoppers had tools to hit the site again and again until they got a bargain. In general, there is a constant struggle between the designers of intermediaries—from Web caches to anonymous communication services—who wish to control a user's transactions is various ways, and merchant sites, that wish to break this control and "own" the user directly.

I'll come back to the effects of network economics on security in Section 22.6.

19.8 What Else Goes Wrong

An important survey of the things that went wrong with First Virtual, one of the first online banks, revealed that the typical problem was an upset customer calling at three in the morning and wanting to speak to someone in Korean about a missing payment. Investigation would typically reveal that the cause was an obscurely broken implementation of one or more Internet protocols, or a mistake made in typing an email address. Solving such problems is not currently a core competence of the typical financial institution [129].

This pattern—that most of the problems come from unanticipated bugs and blunders—was to be expected from other application areas; and it has continued. A number of large online stores, including `Buy.com`, `Staples.com` and Amazon-backed crafts retailer `eZiba.com`, were hit by pricing errors. At `Buy.com`, a coupon meant to be worth $50 off any order of $500 or more actually gave $50 off any purchase, making any item sold for $50 or less free to the buyer. At `eZiba.com`, each customer was offered a $20 voucher; people logged on with multiple names and found that they could use the discount many times [671]. Errors like these are nothing new; there have been numerous cases in the past of a special offer being carelessly designed, or even just being more popular than planned for. The difference is that, on the Net, an error can become widely known very rapidly and lead to large losses.

There have also been some interesting attacks on specific systems. The *Radio Data System* (RDS) adds a data channel to broadcast radio so the receiver can tell which station it is and what sort of content is being broadcast. This enables the radio to switch automatically to the strongest transmitter for your favorite network when you're driving along in your car; you can also program the radio to interrupt you if traffic information appears on another channel. (An RDS radio has two tuners, one of which constantly sweeps the band looking for a higher-strength or higher-priority signal). Pirate radio stations have developed the trick of marking their content falsely as traffic news, so lots of car radios switch to them automatically [306]. This isn't always obvious if the pirate is playing the same general kind of music as the station you were just listening to. It's also not obvious how genuine radio stations could be authenticated; perhaps the FCC would act as a certification authority, and issue certificates along with spectrum licenses. But then how would a genuine station that turned pirate be revoked? The moral is that often it is necessary to protect the integrity of distribution channels; and, more generally, that interesting new features often turn out to be vulnerable to interesting new exploits.

Computer games are another fertile field for finding hacks. An example is Quake, a distributed game whose source code is openly distributed. Some players have exploited their access to the code to modify the Quake client so that they can cheat [633]. This raises a number of questions, particularly with e-commerce applications that employ Java applets or other code that is run on a potentially hostile customer machine. There's no obvious way such applets can protect themselves against virtualization. At the very least, it seems prudent to have a non-Java version of your site. This will not only mean that you can do business with people like me, who leave Java turned off for security reasons; it will also give you a fallback mechanism to block fraud based on bad applets without having to close down your site for redevelopment.

19.9 What Can a Merchant Do?

In general, the advice I give to people concerned about e-commerce risks is that they are not much different from normal business and IT risks.

You should make sure your developers understand the business model; use a structured development methodology; test your code thoroughly; don't be too clever; look around for proven ideas which you can adopt; by all means worry about the firewall through which your internal systems are connected to the Net, but pay particular attention to internal controls to discourage, prevent, and detect insider fraud. Expect that no matter what you do, things will go wrong and may have to be changed quickly. Don't be too greedy; if you put "We guarantee you can't lose money shopping online with us" on your Web page and "Our records are the sole and definitive evidence of all transactions between us" in the small print, you may expect to have the TV crew from a consumer rights program camping on your doorstep one day.

This much is motherhood and apple pie for any company IT director. The main way in which e-commerce appears different—at least as of mid-2000—is the seriously enhanced risk and cost of customers repudiating credit card transactions. There's no obvious fix; but a useful damage limitation strategy is to have a controlled procedure through which customers are invited to complain, rather than going directly to their credit card company on day one. For example, you can advertise a policy of allowing exchanges with a discount off the postage; and if customers do want a refund, ask them to print out and sign a form, and mail it to you by physical post, rather than offering a Web form for the purpose.

Above all, focus on the business risks, and have risk management documentation that you upgrade regularly in consultation with your auditors, insurers, and directors, rather than getting carried away with the latest technical security gizmos. Business is business, and just because there are now highly paid computer scientists designing business processes that used to be the domain of the work study clerks of old, this does not mean that things are any better. The risks associated with the "Net mentality" have to be carefully assessed and managed.

Finally, it may make sense to pay some attention to non-technical issues such as product liability. One critical advantage enjoyed by U.S. e-businesses is that foreign civil judgments aren't enforced by U.S. courts. So an e-business operating from the United States doesn't have to worry about being sued by consumers in faraway countries, even if the local law lets them sue locally, because the judgments they get cannot be enforced. But in Europe, there are international reciprocal agreements: a U.K. retailer sued in a local Greek court can have the judgment enforced in the U.K. On the other hand, U.S. courts are accessible and can give punitive damages, while courts in many European countries are so expensive and give such small awards that product liability suits are rare. These considerations interact with credit card chargeback issues, but are not subsumed by them. They can be so complex that all I'll say is that you should get legal advice: the best location for your business may depend on what you're selling, and to whom.

19.10 Summary

Most of the problems facing online businesses are no different from those facing other organizations, and the network security risks are not much different from those facing traditional businesses. The real increased risks to an e-business have to do with ways in which traditional risk management mechanisms don't scale properly from a world of local physical transactions to one of worldwide, dematerialized ones. Credit card transaction repudiation is the main example at present. There are also significant risks to rapidly growing companies that have hired a lot of new staff but that don't have the traditional internal controls in place.

Research Problems

Most of the research behind the e-commerce protection mechanisms that are already deployed, or about to be, was done around 1994–1996. It may well be time for a second wave now that we can see what has worked, what can work but failed in the marketplace, and where the real problems are.

Further Reading

The early history of the telegraph can be found in a book by Major General RFH Nalder [569], while Tom Standage tells the story of its rapid deployment in Victorian times [729]. There is a survey of organized credit card counterfeiting in [592]. The official specification of SSL is hard to read; a better exposition is in [604]. The SET protocol is described in a book by its chief architect Li Song [509]. The problems of public key certification and infrastructures are analyzed in [42, 268]. Finally, the best book I know on network economics is by Carl Shapiro and Hal Varian [696].

CHAPTER 20

Copyright and Privacy Protection

The DeCSS case is almost certainly a harbinger of what I would consider to be the defining battle of censorship in cyberspace. In my opinion, this will not be fought over pornography, neo-Nazism, bomb design, blasphemy, or political dissent. Instead, the Armageddon of digital control, the real death match between the Party of the Past and Party of the Future, will be fought over copyright.

—JOHN PERRY BARLOW

Be very glad that your PC is insecure—it means that after you buy it, you can break into it and install whatever software you want. What YOU want, not what Sony or Warner or AOL wants.

—JOHN GILMORE

20.1 Introduction

There are a number of reasons to consider technical mechanisms that support copyright and privacy in a single book chapter.

At the political level, there is the conflict alluded to by Barlow in the above quotation. The control of information has been near the center of government concerns since before William Tyndale (one of the founders of the Cambridge University Press) was burned at the stake for printing the Bible in English. The sensitivity continued through the eighteenth-century battles over press censorship, to the more recent doctrine that warfare is about controlling the information space of one's own nation and its competitors. In the last few generations, the great wealth accruing to the owners of literary, film, and music copyright has created another powerful interest in control.

At a system level, both copyright and censorship are access control issues, concerned with limiting access to some information to people in a particular group. In the former case, the group consists of people who have paid for the bits in question; in the latter, they meet some other criterion (such as being over 18, or nonresidents of Singapore, or whatever). Sometimes, they overlap, as with the common convention of restricting online pornography to users who can use a credit card with an "age check" service. (The assumption that all credit card holders are 18 or over may not hold up forever, giving rise to an interesting security failure of the "changing environment" type.) In general, users' real names matter: if identity is no longer sacrosanct, liability for sedition, copyright infringement, and defamation become shaky.

Privacy is also largely an access control issue. It's about being able to limit the number of people who can see who you're exchanging email with, what you're reading and what music you're listening to. In theory, there is no compelling reason why they should be in conflict, and in the pre-electronic world, they usually weren't. Copyright was protected by the cost of small-scale duplication; it was simpler and cheaper to buy a book or a record than to make a single copy, and people who made large numbers of copies could usually be tracked down and prosecuted. The cost barrier to copying was eroded significantly by the photocopier and the cassette recorder, but they didn't change the basic economics. So books, records, and videos can be bought for cash and traded secondhand. But the move to a digital world is changing this. Although there are some systems, such as pay-TV, which depend on a physically tamper-resistant device, most copyright control is moving in the direction of registration. Once you have bought a software product, you're supposed to register as a user, and this business model is spreading to other media—which in turn is undermining privacy.

In this chapter, I'm going to use a technical view of privacy. Confidentiality means keeping information secret because of an obligation owed to a third party, while privacy refers to the ability to control the dissemination of information about oneself. In the privacy applications I've discussed up till now, these tend to overlap. For example, my medical privacy is implemented by imposing on my doctor a duty of confidentiality. But in this chapter I'm interested in the mechanisms I can use to protect my own privacy directly, starting from encrypted electronic mail and going up through online pseudonyms and networks of anonymous remailers to file systems whose owners can plausibly deny knowledge of their contents.

At this technical level, the tension between copyright and privacy becomes acute. Videos and music tracks that are not protected by physically tamper-resistant tokens can in principle be copied and shared; they can end up being traded informally, on a large scale, and without any payment to the copyright owner; and whatever the pressure brought on ISPs to curtail traffic in things like MP3 audio files, the existence of traceless communication systems might ultimately make enforcement efforts futile. On the other hand, a number of existing and proposed electronic distribution systems make encrypted content freely available: to decrypt it, the user must contact a server and buy a key—which usually means providing your name and address. This means that there's enormous amounts of "information exhaust," as one vendor puts it: a central license server knows exactly who bought access to what, and when. Marketers think this is magnificent; privacy advocates are appalled [260].

In addition, a number of the emerging technologies cut both ways. Data hiding techniques can be used to embed copyright marks invisibly in digital video; they can also be used for *steganography*, that is for hiding messages in other messages. The family snapshots that you email to your brother might actually contain a ripped-off track from your favorite band's latest CD. (They could also contain a message organizing demonstrators to picket an international trade conference, so the government interest is never far away.)

20.2 Copyright

The protection of copyright is now an obsession of the film, music, and book publishing industries (often referred to collectively—and perjoratively—by computer industry people as "Hollywood"). But this didn't start with the Internet. There were long and acrimonious disputes arose in many countries over whether blank audio or videocassettes should be subjected to a tax whose proceeds would be distributed to copyright owners. And the issue isn't confined to electronic media; in Britain, several million pounds a year are distributed to authors whose books are borrowed from public lending libraries [629]. Going back to the nineteenth century, there was alarm that the invention of photography would destroy the book publishing trade; and in the sixteenth, the invention of movable type printing was considered to be highly subversive by most of the powers that were, including princes, bishops, and craft guilds.

There is now a lot of work being done on *electronic copyright management systems* (ECMS), of which the most significant fielded example to date is pay-TV. We've already looked at the tamper-resistance aspects of pay-TV systems, and some of the protocol failures. I noted that such systems are highly challenging because the attackers can buy as many access tokens as they like for dismantling and study. But before we worry about high-tech systems, let's look at software protection, as most of the current copyright issues have been played out in the PC and games software markets over the last twenty years or so.

20.2.1 Software

Software for early computers was given away free by the hardware vendors or by users who'd written it. IBM even set up a scheme in the 1960s whereby its users could share programs they had written. (Most of these were useless, as they were too specialized, too poorly documented, or otherwise too hard to adapt.) So protecting software copyright was not an issue. Almost all organizations that owned computers were large and respectable; the software tended to require skilled maintenance; and so they often had full-time system engineers employed by the hardware vendor on-site. There are still sectors which operate on this business model. For example, one supplier of software for bank dealing rooms takes the view that anyone who pirates its code is welcome, as using it without skilled technical support would be a fast way for a bank to lose millions.

But when minicomputers arrived in the 1960s, software costs started to become significant. Hardware vendors began to charge extra for their operating system, and third-party system houses sprang up. To begin with, these mostly sold complete bespoke systems— hardware, software, and maintenance—so piracy was still not much of an issue. By the mid 1970s, some of them had turned bespoke systems into packages: software originally written for one bakery would be parameterized and sold to many bakeries. The main type of copyright dispute in those days was when a programmer left your company to join a competitor, and their code suddenly acquired a number of your features. The question then was whether he'd taken code with him, or reimplemented it. The standard way to resolve such a problem is to look at *software birthmarks*, features of how a particular implementation was done, such as the order in which registers are pushed and popped. This continues to be an issue, and there are various code comparison tools available—many of them developed in universities to detect students cheating on programming assignments. (This thread of research leads to general-purpose plagiarism-detection tools, which can trawl through natural language, as well as code, and typically recognize a passage of text by indexing it according to the least-common words that appear in it [376]; on to systems used by humanities scholars to figure out whether Bacon wrote Shakespeare, and back to tools that try to identify the authors of viruses from their coding style [476].)

With time, people invented more and more things to do with software. So a firm that had bought a minicomputer for stock control (or contracted for time on a bureau service) might be tempted to run a statistical program too to prepare management reports. Meanwhile, the installed base of machines grew large enough for software sharing to happen more than just occasionally. In response, some system houses started to put in copyright enforcement mechanisms. A common one was to check the processor serial number; another was the *time bomb*. In 1981, when I worked for a company selling retail stock control systems, we caused a message to come up every few months saying something like "Fault no. WXYZ—please call technical support." WXYZ was an encrypted version of the licensed customer's serial number, and if the caller claimed to be from that customer we'd give them a password to reenable the system for the next few months. (If not, we'd send round a salesman.) This mechanism could have been defeated easily if the "customer" understood it, but in practice it worked fine—most of the time it was a low-level clerk who encountered the fault message and called our hotline.

Software piracy really started to become an issue when the arrival of microcomputers in the late 1970s and early 1980s created a mass market, and software houses started to produce products that didn't require technical support to install and run. Initial responses varied. In a famous open letter from Bill Gates in 1976, a year after Microsoft was founded, he complained that less than 10% of all microcomputer users had paid them for BASIC [319]. "Who cares if the people who worked on it get paid?" he asked. "Is this fair?" His letter concluded: "Nothing would please me more than being able to hire ten programmers and deluge the hobby market with good software."

Appeals to people's sense of fair play only got so far, and the industry next tackled the obvious difference between minis and micros—the latter had no processor serial numbers. Three general approaches were tried: to add uniqueness on to the machine, to create uniqueness in it, or to use whatever uniqueness happened to exist already by chance.

- The standard way to add hardware uniqueness was a *dongle*—a device, typically attached to the PC's parallel port, which could be interrogated by the software. The simplest just had a serial number; the most common executed a simple challenge-response protocol; while some top-end devices actually performed some critical part of the computation.

- A cheaper and very common strategy was for the software to install itself on the PC's hard disk in a way that was resistant to naive copying. For example, a sector of the hard disk would be marked as bad, and a critical part of the code or data written there. Now if the product were copied from the hard disk using the utilities provided by the operating system for the purpose, the data hidden in the bad sector wouldn't be copied and so the copy wouldn't work. A variant on the same theme was to require the presence of a master diskette which had been customized in some way, such as by formatting it oddly or even burning holes in it with a laser. In general, though, a distinction should be drawn between protecting the copy and protecting the master. It's often a requirement that people should be able to make copies for backup if they wish, but not to make copies of the copies (this is called *copy generation control*).

■ A product I worked on stored the PC's configuration—which cards were present, how much memory, what type of printer—and if this changed too radically, it would ask the user to phone the helpline. It's actually quite surprising how many unique identifiers there are in the average PC; ethernet addresses and serial numbers of disk controllers are only the more obvious ones. Provided you have some means of dealing with upgrades, you can use component details to tie software to a given machine.

A generic attack that works against most of these defenses (or at least those that don't hide critical code somewhere uncopiable) is to go through the software with a debugger and remove all the calls made to the copy protection routines. Many hobbyists did this for sport, and competed to put unprotected versions of software products online as soon as possible after their launch. Even people with licensed copies of the software often got hold of unprotected versions as they were easier to back up and often more reliable generally.

The vendors also used psychological techniques.

■ The installation routine for many business programs would embed the registered user's name and company on the screen, for example in the toolbar. This wouldn't stop a pirate distributing copies registered in a false name, but it could discourage legitimate users from giving casual copies to colleagues.

■ Industry publicists retailed stories of organizations that had come unstuck when they failed to get a critical upgrade of software they hadn't paid for. One of the popular stories was of the U.S. army bases in Germany that didn't pay for the VAX VMS operating system, then got hacked after they didn't get a security patch.

■ If early Microsoft software (Multiplan, Word, or Chart) thought you were running it under a debugger, trying to trace through it, it would put up the message, "The tree of evil bears bitter fruit. Now trashing program disk." It would then seek to track zero on the floppy and go "rrnt, rrnt, rrnt."

In the mid- to late-1980s, the market split. The games market moved in the direction of hardware protection, and ended up dominated by games console products with closed architectures, where the software is sold in proprietary cartridges. Business software vendors, however, generally stopped trying to protect mass-market products using predominantly technical means. There were several reasons.

■ Unless you're prepared to spend money on seriously tamper-resistant dongle hardware that executes some of your critical code, the mechanisms will be defeated by people for whom it's an intellectual challenge, and unprotected code will be anonymously published. Code that isn't protected in the first place is less of a challenge.

■ As processors got faster and code more complex, operating system interfaces became higher level, and software protection routines of the "bad disk sector" variety got harder to write. Now that it's possible to run a Windows NT system on top of Linux using vmware, application software can be completely shielded from machine specifics such as Ethernet addresses. The net effect is an increase in the cost and complexity of both protection and piracy.

■ Protection is a nuisance. Multiple dongles get in the way of, or even interfere with, each other. Software protection techniques tend to make a product less robust and cause problems—as when your hard disk fails and you recover from backup to a new disk. Protection mechanisms can also cause software from different vendors to be unnecessarily incompatible, and in some cases unable to reside on the same machine.

■ Technical support became more and more important as software products became more complex, and you only get it if you pay for the software.

■ The arrival of computer viruses was great for the industry. It forced corporate customers to invest in software hygiene, which in turn meant that casual copying couldn't be condoned so easily. Within a few years, antivirus programs made life much harder for copy protection designers in any case, as nonstandard operating system usage tended to set off virus alarms.

■ There was not much money to be made out of harrassing personal users as they often made only casual use of the product and would throw it away rather than pay.

■ A certain level of piracy was good for business. People who got a pirate copy of a tool and liked it would often buy a regular copy, or persuade their employer to buy one.

■ In Microsoft's case, customer reaction to its scare message was pretty negative.

■ Many vendors preferred not to have to tackle issues such as whether the software was licensed to the user (in which case he could migrate it to a new machine) or to the machine (in which case he could sell the computer secondhand with the software installed). As both practices were common, mechanisms that made one or the other very much harder caused problems. The mechanisms that could easily deal with both (such as dongles) tended to be expensive.

■ Finally, Borland shook up the industry with its launch of Turbo Pascal. Before then a typical language compiler cost about $500 and came with such poor documentation that you had to spend a further $50 on a book to tell you how to use it. Borland's product cost $49.95, was technically superior to the competition, and came with a manual that was just as good as a third party product. (So, like many other people, once I'd heard of it, pirated a copy from a friend, tried it and liked it, I went out and bought it.) 'Pile it high and sell it cheap' simply proved to be a more profitable business model—even for speciality products such as compilers.

The industry then swung to legal solutions. The main initiative was to establish anti-piracy trade organizations in most countries (in the United States, the Software Publishers' Association), which brought a number of high-profile prosecutions against large companies that had been condoning widespread use of pirate PC software. This was followed by harrassing medium and even small businesses with threatening letters demanding details of the company's policy on enforcing copyright—holding out a carrot of approved software audit schemes and a stick of possible raids by enforcement squads. All sorts of tricks were used to get pirates to incriminate themselves. A typical ruse was the *salted list*. For example, one trade directory product I worked on contained details of a number of bogus companies, with phone numbers directed to the publisher's help desk whose staff would ask for the caller's company and check it off against the list of paid subscribers.

Eventually, the industry discovered that the law not only provides tools for enforcement, but sets limits too. The time-honored technique of using time bombs has now been found to be illegal in a number of jurisdictions. In 1993, for example, a software company director in Scunthorpe, England, received a criminal conviction under Britain's Computer Misuse Act for "making an unauthorized modification" to a system after he used a time bomb to enforce payment of an disputed invoice [194]. Many jurisdictions now consider time bombs unacceptable unless the customer is adequately notified of their existence at the time of purchase.

The emphasis is now swinging somewhat back in the direction of technical mechanisms. Site license agreements are enforced using *license servers*, which are somewhat like dongles but are implemented on PCs that sit on a corporate network and limit the number of copies of an application that can run simultaneously. These servers can still be defeated by disassembling the application code, but as code becomes larger this gets harder; combined with the threat of legal action, they are often adequate. Other mechanisms include issuing such frequent updates to software that life becomes tiresome outside the official distribution chain; and (a cynic might say) making the operating system so unreliable that every few months it will crash completely, forcing all software to be reloaded from the distribution media.

The model to which the software industry is converging is thus one that combines technical and legal measures, understanding the limits of both, and accepting that a certain amount of copying will take place (with which you try to leverage fully-paid sales). One of the more revealing dicta of Billionaire Bill is:

> Although about three million computers get sold every year in China, people don't pay for the software. Someday they will, though. And as long as they're going to steal it, we want them to steal ours. They'll get sort of addicted, and then we'll somehow figure out how to collect sometime in the next decade [332].

The latest developments have to do with online registration. If you design your product so that customers interact with your Web site—for example, to download the latest exchange rates, virus signatures or security patches—then you can keep a log of everyone who uses your software. But this can be dangerous. When Microsoft tried it with Registration Wizard in Windows 95, it caused a storm of protest. Also, a colleague found that he couldn't upgrade Windows 98 on a machine on his yacht since it was always offline. But the wind appears to be blowing in this direction.

It's also worth noting that different methods are used to counter different threats. Large-scale commercial counterfeiting may be detected by monitoring product serial numbers registered online; but such operations are found and closed down by using investigative agencies to trace their product back through the supply chains, and people are deterred from getting into the business in the first place using a combination of the seals and other secure packaging techniques discussed in Chapter 12.

That is more or less what's being done in the personal and small business sectors, but with medium and large businesses, the main risk is that fewer legal copies will be purchased than there are machines that run them. The usual countermeasure is to combine legal pressure from software trade associations with site licenses and rewards for whistleblowers. It's significant that companies such as Microsoft make the vast bulk of their sales from business rather than personal customers. This is perhaps the main reason that the industry holds back from using online registration to enforce copyright aggressively against personal users. The potential extra revenues are small given the possible costs of a public backlash. Other considerations are privacy laws (especially in Europe), and the difficulty of tracing people who change addresses or trade PCs secondhand.

To sum up: none of the low-cost protection technologies available at the beginning of the twenty-first century is foolproof, especially against a determined opponent. But by using the right combination of them, a large software vendor can usually get a tolerable result—especially if prices are not too extortionate and the vendor isn't too unpopular. Small software companies are under less pressure, as their products tend to be more specialized, and the risk of copying is lower, so they can often get away with making little or no effort to control copying.

There are also many alternative business models. One is to give away a limited version of the product, and sell online a password that unlocks its full functionality. Unix was popularized by giving it away free to universities, while companies had to pay. A variant on this theme is to give basic software away free to individuals but to charge companies, as Netscape did. An even more radical model is to give software away completely free, and make money from selling services ranging from consultancy and support to advertising on a Web site—as the Linux industry is now doing.

This experience has led many computer people to believe that ultimately the solution for "Hollywood's" problem lies in a change of business model. But before we dive into the world of protecting multimedia content, let's look briefly at a few historical precedents.

20.2.2 Books

Shapiro and Varian present a useful historical lesson in the rise of book publishing [696]. In 1800, there were only 80,000 frequent readers in England; until then, most books were serious philosophical or theological tomes. After the invention of the novel, a mass market emerged for books, and circulating libraries sprung up to service it. The educated classes were appalled, and the printers were frightened that the libraries would deprive them of sales.

But the libraries so whetted people's appetite for books that the number of readers grew to 5,000,000 by 1850. Sales of books soared as people bought books they'd first borrowed from a library. The library movement turned out to have been the printers' greatest ally, and helped create a whole new market for mass-market books.

20.2.3 Audio

Pirates have also been copying music and other audio much longer than software. Paganini was so worried that people would copy his violin concertos that he distributed the scores himself to the orchestra just before rehearsals and performances, and collected them again afterward. (As a result, many of his works were lost to posterity.)

In recent years, there have been one or two flurries of industry concern. When the cassette recorder came along in the 1960s, the record industry lobbied for (and in some countries got) a tax on audiocassettes, to be distributed to copyright holders. Technical measures were also tried. The Beatles' record "Sergeant Pepper" contained a 20 KHz spoiler tone, which should in theory have combined with the 21 KHz bias frequency of the tape to produce a 1 KHz whistle that would spoil the sound. In practice it didn't work, as many record players didn't pick up the spoiler tone. But in practice this didn't matter. Cassettes turned out not to be a huge problem because the degradation in quality is noticeable on home equipment; many people just used them to record music to listen to in their cars. Then, in the 1980s, the arrival of the Sony Walkman made cassettes big business; and although there was some copying, there were also huge sales of prerecorded cassettes, and the music industry cleaned up.

The introduction of *digital audio tape* (DAT) caused the next worry, because a perfect copy of the contents of a CD could be made. The eventual response was to introduce a *serial copy management system* (SCMS)—a single bit in the tape header that would indicate whether a track could be copied or not [410]. The idea was that copies made from a CD would be marked so that they could not be copied again; in this way, people could make copies of CDs they already owned, to listen to on the move, but couldn't make copies of the copies. This didn't work well, as the no-more-copies bit is ignored by many recorders and can be defeated by simple filtering. Again, this didn't matter as DAT didn't become widely used. (CD-ROMs also have a no-copy bit in the track header but this is almost universally ignored.)

Audio copying has recently become a headline concern again, thanks to the popularity of the MP3 format for compressing audio. Previously, digital audio was protected by its size—a CD full of uncompressed music can take 650 Mb. However, MP3 enables people to take an audio CD track of tens of megabytes and squeeze it into a few hundred kilobytes, making it practical to download over a dial-up modem line. Usage in universities is particularly heavy; in 1998, some 40% of the network traffic at MIT was MP3 traffic. Some students have become underground disc jockeys and relay audio streams around campus—without paying royalties to the copyright owners.

The initial response of the industry was to look for technical fixes. Alternative audio compression technologies were developed that did contain copyright protection mechanisms (for example, [483]), but failed to take off. Hollywood is still trying to pressure the computer industry into making platforms on which music copying is hard, but this is not happening.

- First, the PC is an open platform and it's intrinsically easy to copy bit streams inside it. There have been proposals to close the platform, such as by incorporating bus encryption (which I discussed in Section 14.5.2) into cache controller chips, or even the main Intel processor line. But the first step in this direction—a processor serial number in the Pentium III—met with huge public resistance. Attempts to keep DVD proprietary meant preventing Linux PCs from using DVDs, and have led to a fight I'll discuss later. So far all we've seen are hacks, such as encrypting the music stream all the way to the sound card driver software. The response to this is a modified sound card that grabs the deciphered data.

■ Second, the success of new hardware depends on the availability of software, and vice versa. To launch a new platform for audio, it had better be backward-compatible with existing CDs and players. One trick that has been proposed is to encrypt only the least significant bits of the music track, and decode them in the sound card driver in the PC operating system. This way, people with existing CD players can get music, and people with authorized copy protected equipment can get higher quality music. However, the quality is most important with classical tracks, which are not economically important, and in any case the complete signal can be extracted using modified sound cards. Finally, excluding Linux users from next-generation audio will probably lead to the same kind of fight as over DVD.

■ In any case, many CDs have been sold that contain easily reproducible, perfect-quality digital copies—in effect, billions of golden master disks that are completely outside the industry's control.

The next step Hollywood took was to sue, with the main targets being Web sites that allowed MP3s to be shared. Commercial MP3 sites are being bulldozed into setting up subscription channels and generally making their peace with the music industry. But they have been replaced in the firing line by systems such as Napster and Freenet, which enable users who wish to swap tracks to get in touch with each other directly. I'll come back to the potential of these systems when I discuss privacy mechanisms later in the chapter. Meanwhile, I can see no compelling reason why audio protection should develop all that differently from software protection: technical solutions that people found ways to defeat, followed by a legal onslaught that ran out of steam eventually, finally settling down to a mix of technical and legal controls that limit piracy even if it can't be eliminated entirely.

This is not to say that I expect a one-size-fits-all copyright control package to be developed. Just as Microsoft has different needs from a small specialist firm, and uses different methods, so also one can expect rather different controls on the current Top of the Pops than there will be on a specialist cult item such as a CD by the Bonzo Dog Doo-Dah Band.

■ In the former case, the density of listeners is such that a track can spread widely by personal copying, but there is a very short shelf-life. Speed and fashion will be everything. Indeed, sales of fashion merchandise may become much more important than CD sales; as with the Netscape/Linux business model, it may make sense to give the "product" away free and make money on the "maintenance" (tours, T-shirts, fan club . . .).

■ In the latter case, the appeal is timeless but to a scattered minority of enthusiasts, who copy tracks because they feel exploited by having to pay $17.95

for a CD that they already have on vinyl. Because of this, it might not even be possible to sue "violators" in many jurisdictions. So the trick may be slightly keener pricing and/or packaging that appeals to the collector.

I also expect that Hollywood will follow the software industry and adopt a somewhat more mature attitude to copying. After all, 70% of a market worth $100 billion is better than 98% of a market worth $50 billion. And just as a certain amount of copying helped market software, it can help music sales too: the Grateful Dead encouraged bootleg taping because they had learned it didn't harm their sales.

20.2.4 Video and Pay-TV

The early history of videocassettes is very similar to that of audio cassettes. At first Hollywood was terrified, and refused to release movies for home viewing. Again, there were technical measures taken to prevent copying—such as the Macrovision system that adds spurious synchronization pulses to confuse the recording circuitry of domestic VCRs—but again these turned out to be straightforward for technically savvy users to defeat. Then Hollywood became paranoid about video rental stores, just as book publishers had been about libraries: but Video rentals greatly increased the number of VCRs sold, and whetted people's desire to own their favorite movies. VCRs and videocassettes became mass-market products rather than rock stars' toys, and now sales of prerecorded cassettes make up most of the income of firms such as Disney. The business model has changed so that the cinema release is really just advertising for the sales of the video.

And now that many of the world's pre-teens demand that their parents build them a collection of Disney cassettes, just like their friends have, a videocassette pirate must make the packaging look original. This reduces the problem to an industrial counterfeiting one. As with mass-market software before the onset of online registration, or with perfumes and Swiss watches today, enforcement involves sending out field agents to buy cassettes, look for forgeries, trace the supply chain and prosecute the bad guys.

Much more interesting technical protection mechanisms have been built into the last few generations of pay-TV equipment.

The advent of pay-TV, whether delivered by cable or satellite, created a need for *conditional access* mechanisms, to allow station operators to restrict reception of a channel in various ways. If they bought only the rights to screen a movie in Poland then they'd have to block German or Russian viewers within the satellite footprint from watching. Porn channel operators needed to prevent reception in countries like Britain and Ireland with savage censorship laws. Most operators wanted to be able to charge extra for specific events such as boxing matches.

20.2.4.1 Typical System Architecture

A number of systems were developed, and their evolution was determined largely by the hardware cost of deciphering video (for a history of set-top boxes, see [186]). The first-generation systems, available since the 1970s, were crude analog devices which used tricks such as inverting the video signal from time to time, interfering with the synchronization, and inserting spikes to confuse the TV's automatic gain control. They were easy enough to implement, but also easy to defeat; breaking them didn't involve cryptanalysis, just an oscilloscope and some patience.

The second generation of systems appeared in the late 1980s and employed a hybrid of analogue and digital technologies—the broadcast was analogue, the subscriber control was digital. These included systems such as Videocrypt, Eurocrypt, and Nagravision. A typical such system has three components:

- There is a subscription management service at the station, which enciphers the outgoing video, embeds various *entitlement control messages* (ECMs) in it, and issues access tokens such as smartcards to subscribers.

- There is a *set-top box* which converts the cable or satellite signal into one the TV can deal with. This includes descrambling it.

- Finally there is the subscriber smartcard, which personalizes the device and controls which programs the set-top box is allowed to descramble. It does this by interpreting the ECMs and by providing keys to the descrambling circuit in the set-top box.

This arrangement means that the complex, expensive processes such as bulk video scrambling can be done in a mass-produced standard device with a long product life, while security-critical functions—which may need to be replaced in a hurry after a hack—can be sold to the customer in a low-cost token that can easily be replaced. If the set-top box itself had to replaced every time the system was hacked, the economics would be much less attractive.

The set-top box decodes the ECMs from the input data stream, and passes them to the card; the card processes the ECMs to get both control messages (such as "smartcard number 123356: your subscriber hasn't paid, stop working until further notice"); and keys, known as *control words*, that are passed to the set-top box. The set-top box uses the control words to descramble the video and audio streams.

20.2.4.2 *Video Scrambling Techniques*

The most common video scrambling technique was *cut-and-rotate*. This scrambles one line of video at a time by cutting it at a point determined by a control byte and swapping the left and right halves (see Figure 20.1). This involved analogue-to-digital conversion

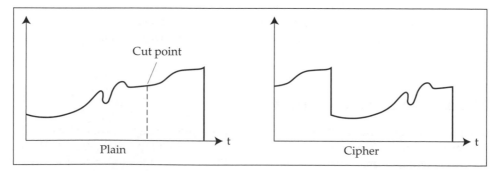

Figure 20.1   Cut-and-rotate scrambling.

Figure 20.2   Scrambled video frame.

of the video signal, storage in a buffer, and digital-to-analogue conversion after rotation, a process that could just about be shoehorned into a low-cost custom VLSI chip using the technology of the mid-1980s.

One systemic vulnerability of systems that encrypt only one line of video at a time was that successive lines of video were usually correlated, so it was often possible to reconstruct the image using signal processing techniques. This was first done by Markus Kuhn in 1995, and required the use of a supercomputer at the University of Erlangen to do in real time. Figure 20.2 shows a frame of enciphered video, and Figure 20.3 the same frame after processing. By the time of writing, it's possible to do this on a powerful PC (though still not quite in real time) [733]. If this attack had been feasible earlier, it would have caused a complete break of the system, because regardless of how well the smartcard managed the keys, the video signal could be retrieved without them. But the scrambling technique lasted (just) long enough; pay-TV operators are now moving their customers to fully digital systems in which attacks using properties of the analogue signal are irrelevant.

The generation of the control bytes is of independent interest. Every half second or so, the smartcard supplies the set-top box with a new control word, and this is loaded into a keystream generator which works as follows. There are two linear feedback shift registers (of lengths 31 and 29 in the Eurocrypt system) which generate long linear sequences. Some of the bits of register 1 are used as address lines to a multiplexer, which selects a bit from register 2; this bit becomes the next bit of the keystream sequence. Each successive byte of output becomes a control byte for the scrambler (see Figure 20.4).

Figure 20.3   Processed video frame.

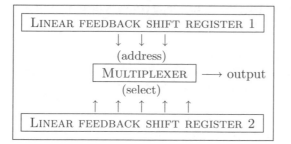

Figure 20.4   The multiplexer generator.

The designers intended that breaking this cipher should involve guessing the key; and as it is 60 bits long a guess would take on average 2^{59} trials, which is uneconomic—as it has to be done about twice a second. But it turns out that the cipher has a shortcut attack. The trick is to guess the contents of register 1, use this address information to place bits of the observed keystream in register 2, and if this causes a clash, reject the current guess for register 1. (I discovered this attack in 1985, and it's what got me interested in cryptography.) Now the high-order four bits or so of each control word are easy to deduce from interline correlations—it's the least-significant bits you really have to work hard for. So you can easily get about half the bits from a segment of keystream, and reconstruct the control word using cryptanalysis. But this computation is still comparable with the full signal processing attack. The stream cipher, like the scrambling technique, may be weak, but it survived (just) long enough. So the pirates had to attack the subscriber management mechanisms.

20.2.4.3 Subscriber Management Techniques

Given a population of set-top boxes that will unscramble broadcast video given a stream of control words, the next problem is to see to it that only paying customers can generate the control words. In general, this can be done with whitelists or blacklists. But the bandwidth available to last-generation pay-TV systems was low—typically, of the order of ten ECMs per second could be sent, or just over half a million a day. Thus, the blacklist approach was the main one. With a subscriber base of five million customers, sending an individual message to each customer would take over a week.

The basic protocol is that the smartcard interprets the ECMs; and if the current program is one the subscriber is allowed to watch, then a MAC is computed on a series of ECMs using a master key held in the card and supplied to the set-top box as the control word:

$$CW = MAC(K; ECM_1, ECM_2, ECM_3, ECM_4)$$

In this way, if a subscriber stops paying, their card can be inactivated by sending an ECM that orders it to stop issuing control words; and it needs access to the ECM stream in order to compute the control words at all.

20.2.4.4 What Went Wrong

The first attacks on this system were protocol attacks. Since the control word sent from the smartcard to the set-top box is the same for every set-top box currently unscrambling the program, it is possible for one person to place a PC between the smartcard and the set-top box, record the stream of control words, and post them to the Internet: other people can video-record the scrambled program, and unscramble it later after downloading the control word file [532]. Servers for this key log attack exist, but they are a minor nuisance to the pay-TV industry; not many viewers are prepared to get a special adapter to connect their PC to their set-top box. Others included *blockers*, which would prevent ECMs addressed to your card from being delivered to it; this way, you could cancel your subscription without the station operator being able to cancel your service. Others exploited a master key leakage: someone bought a second-hand PC, looked out of curiosity to see whether there were any interesting deleted files on the hard disk, and managed to undelete a complete subscriber management system for one pay-TV operator—including embedded master keys.

Once this "low-hanging fruit" had been picked, the commercial pirates turned to reverse-engineering customer smartcards using a series of attacks which I described in Chapter 14. But hardware-level fixes were limited to new card issues, and the operators didn't want to issue a new card more than once a year as it cost several dollars per subscriber, and the subscriptions were usually less than $20 a month. So other defensive techniques had to be found.

Litigation was tried, but it didn't work as well as the operators hoped. A lawsuit was lost against a pirate in Ireland, which for a while became a haven from which pirates sold cards by mail order all over Europe. The industry's lobbying muscle was deployed to bring in European law to override Dublin, but this took years and the losses were getting significant. By the middle of 1995, for example, the main U.K. satellite TV station (Sky-TV) was losing 5% of its revenue to pirate cards.

20.2.4.5 How It Was Fixed

All through the mid-1990s, pirates and the operators engaged in a war of countermeasures and counter-countermeasures. The operators would buy pirate cards, analyze them, and develop all sorts of tricks to cause them to fail. The problem faced by the operators was this: when all the secrets in your system are compromised, how can you still fight back against the pirates?

This might seem impossible to the conventional way of thinking about cryptology, but the operators managed it. One of their more effective techniques was an ECM whose packet contents were executed as code by the smartcard; in this way, the existing card base could be upgraded on the fly, and implementation differences between the genuine and pirate cards could be exploited. Any computation that would give a different answer on the two platforms—even if only as a result of an unintentional timing condition—could be fed into the MAC algorithm and used to make the pirate cards deliver invalid control words.

It's worth looking briefly at how to revoke the access rights of subscribers who stop paying. Each of the subscriber smartcards contains a subscriber key k_i, and a binary tree of intermediate group keys $KGij$ links the subscriber keys to the currently active master key KM (Figure 20.5). Each operational card knows all the group keys in the path between it and the master key. In this scheme, if (say) key $k2$ appears in pirate cards and has to be revoked, the operator will send out a stream of packets that let all the other subscriber cards compute a new master key KM'. The first packet will be $\{KM'\}_{KG12}$, which will let half the subscribers compute KM' at once; then there will be a KM' encrypted under an updated version of $KG11$: $\{KM'\}_{KG'11}$; then this new group key $KG'11$ encrypted under $KG22$; and so on. The effect is that, even with ten million customers, the operator has to transmit fewer than 50 ECMs to do a complete key change. Of course, this isn't a complete solution: operators also need to think about how to deal with pirate cards that contain several subscriber keys, and how leaked keys can by identified without having to go to the trouble of reverse-engineering pirate cards. However, the binary revocation tree is a useful tool in the countermeasures war. (Using individual keys to protect group keys is not really new; Marks recounts how, during World War II, the Special Operations Executive sent its agents *iodoforms*, or open codes, enciphered under their personal keys [523]. When an iodoform was broadcast on the radio, it transmitted an order such as 'blow up a railway bridge' to many agents simultaneously.) Other applications with similar requirements include managing the shared "keys of the day" in naval task forces.

Psychological measures were also used. For example, one cable-TV station broadcast a special offer for a free T-shirt, but prevented legitimate viewers from seeing the 800-number to call; this got it a list of the pirates' customers. Economic factors also made a difference. Pay-TV pirates depend for their success on time-to-market as much as conventional software firms: a pirate who could produce a 99% correct forgery in

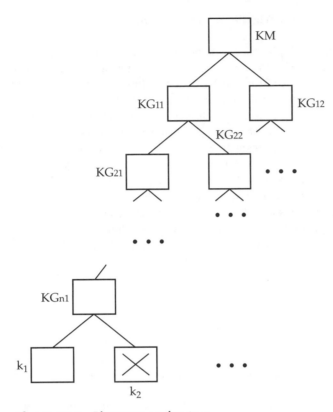

Figure 20.5 Binary revocation tree.

three weeks would wipe out a competitor who produced a 99.9% forgery after three months. So pirate cards also have bugs, and exploiting them efficiently involves an understanding of pirate economics. It's best to let a pirate build up a substantial user base before you pull the plug on him, as this will destroy his credibility with more potential customers than an immediate response would. But if you leave him too long, he may acquire both the financial and technical resources to upgrade his customers to a high-quality forgery.

The main technical lesson learned by the pay-TV industry was to plan in advance for security recovery, and to hide a number of features in its products that weren't used initially but could be activated later. (As usual, the same lesson had been learned years previously by another industry—in this particular case the banknote printers.)

Eventually, the smartcards were made a bit more difficult to forge by including proprietary encryption algorithms in the processor hardware. When the attacker could no longer just read out the algorithm with a probing station, but had to reverse engineer part of the chip, it reduced to a few dozen the number of laboratories with the technical capability to do attacks. Many of these laboratories were drawn into the industry's orbit by consultancy deals or other kinds of sponsorship. Those that remained outside the tent, and appeared to pose a threat, were watched carefully. Vigorous legal enforcement provided the last link in the chain. The industry hunted down the main commercial pirates and put them out of business, whether by having them jailed or by drowning them in litigation.

For example, in the last big pay-TV piracy case in the twentieth century, British pirate Chris Cary was convicted of forging Sky-TV smartcards, whose design he had had reverse engineered by a company in Canada for $105,000. He then sold forgeries through a front company in Ireland, where counterfeit cards were not illegal at the time [568]. Sky TV's security consultants infiltrated a spy into Cary's Dublin sales office, and she quietly photocopied enough documents to prove that the operation was really being run from England [403]. The British police didn't want to prosecute, so Sky brought a private prosecution and had Cary convicted. When he later escaped from jail, Sky's private detectives relentlessly hunted him down and eventually caught him in New Zealand, where he had fled using a passport in a dead person's name [367].

The pay-TV story reinforces the business lesson that one must make the engineering and legal aspects of copyright protection work together. Neither is likely to be adequate on its own. An example of how not to do it comes from the world of DVD.

20.2.5 DVD

The consumer electronics industry introduced the *digital video disk* (DVD), later re-named the *digital versatile disk*, in 1996. As usual, Hollywood took fright and said that unless DVD had a decent copy protection mechanism, first-class movies wouldn't be released for it. So a mechanism called the *content scrambling system* (CSS) was introduced.

There is also a scheme whereby the world is divided into five regions, and disks are supposed to run only on players from some designated list of regions. This was to support the traditional business practice of releasing a movie in the United States first, then in Europe, and so on, in order to minimize the loss if it flops. This region code was the first to be broken and is now increasingly ignored by manufacturers. The globalization of markets for products such as DVDs is destroying the market for DVD players that will play only locally manufactured disks.

This left CSS, which was known to be vulnerable by the time that DVD was launched [601]. One industry story was that the designers had been told to come up with a copy protection scheme in two weeks, to use no more than 3,000 gates, and to limit the keylength to 40 bits so the equipment wouldn't fall foul of U.S. export regulations; another story was that DVD consortium only ever intended to compel player manufacturers to license the CSS patent from Matsushita, a condition of which would be implementation of other copy protection mechanisms [119]. No matter whose fault the design was, it's actually quite curious that their system held up for three years.

The detailed description of CSS is currently the subject of frantic litigation, with numerous injunctions issued in the United States against Web sites that have published the code. This is almost certainly futile, as there are plenty sites outside the United States where you can get it (such as [737]). However, because my publishers are located in the United States and I don't want them spending all my royalties on lawyers, here's a suitably abbreviated description.

CSS is based on a stream cipher which is similar to that in Figure 20.5 except that the multiplexer is replaced with a full adder: each successive keystream bit is obtained by adding together the next two outputs from the shift registers with carry. Combining the xor operations of the shift registers with the add-with-carry of the combiner can actually give a strong cipher, if there are (say) five shift registers with coprime lengths greater than 70 [656]. But in CSS, there are only two registers, with lengths 17 and 25, so there is a 2^{16} shortcut attack of exactly the same kind as the one discussed above. Where the cipher is used to protect keys rather than data, there is a further mangling step; but this only increases the complexity to 2^{25}.

The DVD protocol is as follows. Each player has one or more keys specific to the manufacturer, and each DVD disk has a disk key, kd, encrypted under each of the current manufacturer keys, kmi (409 of them in 1999): $\{kd\}_{km1}, \{kd\}_{km2}, \{kd\}_{km3}, \ldots, \{kd\}_{km409}$. There is also a hash of kd, computed by encrypting it with itself: $\{kd\}_{kd}$. The actual content is protected under sector keys derived from kd. Of course, given that the cipher can be broken with 2^{25} effort, any disk key can be found from a single disk hash.

So CSS contravened Kerckhoffs' principle, in that it depended for its protection on the algorithm remaining secret. The DVD consortium appears not to have understood this, as it hoped to keep enough of the manufacturer keys secret by economic pressure. The idea was that if any manufacturer's master key got leaked, then it wouldn't be used on future disks, so his players wouldn't be able to play new releases. So manufacturers would implement decent tamper resistance—or so it was hoped. But the design of CSS doesn't support this. Given any key in the system, all the others can be found at once. Also, the economics of mass-producing consumer electronics doesn't allow the kind of processors required to give serious tamper protection.

Another set of problems came from the fact that the PC is an open platform. The DVD consortium's chosen method of dealing with this was that people producing DVD player software had to obfuscate their code so that it would be hard to reverse-engineer. Papers duly appeared on tricks for systematic software obfuscation [58]. These tricks may have pushed up the cost of reverse engineering from a few days of effort to a few weeks, but once the CSS design was out, that was it.

An even more serious problem with the openness of the PC came from Linux, the open source PC operating system used by millions of people. The DVD consortium's philosophy and architecture was not consistent with making DVD drivers available to the Linux community. So as PCs with CD drives started being replaced in the stores with PCs fitted with DVD drives, the Linux user community either had to break CSS or give up using Linux in favor of Windows. Under the circumstances, even if every DVD player had contained a pay-TV-grade smartcard processor, it was only a matter of time before someone read it out.[1]

One result of the break is a program (DeCSS) that will unprotect any DVD. The industry's reaction was to reach for their lawyers. Web sites in the United States which host DeCSS get hammered with injunctions, which simply cause the software to become ever

---

[1] This error may well be repeated with the *secure digital music initiative* (SDMI), a proposed replacement for MP3. SDMI will use encrypted audio streams that will be decrypted in the soundcard driver software in the PC operating system. There will also be a watermarking scheme. However, depriving Linux users—who probably include most of the world's computer science and engineering students—access to the latest audio unless they mount the despised Windows operating system is guaranteed to create many capable motivated opponents. The likely watermarking scheme—echo hiding—was already broken in [610] by Fabien Petitcolas.

more widely distributed and make the industry look foolish [491]. There are some quite unpleasant undercurrents, though. For example, copyright law traditionally allows *fair use*, which includes copying parts of a work for the purpose of scholarship, quotation, and even ridicule; the movie industry lawyers seek to squash this for digital media so that copyright holders have completely unfettered control over what happens to a digital work. This would be disastrous for universities, public libraries, and many other bodies, where the exploitation of fair use rights is strongly entrenched. So the battle referred to by Barlow in the quote at the head of this chapter has started.

A leading U.S. authority, Samuelson, takes the view that some copying is beneficial to publishers in a much wider range of industries than just software [665]. A European expert put it more strongly: copyright laws are tolerated only because they are not enforced against the large numbers of petty offenders [610]. It is worth noting that even if Hollywood gets all it wants in the U.S. courts, it's unlikely to get quite the same result in Europe, where copyright law specifically allows reverse engineering for the purpose of building compatible equipment, and where a video rental treaty may protect temporary copies [666]. I'll return to all this in Chapter 21 when we discuss e-policy.

Another point (made for example in [491]) is that small-scale copying of DVDs is uneconomic anyway, as home-burnable DVD disks cost more than prerecorded ones; that large-scale copying in the Far East already happens; and that the real reason for the litigation is that the publication of CSS enables anyone to build a DVD player without paying royalties to the DVD consortium.

Anyway, DVD is following the usual pattern: Hollywood terrified, and refusing to release its best movies; technical measures taken to prevent copying, which got broken; then litigation. A reasonable person might hope that once again the studios will see sense in the end, and make a lot of money from selling DVDs. There will be copying, of course, but it's not entirely trivial yet—even a DSL modem takes hours to send a 4Gb DVD movie to a friend, and PC disk space is also an issue. Eventually, as DVD drives replace CD drives in all PCs, we can expect to see rewriteable DVDs being widely used for backup; and it's completely predictable that whatever new mechanisms are fielded to prevent copying will be circumvented. But I also predict that in 10 years' time, the lineup of DVDs on my shelf will be pretty much the same as my videocassette lineup is today—about 50 prerecorded cassettes and maybe two dozen home-recorded ones, the former bought mostly for the family and the latter being mostly old TV programs that have a direct relevance to my work. I'm sure the industry can live with that.

Meanwhile, strenuous efforts are being made to improve DVD security by fitting the next generation of players with mechanisms based on copyright marking. This is an interesting technology, and worth a look.

20.3 Information Hiding

Hollywood's interest in finding new mechanisms for protecting copyright came together in the mid-1990s with the military's interest in unobtrusive communications and public concerns over government efforts to control cryptography, and started to drive rapid developments in the field of *information hiding*. This largely refers to techniques that enable data to be hidden in other data, such as when a secret message is hidden in an MP3 audio file, or a program's serial number is embedded in the order in which certain instructions are executed.

The Hollywood interest is in *copyright marks*, which can be hidden unobtrusively in digital audio, video, and artwork. These are generally either *watermarks*, which are hidden copyright messages, or *fingerprints*, which are hidden serial numbers.

The privacy interest is in *steganography*, whose purpose is to embed a message in some cover medium in such a way that its very existence remains undetectable. A common conceptual model, proposed by Simmons [700, 707], is as follows. Alice and Bob are in jail, and wish to hatch an escape plan; all their communications pass through the warden, Willie; and if Willie detects any encrypted messages, he will frustrate their plan by throwing them into solitary confinement. So they must find some way of hiding their secret messages in an innocuous-looking covertext. As in the related field of cryptography, we assume that the mechanism in use is known to the warden, so the security must depend solely on a secret key that Alice and Bob have somehow managed to share.

There is some similarity with electronic warfare. First, if steganography is seen as a low-probability-of-intercept communication, then copyright marking is like the related jam-resistant communication technique: it may use much the same methods but in order to resist focused attacks it is likely to have a much lower bit rate. We can think of Willie as the pirate who tries to mangle the audio or video signal in such a way as to cause the copyright mark detector to fail. Second, techniques such as direct sequence spread spectrum, which were originally developed for electronic warfare, are finding wide use in the information hiding community.

Of course, copyright marks don't have to be hidden to be effective. Some TV stations embed their logo in a visible but unobtrusive manner in the corner of the picture, and many ECMS systems have control tags bundled quite visibly with the content. In many cases, this is the appropriate technology. However, in what follows I'll concentrate on hidden copyright marks.

20.3.1 The DVD Marking Concept

A current objective of the DVD consortium is to find a copyright marking scheme that will enforce serial copy management. Videos might be unmarked, marked "never copy," or marked "copy once only"; compliant players would not record a video marked "never copy," and when recording one marked "copy once only" would change its mark to "never copy." Commercially sold videos would be marked "never copy," while TV broadcasts and similar material would be marked "copy once only." In this way, the DVD players available to consumers would allow unlimited copying of home videos and time-shifted viewing of TV programs, but could not easily be abused for commercial piracy. There is an overview of the proposed mechanisms in [119].

The basic idea is simple [504]. For each disk, choose a *ticket*, X, which can be a random number, plus copy control information, plus possibly some information unique to the physical medium, such as the wobble in the lead-in track. Use a one-way hash function h to compute $h(X)$ and then $h(h(X))$. Embed $h(h(X))$ in the video as a hidden copyright mark. See to it that compliant machines look for a watermark, and if they find one will refuse to play a track unless they are supplied with $h(X)$, which they check by hashing it and comparing it with the mark. Finally, arrange things so that a compliant device will record a marked track only if given X, in which case only $h(X)$ is written to the new disk. In this way, a "copy once only" track in the original medium becomes a "copy no more" track in the new medium.

Doing copy generation management using embedded marks, rather than with attached data, has the advantage that it can survive conversion from digital to analogue and back to digital. This leads to a number of problems. First, we need a method of embedding a mark in audio or video, which—even though it might take a lot of effort to embed—can be detected readily and is difficult for an attacker to remove. Second, the detection must be carried out by mass-market equipment, that is, using cheap processors or custom silicon with a limited gate count, and have a low false positive alarm rate [554]. For example, if your legitimate DVD player were to detect a mark in your wedding video by mistake, you'd have to buy a pirate player to watch it.

20.3.2 General Information-Hiding Techniques

Information hiding goes back even further than cryptology, having its roots in camouflage. Probably the first historical mention is in Herodotus who records tricks used during the wars between the Greeks and the Persians—including hiding a message in the belly of a hare carried by a hunter, tattooing it on the shaven head of a slave whose hair was then allowed to grow back, and writing it on the wooden base under the wax of a writing tablet [377]. Francis Bacon proposed a system that embedded a binary message in a book at one bit per letter by alternating between two different fonts [607]. Until quite modern times, most writers considered hiding confidential information much more important than enciphering it [805]. Military organizations still largely hold this view and have used all sorts of technologies, from the microdots used by spies in much of the twentieth century to the low-probability-of-intercept radios discussed in Chapter 16.

When it comes to hiding data in other data, the modern terminology of the subject is as follows [614]. The copyright mark, or in the case of steganography, the *embedded text*, is hidden in the *cover-text* producing the *marked text* or in the case of steganography the *stego-text*. In most cases, additional secret information is used during this process; this is the *marking key* or *stego-key*, and some function of it is typically needed to recover the mark or embedded text. Here, the word "text" can be replaced by "audio," "video," and so on, as appropriate.

A wide variety of embedding schemes have been proposed.

- In many ways the obvious technique is to hide the mark or secret message in the least-significant bits of the audio or video signal. Many public domain steganography tools do this. But it isn't usually a very good strategy, as the hidden data is easy to detect statistically (the least-significant bits are no longer correlated with the rest of the image), and it's trivial to remove or replace. It's also severely damaged by lossy compression techniques.

- A classic technique is to hide the mark or secret message at a location determined by the secret key. This was first invented in classical China. The sender and receiver had copies of a paper mask, which had holes cut out of it at random locations. The sender would place his mask over a blank sheet of paper, write his message in the holes, then remove it and compose a cover message including the characters of the secret embedded message. This trick was reinvented in the sixteenth century by the Italian mathematician Cardan and is now known to cryptographers as the Cardan grille [428].

- A modern implementation of this hides a copyright or other message in a `.gif` format image as follows. A secret key is expanded to a keystream, which selects an appropriate number of pixels. The embedded message is the parity of the color codes for these pixels. In practice, even a quite large number of the pixels in an image can have their color changed to that of a similar one in the palette without any visible effects [413]. However, if all the pixels are tweaked in this way, then the hidden data is easy to remove by just tweaking them again. A better result is obtained if the cover image and embedding method are such that (say) only 10% of the pixels can safely be tweaked. Then, if the warden repeats the process, but with a different key, an independent 10% of the pixels will be tweaked and only 10% of the bits of the hidden data will be corrupted.

- In general, the introduction of noise or distortion—as happens with lossy compression—will introduce errors into the hidden data almost regardless of the embedding method unless some kind of error correcting code is added. A system proposed for banknote marking, Patchwork, uses a repetition code—the key selects two subsets of pixels, one of which is marked by increasing the luminosity and the other by decreasing it. This embeds a single bit; the note is either watermarked using that key, or it isn't [96, 357]. In the general case, one may want to embed more than one bit, and have the embedded data to survive very high levels of induced errors. So a common technique is to use direct sequence spread spectrum techniques borrowed from electronic warfare [748].

- Spread spectrum encoding is often done in a transform space to make its effects less perceptible and more robust against common forms of compression. These techniques are also commonly used in conjunction with perceptual filtering, which emphasizes the encoding in the noisiest or perceptually most significant parts of the image or music track, where it will be least obtrusive, and de-emphasizes it in quiet passages of music or large expanses of color [127].

- Some schemes use the characteristics of particular media, such as a scheme for marking print media by moving text lines up or down by a three-hundredth of an inch [135], or adding extra echoes to music below the threshold of perception [96]. So far, such techniques don't seem to have become as robust, as generic techniques based on keyed embedding using transform spaces, spread spectrum, and perceptual filtering.

Progress in copyright marking and steganography was very rapid in the last few years of the twentieth century. Its history has repeated that of cryptology, but on a much more compressed timescale: people invented marking schemes, which other people broke, and eventually the technology became more mature and robust.

20.3.3 Attacks on Copyright-Marking Schemes

Throughout this book, I've described attacks on cryptographic systems that occasionally involved cryptanalysis, but more often relied on mistaken assumptions, protecting the wrong things, protocol failures, and the opportunistic exploitation of implementation bugs. Copyright marking has been no different.

■ In the beginning, many people assumed that the main market would be watermarking—embedding hidden copyright messages so that ownership of a work could be proved in court. This has turned out to be mistaken. Intellectual property lawyers almost never have any difficulty in proving ownership of an exhibit; and they don't rely on technical measures that might confuse a jury, but on documents such as contracts with bands and model release forms. The legal use of copyright marks may rather be for fingerprints, namely hidden serial numbers.

■ The first large vendor of marking systems—Digimarc—then set up a service to track intellectual property on the Web. This has clearly got some potential, as one the main costs faced by multimedia producers is tracking the copyright of large numbers of images and the royalties due to their owners. However, the Digimarc system could be easily defeated by guessing the master password or by modifying the marking software so that it would overwrite existing marks. They also had a "Marc spider," a bot that crawled the Web looking for marked pictures and reporting them to the copyright owner; but there were a number of ways to defeat this [610].

■ Many marks are simply additive. This opens a whole series of possible vulnerabilities. For example, if all the frames in a video carry the same mark, it is possible to average them to get the mark and then subtract it out. An even simpler attack is to supply some known content to a marking system, and compare its input and output—just like the chosen plaintext attacks possible on some cipher systems. And if a picture, P, with a mark, m, is just $P + m$, then a competitor whose mark is m' might simply claim that the original was $P + m - m'$, and so the published picture $P + m$ was really marked with m'.

■ As usual, many designers ignored Kerckhoffs' principle—that the security of a system should reside in the choice of key, not in the algorithm in use. But this principle applies with greater than usual force when marks are to be used in evidence, as this means disclosing them in court. In fact, as even the marking keys may need to be disclosed, it may be necessary to protect objects with multiple marks. For example, one can have a mark with a secret key that is system wide and that serves to identify which customer re-sold protected content in violation of his license, and a second mark with a unique key that can be disclosed in court when he's prosecuted.

■ There have been various attempts to develop a marking equivalent of public key cryptography, so that (for example) anyone could insert a mark that only one principal could detect, or anyone could detect a mark that only one principal could have inserted. The former seems just about feasible if the mark can be inserted as the cover audio or video is being manufactured [210]. The latter is the case of particular interest to Hollywood. However, it seems a lot harder than it looks, as there is a very general attack. Given a device that will detect the mark, an attacker can remove a mark by applying small changes to the image until the decoder cannot find it anymore [606, 505].

- Some neat steganalysis techniques were developed to break particular embedding schemes. For example, when the mark was added by either increasing or decreasing the luminosity of the image by a small fixed amount, this caused the peaks in the luminosity graph to become twin peaks, which meant that the mark could be filtered out over much of many images [519].

- Another family of attacks exploit the properties of particular media. For example, the typical Web browser, when presented with a series of graphics images, will display them one after another without any gaps; so a marked image can often be chopped up into smaller images, which together will look just like the original when displayed on a Web page but in which a copyright mark won't be detected (see Figure 20.6) [610].

- The most general known attacks on copyright marking schemes involve suitably chosen distortions. Audio marks can be removed by randomly duplicating or deleting sound samples to introduce inaudible jitter; techniques used for click removal and resampling are also powerful mark removers. For images, there is a tool we developed called Stirmark, which introduces the same kind of errors into an image as printing it on a high-quality printer and then scanning it again with a high quality scanner. It applies a minor geometric distortion: the image is slightly stretched, sheared, shifted, and/or rotated by an unnoticeable random amount (see Figure 20.7). This defeated almost all the marking schemes in existence when it was developed, and is now a standard benchmark for copyright mark

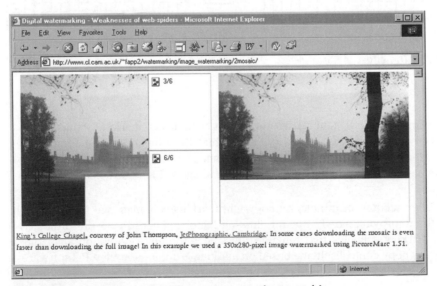

Figure 20.6 The Mosaic attack (courtesy Jet Photographic, http://www.jetphotographic.com).

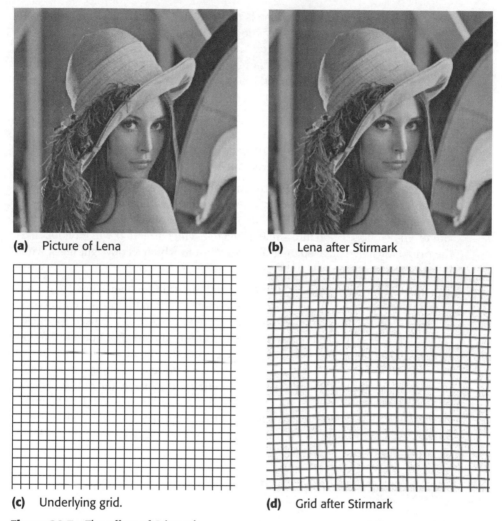

(a) Picture of Lena

(b) Lena after Stirmark

(c) Underlying grid.

(d) Grid after Stirmark

Figure 20.7 The effect of Stirmark.

robustness [610]. In general, it's not clear how to design marking schemes that will resist a *chosen distortion attack*, in which the attacker who understands the marking scheme mangles the content in such a way as to cause maximum damage to the mark while doing minimal damage to the marked content.

For a fuller account of attacks on copyright marking schemes, see [610, 611]. The technology's improving slowly but the limiting factor appears to be the difficulty of designing marking schemes that remain robust once the mark detection algorithm is known. If any copy control scheme based on marking is implemented in PC software or low-cost tamper-resistant processors, it's only a matter of time before the algorithm gets out; then expect to see people writing quite effective unmarking software.

20.3.4 Applications of Copyright-Marking Schemes

The applications of marking techniques are much broader than just DVDs and still pictures distributed on the Net. Radio adverts in the United States are commonly marked with a serial number, to enable auditing agencies to check automatically whether stations are playing them as often as they claim. Color copiers sold in the United States have their serial number hidden in the bit patterns of copies, as a means of detecting currency forgers [797]. Apparently there will be digital watermarks in the new Euro notes, which will shortly replace many European currencies; and there has been a call for proposals from the U.S. Bureau of Engraving and Printing, which wants to do something similar.

While most copyright marks have to be robust to withstand distortion attacks, some applications have been found for marks that are deliberately made as fragile as possible. One proposal highlights any changes made in an image *after* it was applied, and might be useful in assuring the integrity of images to be used in evidence [489]. Another proposed use of fragile watermarking is to hold the tickets for the DVD copy protection scheme [119].

Then there's a class of proposed applications that have to do with convenience or safety, rather than preventing malicious behavior. It has been proposed that music broadcast over the radio should be marked with the CD's number, so that someone who likes it could order the CD automatically by pressing a button. And in medicine, digital versions of X rays often get separated from the patient's details, as the various proprietary file formats get mangled through numerous protocol conversions; this safety problem could be solved by embedding patient details directly in the image.

Finally, perhaps a quarter to a third of information-hiding research doesn't aim at Hollywood's requirements, or those of the Bureau of Engraving and Printing, but at hiding information for privacy purposes.

20.4 Privacy Mechanisms

The technology of privacy includes two types of mechanism: those with which people discharge obligations of confidentiality to third parties, as discussed in Chapter 8, and those which individuals can use to protect their own privacy in the face of surveillance or other intrusion by third parties. The former are more important in the general scheme of things: without the obligations of confidentiality owed to us by doctors, lawyers, bankers, and other service providers, society would be very different. However, the citizen's ability to keep certain things private remains an important backstop, and privacy mechanisms are of much wider importance. To understand why, we have to examine what these mechanisms achieve.

In pre-technological societies, the available protection included not just cryptography in the form of hand ciphers and steganography in the form of prearranged signals, but the fact that two people could walk a short distance away from everyone else and have a conversation that left no hard evidence of what was said. If Alice claimed that Bob had tried to recruit her for an insurrection, then Bob could always claim the converse—that it was Alice who'd proposed to overthrow the king and he who'd refused out of loyalty.

In other words, some communications were *deniable*. Plausible deniability remains an important feature of some communications today, from everyday life up to the highest reaches of intelligence and diplomacy. In some circumstances, it can be implemented by convention: for example, in some countries, a participant in litigation can write a letter marked "without prejudice" to another and propose a settlement; this letter cannot be used in evidence. However, there are many circumstances without such clear and convenient rules, and where the electronic nature of communication means that "just stepping outside for a minute" isn't an available option. What then?

Another issue is anonymity. Until the industrial revolution, most people lived in small villages where everyone knew everyone else's business. For many people, it was a relief to move into a town, where this wasn't the case. Nowadays, the phrase "electronic village" not only captures the way in which electronic communications have shrunk distance, but also for many people the fear that as everything goes online, as data get collected about every transaction, accumulated into marketing profiles and sold, so we will return to something resembling the status quo of the seventeenth century. Everything about us will be known. Of course, if you live in a country such as Germany with fierce data protection laws, then you may be safe (as long as all your business remains in Germany). But as soon as you shop at an online store in the United States, that protection is gone. Is there some way to conduct online business anonymously?

20.4.1 Content Hiding: PGP

One of the best-known and widely used privacy tools is encryption of electronic mail. The market-leading product, *Pretty Good Privacy* (PGP), has done much to raise public awareness of the issues—especially since the U.S. government harassed its author, Phil Zimmermann, and threatened to prosecute him for allegedly breaking U.S. export controls by making encryption software available on the Net.

PGP has a number of features but in its most basic form, each user generates a private/public keypair. To protect a message, you sign a hash of it using your private key, encrypt both the message and the signature with a randomly chosen session key, then encrypt the session key using the public key of each of the intended recipients. Thus, if Alice wants to send an encrypted email to Bob and Charlie, she forms the message:

$$\{KS\}_{KB}, \{KS\}_{KC}, \{M, \text{sig}_{KA}\{h(M)\}\}_{KS}$$

The management of keys is deliberately left to the user, the rationale being that a single centralized certification authority would become such an attractive target that it would likely be cracked or come under legal coercion. The intended mode of operation is that each user collects the public keys of people she intends to correspond with, and bundles them into her *public keyring* which she keeps on her system. The public keys can be authenticated by any convenient method such as by printing them on her business card. To make this easier, PGP supports a *key fingerprint* which is a one-way hash of the public key, presented as a hexadecimal string.

Another mechanism to help users manage trust is that they can sign each others' keys. This may simply be used as an integrity protection mechanism on their public keyrings, but becomes more interesting if the signatures are exported. The set of publicly visible PGP signatures makes up the *web of trust*: the idea is that if Alice wants a public key for Bob, with whom she has not corresponded before, then she might be lucky enough to find a key for Bob signed by Charlie, and a key for Charlie signed by David, whom she already trusts. The resulting *certificate chain:*

$$\text{sig}_{KC}\{KB\}, \text{sig}_{KD}\{KC\}, \text{sig}_{KA}\{KD\}$$

can be taken to be equivalent to the trust relationship she seeks, namely $\text{sig}_{KA}\{KB\}$ provided she is prepared to take the risk of either Charlie or David having been dishonest or incompetent.

Other mechanisms for distributing PGP keys have been developed. One of the most widely used is a series of *key servers* which contain large collections of PGP keys. Some caution is needed, as anyone can put up a key there with any attached email address; keys for addresses such as `president@whitehouse.gov` aren't controlled by the people you might normally associate with them. There was also a book of important public keys published [42]; this also contains information about some bugs in early versions of PGP.

Of course, encrypting email is only part of the solution. In some countries, including Russia, Zimbabwe, and Britain, the police have the power to require you to decrypt ciphertext they seize, or even hand over the key. This power is also available to the civil courts in many countries under subpoena, and to many tax authorities. Other situations in which coercion may be a problem include where soldiers or intelligence agents could be captured; where police power is abused, for example to seize a key on the grounds of a supposed criminal investigation but where in reality they've been bribed to obtain commercially confidential information; and where private individuals may be tortured by robbers into revealing information such as the secret codes for their bank cards and the location of safes [793].

In such circumstances, there is a serious problem with systems where private keys are long-lived. If the taxman seizes your private key while investigating you, then leaves this on a server shared with other government agencies, these agencies now have the power to decrypt any of your old incoming messages which they happen to have stored—and perhaps also to forge your digital signature.

So the latest versions of PGP have separate keypairs for encryption and signature:

- Your public signature verification key is the long-term key which you get people to sign, print on your business card, include in your signature file, and so on.

- You generate a set of time-limited encryption/decryption keypairs and sign the public encryption keys using your long-term signature key.

- You delete your private decryption keys after they expire.

The U.S. Defense Messaging System uses a similar mechanism, but it supports the use of short-lived public encryption keys. Each user has a key server that will provide a fresh encryption key on demand, signed by the user's signing key; once the message is received and decrypted, the decryption key is destroyed.

However, there are limits to what can be done with cryptography alone, and many conventional IT security mechanisms can even endanger privacy [296]. Encryption use may mark your messages for traffic analysis; authentication can identify users unambiguously, removing wriggle room in censorship, defamation, and copyright infringement cases; and in many jurisdictions, naive encryption can be countered by what's called *rubber hose cryptanalysis*—the police simply beat the key out of you. (Countries such as Britain are slightly more civilized; there's now a law there that lets a police officer demand your key and send you to jail if you refuse. I'll discuss this in Chapter 21.)

20.4.2 Content Deniability— Steganography

When the threat model includes coercion, simply destroying old keys may not be enough, as the very existence of protected material can be sufficient to cause suspicion. In such circumstances, more complete plausible deniability can be provided by the use of steganography. If the secret message is well hidden in an innocuous cover object such as an MP3 audio track, then with luck the opponent will never suspect that anything clandestine is taking place.

Stored data is particularly difficult. Most customs authorities have the power to require travellers to decrypt any material found on the hard disk of their laptop in order to check for subversive material, pornography, and the like. There are many crude ways to hide the existence of files, such as having a separate partition on your hard disk that runs Linux, which the customs men probably won't understand—but against a capable opponent such defenses are ineffective, and over time even the customs man will acquire suitable tools. Files can be hidden using steganography tools in larger multimedia files, but this can be inefficient.

This led to the design of the *steganographic file system*, which has the property that a user may provide it with the name of an object, such as a file or directory, together with a password; and if these are correct for an object in the system, access to it will be provided. However, an attacker who does not have the matching object name and password, and lacks the computational power to guess it, can get no information about whether the named object even exists. This is an even stronger property than Bell-LaPadula; Low cannot even demonstrate the existence of High. The user can give the customs man the Low password, and deny that a High password exists; the customs man should never be able to prove that the user lied.

The whole disk is encrypted, and fragments of the files are scattered through it at places that depend on the password, with some redundancy to recover from cases where High data is accidentally overwritten by a Low user [49]. There is an early implementation described in [536]. Of course, a really robust implementation would have to take account of many of the multilevel security issues discussed in Chapter 7, from covert channels to limiting the damage that can be done by malicious code; there are also some peculiarly difficult threats to steganographic systems, such as what happens when successive snapshots of the system are taken by a Low user who then tries to deduce whether any High writes have occurred meanwhile. This problem is still not fully solved, and better implementations would be useful.

20.4.3 Association Hiding—Remailers and the Dining Cryptographers

However, there are limitations to what even steganography can do. As I remarked in several contexts, the opponent often gets most of his information from traffic analysis.

Even if the communications between Alice and Bob are encrypted, and the ciphertext is hidden in MP3 files, and even if on inspection neither Alice's laptop nor Bob's contains any suspicious material—whether because it's hidden on a stego file system or because it was simply memorized and deleted—the mere fact that Alice communicated with Bob may give the game away. This is why criminals set much more store by anonymous communication (such as using prepaid mobile phones) than by encryption. Of course, there are legitimate uses too, such as anonymous helplines for abuse victims, whistleblowers, police informants, and protest groups that want to dig a perfectly legal elephant trap for the government of the day. There's anonymous student feedback for university professors, anonymous refereeing of conference paper submissions, and anonymous HIV tests where you get the results online using a one-time password that came with a test kit you bought for cash. You may want to apply for a job without your current employer finding out, to exchange private email with people who don't use encryption, or fight a harmful cult. There's also the simple matter of preserving privacy in a world where ever more businesses collect and trade personal information. So how can anonymity be assured online?

There are two basic mechanisms, both invented by David Chaum in the 1980s. The first is the *mix* or *anonymous remailer* [177]. This is a device which accepts encrypted messages, strips off the encryption, and then remails them to the address that it finds inside. In its simplest form, if Alice wants to send anonymous email to Bob via Charlie and David, she composes the message:

$$A \longrightarrow C : \{D, \{B, \{M\}_{KB}\}_{KD}\}_{KC}$$

Charlie now strips off the outer wrapper and finds David's address, plus a ciphertext. He sends the ciphertext to David, who decrypts it and finds Bob's address, plus a ciphertext. He sends the ciphertext to Bob, who decrypts it and gets the message M. Of course, an anonymous remailer could be an attractive honey trap for a law enforcement agency or intelligence agency to operate, and so it's common to send messages through a number of successive remailers and arrange things so that most of them would have to conspire to break the traffic.

There are many refinements on this basic technique. In order to prevent an opponent tracking messages through one remailer after another, it's common for message sizes to be fixed; for remailers to batch up messages or to forward them after random delays; and for message replay to be detected. Some allow replies to unknown destinations, and others don't; anonymous replies may be handled by a pseudonym service [531].

Anonymous connections aren't limited to email, but can include any kind of communications service: an experimental U.S. Navy system, called *Onion Routing*—because the messages are nested like the layers of an onion—can be used as a communications primitive on which services such as mail and Web access can be layered [637]. There's also a design for anonymous networks of ISDN digital telephones, which might conceivably be built on top of third-generation mobile services [312, 419]. Indeed, the existence of anonymous communication channels greatly simplifies the design of more complex services with anonymity requirements, such as elections and digital cash [708]; and in the real world they can be usefully implemented by noncryptographic means such as broadcast by access tokens or other low-cost portable devices [732].

While anonymous communications based on remailers provide protection that depends on all sorts of aspects of the implementation—such as whether replay or other chosen-traffic attacks are possible—there is another stronger mechanism that is not so dependent, and thus may be considered the anonymity equivalent of "unconditional security." This was also introduced by Chaum as the *dining cryptographers' problem*, inspired by the "dining philosophers' problem" in distributed systems, discussed in 6.1.4.

Several cryptographers are gathered around a table for dinner, and the waiter informs them that the meal has already been paid for by an anonymous benefactor, who could be one of the participants or the NSA. The cryptographers would like to know who. So pairs of principals share one-time pads, after which each principal outputs a function of her "I paid/I didn't pay" bit, and everyone can later work out the total parity of all such bits. As long as not more than one of the cryptographers says "I paid," even parity means that the NSA paid, while odd parity means that one of the diners paid, even if nobody can figure out who [179]. Various extensions have been proposed, including one in which "dining drug dealers" can auction a consignment of cocaine without revealing the bidders' identities to the other bidders or to the seller. Nobody except buyer and seller know who won the auction; and even the seller is not able to find out the identity of the highest bidder before committing to the sale [732].

Doing anonymity properly is hard. As mentioned above, the anonymous remailer itself might be owned by the enemy. One option is to buy a service from a company whose main business is providing anonymity, of which the most prominent is Zero Knowledge Systems—such a firm has a lot to lose if they are exposed as dishonest or incompetent at their chosen trade. Another is to use remailers operated by cypherpunks or by a research team at a major university. Even then, there are still potential problems. There are all sorts of attacks involving chosen traffic insertion, which may allow powerful opponents (those who can monitor traffic at a large number of places in the Internet) to track relationships between correspondents [359]. Even more service denial attacks are possible on the remailer itself. People who want the service closed down can send large amounts of junk mail to or through the system; they can try to get it into a mail loop with high-volume mailing lists; they may even turn up with a subpoena. The best account of such attacks comes from David Mazières and Frans Kaashoek's experience of running the MIT server [531].

Another possibility is for the mail or Web forwarding functions to be undertaken by the users rather than by a centralized service. *Crowds* is a system in which users group together and do Web page forwarding for each other. In this way, if one of them downloads a subversive Web page, then the secret police have several hundred suspects to deal with [641]. A similar scheme was devised by a well-known CEO who, each morning, helps himself at random to one of the mobile phones of his managers, and has his switchboard forward his calls.

For many purposes, elaborate technical protection mechanisms are unnecessary. There are several online services which enable people to browse the Web anonymously, such as Anonymizer [52]. Users can set up a session with these services and enter the URLs of Web pages they want fetched; the anonymizing service will do this, while filtering those parts of the http protocol (such as cookies) that could reveal the client's identity. Some of the services offer encrypted sessions, in some cases at a premium price. In fact, any Web cache will provide some level of anonymity, because pages are fetched on the user's behalf. However, that does mean that the cache will have some very interesting logs!

Implementing high-quality anonymity is hard, not just for all these reasons but also for those discussed in Section 19.7: merchant sites are forever dreaming up new cache-busting tricks to ensure that customers see their ads and make their identities available, and many of these can break anonymity in one way or another. For a survey of anonymizing services, see [524]; for a discussion of defeating them using Web redirects, Java applets, and so on, see [716, 654]. It is particularly hard to flush the internal state of some browsers, such as Internet Explorer, so care must be taken if the opposition might gain control of your PC later.

However, the most common anonymity services are the Internet cafe and the throwaway Web-based email address. Many places offer Net access for a fixed cash sum per hour, and there are services that offer free email accounts which can be accessed from a browser and are supported by advertising, without any authentication of the users' claims to identity. Some of these services offer SSL-encrypted access for added privacy. Combining the two is a very attractive proposition for the acutely privacy conscious, because, provided you pay cash, there may be no durable record at all linking your electronic persona to your physical person. Of course such services occasionally get abused. There was public alarm in Britain after a neo-nazi downloaded bomb-making information in a London cybercafe, after which he bombed black and Asian districts and a gay bar, killing three people and injuring more than 70 others; but it's unclear that he actually got anything from the anonymity [191]. Of course, cybercafes and throwaway email accounts are useful for all sorts of legitimate purposes.

20.4.4 Association Deniability— Digital Cash

Even if you use a throwaway email account, you may want to shop on the Net, and this usually means giving a credit card number. As I mentioned in the chapter on electronic commerce, the merchants will routinely build a marketing profile of you, indexed by your credit card number (even though this breaches the banks' standard conditions of business). You may be lucky enough to get a credit card in a false name. (This can even be legitimate—in the United States if you work for an organization in the intelligence community, and in Britain if you're entitled to police protection for some reason.) But this still won't stop the transactions that you make being linked together into a profile for the marketers.

This raises the question of whether there is an electronic equivalent of cash—that is, a payment medium that is anonymous, untraceable, and unlinkable. There have been various attempts to do this. Some vendors of electronic purses claim that their products are anonymous, as the purse itself has only a serial number, and the link between it and the customer's name is known only to the issuing bank. (Some of them have got into trouble with advertising and trading standards authorities as their claims weren't all that well founded.) The most interesting protection concept in this space is *digital cash*, another invention by Chaum [178, 180].

In Chapter 6, I explained the underlying technical idea—the blind signature. The customer constructs a banknote according to an agreed format, and presents it to the bank for signature after multiplying it by a suitable random blinding factor. Things are arranged so that after the signature is done, the blinding factor can be removed, leaving a digital coin, or, more accurately, a digital cashier's check whose serial number is not known to the bank. Extra features are needed to ensure that the bank can detect whether a coin has been spent twice [180]; a modern digital cash system is described in [134].

Digital cash has been tried, but so far has not succeeded in the marketplace; the first company to launch it as a product, Digicash Inc., ended up in bankruptcy. The search for applications continues. There have been pilot projects involving road tolls; another possibility is the management of pseudonyms for private online e-commerce [134]; still another is that medical insurance schemes could adopt anonymous health credit cards to protect patient privacy [117].

The basic idea behind all these systems is that a customer's relationship with a merchant can be revealed only by the customer (for example, by showing a receipt). These systems require as part of their infrastructure an anonymous communication system (otherwise, the merchant can just read off the customer's name directly, such as from an email header). This makes them of limited appeal to e-business, and expensive. There are also intrinsic limitations. If, for example, an online transaction involves the shipment of physical goods, there will be a delivery address. If the product is intangible, such as software or audio, the copyright owner may want some means of pursuing you if you distribute copies widely. So the ultimate use of digital cash technology may be in a closed application such as road tolling. Related technologies may be used to protect voters in online elections—a subject to which I'll return in the next chapter.

20.4.5 Other Applications and Issues

The control of meta-information, and applications of anonymity and deniability, surface in a number of other applications.

20.4.5.1 *The Right to Remain Ignorant*

One of the most difficult things to assure in automated systems, whether with the mechanisms described here or those described in Chapter 8, is the right to not know something. The classic example is that in many countries you have the right not to know the outcome of a DNA test that a relative has for an inheritable disease. Your relative does have a right to know, and he may tell others—in theory, he might tell everyone else in the world. This is not just a problem technically, but also for the data protection laws of a number of countries [741].

20.4.5.2 *Location Security*

In the chapter on telecoms security, I mentioned the location security mechanism in GSM—the temporary mobile subscriber identity or TMSI. This turned out to be relatively easy for the police to defeat; and in some countries the phone companies' logs of mobile users' location history were made available to the police anyway (there was a political furor in Switzerland when people realized this was happening there). Many countries, including the United States, have now passed laws or regulations demanding that this information be available on production of a warrant (or even on demand) to the police; there are further requirements such as tracking mobiles which make emergency calls.

Third generation mobile services will provide location information accurate to 250 m, and in Europe at least it looks like there will be a legal requirement for phone companies to keep this for a year in case the police want it. What's more, many businesses plan to offer location-based services, with marketing pitches such as "50c off a Big Mac at the McDonalds you're about to drive past". There are even proposals for authentication schemes in which mobile terminals would only be allowed access to a system if they were in a particular area, such as within the confines of a military base [237].

Thus there appears little prospect that real location security services will be offered in public networks. There's no technical reason for this—in principle, one could use digital coins to pay for network access, and a more elaborate design is presented in [456]—but given business and regulatory pressure it's unlikely to happen. The most one can expect is that users may get medium-grade privacy from each other.

Location privacy mechanisms may, however, be fielded in embedded systems, such as road tolls in Germany, where data protection law prohibits the retention of vehicle details once the vehicle moves out of sight of the toll gantry, unless the toll has not been paid [164]. Of course, it will always be open to individuals to devise their own protection measures, as with the businessman mentioned above who randomly borrows a different mobile phone each day. However, in the absence of such extreme measures, location privacy seems set to be one of the more difficult things to achieve in the years ahead.

20.4.5.3 Peer-to-Peer and Censorship-Resistant Systems

If there were an anonymous channel that couldn't be jammed, then you could use it to send out copyrighted, blasphemous, or libellous material without getting caught. This is one of the central tensions between anonymity, copyright, censorship, and civil liberties.

An early anonymous remailer, `anon.penet.fi`, was closed down following legal action brought by the Scientologists. It had been used to post a message that upset them. This contained an affidavit by a former minister of their church, the gist of which was reported to be an allegation that once members had been fully initiated they were told that the rest of the human race was suffering from false consciousness; that in reality, Jesus was the bad guy and the Devil was the good guy. Well, history has many examples of religions that denounced their competitors as both deluded and wicked; the Scientologists' innovation was to claim that the details were their copyright. They were successful in bringing lawsuits in a number of jurisdictions.

The reaction of the Internet community has included a number of designs for distributed file stores, some of which deliberately use anonymity mechanisms to make this kind of censorship much more difficult. An early proposal was the Eternity Service, designed to provide long-term file storage by distributing file fragments across the Net, encrypted so that the people hosting them would not be able to tell which fragments they had, and reconstruction could only be performed through remailer mechanisms [27]. A modern version of this is Publius[2], which also provides a censor-resistant anonymous

---

[2]For non-U.S. readers: the revolutionaries Alexander Hamilton, John Jay, and James Madison used the pen name Publius when they wrote the Federalist Papers, a collection of 85 articles published in New York State newspapers in 1787–1788 and which helped convince New York voters to ratify the United States Constitution. The reference is to the U.S. right to anonymous political speech.

publishing mechanism [785]. Another successor system is Freenet which seeks to provide communications as well as file storage services [189].

But probably the most heavily used decentralized file-sharing service is Napster [570]. This enables Net users who are online to share MP3 audio files with each other. Rather than keeping the files centrally, which would invite legal action, Napster simply provides an indexing service so that someone wanting a given track can find out who else has got it and is prepared to share or trade. In addition to litigation from Hollywood, Napster has attracted perhaps 10–20 million users and a number of imitators (such as gnutella and mojonation). Given the huge volume of MP3 traffic it has generated, there will be a temptation to use this as cover traffic, and to share other data through the system. This other traffic might be encoded steganographically in MP3 files or simply wrapped so that it appears to be in MP3 format.

These two streams of development—censorship resistance and file sharing—have recently been coalescing into the new discipline of peer-to-peer networking. This burst on the scene in the middle of 2000, and is starting to encompass other issues, such as ad-hoc networks of mobile devices.

Early computer networks were many-to-one (or, as we would now call them, client-server): many terminals connected to one mainframe. The early ARPANET went to the other extreme, with each connected machine being an equal peer of the others. As the ARPANET grew into the Internet, more hierarchy and organization got added, first with services such as DNS and telnet, and later with the development of large commercial Web sites. By now, Tim Berners-Lee's vision of the Web as a person-to-person communications mechanism has been turned into a client-server model in which people's PCs act as more-or-less dumb terminals for large Web servers.

Peer-to-peer networking is often seen as a return to basics. The participating machines become equals once more, and can all communicate with each other. The driving forces are not just copyright and censorship, though. The rapid growth of the net has left DNS behind; there are now simply not enough IP addresses. Most dial-up Web users are now allocated a temporary IP address by their ISP, so applications that enable users to talk to each other, such as ICQ, have had to invent their own naming systems that function despite the intermittent connectivity of the principals.

Another reason for interest in peer-to-peer networking is the arrival of ad-hoc mobile network technologies such as Bluetooth. Within a few years, you will probably have a personal network of dozens of devices: your organizer, your mobile phone, your heart monitor, your PC at home, your burglar alarm—and some of these will make transient connections to things such as train ticket dispensers and the laser printer in a client's office. Centralised administration of such networks will be impossible (thank goodness), and the current Internet infrastructure (such as DNS) will probably not be able to cope. The way forward appears to be for principals to use many infrastructures, rather than just one, and to tailor the infrastructure to the application. Some infrastructures may be hierarchical (as with ICQ) while others may be decentralized for extreme survivability (as with censorship-resistant systems) and yet others may be transient (as with ad-hoc networks).

We have recently started to realize that many of the techniques developed for systems like Eternity and Publius, plus those developed for secure ad-hoc networking such as [731] and [732], can bring quite a lot to this party. The field is young and vigorous; a collection of papers should appear shortly as 'Peer-to-peer: Harnessing the disruptive potential of collaborative networking', edited by Andy Oram and published by O'Reilly. (I got an advance copy of this too late to include it in this book's bibliography.)

20.4.5.4 Subversive Group Computing

An interesting engineering problem is the extent to which it's possible to integrate the technologies discussed here to provide systems that are highly resistant to all kinds of surveillance and coercion. This problem has been called *subversive group computing* and may be thought of as the set of technologies necessary for a subversive group—say, for example, a Tibetan group wishing to throw off Chinese rule. The threat model here involves not just pervasive surveillance and determined service denial attacks, but also the regular subversion of group members.

One can imagine a "covert superhighway" that would enable group members to communicate with each other using anonymity mechanisms; distributed file stores for propaganda that would otherwise be suppressed; steganographic file systems to help group members appear innocuous if caught; and—as a backstop—a cell mechanism to limit the damage that could be done by a group member who is "turned." Such a hypothetical system might be thought of as a generalization of the mechanisms for enabling a group of servers to withstand and recover from an integrity failure of one of their number, such as AT&T's Rampart and IBM's Proactive Security, which we discussed above in 6.2.2.

There's an obvious direct interest in such techniques not just for national liberation groups and counterintelligence agencies, but also from the point of view of public policy generally, as they will set the technical limits of both privacy and surveillance. And, if recent history is any guide, they are likely to be at least as much driven by the desire to evade, or enforce, copyright as by any particular political liberation agenda. It's likely that these technologies will also find some wider criminal use, but as Whitfield Diffie puts it, "If you campaign for liberty, you're likely to find yourself drinking in bad company at the wrong end of the bar."

20.4.5.5 Abuse

Finally we turn to the more common kinds of abuse, such as spam, mail bombing, and harassment generally. In meatspace, such harassment is controlled by social pressures and at the extreme by physical confrontation: you can shut your house door in the face of an unwanted salesman. The same holds for cash transactions. If you grab a banana from a market stall and run off without paying, the stallholder can run after you.

One of the critical ways cyberspace is different is that these physical aspects of security and control are absent, and especially so if users can shelter behind unbreakable anonymity. For this reason, a number of people have proposed *identity escrow* schemes under which Net users have pseudonyms that normally provide identity protection but that can be removed by order of a court [155].

A contending view is that, given the ease with which people can get throwaway email addresses, and log on through cybercafes or via prepaid mobile phones, anonymity will continue to exist and will occasionally be a factor in abuse; and given our experience of real-world abuse so far, other mechanisms are likely to be at least as effective as tracing the perpetrators.

Unsolicited commercial email—*spam*—is our main teacher when it comes to abuse. It's routine for spammers to hide the source address of their product to prevent counterattacks by irritated Net users. Throwaway email addresses are one technique they use; another is simple mail forgery. A number of strategies have been adopted to manage it. Many of the most effective systems use a system of *bait addresses*, which are publicized on newsgroups and mailing lists so that spammers will add them to their lists; addresses from which spam is sent to the bait addresses are then blacklisted. A particularly effective variant on this theme adds a delay of a few hours to all messages received from unknown hosts, in order to see if they turn up at a bait address meanwhile [411].

Another technique is *rate control:* an ISP may limit the number of email messages that a subscriber can send. One supplier of anonymity services, Zero Knowledge Systems, has decided against identity escrow and in favor of rate control, plus the cancellation of pseudonyms from which abusive or illegal material is sent [821]. (An interesting footnote here is that De Montfort University in Britain has blocked Zero Knowledge at its firewall on the grounds that it can no longer enforce its policy of blocking pornographic materials. A debate over academic freedom is brewing.) This doesn't provide a huge disincentive, as the nym can't be traced back to its purchaser, and he can simply buy a new one. We'll just have to see how this pans out in practice.

Spam interacts with protection mechanisms in various ways. A notable one is that spammers sometimes use remailer services to conceal themselves, so it's routine for anonymity services to implement rate control (this also makes it more difficult to attack the system by sending large volumes of traffic to a single pseudonym and trying to see where the traffic goes). Another is the *reverse mail bomb:* by forging spam (or other offensive messages) that appear to come from your victim, you cause him to be deluged with angry messages from recipients.

Finally, many of the real difficulties ISPs have in tracking down the perpetrators of abuse are not due to people hiding behind remailers, but have to do with real-world problems. Examples are the difficulty of establishing responsibility when abusive traffic comes from a phone line in a multi-occupied student house, or when someone accesses a dial-up account on a free ISP from a phone whose calling line ID has been blocked. ISPs also often keep quite inadequate logs, and hence can't trace abusive traffic later. So, in practice, as opposed to theory, anonymity is already pretty widespread [190].

Abuse—whether technical, social, or even criminal—is not going to go away, and means of reducing its impact and holding the culprits responsible will continue to be an issue. For example, the view of U.K. ISPs is that, "Anonymity should be explicitly supported by relevant tools, rather than being present as a blanket status quo, open to use and misuse" [190]. The detailed design of these tools is likely to remain contentious for some time.

20.5 Summary

Some of the most difficult security engineering problems at the beginning of the twenty-first century have to do with copyright and privacy. In the absence of affordable tamper-proof devices, will the enforcement of intellectual property rights necessarily mean detailed monitoring of who reads which book, who listens to which music, and who runs which software? If the tools are made available to enable people to prevent monitoring, will this imply large-scale piracy of copyrighted matter?

This may at first sight seem to be the modern equivalent of the old philosophers' question of what happens when an irresistible cannon ball meets an immovable post— both can't exist in the universe at the same time. But, as always, it's not that simple. The problems facing Hollywood, and the problems of defending one's private space against intrusion, are more subtle and will involve the judicious combination of a range of tools. These tools have the feature that they manage meta-information: the source of a message, its destination, whether it's been paid for, whether copying is allowed, whether it should no longer be readable after a certain date, and so on. By a choice of suitable mechanisms, some quite subtle combinations of properties can be engineered.

That's not to say that there will be no conflict between copyright and privacy—merely that governments that rush to infringe personal liberties at the behest of the film and music industries fail to understand the problems, and deserve to have their legislation overturned by the judiciary. Also, the headline nature of large-scale copyright piracy should not deflect managers and policymakers from other serious real-world abuses, such as spam and harassment generally.

This seems an appropriate note to finish the technical part of this book. Part 3 will deal with issues of policy, assurance, economics, and management.

Research Problems

There are many interesting research problems in copyright management. Some of them I've already touched on, such as whether much cheaper tamper-proof hardware tokens can be built. Others are the subject of intense activity, such as better ways of embedding copyright marks in digital pictures and sound. There are also business modelling issues, which seem to have got little attention. For example, could we reuse the work done on modelling epidemic thresholds for computer viruses to find out how much it's economic to spend on combatting various kinds of content piracy?

Privacy is also an active field of research and innovation. Perhaps the most difficult problems have to do with preventing the abuse of anonymous services, particularly by people whose goal is to close down an anonymous service by abusing it deliberately.

Further Reading

Software copy protection techniques are discussed at length in [356]; there's a brief history of technical protection mechanisms for audio and video in [307]; and a racy account of the coevolution of attack and defense in pay-TV systems in [532]. More information about pay-TV, and the available information on DVD, can be found at various Web sites (which may move because of legal harassment); a lawyer's view can be found at [361].

There is an overview of information hiding techniques, including steganography and copyright marking, in a special issue of the Proceedings of the IEEE [515]; for attacks on marking schemes in particular, see [610, 611]. For more detail, there's a recent book on the subject [443]. Kahn is, as usual, good historical background reading [428]. The best introduction to anonymous remailers is probably [531]. Finally, ongoing research work can be found in the proceedings of the workshops on information hiding [28, 59, 613].

PART

Three

In the final section of the book, I cover three themes: politics, management, and assurance. Given that we now have some idea how to provide protection, the three big questions are: what are you allowed to do? how do you go about organizing it? and how do you know when you're done?

There has been much public debate recently about whether cryptography should be controlled in the interests of law enforcement. The evolution of U.S. and European law and policy on cryptography makes an interesting tale, but I'll cover it at some speed. It's only the tip of an iceberg.

Other places at which security engineering is coming into conflict with politics abound. In what circumstances should legal recognition be given to digital signatures? What sort of mechanisms are feasible to protect people from inappropriate material on the Web (and who's to say what's inappropriate in any case)? What are the implications for commercial system designers of the threat of "information warfare" by hostile powers or substate groups? And how will individual privacy be protected? This last question is being answered quite differently in the United States and Europe. In the former, it's left to corporate "self-regulation," while in the latter, the experience of World War II has led to privacy being entrenched as a constitutional principle. "Data protection," as it's called in Europe, threatens a major ruction between the two continents. Successive U.S. administrations have tended to see privacy as something on which "a deal could be done" or that could be fudged or just swept under the carpet—not realizing that Germans can be as inflexible on data protection as many Americans are on gun control.

Our next chapter is about management. This has become a dirty word in the information security world; there are endless vapid articles written in "managementese" that say nothing at great length. But management issues are important. Organizational and economic incentives often determine whether secure systems get built.

A large number of systems have failed because the protection was tacked on as an afterthought, or because the real purpose of the system was not its advertised purpose, or because the people who controlled the system design were not the people who suffered when it failed. Economics provides a number of insights; for example, security engineers often work with imperfect information, and network externalities are particularly savage. The management of residual risk, and the retention of organizational know-how, are two of the other problems that frequently cause expensive failures.

Assurance is a huge political can of worms. On the face of it, it's just an engineering issue. How do you go about finding convincing answers to the questions: are we building the right system? and, are we building it right? These questions are familiar from software engineering (which can teach us a lot), but they acquire new meaning when systems are exposed to hostile attack. Also, most of the organizational structures within which assurance claims can be made, or certified, are poisoned one way or another. Claims about system security properties are often thinly veiled assertions of power and control, so it should surprise no one if the results of evaluation by equipment makers, insurers' laboratories, military agencies, and academic attackers are very different. So it's really important for the security engineer to set out at the start of a project not just what the objective is, but the criteria by which it will be judged a success or a failure.

E-Policy

Experience should teach us to be most on our guard to protect liberty when the government's purposes are beneficient.... The greatest dangers to liberty lurk in insidious encroachment by men of zeal, well meaning but without understanding.

—SUPREME COURT JUSTICE LOUIS BRANDEIS

The arguments of lawyers and engineers pass through one another like angry ghosts.

—NICK BOHM, BRIAN GLADMAN, AND IAN BROWN [124]

21.1 Introduction

Information security is about power. It's about determining who will be able to grant (or deny) the use of a resource. In the past the implications went largely unexamined and uncontested. Banks built systems that failed in their favor, rather than the customers'; hospitals harvested patient data for management and research, without telling their patients; and governments bullied phone companies into making their networks easy to tap. But since the early 1990s, many of these assumptions have begun to be challenged. Contributory factors include increased public awareness, the greater importance of IT in people's lives and businesses, and the fact that computing power is now more distributed. Cheap computers meant that small businesses could balance their bank account and check their interest calculations, making it harder for the bank manager to quietly add a percent or two to the agreed rate; the contempt that many health insurers and hospitals had for medical privacy was exposed once family doctors started competing for control of the electronic health record; and wiretapping became an issue once ubiquitous PCs, email, and encryption software made it practical for individuals to defeat some kinds of government surveillance.

The role of government in e-commerce and the Internet generally has become a source of much argument. For much of the 1990s, the debate was dominated by *key escrow*—the view (held by the governments of the United States, France, Russia, and, after 1996, Britain) that copies of encryption keys should be given to the government for the convenience of law enforcement and national intelligence agencies. The opposing position—held by the governments of countries such as Germany and Ireland, Britain until 1996, and almost all of the IT industry—was that it was better to leave the development of the Internet to technological and market forces.

I'll delve into some of the arguments shortly. However, at the beginning of the twenty-first century, the places where government policy meets information security are multiplying. How are government services, from welfare payments through the court system to passports and tax collection, to be organized in a society that increasingly expects everything to be available at once and online? How can government avoid deepening the social exclusion of the poor, the old, and ethnic minorities—who may be the last to go online? Should elections be conducted online, and if so what should we do to make fraud, corruption, and coercion at least as hard as they are now? When automating government, will we replace an inefficient tiresome mess with an automated inefficient tiresome mess?

Government departments, like businesses, are struggling to stake out territory in cyberspace. Key escrow was just one of the earliest land grabs, and was unsurprising given that intelligence agencies are among the most technically sophisticated public-sector organizations. An unfortunate side effect is that, in many countries, the debate over who should have access to cryptographic keys has not only soured government relations with local IT communities, but has also enabled the agencies to take a dominant position in IT policy. In Britain, for example, the mantle of "national technical authority" for such matters is worn jealously by CESG, a department of the signals intelligence agency GCHQ. So it's policy that all state sector keys be escrowed. This will raise serious concerns about any online system for elections. Of course the agencies will want to know who votes for Sinn Féin in Northern Ireland; but if it's too easy for them to find out, then the legitimacy of the province's government will be undermined, and this is likely to cause more deaths than any tactical intelligence failure. Many people consider that letting espionage agencies set national computer security policy amounts to putting the fox in charge of the henhouse. But what's the alternative? What sort of political control should be exercised over the agencies, and how are they to be held accountable? Where and how are alternative public-sector centers of expertise in information security (and IT generally) to be built?

So the first policy issue we need to look at is the whole question of how wiretaps, traffic analysis, and cryptography are to be regulated.

21.2 Cryptography Policy

Millions of words have been written in the last few years on cryptography policy and related issues. In this section, all I can reasonably try to do is to place the debate in context, sketch the broad outlines, and provide pointers to primary sources.

Although restrictions on cryptography had existed for years and greatly irritated civilian users such as the banking industry, they shot to the headlines in 1993 when the new administration of Bill Clinton astonished the IT industry with the *Escrowed Encryption Standard* (EES), more popularly known as the *Clipper chip*. This was a proposed replacement for DES, with a built-in back-door key that enabled government agencies to decipher any traffic. (I explained the technical aspects in 14.5.3.) However, Clipper is even more important as the issue that politicized cryptography and information security generally.

U.S. opinion polarized with the government taking the view that since cryptography is about keeping messages secret, it could be used by criminals to prevent the police gathering evidence from wiretaps; the IT industry (with a few exceptions) took the conflicting view that cryptography was the only means of protecting electronic commerce, and was thus vital to the future development of the Net. Civil liberties groups lined up with the industry, and claimed that cryptography would be the critical technology for privacy. By 1994, the NSA had concluded that it faced a war with Microsoft, which it would lose, so it handed off the policy lead to the FBI, while continuing to direct matters from behind the scenes.

The debate rapidly became tangled up with export controls on weapons, the means by which cryptography was traditionally controlled. U.S. software firms were not allowed to export products containing cryptography that was seen as too hard to break (usually interpreted as meaning a keylength of over 40 bits). A U.S. software author, Phil Zimmermann, was hauled up before a grand jury for arms trafficking after a program he wrote—PGP—"escaped" on to the Internet. He immediately became a folk hero and made a fortune as his product grabbed market leadership. The conflict became international: the U.S. State Department invested significant effort in persuading other countries to control cryptography too.

The results were mixed. Some countries that had oppressive regimes within living memory, such as Germany and Japan, resisted American blandishments. Others, such as Russia, seized the excuse to pass harsh crypto control laws. France relaxed a traditional prohibition on non-government use of crypto; while Britain went from a liberal, laissez-faire policy under John Major in the mid-1990s to a draconian law under Tony Blair in 2000—the *Regulation of Investigatory Powers* (RIP) Act.

Throughout this process, the means of compulsion applied by governments (outside the Russia/Zimbabwe end of the spectrum) have become progressively more subtle. Outright criminalization has given way to a grab-bag of economic and legal incentives. But, overall, the popular view of the crypto policy struggle has been one in which the Forces of Light (privacy advocates and IT companies) have slowly overcome the Forces of Darkness (policemen and spies) in a Manichean struggle for the Soul of the Internet.

Reality is, as always, a bit more complicated. It may be useful to step back and try to place the debate in its historical context.

21.2.1 The History of Police Wiretapping

Since the earliest states arose, their rulers have tried to control communications. In classical times, this was done by checks on couriers at customs posts. From the Middle Ages, many kings either granted a monopoly of postal services to a trusted nobleman or made them the property of the state. The letter-opening and code-breaking facilities of early modern states, the so-called *Black Chambers*, are described in Kahn [428].

The invention of electronic communications brought forth a defensive and indeed atavistic response, one very reminiscent of the recent crypto policy debate. In most of Europe, the telegraph service was set up as part of the Post Office and was always owned by the government. Even where it wasn't, regulation was usually so tight that the industry's growth was severely hampered, leaving America with a clear competitive advantage. A profusion of national rules, which sometimes clashed with each other, so exasperated Europeans that the *International Telegraph Union* (ITU) was set up in 1865 [729]. This didn't satisfy everyone. In Britain, the telegraph industry was nationalized by Gladstone in 1869. (This experience was so traumatic for both government and business that the next significant nationalizations in Britain were not until after 1945.)

The invention of the telephone further increased government interest in surveillance. Resistance, both legal and technical, has a long history. In the United States, the Supreme Court ruled in 1928 in *Olmstead vs. United States* that wiretapping didn't violate the Fourth Amendment provisions on search and seizure, as there was no physical breach of a dwelling; Judge Brandeis famously dissented. In 1967, the Court reversed itself in *Katz vs. United States*, ruling that the amendment protects people, not places. The following year, Congress legalized Federal wiretapping (in Title III of the Omnibus Crime Control and Safe Streets Act) following testimony on the scale of organized crime in the United States. In 1978, following an investigation into the Nixon administration's abuses, Congress passed the Federal Intelligence Surveillance Act (FISA), which places controls on wiretapping for national security. In 1986, the Electronic Communications Protection Act (ECPA) relaxed the Title III warrant provisions. By the early 1990s, the spread of deregulated services, from mobile phones to call forwarding, had started to undermine the authorities' ability to implement wiretaps, as did technical developments such as out-of-band signalling and adaptive echo cancellation in modems. By 1994, the Communications Assistance for Law Enforcement Act (CALEA) required all communications companies to make their networks tappable in ways approved by the FBI. By 1999, over 2,450,000 telephone conversations were legally tapped following 1,350 court orders [272, 533]. The relevant law is 18 USC (US Code) 2510-2521 [759] for telco services. (The Cable Act of 1984 regulates wiretaps for cable modems and is much more restrictive—so the administration wants it watered down [439].)

It must by noted that, according to some serious analysts, there are at least as many unauthorized wiretaps as authorized ones [250]. In some countries the figures can be distorted by wiretapping being uncontrolled if one of the equipment owners consents—so that calls from phone boxes are free to market.

But even if the official figures have to be doubled or tripled, it's still clear that democratic regimes make very much less use of wiretapping than authoritarian ones. For example, lawful wiretapping amounted to 63,243 line-days in the United States in 1999, or an average of just over 173 taps in operation on an average day. The former East Germany had some 25,000 telephone taps in place, despite having a fraction of the U.S. population [295]. There was also extensive use of technical surveillance measures, such as room bugs and body wires. (It's hardly surprising that nudist resorts became extremely popular in that country.)

It's also worth noting that the incidence of wiretapping is highly variable in the developed democracies. In the United States, for example, only about half the states use it; and for many years, the bulk of the taps were in the "Mafia" states of New York, New Jersey, and Florida (though recently, Pennsylvania and California have caught up) [372]. There is similar variation in Europe. Wiretaps are very common in the Netherlands, despite Dutch liberalism on other issues [147]: they have up to 1,000 taps on the go at once, with a tenth of America's population. In a homicide investigation there, for example, it's routine to tap everyone in the victim's address book for a week to monitor how they react to the news of the death. In Britain, wiretaps are supposed to need a ministerial warrant, and are rarer; but police use bugs and similar techniques quite a lot in serious cases. To some extent, the technologies are interchangeable.

The cost of wiretapping is a serious issue. Before CALEA was introduced, in 1993, U.S. police agencies spent only $51.7 million on wiretaps—perhaps a good estimate of their value before the issue became politicized [372]. The implementation of CALEA has supposedly cost over $500 million, even though it doesn't cover ISPs. This raises some obvious policy questions. Is it worth it? Should agencies cut back on wiretapping, and spend the money on more cops instead? Or will they try to expand its use to amortize their costs? Once you start molding an infrastructure to meet requirements other than cost and efficiency, someone has to pay; and as the infrastructure gets more complex, the bills keep on mounting.

21.2.2 The History of Traffic Analysis

However, the bulk of police communications intelligence in developed democratic countries does not come from the surveillance of content, but from the analysis of telephone toll records and other communications data. I examined in the chapter on telecomms security how criminals go to great lengths to bury their signals in innocuous traffic using techniques such as prepaid mobile phones and PBX hacking, and the techniques used by the police to trace networks of criminal contexts nonetheless.

Again, this is nothing new. Rulers have long used their control over postal services to track the correspondents of potential subversives, even when the letters weren't opened. The introduction of postage stamps in 1840 was an advance for privacy as it made it much easier to send a letter anonymously. Some countries got so worried about the threat of sedition and libel that they passed laws requiring a return address to be written on the back of the envelope. The development of the telegraph, on the other hand, was an advance for surveillance; messages were logged by sender, receiver and word count, so traffic totals could be compiled, and were found to be an effective indicator of economic activity [729]. World War I brought home to the combatants the value of the intelligence that could be gleaned from listening to the volume of enemy radio traffic, even when it couldn't conveniently be deciphered [428, 569]. Later conflicts reinforced this.

By the late twentieth century, traffic analysis provided the bulk of police communications intelligence. For example, in the United States, there were 1,329 wiretap applications approved in 1998 (the last year for which comparable statistics were available at the time of writing), while there were 4,886 warrants (plus 4,621 extensions) for *pen registers* (devices that record all the numbers dialed from a particular phone line) and 2,437 warrants (plus 2,770 extensions) for *trap-and-trace* devices (which record the calling-line ID of incoming calls, even if the caller tries to block it). In other words, there were 11 times as many warrants for communications data as for content. This pattern has been stable for years, and across many countries. Why should this be?

Wiretaps are so expensive to listen to and transcribe that most police forces with restricted budgets use them only as a weapon of last resort; in contrast, the numbers a suspect calls, and that call him, give a rapid overview of his pattern of contacts. Also, while wiretaps usually have fairly strict warrantry requirements, most countries impose few or no restrictions on the police use of communications data. In the United States, no warrants were required until ECPA. Even after that, they have been easy to get: under 18 USC 3123 [759], the investigative officer merely has to certify to the court "that the information likely to be obtained by such installation and use is relevant to an ongoing criminal investigation." This can be any crime—felony or misdemeanor—and under either federal or state law. Unlike with wiretaps, the court has no power to deny a warrant once a formally correct application has been made, and there is no court supervision once the order has been granted. Since the passage of CALEA, warrants are still required for such communications data as the addresses to which the subscriber has sent e-mail messages, but basic toll records can be obtained under subpoena—and the subscriber need not be notified. So the above figures for pen register and trap-and-trace warrants almost certainly understate the extent of law enforcement traffic analysis. In any case, both phone and computer service records can be provided to bodies other than law enforcement agencies under 18 USC 2703(c); thus, for example, we find Virginia and Maryland planning to use mobile phone tracking data to monitor congestion on the Capital Beltway [710]. Toll data use for marketing purposes was also expressly envisioned by Congress when this law was passed.

In Britain, files of telephone toll tickets were provided by the phone company to the police without any control whatsoever until European law forced the government to regulate the practice in the RIP Act in 2000. Since then, comms data requires only a notice from a senior police officer to the phone company or ISP, not a warrant.

The issue of controlling access to communications data is gradually becoming a live one. The major problem is that comms data and content are becoming more and more intermixed, as what's content at one level of abstraction is often comms data at the next. A good example comes from Web URLs. On the face of it, a URL is just the address of a Web page to be fetched, but a URL such as `http://www.google.com/search?q=marijuana+cultivation+UK` contains the terms entered into a search engine as well as the search engine's name. Clearly there are many policemen who would like a list of everyone who submitted such an enquiry. Equally clearly, giving this sort of data to the police on anything like a large scale would have a chilling effect on online discourse. It would most likely be found unconstitutional in many jurisdictions.

In fact, when the U.K. government was pushing the RIP bill through Parliament, it tried to entrench a definition that would include URLs (while disclaiming that this was the intention). The news that the police would have unrestricted access to the URLs each user enters—their *clickstream*—caused a public outcry against "Big Browser," so the definition of communications data was trimmed. For general Internet traffic, it now means IP addresses, but it also includes email addresses and the location of mobile phones. All this can be demanded with only a notice from a senior police officer.

Other countries will use different definitions. For example, the U.S. Court of Appeals recently ruled that the cell in which a mobile is located is sufficient, and that to require triangulation on the device (an interpretation the police had wanted) would invade privacy [760]. Also, even cell-granularity location information would not be available under the lower standards applied to pen register warrants. Pen register warrants were also found insufficient for *post-cut-through* dialed digits, as there is no way to distinguish in advance between digits dialed to route calls and digits dialed to access or to give information. In practice, this means that if a target of investigation in the United States goes to a convenience store and buys a phone card for a few dollars, the police can't get a list of whom he calls unless they obtain a full wiretap warrant. They are entitled only to the digits the suspect dials to contact the phone card operator, not the digits he dials afterward to be connected.

The proliferation of different national standards of what is content and what is communications data may have significant effects on politics and on engineering.

Finally, the analysis of call data is only one aspect of a much wider issue: law enforcement *data matching*, which means the processing of data from numerous sources. The earliest serious use of multiple source data appears to have been in Germany in the late 1970s, to track down safe houses used by the Baader Meinhof terrorist group. Investigators looked for rented apartments with irregular peaks in utility usage, and for which the rent and electricity bills were paid by remote credit transfer from a series of different locations. This worked: it yielded a list of several hundred apartments, among which were several safe houses. The tools to do this kind of analysis are now shipped with a number of the products used for traffic analysis and for the management of major police investigations. The extent to which they're used depends on the local regulatory climate; there have been debates in Britain over police access to databases of the prescriptions filled by pharmacists for the National Health Service, while in America, doctors are alarmed at the frequency with which personal health information is subpoenaed from health insurance companies by investigators. There are also practical limits imposed by the cost of understanding the many proprietary data formats used by commercial and government data processors. But it's common for police to have access at least to utility data such as electricity bills (which get trawled to find marijuana growers); and in the long term, absolutely anything that gets monitored and logged is potentially liable to be subpoenaed. In both Britain and America, regulations being proposed or introduced at the beginning of 2001 will give the police much increased power to demand personal data electronically.

21.2.3 Communications Intelligence on Foreign Targets

I covered the technical aspects of signals intelligence in Chapter 16; now is the time to look briefly at the political and organizational aspects.

The bulk of communications intelligence, whether involving wiretaps, traffic analysis, or other techniques, is not conducted for law enforcement purposes but for foreign intelligence. In the United States, the main agency responsible for this is the National Security Agency, the NSA, whose budget (though classified) is certainly in the billions, given its huge facilities and its tens of thousands of employees. The NSA completely dwarfs law enforcement's 150–200 active wiretaps. The situation is similar in other countries; Britain's Government Communications Headquarters (GCHQ) has thousands of employees and an acknowledged budget of £650 million (about a billion dollars), while for many years one single police officer at New Scotland Yard handled the administration of all the police wiretaps in London (and ran the computer crime squad, too).

Information has steadily trickled out about the scale and effectiveness of modern signals intelligence operations. Kahn's influential history of cryptography laid the groundwork, by describing much of what happened prior to the start of World War II [428]; an anonymous former NSA analyst, later identified as Perry Fellwock, revealed the scale of NSA operations in 1972 [288]. "Information gathering by NSA is complete," he wrote. "It covers what foreign governments are doing, planning to do, have done in the past: what armies are moving where and against whom; what air forces are moving where, and what their capabilities are. There really aren't any limits on NSA. Its mission goes all the way from calling in the B-52s in Vietnam to monitoring every aspect of the Soviet space program."

While Fellwock's motive was opposition to Vietnam, the next major whistleblower was a British wartime codebreaker, Frederick Winterbotham, who wanted to write a memoir of his wartime achievements and, as he was dying, was not bothered about prosecution. In 1974, he revealed the Allies' success in breaking German and Japanese cipher systems during that war [806], which led to many further books on World War II sigint [188, 429, 800]. Thereafter there was a slow drip of revelations by investigative journalists, quite of few of whose sources were concerned about corruption or abuse of the facilities by officials monitoring targets they should not have, such as domestic political groups. For example, whistleblower Peg Newsham revealed that the NSA had illegally tapped a phone call made by Senator Strom Thurmond [157, 158]. James Bamford pieced together a fair amount of information on the NSA from open sources and by talking to former employees [70]. But the most substantial source on the organization and methods of the signals intelligence of the United States and allies was put together by New Zealand journalist Nicky Hager [368] following the New Zealand intelligence community's failure to obey an order from its Prime Minister to downgrade intelligence cooperation with the NSA.

The end of the Cold War meant that the agencies had to find new reasons to justify their budgets, and a common theme was developing economic intelligence operations against competitor countries. This has accelerated the flow of information about sources and methods. The most high-profile exposé of U.S. economic espionage was made in a report to the European parliament [278], which is concerned that now the USSR has evaporated, and intelligence is acquiring an economic focus, European Union member nations are now the main targets [160].

The picture that emerges from these sources is of a worldwide signals intelligence collection system, known as *Echelon*, and run jointly by the WASP countries (the United States, Britain, Canada, Australia, and New Zealand). Data, faxes, and phone calls get collected at a large number of nodes, including international communications cables that land in member countries (or are tapped clandestinely underwater), observation of traffic to and from commercial communications satellites, special sigint satellites that collect traffic over potentially hostile countries, and listening posts in member states' embassies [278]. The collected traffic is searched in real time by computers known as *dictionaries* according to criteria such as the phone numbers or IP addresses of the sender or receiver, and keyword searches on the contents of email. These search criteria are entered by member countries' intelligence analysts; the dictionaries then collect the traffic satisfying them and ship it back to the analyst. Echelon appears to work very much like a Web search engine, except that instead of searching Web pages it searches through the world's phone and data network traffic in real time.

A number of points here are worth bearing in mind.

- First, modern military operations would be much more difficult without signals intelligence, and in many cases they would be suicidal. The combatant with the better understanding of the other side's radar and communications has a decisive advantage when it comes to jamming and deception. Without an ability to conduct electronic warfare, a state will be unlikely to be competitive in air or naval warfare or in tank battles on the ground. Even guerilla warfare is less likely to be effective if the occupation forces can deny the guerilla the use of modern communications. So it's not surprising that most of the personnel at NSA are military, and its director has always been a serving general. A large proportion of its work concerns the identification and analysis of the radars, telemetry, weapons guidance, electronic countermeasures, and other such resources of countries that are hostile or potentially so.

- Second, the proliferation of cordless phones, radio LANs and other radio-based technologies, plus the fact that everything is going online, present the agencies with a cornucopia of new information sources [560]. Times have never been so good—regardless of the outcome of policy debates over cryptography.

- Third, even with a budget of billions of dollars a year and tens of thousands of staff, not even the NSA can collect all the electronic communications everywhere in the world. The world described by Fellwock is no more. Sprint's budget is bigger than the NSA's, and is largely spent on low-cost commercial products rather than high-cost classified ones, so it can put in lines much faster than the NSA can tap them. And even if the NSA were only interested in, say, the U.K. university system—and could manage to tap the network access point of every British university—it still couldn't ship all the bits across the Atlantic to Fort Meade, as there just isn't enough transatlantic bandwidth. The task of tapping all the data streams of all the corporations in Japan would be an order of magnitude harder. Thus, the central problem facing intelligence agencies is the same as that facing the police: traffic selection. Although in the old days it was possible to record all telephone and data traffic across the Atlantic, even this would be too expensive nowadays, because communications bandwidth is growing in scale and falling in cost much more rapidly than data storage capacity. The critical question then is whether traffic selection can be done in real time [490].

- Fourth, although other countries may complain about U.S. sigint collection, for them to moralize about it is hypocritical. Other countries also run intelligence operations, and are often much more aggressive in conducting economic and other nonmilitary espionage. The real difference between the WASP countries and the others is that no-one else has built this "system-of-systems." Indeed, there appear to be network effects at work in the economics of sigint as in so many other online activities. The value of a network grows faster than its size, and intelligence networks appear to be no different from phone networks, banking networks, or the Internet itself. The more you tap, the cheaper it gets. There have thus been moves to construct a "European Echelon" involving the police and intelligence agencies of continental European countries [269, 280].

Signals intelligence is necessary for a nation's survival, but potentially dangerous—just like the armed forces it serves. An army can be a good servant, but is likely to be an intolerable master. The issue is not whether such resources should exist, but how they are to be held accountable. In the United States, hearings by Senator Church in 1975 detailed a number of abuses, such as the illegal monitoring of U.S. citizens [185]. Foreign intelligence gathering is now regulated by U.S. law in the form of 50 USC 1801–1811 [759]. This isn't perfect; its requirements are much more lax than those on domestic wiretapping, and in many cases the president can simply authorize collection rather than getting a warrant. Also, there are known loopholes. One is collaboration with friendly services overseas. When Margaret Thatcher wanted to spy on one of her cabinet ministers, she got the work done by the Canadians [322]; and if the U.S. president really wanted to wiretap a senator there's no doubt he could simply ask Britain's GCHQ to do the job—for them, it would be a perfectly legal foreign intelligence task. And Americans are lucky: in most countries, the oversight of intelligence isn't even discussed.

However, there's a much more serious consequence of poor control and accountability than the occasional political abuse. This is the proliferation of intelligence bureaucracies that turn out to be largely useless once the shooting starts. It became a commonplace in Washington during the Cold War that the agencies hated each other much more than they hated the Russians. In Britain, one of the most vicious intelligence battles was not against the IRA, but between the police and MI5 over who would take the lead in the fight against the IRA. There are numerous accounts of intelligence inefficiency and infighting by well-placed insiders, such as Jones [425]. It is in this context of bureaucratic turf wars that we should approach the whole question of key escrow.

21.2.4 The History of Crypto Policy

Many countries made laws in the mid-nineteenth century banning the use of cryptography in telegraph messages, and some even forbade the use of languages other than those on an approved list. Prussia went as far as to require telegraph operators to keep copies of the plaintext of all messages [729]. Sometimes, the excuse was law enforcement—preventing people obtaining horse race results or stock prices in advance of the "official" transmissions—but the real reason was concern about national security. This pattern was to repeat itself again in the twentieth century.

After the immense success that the Allies had during World War II with cryptanalysis and signals intelligence in general, the U.K. and U.S. governments made an agreement to continue intelligence cooperation. This is known as the UKUSA agreement, although the other WASP countries quickly joined it. Although made in 1947, its existence was acknowledged only in 1999. Throughout much of this period, the member nations operated a crypto policy whose main goal was to prevent the proliferation of cryptographic equipment and know-how. Its outlines were vaguely visible to those of us who worked in industries such as banking; more recently, articles written by former insiders have fleshed out the details.

21.2.4.1 Export Control

Until the 1980s, almost the only makers of cryptographic equipment were companies selling into government markets. They could, by and large, be trusted not to sell anything overseas that would upset their major customers at home. This was reinforced by export controls, which were operated "in as covert a way as possible, with the minimum of open guidance to anyone wanting, for example, an export licence. Most things were done in behind-the-scenes negotiation between the officials and a trusted representative of the would-be exporter" [82].

In these negotiations, the authorities would try to steer applicants toward using weak cryptography where possible; and where confronted with a more sophisticated user, would try to see to it that systems had a "back door" (known in the trade as a *red thread*) that would give access to traffic. Anyone who tried to sell decent crypto domestically could be dissuaded by various means. A large company would be threatened with loss of government contracts; a small one, could be strangled with red tape as it tried to get telecoms and other product approvals. The problem encompassed more than cryptography, as controls designed for mainframes were overtaken by technology. By the mid-1980s, the computers that kids had in their bedrooms were considered to be munitions, and manufacturers ended up doing lots of paperwork for export orders. This pleased the bureaucrats, as it gave them jobs and power. Of course, the power was often abused. In one case, an export order for a large number of British-made home computers to the school system in Yugoslavia was blocked at the insistence of the U.S. authorities, on the grounds that it contained a U.S. microprocessor; a U.S. firm was promptly granted a license to export into this market. Although incidents like this brought the system into disrepute, it persists to this day.

By the early 1970s, the development of ATMs and other electronic banking applications created a significant market for standardized, reasonable-quality cryptographic protection. Part of the solution was to run crypto policy along the same lines as controls on missile technology exports—to let just enough out to prevent companies in other countries developing viable markets. Whenever crypto controls got so onerous that banks in somewhere like Brazil or South Africa started having crypto equipment custom-built by local electronics firms, export licensing would ease up until the threat had passed.

The other part of the solution lay in control of standards for banking crypto. A problem that worried the NSA in the 1970s was that many countries were still using cipher machines that could be broken using the techniques developed in World War II (and these weren't just poor countries: the South Africans used rotor machines up till the mid-1980s and the Swiss till the early 1990s). How could a decent cipher be provided for the banking industry, not just in America but overseas, without its being adopted by foreign governments and thus adding hugely to the costs of intelligence collection?

21.2.4.2 DES and Crypto Research

The solution was the Data Encryption Standard (DES). At the time, as I mentioned in 5.4.3.2, there was a good deal of controversy about whether 56 bits were enough. We now know that this was deliberate. The NSA did not at the time have the machinery needed to do DES keysearch; that came later. But by giving the impression that it did, it managed to stop most foreign governments adopting it. The rotor machines continued in service, in many cases reimplemented using microcontrollers, and the traffic continued to be harvested. Intelligence targets who encrypted their important data with such ciphers merely solved the NSA's traffic selection problem.

A second initiative was to undermine academic research in cryptology. In the 1970s, this was done directly by harassing the people involved; by the 1980s, it had evolved into the subtler strategy of claiming that published research work was all old hat. The agencies opposed crypto research funding, essentially by saying, "We did all that stuff 30 years ago; why should the taxpayer pay for it twice?" The insinuation that DES may have had a trapdoor inserted into it fitted well with this play. (A side effect we still live with is that the crypto and computer security communities got separated from each other in the early 1980s, as the NSA worked to suppress one and build up the other. This has significant costs today for all players, including the NSA. Another cost is that, whenever the NSA makes a mistake, as with the design of Clipper, it gets more harshly judged. What goes around, comes around.)

By the mid-1990s, this line had become exhausted. Agency blunders in the design of various key escrow systems showed that they have no special expertise in cryptology compared with the open research community; and as attempts to influence the direction of academic research by interfering with funding have become less effective, they have become much less common.

21.2.4.3 Clipper

Crypto policy came into the open in 1993 with the launch of the Clipper chip. The immediate stimulus for Clipper was the proposed introduction by AT&T to the U.S. domestic market of a high-grade encrypting telephone that would have used Diffie-Hellman key exchange and triple-DES to protect traffic. The government's response was that it could use its huge buying power to ensure the success of a different standard in which spare keys would be available to the agencies to decrypt traffic. This led to a public outcry, and Clipper was withdrawn.

Several more attempts were made to promote the use of cryptography with government access to keys in various guises. Key escrow acquired various new names, such as *key recovery*; certification authorities that kept copies of their clients' private decryption keys became known as *Trusted Third Parties* (TTPs)—somewhat emphasizing the NSA definition of a trusted component as one that can break security. Much of the policy leverage had to do with export licensing; as the typical U.S. software firm exports most of its product, and as maintaining a separate product line for export is expensive, many firms could be dissuaded from offering strong cryptography by prohibiting its export. Products with "approved" key escrow functionality were then granted preferential U.S. export license treatment. (The history of this struggle is still to be fully written, but a first draft is available from Diffie and Landau [250]; and many of the U.S. source documents, obtained under FOIA, have been published in [684].)

One of the engineering lessons from this whole process is that doing key escrow properly is hard. Making two-party security protocols into three-party protocols increases the complexity and the risk of serious design errors; and centralizing the escrow databases creates huge targets [3]. Where escrow is required, it's usually better done with simple local mechanisms. In one army, the elegant solution is that every officer must write down her passphrase on a piece of paper, put it into an envelope, stamp it "Secret" and hand it to her commanding officer, who puts it in the office safe. That way, the keys are kept in the same place as the documents whose electronic versions they protect, and there's no central database for an airplane to bomb or a spy to steal. (If you have been following the key escrow debate, you may have been conditioned to object, "But a soldier could deposit a false key and then desert and try to sell back the right one." I posed this question to my informant, and he looked at me as if I was crazy. I now believe this objection is indeed crazy, or at best clutching at straws. Anyone, soldier or programmer, can take paper documents and try to ransom them. In practice, it's so rare an event that nobody bothers about it.)

21.2.4.4 European Initiatives

In Europe, things have been somewhat more confused. Here's a brief summary (there is an extensive survey at [472]). International arms control agreements (COCOM and Wassenaar) bind most governments to implement export controls on cryptographic equipment; and countries that are member states of the European Union are also bound by an EU regulation on the export of *dual-use goods*—goods that have both civilian and military uses. But European bodies have been cool toward crypto control, and national implementations vary. U.K. law doesn't control export of intangibles, so crypto software could be exported electronically; the Belgian government would grant licenses for almost anything; and Switzerland remained a major exporter of crypto equipment. Domestic controls also varied. The French government started from a position of prohibiting most civilian cryptography, and moved to almost complete liberalization, while Britain went the other way.

In 1996, one of the last acts of the outgoing Major government in Britain was to propose that key escrow be mandatory. The opposition Labour party made a ringing denunciation of this: "Attempts to control the use of encryption technology are wrong in principle, unworkable in practice, and damaging to the long-term economic value of the information networks" [197]. Once in power, though, their view changed rapidly and the new RIP Act allows a policeman to demand any crypto key that's been in your possession. If you refuse you can get two years, and if you tell anyone that it's been seized you can get five. One intended effect was 'escrow by intimidation'—to bully companies into using key escrow to ensure they could comply with law enforcement demands for keys. However an attempt to make company directors liable to go to prison if keys couldn't be produced was defeated by industry lobbying. For the history of the RIP bill, see [304].

Another thread running through European crypto policy initiatives has been the attempt to link key escrow to other initiatives and standards. For example, the European Electronic Signature Directive forces member states to grant higher-quality recognition of digital signatures made using approved products; in at least one country, it was proposed that this would mean products supporting escrow. And, as noted in the chapter on telecomms fraud, law enforcement access was built into the standards for third-generation mobile services.

21.2.4.5 Red Threading and the Crypto AG Case

Quite often, key escrow has been implemented without the knowledge of the users. The Swedish government got upset when it learned that the "export version" of Lotus Notes, which it used widely in public service, had its cryptography deliberately weakened to allow NSA access; and at least one (U.S. export approved) cipher machine has broadcast its plaintext in the clear in the VHF band. But the most notorious example was the Bühler case.

Hans Bühler worked as a salesman for the Swiss firm Crypto AG, which was a leading supplier of cryptographic equipment to governments without the technical capability to build their own. He was arrested in Iran in 1992, and the authorities accused him of selling them cipher machines that had been tampered with so that the Great Satan could get at the plaintext. After he had spent some time in prison, Crypto AG paid 1.44 billion Rials—about $1 million U.S.—to bail him out; then he was fired after he got back to Switzerland. Bühler later alleged on Swiss radio and TV that the firm was secretly controlled by the German intelligence services, and that it had been involved in intelligence work for years [143]. The interpretation commonly put on this was that ultimate control resided with the NSA (the founder of Crypto, Boris Hagelin, had been a lifelong friend of William Friedman, the NSA's chief scientist) and that equipment was routinely red-threaded [517]. A competing interpretation is that these allegations were concocted by the NSA to undermine the company, as it was one of the third world's few sources of cryptographic equipment. Bühler's story is told in [740].

What should an ordinary security engineer—one not involved in the intelligence business—make of all this?

21.2.5 Discussion

When the key escrow debate got going in Britain in 1994–1995, I took a line that was unpopular at the time with both the pro-escrow and the anti-escrow lobbies. The pro-escrow people said that because crypto provided confidentiality, and confidentiality could help criminals, there had to be some way to defeat it. The anti-escrow lobby said that because crypto was necessary for privacy, there must not be a way to defeat it. I argued in [21] that essentially all the premises behind these arguments were wrong. Most crypto applications (in the real world, as opposed to academia) are about authentication, rather than confidentiality; they help the police rather than hinder them. As for criminals, they require unobtrusive communications—and encrypting a phone call is a good way to bring yourself to the attention of the agencies. As for privacy, most violations result from abuse of authorized access by insiders. Finally, a much more severe problem for police or auditors investigating electronic crimes is to find acceptable evidence, for which decent authentication can be helpful.

Events since have largely borne out this initially contrarian view. For most of the 1990s, I helped organize an annual conference on white collar crime in Cambridge, and organized regular sessions and workshops on key escrow and related issues. These turned out to be of almost no interest to the policemen and prosecutors who formed the bulk of our audience; they headed off to the bar as soon as the session on wiretaps and crypto got going. Most police forces took an interest in the subject only once they were told to. In many countries, including the United States and Britain, the lead agency on crypto policy is a law enforcement one (the FBI and the National Criminal Intelligence Service, respectively), but this is simply a front for the intelligence community—as was admitted in an unguarded moment in 1996 by the U.K. representative on the European body responsible for crypto policy [378].

21.2.5.1 Law Enforcement or Intelligence?

The use of law enforcement as a cover is a source of continuing problems. The aims and objectives of policemen and spies are not quite identical, and confusing them has clouded matters. It is perhaps an oversimplification that the former try to prevent crimes at home, while the latter try to commit them abroad; but such aphorisms bring out some of the underlying tension. For example, policemen want to preserve evidence, while spies like to be able to forge or repudiate documents at will. During the discussions on a European policy toward key escrow ("Euroclipper") that led up to the Electronic Signature Directive, the German government demanded that only confidentiality keys should be escrowed, not signature keys, whereas Britain wanted signature keys to be escrowed as well. The British view followed the military doctrine that deception is at least as important as eavesdropping, while the Germans supported the police doctrine of avoiding investigative techniques that undermine the value of any evidence subsequently seized.

Key escrow can also, like the system for classifying official documents, help provide plausible deniability for official wrongdoing. The key management system used in the U.K. civil service distributes signature keys to end users encrypted under escrowed confidentiality keys [50]. So if an embarrassing electronic document is leaked to the press, the government can claim that it was forged by the departmental security officer—the person responsible for preventing leaks, who is also the person with access to escrowed keys. Depending on your point of view, this is either a brilliant piece of security engineering, whose inventor should get a medal, or a wicked and perverted design whose inventor should get jail time for undermining public accountability and the principles of freedom of information.

Quite apart from signing key issues, the intelligence community appears to be the main beneficiary of crypto control. It's not just that wiretaps are the most economic way to keep an eye on guys like Saddam Hussein. If a significant proportion of data traffic were encrypted, then the automated keyword searching done by systems such as Echelon would be largely frustrated. Spooks are also aware that large numbers of new network infrastructures are built each year, and if cryptography isn't built in at the start, it may well be too expensive to retrofit it later. Therefore, each year that the NSA can hold the line on crypto controls means hundreds of networks that will be open to surveillance for decades in the future. Whether this will work for the long-term benefit of the United States and Europe, leave us terribly exposed in twenty years' time once China starts to compete as a superpower, or even lead to destabilizing conflicts on economic espionage between the United States and Europe, is a question that doesn't get debated much.

This is not to say that the police have no use for wiretaps. Although many police forces get by quite happily without them, and many of the figures put forward by the pro-wiretap lobby are dishonest [250], there are some occasions when wiretapping can be economic as an investigative tool. The Walsh report—by a senior Australian intelligence officer—gives a unusually balanced examination of the issues [787]. Walsh compared the operational merits of wiretaps, bugs, and physical surveillance, and pointed out that wiretaps were either the cheapest or the only investigative technique in some circumstances; but he still felt that compelling disclosure of crypto key material to the government was likely to be ineffective. "The invocation of the principle of non-self-incrimination may well represent the polite end of the possible range of responses," he drily remarked. Among his findings were that there is "no compelling reason or virtue to move early on regulation or legislation concerning cryptography." But he did recommend that police and intelligence agencies be allowed to hack into target computers to obtain access or evidence.[1] Although there will be some policing costs associated with technological advances, there will also be opportunities: for example, to infect a suspect's computer with software that will turn it into a listening device. In general, the police—like the intelligence services—are reaping a rich harvest from modern technology.

Overall, the net effect on law enforcement of the key escrow debate has been negative; it has eroded both public trust and operational effectiveness. In the intelligence community, too, many officers deeply regret having launched the Clipper initiative. Before it, cryptography was largely unknown: a few mathematicians studied it academically, and it was used in cash machines and pay-TV decoders, but public awareness of communications security was low. (When I first wrote some email encryption software in 1985, there was almost no interest.) That has now changed. Not only do many more criminals use anonymous communications channels, such as prepaid mobiles, but many countries that previously bought weak or red-threaded cipher machines for their military and diplomats have now started to develop local expertise and products. However, as the saying goes, "Policy has no reverse gear."

21.2.5.2 *Carnivore*

As of summer 2000, the direction of policy on wiretaps, traffic analysis, and crypto control is acquiring two main features, The first is the blurring of the line between intelligence and law enforcement. There has always been some overlap, especially in counterespionage and terrorism cases. In some countries, such as the United States, there are agencies explicitly endowed with both functions (the FBI—though note that in 1998, for example, only 45 of its 12,730 convictions involved what the Justice Department classified as internal security or terrorism matters [751]). In others, there have been huge turf fights. I mentioned the one in Britain over whether the police or MI5 should deal with the IRA; since the Northern Ireland peace treaty, the same fight has been repeated over computer crime. The end of the Cold War, and of many regional insurgencies, has left a lot of well-connected agencies desperately looking for new lines of business.

The second thread is more intrusive surveillance at ISPs. Tapping data traffic is harder than tapping voice used to be; modern modems use adaptive echo cancellation that makes passive interception of the local loop more difficult, while interception elsewhere faces several obstacles such as transient IP addresses given to dial-up customers and the increasingly distributed nature of packetized traffic. Both Russia and Britain have introduced laws requiring ISPs to attach black boxes to their networks for surveillance purposes, while in the United States the FBI has a device called Carnivore that performs

---

[1] The Walsh report has an interesting publishing history. Originally released in 1997 as an unclassified document, it was withdrawn three weeks later after people asked why it wasn't yet on sale in the shops. It was then republished in redacted form. But in 1998, researchers found unexpurgated copies in a number of public and university libraries, which had received legal deposit copies and had been insufficiently diligent in finding and returning them. These were published on the Web, and the redacted parts drew attention at once to the issues the government considered sensitive. As late as 1999, the Australian government was still trying to suppress the report [787].

this function. So-called because it's supposed to "get the meat" out of a digital wiretap, Carnivore is documented extensively at [717].

The thinking behind Carnivore was that legal solutions were becoming ineffective, as the technology changes too quickly; and that the standard tools used by ISPs to monitor their networks for diagnostic purposes got only parts of the needed information, or too much (which conflicted with legal requirements for minimization). It was preferable to have a technological solution based on a general-purpose platform whose software could be upgraded as needed. In fact, Carnivore can be configured remotely, which some ISPs don't like. What's more, the operator is completely trusted; pressing a single button causes all TCP traffic to be collected, and the device lacks the audit trails needed for establishing individual accountability. There are a number of serious problems, such as dealing with non-standard ISP equipment and with services layered on top of other services, such as webmail. No doubt Carnivore and its foreign equivalents will continue to evolve, and the growing complexity of the ISP business will keep their maintainers busy.

At least in the United States, the better legal supervision of wiretaps means that Carnivore isn't preplaced but is installed only after a court has granted a warrant; and the number of deployments each month can still be counted on the fingers of one hand. In the U.K. and the Netherlands, it looks like similar devices will be installed at all major ISPs to monitor traffic continuously [147]; in Russia, they already have been.

21.2.5.3 Underlying Policy Problems

What are we to make of a huge effort to build a capability that's used only rarely? I am afraid that many of the disputes in e-policy involve what Freudians might call a *displacement activity:* inability to solve a hard problem causes frustration, which is vented by energetically solving an irrelevant but easier one. In England, for example, it has been notorious since at least the time of Queen Elizabeth the First that rich, successful criminals are almost never prosecuted. They usually get caught only when their businesses collapse, as with the Barings and Maxwell cases discussed in Section 9.2.3 (and even then, Leeson was prosecuted in Singapore rather than London, while Maxwell's crimes were detected only after his suicide.) In my own professional practice, I have long since given up reporting crooked bankers to the police: there has been no prosecution of a senior banker that anyone can remember. In the United States, about a thousand bankers at the grade of vice president and up get prosecuted every year, and over a third get jail time. This isn't a matter of British virtue, or American vice, but has to do with how the two law enforcement systems are organized. U.S. police officers get promoted if they win high-profile convictions, so the relevant U.S. agecies such as the FBI, the Secret Service and local DAs' offices compete to put bent bankers in jail. In contrast, their British counterparts depend for promotion on establishment patronage; and raiding a prominent person for anything short of murder is career death. Thus, U.K. agencies compete to pass the buck and look the other way. Now as high-value crimes by smart crooks are precisely the minority of crimes in which wiretaps are often economic, the U.K. government's public arguments about police surveillance powers seem even thinner.

Displacement activity isn't limited to communications intelligence issues. A lot of noise has been made about Internet-based child sex offenses, and especially kiddieporn.

Yet the number of such cases is small; and even in a high-profile case involving what the judge called the "very worst possible type" of material—against former pop idol Gary Glitter—the court thought a four-month sentence appropriate. Most offenders get away with fines or community service [12]. So it's hardly the most serious of crimes, and as the use of computers by child porn networks goes back to the 1980s, it's hardly a new one either. What's more, when you talk to people involved in child protection, it becomes clear that there are thousands of really serious cases of child abuse every year in Britain, usually involving abuse by family members, abuse of young persons with learning difficulties, abuse of children in local authority care, and under-age prostitution. For various political reasons, the police don't always find it convenient to crack down on these crimes; and as for the charities, the end of the orphanage system has left them dependent on local government for permission to place vulnerable children in care. Still, children's organizations spend their charitable funds campaigning against the evils of the Net [168], rather than lobbying for the respectable middle-class customers of 13-year-old prostitutes to be sent down for child rape [528]. (There are some interesting reflections on attitudes to sex offenders, and the transference mechanisms involved, at [215]. It appears that, just as the end of universal belief in God left a surveillance vacuum which governments have rushed to fill, so also the death of the devil has left a vacancy. The greatest hysteria about child sex abuse is whipped up in the very neighborhoods where the abuse of girls by their stepfathers or stepbrothers is routine. People transfer to 'the devil' their own darkest fears and childhood traumas.)

The implication of all this for the security engineer is that you have to think hard about the risk that your product or service will become the target of hysterical abuse by ineffective or corrupt public servants, or by ignorant and hypocritical self-publicists. You can't ignore the social and political context of what you're trying to build.

21.3 Copyright

In Chapter 20, I suggested that the 1990s debate on crypto policy is likely to be a test run for an even bigger battle, which will be over anonymity, censorship, and copyright. I looked at some of the technical aspects in that chapter, and discussed a number of the business and political aspects that were integral to that story. The context is not just copyright though. Mechanisms such as anonymous remailers and highly distributed file stores allow people to exercise their right to anonymous political speech, and also let them publish material that is defamatory or seditious with a decreased likelihood of being caught and punished. Thus, the copyright enforcement lobby has some powerful potential allies.

There are geopolitical aspects, too. In most countries, there is no right to free speech (let alone anonymous political speech), as enjoyed in the United States; and even in European countries, the laws on defamation and sedition can be savage. There have also been high-profile cases in which courts in countries with laws against hate speech, such as France and Germany, have looked for ways to censor U.S. online services. As I write, a court in Paris has just given Yahoo three months to prevent its French subscribers having access to auctions of Nazi memorabilia, which are illegal in France. And at the Global Internet Project conference in Berlin, in November 2000, I heard the German federal justice minister proclaim that her greatest achievement in office was stopping Books Online shipping copies of "Mein Kampf" to addresses in Germany. Speaking through an interpreter, she assured us that she would not rest until they stopped shipping it in Arizona, too. (Given that the copyright of "Mein Kampf" is owned by the government of the state of Bavaria, they may have the right to end its publication by boring, old-fashioned legal means; perhaps denouncing the Evils of the Internet is thought more attractive to the voters.)

If, as Leslie Lamport said, you know you have a distributed system when the crash of a computer you've never heard of stops you from getting any work done, then you also know you're living in the global village when a judge in a country you've never heard of can try to close down your business—or at least dictate onerous conditions on how you conduct it in your own country. (Being based in the United States, which is isolated from international enforcement of court judgments, gives you some protection—as discussed in Section 19.9.) I don't think anyone has ever considered the distributed systems aspects of international law, but there could be an interesting PhD thesis in it.

Of course, it cuts both ways: third world despots and Asian strongmen denounce the freedom of speech on the Internet as "neo-imperialism." And most European countries have a more liberal view of pornography than most Americans are comfortable with. It remains to be seen whether the Internet of 2020 will have U.S. rules on freedom of speech and European rules on porn, or the other way round.

Because of the lack of consensus on issues such as obscenity and sedition, the most likely way for controls to be introduced will be copyright. Chapter 20 described how successive technologies such as audiocassettes and videocassettes arrived on the market, caused panic among copyright owners, but turned into profitable lines of business once Hollywood had learned to manage them. PC software followed exactly the same model, only more rapidly. Pay-TV was slightly different, as the use of tamper-resistant subscriber tokens, plus aggressive legal pursuit of token forgers, enabled piracy to be kept in the single percentage figures. Hollywood is now trying to get DVD to follow the pay-TV path; however, thanks to design and other errors, this looks to be slipping from their grasp. It now looks like DVDs will follow the same model as PC software or videocassettes, and will be the future distribution medium for both.

The issue is by no means a straight fight between copyright and privacy. As noted in Chapter 20, the doctrine of fair use allows people to copy parts of a work for purposes ranging from scholarship to ridicule. The possible abolition of fair use has alarmed universities and libraries. Pamela Samuelson expresses a common sentiment: "Why would the Clinton administration want to transform the emerging information superhighway into a publisher-dominated toll road" [667]?

21.3.1 DMCA

Following heavy lobbying, a treaty was made in Geneva in 1996 under the auspices of the *World Intellectual Property Oragnization* (WIPO), with signatory states obliged to harmonize the treatment of digital copyright. The implementation in the United States was the *Digital Millennium Copyright Act* (DMCA) of 1998. This prohibits the alteration of any electronic *copyright management information* (CMI) bundled with digital content, such as details of ownership and licensing; and outlaws the manufacture, importation, sale or offering for sale of anything primarily designed to circumvent copyright protection technology. There are specific exemptions for people engaged in encryption research, for libraries, and to detect and disable the kind of snitchware discussed in Section 18.3.2.4.

DMCA also provides some limited protection for ISPs that unknowingly host copyright material on Web sites that has been posted by their clients or other third parties. A condition is "Notice and Take Down": when a copyright owner notifies an ISP of a violation, the offending material must be removed. To prevent this being abused, there is also a provision for "Notice and Put Back": if the subscriber files a proper "counter notice," attesting to its lawful use of the material, then the ISP must promptly notify the copyright owner and restore the material within 14 business days, unless the matter has been referred to a court.

The exemptions for libraries are the focus of continuing debate, as digital access will mean only limited access, unless you own a copy of the work; and libraries will have to negotiate terms for fair access for all reasonably expected purposes, in the face of initial licensing conditions and fees that that may be far too high. (These issues are discussed at [513].) Particularly intractable problems are raised by legal deposit libraries, such as the Library of Congress and its counterparts elsewhere. Traditionally, the grant of copyright in many countries was conditional on the copyright owner's depositing one or more copies of the work in a national archive. This serves a number of purposes ranging from helping the courts resolve copyright disputes, through access by future generations of scholars, to the supply of obscure books through library loan schemes. But how can we preserve digital works that may use proprietary platforms, have copy-protection schemes, and may even require occasional online access to a license server? However, the first big test of DMCA looks to be the reverse-engineering of DVD CSS, which is currently making its way through the U.S. courts.

21.3.2 The Forthcoming European Directive and UCITA

In Europe, there is already a Conditional Access Directive that obliges EU member states to outlaw devices that enable unauthorized access to services such as pay-TV and Internet subscription sites. As with DMCA, there are exemptions for bona fide research. A difference is that the Conditional Access Directive protects measures that control access to a service, not those that control access to a work.

The protection of works should arrive in the form of a Copyright Directive, which at the time of writing is still the subject of debate. There has been vigorous lobbying on the one hand from Hollywood and on the other from libraries. It looks like the directive will have broadly the same effect as DMCA, though the details will be up to member countries. (For a discussion of the proposed directive and a comparison with DMCA, see [468].) The sort of argument being considered by the European Commission is that if a rights holder could object to circumvention in cases where a claim based upon copyright law would not succeed, the effective "reach" of copyright holders would expand. What's more, some companies are already packaging copyright control mechanisms with other kinds of protection, such as accessory control in the computer games industry. It seems unreasonable to just grant copyright holders and gaming console vendors any right for which they can devise a protection mechanism, and to criminalize defeats of such mechanisms, however ineffective or inappropriate they are.

Also, existing European law allows reverse-engineering for interoperability—to ensure that the program can work with other programs—while DMCA adds the restriction that there must not be a readily available commercial alternative for that purpose. The general European view, following the reverse-engineering of the DVD CSS (which was necessary for the Linux community), is that the DMCA provisions are too tightly drawn. (This means that even if Hollywood wins the U.S. case, there should be a safe haven for Linux developers in Europe.)

Another issue in the United States is the *Uniform Computer Information Transactions Act* (UCITA), a model law sponsored by the National Council of Commissioners on Uniform State Laws (NCCUSL), which will be introduced in state legislatures nation wide. UCITA will update the U.S. Uniform Commercial Code to cover digital trade, and will govern contracts between manufacturers and consumers regarding nearly all "transactions in information." This means everything from stories, computer programs, images, music, and Web pages to online databases and interactive games. UCITA will significantly extend federal copyright law. Many states are unhappy with it; it will replace copyright law with contract law in many cases, undercut fair use, outlaw reverse-engineering even for interoperability, and enable shrink-wrap/click-on licenses to bind users to contracts before they can even read the conditions. It could have severe consequences for everyone from open source software authors to universities [608].

It's by now inevitable that there will be important differences between the laws in the United States and Europe, which may have a significant effect on security designs. Also, at the level of fine structure, the issues look set to be fought out in dozens of individual state and national legislatures. This might work in Hollywood's favor, as it has the money and organizational resources to lobby in dozens of places at once. But it also increases the likelihood that a spectacular loss somewhere will create a haven, just as Ireland became a safe haven for pay-TV smartcard cloning in the early 1990s.

21.4 Data Protection

Data protection is a term used in Europe to mean the protection of personal information from inappropriate use. Personal information generally means any data kept on an identifiable human being, or *data subject*, such as bank account details and credit card purchasing patterns. It corresponds roughly to the U.S. term *computer privacy*. The difference in terminology is accompanied by a major difference in law and in attitudes. In fact, this may become one of the thorniest problems in e-policy in the first decade of the twenty-first century, as well as a serious complication for people setting up e-businesses.

European law gives data subjects the right to inspect personal data held on them, have them changed if inaccurate, understand how they're processed, and in many cases prevent them being passed on to other organizations without their consent. This means, for example, that people who have been refused credit can see not just their files but also the credit-scoring algorithms used to make the decision; and if a U.S. bank doesn't like that, tough. There are exemptions for national security, but not for all police data. Most commercial data are covered, and there are particularly stringent controls on data relating to intimate matters such as health, religion, race, sexual life, and political affiliations. Finally, recent law prescribes that personal data may not be sent to organizations in countries whose laws do not provide comparable protection. In practice, that means America, where legal protections on privacy are fragmentary.

The implication for the engineer designing an e-commerce application is that once the relevant European law has been tested all the way to the European court—which might be in 2004 or 2005—it may be illegal for you to process data about your European customers in a facility on U.S. soil. One solution may be to put your servers in a European country with lax enforcement, such as Britain or Iceland; but there is a growing body of case law that constrains European governments' freedom to turn a blind eye. If your business model involves collecting large amounts of personal information about buying habits, news-reading patterns, and so on, then you could be in trouble even in London or Reykjavik.

Another solution favored by many business is *coercive consent*, which means you insist that customers agree to their personal data being shared before doing business with them. This tends to work at present (it's how U.S. medical insurers get away with their abuses) but isn't guaranteed for ever. The click-on no-privacy agreement on your Web site might be deemed an unfair contract term by a court; and in some countries, it will be invalid if the customer is a minor or the information relates to an intimate matter such as health.

European privacy law didn't spring full-formed from the brow of Zeus, though, and it may be helpful to look at its origins.

21.4.1 European Data Protection: History

Technofear isn't a late twentieth-century invention. As early as 1890, Warren and Brandeis warned of the threat to privacy posed by "recent inventions and business methods," specifically photography and investigative journalism [792]. Years later, after large retail businesses started using computers in the 1950s and banks followed in the early 1960s, people started to worry about the social implications if all a citizen's transactions could be collected, consolidated, and analyzed. In Europe, big business escaped censure by making the case that only government could afford enough computers to be a serious privacy threat. It was realized that it was possible, economic and rational for government to extend its grasp by using the personal data of all citizens as a basis for prognosis; and given the recent memory of the Gestapo in most European countries, this became a human rights issue. A patchwork of data protection laws began to appear, starting with the German state of Hesse in 1969. Because of the rate at which technology changes, the successful laws have been technology-neutral. Their common theme was a regulator (whether at national or state level), to whom users of personal data had to report and who could instruct them to cease and desist from inappropriate processing. The practical effect was usually that the general law became expressed through a plethora of domain-specific codes of practice.

Over time, processing by multinational businesses became an issue, and it became clear that purely local or national initiatives were likely to be ineffective against them. Following a voluntary code of conduct promulgated by the OECD in 1980 [598], data protection was entrenched by a Council of Europe convention in January 1981, which entered into force in October 1985 [206]. Although, strictly speaking, this convention was voluntary, many states signed on for fear of losing access to data-processing markets. It was founded in the European Convention on Human Rights, and required signatory states to pass domestic legislation to implement at least certain minimum safeguards. Data had to be obtained lawfully, and processed fairly, and states had to ensure that legal remedies were available when breaches occurred.

The quality of implementation varied widely. In Britain, for example, Margaret Thatcher unashamedly did the least possible to comply with European law. A data protection body was established, but starved of funds and technical expertise; and many exemptions were provided for favored constituencies. Though not for journalists; if you kept notes on your laptop which identified people, you were formally liable to give copies of this information to the data subjects on demand. In hard-line privacy countries such as Germany the data protection bodies became serious law enforcement agencies. Many non-European-union countries, such as Australia, Canada, Iceland and Switzerland, passed comparable privacy laws in the 1980s and early 1990s. Some, like Switzerland, went for the German model, while others, like Iceland, followed the British one.

By the early 1990s, it was clear that the difference between national implementations, exacerbated by the accretion of case law, was erecting barriers to trade. For many businesses, the solution was to avoid controls altogether by moving (or outsourcing) their data processing to the United States. The growing tensions led in 1995 [279] to a new Data Protection Directive. This sets higher minimum standards than most countries had required before, with particularly stringent controls on highly sensitive data such as health, religion, race, and political affiliation. It also prevents personal information being shipped to "data havens" such as the United States, unless there are comparable controls in place. The directive could prove to be a serious headache for new business models, such as application rental [182].

21.4.2 Differences between Europe and the United States

The history in the United States is, basically, that business managed to persuade government to leave privacy largely to "Self-regulation" (for more on U.S. history on this topic, see [572]). Although there is a patchwork of state and federal laws, they are application-specific and highly fragmented. In general, privacy in federal government records and in communications is fairly heavily regulated, while health and business data are largely uncontrolled. One or two islands of regulation, do exist, such as the Fair Credit Reporting Act of 1970, which governs disclosure of credit information, and is broadly similar to European rules; and the Video Privacy Protection Act or "Bork Bill," enacted after a Washington newspaper published Judge Robert Bork's video rental history following his nomination to the U.S. Supreme Court.

Attitudes also differ. According to Westin, about twenty-five percent of Americans are "privacy fundamentalists," favoring legislative standards; twenty percent are unconcerned, and will readily pass on their personal information for minor benefits; while the majority, fifty-five percent, are pragmatists who take privacy decisions case by case. But there is a growing feeling that people have lost control of the uses to which their personal information is put. This still lags behind Europe, where privacy is seen as a fundamental human right that requires vigorous legislative support [802].

Clearly, the stage is set for a major conflict between Europe and the United States on data protection. U.S. policymakers have failed to appreciate the severity of the problem; a common view on Capitol Hill is that, "It's just a spiteful retaliation for the Helms-Burton Act, and we can negotiate some deal on it." Their current hope for a deal is the *safe haven* concept, that U.S. data processors can simply enter into a contract with their European customer or subsidiary to the effect that data will be processed in accordance with European law. Some firms have already done this, led by Citibank which uses such an arrangement to process German cardholder data in South Dakota. But this creates severe practical enforcement problems for EU citizens who feel that their rights have been violated, and may well fail when tested in court. For a discussion, see [802].

21.4.3 Current Trends

The European regulatory drive toward data thrift is counter to the direction in which commerce is developing. Quite apart from the law enforcement surveillance techniques discussed in the first section of this chapter, e-businesses are developing all sorts of customer tracking and marketing tools from cookies to clicktrails, wallets to IPR enforcement tools, and snitchware that enables software vendors to monitor customers' hard drives remotely. The information flow is one-way, in the sense that you retain essentially, no rights over personal information once surrendered; yet businesses will only license their software to you rather than sell it. Some writers have expressed the fear that, regardless of any regulatory efforts, technology will land us in a world in which there is no place to hide [323].

An extreme version of this view is taken by David Brin [139]. He argues that pervasive surveillance technologies will inevitably be available to the authorities, and the only real question is whether they will be available to the rest of us, too. He paints a choice between two futures—one in which the citizens live in fear of an East German-style police force, and one in which officials are held to account by public scrutiny. The cameras will exist: will they be surveillance cams or Web cams?

There are some successful experiments in openness. The U.S. Freedom of Information Act may be the most conspicuous, but there are others, such as the practice (in Iceland and in some Swiss cantons) of publishing tax returns—a practice that greatly cuts evasion as rich men fear the loss of social status that an artificially low declared income would bring.

Underlying such considerations is a growing understanding of the economics of privacy. The basic problem is that for the data subject, the value of personal data is its marginal cost, while for the collector it's the average cost. Thus collectors are going to pay more to get data than most users will pay to deny it to them. Another economic aspect is that, if privacy is left to technology, it will be a cost that falls largely on the data subject; but if it's done by regulation, it will fall more on the collector [323]. One ray of hope is that the data that people want to keep private and the data that marketers want to collect are often not the same commodity. Personal secrets tend to be long term (such as a treatment for alcoholism ten years ago), while marketing data is short term

(how much can I increase the probability of selling this person an airplane seat today if I cut the price 20%?)

Perhaps part of the solution will come from tools such as online auctions. But there are many places where Web cams will probably always be considered unacceptable, such as corporate research and development labs, attorneys' offices and doctors' consulting rooms. Defining the boundary will no doubt involve a lot of pushing and shoving.

The evolution of this issue over the next few years will be of great interest to security engineers. The issue will not be limited to the collection of data, but also to its collation. For example, while U.S. felony convictions remain on the record forever, many European countries have laws governing rehabilitation of offenders, under which most convictions disappear after a period of time that depends on the severity of the offence. But how can such laws be enforced now that Web search engines exist? The German response is that if you want to cite a criminal case, you're supposed to get an officially deidentified transcript from the court. But if electronic newspaper archives are searchable online, what good will this do—unless the identities of all offenders are blocked from electronic reporting? Recently, for example, there has been much debate over the monitoring of former child sex offenders, with laws in some states requiring that offender registers be publicly available. Riots occurred in England following the naming of some former offenders by a Sunday newspaper. There's a long list of similar issues, from the permissible uses of electoral rolls and lists of people who have been naturalized to whether it is permissible to index certain types of publicly available information. The upshot is that even if data is public, its use can still cause offenses under European privacy law.

This causes peculiar difficulties in the United States, where courts have consistently interpreted the First Amendment to mean that you can't stop the repetition of true statements in peacetime except in a small number of cases, of which the classic example is a regulated profession such as securities trading. Perhaps marketing will end up a regulated profession; or perhaps the penalties for the repetition of untrue statements can be made high enough to cause people to take care. Neither seems likely at present in mass markets, although the rich and famous can extract substantial damages for libel in many countries' courts. I await with interest the first case in which someone bankrupts a search engine operator for bringing to public attention an expired conviction for drug use.

It's possible that America will enact privacy legislation that's sufficiently mid-Atlantic to prevent a trade war on the issue; Al Gore promised an "Electronic Bill of Rights" to protect people against the misuse of computerized personal information of all types. It's conceivable that, like the Internet, privacy intrusions will suddenly reach a critical mass, and public opinion in the United States will compel politicians to override business interests and pass European-style data protection laws. It's also conceivable that Europeans will come to share the view of American privacy pragmatists—that though a few unlucky people may have terrible experiences, the worst that will happen to the average family is an armful of junk mail each week with which they can light the barbecue. But it's also possible that Europe might become more fundamentalist still, perhaps in reaction to U.S. e-commerce practices. Thus, although the two markets might converge, there is a real risk that they won't; and neither is small enough to ignore.

In the meantime, it is prudent for the e-commerce designer to ensure that business processes and systems can comply with the European way of doing things as well as the American one.

21.5 Evidential Issues

I mentioned the European Electronic Signature Directive, which forces member states to grant higher-quality recognition of digital signatures made using approved products; that there were attempts to link this approval to approved key escrow mechanisms; and that there were attempts to force the escrow of signature keys as well, which could have undermined the value of digital evidence.

But these are neither the beginning nor the end of the evidential issues confronting the security engineer. Designing a system whose functions include the production of evidence is a lot harder that it seems at first.

21.5.1 Admissibility of Evidence

When courts were first confronted with computer evidence in the 1960s, there were various concerns about the reliability, both in a technical sense and in the legal sense of whether it was inadmissible on the grounds that it was hearsay. Different legislatures tackled this differently. In some, computer evidence is deemed to be admissible, but can be challenged in court by the other side; in others, it can't even be presented unless accompanied by a certificate stating that the computer was working properly. (This can cause problems when the evidence comes from a machine that has been hacked.) In the United States, most of the law is found in the Federal Rules of Evidence, while in Britain it's in the Police and Criminal Evidence Act 1984 and the Civil Evidence Act 1995.

In many cases, evidence can be derived only from the operation of a machine as it's operated in the normal course of business, and this can cause problems if a requirement for evidence hasn't been anticipated by the engineer. For example, in one case in my own experience, a woman was accused of stealing a debit card from the mail, and the police wanted to ascertain whether a torn-off corner of a PIN mailer found in her purse would activate the stolen card. They got the branch manager to put the card into a statement printer in the branch office, entered the PIN, and the card was confiscated. The manager testified that the way the card was confiscated showed that it was because the account had been closed rather than because the PIN was wrong. The court ruled this evidence to be inadmissible. The law on this subject changes regularly, though.

21.5.2 Reliability of Evidence

Even where the local formalities can be observed, computer forensics pose complex and nontrivial engineering problems. Even to the experienced systems administrator, securing evidence of an intrusion in a timely and nondestructive manner is hard. As operating systems get ever more complex, they become less deterministic, and their logging and other features more opaque. The response of the law enforcement community has been tools that will take a mirror image copy of a hard disk for subsequent examination. This isn't the end of the story, though, because of the complexity and quantity of data, and the multiple interpretations that are often possible. Application file formats usually aren't adequately documented, and may contain bugs or features which their creators are unwilling to discuss, because they would embarrass or even incriminate them. New gadgets, such as palmtop computers with closed operating systems, and SIM cards for which the suspect won't divulge the password, can force the practitioner to resort to the kind of reverse-engineering tricks described in Chapter 14. Things are made worse by the technical incompetence of judges and other lawyers; the common result is that arguments (and judgments) confuse fact, conjecture, assumption, inference and opinion.

The signal-to-noise ratio of the court system is especially low when a case hinges on a technical matter. Often, the only safeguard against injustice lies in the adversarial system itself. Recall the Munden case described in 9.4.3. A man was falsely accused and wrongly convicted of attempted fraud after he complained of unauthorized withdrawals from his bank account. Rational argument having failed, the way in which the appeal was won was tactical—getting an order requiring the bank to open its systems to the defense expert, as it had done for the prosecution. When the bank refused, the defendant's bank statements were ruled inadmissible, and the prosecution case collapsed. Thus, if a system is to be useful as a source of evidence, then it must be designed to withstand examination by hostile experts. I'll have more to say on this in Chapter 23.

The hostile expert problem isn't something we can expect to go away anytime soon. In countries where experts are appointed by the court, the risk is that they will be from the developer community, and so may have an interest in defending the system that they are supposed to be examining dispassionately. In general, we can expect computer forensics to remain a hard problem.

21.5.3 Electronic Signatures

In this generally unsatisfactory environment, many people hope that things can be simplified by gee-whiz technologies such as *electronic signatures*. This term encompasses (among other things) cryptographic digital signatures and alternative technologies such as tablets on which users scribble copies of their manuscript signatures to record assent to a document. In some cases, such as the U.S. Electronic Signatures in Global and National Commerce Act, the objective is to give legal force to any "sound, symbol, or process" by which a consumer assents to something. By pressing a telephone keypad ("Press 0 to agree or 9 to terminate this transaction"), clicking a hyperlink to enter a Web site, or clicking "Continue" on a software installer, the consumer consents to be bound to an electronic contract [709].

In many jurisdictions, this is already the case. In both the United States and England, the defining attribute of a signature is the signer's intent, and a plaintext name at the bottom of an email message has legal force. It may be easy to forge, but then so are the manuscript signatures that have been used for centuries [810, 811].

However, as I discussed in the section on handwritten signatures (13.2) there are many specific requirements that particular types of transaction—real estate, patent, copyright—be in writing, and these can hold up the adoption of online systems. Some countries, like Australia, have simply passed laws stating that electronic writing is OK wherever manuscript writing was required in the past; others, like Britain, have passed laws giving the government the power to issue regulations causing this to happen; still others, such as Germany, have made laws giving effect to digital signatures provided they meet laid-down technical standards. Such laws often suffer from multiple objectives.

Britain, for example, wants to promote the use of software and systems that support key escrow, while Germany wants to support its smartcard industry.

The laws passed in various American states are less tainted with ulterior motives, but still create a confusing and contradictory mosaic. Sometimes, digital signatures are enabled for general use, and sometimes for limited purposes such as communicating with the state government. Sometimes they're technology specific and sometimes they're not. For surveys of digital signature laws, see [68, 335].

Efforts are now underway to sort out the mess. The European Union issued an Electronic Signature Directive, which came into force in January 2000, that requires member states to introduce compatible legislation to recognize digital signatures as the legal equivalent of manuscript signatures. The directive sets out two different standards: an *electronic signature* means data attached to or logically associated with other electronic data and that serve as a method of authentication, while an *advanced electronic signature* must also:

- Be uniquely linked to the signatory.
- Be capable of identifying the signatory.
- Be created using means that the signatory can maintain under his sole control.
- Be linked to the data to which it relates in such a manner that any subsequent change of the data is detectable.

The basic idea is that an electronic signature includes a name typed at the bottom of an email, or a push of a Web page button to assent to a deal, while the advanced variety means use of a digital signature or biometric device. Lawmakers and people writing contracts should therefore be able to distinguish, using terms that are uniform across Europe, between weak and strong signature mechanisms.

One embarrassing problem is that the third of these requirements can't be met by currently available consumer electronics technology. Given the large number of ways in which a PC can be subverted, it would be very imprudent to have a signing key on your PC that could bind you for more than a small sum of money. Smartcards don't help; a villain who can write a virus to infect your PC and sign messages with a key in your browser software can just as easily infect the device driver of your smartcard reader to get the bogus message signed next time you insert the card. Also, if the card can be used in a parking meter as well as to mortgage your house, then you are extending to the parking meter the level of trust you'd normally restrict to your spouse or your lawyer. In the absence of secure platforms, some protection can be got from the traditional practice of having separate cards or other tokens for different types of transaction, so that the customer can keep the valuable ones under lock and key. (But personally I don't see any benefit in having an electronic means of performing a transaction I do at intervals of many years such as mortgaging my house.)

In the words of Bohm, Brown and Gladman, "It is of course no fatal reproach to the Directive that it should thus deliver thunder with no lightning; and it could be excused on the basis that the law will for once be ahead of events" [124]. However, there's enough wriggle room for countries to tack on interpretations and regulations that will deem products from their own smartcard or other suppliers to be adequate; and the current indications are that a moderately good smartcard will do, even if it's used with an insecure PC. (I'll discuss this in more detail in Section 23.3.3.1 below.) Businesses in other countries will then have to accept the resulting "advanced" signatures as valid. So what sort of risks will people run once we have digital signatures that are considered by judges to be totally secure even although they aren't?

21.5.4 Burden of Proof

There is an even deeper problem with most digital signature laws (including those of many U.S. states). This is that they create a presumption that a digital signature meeting certain criteria (authorized type of smartcard, public key certified by licensed TTP, whatever) is valid. This flies in the face of traditional business practice, in which the risk that a signature is forged falls on the party who relies on it rather than on the party who made it.

If a bank debits your account with payment of a check that you did not sign, it has no authority for the debit and must credit the money back to you. In general, if someone wishes to enforce a document against you on the basis that you signed it, and you deny that you signed it, then it is for them to prove that the signature was made or authorized by you. This means that banks and merchants can decide for themselves how much care to take when verifying signatures; if they decide to verify signatures only for amounts over $1,000, or even $10,000, that is their concern, and has nothing to do with the customer. I discussed the error rates of handwritten signatures at 13.2; in practice the associated risks are manageable. In Chapter 19, I explained that essentially the same happens with credit cards, although there the customer typically bears the first $50 of the risk and in return gets the ability to pursue a claim against the card issuer if the merchant goes bust or otherwise fails to deliver.

It is understandable that banks and merchants would like to offload their exposure, and digital signature laws have been held out as a means of doing this. As described in Chapter 19, VISA and MasterCard went as far as to design the SET protocol to support credit card payment via digital signatures; and a number of governments dangled the bait of a presumption of validity of digital signatures as a way to get key escrow adopted [132].

Clearly, this is a bad thing from the customer's point of view. What's less obvious is that any temptation for the banks to use new technical security measures to dump risks on the customer should also be resisted in the wider interest of public confidence in electronic commerce and of the banking industry itself. This isn't just a digital signature issue. In the U.K., when it turned out that people who'd accessed electronic services at Barclays Bank via a public terminal could be hacked by the next user pressing the Back button on the browser, the bank tried to blame customers for not clearing their Web caches [747]. If opposing that in court, I'd have great fun finding out how many of Barclays' branch managers knew what a cache is, and the precise date on which the bank's directors had it brought to their attention that such knowledge is now essential to the proper conduct of retail banking business.

It is predictable that such risk dumping will reduce the motivation banks have to build secure systems, and will in time lead to injustices that neither the courts nor public opinion will tolerate. Recall that banks in some countries dumped the risks of ATM systems on customers, and claimed that any customers who complained of "phantom withdrawals" were mistaken or lying, then were greatly inconvenienced when the courts destroyed their fiction by sending ATM fraudsters to jail. The banks seem to be slow learners, and the ATM mistakes are likely to be repeated on a very much grander scale if digital signatures made by customers start being accepted as gospel in business-to-consumer e-commerce transactions.

Even in advance of the deployment of digital signatures, a number of banks have adopted electronic banking terms and conditions under which their records of a transaction are definitive; they are already getting into trouble under consumer law and truth-in-advertising regulations. These issues are discussed in detail in [124].

Business-to-business is a different matter, and as discussed in 19.5.4 there have been systems fielded for some years that use digital signatures in applications such as inter-bank funds transfer, registration of securities, and bills of lading. This appears likely to be the main application of digital signature technology, at least in the short term. One might assume that large businesses either have the expertise to secure the systems that they use to generate signatures or to pay others to do so. But disputes will still arise, especially with small businesses that don't have these resources. The liability for a forged digital signature could be particularly difficult for the courts to pin down, given the refusal of most software companies to accept any liability at all for security failures and even just plain bugs in their products. Therefore, the prudent thing for an e-commerce system designer to do is to set out in the subscribers' contract a procedure for dispute resolution, which should be sufficiently fair to withstand furious legal challenges once the first frauds occur.

21.6 Other Public Sector Issues

A whole grab-bag of other public sector information security issues are appearing. They vary from one country to another; I'll just give a few examples.

21.6.1 Service Delivery

A typical government department, such as a welfare agency or a passport office, has the operation and maintenance of a large distributed system as its core business function. Yet governments have usually been bad at conceiving and implementing large IT projects. Many of the reasons are well known. The civil service doesn't pay very well, so can't usually compete for the brightest IT staff; many government departments have traditional ways of doing things that don't automate well; planning and purchasing cycles are long compared with technology cycles; the managerial culture is more risk-averse than is ideal; and outside a few specialized functions, it isn't easy to set up a dozen competing organizations and just let the market sort them out. Many of the things I've seen go wrong with public sector projects have at their heart the culture clash between the computer business and the civil service. This problem cuts both ways, of course: civil servants tend to see computer people as impossibly ambitious and pushy people who want to disturb time-honored political fudges and eliminate discretionary powers in the interests of automation.

This clash will worsen as the growth of the Net places more severe strains on civil service administrative capabilities. The political leadership expects that government services will be delivered online, and that service levels will rise to somewhere near those of the private sector. The voters expect no less. Yet often automation makes problems worse. In Britain, for example, the National Health Service suppresses demand for healthcare in a number of ways that doctors have evolved over time, such as by making it difficult to get appointments to see a specialist. Recently, ministers have started to insist that patients be able to book a specialist appointment over the phone, and the predictable result is a sudden rise in demand with no corresponding increase in supply. In the absence of a working price mechanism, this is a recipe for chaos. Already, we see signs of specialist doctors heading for early retirement as a response to rising pressure to treat more patients.

The relevance for the security engineer is that many things that are claimed to be impossible on "security" or "privacy" grounds are really demand-suppression issues. A lack of sensitivity to this can make a sale of your "solution" unlikely, or its side effects unpleasant. So you should always try to dig beneath the surface excuses and find out what your prospective clients' real concerns are.

21.6.2 Social Exclusion and Discrimination

A separate set of issues cluster around the delivery of government services to the poor and the old, in the belief that they are much less likely to be online and therefore face a reduced quality of support. The British government, for example, wants public-access Internet terminals made available in libraries and post offices [758]. In effect, this will provide subsidized public-sector competition for Internet cafes.

We'll just have to wait and see whether this catches on. But while Internet use has tended in the past to be the preserve of young affluent white males, it's not altogether clear that this will continue. Women and seniors are among the fastest-growing sectors of Net usage, and the integration of mail and browser facilities into satellite TV is bringing the Net to Joe Sixpack too. Perhaps the interesting question for the security engineer is the extent to which public terminals open up interesting new attacks. We saw in 21.5.4 how systems can be attacked using information kept in caches and the like; there are many pitfalls here.

Another security engineering issue related to equality of access is that many of the assumptions embedded in protection mechanisms can discriminate in ways that may be illegal or at least undesirable. Section 13.8 described how many biometric authentication systems may be regressive, in that the elderly and manual workers can suffer higher error rates with fingerprint readers, and that disabled people with no fingers, or no eyes, risk exclusion if fingerprint or iris scanning systems become widespread. Blind people are already seriously prejudiced in their use of the Web by many of the tricks used by website designers to prevent their pages being scanned by comparison shopping bots—which from the site owner's viewpoint is a security measure.

Intrusion detection systems are another contentious area; as discussed in 18.5.2, automatic systems that detect fraud, or bogus insurance claims, or airline passengers likely to be terrorists, often end up discriminating against some ethnic or social group. Another issue is that systems designed for, and by, college-educated computer scientists are often too hard for less educated people to use. The attitude that users are a nuisance must be vigorously resisted; secure systems, like any other systems, need to be designed for the people who will actually use them. Replacing the word "user" with "customer" or "citizen" is a small step in the right direction.

21.6.3 Revenue Protection

One of the most high-profile concerns is that a combination of anonymous remailers, digital cash and offshore tax havens might make the task of collecting taxes impossible, leading to the breakdown of the system of nation states. This is perhaps most cogently expressed by Neal Stephenson [736] but has found echoes in much other commentary. This tends to ignore the fact that many countries get most of their revenue from sales taxes and customs duties; European readers used to paying over $5 a gallon for gas and $20 for a bottle of whisky will be much more sceptical about this vision.

21.6.4 Elections

Finally, the most fundamental process in any democracy is the conduct of elections. If this is undermined, the whole structure may collapse. I sincerely hope that the election of security chief Vladimir Putin as the president of Russia had nothing to do with the fact that the national electoral reporting system is run by FAPSI, a Russian signals intelligence agency formed in 1991 as the successor to the KGB's 8th and 16th directorates. Its head, General Starovoitov, was reported to be an old KGB type; his agency reported directly to President Yeltsin, who chose Putin as his successor [327, 430].

I would certainly be concerned if Britain were to introduce an electronic election system, and if CESG, the part of GCHQ that is our "national technical authority" for information protection, had anything to do with its design or audit. I mentioned in the introduction to this chapter that the U.K. policy of escrowing all public sector keys could cause serious problems here: even if the agencies don't actually manipulate the result, they will be sorely tempted to find out who voted for parties such as Sinn Féin. But where are the alternative centers of expertise?

The situation in the United States is perhaps not so worrying, because control over elections is very widely distributed, with accreditation state by state and hundreds of legacy systems in the field. But complacency isn't advisable. The sheer cost of obtaining accreditation in fifty states (over $100,000 a state to have design and source code checked by an independent expert) will limit the number of companies that can make a serious bid to provide the online successors to the current local systems. The disputes over the 2000 election may also drive state legislators to embrace "modern" online systems without stopping to think. If one or two companies end up controlling voting in all or most of the states, they will bear close watching.

21.7 Summary

Governments and public policy concerns generally are intruding more and more into the work of the security engineer. The legal controls on cryptography in many countries are just the most obvious example. Although misguided, these controls have a number of pernicious and unobvious effects, of which the worst may be the erosion of the boundary between law enforcement and intelligence. Other boundaries whose erosion could threaten civil liberties include those between traffic analysis and wiretaps for content, between copyright and censorship, and between mechanisms that enforce copyright and those that do other things as well, such as accessory control. Working for increased transparency might be more strategic than taking issue with particular technologies.

There are many other issues though. The engineer must pay attention to the protection of personal data, the quality of evidence a system produces, copyright law issues, social exclusion and discrimination. There are also some mechanisms that we really must get right, such as the integrity of the systems used to record and tally votes in elections.

Research Problems

Technopolicy issues tend to involve a complex interplay between science, engineering, applied psychology, law and economics. There is altogether too little serious cross-disciplinary research; the apothegm at the head of this chapter captures well the problem that people from these different disciplines often talk at cross purposes. Debates on issues such as key escrow are slowly building a body of people with experience in talking to both computer scientists and lawyers; and electronic commerce leads computer scientists to talk to economists. Initiatives that speed up this process are almost certainly a good thing; bringing in psychologists, historians of science, and others would also be positive. It's not clear is how to do this within the current structures of academic and industrial research organizations.

Further Reading

It's extraordinarily easy for technopolicy arguments to get detached at one or more corners from reality; and many of the nightmares conjured up to get attention and money (such as credit card transactions being intercepted on the Internet) are really the modern equivalent of the monsters that appeared on medieval maps to cover up the cartographer's ignorance. An engineer who wants to build things that work and last has a duty not to get carried away. For this reason, it's particularly important to dig out primary sources—material written by experienced insiders such as R.V. Jones [425] and Gerard Walsh [787], books by people with a long involvement in the policy process such as Whitfield Diffie and Susan Landau [250], government reports that were influential in policy formation such as the NRC study on cryptography policy [580], and compilations of primary materials, such as [684].

There's also useful material at the Web sites of organizations such as EPIC [266], EFF [264], FIPR [304], CDT [173], the Privacy Exchange [628], and on mailing lists such as politech [619] and ukcrypto [755].

The best book I know on computer forensics is by Tony Sammes and Brian Jenkinson [664]; and there's a nice article by Peter Sommer on the forensics and evidential issues that arose when prosecuting some U.K. youngsters who hacked the USAF Rome airbase [722]. The Department of Justice's "Guidelines for Searching and

Seizing Computers" also bear some attention [245]. For collections of computer crime case histories, see Peter Neumann [590], Dorothy Denning [235], and Donn Parker [602].

On the topic of data protection, there is a huge literature, but no concise guide that I know of. [802] Alan Westin provides a good historical overview, with a perspective on the coming collision between Europe and the United States. Simson Garfinkel [330] and Michael Froomkin [323] survey U.S. privacy and surveillance issues.

There's now quite a literature on electronic voting. The issues are largely the same as with voting by mail or by phone, but not quite. An influential survey of the requirements, and of the things that can go wrong, is by Mike Shamos [693]; while Roy Saltman (for many years the authority at NIST) discusses things that have gone wrong in the United States and various NIST recommendations, in [663]. There's a report on the feasibility of Internet voting from the State of California at [152]. Finally, Lorrie Cranor has a useful link farm on electronic voting at [209].

CHAPTER 22

Management Issues

My own experience is that developers with a clean, expressive set of specific security requirements can build a very tight machine. They don't have to be security gurus, but they have to understand what they're trying to build and how it should work.

—RICK SMITH

One of the most important problems we face today, as techniques and systems become more and more pervasive, is the risk of missing that fine, human point that may well make the difference between success and failure, fair and unfair, right and wrong ... no IBM computer has an education in the humanities.

—TOM WATSON

Management is that for which there is no algorithm. Where there is an algorithm, it's administration.

—ROGER NEEDHAM

22.1 Introduction

To this point, I've outlined a variety of security applications, techniques, and concerns. If you're a working IT manager, paid to build a secure system, you will by now be looking for a systematic way to select protection aims and mechanisms. This brings us to the topics of system engineering, risk analysis, and threat assessment.

The experience of the business schools is that management training should be conducted largely through the study of case histories, stiffened with focused courses on basic topics such as law, economics, and accounting. I have followed this model in this book. We went over the fundamentals, such as protocols, access control and crypto, and then looked at a lot of different applications. Now we have to pull the threads together and discuss how a security engineering problem should be tackled. Organizational issues matter here as well as technical ones. It's important to understand the capabilities of the staff who'll operate your control systems, such as guards and auditors, to take account of the managerial and work-group pressures on them, and get feedback from them as the system evolves.

22.2 Managing a Security Project

The core of the security project manager's job is usually requirements engineering—figuring out what to protect and how. When doing this, it is critical to understand the trade-off between risk and reward. Security people have a distinct tendency to focus too much on the former and neglect the latter. If the client has a turnover of $10 million, profits of $1 million and theft losses of $150,000, the security consultant may make a pitch about "how to increase your profits by 15%" when often what's really in the shareholders' interests is to double the turnover to $20 million, even if this triples the losses to $450,000. Assuming the margins remain the same, the profit is now $1.85 million, an increase of 85%. The point is, don't fall into the trap of believing that the only possible response to a vulnerability is to fix it; and distrust the sort of consultant who can talk only about "tightening security." Often, it's too tight already.

22.2.1 A Tale of Three Supermarkets

My thumbnail case history to illustrate this point concerns three supermarkets. Among the large operational costs of running a supermarket are the salaries of the checkout and security staff, and the stock shrinkage due to theft. Checkout delays are also a significant source of aggravation: just cutting the number of staff isn't an option, and working them harder might mean more shrinkage. What might technology do to help?

One supermarket in South Africa decided to automate completely. All produce would carry an RF tag, so that an entire shopping cart could be scanned automatically. If this had worked, it would have killed both birds with one stone: the same RF tags could have been used to make theft very much harder. Though there was a pilot, the idea couldn't compete with barcodes. Customers had to use a special cart, which was large and ugly, and the RF tags also cost money.

Another supermarket in a European country believed that much of their losses were due to a hard core of professional thieves, and thought of building a face recognition system to alert the guards whenever one of these habitual villains came into a store. But current technology can't do that with low enough error rates to be useful. In the end, the chosen route was civil recovery. When a shoplifter is caught, then even after the local magistrates have fined him about the price of a lunch, the supermarket goes after him in the civil courts for wasted time, lost earnings, attorneys' fees and everything else they can think of; and then armed with a judgment for about the price of a car they go round to his house and seize all his furniture. So far so good. But their management got too focused on cutting losses rather than increasing sales. In the end, they started losing market share and saw their stock price slide. Diverting effort into looking for a security-based solution was probably a symptom of their decline rather than a cause, but may well have contributed to it.

The supermarket that appears to be doing best is Waitrose in England which has introduced self-service scanning. When you go into the store you swipe your store card in a machine that dispenses a portable barcode scanner. You scan the goods as you pick them off the shelves and put them into your shopping bag. At the checkout, you hand back the scanner, get a printed list of everything you bought, swipe your credit card, and head for the parking lot. This might seem rather risky—but then so did the self-service supermarket back in the days when traditional grocers' shops stocked all the goods behind the counter. In fact, there are a number of subtle control mechanisms at work. Limiting the service to store cardholders not only enables the managers to exclude known shoplifters, but also helps market the store card. By having a card, you acquire a trusted status visible to any neighbors you meet while shopping; conversely, losing your card (whether by getting caught stealing, or, more likely, falling behind on your payments) could be embarrassing. And trusting people removes much of the motive for cheating, as there's no kudos in beating the system. Of course, should the guard at the video screen see a customer lingering suspiciously near the racks of hundred-pound wines, it can always be arranged for the system to "break" as the suspect gets to the checkout, which gives the staff a non-confrontational way to recheck the bag's contents.

22.2.2 Balancing Risk and Reward

The purpose of business is profit, and profit is the reward for risk. Security mechanisms can often make a significant difference to the risk/reward equation, but, ultimately, it's the duty of a company's board of directors to get the balance right. In this *risk management* task, they may draw on all sorts of advice—lawyers, actuaries, security engineers—as well as listen to their marketing, operations, and financial teams. A sound corporate risk management strategy involves much more than the operational risks from attacks on information systems; there are non-IT operational risks (such as fires and floods) as well as legal risks, exchange rate risks, political risks, and many more. Company bosses need the big picture view to make sensible decisions, and a difficult part of their task is to see to it that advisers from different disciplines work together just closely enough, but no more.

Advisers need to understand each others' roles, and work together rather than try to undermine each other; but if the company boss doesn't ask hard questions and stir the cauldron a bit, then the advisers may cosy up with each other and entrench a consensus view that steadily drifts away from reality. One of the most valuable tasks the security engineer is called on to perform (and the one needing the most diplomatic skill) is when you're brought in to contribute, as an independent outsider, to challenging this sort of groupthink. In fact, on perhaps a third of the consulting assignments I've done, there's at least one person at the client company who knows exactly what the problem is and how to fix it—they just need a credible mercenary to beat up on the majority of colleagues who're averse to change. (This is one reason why famous consulting firms that exude an air of quality and certainty often have a competitive advantage over specialists; however, in the cases where specialists are needed, but the work is given to "suits," some fairly spectacular things can go wrong.)

Although the goals and management structures in government may be slightly different, exactly the same principles apply. Risk management is often harder because people are more used to an approach based on compliance with a set of standards (such as the Orange Book) rather than case-by-case requirements engineering. James Coyne and Norman Kluksdahl present in [208] a classic case study of information security run amok at NASA. There, the end of military involvement in Space Shuttle operations led to a security team being set up at the Mission Control Center in Houston to fill the vacuum left by the DoD's departure. This team was given an ambitious charter; it became independent of both the development and operations teams; its impositions became increasingly unrelated to budget and operational constraints; and its relations with the rest of the organization became increasingly adversarial. In the end, it had to be overthrown or nothing would have got done.

22.2.3 Organizational Issues

Although this chapter is about management, I'm not so much concerned with how you train and grade the guards as with how you build a usable system. However, you need to understand the guards (and the auditors, and the checkout staff, and . . .) or you won't be able to do even a halfway passable job. Many systems fail because their designers make unrealistic assumptions about the ability, motivation, and discipline of the people who will operate it. This isn't just a matter of one-off analysis. For example, an initially low rate of fraud can cause people to get complacent and careless, until suddenly things explode. Also, an externally induced change in the organization—such as a merger or acquisition—can undermine control.

A surprising number of human frailties express themselves through the way people behave in organizations, and for which you have to make allowance in your designs.

22.2.3.1 The Complacency Cycle
and the Risk Thermostat

The effects of organizational complacency are well illustrated by phone fraud in the United States. There is a seven-year cycle: in any one year there will be one of the "Baby Bells" that is getting badly hurt. This causes its managers to hire experts, clean things up, and get everything under control, at which point another of them becomes the favored target. Over the next six years, things gradually slacken off, then it's back to square one.

Some interesting and relevant work has been done on how people manage their exposure to risk. Adams studied the effect of mandatory seat belt laws, and established that these laws don't actually save lives: they just transfer casualties from vehicle occupants to pedestrians and cyclists. Seat belts make drivers feel safer, so they drive faster to bring their perceived risk back up to its previous level. Adams calls this a *risk thermostat* and the model is borne out in other applications too [8, 9]. The complacency cycle can be thought of as the risk thermostat's corporate manifestation. No matter how these phenomena are described, risk management remains an interactive business that involves the operation of all sorts of feedback and compensating behavior. The resulting system may be stable, as with road traffic fatalities; or it may oscillate, as with the Baby Bells.

The feedback mechanisms may provide a systemic limit on the performance of some risk reduction systems. The incidence of attacks, or accidents, or whatever the organization is trying to prevent, will be reduced to the point at which "there are not enough attacks"—as with the alarm systems described in Chapter 10 and the intrusion detection systems discussed in Section 18.5.3. Perhaps systems will always reach an equilibrium at which the sentries fall asleep, or real alarms are swamped by false ones, or organizational budgets are eroded to (and past) the point of danger. It is not at all obvious how to use technology to shift this equilibrium point.

Risk management may be one of the world's largest industries. It includes not just security engineers but also fire and casualty services, insurers, the road safety industry and much of the legal profession. Yet it is startling how little is really known about the subject. Engineers, economists, actuaries and lawyers all come at the problem from different directions, use different language and arrive at quite incompatible conclusions. There are also strong cultural factors at work. For example, if we distinguish *risk* as being where the odds are known but the outcome isn't, from *uncertainty* where even the odds are unknown, then most people appear to be more uncertainty-averse than risk-averse. Where the odds are directly perceptible, a risk is often dealt with intuitively; but where the science is unknown or inconclusive, people are liberated to project all sorts of fears and prejudices. So perhaps the best medicine is education. Nonetheless, there are some specific things that the security engineer should either do, or avoid.

22.2.3.2 Interaction with Reliability

A significant cause of poor internal control in organizations is that the systems are insufficiently reliable, so lots of transactions are always going wrong and have to be corrected manually. A high tolerance of chaos undermines control, as it creates a high false alarm rate for many of the protection mechanisms. It also tempts staff: when they see that errors aren't spotted, they conclude that theft won't be either.

A recurring theme is the correlation between quality and security. For example, it has been shown that investment in software quality will reduce the incidence of computer security problems, regardless of whether security was a target of the quality program or not; and that the most effective quality measure from the security point of view is the code walk-through [292]. It seems that the knowledge that one's output will be read and criticized has a salutary effect on many programmers.

Reliability can be one of your biggest selling points when trying to get a client's board of directors to agree on protective measures. Mistakes cost business a lot of money; no one really understands what software does; if mistakes are found, the frauds should be much more obvious; and all this can be communicated to top management without embarrassment on either side.

22.2.3.3 Solving the Wrong Problem

Faced with an intractable problem, it is common for people to furiously attack a related but easier one. We saw the effects of this in the public policy context in 21.2.5.3.

Displacement activity is also common in the private sector. An example comes from the smartcard industry. As discussed in Section 14.7.2, the difficulty of protecting smartcards against microprobing attacks has led the industry to concentrate on securing other things instead. Even programming manuals are available only under *nondisclosure agreements* (NDA) even plant visitors have to sign an NDA at reception; much technical material isn't available at all; and vendor facilities have almost nuclear-grade physical security. Physical security overkill may impress naive customers—but almost all of the real attacks on fielded smartcard systems used probing attacks rather than any kind of inside information.

One organizational driver for this is an inability to deal with uncertainty. Managers prefer approaches that can be implemented by box-ticking their way down a checklist, and if an organization needs to deal with an ongoing risk, then some way must be found to keep it as a process and to stop it turning into a due-diligence checklist item. But there will be constant pressure to replace processes with checklists, as they demand less management attention and effort. I noted in Section 7.6.6 that bureaucratic guidelines for military systems had a strong tendency to displace critical thought; instead of thinking through a system's security requirements, designers just reached for their checklists. Commercial systems are not much different.

Another organizational issue is that when exposures are politically sensitive, some camouflage may be used. The classic example is the question of whether attacks come from insiders or outsiders. We've seen in system after system that the insiders are the main problem, whether because some of them are malicious or because most of them are careless. But it's imprudent to enforce controls too overtly against line managers and IT staff, as this will alienate them and it's often hard to get them to manage the controls themselves. It's also hard to sell a typical company's board of directors on the need for proper defenses against insider attack, as this means impugning the integrity and reliability of the staff who report to them.

Thus, a security manager will often ask for, and get, lots of money to defend against nonexistent "evil hackers" so that she can spend most of it on controls to manage the real threat, namely dishonest or careless staff. I would be cautious about this strategy, because protection mechanisms without clear justifications are likely to be eroded under operational pressure—especially if they are seen as bureaucratic impositions. Often, it will take a certain amount of subtlety and negotiating skill, and controls will have to be marketed as a way of reducing errors and protecting staff. Bank managers love dual-control safe locks because they understand that it reduces the risk that their families will be taken hostage; and requiring two signatures on transactions over a certain limit means that there are extra shoulders to take the burden when something goes wrong. But such consensus on the need for protective measures is usually lacking elsewhere.

22.2.3.4 Incompetent or Inexperienced Security Managers

The situation is bad enough even with a competent IT security manager, who has to use all sorts of guile to raise money for an activity that many of her management colleagues will tend to regard as a pure cost. In real life, the situation is even worse. In many traditional companies, promotions to top management jobs are a matter of seniority and contacts; so if you want to get to be the CEO, you'll have to spend maybe 20 or 30 years in the company without offending too many people. Being a security manager is absolutely the last thing you want to do, as it will mean saying no to people all the time. It's hardly surprising that the average tenure of computer security managers at U.S. government agencies is only seven months [384].

Things are complicated by reorganizations, in which central computer security departments may be created and destroyed every few years, while the IT audit function oscillates between the IT department, the internal audit department, and outside auditors or consultants. The security function is even less likely than other business processes to receive sustained attention and analytic thought, and more likely to succumb to a box-ticking due diligence mentality.

22.2.3.5 *Moral Hazard*

Companies often design systems so that the risk gets dumped on third parties. I mentioned in Chapter 21 that one of the attractions of digital signatures is that they can allow the risk associated with a forged signature to be transferred from the relying party to the alleged signer; thus, for example, transferring much of the risk associated with online banking from the bank to the customer. I also discussed in Chapter 9, how banks in some countries claimed that their automatic teller machines could not possibly make mistakes, so that any disputes must be the customer's fault.

In addition to the public policy aspects, and macroeconomic effects which I'll come to in Section 22.6, this has effects on the dumping company internally. It creates a *moral hazard*, by removing the incentives for people to take care, and for the company to invest in appropriate risk management techniques. Worse, a company whose policy is to deny vigorously that some particular type of fraud is possible leaves itself open to staff who defraud it knowing that a prosecution would be too embarrassing.

A slightly different kind of moral hazard is created when people who make system design decisions are unlikely to be held accountable for their actions. There are many possible causes. IT staff turnover could be high, with much reliance placed on contract staff; a rising management star with whom nobody wishes to argue can be involved as a user in the design team; or imminent business process re-engineering may turn loyal staff into surreptitious job seekers. In any case, when you design a secure system, it's a good idea to look at your colleagues and ask yourself which of them will shoulder the blame three years later when things go wrong. Another common incentive failure occurs when one part of an organization takes the credit for the profit generated by some process, while another part picks up the bills when things go wrong. Very often the marketing department gets the praise for increased sales, while the finance department is left with the bad debts. One might think that they would between them strike a balance between risk and reward, but this is very often not so. The case of the three supermarkets, mentioned above, is just one example of many. Companies may swing wildly over a period of years from being risk takers to being excessively risk averse, and (less often) back again. Adams documents in [9] that risk taking and risk aversion are strongly associated with different personality types: the former tend to be individualists, a company's entrepreneurs, while the latter tend to be hierarchists. As the latter usually come to dominate bureaucracies, it is not surprising that stable, established organizations tend to be much more risk averse than rational economics would dictate.

Which tools and concepts can help cut through the fog of bureaucratic infighting and determine a system's protection requirements from first principles?

The rest of this chapter will be organized as follows. The next section will look at basic methodological issues, such as top-down versus iterative development. After that, I'll explain how these apply to the specific problem of security requirements engineering. Having set the scene, I'll then return to risk management and look at technical tools. Then I'll talk about some of the economic issues, and finally discuss the things that go wrong.

22.3 Methodology

Large software projects usually take longer than planned, cost more than budgeted for, and have more bugs than expected. (This is sometimes known as "Cheops' law" after the builder of the Great Pyramid.) By the 1960s, people had started talking about the *software crisis*, although the word crisis is hardly appropriate for a starte of affairs that has now lasted (like computer insecurity) for two generations. Anyway, the term *software engineering* was proposed by Brian Randell in 1968, and defined to be:

> Software engineering is the establishment and use of sound engineering principles in order to obtain economically software that is reliable and works efficiently on real machines.

This encompassed the hope that the problem could be solved in the same way that one builds ships and aircraft, with a proven scientific foundation and a set of design rules [583]. Since then, much progress has been made, though never as much as one would like.

Software engineering is about managing complexity, of which there are two kinds. One is the *incidental complexity* involved in programming using inappropriate tools, such as the assembly languages that were all that some early machines supported; programming a modern application with a graphical user interface in such a language would be impossibly tedious and error-prone. The other is the *intrinsic complexity* of dealing with large and complex problems. A bank's administrative systems, for example, may involve tens of millions of lines of code and be too complex for any one person to understand.

Incidental complexity is largely dealt with using technical tools. The most important of these are high-level languages that hide much of the drudgery of dealing with machine-specific detail and enable the programmer to develop code at an appropriate level of abstraction. There are also formal methods that enable particularly error-prone design and programming tasks to be checked. The obvious security engineering example is provided by the BAN logic for verifying cryptographic protocols, which I described in Section 2.7.

Intrinsic complexity usually requires methodological tools that focus on dividing up the problem into manageable subproblems, and restricting the extent to which these subproblems can interact. Many tools are available on the market to help you do this; which you use may well be a matter of your client's policy. But there are basically two approaches: top-down and iterative.

22.3.1 Top-Down Design

The classical model of system development is the *waterfall model* developed by Winston Royce in 1970 for the U.S. Air Force [653]. The idea is that you start from a concise statement of the system's requirements, elaborate this into a specification, implement and test the system's components, integrate and test them as a system, then roll out the system for live operation (see Figure 22.1).

The idea is that the requirements are written in the user language, and the specification in technical language; the unit testing checks the units against the specification, and the system testing checks whether the requirements are met. At the first two steps in this chain there is feedback on whether you're building the right system (*validation*) and at the next two on whether you're building it right (*verification*). There may be more than four steps; a common elaboration is to have a sequence of *refinement* steps as the requirements are developed into ever more detailed specifications. But that's by the way.

The critical thing about the waterfall model is that development flows inexorably downward from the first statement of the requirements to the deployment of the system in the field. Although there is feedback from each stage to its predecessor, there is no system-level feedback from, say, system testing to the requirements. Therein lie the waterfall model's strengths, and also its weaknesses.

The strengths of the waterfall model are that it compels early clarification of system goals, architecture, and interfaces; it makes the project manager's task easier by providing definite milestones to aim at; it increases cost transparency by enabling separate charges to be made for each step, and for any late specification changes; and it's compatible with a wide range of tools. Where it can be made to work, it's usually the best approach. The critical question is whether the requirements are known in detail in advance of any development or prototyping work. Sometimes, this is the case, such as when writing a compiler or (in the security world) designing a tamper-resistant cryptographic processor to implement a known transaction set and pass a certain level of FIPS evaluation.

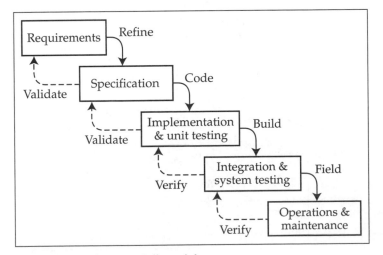

Figure 22.1 The waterfall model.

But, often, the detailed requirements aren't known in advance, so an iterative approach is necessary. There are quite a few possible reasons for this. Perhaps the requirements aren't understood yet by the customer, and a prototype is necessary to clarify them rather than more discussion; the technology may be changing; the environment could be changing; or a critical part of the project may involve the design of a feature, such as a human-computer interface, which we know from experience will involve several prototypes. (No matter how well engineered the internals of a protection system, user interface problems are to be expected, and a pilot is advisable if the business model allows it.)

22.3.2 Iterative Design

Many development projects just need an iterative approach to development, but the iteration might never terminate satisfactorily. You could build a prototype for the client who would play with it, then say, "No, I want it this way instead." Then you would build another one, come up against another objection, and never get anything fielded at all.

There are two common ways to deal with this. The first is Barry Boehm's *spiral model* in which development proceeds through a pre-agreed number of iterations. In each of these, a prototype is built and tested, with managers being able to evaluate the risk at each stage so they can decide whether to proceed with the next iteration or to cut their losses. It's called the spiral model because the process is often depicted as shown in Figure 22.2.

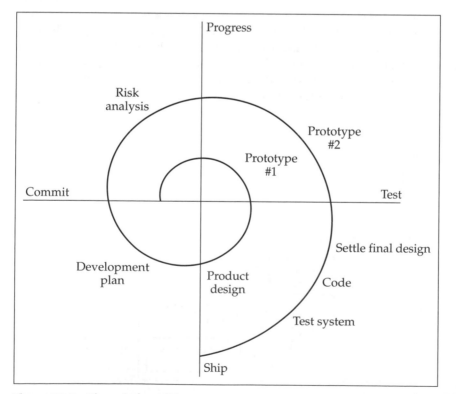

Figure 22.2 The spiral model.

The other common model is *evolutionary development*. This has become increasingly important, because it's how the packaged software industry works, and has recently been popularized under the name of "extreme programming." Unfortunately, it tends to be neglected in academic courses and books on software engineering.

As the world moves from bespoke software developed in formal projects to packages whose owners put in more and more features to appeal to ever wider markets, software products become so complex that they cannot be economically developed (or redeveloped) from scratch. Indeed, Microsoft has tried more than once to rewrite Word, but gave up each time. (Perhaps the best book on the evolutionary development model is by Steve Maguire, a Microsoft manager [521].) In this view of the world, products aren't the result of a project but of a process, which involves continually modifying previous versions.

The critical point about evolutionary development is that just as each generation of a biological species has to be viable for the species to continue, so each generation of an evolving software product must be viable. The core technology for this is *regression testing*. At regular intervals—perhaps once a day—all the teams working on different features of a product upgrade check in their code, and it gets compiled to a *build*, which is then tested automatically against a large set of inputs. This step checks whether things that used to work still work, and that old bugs that had been removed haven't found their way back in. Of course, it's always possible that a build just doesn't work at all, and there may be quite long disruptions as a major change is implemented. Thus, we consider the current "generation" of the product to be the last build that worked. One way or another, we always have viable code that we can ship for beta testing or whatever our next stage is.

The technology of testing is probably the biggest practical improvement in software engineering during the 1990s. Before automated regression tests were widely used, engineers reckoned that 15% of bug fixes either introduced new bugs or reintroduced old ones [7]. But automated testing is less useful for the security engineer, for a number of reasons. Security properties are more diverse, and security engineers are fewer in number, so we haven't had as much investment in tools; moreover, the available tools are much more fragmentary and primitive than those available to the general software engineering community. Many of the flaws that we want to find and fix—such as stack overflow attacks—tend to appear in new features rather than to reappear in old ones. Specific types of attack are also often easier to fix using specific remedies, such as the canary mentioned in Section 4.4.5 in the case of stack overflow. And many security flaws result from subtle bugs that cross a system's levels of abstraction, such as when specification errors interact with user interface features—the sort of problem for which it's difficult to devise automated tests. But regression testing is still important. It finds functionality that has been affected by a change but that is not fully understood.

Much the same applies to safety-critical systems, which are similar in many respects to secure systems. Some useful lessons can be drawn from them.

22.3.3 Lessons from Safety-Critical Systems

Critical computer systems can be defined as those in which a certain class of failure is to be avoided if at all possible. Depending on the class of failure, they may be safety-critical, business-critical, security-critical, critical to the environment, or whatever. Obvious examples of the safety-critical variety include flight controls and automatic braking systems. There is a large literature on this subject, and a lot of methodologies have been developed to help manage risk intelligently.

Overall, these methodologies tend to follow the waterfall view of the universe. The usual procedure is to identify hazards and assess risks; decide on a strategy to cope with them (avoidance, constraint, redundancy ...); trace the hazards down to hardware and software components which are thereby identified as critical; identify the operator procedures which are also critical and study the various applied psychology and operations research issues; and, finally, decide on a test plan and get on with the task of testing. The outcome of the testing is not just a system you're confident to run live, but a *safety case* to justify running it.

The safety case will provide the evidence, if something does go wrong that you exercised due care; it will typically consist of the hazard analysis, the documentation linking this to component reliability and human factor issues, and the results of tests (both at component and system levels), which show that the required failure rates have been achieved.

The ideal system design avoids hazards entirely. A good illustration comes from the motor-reversing circuits shown in Figure 22.3. In the first design on the left, a double-pole, double-throw switch reverses the current passing from the battery through the motor. However, this has a potential problem: if only one of the two poles of the switch moves, the battery will be short-circuited, and a fire may result. The solution is to exchange the battery and the motor, as in the modified circuit on the right. There, a switch failure will short out only the motor, not the battery.

Hazard elimination is useful in security engineering, too. Recall the example in the early design of SWIFT in Section 9.3.1: there, the keys used to authenticate transactions between one bank and another were exchanged between the banks directly. In this way, SWIFT personnel and systems did not have the means to forge a valid transaction, and had to be trusted much less. In general, minimizing the trusted computing base is, to a large extent, an exercise in hazard elimination.

Once as many hazards as possible have been eliminated, the next step is to identify failures that could cause accidents. A common top-down way of identifying the things that can go wrong is to conduct a *fault tree analysis:* a tree is constructed whose root is the undesired behavior and whose successive nodes are its possible causes. This carries over in a fairly obvious way to security engineering; Figure 22.4 shows an example of

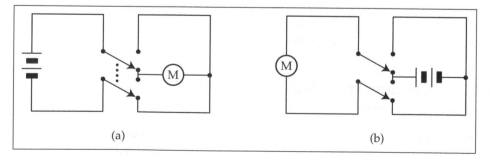

Figure 22.3 Hazard elimination in motor-reversing circuit.

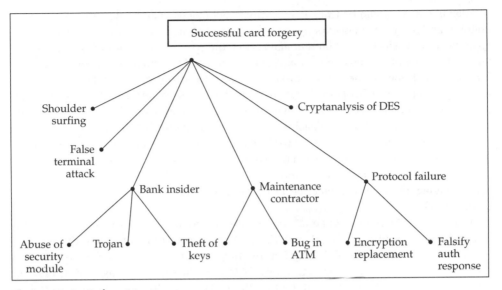

Figure 22.4   A threat tree.

a fault tree (or *threat tree*, as it's often called in security engineering) for fraud from automatic teller machines. Threat trees are standard practice in the U.S. Department of Defense.

Here's how a threat tree works. You start out from each undesirable outcome, and work backward by writing down each possible immediate cause. You work backward from there by adding each precursor condition, and recurse. Then, working around the tree's leaves, you should be able to see each combination of technical attack, operational blunder, physical penetration, and so on, which would break security. Note that this can amount to an attack manual for the system, and so it may be highly classified. Nonetheless, it must exist; and if the system evaluators or accreditors can find any significant other attacks, they may fail the product.

Returning to the safety-critical world, another way of doing the hazard analysis is *failure modes and effects analysis* (FMEA), pioneered by NASA, which is bottom-up rather than top-down. This involves tracing the consequences of a failure of each of the system's components all the way up to the effect on the mission. This is often useful in security engineering; it's a good idea to have a clear picture of the consequences of a failure of any one of your protection mechanisms.

A really thorough analysis of failure modes may combine top-down and bottom-up approaches, and there are various ways to manage the resulting mass of data. For example, you can construct a matrix of hazards against safety mechanisms; and if the safety policy is that each serious hazard must be constrained by at least two independent mechanisms, then you can check that there are two entries in each of the relevant columns. In this way, you can demonstrate graphically that, in the presence of the hazard in question, at least two failures will be required to cause an accident. This methodology goes across unchanged to security engineering, as I'll explain below.

The safety-critical systems community has a number of techniques for dealing with failure and error rates. Component failure rates can be measured statistically; the number of bugs in software can be tracked by various techniques, which I describe in the next chapter; and there is a lot of experience with the probability of operator error at different types of activity. The telegraphic summary is that the error rate depends on the familiarity and complexity of the task, the amount of pressure, and the number of cues to success. Where a task is simple, performed often, and there are strong cues to success, the error rate might be 1 in 100,000 operations. However, when a task is performed for the first time in a confusing environment, where logical thought is required and the operator is under pressure, then the odds can be against successful completion of the task. Designers of systems such as nuclear reactors are well aware (at least since Three Mile Island) that it's when the red lights go on for the first time that the worst mistakes get made. Similarly, in security systems, it tends to be the important but rarely performed tasks, such as getting senior managers to set up master crypto keys, where the most egregious blunders can be expected.

A classic example was when a bank wanted to create a set of three master keys to link its cash machine network to VISA, and needed a terminal to drive the security module [20]. A contractor obligingly lent the bank a laptop PC, together with software that emulated the desired type of terminal. With this, the senior managers duly created the required keys and sent them off to VISA. None of them realized that most PC terminal emulation software packages can be set to log all the transactions passing through, and this is precisely what the contractor did. He captured the clear zone key as it was created, and later used it to decrypt the bank's master PIN key.

When doing security requirements engineering, special care has to be paid to the skill level of the staff who will perform each critical task, and estimates must be made of the likelihood of error. Be cautious here: an airplane designer can rely on a fairly predictable skill level from anyone with a commercial pilot's licence; and a shipbuilder knows the strengths and weaknesses of a sailor in the Navy. The security engineer usually has no such luck. Many security failures remind me of a remark made by a ranger at Yosemite National Park about the devices provided to prevent bears from getting at campers' food supplies: that it's an impossible engineering problem because the brighter bears are smarter than the dumber campers.

There are also testability issues. A common problem with redundant systems is *fault masking:* if the output is determined by majority voting between three processors, and one of them fails, then the system will continue to work fine, but its safety margin will have been eroded. Several airplane crashes have resulted from flying a craft with one of the navigation or flight control systems dysfunctional; although pilots may be intellectually aware that their display is unreliable, their reaction under pressure will be to rely on it rather than to check it against other instruments. A further failure can then be catastrophic. A security example is the ATM problem mentioned in Section 9.4.2 where a bank issued all its customers with the same PIN. In that cases, the fault got masked by the handling precautions applied to PINs, which ensured that even the bank's security and audit staff get hold of only the PIN mailer for their own personal account. Clearly, some thought is needed about how faults can remain visible and testable even when their immediate effects are masked.

The final lesson from safety-critical systems is that, although there will be a safety requirements specification and safety test criteria as part of the safety case for the lawyers or regulators, it is good practice to integrate the safety case with the general requirements and test documentation. If the safety case is a separate set of documents, then it's easy to sideline it after approval is obtained, and thus fail to maintain it properly. If, on the other hand, it's an integral part of the product's management, not only will it likely get upgraded as the product is, but it is also much more likely to be taken heed of by experts from other domains who might be designing features with possible interactions.

As a general rule, safety must be built in as a system is developed, not retrofitted; the same goes for security. The main difference is in the failure model. Rather than the effects of random failure, we're dealing with a hostile opponent who can cause some of the components of our system to fail at the least convenient time and in the most damaging way possible. In effect, our task is to program a computer which gives answers that are subtly and maliciously wrong at the most inconvenient moment possible. This has been referred to as "programming Satan's computer," to distinguish it from the more common problem of programming Murphy's [48]. This provides an insight into one of the reasons security engineering is hard: Satan's computer is hard to test [682].

22.4 Security Requirements Engineering

In Chapter 7, I defined a security policy model to be a concise statement of the protection properties that a system, or generic type of system, must have. This was driven by the threat model, which I introduced in Chapter 3 and sets out the attacks and failures with which the system should be able to cope. The security policy model is further refined into a *security target*, which is a more detailed description of the protection mechanisms that a specific implementation provides, and how they relate to the control objectives. The security target forms the basis for testing and evaluation of a product. The policy model and the target together may be referred to loosely as the *security policy*, and the process of developing a security policy and obtaining agreement on it from the system owner is the process of *requirements engineering*.

Requirements engineering is the most critical task of managing secure system development, and is also the hardest. It's where "the rubber hits the road." It's at the intersection of the most difficult technical issues, the most acute bureaucratic power struggles, and the most determined efforts at blame avoidance. The available methodologies have consistently lagged behind those available to the rest of the system engineering world [77].

In my view, the critical insight is that the process of generating a security policy and a security target is not essentially different from the process of producing code. Depending on the application, you can use a top-down, waterfall approach, a limited iterative approach such as the spiral model, or a continuing iterative process such as the evolutionary model. In each case, we need to build in the means to manage risk and have the risk assessment drive the policy development or evolution.

Risk management must also continue once the system has been deployed. It's notoriously hard to tell what a new invention will be useful for; attacks are just as difficult to predict. Phone companies spent the 1970s figuring out ways to stop phone phreaks getting free calls; as it turned out, the real problem was crooks abusing the system to make calls that would be hard for the police to trace. Some people worried about crooks hacking bank smartcards, and put in lots of back-end protection for the early electronic purses; but the attacks came on pay-TV smartcards instead. Other people worried about the security of credit card numbers used in transactions on the Net, only to learn that the real threat to online businesses was not hackers but refunds and disputes. As they say, "The street finds its own uses for things." The point is, don't expect to get the protection requirements completely right at the first attempt. In many cases, the policy and mechanisms were set when a system was first built, then undermined as the environment (and the product) evolved, but the protection did not. There must be a mechanism for monitoring, and acting on, changing protection requirements.

In this section, unlike in the previous one, I'll describe the case of evolving protection requirements first, as it is both more common and easier to manage.

22.4.1 Managing Requirements Evolution

Most of the time, security requirements have to be tweaked for one of four reasons. First, we might need to fix a bug. Second, we may want to improve the system; as we get more experience of the kind of attacks that happen, we will want to tune the controls. Third, we may want to deal with an evolving environment; for example, if an online ordering system that was previously limited to a handful of major suppliers is to be extended to all of a firm's suppliers, then the controls are likely to need review. Finally, there may be a change in the organization; firms are continually undergoing mergers, management buyouts, business process re-engineering, you name it.

Of course, any of these could result in such a radical change that we would consider it to be a redevelopment rather than an evolution. The dividing line between the two is inevitably vague, but as I'll explain, many evolutionary ideas carry over into one-off projects.

22.4.1.1 Bug Fixing

Most security enhancements fall into the category of bug fixes or product tuning. Fortunately, they are usually the easiest to cope with, provided that the right structures are in place.

If you sell software that's at all security-critical—and most anything that can communicate with the outside world is potentially so—then the day will come when you get a report of a vulnerability or even an attack. In the old days, vendors could take months to respond with a new version of the product, or would do nothing at all but issue a warning (or even a denial). Public expectations are higher nowadays. With mass-market products, you can expect press publicity; even with more specialized products there is a risk of press coverage. In short, you had better have a plan to deal with it. This will have four components: monitoring, repair, distribution, and reassurance.

First, be sure to learn of vulnerabilities as soon as you can—and preferably no later than the press (or the bad guys) do. Listening to customers is important; provide an efficient way for them to report bugs. Consider offering an incentive, such as points toward their next upgrade, lottery tickets, or even cash. Then make someone responsible for monitoring these reports, and for reading relevant mailing lists, such as bugtraq [144].

Second, be able to respond appropriately. In organizations such as banks with time-critical processing requirements, it's normal for one member of each product team to be on call via a pager in case something goes wrong at three in the morning and needs fixing immediately. This might be excessive for a small software company, but you should still know the home phone numbers of people whose skills might be needed urgently; see to it that there's more than one person with each critical skill; and have supporting procedures. For example, emergency bug fixes must be run through the full testing process as soon as possible. And the documentation must be upgraded, too; this is critical for evolutionary security improvement, but too often ignored. When the bug fix changes the requirements, you need to fix their documentation, too (and perhaps your threat model, and even top-level risk management paperwork).

Third, be able to distribute the patch or other repair to your customers rapidly. This must be planned in advance. The details will vary depending on your product: if you have only a few dozen customers running your code on servers at data centers that are staffed 24/7, then it may be very easy, but if it involves patching millions of copies of consumer software a lot of care will be needed. It may seem simple enough to get your customers to visit your Web site once a day and check for upgrades, but to do this safely there are a surprising number of details you have to get right. Will the server be able to cope with the increased traffic? Have you given your customers adequate legal notification that their software might be changed under their feet? Could an opponent—such as a disgruntled former employee—hijack the mechanism and trash your entire customer base?

Finally, have a plan for dealing with the press. The last thing you need is for dozens of journalists to call and be stonewalled by your switchboard operator as you struggle madly to fix the bug. Have a set of press release templates for incidents of varying severity on file in your word processor, so that all you have to do is pick the right one and fill in the details. The release can then ship as soon as the first (or perhaps the second) journalist calls.

22.4.1.2 Control Tuning and Corporate Governance

The main process by which organizations such as banks develop their bookkeeping systems and their other internal controls is by tuning them in the light of experience. A bank with 25,000 employees might be firing about one staff member a day for petty theft or embezzlement, and, traditionally, it's the internal audit department that will review the loss reports and recommend system changes to reduce the incidence of the most common scams. I gave some examples in 9.2.3.

It is important for the security engineer to have some knowledge of internal controls. There is a shortage of books on this subject: audit is largely learned on the job, but know-how is also available via courses and through accounting standards documents. There is a survey of internal audit standards by Janet Colbert and Paul Bowen [193]; the most influential is the Risk Management Framework from the *Committee of Sponsoring Organizations* (COSO), a group of U.S. accounting and auditing bodies [196]. This is the yardstick by which your system will be judged if it's used in the U.S. public sector or by companies quoted on U.S. equity markets.

The COSO model is targeted not just on internal control but on the reliability of financial reporting and compliance with laws and regulations. Its basic process is an evolutionary cycle: in a given environment, you assess the risks, design controls, monitor their performance, and then go round the loop again. COSO emphasizes soft aspects of corporate culture more than hard system design issues, and may be seen as a guide to managing and documenting the process by which your system evolves. However, its core consists of the internal control procedures whereby senior management check that their control policies are being implemented and achieving their objectives, and modify them if not.

It is also worthwhile for the security engineer to learn about the more specialized information systems audit function. The IS auditor should not have line responsibility for security, or there will be a conflict of interest: she should not be asked to assess systems that she designed or for whose operation she is responsible. Rather, she should monitor how things are done, look into things that are substandard or appear suspicious, and suggest improvements. Much of the technical material is common with security engineering; if you have read and understood this book so far, you should be able to get well over 50% on the Certified Information Systems Auditor (CISA) exam (details are at [408]). The Information Systems Audit and Control Association, which administers CISA, has a refinement of COSO known as the *Control OBjectives for Information and related Technology* (COBIT) which is more attuned to IT needs, more international, and more accessible than COSO (it can be downloaded from [407]). COBIT covers much more than engineering requirements, as issues such as personnel management, change control, and project management are also the internal auditor's staples. (The working security engineer needs to be familiar with this material, too.)

These general standards are necessarily rather vague. They provide the engineer with a context and a top-level checklist, but rarely offer any clear guidance on specific measures. For example, COBIT 5.19 states: 'Regarding malicious software, such as computer viruses or trojan horses, management should establish a framework of adequate preventative, detective and corrective control measures'. More concrete standards are often developed to apply such general principles to specific application areas. For example, when I was working in banking security in the 1980s, I relied on guidelines from the Bank for International Settlements [71]. Where such standards exist, they are often the ultimate fulcrum of security evolutionary activity.

It's a good idea to have high-bandwidth channels of communication to your client's internal audit department. But it's not a good idea to rely on them completely for feedback. Usually, the people who know most about how to break the system are the staff who actually use it. Ask them.

22.4.1.3 Evolving Environments and the Tragedy of the Commons

I've described a number of systems that broke after their environment changed, and where appropriate changes to the protection mechanisms were skimped, avoided, or forgotten. Card-and-PIN technology that worked fine with ATMs became vulnerable to false terminal attacks when used with retail point-of-sale terminals; smartcards that were perfectly good for managing credit card numbers and PINs in point-of-sale applications were inadequate to keep out the pay-TV pirates; and even very basic mechanisms such as authentication protocols had to be redesigned for systems where the main threat was internal rather than external. Military environments evolve particularly rapidly in wartime, as attack and defence coevolve; R.V. Jones attributes much of the Allies' relative success in electronic warfare in World War II to the fact that the Germans used a rigid top-down development methodology, which resulted in beautifully engineered equipment, but six months too late [424].

Changes in the application aren't the only problem. An operating system upgrade may introduce a whole new set of bugs into the underlying platform. Changes of scale as businesses become 'e-' can alter the cost-benefit equation, as can the fact that many system users may be in foreign jurisdictions with ineffective computer crime laws (or none at all). Also, attacks that were known by experts for many years to be possible, but that were ignored because they didn't happen in practice, can suddenly start to happen—a good example being the distributed denial-of-service attack.

When you own the system, things are merely difficult. You manage risk by ensuring that someone in the organization has responsibility for maintaining its security rating; this may involve an annual review driven by your internal audit bureaucracy, or be an aspect of change control. Maintaining organizational memory is hard, thanks to the high turnover of both IT and security staff, which I discussed in Section 22.2.3.4.

That's tough enough, but where many of the really intractable problems arise is where no one owns the system at all. The responsibility for established standards, such as how ATMs check PINs, is diffuse. In that case, the company that developed most of the standards (IBM) lost its leading industry role; its successor, Microsoft, is not interested in that market. Cryptographic equipment is sold by a number of specialist firms. Although VISA used to certify equipment, it stopped in about 1990, and Mastercard never got into that business, so there was no one person or company in charge. Each player—equipment maker or bank—had a motive to push the boundaries just a little bit further, in the expectation that when eventually something did go wrong, it would happen to somebody else.

This problem is familiar to economists, who call it the *tragedy of the commons* [507]. If a hundred peasants are allowed to graze their sheep on the village common, where the grass is finite, then whenever another sheep is added, its owner gets almost the full benefit while the other ninety-nine suffer only a very small disadvantage from the decline in the quality of the grazing. Thus, they aren't motivated to object, but rather to add another sheep of their own to get as much of the declining resource as they can. The result is a dustbowl. In the world of agriculture, this problem is tackled by community mechanisms, such as getting the parish council set up a grazing control committee. The cowherds in tenth-century Saxon villages were already well-enough organized to do this; one of the challenges facing us is to devise some mix of technical and organizational controls that will give us a comparable result, only on the larger scale of the Internet.

22.4.1.4 *Organizational Change*

Organizational issues are not just a contributory factor in security failure, as with the loss of organizational memory and the lack of community mechanisms for monitoring changing threat environments. They can often be a primary cause.

In the early 1990s, management fashion was for *business process re-engineering*, which often meant using changes in business computer systems to compel changes in the way people worked. There have been some well-documented cases in which poorly designed systems interacted with resentful staff to cause a disaster.

Perhaps the best known case is that of the London Ambulance Service. It had a manual system whereby incoming emergency calls were written on forms and sent by conveyer belt to three controllers, who allocated vehicles and passed the form to a radio dispatcher. Industrial relations were poor, and there was pressure to cut costs; managers got the idea of solving all these problems by automating. Lots of things went wrong, and as the system was phased in it became clear that it couldn't cope with established working practices, such as crew taking the "wrong" ambulance (staff had favorite vehicles with senior members getting the better ones). Managers didn't want to know, and forced the new system into use on October 26, 1992, by reorganizing the room so that controllers and dispatchers had to use terminals rather than paper.

The result was meltdown. A number of positive feedback loops became established that caused the system progressively to lose track of vehicles. Exception messages built up, scrolled off screen, and were lost; incidents were held as allocators searched for vehicles; as the response time stretched, callbacks from patients increased (the average ring time for emergency callers went over 10 minutes); as congestion increased, the ambulance crews got frustrated, pressed the wrong buttons on their new data terminals, couldn't get a result, tried calling on the voice channel, and increased the congestion; as more and more crews fell back on the methods they understood, they took the wrong vehicles even more often; many vehicles were sent to an emergency, or none; and, finally, the whole service collapsed. It's estimated that perhaps 20 people died as a direct result of not getting paramedic assistance in time. By the afternoon on the 26th, it was the major news item; the government intervened, and on the following day the system was switched back to semi-manual operation.

This is only one of many such disasters, but it's particularly valuable to the engineer as it was extremely well documented by the resulting public inquiry [723]. In my own professional experience, I've seen cases where similar attempts to force through changes in corporate culture by replacing computer systems have so undermined morale that honesty became a concern. (Much of my consulting work has had to do with environments placed under stress by corporate reorganization or even by national political crises.)

In extreme cases, a step change in the environment brought on by a savage corporate restructuring will be more like a one-off project than an evolutionary change. There will often be some useful base to fall back on, such as an understanding of external threats; but the internal threat environment may become radically different. This is particularly clear in banking. Fifteen years ago, bank branches were run by avuncular managers and staffed by respectable middle-aged ladies who expected to spend their entire working lives there. Today, the managers have been replaced by product sales specialists, and the teller staff are youngsters earning near-minimum wages who turn over every year or so. It's simply not the same business.

22.4.2 Managing Project Requirements

This brings us to the much more difficult problem of how to do security requirements engineering for a one-off project. The most common example might be building an e-commerce application from scratch, whether for a start-up or for an established business that wants to create new distribution channels.

Building things from scratch is an accident-prone business and there are many cases in which large software projects crashed and burned. The problems appear to be very much the same whether the disaster is a matter of safety, of security, or of the software simply never working at all; so security people can learn a lot from the general software engineering literature.

The classic study of large software project disasters was written by Bill Curtis, Herb Krasner, and Neil Iscoe [212]. They found that failure to understand the requirements was mostly to blame: a thin spread of application domain knowledge typically led to fluctuating and conflicting requirements, which in turn caused a breakdown in communication. They suggested that the solution was to find an "exceptional designer" with a thorough understanding of the problem who would assume overall responsibility.

The millennium bug gives another useful data point, which many writers on software engineering still have to digest. If one accepts that many large commercial and government systems actually needed extensive repair work, and the conventional wisdom that a significant proportion of large development projects are late or never delivered at all, then the prediction of widespread chaos at the end of 1999 was inescapable. But it didn't happen. Certainly, the risks to the systems used by small and medium-sized firms were overstated [37]; nevertheless, the systems of some large firms whose operations are critical to the economy, such as banks and utilities, did need substantial fixing. But despite the conventional wisdom, there have been no reports of significant organizations going belly-up. This appears to support Curtis, Krasner, and Iscoe's thesis. The requirement for Y2K bug fixes was known completely: "I want this system to keep on working, just as it is now, through into 2000 and beyond."

As a requirements engineer, you need to acquire a comprehensive knowledge of the application, as well as of the people who might attack it and the kind of tools they might use. If domain experts are available, well and good. When interviewing them, try to distinguish tasks that are done for a purpose, as opposed to those that are just "how things are done around here." Probe constantly for the reasons why things are done as they are, and be sensitive to after-the-fact rationalizations. Focus particularly on the things that are going to change. For example, if dealing with customer complaints depends on whether the customer is presentable or not, and your job is to take this business online, then ask the experts what alternative controls might work in a world where it's much harder to tell a customer's age, sex, and social class. (This should probably have been done round about the time of the civil rights movement in the 1960s, but better late than never.)

When tackling a new application, dig into its history. I've tried to do that throughout this book, and bring out the way in which problems repeat. To find out what electronic banking will be like in the twenty-first century, it's a good idea to know what it was like in the nineteenth; human nature doesn't change much. Historical parallels will also make it much easier for you to sell your proposal to your client's board of directors.

You will likely find that a security requirements specification for a new project requires iteration, so it's more likely to be spiral model than waterfall model. In the first pass, you'll describe the new application and how it differs from any existing applications for which loss histories are available, set out a model of the risks as you perceive them, and draft a security policy (I'll have more to say on risk analysis and management in the next section). In the second pass, you might get comments from your client's middle management and internal auditors, while meantime you scour the literature—from internal audit guidelines to books like this one—for useful checklist items and ideas you can recycle. The outcome of this will be a revised, more quantitative risk model, a security policy, and a security target that sketches how the policy will be implemented in real life. It will also set out how a system can be evaluated against these criteria. In the third pass, the documentation will circulate to a wider group of people, including your client's senior management, external auditors, insurers and perhaps an external evaluator.

22.4.3 Parallelizing the Process

Often, there isn't an expert to hand, as when something is being done for the first time, or when you're building a competitor to a proprietary system whose owners won't share their loss history with you. An interesting question to ask is how to brainstorm a specification just by trying to think of all the things that could go wrong. The common industry practice is to hire a single consulting firm to draw up a security target; but the experience I described in Section 10.3.3 suggested that using several experts in parallel would be better. People with backgrounds in crypto, access control, internal audit, and so on will see a problem from different angles. There is also an interesting analogy with the world of software testing, where it is more cost-efficient to test in parallel rather than in series: each tester has a different focus in the testing space, and will find some subset of flaws faster than the others. (I'll introduce a more quantitative model of this in the next chapter.)

The preceding motivated me to carry out an experiment in 1999 to see if a high-quality requirements specification could be assembled quickly by getting a lot of different people to contribute drafts. The idea was that most of the possible attacks would be considered in at least one of them. Thus, in one of our university exam questions, I asked what would be a suitable security policy for a company planning to bid for the license for a public lottery.

The results are described in [36]. The model answer was that attackers, possibly in cahoots with insiders, would try to place bets once the result of the draw was known, whether by altering bet records or forging tickets; or would place bets without paying for them; or would operate bogus vending stations that would pay small claims but disappear if a client won a big prize. The security policy that follows logically from this is that bets should be registered online with a server that is secured prior to the draw, both against tampering and against the extraction of sufficient information to forge a winning ticket; that there should be credit limits for genuine vendors; and that there should be ways of identifying bogus vendors.

Valuable and original contributions from the students came at a number of levels, including policy goal statements, discussions of particular attacks, and arguments about the merits of particular protection mechanisms. At the policy level, there were a number of shrewd observations on the need to maintain public confidence and the threat from senior managers in the operating company. At the level of technical detail, one student discussed threats from refund mechanisms, while another looked at attacks on secure time mechanisms, and observed that the use of the radio time signal in lottery terminals would be vulnerable to jamming (this turned out to be a real vulnerability in one existing lottery).

The students also came up with quite a number of routine checklist items of the kind that designers often overlook, such as "tickets must be associated with a particular draw." This might seem obvious, but a protocol design that used a purchase date, ticket serial number, and server-supplied random challenge as input to a MAC computation might appear plausible to a superficial inspection. Experienced designers appreciate the value of such checklists.

The lesson to be learned from this case study is that requirements engineering, like software testing, is susceptible to a useful degree of parallelization. If your target system is something novel, then instead of paying a single consultant to think about it for twenty days, consider getting fifteen people with diverse backgrounds to think about it for a day each, then have a consultant spend a week hammering their ideas into a single coherent document.

22.5 Risk Management

Whether a threat model and security policy evolve or are developed in a one-off project, at their heart lie business decisions about priorities—how much to spend on protection against what. This is risk management, and it should be done within the broader framework of managing non-IT risks.

A number of firms sell methodologies for this. Some come in the form of do-it-yourself PC software, while others are part of a package of consultancy services. Which one you use may be determined by your client's policies; for example, if you're selling anything to the U.K. government, you're likely to have to use a system called CRAMM. The basic purpose of such systems is to prioritize security expenditure, while at the same time provide a financial case for it to senior management.

The most common technique is to calculate the *annual loss expectancy* (ALE) for each possible loss scenario. This is the expected loss multiplied by the number of incidents expected in an average year. A typical ALE analysis for a bank's computer systems might consist of several hundred entries, including items such as those listed in Figure 22.5. Note that accurate figures are likely to be available for common losses (such as "Teller takes cash"), while for the uncommon, high-risk losses such as a large funds transfer fraud, the incidence is largely guesswork.

ALEs have been standardized by NIST as the technique to use in U.S. government procurements [602]. But in real life, the process of producing such a table is all too often just iterative guesswork. The consultant lists all the threats she can think of, attaches notional probabilities, works out the ALEs, adds them all up, and gets a ludicrous result, such as that the bank's ALE is greater than all its noninterest income. She then tweaks

Loss type	Amount	Incidence	ALE
SWIFT fraud	$50,000,000	.005	$250,000
ATM fraud (large)	$250,000	.2	$100,000
ATM fraud (small)	$20,000	.5	$10,000
Teller takes cash	$3,240	200	$648,000

Figure 22.5 Example of Annual Loss Expectancies.

the total down to the amount that will justify the largest security budget she thinks the board of directors will stand for (or which her client, the chief internal auditor, has told her is politically possible). The loss probabilities are then massaged to give the right answer. (Great invention, the spreadsheet.) I'm sorry if this sounds a bit cynical, but it's what happens more often than not. The point is, ALEs may be of some value, but they shouldn't be elevated into a religion.

Insurance can be of some help in managing large but unlikely risks. But the insurance business is not completely scientific either. For years, the annual premium for bankers' bond insurance, which covered both computer crime and employee disloyalty, was 0.5% of the sum insured. This represented pure profit for Lloyds of London, the firm that wrote the policies. Then there was a large claim, and the premium doubled to 1% per annum. Such policies may have a deductible of between $50,000 and $10,000,000 per incident, so they remove only a small number of very large risks from the equation. There is a substantial benefit in having an experienced insurance assessor check out the computer system and suggest security enhancements; but this can be arranged for much less than the six-figure sum that a typical bank might pay for coverage.

The main reason that large companies take out computer crime coverage—and do many other things—is due diligence. The risks being tackled may seem on the surface to be operational, but are often actually legal, regulatory, and PR risks. Usually, they are managed by "following the herd"—being just another one of the millions of gnu on the African veld, to reuse my metaphor for Internet security. This is one reason that computer security is such a fashion-driven business. During the mid-1980s, hackers were the main concern, and firms selling dial-back modems did a booming business. From the late 1980s, viruses took over the corporate imagination, and antivirus software made some people rich. Recently, with all the fanfare about e-business, the firewall has become the new star product. These are the threats, and the products, that are seen by corporate CEOs on TV and in the financial press. Amidst all this noise, the security professional must retain a healthy scepticism and strive to understand what the real threats are.

Ultimately, knowing what computer and communications security is appropriate in a particular application comes down to judgment. Sooner or later, the client's CEO must choose one of the options, and the best you can do is to give a competent and honest assessment of the pros and cons.

22.6 Economic Issues

Many of the problems that confront the security engineer have their origin in economics. Consultants often explain that the reason a design, for which they were responsible failed was that "the client didn't want a secure system, but just the most security I could fit on the product in one week on a budget of $10,000." It's important to realize that this isn't just management stupidity.

I first discussed network effects in Section 19.6. Networks with more users are more valuable to each user, leading to strong positive feedback and, very often, a huge first-mover advantage. This is the origin of the philosophy of, "We'll ship it on Tuesday and get it right by version 3." Although often attributed by cynics to Microsoft, this is often perfectly rational economic behavior in markets where network economics apply.

Network economics has many other effects on the security management process. Rather than using a standard, well-analyzed, and tested solution, companies often prefer a proprietary, obscure one to increase customer lock-in and to increase the problems for competitors who try to create compatible products. Where possible, they will use patented algorithms (even if these are not much good) as a means of imposing licensing conditions on manufacturers—recall from Section 20.2.5 how the DVD Content Scrambling System was used as a means of requiring manufacturers of compatible equipment to agree to a whole list of copyright protection measures (and how this appears to have failed because it would have prevented the Linux operating system from running on next-generation PCs). Network owners and builders will appeal to the developers of the next generation of applications by arranging for the bulk of the support costs to fall on users rather than developers—even if this makes effective security administration impractical. Security engineers need to study network economics texts, such as Shapiro and Varian [696], to understand how the various plays that companies make to entrench monopolies, or to overturn them, interact with protection mechanisms.

There are also local economic issues. Security is about power, and a design will usually serve the perceived interests of whoever pays for the design work to be done. I described, in Chapter 8, how medical payment systems that are designed by insurers rather then by healthcare providers fail to protect patient privacy whenever this conflicts with the insurer's wish to maximize information about its clients. Chapter 9 described how banks in many countries managed for years to get their customers to bear the risk and cost of fraud; and Chapter 21 explained how some digital signature laws transfer the risk of forged signatures from the person who relies on the signature to the person alleged to have made it. Section 22.4.1.3 in this chapter explained the tragedy of the commons, where many players can dump their risks into a common pool, so that each gets a large benefit from taking a shortcut but suffers only a small share of the loss when something goes wrong; the result is that standards can decline rapidly.

A particularly topical case of the tragedy of the commons comes from the recent spate of distributed denial-of-service attacks whose technical aspects I discussed in Section 18.2.2.3. In these attacks, vandals hack a number of PCs and install attack software that bombards the target with more message traffic than it can handle. The probability of becoming a victim of such an attack is so low that most normal users quite rationally ignore it, so they don't bother to protect their PCs properly. Then, just as a common pasture gets overgrazed, so the Internet becomes increasingly insecure—and with more and more people installing high-bandwidth, always-on Internet connections, the insecurity will get worse. Jean Camp and Catherine Wolfram have drawn an interesting parallel between Internet insecurity and environmental pollution in [156].

The best way to manage such situations would be for the risks to fall on the parties most able to manage them. This is an established general principle in tort law, but enough industries and applications manage to escape it one way or another. In the case of distributed denial-of-service attacks, there would be little point in victims suing whichever random users had been hacked, as most home PC users are clueless about security; and, in any case, the risk of being the unlucky individual who got hacked and then sued would be low. Hal Varian has suggested that the hacked users' Internet service provider should carry much of the risk [771]. This would create the needed incentive for firewalls to police not just incoming traffic, but outgoing traffic as well. This is the thinking behind a strategy, which I described in passing in Section 6.2.4, of responding to a service denial attack on a Web site by replicating the site to a more capable, distributed server. As the use of such services can be rented, the necessary economic incentives can be implemented in a more-or-less transparent way. (For further details, see [816].)

In practice the driving forces behind security design usually have nothing to do with an altruistic desire to protect the end-users' privacy and to reduce the risk that they will be defrauded. The motives are much more likely to be the desire to grab a monopoly, to charge different prices to different users for essentially the same service, and to dump risk. Often, this is perfectly rational. Sometimes it isn't; British banks that dumped the risk of ATM fraud on their customers installed many security mechanisms so that in case of dispute they could argue in court that they had exercised due diligence; they ended up spending more on ATM security than U.S. banks, which had always borne the liability and for which security was a rational matter of risk management [19].

In an ideal world, the removal of perverse economic incentives to create insecure systems would depoliticize most issues. Security engineering would then be a matter of rational risk management rather than risk dumping. But don't hold your breath.

22.7 Summary

Developing a security requirements specification is often the most difficult part of the entire engineering process. Like developing the system itself, it can involve a one-off project, be a limited iterative process, or be a matter of continuous evolution. Evolution is easiest to manage, though it is complicated by changes of scale, environment, and business structures. Doing it from scratch for a completely new system is hardest and most error-prone, but there are still some useful techniques and lessons that can be borrowed from elsewhere.

In the absence of anything better, I suggest to the project manager engaged in building an application with some nontrivial protection requirements that you make a best effort to understand precisely what these properties are, build them into the specification, and then use whatever methodology you would use normally to follow them through implementation, testing, and deployment. But assume that you won't get it right first time. Make sure that you have some institutional means of capturing feedback on what goes wrong and how the environment is changing, so that you can feed this back into the process of enhancing and maintaining the system. Security must be an integral part of how you manage the system lifecycle.

Research Problems

The issues discussed in this chapter are among the most important—and most difficult—of any in our field. Ironically, they tend to receive little attention, because they lie at the boundaries with software engineering, applied psychology, economics, and management. Each of these interfaces appears to be a potentially very productive area of research—if you have the necessary background. When building systems to be robust in the face of malice, you must also build them so that they remain robust in the face of normal human behavior, and hopefully are able to tell the difference between the two often enough to do something useful.

Further Reading

Literature on managing the development of information systems is large, diffuse, and multidisciplinary. There are classics that everyone should read, such as Fred Brooks' *Mythical Man-Month* [140] and Nancy Leveson's *Safeware* [498]. Standard textbooks on software engineering, such as those by Roger Pressman [622] and Hans van Vliet [767] cover the basics of project management and requirements engineering. The economics of the software lifecycle are discussed by Fred Brooks and Barry Boehm [123]. The Microsoft approach to managing software evolution is described by Steve McGuire [521]. There are useful parallels to other engineering disciplines. An interesting book by Henry Petroski discusses the history of bridge building, why bridges fall down, and how civil engineers learned to learn from the collapses: what tends to happen is that an established design paradigm is stretched and stretched until it suddenly fails for some unforeseen reason [612]. For a survey of risk management methods and tools, see Richard Baskerville [77] or Donn Parker [602]; there are some interesting case histories at IFCI [402]. Computer system failures are another necessary subject of study; the best source is the comp.risks newsgroup, of which a selection has been collated and published in print by Peter Neumann [590].

Organizational aspects are discussed at length in the business school literature, but this can be bewildering to the outsider. A critical guide to the literature is provided by John Micklethwait and Adrion Wooldridge, who draw out a number of highly relevant tensions, such as the illogicality of management gurus who tell managers to make their organizations more flexible by firing people, while at the same time preaching the virtues of trust [550]. Familiarity with this material is useful for predicting the protection consequences of your client's latest reorganizational fashion. Finally, the best books I know for material on the underlying economics are a popular synopsis by Carl Shapiro and Hal Varian [696], and a standard textbook by Hal Varian [770].

CHAPTER 23

System Evaluation and Assurance

If it's provably secure, it probably isn't.
—LARS KNUDSEN

I think any time you expose vulnerabilities it's a good thing.
—U.S. ATTORNEY GENERAL JANET RENO [642]

23.1 Introduction

I've covered a lot of material in this book, some of it quite difficult. But I've left the hardest topics to the last. These are the questions of *assurance*, whether the system will work, and *evaluation*, how you convince other people of this.

Fundamentally, assurance comes down to the question of whether capable, motivated people have beat up on the system enough. But how do you define enough? And how do you define the system? How do you deal with people who protect the wrong thing, because their model of the requirements is out-of-date or plain wrong? And how do you allow for human failures? Many systems can be operated just fine by alert experienced professionals, but are unfit for purpose because they're too tricky for ordinary folk to use or are intolerant of error.

But if assurance is hard, evaluation is even harder. It's about how you convince your boss, your clients—and, in extremis, a jury—that the system is indeed fit for purpose; that it does indeed work (or that it did work at some particular time in the past). The reason that evaluation is both necessary and hard is that, often, one principal carries the cost of protection while another carries the risk of failure. This creates an obvious tension, and third-party evaluation schemes such as the Common Criteria are marketed as a means of making it more transparent.

23.2 Assurance

A working definition of *assurance* could be "our estimate of the likelihood that a system will not fail in some particular way." This estimate can be based on a number of factors, such as the process used to develop the system; the identity of the person or team who developed it; particular technical assessments, such as the use of formal methods or the deliberate introduction of a number of bugs to see how many of them are caught by the testing team; and experience—which ultimately depends on having a model of how reliability grows (or decays) over time as a system is subjected to testing, use, and maintenance.

23.2.1 Perverse Economic Incentives

A good starting point for the discussion of assurance is to look at the various principals' motives. As a preliminary let's consider the things for which we may need assurance:

- *Functionality* is important and often neglected. It's all too common to end up protecting the wrong things or protecting the right things in the wrong way. Recall from Chapter 8, for example, how the use of the Bell-LaPadula model in the healthcare environment caused more problems than it solved.

- *Strength of mechanisms* has been much in the news, thanks to U.S. export controls on crypto. Many products, such as DVD, were shipped with 40-bit keys and were thus intrinsically vulnerable. Strength of mechanisms is independent of functionality, but can interact with it. For example, in Chapter 14, I remarked how the difficulty of preventing probing attacks on smartcards led the industry to protect other, relatively unimportant things such as the secrecy of chip masks.

- *Implementation* is the traditional focus of assurance. This involves whether, given the agreed functionality and strength of mechanisms, the product has been implemented correctly. As we've seen, most real-life technical security failures are due to programming bugs—stack overflow vulnerabilities, race conditions, and the like. Finding and fixing them absorbs most of the effort of the assurance community.

- *Usability* is the missing factor—one might even say the spectre at the feast. Perhaps the majority of system-level (as opposed to purely technical) failures have a large human interface component. It is very common for secure system designers to tie up the technical aspects of protection tightly, without stopping to consider human frailty. There are some notable exceptions. The bookkeeping systems described in Chapter 9 are designed to cope with user error; and the security printing technologies discussed in Chapter 12 are often optimized to make it easier for untrained and careless people to spot forgeries. But usability concerns developers as well as users. A developer usability issue, mentioned in Chapter 4 is that the access controls provided with commodity operating systems often aren't used, as it's so much simpler to make code run with administrator privilege.

These four factors are largely independent, and the system builder has to choose an appropriate combination of them to aim at. A personal computer user, for example, might want high usability, medium assurance (because high would be expensive, and we can live with the odd virus), high strength of mechanisms (they don't cost much more), and simple functionality (as usability is more important). But the market doesn't deliver this, and a moment's thought will indicate why.

Commercial platform vendors go for rich functionality (rapid product versioning prevents the market being commoditized, and complementary vendors that grab too much market share can be undermined), low strength of mechanisms (except for cryptography where the escrow debate has led vendors to regard strong crypto as an essential marketing feature), low implementation assurance (so the military-grade crypto is easily defeated by Trojan horses), and low usability (application programmers matter much more than customers, as they enhance network externalities).

In Chapter 22, I described why this won't change any time soon. The strategy of "ship it Tuesday and get it right by version 3" isn't a personal moral defect of Bill Gates, as some of his critics allege, but is dictated by the huge first-mover advantages inherent in the economics of networks. And mechanisms that compelled application developers to use operating system access controls would alienate them, raising the risk that they might write their code for competitors' platforms. Thus, the current insecurity of commercial systems is perfectly rational from the economists' viewpoint, however undesirable from the users'.

Government agencies' ideals are also frustrated by economics. Their dream is to be able to buy commercial off-the-shelf products, replace a small number of components (such as by removing commercial crypto and plugging in Fortezza cards in its place), and end up with something they can use with existing defense networks. That is, they want Bell-LaPadula functionality (never mind that it fails to support mechanisms some of the vendors' other customers need) and high implementation assurance. There is little concern with usability, as a trainable and disciplined workforce is assumed (however wrongly), and low strength of crypto is preferred so as to limit the benefits that potential enemies can gain from otherwise high-assurance systems being on the market. This wish list is unrealistic given not just the cost of high assurance (which I'll discuss shortly), but also the primacy of time-to-market, the requirement to appease the developer community, and the need for frequent product versioning to prevent the commoditization of markets. Also, larger networks usually swamp smaller ones; so a million government computer users can't expect to impose their will on 100 million users of Microsoft Office.

The dialogue between user advocates, platform vendors, and government is probably condemned to remain a dialogue of the deaf. But that doesn't mean there's nothing more of interest to say on assurance.

23.2.2 Project Assurance

Assurance is a process very much like the development of code or documents. Just as you will have bugs in your code and in your specification, you will also have bugs in your test procedures. So assurance can be done as a one-off project or be the subject of continuous evolution. An example of the latter is given by the huge databases of known computer viruses that anti-virus software vendors accumulate over the years to do regression-testing of their products. Assurance can also involve a combination, as when a step in an evolutionary development is managed using project techniques and is tested as a feature before being integrated and subjected to system-level regression tests. Here, you also have to find ways of building feature tests into your regression test suite.

Nonetheless, it's helpful to look first at the project issues, then at the evolutionary issues.

23.2.2.1 Security Testing

In practice, security testing usually comes down to reading the product documentation, reviewing the code, then performing a number of tests. (This is known as *white-box testing*, as opposed to *black-box testing*, for which the tester has the product but not the design documents or source code). The process is:

1. First look for any obvious flaws, the definition of which will depend on the tester's experience.

2. Then look for common flaws, such as stack-overwriting vulnerabilities.

3. Then work down a list of less common flaws, such as those described in the various chapters of this book.

The process is usually structured by the requirements of a particular evaluation environment. For example, it might be necessary to show that each of a list of control objectives was assured by at least one protection mechanism; in some industries, such as bank inspection, there are more or less established checklists (see, for example, [72]).

23.2.2.2 Formal Methods

In Chapter 2, I gave an example of a formal method: the BAN logic that can be used to verify certain properties of cryptographic protocols. The working engineer's take on formal methods may be that they're widely taught in universities, but not used anywhere in the real world. This isn't quite true in the security business. There are problems—such as in designing crypto protocols—where intuition is often inadequate and where formal verification can be helpful. Military purchasers go further, and require the use of formal methods as a condition of higher levels of evaluation under the Orange Book and the Common Criteria. I'll discuss this further below. For now, it's enough to say that this restricts high evaluation levels to relatively small and simple products, such as line encryption devices and operating systems for primitive computers such as smartcards. Even so, formal methods aren't infallible. Proofs can have errors, too; and often the wrong thing gets proved [673]. The quote by Knudsen at the head of this chapter refers to the large number of breaks of cryptographic algorithms or protocols that had previously been proven secure. These breaks generally occur because one of the proof's assumptions is unrealistic, or has become so over time.

23.2.2.3 *Quis Custodiet?*

Just as mistakes can be made by theorem provers and by testers, so they can also be made by people who draw up checklists of things for the testers to test (and by the security textbook writers from whose works the checklist writers draw). This is the old problem of *quis custodiet ipsos custodes*, as the Romans more succintly put it: who shall watch the watchmen?

There are a number of things one can do, few of which are likely to appeal to the organization whose goal is a declaration that a product is free of faults. The obvious one is *fault injection*, whereby a number of errors are deliberately introduced into the code at random. If there are 100 such errors, and the tester finds 70 of them, plus a further 70 that weren't deliberately introduced, then once the 30 remaining deliberate errors are removed, you can expect that there are 30 bugs left that you don't know about. (This assumes that the unknown errors are distributed the same as the known ones; reality will almost always be worse than this [133].)

Even in the absence of deliberate bug insertion, a rough estimate can be obtained by looking at which bugs are found by which testers. For example, I had Chapter 7 of this book reviewed by a fairly large number of people, as I took a draft of it to a conference on the topic. Given the bugs they found, and the number of people who reviewed the other chapters, I'd estimate that there are maybe three dozen errors of substance left in the book. The sample sizes aren't large enough in this case to justify more than a guess, but where they are large enough, we can use statistical techniques, which I'll describe shortly.

Another factor is the rate at which new attacks are discovered. In the university system, we train graduate students by letting them attack stuff; new vulnerabilites and exploits end up in research papers, which bring fame and, ultimately, promotion. The mechanics in government agencies and corporate labs are slightly different, but the overall effect is the same: a large group of capable, motivated people look for new exploits. Academics usually publish, government scientists usually don't, and corporate researchers sometimes do. So you need some means of adding new procedures to your test suite as fresh ideas come along, and to bear in mind that it will never be complete.

Finally, we get feedback from the rate at which instances of known bugs are discovered in products once they're fielded. This also provides valuable input for reliability growth models.

23.2.3 Process Assurance

In recent years, less emphasis has come to be placed on assurance measures focused on the product, such as testing, and more on process measures, such as who developed the system. As anyone with experience of system development knows, some programmers produce code with an order of magnitude fewer bugs than others. Also, some organizations produce much better quality code than others. This is the subject of much attention in the industry.

Some of the differences between high-quality and low-quality development teams are amenable to direct management intervention. Perhaps the most notable is whether people are responsible for correcting their own bugs. In the 1980s, many organizations interpreted the waterfall model of system development to mean that one team wrote the specification, another wrote the code, yet another did the testing (including some bug fixing), while yet another did the maintenance (including the rest of the bug fixing). The teams communicated with each other only by means of the project documentation. This was justified on the grounds that it is more efficient for people to concentrate on a single task at a time; interrupting a programmer to ask him to fix a bug in code he wrote six months ago and had forgotten about could cost a day's productivity, while getting a maintenance programmer to do it might cost only an hour.

But the effect was that the coders produced megabytes of buggy code, and left it to the poor testers and maintenance people to clear up after them. Over time, both quality and productivity sagged. Industry analysts have ascribed IBM's near-death experience in the early 1990s, which cost over $100 billion in asset value, to this [169]. For its part, Microsoft considers that one of its most crucial lessons learned as it struggled with the problems of writing ever larger programs was to have a firm policy that "if you wrote it, you fix it." Bugs should be fixed as soon as possible; and even though they're as inevitable as death and taxes, programmers should never give up trying to write clean code.

Many other controllable aspects of the organization can have a significant effect on output quality, ranging from how bright your hires are to how you train them and the work habits you inculcate. (See Maguire for an extended discussion of Microsoft policy [521].)

For some years, internal auditors have included process issues while evaluating the quality of security code. This is harder to do than you might think, because a large part of an organization's quality culture is intangible. While some rules (such as "fix your own bugs") seem to be fairly universal, imposing a large number of specific rules would induce a bureaucratic box-ticking culture, rather than a dynamic competitive one. Consequently, recent work has aimed for a more holistic assessment of a team's capability; the lead contender is the *Capability Maturity Model* (CMM) from the Software Engineering Institute at Carnegie-Mellon University.

CMM is based on the idea that, as a team acquires experience, it can progress through a series of levels. The model has five levels—initial, repeatable, defined, managed, and optimizing—with a list of new things to be added as you go up the hierarchy. Thus, for example, project planning must be introduced to move up from initial to repeatable, and peer reviews to make the transition from repeatable to defined. There is a fuller description and bibliography in [767]; several attempts have been made to adapt CMM to security work, and a significant number of vendors already use it [545, 822].

An even more common process assurance approach is the ISO 9001 standard. The essence of this standard is that a company must document its processes for design, development, testing, documentation, audit, and management control, generally. For more detail, see [767]; there is now a whole industry of consultants helping companies get ISO 9001 certification. At its best, it can provide a framework for incremental process improvement; companies can monitor what goes wrong, trace it back to its source, fix it, and prevent it happening again. At its worst, it can be an exercise in box-ticking which merely replaces chaos with more bureaucratic chaos.

Many writers have remarked that organizations have a natural cycle of life, just as people do. Joseph Schumpeter argued that economic depressions perform a valuable societal function of clearing out companies that are past it or just generally unfit, in much the same way that fires rejuvenate forests. Successful companies become complacent and bureaucratic, so that some insiders opt for the good life while others leave (it used to be commonly said that the only people who ever left IBM were the good ones). Too rapid growth also brings problems: Microsoft insiders blame many of the current problems on the influx of tens of thousands of new hires in the late 1990s, many of whom were motivated more by the prospect of making millions from stock options than by the mission to write good code and get it running on every computer in the known universe.

The cycle of corporate birth, death, and reincarnation turns much more quickly in the computer industry than elsewhere, thanks to the combination of technological progress and multiple network externalities. The telecoms industry is suffering severe trauma as the computer and communications industries merge and the phone companies' 15-year product cycles have to shorten to 15 months to keep up with Microsoft. The security industry is starting to feel the same pressures. Teams that worked steadily for decades on cost-plus contracts to develop encryptors or MLS systems for the military have suddenly been exposed to ferocious technological and market forces, and have been told to build completely different things. Some have succeeded, as with the MLS supplier TIS, which reinvented itself as a firewall vendor; others have failed and disappeared. Thus, the value of a team of MLS "graybeards" is questionable. In any case, expert teams usually depend on one or two key gurus, and when they go off to do a startup, the team's capability can evaporate overnight.

Schemes such as ISO 9001 and CMM would be more convincing if there were some effective means of taking certification away from teams that had lost their stars, their sparkle, or their relevance. It is tempting to think that a solution might lie in the sort of ranking system used in food guides, where declaring a new establishment to be "the best Asian restaurant in San Francisco" entails dislodging the previous holder of this title. Of course, if certification were a more perishable asset, it would have to confer greater market advantage for companies to invest the same amount of effort in getting it. This may be feasible: the restaurant guide system works, and academic peer review works somewhat along the same lines.

23.2.4 Assurance Growth

Another aspect of process-based assurance is that most customers are not so much interested in the development team as in its product. But most software today is packaged rather than bespoke, and is developed by a process of continual evolutionary enhancement rather than in a one-off project. What, then, can usefully be said about the assurance level of evolving products?

The quality of such a product can reach equilibrium if the rate at which new bugs are introduced by product enhancements equals the rate at which old bugs are found and removed. But there's no guarantee that this will happen. (There are second-order effects, such as *senescence*, when repeated enhancement makes code so complex that its underlying reliability and maintainability drop off, but I'll ignore them for the sake of simplicity.)

While controlling the rate at which bugs are introduced will depend on the kind of development controls I've already described, measuring the rate at which they are removed requires different tools—models of how the reliability of software (and systems in general) improves under testing.

A lot is known about reliability growth, as it's of interest to many more people than just software engineers.

Where the tester is trying to find a single bug in a system, a reasonable model is the Poisson distribution: the probability, p, that the bug remains undetected after t statistically random tests is given by $p = e^{-Et}$, where E depends on the proportion of possible inputs that it affects [506]. Where the reliability of a system is dominated by a single bug—as when we're looking for the first, or last, bug in a system—reliability growth can be exponential.

But extensive empirical investigations have shown that in large and complex systems, the likelihood that the t-th test fails is not proportional to e^{-Et} but to k/t for some constant k, so the system's reliability grows very much more slowly. This phenomenon was first noticed and documented in the bug history of IBM mainframe operating systems [7], and has been confirmed in many other studies [514]. As a failure probability of k/t means a *mean time between failure* (MTBF) of about t/k, reliability grows linearly with testing time. This result is often stated by the safety-critical systems community as, 'If you want a mean time between failure of a million hours, then you have to test for (at least) a million hours' [150]. This has been one of the main arguments against the development of complex, critical systems that can't be fully tested before use, such as ballistic missile defense.

The reason for the k/t behavior emerged in [105], and was proved under much more general assumptions in [133]. The latter uses techniques of statistical thermodynamics, and its core idea is that where a population of bugs with individual survival probabilities $p_i = e^{-E_i t}$ is large enough for certain statistical assumptions to hold, and they are eliminated over a long period of time, then the $e^{-E_i t}$ statistics of the individual bugs sum to k/t for the whole system. If they were eliminated any more slowly than this, the software would never work at all; and if they were eliminated any more quickly, the product would rapidly become bug-free—which, as we know, it usually doesn't.

This model gives a number of other interesting results. Under assumptions that are often reasonable, it is the best possible: the rule that you need a million hours of testing to get a million hours MTBF is inescapable, up to some constant multiple that depends on the initial quality of the code and the scope of the testing. This amounts to a proof of a version of Murphy's Law, that the number of defects that survive a selection process is maximized.

The model is similar to mathematical models of the evolution of a biological species under selective pressure. The role of bugs is played, roughly, by genes that reduce fitness. But some of the implications are markedly different. Murphy's Law, that the number of defects that survive a selection process is maximized, may be bad news for the engineer, but it's good news for biological species. While software testing removes the minimum possible number of bugs, consistent with the tests applied, biological evolution enables a species to adapt to a changed environment at a minimum cost in early deaths, meanwhile preserving as much diversity as possible. This diversity helps the species survive future environmental shocks. For example, if a population of rabbits is preyed on by snakes, the rabbits will be selected for alertness rather than speed. The variability in speed will remain, so if foxes arrive in the neighborhood, the rabbit population's average running speed will rise sharply under selective predation. More formally, the *fundamental theorem of natural selection* says that a species with a high genic variance can adapt to a changing environment more quickly. But when Fisher proved this in 1930 [297], he was also proving that complex software will exhibit the maximum possible number of bugs when it is migrated to a new environment.

The evolutionary model also points to fundamental limits on the reliability gains to be had from reusable software components such as objects or libraries; well-tested libraries simply mean that overall failure rates will be dominated by new code. It also explains the observation of the safety-critical systems community that test results are often a poor performance indicator [506]: the failure time measured by a tester depends only on the initial quality of the program, the scope of the testing and the number of tests, so it gives virtually no further information about the program's likely performance in another environment. There are also some results that are unexpected, but obvious in retrospect. For example, each bug's contribution to the overall failure rate is independent of whether the code containing it is executed frequently or rarely—intuitively, code that is executed less is also tested less. Finally, as mentioned in Section 22.4.3, it is often more economic for different testers to work on a program in parallel rather than in series.

In short, complex systems become reliable only following prolonged testing. Thus, this book may be pretty reliable once thousands of people have read it and sent me bug reports; but if there's a second edition with a lot of new material, I can expect new bugs to creep in too. As for mass-market software, its wide use enables rapid debugging in principle; but, in practice, the constant new versions dictated by network economics place severe limits on what may reasonably be expected.

There appears to be no reason why these results don't go across in their entirety if a bug is defined to be a defect that causes a security vulnerability, rather than just any old defect—just as long as the number of bugs is large enough to do statistics.

23.2.5 Evolution and Security Assurance

Evolutionary growth of reliability may be much worse for the software engineer than for a biological species, but for the security engineer it's worse still.

Rather than going into the detailed mathematics, let's take a slightly simplified example. Suppose a large and complex product such as Win2K has a million bugs, each with an MTBF of a billion hours. Also suppose that Paddy works for the Irish Republican Army, and his job is to break into the British Army's computer to get the list of informers in Belfast, while Brian is the army assurance guy whose job is to stop Paddy. So he must learn of the bugs before Paddy does.

Paddy also has a day job, so he can only do 1,000 hours of testing a year. Brian, on the other hand, has full Windows source code, dozens of PhDs, control of the commercial evaluation labs, an inside track on CERT, an information-sharing deal with other UKUSA member states, and he runs the government's scheme to send consultants to critical industries such as power and telecoms to find out how to hack them (pardon me, to advise them how to protect their systems). Brian does ten million hours a year of testing.

After a year, Paddy finds a bug, while Brian has found 10,000. But the probability that Brian has found Paddy's bug is only 1%. Even if Brian declares martial law, drafts all Britain's 50,000 computer science graduates to a concentration camp in Gloucestershire, and sets them trawling through the Windows source code, he'll still only get 100 million hours of testing done each year. After ten years, he will find Paddy's bug. But by then

Paddy will have found nine more, and it's unlikely that Brian will know of all of them. Worse, Brian's bug reports will have become such a firehose that Bill will have killfiled them.

In other words, Paddy has thermodynamics on his side. Even a very moderately resourced attacker can break anything that's at all large and complex. There is nothing that can be done to stop this, as long as there are enough different security vulnerabilities to do statistics. The ray of hope is that, if all your vulnerabilities are, say, stack overflows, and you start using a new compiler that traps them, then for modelling purposes, there was only a single vulnerability, and you escape the statistical trap.

23.3 Evaluation

A working definition of *evaluation* is "the process of assembling evidence that a system meets, or fails to meet, a prescribed assurance target." (Evaluation often overlaps with testing, and is sometimes confused with it.) As I mentioned, this evidence might be needed only to convince your boss that you've completed the job. But, often, it is needed to reassure principals who will rely on the system that the principal who developed it, or who operates it, has done a workmanlike job. The fundamental problem is the tension that arises when the party who implements the protection and the party who relies on it are different.

Sometimes the tension is simple and visible, as when you design a burglar alarm to standards set by insurance underwriters, and have it certified by inspectors at the insurers' laboratories. Sometimes it's still visible but more complex, as when designing to government security standards that try to reconcile dozens of conflicting institutional interests, or when hiring your company's auditors to review a system and tell your boss that it's fit for purpose. It is harder when multiple principals are involved; for example, when a smartcard vendor wants an evaluation certificate from a government agency (which is trying to encourage the use of some feature such as key escrow that is in no one else's interest), in order to sell the card to a bank, which in turn wants to use it to dump the liability for fraud on to its customers. That may seem all rather crooked; but there may be no clearly criminal conduct by any of the people involved. The crookedness may be an emergent property that arises from managers following their own personal and departmental imperatives.

For example, managers often buy products and services that they know to be suboptimal or even defective, but which are from big-name suppliers. This is known to minimize the likelihood of getting fired when things go wrong. Corporate lawyers don't condemn this as fraud, but praise it as due diligence. The end result may be that the relying party, the customer, has no say whatsoever, and will find it hard to get redress against the bank, the vendor, the evaluator, or the government when things go wrong.

Another serious and pervasive problem is that the words "assurance" and "evaluation" are often interpreted to apply only to the technical aspects of the system, and ignore usability (not to mention the even wider issues of appropriate internal controls and good corporate governance). Company directors also want assurance—that the directed procedures are followed, that there are no material errors in the accounts, that applicable laws are being complied with, and dozens of other things. But many evaluation schemes (especially the Common Criteria) studiously ignore the human and organizational elements in the system. If any thought is paid to them at all, the evaluation of these elements is considered to be a matter for the client's IT auditors, or even for a system administrator setting up configuration files. All that said, I'll focus on technical evaluation in what follows.

It is convenient to break evaluation into two cases. The first is where the evaluation is performed by the relying party; this includes insurance assessments, the independent verification and validation done by NASA on mission-critical code, and the previous generation of military evaluation criteria, such as the Orange Book. The second is where the evaluation is done by someone other than the relying party. Nowadays, this often means the Common Criteria evaluation process.

23.3.1 Evaluations by the Relying Party

In Chapter 10, I discussed many of the concerns that insurers have with burglar alarm systems, and the considerations that go into approving equipment for use with certain sizes of risk. The approval process itself if simple enough; the insurance industry operates laboratories where tests are conducted. These might involve a fixed budget of effort (perhaps one person for two weeks, or a cost of $15,000). The evaluator starts off with a fairly clear idea of what a burglar alarm should and should not do, spends the budgeted amount of effort looking for flaws, and writes a report. The laboratory then either approves the device, turns it down, or demands some changes.

In Section 7.4, I described another model of evaluation, that done from 1985–2000 at the NSA's National Computer Security Center on computer security products proposed for U.S. government use. These evaluations were conducted according to the Orange Book, the Trusted Computer Systems Evaluation Criteria [240]. The Orange Book and its supporting documents set out a number of evaluation classes:

C1: Discretionary access control by groups of users. In effect, this is considered to be equal to no protection.

C2: Discretionary access control by single users; object reuse; audit. C2 corresponds to carefully configured commercial systems; for example, C2 evaluations were given to IBM mainframe operating systems with RACF, and to Windows NT. (Both of these were conditional on a particular version and configuration; in NT's case, for example, it was restricted to diskless workstations).

B1: Mandatory access control. All objects carry security labels, and the security policy (which means Bell-LaPadula or a variant) is enforced independently of user actions. Labeling is enforced for all input information.

B2: Structured protection. As B1, but there must also be a formal model of the security policy that has been proved consistent with security axioms. Tools must be provided for system administration and configuration management. The TCB must be properly structured and its interface clearly defined. Covert channel analysis must be performed. A trusted path must be provided from the user to the TCB. Severe testing, including penetration testing, must be carried out.

B3: Security domains. As B2, but the TCB must
be minimal; it must mediate all access requests, be tamper-resistant, and be able to withstand formal analysis and testing. There must be real-time monitoring and alerting mechanisms, and structured techniques must be used in implementation.

A1: Verification design. As B3, but formal techniques must be used to prove the equivalence between the TCB specification and the security policy model.

The evaluation class of a system determines what spread of information may be processed on it. The example I gave in Section 7.5.2 was that a system evaluated to B3 may in general process information at Unclassified, Confidential, and Secret, or at Confidential, Secret, and Top Secret. (The complete rule set can be found in [244].) Although these ratings will cease to be valid after the end of 2001, they have had a decisive effect on the industry.

The business model of Orange Book evaluations followed traditional government service work practices. A government user would want some product evaluated; the NSA would allocate people to do it; they would do the work (which, given traditional civil service caution and delay, could take two or three years); the product, if successful, would join the evaluated products list; and the bill would be picked up by the taxpayer. The process was driven and controlled by the government—the party that was going to rely on the results of the evaluation—while the vendor was the supplicant at the gate. Because of the time the process took, evaluated products were usually one or two generations behind current commercial products, and often an order of magnitude more expensive.

The Orange Book wasn't the only evaluation scheme running in America. I mentioned in Section 14.4 the FIPS 140-1 scheme for assessing the tamper-resistance of cryptographic processors; this uses a number of independent laboratories as contractors. Independent contractors are also used for *Independent Verification and Validation* (IV&V), a scheme set up by the Department of Energy for systems to be used in nuclear weapons, and later adopted by NASA for manned space flight, which has many similar components (at least at the rocketry end of things). In IV&V, there is a simple evaluation target: zero defects. The process is still driven and controlled by the relying party—the government. The IV&V contractor is a competitor of the company that built the system, and its payments are tied to the number of bugs found.

Other governments had similar schemes. The Canadians had the *Canadian Trusted Products Evaluation Criteria* (CTPEC), while a number of European countries developed the *Information Technology Security Evaluation Criteria* (ITSEC). The idea was that a shared evaluation scheme would help European defense contractors compete against U.S. suppliers, with their larger economies of scale; Europeans would no longer be required to have separate certification in Britain, France, and Germany. ITSEC combined ideas from the Orange Book and IV&V processes, in that there were a number of different evaluation levels; and for all but the highest of these levels, the work was contracted out. However, ITSEC introduced a pernicious innovation: the evaluation was not paid for by the government but by the vendor seeking an evaluation on its product.

This was the usual civil service idea of killing several birds with one stone: saving public money and at the same time promoting a more competitive market. As usual, the stone appears to have done more damage to the too-clever hunter than to either of the birds.

This change in the rules provided the critical perverse incentive. It motivated the vendor to shop around for the evaluation contractor who would give its product the easiest ride, whether by asking fewer questions, charging less money, taking the least time, or all of these. (The same may happen with FIPS 140-1 now that commercial companies are starting to rely on it for third-party evaluations.) To be fair, the potential for this was realized, and schemes were set up whereby contractors could obtain approval as a *commercial licensed evaluation facility* (CLEF). The threat that a CLEF might have its license withdrawn was intended to offset the commercial pressures to cut corners.

23.3.2 The Common Criteria

This sets the stage for the Common Criteria. The original goal of the Orange Book was to develop protection measures that would be standard in all major operating systems, not an expensive add-on for captive government markets (as Orange Book evaluated products became). The problem was diagnosed as too-small markets, and the solution was to expand them. Because defense contractors detested having to obtain separate evaluations for their products in the United States, Canada, and Europe, agreement was reached to scrap the national evaluation schemes and replace them with a single standard. The work was substantially done in 1994–1995, and the European model won out over the U.S. and Canadian alternatives. As with ITSEC, evaluations under the Common Criteria, at all but the highest levels are done by CLEFs, and are supposed to be recognized in all participating countries (though any country can refuse to honor an evaluation if it says its national security is at stake); and vendors pay for the evaluations.

There are some differences. Most crucially, the Common Criteria have much more flexibility than the Orange Book. Rather than expecting all systems to conform to Bell-LaPadula, a product is evaluated against a *protection profile*, which, at least in theory, can be devised by the customer. This doesn't signify that the Department of Defense has abandoned multilevel security as much as an attempt to broaden the tent, get lots of commercial IT vendors to use the Common Criteria scheme, and thus defeat the perverse economic incentives described in Section 23.2.1 above. The aspiration was to create a bandwagon effect, which would result in the commercial world adapting itself somewhat to the government way of doing things.

23.3.2.1 Common Criteria Terminology

To discuss the Common Criteria in detail, I need to introduce some more jargon. The product under test is known as the *target of evaluation* (TOE). The rigor with which the examination is carried out is the *evaluation assurance level* (EAL); it can range from EAL1, for which functional testing is sufficient, all the way up to EAL7, for which thorough testing is required as well as a formally verified design. The highest evaluation level commonly obtained for commercial products is EAL4, although there is one smartcard operating system with an EAL6 evaluation (obtained, however, under ITSEC rather than under CC).

A *protection profile* is a set of security requirements, their rationale, and an EAL. The profile is supposed to be expressed in an implementation-independent way to enable comparable evaluations across products and versions. A *security target* (ST) is a refinement of a protection profile for a given target of evaluation. In addition to evaluating a product, one can evaluate a protection profile (the idea is to ensure that it's complete, consistent, and technically sound) and a security target (to check that it properly refines a given protection profile). When devising something from scratch, the idea is to first create a protection profile, and evaluate it (if a suitable one doesn't exist already), then do the same for the security target, then finally evaluate the actual product. The result of all this is supposed to be a registry of protection profiles and a catalogue of evaluated products.

A protection profile should describe the environmental assumptions, the objectives, and the protection requirements (in terms of both function and assurance), and break them down into components. There is a stylized way of doing this. For example, FCO_NRO is a functionality component (hence F) relating to communications (CO), and it refers to nonrepudiation of origin (NRO). Other classes include FAU (audit), FCS (crypto support), and FDP, which means data protection (this isn't data protection as in European law, but refers to access control, Bell-LaPadula information flow controls, and related properties). The component catalogue is heavily biased toward supporting MLS systems.

There are also catalogues of:

- Threats, such as T.Load_Mal—"Data loading malfunction: an attacker may maliciously generate errors in set-up data to compromise the security functions of the TOE."

- Assumptions, such as A.Role_Man—"Role management: management of roles for the TOE is performed in a secure manner" (in other words, the developers, operators and so on behave themselves).

- Organizational policies, such as P.Crypt_Std—"Cryptographic standards: cryptographic entities, data authentication, and approval functions must be in accordance with ISO and associated industry or organizational standards."

- Objectives, such as O.Flt_Ins—"Fault insertion: the TOE must be resistant to repeated probing through insertion of erroneous data."

- Assurance requirements, such as ADO_DEL.2—"Detection of modification: the developer shall document procedures for delivery of the TOE or parts of it to the user."

I mentioned that a protection profile will contain a *rationale*. This typically consists of tables showing how each threat is controlled by one or more objectives, and, in the reverse direction, how each objective is necessitated by some combination of threats or environmental assumptions, plus supporting explanations. It will also justify the selection of an assurance level and requirements for strength of function.

The fastest way to get the hang of this is to read a few of the existing profiles, such as that for smart cards [579]. As with many protection profiles, this provides a long list of things that can go wrong and things that a developer can do to control them, and so is a useful checklist. The really important aspects of card protection, though, are found in O.Phys_Prot, "Physical protection: the TOE must be resistant to physical attack or be able to create difficulties in understanding the information derived from such an attack" [p. 24]. An inexperienced reader might not realize that this objective is the whole heart of the matter; and as explained in Chapter 14, it's extremely hard to satisfy. (There's an admission on pp. 100–101 that competent attackers will still get through, but this is couched in terms likely to be opaque to the lay reader.) In general, the Criteria and the documents generated using them are unreadable, and this undermines the value they were intended to bring to the nonspecialist engineer.

Still, the Common Criteria can be useful to the security engineer in that they provide such extensive lists of things to check. They can also provide a management tool for keeping track of all the various threats and ensuring that they're all dealt with (otherwise, it's very easy for one to be forgotten in the mass of detail). But if the client insists on an evaluation—especially at higher levels—then these lists are apt to turn from a help into a millstone. Before accepting all the costs and delays this will cause, it's important to understand what the Common Criteria don't do.

23.3.2.2 *What the Common Criteria Don't Do*

The documents admit that the Common Criteria don't deal with administrative security measures, nor "technical-physical" aspects such as Emsec, nor crypto algorithms, nor the evaluation methodology, nor how the standards are to be used. The documents claim not to assume any specific development methodology (but then go on to assume a waterfall approach). There is a nod in the direction of evolving the policy in response to experience, but reevaluation of products is declared to be outside the scope. Oh, and there is no requirement for evidence that a protection profile corresponds to the real world; and I've seen a few that studiously ignore published work on relevant vulnerabilities. In other words, the Criteria avoid all the hard and interesting bits of security engineering, and can easily become a cherry pickers' charter.

The most common specific criticism (apart from cost and bureaucracy) is that the Criteria are too focused on the technical aspects of design. For example, in ADO_DEL.2 (and elsewhere) we find that procedures are seen as secondary to technical protection (the philosophy is to appeal to procedures where a technical fix isn't available). But, as explained in Section 12.6, when evaluating a real system, you have to assess the capability and motivation of the personnel at every stage in the process. This is fundamental, not something that can be added on afterward.

Even more fundamental, is that business processes should not be driven by the limits of the available technology (and especially not by the limitations of the available expensive, out-of-date military technology). System design should be driven by business requirements; and technical mechanisms should be used only where they're justified, not just because they exist. In particular, technical mechanisms shouldn't be used where the exposure is less than the cost of controlling it, or where procedural controls are cheaper. Remember why Samuel Morse beat the dozens of other people who raced to build electric telegraphs in the early nineteenth century. They tried to build modems, so they could deliver text from one end to the other; Morse realized that, given the technology then available, it was cheaper to train people to be modems.

So much for the theory of what's wrong with the Criteria. As always, the practical vulnerabilities are different, and at least as interesting.

23.3.3 What Goes Wrong

In none of the half-dozen or so affected cases I've been involved in has the Common Criteria approach proved satisfactory. (Perhaps that's because I can called in only when things go wrong—but my experience still indicates a lack of robustness in the process.)

One of the first points that must be made is that the CLEFs that do the evaluations are beholden for their registration to the local intelligence agency, and their staff must all have clearances. This leaves open a rather wide path toward what one might call *institutional corruption.*

Corruption doesn't have to involve money changing hands or even an explicit exchange of favors. For example, when the Labor party won the 1997 election in Britain, I soon received a phone call from an official at the Department of Trade and Industry. He wanted to know whether I knew any computer scientists at the University of Leeds, so that the department could award my group some money to do collaborative research with them. It transpired that the incoming science minister represented a constituency in Leeds. This does not imply that the minister told his officials to find money for his local university; almost certainly it was an attempt by the officials to schmooze him.

23.3.3.1 Corruption, Manipulation, and Inertia

This preemptive cringe, as one might call it, appears to play a large part in the conduct of the evaluation labs. The most egregious example in my experience occurred in the British National Health Service. The service had agreed, under pressure from the doctors, to encrypt traffic on the health service network; GCHQ made no secret of its wish that key escrow products be used. Trials were arranged; one of them used commercial encryption software from a Danish supplier that had no key escrow, and cost £3,000, while the other used software from a U.K. defense contractor that had key escrow, and cost £100,000. To GCHQ's embarrassment, the Danish software worked, but the British supplier produced nothing that was usable. The situation was quickly salvaged by having a company with a CLEF license evaluate the trials. In its report, it claimed the exact reverse: that the escrow software worked fine, while the foreign product had all sorts of problems. Perhaps the CLEF was simply told what to write; it's just as likely that the staff wrote what they knew GCHQ wanted to read.

Sometimes, an eagerness to please the customer becomes apparent. In the context of the Icelandic health database (Section 8.3.4.1 above), its promoters wanted to defuse criticism from doctors about its privacy problems, so they engaged a British CLEF to write a protection profile for them. This simply repeated, in Criteria jargon, the promoters' original design and claims; it studiously avoided noticing flaws in this design, which had already been documented and even discussed on Icelandic TV [38].

Sometimes the protection profiles might be sound, but the way they're mapped to the application isn't. For example, European governments and IT vendors are currently working on regulations for the "advanced electronic signatures," which, as mentioned in Section 21.2.4.4, will shortly have to be recognized as the equivalent of handwritten signatures in all EU member states. The present proposal is that the signature creation device should be a smartcard evaluated to above level EAL4. (The profile [579] is for

EAL4 augmented, which, as mentioned, is sufficient to keep out all attackers but the competent ones.) But no requirements are proposed for the PC that displays to you the material that you think you are signing. The end result will be a "secure" (in the sense of non-repudiable) signature on whatever the virus or Trojan in your PC sent to your smartcard.

Of course, insiders figure out even more sophisticated ways to manipulate the system. A nice example comes from how the French circumvented British and German opposition to the smartcard-based electronic tachograph described in Section 10.4. They wrote a relaxed protection profile and sent it to a British CLEF to be evaluated. The CLEF was an army software company; whatever their knowledge of MLS, they knew nothing about smartcards. But this didn't lead them to turn down the business. They also didn't know that the U.K. government was opposed to approval of the protection profile. Thus, Britain was left with a choice between accepting defective road safety standards as a fait accompli, and undermining confidence in the Common Criteria.

Given all the corruption, greed, incompetence, and manipulation, it's like a breath of fresh air to find some good, old-fashioned bureaucratic inertia. An example is the healthcare protection profile under development for the U.S. government. Despite all the problems with using the MLS protection philosophy in healthcare, which I discussed in Chapter 9, that's what the profile ended up using [34]. It assumed that no users would be hostile (despite the fact that almost all attacks on health systems are from insiders), and insisted that multiple levels be supported, even though, as described in Chapter 9, levels don't work in that context. It also provided no rules as to how classifications or compartments should be managed, but left access control policy decisions to the catch-all phrase "need to know."

23.3.3.2 Underlying Problems

In general, the structure of the Common Criteria is strongly oriented toward MLS systems and to devices that support them, such as government firewalls and encryption boxes. This is unsurprising given the missions of the agencies that developed them. They assume trained obedient users, small systems that can be formally verified, uniform MLS-type security policies, and an absence of higher-level attacks, such as legal challenges. This makes them essentially useless for most of the applications one finds in the real world.

As for the organizational aspects, I mentioned in 23.2.3 that process-based assurance systems fail if accredited teams don't lose their accreditation when they lose their sparkle. This clearly applies to CLEFs. Even if CLEFs were licensed by a body independent of the intelligence community, many would deteriorate as key staff leave or as skills don't keep up with technology; and as clients shop around for easier evaluations, there will inevitably be grade inflation. Yet, at present, I can see no usable mechanism whereby a practitioner with very solid evidence of incompetence (or even dishonesty) can challenge a CLEF and have it removed from the list. In the absence of sanctions for misbehavior, institutional corruption will remain a serious risk.

When presented with a new security product, the engineer must always consider whether the sales rep is lying or mistaken, and how. The Common Criteria were supposed to fix this problem, but they don't. When presented with a product from the evaluated list, you have to ask how the protection profile was manipulated and by whom; whether the CLEF was dishonest or incompetent; what pressure from which government was applied behind the scenes; and how your rights are eroded by the certificate.

For example, if you use an unevaluated product to generate digital signatures, then a forged signature turns up and someone tries to use it against you, you might reasonably expect to challenge the evidence by persuading a court to order the release of full documentation to your expert witnesses. A Common Criteria certificate might make a court very much less ready to order disclosure, and thus could severely prejudice your rights. In fact, agency insiders admit after a few beers that the main issue is "confidence"—that is, getting people to accept systems as secure even when they aren't.

A cynic might suggest that this is precisely why, in the commercial world, it's the vendors of products that rely on obscurity and that are designed to transfer liability (such as smartcards), to satisfy due-diligence requirements (such as firewalls) or to impress naive users (such as PC access control products), who are most enthusiastic about the Common Criteria. A really hard-bitten cynic might point out that since the collapse of the Soviet Union, the agencies justify their existence by economic espionage, and the Common Criteria signatory countries provide most of the interesting targets. A false U.S. evaluation of a product that is sold worldwide may compromise 250 million Americans; but as it will also compromise 400 million Europeans and 100 million Japanese, the balance of advantage lies in deception. The balance is even stronger with small countries such as Britain, which has fewer citizens to protect and more foreigners to attack. In addition, agencies get brownie points (and budgets) for foreign secrets they steal, not for local secrets that foreigners didn't manage to steal.

An economist, then, is unlikely to trust a Common Criteria evaluation. Perhaps I'm one of the cynics, but I tend to view them as being somewhat like a rubber crutch. Such a device has all sorts of uses, from winning a judge's sympathy through wheedling money out of a gullible government to smacking people round the head. (Just don't try to put serious weight on it!)

Fortunately, the economics discussed in Section 23.2.1 should limit the uptake of the Criteria to sectors where an official certification, however irrelevant, erroneous, or mendacious, offers some competitive advantage.

23.4 Ways Forward

In his classic book, *The Mythical Man-Month*, Brooks argues compellingly that there is no "silver bullet" to solve the problems of software projects that run late and over budget [140]. The easy parts of the problem, such as developing high-level languages in which programmers can work much better than in assembly language, have been done. The removal of much of the accidental complexity of programming means that the intrinsic complexity of the application is what's left. I discussed this in Chapter 22, in the general context of system development methodology; the above discussion should convince you that exactly the same applies to the problem of assurance and, especially, to evaluation.

A more realistic approach to evaluation and assurance would look not just at the technical features of the product but at how it behaves in real applications. Usability is ignored by the Common Criteria, but is in reality all-important; a U.K. government email system that required users to reboot their PC whenever they changed compartments frustrated users so much that they made informal agreements to put everything in common compartments—in effect wasting a nine-figure investment. (Official secrecy will no doubt continue to protect the guilty parties from punishment.) The kind of features I described in the context of bookkeeping systems in Chapter 9, which are designed to limit the effects of human frailty, are also critical. In most applications, we must assume that people are always careless, usually incompetent, and occasionally dishonest.

It's also necessary to confront the fact of large, feature-rich programs that are updated frequently. Network economics cannot be wished away. Evaluation and assurance schemes, such as the Common Criteria, ISO9001, and even CMM, try to squeeze a very volatile and competitive industry into a bureaucratic straightjacket, to provide purchasers with the illusion of stability. If such stability did exist, the whole industry would flock to it; but the best people can do is flock to brands, such as IBM in the 1970s and 1980s, and Microsoft now. The establishment and maintenance of these brands involves huge market forces; security plays a small role.

I've probably given you enough hints by now about how to cheat the system and pass off a lousy product as a secure one—at least long enough for the problem to become someone else's. In the remainder of this book, I'll assume that you're making an honest effort to protect a system and that you want risk reduction, rather than due diligence or some other kind of liability dumping. In many cases, it's the system owner who loses when the security fails; I've cited a number of examples earlier (nuclear command and control, pay-TV, prepayment utility meters, etc.) and they provide some of the more interesting engineering examples.

When you really want a protection property to hold it is vital that the design be subjected to hostile review. It will be eventually, and it's better if it's done before the system is fielded. As discussed in one case history after another, the motivation of the attacker is almost all-important; friendly reviews, by people who want the system to pass, are essentially useless, compared with contributions by people who are seriously trying to break it.

23.4.1 Semi-Open Design

One way of doing this is, to hire multiple experts from different consultancy firms or universities. Another is to use multiple different accreditation bodies: I mentioned in 21.6.4 how voting systems in the United States are vetted independently in each state; and in the days before standards were imposed by organizations such as VISA and SWIFT, banks would build local payment networks, with each of them having the design checked by its own auditors. Neither approach is infallible, though; there are some really awful legacy voting and banking systems.

Another, very well established, technique is what I call *semi-open design*. Here, the architectural-level design is published, even though the implementation details may not be. Examples that I've given include the smartcard banking protocol discussed in Section 2.7.1, and the nuclear command and control systems mentioned in Chapter 11.

Another approach to semi-open design is to use an openly available software package, which anyone can experiment with. This can be of particular value when the main threat is a legal attack. It is unreasonable to expect a court to grant access to the source code of a spreadsheet product such as Excel, or even to accounting software sold by a medium-sized vendor; the opposing expert will just have to buy a copy, experiment with it, and see what she can find. You just have to take your chances that a relevant bug will be found in the package later, or that some other feature will turn out to undermine the evidence that it produces.

23.4.2 Open Source

Open source extends the philosophy of openness from the architecture to the implementation detail. A number of security products have publicly available source code, of which the most obvious is the PGP email encryption program. The Linux operating system and the Apache Web server are also open source, and are relied on by many people to protect information. There is also a drive to adopt open source in government.

Open source software is not entirely a recent invention; in the early days of computing, most system software vendors published their source code. This openness started to recede in the early 1980s when pressure of litigation led IBM to adopt an "object-code-only" policy for its mainframe software, despite bitter criticism from its user community. The pendulum now seems to be swinging back.

There are a number of strong arguments in favor of open source, and a few against. The strongest argument is that if everyone in the world can inspect and play with the software, then bugs are likely to be found and fixed; in Eric Raymond's famous phrase, "To many eyes, all bugs are shallow" [634]. This is especially so if the software is maintained in a cooperative effort, as Linux and Apache are. It may also be more difficult to insert backdoors into such a product.

Arguments against open source center on the fact that once software becomes large and complex, there may be few or no capable motivated people studying it, hence major vulnerabilities may take years to be discovered. A recent example was a programming bug in PGP versions 5 and 6, which allowed an attacker to add an extra escrow key without the keyholder's knowledge [690], and which was fielded for several years before it was spotted. (The problem may be that PGP is being developed faster than people can read the code; that many of the features with which it's getting crammed are uninteresting to the potential readers; or just that now that it's a commercial product, people are not so motivated to do verification work on it for free.)

There have also been backdoor "maintenance passwords" in products such as sendmail that persisted for years before they were removed. The concern is that there may be attackers who are sufficiently motivated to spend more time finding bugs or exploitable features in the published code than the community of reviewers are. In fact, it can be worse than this; as noted in Section 23.2.4, different testers find different bugs, because their test focus is different, so it's quite possible that even once a product had withstood 10,000 hours of community scrutiny, a foreign intelligence agency that invested a mere 100 hours might find a new exploitable vulnerability. Given the cited reliability growth models, the probabilities are easy enough to work out.

Other arguments against open source include the observation that active open source projects add functionality and features at dizzying speed compared to closed software, which can open up nasty feature interactions; that there had better be consensus about what the security is trying to achieve; and that there are special cases, such as when protecting smartcards against various attacks, where a proprietary encryption algorithm embedded in the chip hardware can force the attacker to spend significantly more effort in reverse engineering.

So where is the balance of benefit? Eric Raymond's influential analysis of the economics of open source software [635] suggests that there are five criteria for whether a product would be likely to benefit from an open source approach: where it is based on common engineering knowledge, rather than proprietary techniques; where it is sensitive to failure; where it needs peer review for verification; where it is sufficiently business-critical that users will cooperate in finding and removing bugs; and where its economics include strong network effects. Security passes all these tests, and indeed the long-standing wisdom of Kerckhoffs is that cryptographic systems should be designed in such a way that they are not compromised if the opponent learns the technique being used [454]. There is increasing interest in open source from organizations such as the U.S. Air Force [688, 689].

It's reasonable to conclude that while an open source design is neither necessary nor sufficient, it is often going to be helpful. The important questions are how much effort was expended by capable people in checking and testing the code—and whether they tell you everything they find.

23.4.3 Penetrate-and-Patch, CERTs, and bugtraq

Penetrate-and-patch is the name given dismissively in the 1970s and 1980s to the evolutionary procedure of finding security bugs in systems and then fixing them; it was widely seen at that time as inadequate, as more bugs were always found. At that time, people hoped that formal methods would enable bug-free systems to be constructed. With the realization that such systems are too small and limited for most applications, iterative approaches to assurance are coming back into vogue, along with the question of how to manage them.

Naturally, there's a competitive element to this. The U.S. government's wish is that vulnerabilities in common products such as operating systems and communications software should be reported first to authority, so that they can be exploited for law enforcement or intelligence purposes if need be, and that vendors should ship patches only after unauthorized persons start exploiting the hole. Companies such as Microsoft share source code and vulnerability data with intelligence agency departments engaged in the development of hacking tools, and the computer emergency response teams (CERTs) in many countries are funded by defense agencies. In addition, many feel that the response of CERTs is somewhat slow. The alternative approach is open reporting of bugs as they're found—as happens on a number of mailing lists, notably bugtraq.

Neither approach is fully satisfactory. In the first case, you never know who saw the vulnerability report before you did; and in the second case, you know that anyone in the world could see it and use it against you before a patch is shipped. Perhaps a more sensible solution was proposed in [631], under which a researcher who discovers a vulnerability should first email the software maintainer. The maintainer will have 48 hours to acknowledge receipt, failing which the vulnerability can be published; the maintainer will have a further five days to actually work on the problem, with a possibility of extension by mutual negotiation. The resulting bug fix should carry a credit to the researcher. Just before this book went to press, CERT agreed to start using this procedure, only with a delay of 45 days for the vendor to design and test a fix [174].

This way, software companies have a strong incentive to maintain an attentive and continually staffed bug-reporting facility, and in return will get enough time to test a fix properly before releasing it; researchers will get credits to put on their CVs; users will get bug fixes at the same time as bug reports; and the system will be very much harder for the agencies to subvert.

23.4.4 Education

Perhaps as an academic, I'm biased, but I feel that the problems and technologies of system protection need to be much more widely understood. I have seen case after case in which the wrong mechanisms were used, or the right mechanisms were used in the wrong way. It has been the norm for protection to be got right only at the fifth or sixth attempt. With a slightly more informed approach, it might have been the second or third. Security professionals unfortunately tend to be either too specialized and focused on some tiny aspect of the technology, or else generalists who've never been exposed to many of the deeper technical issues. But blaming the problem on the training we currently give to students—whether of computer science, business administration, or law—is too easy; the hard part is figuring out what to do about it. This book isn't the first step, and certainly won't be the last word—but I hope it will be useful.

23.5 Summary

Sometimes the hardest part of a security engineering project is knowing when you're done. A number of evaluation and assurance methodologies are available to help. In moderation they can be very useful, especially to the start-up firm whose development culture is still fluid and is seeking to establish good work habits and build a reputation. But the assistance they can give has its limits, and overuse of bureaucratic quality control tools can do grave harm. I think of them as like salt: a few shakes on your fries can be a good thing, but a few ounces definitely are not.

But although the picture is gloomy, it doesn't justify despondency. As people gradually acquire experience of what works, what gets attacked and how, and as protection requirements and mechanisms become more part of the working engineer's skill set, things gradually get better. Security may be got right only at the fourth pass, but that's better than never—which was typical 15 years ago.

Life is chaotic. Success means coping with it. Complaining too much about it is the path to failure.

Research Problems

We could do with some new ideas on how to manage evaluation. Perhaps it's possible to apply some of the tools that economists use to deal with imperfect information, from risk-pricing models to the theory of the firm. It would also be helpful if we had better statistical tools to measure and predict failure.

Further Reading

An entire industry is devoted to promoting the assurance and evaluation biz, supported by mountains of your tax dollars. Its enthusiasm can even have the flavor of religion. Unfortunately, there are nowhere near enough people writing heresy.

CHAPTER 24

Conclusions

We are in the middle of a change in how security is done.

Ten years ago, the security manager of a large company was usually a retired soldier or policeman, for whom 'computer security' was a relatively unimportant speciality which he left to the computer department, with occasional help from outside specialists. In ten years' time, his job will be occupied by a systems person; she will consider locks and guards to be a relatively unimportant speciality which she'll farm out to a facilities management company, with an occasional review by outside specialists.

Ten years ago, security technology consisted of an archipelago of mutually suspicious islands—the cryptologists, the operating system protection people, the burglar alarm industry, right through to the chemists who did funny banknote inks. We all thought that the world ended at our shore. In ten years' time, security engineering will be an established discipline; the islands are being joined up by bridges, and practitioners will need to be familiar with all of them. The banknote ink man who doesn't understand digital watermarks, and the cryptologist who's only interested in communications confidentiality mechanisms, will be poor value as employees.

Ten years ago, information security was said to be about 'confidentiality, integrity and availability'. In ten years' time, this list of priorities will be the other way round (as it already is in many applications). Security engineering will be about ensuring that systems are predictably dependable in the face of all sorts of malice, and particularly in the face of service denial attacks. They will also have to be resilient in the face or error and mischance. So tolerance of human carelessness and incompetence will be at least as important as tolerating dishonesty, and this will mean paying close attention to economic and institutional issues as well as technical ones. The ways in which real systems will provide this dependability will be much more diverse than today: tuning the security policy to the application will be an essential part of the engineering art.

Ten years ago, the better information security products were the domain of government. They were designed in secret and manufactured in small quantities by cosseted cost-plus defense contractors. Already, commercial uses dwarf government ones, and in ten years' time the rough and tumble of the marketplace will have taken over completely.

Ten years ago, government policy toward information security was devoted to maintaining the effectiveness of huge communications intelligence networks built up during the Cold War. It was run in secret and along the same lines as the nuclear or missile technology non-proliferation policy: only enough could be exported to prevent the development of competent manufacturers in other countries, and control had to be maintained at all times by vetting end-users and enforcing export licensing. Already, it is becoming clear that crypto controls are almost irrelevant to real policy needs. Issues such as data protection, consumer protection and even online voting are more important. In ten years' time, information protection issues will be pervasive throughout government operations from tax collection through market regulation, and many decisions taken hastily now, at the behest of empire-building police agencies, will have to be changed at some expense.

The biggest challenge though is likely to be systems integration and assurance. Ten years ago, the inhabitants of the different islands in the security archipelago all had huge confidence in their products. The cryptologists believed that certain ciphers couldn't be broken; the smartcard vendors claimed that probing out crypto keys held in their chips was absolutely physically impossible; and the security printing people said that holograms couldn't be forged without a physics PhD and $20 million worth of equipment. At the system level, too, there was much misplaced confidence. The banks claimed that their automatic teller machines could not even conceivably make a mistaken debit; the multilevel secure operating systems crowd sold their approach as the solution for all system protection problems; and people assumed that a security evaluation done by a laboratory licensed by a developed country's government would be both honest and competent. These comfortable old certainties have all evaporated.

Many things will make the job more complicated. The distinction between outsiders and insiders used to be central to the business, but as everything gets connected, it's disappearing fast. Protection used to be predicated on a few big ideas and on propositions that could be stated precisely, while now the subject is much more diverse and includes a lot of inexact and heuristic knowledge. The system life-cycle is also changing: in the old days, a closed system was developed in a finite project, while now systems evolve and accumulate features without limit. Changes in the nature of work are significant: while previously a bank's chief internal auditor would remember all the frauds of the previous thirty years and prevent the data processing department repeating the errors that had caused them, the new corporate culture of transient employment and "perpetual revolution" (as Mao Tse-Tung described it) has all but destroyed corporate memory. Finally, there are the economics of networked information systems: strong externalities dictate that time-to-market will remain much more important than quality.

The net effect of all these changes is that the protection of information in computer systems is no longer a scientific discipline, but an engineering one.

The security engineer of the twenty-first century will be responsible for systems that evolve constantly and face a changing spectrum of threats. She will have a large and constantly growing toolbox. A significant part of her job will be keeping up to date technically: understanding the latest attacks, learning how to use new tools, and keeping up on the legal and policy fronts. Like any engineer, she'll need a solid intellectual foundation; she will have to understand the core disciplines such as cryptology, access control, information flow, networking and signal detection. She'll also need to understand the basics of management: how accounts work, the principles of finance and the business processes of her client. But most important of all will be the ability to manage technology and play an effective part in the process of evolving a system to meet changing business needs. The ability to communicate with business people, rather than just with other engineers, will be vital; and experience will matter hugely.

I don't think anybody with this combination of skills is likely to be unemployed—or bored—anytime soon.

Bibliography

I intend to keep a collection of links at the book's web page, `http://www.ross-anderson.com`. Please check out this page if a link you wish to follow is out of date.

[1] M Abadi, "Explicit Communications Revisited: Two New Attacks on Authentication Protocols," in *IEEE Transactions on Software Engineering*, v 23 no 3 (Mar 1997), pp 185–186.

[2] M Abadi, RM Needham, "Prudent Engineering Practice for Cryptographic Protocols," *IEEE Transactions on Software Engineering*, v 22 no 1 (Jan 1996) pp 6–15; also as DEC SRC Research Report no 125 (June 1 1994) at `ftp://gatekeeper.pa.dec.com/pub/DEC/SRC/research-reports/SRC-125.pdf`.

[3] H Abelson, RJ Anderson, SM Bellovin, J Benaloh, M Blaze, W Diffie, J Gilmore, PG Neumann, RL Rivest, JI Schiller, B Schneier, "The Risks of Key Recovery, Key Escrow, and Trusted Third-Party Encryption," in *World Wide Web Journal*, v 2 no 3 (Summer 1997), pp 241–257.

[4] DG Abraham, GM Dolan, GP Double, JV Stevens, "Transaction Security System," in *IBM Systems Journal*, v 30 no 2 (1991), pp 206–229.

[5] A Abulafia, S Brown, S Abramovich-Bar, "A Fraudulent Case Involving Novel Ink Eradication Methods," in *Journal of Forensic Sciences* v 41 (1996), pp 300–302.

[6] N Achs, "VISA Confronts the Con Men," *Cards International* (Oct 20, 1992) pp 8–9.

[7] EN Adams, "Optimizing Preventive Maintenance of Software Products," *IBM Journal of Research & Development*, v 28 no 1 (1984), pp 2–14.

[8] J Adams, "Cars, Cholera, and Cows: The Management of Risk and Uncertainty," in *Policy Analysis*, no 335, Cato Institute, Washington (1999), at `http://www.cato.org/pubs/pas/pa-335es.html`.

[9] J Adams, *Risk*, University College London Press (1995), ISBN 1-85728-067-9.

[10] Y Adini, Y Moses, S Ullman, "Face recognition: The Problem of Compensating for Changes in Illumination Direction," in *IEEE Transactions on Pattern Analysis and Machine Intelligence*, v 19 no 7 (July 1997), pp 721–732.

[11] C Ajluni, "Two New Imaging Techniques Promise to Improve IC Defect Identification," in *Electronic Design*, v 43 no 14 (July 10, 1995), pp 37–38.

[12] Y Akdeniz, "Regulation of Child Pornography on the Internet" (Dec 1999), at `http://www.cyber-rights.org/reports/child.htm`.

[13] Alliance to Outfox Phone Fraud, `http://www.bell-atl.com/security/fraud/`.

[14] American Society for Industrial Security, `http://www.asisonline.org`.

[15] E Amoroso, *Fundamentals of Computer Security Technology*, Englewood Cliffs, NJ: Prentice Hall (1994), ISBN 0-13-10829-3.

[16] J Anderson, *Computer Security Technology Planning Study*, ESD-TR-73-51, U.S. Air Force Electronic Systems Division (1973), `http://csrc.nist.gov/publications/history/index.html`.

[17] M Anderson, C North, J Griffin, R Milner, J Yesberg, K Yiu, "Starlight: Interactive Link," in *12th Annual Computer Security Applications Conference* (1996) proceedings, published by the IEEE, ISBN 0-8186-7606-XA, pp 55–63.

[18] RJ Anderson, "Solving a Class of Stream Ciphers," in *Cryptologia*, v XIV no 3 (July 1990), pp 285–288.

[19] RJ Anderson, "Why Cryptosystems Fail," in *Communications of the ACM*, v 37 no 11 (Nov 1994), pp 32–40; earlier version at `http://www.cl.cam.ac.uk/users/rja14/wcf.html`.

[20] RJ Anderson, "Liability and Computer Security: Nine Principles," in *Computer Security—ESORICS 94*, Springer LNCS, v 875, pp 231–245.

[21] RJ Anderson, "Crypto in Europe—Markets, Law, and Policy," in *Cryptography: Policy and Algorithms*, Springer LNCS, v 1029, pp 75–89.

[22] RJ Anderson, "Clinical System Security—Interim Guidelines," in *British Medical Journal*, v 312 no 7023 (Jan 13, 1996), pp 109–111; `http://www.cl.cam.ac.uk/ftp/users/rja14/guidelines.txt`.

[23] RJ Anderson, "Security in Clinical Information Systems," British Medical Association (1996), ISBN 0-7279-1048-5.

[24] RJ Anderson, "A Security Policy Model for Clinical Information Systems," in *Proceedings of the 1996 IEEE Symposium on Security and Privacy*, pp 30–43; `http://www.cl.cam.ac.uk/users/rja14/policy11/policy11.html`.

[25] RJ Anderson, "An Update on the BMA Security Policy," in [29], pp 233–250; `http://www.cl.cam.ac.uk/ftp/users/rja14/bmaupdate.ps.gz`.

[26] RJ Anderson, C Manifavas, C Sutherland, "NetCard—A Practical Electronic Cash Scheme," in *Security Protocols* (1996), Springer LNCS, v 1189, pp 49–57.

[27] RJ Anderson, "The Eternity Service," in *Proceedings of Pragocrypt 96* (GC UCMP, ISBN 80-01-01502-5), pp 242–252.

[28] RJ Anderson (ed), *Proceedings of the First International Workshop on Information Hiding* (1996), Springer LNCS, v 1174.

[29] RJ Anderson (ed), *Personal Medical Information—Security, Engineering and Ethics*, Springer-Verlag (1997), ISBN 3-540-63244-1.

[30] RJ Anderson, "GSM hack—Operator Flunks the Challenge," in `comp.risks` v 19.48: `http://catless.ncl.ac.uk/Risks/19.48.html`.

[31] RJ Anderson, "On the Security of Digital Tachographs," in *Computer Security—ESORICS 98*, Springer LNCS, v 1485, pp 111–125; `http://www.cl.cam.ac.uk/ftp/users/rja14/tacho5.ps.gz`.

[32] RJ Anderson, "Safety and Privacy in Clinical Information Systems," in *Rethinking IT and Health*, J Lenaghan (ed.), IPPR (Nov 1998), (ISBN 1-86030-077-4), pp 140–160.

[33] RJ Anderson, "The DeCODE Proposal for an Icelandic Health Database"; partly published in *Læknabladhidh* (the *Icelandic Medical Journal*), v 84 no 11 (Nov 1998), pp 874–875; full text available from `http://www.cl.cam.ac.uk/users/ rja14/#Med`.

[34] RJ Anderson, "Healthcare Protection Profile—Comments," panel position paper at NISSC 1998; at `http://www.cl.cam.ac.uk/ftp/users/rja14/healthpp.pdf`.

[35] RJ Anderson, "The Formal Verification of a Payment System," chapter in *Industrial Strength Formal Methods: A Practitioner's Handbook*, MG Hinchey and JP Bowen (eds), Springer Verlag (Sept 1999, 1-85233-640-4), pp 43–52.

[36] RJ Anderson, "How to Cheat at the Lottery (or, Massively Parallel Requirements Engineering)," in *15th Annual Computer Security Application Conference* (1997); proceedings published by IEEE Computer Society, ISBN 0-7695-0346-2, pp xix–xxvii; at `http://www.cl.cam.ac.uk/~rja14/lottery/lottery.html`.

[37] RJ Anderson, "The Millennium Bug—Reasons Not to Panic," at `http://www.ftp.cl.cam.ac.uk/ftp/users/rja14/y2k.html`.

[38] RJ Anderson, "Comments on the Security Targets for the Icelandic Health Database," at `http://www.cl.cam.ac.uk/ftp/users/rja14/iceland-admiral.pdf`.

[39] RJ Anderson, SJ Bezuidenhoudt, "On the Reliability of Electronic Payment Systems," in *IEEE Transactions on Software Engineering*, v 22 no 5 (May 1996), pp 294–301; `http://www.cl.cam.ac.uk/ftp/users/rja14/meters.ps.gz`.

[40] RJ Anderson, E Biham, LR Knudsen,"Serpent: A Proposal for the Advanced Encryption Standard," submitted to NIST as an AES candidate; a short version of

the paper appeared at the AES conference, August 1998; both papers available at [41].

[41] RJ Anderson, E Biham, L Knudsen, "The Serpent Home Page," `http://www.cl.cam.ac.uk/~rja14/serpent.html`.

[42] RJ Anderson, B Crispo, JH Lee, C Manifavas, V Matyás, FAP Petitcolas, *The Global Internet Trust Register*, MIT Press (1999), (ISBN 0-262-51105-3); `http://www.cl.cam.ac.uk/Research/Security/Trust-Register/`.

[43] RJ Anderson, MG Kuhn, "Tamper Resistance—A Cautionary Note," in *Proceedings of the Second Usenix Workshop on Electronic Commerce* (Nov 1996), pp 1–11; `http://www.cl.cam.ac.uk/users/rja14/tamper.html`.

[44] RJ Anderson, MG Kuhn, "Low-Cost Attacks on Tamper-Resistant Devices," in *Security Protocols—Proceedings of the 5th International Workshop* (1997), Springer LNCS, v 1361, pp 125–136.

[45] RJ Anderson, MG Kuhn, "Soft Tempest—An Opportunity for NATO," at *Protecting NATO Information Systems in the 21st Century*, Washington, DC, Oct 25–26, 1999.

[46] RJ Anderson, JH Lee, "Jikzi: A New Framework for Secure Publishing," in *Security Protocols 99*, Springer LNCS, v 1976, pp 21–36.

[47] RJ Anderson, RM Needham, "Robustness Principles for Public Key Protocols," in *Advances in Cryptology—Crypto 95*, Springer LNCS, v 963, pp 236–247; `http://www.cl.cam.ac.uk/ftp/users/rja14/robustness.ps.gz`.

[48] RJ Anderson, RM Needham, "Programming Satan's Computer" in *Computer Science Today*, Springer, Lecture Notes in *Computer Science*, v 1000 (1995), pp 426–441; `http://www.cl.cam.ac.uk/ftp/users/rja14/satan.ps.gz`.

[49] RJ Anderson, RM Needham, A Shamir, "The Steganographic File System," in *Proceedings of the Second International Workshop on Information Hiding*, Springer LNCS, v 1525, pp 74–84.

[50] RJ Anderson, MR Roe, "The GCHQ Protocol and Its Problems," in *Advances in Cryptology—Eurocrypt 97*, Springer LNCS, v 1233, pp 134–148; `http://www.cl.cam.ac.uk/ftp/users/rja14/euroclipper.ps.gz`.

[51] CM Andrew, V Mitrokhin, *The Sword and the Shield: The Mitrokhin Archive and the Secret History of the KGB*, New York: Basic Books (1999), ISBN 0-46500310-9.

[52] `http://www.anonymizer.com`.

[53] JC Anselmo, "U.S. Seen More Vulnerable to Electromagnetic Attack," in *Aviation Week and Space Technology*, v 146 no 4 (July 28, 1997), p 67.

[54] T Appleby, "Chilling Debit-Card Scam Uncovered," in *The Globe & Mail* (Dec 12, 1999), p 1.

[55] U.S. Army, *Electromagnetic Pulse (EMP) and Tempest Protection for Facilities*, Hyattsville, Md: Corps of Engineers Publications Depot (1990).

[56] "ASPECT—Advanced Security for Personal Communications Technologies," at `http://www.esat.kuleuven.ac.be/cosic/aspect/index.html`.

[57] D Aubrey-Jones, "Internet—Virusnet?" in *Network Security* (Feb 1997), pp 15–19.

[58] D Aucsmith, "Tamper-Resistant Software: An Implementation," in [28], pp 317–333.

[59] D Aucsmith (ed), *Proceedings of the Second International Workshop on Information Hiding* (Portland, Oregon: Apr 1998), Springer LNCS, v 1525.

[60] B Audone, F Bresciani, "Signal Processing in Active Shielding and Direction-Finding Techniques," *IEEE Transactions on Electromagnetic Compatibility*, v 38 no 3 (Aug 1996), pp 334–340.

[61] D Austin, "Barclays Winning Card Fraud War," in *Banking Technology* (Apr 1994), p 5.

[62] D Austin, "Flood warnings," in *Banking Technology* (Jul–Aug 1999), pp 28–31.

[63] "Computer Combat Rules Frustrate the Pentagon," in *Aviation Week and Space Technology*, v 147 no 11 (Sept 9, 1997), pp 67–68.

[64] J Bacon, *Concurrent Systems*, Addison-Wesley (1997), ISBN 0-201-17767-6.

[65] J Bacon, K Moody, J Bates, R Hayton, CY Ma, A McNeil, O Seidel, M Spiteri, "Generic Support for Distributed Applications," in *IEEE Computer* (Mar 2000), pp 68–76.

[66] L Badger, DF Sterne, DL Sherman, KM Walker, SA Haghighat, "Practical Domain and Type Enforcement for UNIX," in *Proceedings of the 1995 IEEE Symposium on Security and Privacy*, pp 66–77.

[67] M Baggott, "The Smart Way to Fight Fraud," *Scottish Banker* (Nov 1995), pp 32–33.

[68] SA Baker, PR Hurst, *The Limits of Trust*, Kluwer Law International (1998), ISBN 9-0411-0639-1.

[69] D Balfanz, EW Felten, "Hand-Held Computers Can Be Better Smart Cards," in *Eighth USENIX Security Symposium* (1999), ISBN 1-880446-28-6, pp 15–23.

[70] J Bamford, *The Puzzle Palace: A Report on NSA, America's Most Secret Agency*, New York: Houghton-Mifflin (1982, 3rd printing, revised edition due out shortly), ISBN 0-395-31286-8.

[71] Bank for International Settlements, *Security and Reliability in Electronic Systems for Payments*, British Computer Society (1982).

[72] Bank for International Settlements, `http://www.bis.org/`.

[73] "Card Fraud: Banking's Boom Sector," in *Banking Automation Bulletin for Europe* (Mar 1992), pp 1–5.

[74] RL Barnard, *Intrusion Detection Systems*, Butterworths (1988), ISBN 0-409-90030-3.

[75] A Barnett, "Britain's UFO Secrets Revealed," in *The Observer* (June 4, 2000); at

http://www.observer.co.uk/uk_news/story/
0,6903,328010,00.html.

[76] J Barr, "The Gates of Hades," in *Linux World* (Apr 2000); at http://
www.linuxworld.com/linuxworld/lw-2000-04/lw-04-vcontrol_3.
html.

[77] R Baskerville, "Information Systems Security Design Methods: Implications for
Information Systems Development," in *ACM Computing Surveys*, v 26 (1994),
pp 375–414.

[78] PJ Bass, "Telephone Cards and Technology Development as Experienced by GPT
Telephone Systems," in *GEC Review*, v 10 no 1 (1995), pp 14–19.

[79] "Great Microprocessors of the Past and Present," at http://
www.cs.uregina.ca/~bayko/cpu.html.

[80] F Beck, *Integrated Circuit Failure Analysis—A Guide to Preparation
Techniques*, New York: John Wiley & Sons, Inc. (1998), ISBN 0-471-97401-3.

[81] J Beck, "Sources of Error in Forensic Handwriting Examination," in *Journal of
Forensic Sciences*, v 40 (1995), pp 78–87.

[82] HA Beker, C Amery, "Cryptography Policy," at http://www.baltimore.com/
library/whitepapers/mn_cryptography.html.

[83] HJ Beker, JMK Friend, PW Halliden, "Simplifying Key Management in Electronic
Fund Transfer Point-of-Sale Systems," in *Electronics Letters*, v 19 (1983),
pp 442–443.

[84] H Beker, F Piper, *Cipher Systems*, Northwood (1982).

[85] H Beker, M Walker, "Key Management for Secure Electronic Funds Transfer in a
Retail Environment," in *Advances in Cryptology—Crypto 84*, Springer LNCS,
v 196, pp 401–410.

[86] DE Bell, L LaPadula, "Secure Computer Systems," ESD-TR-73-278, Mitre
Corporation; v I and II (Nov 1973), v III (Apr 1974).

[87] M Bellare, J Kilian, P Rogaway, "The Security of Cipher Block Chaining," in
Advances in Cryptology—Crypto 94, Springer LNCS, v 839, pp 341–358.

[88] M Bellare, P Rogaway, "Optimal Asymmetric Encryption," in *Advances in
Cryptology—Eurocrypt 94*, Springer LNCS, v 950, pp 103–113; see also RFC
2437, http://sunsite.auc.dk/RFC/rfc/rfc2437.html.

[89] SM Bellovin, "Packets Found on an Internet," in *Computer Communications
Review*, v 23 no 3 (July 1993), pp 26–31.

[90] SM Bellovin, "Defending against Sequence Number Attacks," RFC 1948
(May 1996); at http://sunsite.auc.dk/RFC/rfc/rfc1948.html.

[91] SM Bellovin, "Debit-Card Fraud in Canada," in comp.risks, v 20.69; at
http://catless.ncl.ac.uk/Risks/20.69.html.

[92] SM Bellovin, "Permissive Action Links," at http://
www.research.att.com/~smb/nsam-160/pal.html.

[93] SM Bellovin, "ICMP Traceback Messages," Internet draft (Mar 2000), at
      `http://search.ietf.org/internet-drafts/draft-bellovin-itrace-00.txt`.

[94] SM Bellovin, WR Cheswick, *Firewalls and Internet Security: Repelling the Wily Hacker*, Reading, MA: Addison-Wesley (1994), ISBN 0-201-63357-4.

[95] M Benantar, R Guski, KM Triodle, "Access Control Systems: From Host-Centric to Network-Centric Computing," in *IBM Systems Journal*, v 35 no 1 (1996), pp 94–112.

[96] W Bender, D Gruhl, N Morimoto, A Lu, "Techniques for Data Hiding," in *IBM Systems Journal*, v 35 no 3–4 (1996), pp 313–336.

[97] T Benkart, D Bitzer, "BFE Applicability to LAN Environments," in *Seventeenth National Computer Security Conference* (1994); Proceedings published by NIST, pp 227–236.

[98] F Bergadano, B Crispo, G Ruffo, "Proactive Password Checking with Decision Trees," in *4th ACM Conference on Computer and Communications Security* (1997); Proceedings published by the ACM, ISBN 0-89791-912-2, pp 67–77.

[99] T Berson, G Barksdale, "KSOS: Development Methodology for a Secure Operating System," *AFIPS Conference proceedings* (1979).

[100] K Biba, *Integrity Considerations for Secure Computer Systems*, Mitre Corporation MTR-3153 (1975).

[101] E Biham, A Biryukov, "Cryptanalysis of Skipjack Reduced to 31 Rounds Using Impossible Differentials," in *Advances in Cryptology—Eurocrypt 97*, Springer LNCS, v 1592, pp 12–23.

[102] E Biham, A Shamir, *Differential Cryptanalysis of the Data Encryption Standard*, Springer (1993), ISBN 0-387-97930-1.

[103] E Biham, A Shamir, "Differential Fault Analysis of Secret Key Cryptosystems," in *Advances in Cryptology—Crypto 97*, Springer LNCS, v 1294, pp 513–525.

[104] A Biryukov, A Shamir, D Wagner, "Real-Time Cryptanalysis of A5/1 on a PC," in *Fast Software Encryption* (2000).

[105] Bishop and Bloomfield, "A Conservative Theory for Long-Term Reliability-Growth Prediction," in *IEEE Transactions on Reliability*, v 45 no 4 (Dec 1996), pp 550–560.

[106] DM Bishop, "Applying COMPUSEC to the Battlefield," in *17th Annual National Computer Security Conference* (1994), pp 318–326.

[107] M Bishop, M Dilger, "Checking for Race Conditions in File Accesses," in *Computing Systems USENIX*, v 9 no 2 (Spring 1996), pp 131–152.

[108] Wolfgang Bitzer, Joachim Opfer, "Schaltungsanordnung zum Messen der Korrelationsfunktion zwischen zwei vorgegebenen Signalen" [Circuit arrangement for measuring the correlation function between two provided signals]. German Patent DE 3911155 C2, Deutsches Patentamt, November 11, 1993.

[109] J Blackledge, "Making Money from Fractals and Chaos: Microbar," in *Mathematics Today*, v 35 no 6 (Dec 1999), pp 170–173.

[110] RD Blackledge, "DNA versus Fingerprints," in *Journal of Forensic Sciences*, v 40 (1995), p 534.

[111] GR Blakley, "Safeguarding Cryptographic Keys," in *Proceedings of NCC AFIPS* (1979), pp 313–317.

[112] B Blakley, R Blakley, RM Soley, *CORBA Security: An Introduction to Safe Computing with Objects*, Reading, MA: Addison-Wesley (1999), ISBN 0-201-32565-9.

[113] M Blaze, "Protocol Failure in the Escrowed Encryption Standard," in *Second ACM Conference on Computer and Communications Security* (Nov 2–4, 1994), Fairfax, VA: Proceedings published by the ACM ISBN 0-89791-732-4, pp 59–67; at http://www.crypto.com/papers/.

[114] M Blaze, SM Bellovin, "Tapping, Tapping on My Network Door," in *Communications of the ACM* (Oct 2000), Inside Risks 124; at http://www.crypto.com/papers/carnivore-risks.html.

[115] M Blaze, J Feigenbaum, J Lacy, "Decentralized Trust Management," in *Proceedings of the 1996 IEEE Symposium on Security and Privacy*, pp 164–173.

[116] D Bleichenbacher, "Chosen Ciphertext Attacks against Protocols Based on the RSA Encryption Standard PKCS #1," in *Advances in Cryptology—Crypto 98*, Springer LNCS, v 1462, pp 1–12.

[117] G Bleumer, M Schunter, "Digital Patient Assistants: Privacy vs Cost in Compulsory Health Insurance," in *Health Informatics Journal*, v 4 nos 3–4 (Dec 1998), pp 138–156.

[118] B Blobel, "Clinical Record Systems in Oncology. Experiences and Developments on Cancer Registers in Eastern Germany," in [29], pp 39–56.

[119] JA Bloom, IJ Cox, T Kalker, JPMG Linnartz, ML Miller, CBS Traw, "Copy Protection for DVD Video," in *Proceedings of the IEEE*, v 87 no 7 (July 1999), pp 1267–1276.

[120] ER Block, *Fingerprinting*, Franklin Wells (1970), SBN 85166-435-0.

[121] S Blythe, B Fraboni, S Lall, H Ahmed, U de Riu, "Layout Reconstruction of Complex Silicon Chips," in *IEEE Journal of Solid-State Circuits*, v 28 no 2 (Feb 1993), pp 138–145.

[122] WE Boebert, RY Kain, "A Practical Alternative to Hierarchical Integrity Policies," in *8th National Computer Security Conference* (1985), Proceedings published by NIST, p 18.

[123] BW Boehm, *Software Engineering Economics*, Englewood Cliffs, NJ: Prentice Hall (1981), ISBN 0-13-822122-7.

[124] N Bohm, I Brown, B Gladman, "Electronic Commerce—Who Carries the Risk of Fraud?" *Journal of Information Law & Technology*, v 3 (2000); http://elj.warwick.ac.uk/jilt/00-3/bohm.html.

[125] MK Bond, "Attacks on Cryptoprocessor Transaction Sets," *to be submitted to CHES 2001*.

[126] D Boneh, RA Demillo, RJ Lipton, "On the Importance of Checking Cryptographic Protocols for Faults," in *Advances in Cryptology—Eurocrypt 97*, Springer LNCS, v 1233, pp 37–51.

[127] L Boney, AH Tewfik, KN Hamdy, "Digital Watermarks for Audio Signals," in *Proceedings of the 1996 IEEE International Conference on Multimedia Computing and Systems*, pp 473–480.

[128] V Bontchev, "Possible Macro Virus Attacks and How to Prevent Them," in *Computers and Security*, v 15 no 7 (1996), pp 595–626.

[129] NS Borenstein, "Perils and Pitfalls of Practical Cybercommerce," in *Communications of the ACM*, v 39 no 6 (June 1996), pp 36–44.

[130] E Bovenlander, talk on smartcard security, Eurocrypt 97, reported in [44].

[131] E Bovenlander, RL van Renesse, "Smartcards and Biometrics: An Overview," in *Computer Fraud and Security Bulletin* (Dec 1995), pp 8–12.

[132] C Bowden, Y Akdeniz, "Cryptography and Democracy: Dilemmas of Freedom," in *Liberating Cyberspace: Civil Liberties, Human Rights, and the Internet*, Pluto Press (1999), pp 81–125.

[133] RM Brady, RJ Anderson, RC Ball, *Murphy's Law, the Fitness of Evolving Species, and the Limits of Software Reliability*, Cambridge University Computer Laboratory Technical Report no. 471 (1999).

[134] S Brands, *Rethinking Public Key Infrastructures and Digital Certificates—Building in Privacy*, MIT Press (2000), ISBN 0-262-02491-8.

[135] JT Brassil, S Low, NF Maxemchuk, "Copyright Protection for the Electronic Distribution of Text Documents," in *Proceedings of the IEEE*, v 87 no 7 (July 1999), pp 1181–1196.

[136] M Brelis, "Patients' Files Allegedly Used for Obscene Calls," in *Boston Globe*, (Apr 11, 1995); also in comp.risks, v 17 no 7.

[137] DFC Brewer, MJ Nash, "Chinese Wall Model," in *Proceedings of the 1989 IEEE Computer Society Symposium on Security and Privacy*, pp 215–228.

[138] M Briceno, I Goldberg, D Wagner, "An Implementation of the GSM A3A8 Algorithm," at http://www.scard.org/gsm/a3a8.txt.

[139] D Brin, *The Transparent Society: Will Technology Force Us to Choose between Privacy and Freedom?* Perseus Press (1999), ISBN 0-73820144-8.

[140] F Brooks, *The Mythical Man-Month: Essays on Software Engineering*, Addison-Wesley (1995), ISBN 0-201-83595-9.

[141] D Brown, "Techniques for Privacy and Authentication in Personal Communications Systems," in *IEEE Personal Communications*, v 2 no 4 (Aug 1995), pp 6–10.

[142] R Buderi, *The Invention That Changed the World*, Simon & Schuster, New York, (1996); ISBN 0-684-81021-2.

[143] H Buehler, interview with Swiss Radio International, (July 4, 1994); at `http://www.funet.fi/pub/crypt/mirrors/idea.sec.dsi.unimi.it/rpub.cl.msu.edu/crypt/docs/hans-buehler-crypto-spy.txt`.

[144] `http://archives.neohapsis.com/archives/bugtraq/`.

[145] Bundesamt für Sicherheit in der Informationstechnik (German Information Security Agency), "Schutzmaßnahmen gegen Lauschangriffe" [Protection against bugs], *Faltblätter des BSI*, v 5, Bonn (1997); `http://www.bsi.bund.de/literat/faltbl/laus005.htm`.

[146] J Bunnell, J Podd, R Henderson, R Napier, J Kennedy-Moffatt, "Cognitive, Associative and Conventional Passwords: Recall and Guessing Rates," in *Computers and Security*, v 16 no 7 (1997), pp 645–657.

[147] Buro Jansen & Janssen, "Making Up the Rules: Interception versus Privacy," (Aug 8, 2000), at `http://www.xs4all.nl/~respub/crypto/english/`.

[148] M Burrows, M Abadi, RM Needham, "A Logic of Authentication," in *Proceedings of the Royal Society of London A*, v 426 (1989), pp 233–271; earlier version published as DEC SRC Research Report 39, `ftp://gatekeeper.pa.dec.com/pub/DEC/SRC/research-reports/SRC-039.pdf`.

[149] C Busch, F Graf, S Wolthusen, A Zeidler, "A System for Intellectual Property Protection," Fraunhofer Institute, at `http://www.igd.fhg.de/igd-a8`.

[150] RW Butler, GB Finelli, "The Infeasibility of Experimental Quantification of Life-Critical Software Reliability," in *ACM Symposium on Software for Critical Systems* (1991), ISBN 0-89791-455-4, pp 66–76.

[151] "Long Distance Phone Scam Hits Internet Surfers," in `businessknowhow.com`, at `http://www.businessknowhow.com/newlong.htm`.

[152] California Secretary of State, "A Report on the Feasibility of Internet Voting" (Jan 2000), at `http://www.ss.ca.gov/executive/ivote/`.

[153] J Calvert, P Warren, "Secrets of McCartney Bank Cash Are Leaked," in *The Express* (Feb 9, 2000), pp 1–2.

[154] JL Cambier, "Biometric Identification in Large Population," in *Information Security Bulletin*, v 5 no 2 (Mar 2000), pp 17–26.

[155] J Camenisch, JM Piveteau, M Stadler, "An Efficient Fair Payment System," in *3rd ACM Conference on Computer and Communications Security* (1996); Proceedings published by the ACM, ISBN 0-89791-829-0, pp 88–94.

[156] LJ Camp, C Wolfram, "Pricing Security," Third Information Survivability Workshop, Boston, (Oct 2000).

[157] D Campbell, "Somebody's Listening," in *The New Statesman* (Aug 12, 1988), pp 1, 10–12; at `http://jya.com/echelon-dc.htm`.

[158] D Campbell, "Making History: The Original Source for the 1988 First Echelon Report Steps Forward" (Feb 25, 2000); at `http://cryptome.org/echelon-mndc.htm`.

[159] JC Campbell, N Ikegami, *The Art of Balance in Health Policy—Maintaining*

Japan's Low-Cost, Egalitarian System, Cambridge University Press (1998), ISBN 0-521-57122-7.

[160] D Campbell, P Lashmar, "The New Cold War: How America Spies on Us for Its Oldest Friend—the Dollar," in *The Independent* (July 2, 2000); at `http://www.independent.co.uk/news/World/Americas/2000-07/coldwar020700.shtml`.

[161] JP Campbell, "Speaker Recognition: A Tutorial," in *Proceedings of the IEEE*, v 85 no 9 (Sept 1997), pp 1437–1462.

[162] C Cant, S Wiseman, "Simple Assured Bastion Hosts," in *13th Annual Computer Security Application Conference* (1997); Proceedings published by IEEE Computer Society, ISBN 0-8186-8274-4ACSAC, pp 24–33.

[163] "Dark Horse in Lead for Fingerprint ID Card," *Card World Independent* (May 1994), p 2.

[164] "German A555 Takes Its Toll," in *Card World International* (Dec 1994–Jan 1995), p 6.

[165] "High Tech Helps Card Fraud Decline," in *Cards International*, no 117 (Sept 29, 1994).

[166] "VISA Beefs Up Its Anti-Fraud Technology," in *Cards International*, no 189 (Dec 12, 1997), p 5.

[167] JM Carlin, "UNIX Security Update," at *USENIX Security 93*, pp 119–130.

[168] J Carr, "Doing Nothing Is Just Not an Option," in *The Observer* (June 18, 2000), at `http://www.fipr.org/rip/index.html`.

[169] J Carroll, *Big Blues: The Unmaking of IBM*, New York: Crown Publishers (1993), ISBN 0-517-59197-9.

[170] II Carter, "Car Clock Fixer Jailed for Nine Months," in *The Guardian* (Feb 15, 2000), p 13.

[171] R Carter, "What You Are . . . Not What You Have," in *International Security Review Access Control*, Special Issue (Winter 1993–1994), pp 14–16.

[172] S Castano, M Fugini, G Martella, P Samarati, *Database Security*, Reading, MA: Addison-Wesley (1994), ISBN 0-201-59375-0.

[173] Center for Democracy and Technology, `http://www.cdt.org/`.

[174] 'The CERT Coordination Center Vulnerability Disclosure Policy;' http://www.cert.org/faq/vuldisclosurepolicy.html

[175] DW Chadwick, PJ Crook, AJ Young, DM McDowell, TL Dornan, JP New, "Using the Internet to Access Confidential Patient Records: A Case Study," in *British Medical Journal*, v 321 (Sep 9, 2000), pp 612–614; at `http://bmj.com/cgi/content/full/321/7261/612`.

[176] L Chapman, *Your Disobedient Servant*, New York: Penguin Books (1979).

[177] D Chaum, "Untraceable Electronic Mail, Return Addresses, and Digital Pseudonyms," in *Communications of the ACM*, v 24 no 2 (Feb 1981).

[178] D Chaum, "Blind Signatures for Untraceable Payments," in *Crypto 82*, Plenum Press (1983), pp 199–203.

[179] D Chaum, "The Dining Cryptographers' Problem: Unconditional Sender and Recipient Untraceability," in *Journal of Cryptology*, v 1 (1989) pp 65–75.

[180] D Chaum, A Fiat, M Naor, "Untraceable Electronic Cash," in *Advances in Cryptology—CRYPTO '88*, Springer LNCS, v 403, pp 319–327.

[181] R Chellappa, CL Wilcon, S Sirohey, "Human and Machine Recognition of Faces: A Survey," in *Proceedings of the IEEE*, v 83 no 5 (May 1995), pp 705–740.

[182] HJ Choi, private discussion with author.

[183] B Christianson, et al. (ed), "Security Protocols—5th International Workshop," Springer LNCS, v 1360 (1998).

[184] B Christianson, et al. (ed), "Security Protocols—6th International Workshop," Springer LNCS, v 1550 (1999).

[185] F Church (chairman), "Intelligence Activities—Senate Resolution 21," U.S. Senate, 94th Congress, First Session, at `http://cryptome.org/nsa-4th.htm`.

[186] WS Ciciora, "Inside the Set-Top Box," in *IEEE Spectrum*, v 12 no 4 (Apr 1995), pp 70–75.

[187] D Clark, D Wilson, "A Comparison of Commercial and Military Computer Security Policies," in *Proceedings of the 1987 IEEE Symposium on Security and Privacy*, pp 184–194.

[188] R Clark, *The Man Who Broke Purple*, New York, Little Brown (1977), ISBN 0-316-14595-5.

[189] I Clarke, "The Free Network Project Homepage," at `http://freenet.sourceforge.net/`.

[190] R Clayton, G Davies, C Hall, A Hilborne, K Hartnett, D Jones, P Mansfield, K Mitchell, R Payne, N Titley, D Williams, "LINX Best Current Practice—Traceability," Version 1.0 (May 18, 1999), at `http://www.linx.net/noncore/bcp/traceability-bcp.html`.

[191] S Clough, "Bombings 'Inspired by Atlanta Attack,'" in *Daily Telegraph* (June 6, 2000); at `http://www.telegraph.co.uk:80/`.

[192] FB Cohen, *A Short Course on Computer Viruses*, New York: John Wiley & Sons, Inc. (1994), ISBN 0-471-00769-2.

[193] JL Colbert, PL Bowen, "A Comparison of Internal Controls: COBIT, SAC, COSO and SAS 55/78," at `http://www.isaca.org/bkr_cbt3.htm`.

[194] A Collins, "Court Decides Software Time-Locks Are Illegal," in *Computer Weekly* (Aug 19, 1993), p 1.

[195] D Comer, "Cryptographic Techniques—Secure Your Wireless Designs," in *EDN* (Jan 18, 1996), pp 57–68.

[196] Committee of Sponsoring Organizations of the Treadway Commission (CSOTC), "Internal Control—Integrated Framework" (COSO Report, 1992); from `http://www.coso.org/`.

[197] "Communicating Britain's Future," at `http://www.fipr.org/polarch/labour.html`.

[198] "Kavkaz-Tsentr Says Russians Hacking Chechen Web Sites"; "'Information War' Waged on Web Sites over Chechnya," in *Communications Law in Transition* Newsletter, v 1 no 4 (Feb 2000), at `http://pcmlp.socleg.ox.ac.uk/transition/issue04/russia.htm`.

[199] Computer Emergency Response Team Coordination Center, at `http://www.cert.org/`.

[200] "Telecoms Fraud in the Cellular Market: How Much Is Hype and How Much Is Real?" in *Computer Fraud and Security Bulletin* (June 1997), pp 11–14.

[201] Computer Privacy Digest, v 17 no 7 (Sept 15, 2000).

[202] JB Condat, "Toll Fraud on French PBX Systems," in *Computer Law and Security Report*, v 10 no 2 (Mar/Apr 1994), pp 89–91.

[203] J Connolly, "Operation Chain Link: The Deployment of a Firewall at Hanscom Air Force Base," *Twelfth Annual Computer Security Applications Conference* (1996); Proceedings published by the IEEE, ISBN 0-8186-7606-X, pp 170–177.

[204] E Constable, "American Express to Reduce the Risk of Online Fraud".

[205] D Coppersmith, "The Data Encryption Standard (DES) and Its Strength against Attacks," IBM report RC 18613 (81421).

[206] Council of Europe, "Convention for the Protection of Individuals with Regard to Automatic Processing of Personal Data," European Treaty Series, no. 108 (Jan 28, 1981); at `http://www.privacy.org/pi/intl_orgs/coe/dp_convention_108.txt`.

[207] C Cowan, C Pu, D Maier, H Hinton, J Walpole, P Bakke, S Beattie, A Grier, P Wagle, Q Zhang, "StackGuard: Automatic Adaptive Detection and Prevention of Buffer-Overflow Attacks," *7th USENIX Security Conference* (1998), pp 63–77.

[208] JW Coyne, NC Kluksdahl, "'Mainstreaming' Automated Information Systems Security Engineering (A Case Study in Security Run Amok)," in *Second ACM Conference on Computer and Communications Security* (1994); Proceedings published by the ACM, ISBN 0-89791-732-4, pp 251–257; at `http://www.acm.org/pubs/contents/proceedings/commsec/191177/`.

[209] L Cranor, "Lorrie Cranor's Electronic Voting Hot List," at `http://www.ccrc.wustl.edu/~lorracks/sensus/hotlist.html`.

[210] S Craver, "On Public-Key Steganography in the Presence of an Active Warden," in *Proceedings of the Second International Workshop on Information Hiding* (1998), Springer LNCS, v 1525, pp 355–368.

[211] B Crispo, M Lomas, "A Certification Scheme for Electronic Commerce," in *Security Protocols* (1996), Springer LNCS, v 1189, pp 19–32.

[212] W Curtis, H Krasner, N Iscoe, "A Field Study of the Software Design Process for Large Systems," in *Communications of the ACM*, v 31 no 11 (Nov 1988), pp 1268–1287.

[213] J Daemen, L Knudsen, V Rijmen, "The Block Cipher SQUARE," in *Fourth*

International Workshop on Fast Software Encryption, Springer LNCS, v 1267 (1997), pp 149–165; at `http://www.esat.kuleuven.ac.be/~rijmen/square/`.

[214] "Beating the Credit Card Telephone Fraudsters," in *Daily Telegraph* (Oct 9, 1999), at `http://www.telegraph.co.uk:80/`.

[215] T Dalrymple, "The Sinister Ethos of the Baying Mob," in *The Sunday Telegraph* (Aug 13, 2000), at `http://www.dailytelegraph.co.uk`.

[216] M Darman, E le Roux, "A New Generation of Terrestrial and Satellite Microwave Communication Products for Military Networks," in *Electrical Communication* (Q4 1994), pp 359–364.

[217] Data Protection Commissioners of EU and EES countries and Switzerland, two statements, *20th International Conference on Data Protection,* Santiago de Compostela, (Sept 16–18, 1998); at `http://www.dataprotection.gov.uk/20dpcom.html`.

[218] J Daugman, "High Confidence Visual Recognition of Persons by a Test of Statistical Independence," in *IEEE Transactions on Pattern Analysis and Machine Intelligence,* v 15 no 11 (Nov 1993), pp 1148–1161.

[219] J Daugman, "Biometric Decision Landscapes," Technical Report No. TR482, University of Cambridge Computer Laboratory.

[220] C Davies, R Ganesan, "BApasswd: A New Proactive Password Checker," in *16th National Computer Security Conference* (1993); proceedings published by NIST, pp 1–15.

[221] DW Davies, WL Price, *Security for Computer Networks,* New York: John Wiley & Sons, Inc. (1984).

[222] G Davies, *A History of Money from Ancient Times to the Present Day,* University of Wales Press (1996); ISBN 0-7083-1351-5; related material at `http://www.ex.ac.uk/%7ERDavies/arian/llyfr.html`.

[223] H Davies, "Physiognomic Access Control," in *Information Security Monitor,* v 10 no 3 (Feb 1995), pp 5–8.

[224] D Davis, "Compliance Defects in Public-Key Cryptography," in *Sixth USENIX Security Symposium Proceedings* (July 1996), pp 171–178.

[225] D Davis, R Ihaka, P Fenstermacher, "Cryptographic Randomness from Air Turbulence in Disk Drives," in *Advances in Cryptology—Crypto 94,* Springer LNCS, v 839, pp 114–120.

[226] D Dean, EW Felten, DS Wallach, "Java Security: From HotJava to Netscape and Beyond," in *Proceedings of the 1996 IEEE Symposium on Security and Privacy,* IEEE Computer Society Press, pp 190–200.

[227] C Deavours, D Kahn, L Kruh, G Mellen, B Winkel, *Cryptology—Yesterday, Today, and Tomorrow,* Artech House (1987), ISBN 0-89006-253-6.

[228] C Deavours, D Kahn, L Kruh, G Mellen, B Winkel, *Selections from Cryptologia—History, People and Technology,* Artech House (1997), ISBN 0-89006-862-3.

[229] C Deavours, L Kruh, *Machine Cryptography and Modern Cryptanalysis*, Artech House (1985), ISBN 0-89006-161-0.

[230] B Demoulin, L Kone, C Poudroux, P Degauque, "Electromagnetic Radiation of Shielded Data Transmission Lines," in [301], pp 163–173.

[231] I Denley, S Weston-Smith, "Implementing Access Control to Protect the Confidentiality of Patient Information in Clinical Information Systems in the Acute Hospital," in *Health Informatics Journal*, v 4 nos 3–4 (Dec 1998), pp 174–178.

[232] I Denley, S Weston-Smith, "Privacy in Clinical Information Systems in Secondary Care," in *British Medical Journal*, v 318 (May 15, 1999), pp 1328–1331.

[233] DE Denning, "The Lattice Model of Secure Information Flow," in *Communications of the ACM*, v 19 no 5, pp 236–243.

[234] DE Denning, *Cryptography and Data Security*, Addison-Wesley (1982), ISBN 0-201-10150-5.

[235] DE Denning, *Information Warfare and Security*, Addison-Wesley (1999), ISBN 0-201-43303-6.

[236] DE Denning, "Activism, Hacktivism, and Cyberterrorism: The Internet as a Tool for Influencing Foreign Policy," InfowarCon 2000, at http://www.nautilus. org/info-policy/workshop/papers/denning.html.

[237] DE Denning, PH MacDoran, "Location-Based Authentication: Grounding Cyberspace for Better Security," in *Computer Fraud and Security Bulletin* (Feb 1996), pp 12–16.

[238] DE Denning, J Schlorer, "Inference Controls for Statistical Databases," in *IEEE Computer*, v 16 no 7 (July 1983), pp 69–82.

[239] DE Denning, *Information Warfare and Security*, Readings, MA: Addison Wesley (1998), ISBN 0-201-43303-6.

[240] Department of Defense, "Department of Defense Trusted Computer System Evaluation Criteria," DoD 5200.28-STD (Dec 1985).

[241] Department of Defense, "A Guide to Understanding Covert Channel Analysis of Trusted Systems," NCSC-TG-030 (Nov 1993).

[242] Department of Defense, "Password Management Guideline," CSC-STD-002-85 (1985).

[243] Department of Defense, "A Guide to Understanding Data Remanence in Automated Information Systems," NCSC-TG-025 (1991).

[244] Department of Defense, "Technical Rationale behind CSC-STD-003-85: Computer Security Requirements," CSC-STD-004-85 (1985).

[245] Department of Justice, "Guidelines for Searching and Seizing Computers" (1994); at http://www.epic.org/security/computer_search_guidelines. txt.

[246] Y Desmedt, Y Frankel, "Threshold Cryptosystems," in *Advances in Cryptology—Proceedings of Crypto 89*, Springer LNCS, v 435, pp 307–315.

[247] J Dethloff, "Special Report: Intellectual Property Rights and Smart Card Patents: The Past, the Present, the Future," in *Smart Card News* (Feb 1996), pp 36–38.

[248] W Diffie, ME Hellman, "New Directions in Cryptography," in *IEEE Transactions on Information Theory*, v 22 no 6 (Nov 1976), pp 644–654.

[249] W Diffie, ME Hellman, "Exhaustive Cryptanalysis of the NBS Data Encryption Standard," in *Computer*, v 10 no 6 (June 1977), pp 74–84.

[250] W Diffie, S Landau, *Privacy on the Line—The Politics of Wiretapping and Encryption*, MIT Press (1998), ISBN 0-262-04167-7.

[251] E Dijkstra, "Solution of a Problem in Concurrent Programming Control," in *Communications of the ACM*, v 8 no 9 (1965), p 569.

[252] The Discount Long Distance Digest, at `http://www.thedigest.com/shame/`.

[253] D Dittrich, "Distributed Denial of Service (DDoS) Attacks/Tools," at `http://staff.washington.edu/dittrich/misc/ddos/`; see also `http://www.washington.edu/People/dad/`.

[254] RC Dixon, *Spread Spectrum Systems with Commercial Applications*, New York: John Wiley & Sons, Inc. (1994), ISBN 0-471-59342-7.

[255] H Dobbertin, "Cryptanalysis of MD4," *Journal of Cryptology*, v 11 no 4 (1998), pp 253–270.

[256] B Dole, S Lodin, E Spafford, "Misplaced Trust: Kerberos 4 Session Keys," in *Internet Society Symposium on Network and Distributed System Security*; proceedings published by the IEEE, ISBN 0-8186-7767-8, pp 60–70.

[257] "Dotcom Executives 'More Likely to Have Dark Pasts'," C Daniel, *Financial Times*, (Oct 23, 2000); `http://www.ft.com`.

[258] I Drury, "Pointing the Finger," in *Security Surveyor*, v 27 no 5 (Jan 1997), pp 15–17.

[259] Wim van Eck, "Electromagnetic Radiation from Video Display Units: An Eavesdropping Risk?" in *Computers & Security*, v 4 (1985), pp 269–286.

[260] *The Economist*, "Digital Rights and Wrongs" (July 17, 1999); see www.economist.com.

[261] *The Economist*, "Living in the Global Goldfish Bowl," (Dec 18–24, 1999), Christmas special; see www.economist.com.

[262] A Edwards, "BOLERO, a TTP project for the Shipping Industry," in *Information Security Technical Report*, v 1 no 1 (1996), pp 40–45.

[263] M Eichin, J Rochlis, "With Microscope and Tweezers: An Analysis of the Internet Virus of November 1988," in *Proceedings of the 1989 IEEE Symposium on Security and Privacy*, pp 326–343.

[264] Electronic Frontier Foundation, `http://www.eff.org`.

[265] Electronic Frontier Foundation, *Cracking DES: Secrets of Encryption Research, Wiretap Politics, and Chip Design* EFF (1998); ISBN 1-56592-520-3; at `http://cryptome.org/cracking-des.htm`.

[266] Electronic Privacy Information Center, `http://www.epic.org`.

[267] JH Ellis, *The History of Non-Secret Encryption*, at `http://www.cesg.gov.uk/about/nsecret/ellis.htm`.

[268] C Ellison, B Schneier, "Ten Risks of PKI: What You're Not Being Told about Public Key Infrastructure," in *Computer Security Journal*, v XIII no 1 (2000); also at `http://www.counterpane.com/pki-risks.html`.

[269] *Enfopol Papiere*, Telepolis archiv special (1998/1999), at `http://www.heise.de/tp/deutsch/special/enfo/default.html`.

[270] P Enge, T Walter, S Pullen, CD Kee, YC Chao, YJ Tsai, "Wide Area Augmentation of the Global Positioning System," in *Proceedings of the IEEE*, v 84 no 8 (Aug 1996), pp 1063–1088.

[271] EPIC, "Approvals for Federal Pen Registers and Trap and Trace Devices 1987–1998," at `http://www.epic.org/privacy/wiretap/stats/penreg.html`.

[272] EPIC, "Report of the Director of the Administrative Office of the United States Courts," at `http://www.epic.org/privacy/wiretap/stats/1999-report/wiretap99.pdf`.

[273] J Epstein, H Orman, J McHugh, R Pascale, M Branstad, A Marmor-Squires, "A High-Assurance Window System Prototype," in *Journal of Computer Security*, v 2 no 2–3 (1993), pp 159–190.

[274] J Epstein, R Pascale, "User Interface for a High-Assurance Windowing System," in *9th Annual Computer Security Applications Conference* (1993); proceedings published by the IEEE, ISBN 0-8186-4330-7, pp 256–264.

[275] T Escamilla, *Intrusion Detection—Network Security beyond the Firewall*, New York: John Wiley & Sons, Inc. (1998), ISBN 0-471-29000-9.

[276] J Essinger, *ATM Networks—Their Organization, Security, and Future*, Elsevier (1987).

[277] A Etzioni, *The Limits of Privacy*, New York: Basic Books (1999), ISBN 0-465-04089-6.

[278] European Parliament, "Development of Surveillance Technology and Risk of Abuse of Economic Information," Luxembourg (Apr 1999), PE 166.184/Part3/4, at `http://www.gn.apc.org/duncan/stoa.htm`.

[279] European Union, "Directive on the Protection of Individuals with Regard to the Processing of Personal Data and on the Free Movement of Such Data," Directive 95/46/EC, at `http://www.privacy.org/pi/intl_orgs/ec/eudp.html`.

[280] European Union, "Draft Council Resolution on the Lawful Interception of Telecommunications in Relation to New Technologies" 6715/99 (Mar 15, 1999), at `http://www.fipr.org/polarch/enfopol19.html/`; for background, see `http://www.fipr.org/polarch/`.

[281] G Faden, "Reconciling CMW Requirements with Those of X11 Applications," in *Proceedings of the 14th Annual National Computer Security Conference* (1991).

[282] M Fairhurst, "The Hedge End Experiment," in *International Security Review*, no 85 (Summer 1994), p 20.

[283] M Fairhurst, "Signature Verification Revisited: Promoting Practical Exploitation of Biometric Technology," in *Electronics and Communication Engineering Journal*, v 9 no 6 (Dec 1997), pp 273–280.

[284] *Federal Trade Commission v Audiotex Connection, Inc.*, and others, at `http://www.ftc.gov/os/1997/9711/Adtxamdfcmp.htm`.

[285] Federal Trade Commission, "ID Theft: When Bad Things Happen to Your Good Name," at `http://www.consumer.gov/idtheft/`.

[286] Federation of American Scientists, `http://www.fas.org`.

[287] H Federrath, J Thees, "Schutz der Vertraulichkeit des Aufenthaltsorts von Mobilfunkteilnehmern," in *Datenschutz und Datensicherheit* (June 1995), pp 338–348.

[288] P Fellwock (using pseudonym Winslow Peck), "U.S. Electronic Espionage: A Memoir," in *Ramparts*, v 11 no 2 (Aug 1972), pp 35–50; at `http://jya.com/nsa-elint.htm`.

[289] JS Fenton, "Information Protection Systems," PhD thesis, Cambridge University, 1973.

[290] N Ferguson, B Schneier, "A Cryptographic Evaluation of IPSEC," at `http://www.counterpane.com/ipsec.html`.

[291] D Ferraiolo, R Kuhn, "Role-Based Access Controls," in *15th National Computer Security Conference* (1992); proceedings published by NIST, pp 554–563.

[292] PFJ Fillery, AN Chandler, "Is Lack of Quality Software a Password to Information Security Problems?" in *IFIP SEC 94*, paper C8.

[293] "Psychologists and Banks Clash over Merits of Photographs on Cards," in *Financial Technology International Bulletin*, v 13 no 5 (Jan 1996), pp 2–3.

[294] D Fine, "Why Is Kevin Lee Poulsen Really in Jail?" at `http://www.well.com/user/fine/journalism/jail.html`.

[295] B Fischer, talk given at Cryptologic History Symposium, NSA (Oct 1999); reported in *Cryptologia*, v 24 no 2 (Apr 2000), pp 160–167.

[296] S Fischer-Hubner, "Towards a Privacy-Friendly Design and Use of IT-Security Mechanisms," in *17th National Computer Security Conference* (1994); proceedings published by NIST, pp 142–152.

[297] RA Fisher, *The Genetical Theory of Natural Selection*, Oxford: Clarendon Press (1930); 2nd ed., New York: Dover Publications (1958).

[298] J Flanagan, "Prison Phone Phraud (or The RISKS of Spanish)," reporting University of Washington staff newspaper, in `comp.risks`, v 12.47; at `http://catless.ncl.ac.uk/Risks/20.69.html`.

[299] M Fleet, "Five Face Sentence over Notes That Passed Ultraviolet Tests," in *The Daily Telegraph* (Dec 23, 1999), at `http://www.telegraph.co.uk:80/`.

[300] SN Foley, "Aggregation and Separation as Noninterference Properties," in *Journal of Computer Security*, v 1 no 2 (1992), pp 158–188.

[301] Fondazione Ugo Bordoni, Symposium on Electromagnetic Security for Information Protection, Rome, Italy (Nov 21–22, 1991).

[302] S Forrest, SA Hofmeyr, A Somayaji, "Computer Immunology," in *Communications of the ACM*, v 40 no 10 (Oct 1997), pp 88–96.

[303] DS Fortney, JJ Lim, "A Technical Approach for Determining the Importance of Information in Computerized Alarm Systems," in *17th National Computer Security Conference* (1994); proceedings published by NIST, pp 348–357.

[304] The Foundation for Information Policy Research, `http://www.fipr.org`.

[305] B Fox, "How to Keep Thieves Guessing," in *New Scientist* (June 3, 1995), p 18.

[306] B Fox, "Do Not Adjust Your set ... We Have Assumed Radio Control," in *New Scientist* (Jan 8, 2000), at `http://www.newscientist.com/ns/20000108/newsstory6.html`.

[307] B Fox, "The Pirate's Tale," in *New Scientist* (Dec 18, 1999), at `http://www.newscientist.com/ns/19991218/thepirates.html`.

[308] D Fox, "IMSI-Catcher," in *Datenschutz und Datensicherheit*, v 21 no 9 (Sept 1997), p 539.

[309] D Foxwell, "Off-the-Shelf, on to Sea," in *International Defense Review*, v 30 (Jan 1997), pp 33–38.

[310] D Foxwell, M Hewish, "GPS: Is It Lulling the Military into a False Sense of Security?" in *Jane's International Defense Review* (Sept 1998), pp 32–41.

[311] LJ Fraim, "SCOMP: A Solution to the Multilevel Security Problem," in *IEEE Computer*, v 16 no 7 (July 1983), pp 26–34.

[312] E Franz, A Jerichow, "A Mix-Mediated Anonymity Service and Its Payment," in *ESORICS 98*, Springer LNCS, v 1485, pp 313–327.

[313] T Fraser, "LOMAC: Low Water-Mark Integrity Protection for COTS Environments," in *Proceedings of the 2000 IEEE Symposium on Security and Privacy*, IEEE Computer Society Press, pp 230–245.

[314] "Banks Fingerprint Customers to Cut Cheque Fraud," in *Fraud Watch*, no 1 (1997), p 9.

[315] "Chip Cards Reduce Fraud in France," in *Fraud Watch*, no 1 (1996), p 8.

[316] "Counterfeit and Cross-Border Fraud on Increase Warning," in *Fraud Watch*, no 1 (1996), pp 6–7.

[317] "Finger Minutiae System Leaps the 1:100,000 False Refusal Barrier," in *Fraud Watch*, no 2 (1996), pp 6–9.

[318] "Widespread Card Skimming Causes European Concern," in *Fraud Watch*, no 3 (1997), pp 1–2.

[319] P Freiberger, M Swaine, *Fire in the Valley—The Making of the Personal Computer*, New York: McGraw-Hill (1999), ISBN 0-07-135892-7.

[320] M Freiss, *Protecting Networks with Satan*, O'Reilly & Associates (1997), ISBN 1-56592-425-8.

[321] J Frizell, T Phillips, T Groover, "The Electronic Intrusion Threat to National Security and Emergency Preparedness Telecommunications: An Awareness Document," in *17th National Computer Security Conference* (1994); proceedings published by NIST, pp 378–399.

[322] M Frost, "Spyworld: Inside the Canadian & American Intelligence Establishments," Diane Publishing Co (1994), ISBN 0-78815791-4.

[323] AM Froomkin, "The Death of Privacy," in *Stanford Law Review*, v 52, pp 1461–1543, at http://www.law.miami.edu/~froomkin/articles/privacy-deathof.pdf.

[324] DA Fulghum, "Communications Intercepts Pace EP-3s," in *Aviation Week and Space Technology*, v 146 no 19 (May 5, 1997), pp 53–54.

[325] S Furber, *ARM System Architecture*, Addison-Wesley (1996), ISBN 0-210-40352-8.

[326] HF Gaines, *Cryptanalysis—A Study of Ciphers and Their Solution*, Dover, ISBN 486-20097-3 (1939, 1956).

[327] M Galecotti, "Russia's Eavesdroppers Come Out of the Shadows," in *Jane's Intelligence Review*, v 9 no 12 (Dec 1997), pp 531–535.

[328] F Galton, "Personal Identification and Description," in *Nature* (June 21, 1888), pp 173–177.

[329] T Gandy, "Brainwaves in Fraud Busting," *Banking Technology* (Dec 1995/Jan 1996), pp 20–24.

[330] S Garfinkel, *Database Nation*, O'Reilly & Associates (2000), ISBN 1-56592-653-6.

[331] S Garfinkel, G Spafford, *Practical UNIX and Internet Security*, O'Reilly & Associates (1996), ISBN 1-56592-148-8.

[332] W Gates, W Buffett, "The Bill & Warren Show," in *Fortune* (July 20, 1998).

[333] General Accounting Office, U.S., "Medicare—Improvements Needed to Enhance Protection of Confidential Health Information," GAO/HEHS-99-140; at http://www.gao.gov/AIndexFY99/abstracts/he99140.htm.

[334] E German, "Problem Idents," at http://onin.com/fp/problemidents.html.

[335] A Gidari, JP Morgan, "Survey of State Electronic & Digital Signature Legislative Initiatives," at http://www.ilpf.org/digsig/digrep.htm.

[336] D Gifford, A Spector, "The CIRRUS Banking Network," in *Communications of the ACM*, v 28 no 8 (Aug 1985), pp 797–807.

[337] AA Giordano, HA Sunkenberg, HE de Pdero, P Stynes, DW Brown, SC Lee, "A Spread-Spectrum Simulcast MF Radio Network," in *IEEE Transactions on Communications*, v TC-30 no 5 (May 1982), pp 1057–1070.

[338] WN Goetzmann, "Financing Civilization," at http://viking.som.yale.edu/will/finciv/chapter1.htm.

[339] J Goguen, J Meseguer, "Security Policies and Security Models," in *Proceedings of*

the 1982 IEEE Computer Society Symposium on Research in Security and Privacy, pp 11–20.

[340] I Goldberg, D Wagner, "Randomness and the Netscape Browser," in *Dr. Dobbs Journal*, no 243 (Jan 1996), pp 66–70.

[341] L Goldberg, "Recycled Cold-War Electronics Battle Cellular Telephone Thieves," in *Electronic Design*, v 44 no 18 (Sept 3, 1996), pp 41–42.

[342] O Goldreich, *"Foundations of Cryptography" (fragments of a book)*, at `http://www.toc.lcs.mit.edu/~oded/homepage.html`.

[343] O Goldreich, "Modern Cryptography, Probabilistic Proofs, and Pseudorandomness," in Springer (1999), ISBN 3-540-64766-X.

[344] D Gollmann, *Computer Security*, New York: John Wiley & Sons, Inc. (1999), ISBN 0-471-97884-2.

[345] D Gollmann, "What Is Authentication?" in *Security Protocols*, Springer LNCS, v 1796 (2000), pp 65–72.

[346] L Gong, *Inside Java 2 Platform Security: Architecture, API Design, and Implementation*, Addison-Wesley (1999), ISBN 0-201-31000-7.

[347] KE Gordon, RJ Wong, "Conducting Filament of the Programmed Metal Electrode Amorphous Silicon Antifuse," in *Proceedings of International Electron Devices Meeting* (Dec 1993); reprinted as pp 6–3 to 6–10, *QuickLogic Data Book* (1994).

[348] J Gough, *Watching the Skies—A History of Ground Radar for the Air Defence of the United Kingdom by the Royal Air Force from 1946 to 1975*, London: Her Majesty's Stationery Office (1993), ISBN 0-11-772723-7.

[349] RM Graham, "Protection in an Information Processing Utility," in *Communications of the ACM*, v 11 no 5 (May 1968), pp 365–369.

[350] FT Grampp, RH Morris, "UNIX Operating System Security," in *AT&T Bell Laboratories Technical Journal*, v 63 no 8 (Oct 1984), pp 1649–1672.

[351] RD Graubart, JL Berger, JPL Woodward, "Compartmented Mode, Workstation Evaluation Criteria, Version 1," Mitre MTR 10953 (1991); also published by the Defense Intelligence Agency as Document DDS-2600-6243-91.

[352] J Gray, P Helland, P O'Neil, D Shasha, "The Dangers of Replication and a Solution," in *SIGMOD Record*, v 25 no 2 (1996), pp 173–182.

[353] J Gray, P Syverson, "A Logical Approach to Multilevel Security of Probabilistic Systems," in *Distributed Computing*, v 11 no 2 (1988), pp 73–90.

[354] T Greening, "Ask and Ye Shall Receive: A Study in Social Engineering," in *SIGSAC Review*, v 14 no 2 (Apr 1996), pp 9–14.

[355] A Griew, R Currell, *A Strategy for Security of the Electronic Patient Record*, Aberystwyth: Institute for Health Informatics, University of Wales (Mar 1995).

[356] D Grover, *The Protection of Computer Software—Its Technology and Applications*, Cambridge: British Computer Society/Cambridge University Press (1992), ISBN 0-521-42462-3.

[357] D Gruhl, W Bender, "Information Hiding to Foil the Casual Counterfeiter," in

Proceedings of the Second International Workshop on Information Hiding (Portland, Oregon, Apr 1998), Springer LNCS, v 1525, pp 1–15.

[358] LC Guillou, M Ugon, JJ Quisquater, "The Smart Card—A Standardized Security Device Dedicated to Public Cryptology," in [702], pp 561–613.

[359] C Gülcü, G Tsudik, "Mixing E-mail with Babel," in *Proceedings of the Internet Society Symposium on Network and Distributed System Security* (1996); proceedings published by the IEEE, ISBN 0-8186-7222-6, pp 2–16.

[360] R Gupta, SA Smolka, S Bhaskar, "On Randomization in Sequential and Distributed Algorithms," in *ACM Computing Surveys*, v 26 no 1 (Mar 1994), pp 7–86.

[361] J Gurnsey, *Copyright Theft*, Aslib (1997), ISBN 0-566-07631-4.

[362] P Gutman, "Secure Deletion of Data from Magnetic and Solid-State Memory," in *Sixth USENIX Security Symposium Proceedings* (July 1996), pp 77–89.

[363] P Gutman, "Software Generation of Practically Strong Random Numbers," in *Seventh USENIX Security Symposium Proceedings* (Jan 1998), pp 243–257.

[364] S Haber, WS Stornetta, "How to Time-Stamp a Digital Document," in *Journal of Cryptology*, v 3 no 2 (1991), pp 99–111.

[365] S Haber, WS Stornetta, "Secure Names for Bit-Strings," in *4th ACM Conference on Computer and Communications Security*; proceedings published by the ACM, ISBN 0-89791-912-2CCS 97, pp 28–35.

[366] W Hackmann, "Asdics at War," in *IEE Review*, v 46 no 3 (May 2000), pp 15–19.

[367] "Chris Carey Arrested in New Zealand," in *Hack Watch News* (Jan 1, 1999), at `http://www.iol.ie/~kooltek/legal.html`.

[368] N Hager, *Secret Power—New Zealand's Role in the International Spy Network*, Craig Potton Publishing (1996), ISBN 0-908802-35-8.

[369] PS Hall, TK Garland-Collins, RS Picton, RG Lee, *Radar*, Brassey's New Battlefield Weapons Systems and Technology Series, v 9, ISBN 0-08-037711-4.

[370] H Handschuh, P Paillier, J Stern, "Probing Attacks on Tamper-Resistant Devices," in *Cryptographic Hardware and Embedded Systems—CHES 99*, Springer LNCS, v 1717, pp 303–315.

[371] R Hanley, "Millions in Thefts Plague New Jersey Area," in *The New York Times* (Feb 9, 1981), p A1.

[372] R Hanson, "Can Wiretaps Remain Cost-Effective?" in *Communications of the ACM*, v 37 no 12 (Dec 1994), pp 13–15.

[373] MA Harrison, ML Ruzzo, JD Ullman, "Protection in Operating Systems," in *Communications of the ACM*, v 19 no 8 (Aug 1976), pp 461–471.

[374] A Hassey, M Wells, "Clinical Systems Security—Implementing the BMA Policy and Guidelines," in [29], pp 79–94.

[375] Health and Safety Executive, Nuclear Safety Reports at `http://www.hse.gov.uk/nsd/`, especially "HSE Team Inspection of the

Control and Supervision of Operations at BNFL's Sellafield Site,"
`http://www.hse.gov.uk/nsd/team.htm`.

[376] N Heintze, "Scalable Document Fingerprinting," in *Second USENIX Workshop on Electronic Commerce* (1996), ISBN 1-880446-83-9, pp 191–200.

[377] Herodotus, *Histories*, Book 1, 123.4, Book 5 35.3, and Book 7 239.3.

[378] "Interview with David Herson—SOGIS," (Sept 25, 1996), in *Ingeniørennet*, at `http://www.ing.dk/redaktion/herson.htm`.

[379] A Herzberg, M Jokabsson, S Jarecki, H Krawczyk, M Yung, "Proactive Public Key and Signature Systems," *4th ACM Conference on Computer and Communications Security* (1997), pp 100–110.

[380] RA Hettinga, "Credit Card Fraud Higher, Credit Card Fraud Lower," in `nettime` (Mar 22, 2000), at `http://www.nettime.org/nettime.w3archive/200003/msg00184.html`.

[381] M Hewish, "Combat ID Advances on All Fronts," in *International Defense Review*, v 29 (Dec 1996), pp 18–19.

[382] Hewlett-Packard, "IA-64 Instruction Set Architecture Guide," at `http://devresource.hp.com/devresource/Docs/Refs/IA64ISA/index.html`.

[383] HJ Highland, "Electromagnetic Radiation Revisited," in *Computers & Security*, v 5 (1986), pp 85–93, 181–184.

[384] HJ Highland, "Perspectives in Information Technology Security," in *Proceedings of the 1992 IFIP Congress, Education and Society*, IFIP A-13, v II (1992), pp 440–446.

[385] TF Himdi, RS Sandhu, "Lattice-Based Models for Controlled Sharing of Confidential Information in the Saudi Hajj System," in *13th Annual Computer Security Applications Conference*, San Diego, CA (Dec 8–12, 1997); proceedings published by the IEEE Computer Society, ISBN 0-8186-8274-4; pp 164–174.

[386] J Hoffman, "Implementing RBAC on a Type-Enforced System," in *13th Annual Computer Security Applications Conference*, San Diego, CA (Dec 8–12, 1997); proceedings published by the IEEE Computer Society, ISBN 0-8186-8274-4; pp 158–163.

[387] P Hollinger, "Single Language for Barcode Babel," in *Financial Times* (July 25, 2000), p 15.

[388] C Holloway, "Controlling the Use of Cryptographic Keys," in *Computers and Security*, v 14 no 7 (1995), pp 587–598.

[389] DI Hopper, "Authorities Sue Adult Web Sites," in *The Washington Post* (Aug 23, 2000); at `http://www.washingtonpost.com/`.

[390] G Horn, B Preneel, "Authentication and Payment in Future Mobile Systems," in *ESORICS 98*, Springer LNCS, v 1485, pp 277–293; journal version in *Journal of Computer Security*, v 8 no 2–3 (2000), pp 183–207.

[391] JD Horton, R Harland, E Ashby, RH Cooper, WF Hyslop, DG Nickerson, WM

Stewart, OK Ward, "The Cascade Vulnerability Problem," in *Journal of Computer Security*, v 2 no 4 (1993), pp 279–290.

[392] JD Howard, "An Analysis of Security Incidents on the Internet 1989–1995," PhD thesis (1997), Carnegie Mellon University, at `http://www.cert.org/research/JHThesis/Start.html`.

[393] D Howell, "Counterfeit Technology Forges Ahead," in *The Daily Telegraph* (Mar 22, 1999), at `http://www.telegraph.co.uk:80/`.

[394] N Htoo-Mosher, R Nasser, N Zunic, J Straw, "E4 ITSEC Evaluation of PR/SM on ES/9000 Processors," in *19th National Information Systems Security Conference* (1996), proceedings published by MST, pp 1–11.

[395] Q Hu, JY Yang, Q Zhang, K Liu, XJ Shen, "An Automatic Seal Imprint Verification Approach," in *Pattern Recognition*, v 28 no 8 (Aug 1995), pp 251–266.

[396] G Huber, "CMW Introduction," in *ACM SIGSAC*, v 12 no 4 (Oct 1994), pp 6–10.

[397] IBM, '*IBM 4758 PCI Cryptographic Coprocessor—CCA Basic Services Reference and Guide*, Release 1.31 for the IBM 4758-001, available through `http://www.ibm.com/security/cryptocards/`.

[398] "Role of Communications in Operation Desert Storm," *IEEE Communications Magazine*, Special Issue, v 30 no 1 (Jan 1992).

[399] *IEEE Carnahan Conference*, at `http://www.carnahanconference.com/`.

[400] *IEEE Electronics and Communications Engineering Journal*, v 12 no 3 (June 2000), special issue on UMTS.

[401] *IEEE Spectrum*, special issue on nuclear safekeeping, v 37 no 3 (Mar 2000).

[402] IFCI, "Real Cases," at `http://risk.ifci.ch/Realcases.htm`.

[403] "Ex-Radio Chief 'Masterminded' TV Cards Scam," in *The Independent* (Feb 17, 1998); see also, "The Sinking of a Pirate," *Sunday Independent* (Mar 1, 1998).

[404] Intel Corporation, *Intel Architecture Software Developer's Manual, Volume 1: Basic Architecture*, Order number 243190 (1997).

[405] "New England Shopping Mall ATM Scam Copied in UK," in *Information Security Monitor*, v 9 no 7 (June 1994), pp 1–2.

[406] "Pink Death Strikes at US West Cellular," in *Information Security Monitor*, v 9 no 2 (Jan 1994), pp 1–2.

[407] Information Systems Audit and Control Association, "Control Objectives for Information and related Technology," at `http://www.isaca.org/cobit.htm`.

[408] Information Systems Audit and Control Association, "Exam Preparation Materials," available from ISACA, at `http://www.isaca.org/cert1.htm`.

[409] International Atomic Energy Authority (IAEA), "The Physical Protection of Nuclear Material and Nuclear Facilities," INFCIRC/225/Rev. 4, at `http://www.iaea.org/worldatom/program/protection/index.shtml`.

[410] International Electrotechnical Commission, *Digital Audio Interface*, IEC 60958, Geneva (Feb 1989).

[411] I Jackson, personal communication with the author.

[412] L Jackson, "BT Forced to Pay Out Refunds after Free Calls Fraud," in *The Sunday Telegraph* (Feb 9, 1997); at http://www.telegraph.co.uk:80/.

[413] G Jagpal, "Steganography in Digital Images," undergraduate thesis, Selwyn College, Cambridge University (1995).

[414] AK Jain, R Bolle, S Pankanti, *Biometrics—Personal Identification in Networked Society*, Kluwer (1991), ISBN 0-7923-8346-1.

[415] AK Jain, L Hong, S Pankanti, R Bolle, "An Identity-Authentication System Using Fingerprints," in *Proceedings of the IEEE*, v 85 no 9 (Sept 1997), pp 1365–1388.

[416] S Jajodia, W List, G McGregor, L Strous (eds), *Integrity and Internal Control in Information Systems, Volume 1: Increasing the Confidence in Information Systems*, Chapman & Hall (1997), ISBN 0-412-82600-3.

[417] M Jay, "ACPO's Intruder Policy—Underwritten?" in *Security Surveyor*, v 26 no 3 (Sept 1995), pp 10–15.

[418] N Jefferies, C Mitchell, M Walker, "A Proposed Architecture for Trusted Third-Party Services," in *Cryptography: Policy and Algorithms*, Springer LNCS, v 1029, pp 98–104; also appeared at the Public Key Infrastructure Invitational Workshop at MITRE, VA (Sept 1995) and PKS '96 in Zürich (Oct 1, 1996).

[419] A Jerichow, J Müller, A Pfitzmann, B Pfitzmann, M Waidner, "Real-Time Mixes: A Bandwidth-Efficient Anonymity Protocol," in *IEEE Journal on Special Areas in Communications*, v 16 no 4 (May 1998), pp 495–509.

[420] John Young Architect, http://www.jya.com.

[421] K Johnson, "One Less Thing to Believe In: Fraud at Fake Cash Machine," in *The New York Times* (May 13, 1993), p 1.

[422] RG Johnson, ARE Garcia, "Vulnerability Assessment of Security Seals," in *Journal of Security Administration*, v 20 no 1 (June 1997), pp 15–27; http://lib-www.lanl.gov/la-pubs/00418796.pdf; more at http://pearl1.lanl.gov/seals/.

[423] P Jones, "Protection Money," in *Computer Business Review*, v 4 no 12 (Dec 1996), pp 31–36.

[424] RV Jones, *Most Secret War*, Wordsworth Editions (1978, 1998), ISBN 1-85326-699-X.

[425] RV Jones, *"Reflections on Intelligence,"* Octopus (1989), ISBN 0-7493-0474-X.

[426] A Jøsang, K Johannesen, "Authentication in Analogue Telephone Access Networks," in *Pragocrypt 96;* proceedings published by CTU Publishing House, Prague, ISBN 80-01-01502-5; pp 324–336.

[427] *Dorothy Judd v Citibank*, 435 NYS, 2d series, pp 210–212, 107 Misc.2d 526.

[428] D Kahn, *The Codebreakers*, New York: Macmillan (1967).

[429] D Kahn, *Seizing the Enigma*, New York: Houghton Mifflin (1991), ISBN 0-395-42739-8.

[430] D Kahn, "Soviet Comint in the Cold War," in *Cryptologia*, v XXII no 1 (Jan 1998), pp 1–24.

[431] M Kam, G Fielding, R Conn, "Writer Identification by Professional Document Examiners," in *Journal of Forensic Sciences*, v 42 (1997), pp 778–786.

[432] M Kam, G Fielding, R Conn, "Effects of Monetary Incentives on Performance of Nonprofessionals in Document Examination Proficiency Tests," in *Journal of Forensic Sciences*, v 43 (1998), pp 1000–1004.

[433] MS Kamel, HC Shen, AKC Wong, RI Campeanu, "System for the Recognition of Human Faces," in *IBM Systems Journal*, v 32 no 2 (1993), pp 307–320.

[434] MH Kang, IS Moskowitz, "A Pump for Rapid, Reliable, Secure Communications," in *1st ACM Conference on Computer and Communications Security* (Nov 3–5, 1993), Fairfax, VA; proceedings published by the ACM, ISBN 0-89791-629-8, pp 118–129.

[435] MH Kang, JN Froscher, J McDermott, O Costich, R Peyton, "Achieving Database Security through Data Replication: The SINTRA Prototype," in *17th National Computer Security Conference* (1994), pp 77–87.

[436] MH Kang, IS Moskowitz, DC Lee, "A Network Pump," in *IEEE Transactions on Software Engineering*, v 22 no 5 (May 1996), pp 329–338.

[437] MH Kang, IS Moskowitz, B Montrose, J Parsonese, "A Case Study of Two NRL Pump Prototypes," in *12th Annual Computer Security Applications Conference*, San Diego, CA, (Dec 9–13, 1996); proceedings published by the IEEE, ISBN 0-8186-7606-X, pp 32–43.

[438] MH Kang, JN Froscher, IS Moskowitz, "An Architecture for Multilevel Secure Interoperability," in *13th Annual Computer Security Applications Conference*, San Diego, CA, (Dec 8–12, 1997); proceedings published by the IEEE Computer Society, ISBN 0-8186-8274-4; pp 194–204.

[439] CS Kaplan, "Privacy Plan Likely to Kick Off Debate," in *The New York Times* (July 28, 2000), at `http://www.nytimes.com/`.

[440] PA Karger, VA Austell, DC Toll, "*A New Mandatory Security Policy Combining Secrecy and Integrity*," IBM Research Report RC 21717 (97406) (Mar 15, 2000).

[441] F Kasiski, *Die Geheimschriften und die Dechiffrier-Kunst*, Berlin: Mittler & Sohn (1863).

[442] KASUMI Specification, ETSI/SAGE, v 1 (Dec 23, 1999), at `http://www.etsi.org/dvbandca/`.

[443] S Katzenbeisser, FAP Petitcolas, *Information Hiding—Techniques for Steganography and Digital Watermarking*, Artech House (2000), ISBN 1-58053-035-4.

[444] C Kaufman, R Perlman, M Speciner, *Network Security—Private Communication in a Public World*, Prentice Hall 1995, ISBN 0-13-061466-1.

[445] DT Keitkemper, SF Platek, KA Wolnik, "DNA versus Fingerprints," in *Journal of Forensic Sciences*, v 40 (1995), p 534.

[446] J Kelsey, B Schneier, D Wagner, "Protocol Interactions and the Chosen Protocol Attack," in *Security Protocols—Proceedings of the 5th International Workshop* (1997), Springer LNCS, v 1361, pp 91–104.

[447] J Kelsey, B Schneier, D Wagner, C Hall, "Cryptanalytic Attacks on Pseudorandom Number Generators," in *Fifth International Workshop on Fast Software Encryption* (1998), Springer LNCS, v 1372, pp 168–188.

[448] R Kemmerer, "Shared Resource Matrix Methodology: An Approach to Identifying Storage and Timing Channels," in *IEEE Transactions on Computer Systems*, v 1 no 3 (1983), pp 256–277.

[449] R Kemmerer, C Meadows, J Millen, "Three Systems for Cryptographic Protocol Analysis," in *Journal of Cryptology*, v 7 no 2 (Spring 1994), pp 79–130.

[450] R Kemp, N Towell, G Pike, "When Seeing Should Not Be Believing: Photographs, Credit Cards and Fraud," in *Applied Cognitive Psychology*, v 11 no 3 (1997), pp 211–222.

[451] MG Kendall, B Babington-Smith, "Randomness and Random Sampling Numbers," part 1 in *Journal of the Royal Statistical Society*, v 101, pp 147–166; part 2, in *Supplement to the Journal of the Royal Statistical Society*, v 6 no 1, pp 51–61.

[452] JO Kephardt, SR White, "Measuring and Modeling Computer Virus Prevalence," in *Proceedings of the 1993 IEEE Symposium on Security and Privacy*, pp 2–15.

[453] JO Kephardt, SR White, DM Chess, "Epidemiology of Computer Viruses," in *IEEE Spectrum*, v 30 no 5 (May 1993), pp 27–29.

[454] A Kerckhoffs, "La Cryptographie Militaire," in *Journal des Sciences Militaires* (Jan 9, 1883), pp 5–38; at `http://www.cl.cam.ac.uk/users/fapp2/kerckhoffs/`.

[455] PJ Kerry, "EMC in the New Millennium," in *Electronics & Communication Engineering Journal*, v 12 no 2, pp 43–48.

[456] D Kesdogan, H Federrath, A Jerichow, "Location Management Strategies Increasing Privacy in Mobile Communication," in *12th International Information Security Conference* (1996), Samos, Greece; proceedings published by Chapman & Hall, ISBN 0-412-78120-4, pp 39–48.

[457] J Kilian, P Rogaway, "How to Protect DES against Exhaustive Key Search," in *Advances in Cryptology—Crypto 96*, Springer LNCS, v 1109, pp 252–267.

[458] J King, "Bolero—A Practical Application of Trusted Third-Party Services," in *Computer Fraud and Security Bulletin* (July 1995), pp 12–15.

[459] Kingpin, "iKey 1000 Administrator Access and Data Compromise," in *bugtraq* (July 20, 2000), at `http://www.L0pht.com/advisories.html`.

[460] DV Klein, "Foiling the Cracker: A Survey of, and Improvements to, UNIX

Password Security," *Proceedings of the USENIX Security Workshop*, Portland, OR: USENIX Association (Summer 1990); `http://www.deter.com/unix/`.

[461] RL Klevans, RD Rodman, *Voice Recognition*, Artech House (1997), ISBN 0-89006-927-1.

[462] HM Kluepfel, "Securing a Global Village and Its Resources: Baseline Security for Interconnected Signaling System #7 Telecommunications Networks," in *First ACM Conference on Computer and Communications Security* (1993); proceedings published by the ACM, ISBN 0-89791-629-8, pp 195–212; later version in *IEEE Communications Magazine*, v 32 no 9 (Sept 1994), pp 82–89.

[463] N Koblitz, *A Course in Number Theory and Cryptography*, Springer Graduate Texts in Mathematics, no 114 (1987), ISBN 0-387-96576-9.

[464] ER Koch, J Sperber, *Die Datenmafia*, Rohwolt Verlag (1995), ISBN 3-499-60247-4.

[465] M Kochanski, "A Survey of Data Insecurity Devices," in *Cryptologia*, v IX no 1, pp 1–15.

[466] P Kocher, "Timing Attacks on Implementations of Diffie-Hellman, RSA, DSS, and Other Systems," in *Advances in Cryptology—Crypto 96*, Springer LNCS, v 1109, pp 104–113.

[467] P Kocher, "Differential Power Analysis," in *Advances in Cryptology—Crypto 99*, Springer LNCS, v 1666, pp 388–397; a brief version was presented at the rump session of Crypto 98.

[468] KJ Koelman, "A Hard Nut to Crack: The Protection of Technological Measures," in *European Intellectual Property Review* (2000), pp 272–288; at `http://www.ivir.nl/Publicaties/koelman/hardnut.html`.

[469] S Kokolakis, D Gritzalis, S Katsikas, "Generic Security Policies for Health Information Systems," in *Health Informatics Journal*, v 4 nos 3–4 (Dec 1998), pp 184–195.

[470] O Kömmerling, MG Kuhn, "Design Principles for Tamper-Resistant Smartcard Processors," in *USENIX Workshop on Smartcard Technology;* proceedings published by USENIX (1999), ISBN 1-880446-34-0, pp 9–20.

[471] A Kondi, R Davis, "Software Encryption in the DoD," in *20th National Information Systems Security Conference* (1997); proceedings published by NIST, pp 543–554.

[472] BJ Koops, "Crypto Law Survey," at `http://cwis.kub.nl/~frw/people/koops/lawsurvy.htm`; see also his thesis "The Crypto Controversy: A Key Conflict in the Information Society," The Hague: Kluwer Law International (1999), ISBN 90-411-1143-3.

[473] DP Kormann, AD Rubin, "Risks of the Passport Single Signon Protocol," in *Computer Networks* (July 2000); at `http://avirubin.com/vita.html`.

[474] H Krawczyk, M Bellare, R Canetti, "HMAC: Keyed-Hashing for Message Authentication," RFC 2104 (Feb 1997); at `http://www.faqs.org/rfcs/rfc2104.html`.

[475] HM Kriz, "Phreaking recognized by Directorate General of France Telecom," in *Chaos Digest* 1.03 (Jan 1993).

[476] I Krsul, EH Spafford, "Authorship Analysis: Identifying the Author of a Program," in *Computers and Security*, v 16 no 3 (1996), pp 233–257.

[477] MG Kuhn, "Cipher Instruction Search Attack on the Bus-Encryption Security Microcontroller DS5002FP," in *IEEE Transactions on Computers*, v 47 no 10 (Oct 1998), pp 1153–1157.

[478] MG Kuhn, RJ Anderson, "Soft Tempest: Hidden Data Transmission Using Electromagnetic Emanations," in *Proceedings of the Second International Workshop on Information Hiding* (Portland, Apr 1998), Springer LNCS, v 1525, pp 126–143.

[479] MG Kuhn, private communication with the author.

[480] R Kuhn, P Edfors, V Howard, C Caputo, TS Philips, "Improving Public Switched Network Security in an Open Environment," in *Computer* (Aug 1993), pp 32–35.

[481] "L0phtCrack 2.52 for Win95/NT," at `http://www.l0pht.com/l0phtcrack/`.

[482] RJ Lackey, DW Upmal, "Speakeasy: The Military Software Radio," in *IEEE Communications Magazine*, v 33 no 5 (May 1995), pp 56–61.

[483] J Lacy, SR Quackenbush, A Reibman, JH Snyder, "Intellectual Property Protection Systems and Digital Watermarking," in *Proceedings of the Second International Workshop on Information Hiding* (Portland, OR: Apr 1998), Springer LNCS, v 1525, pp 158–168.

[484] Lamarr/Antheil Patent Story Home Page, `http://www.ncafe.com/chris/pat2/index.html`; contains U.S. patent no 2,292,387 (HK Markey et al., Aug 11, 1942).

[485] G Lambourne, *The Fingerprint Story*, Harrap (1984), ISBN 0-245-53963-8.

[486] L Lamport, "Time, Clocks and the Ordering of Events in a Distributed System," in *Communications of the ACM*, v 21 no 7 (July 1978), pp 558–565.

[487] L Lamport, R Shostack, M Peace, "The Byzantine Generals' Problem," in *ACM Transactions on Programming Languages and Systems*, v 4 no 3 (1982), pp 382–401.

[488] B Lampson, "A Note on the Confinement Problem," in *Communications of the ACM*, v 16 no 10 (Oct 1973), pp 613–615.

[489] P Lamy, J Martinho, T Rosa, MP Queluz, "Content-Based Watermarking for Image Authentication," in *Proceedings of the Third International Workshop on Information Hiding* (1999), Springer LNCS, v 1768, pp 187–198.

[490] S Landau, S Kent, C Brooks, S Charney, D Denning, W Diffie, A Lauck, D Miller, P Neumann, D Sobel, "Codes, Keys, and Conflicts: Issues in U.S. Crypto Policy," *Report of the ACM U.S. Public Policy Committee* (June 1994).

[491] R Landley, "Son of DIVX: DVD Copy Control," Motley Fool, `http://www.fool.com/portfolios/rulemaker/2000/rulemaker000127.htm`.

[492] P Landrock, "Roles and Responsibilities in BOLERO," in *TEDIS EDI Trusted Third Parties Workshop* (1995); proceedings published as ISBN 84-7653-506-6, pp 125–135.

[493] CE Landwehr, AR Bull, JP McDermott, WS Choi, "A Taxonomy of Computer Program Security Flaws, with Examples," U.S. Navy Report NRL/FR/5542–93-9591 (Nov 19, 1993).

[494] D Lane, "Where Cash is King," in *Banking Technology* (Oct 1992), pp 38–41.

[495] J Leake, "Workers Used Forged Passes at Sellafield," in *Sunday Times* (Apr 2, 2000), p 6.

[496] HC Lee, RE Guesslen (eds), *Advances in Fingerprint Technology*, Elsevier (1991), ISBN 0-444-01579-5.

[497] AK Lenstra, HW Lenstra, "The Development of the Number Field Sieve," in *Springer Lecture Notes in Mathematics*, v 1554 (1993), ISBN 0-387-57013-6.

[498] NG Leveson, *Safeware—System Safety and Computers*, Addison-Wesley (1994), ISBN 0-201-11972-2.

[499] A Lewcock, "Bodily Power," in *Computer Business Review*, v 6 no 2 (Feb 1998), pp 24–27.

[500] O Lewis, "Re: News: London Mailbomber Used the Net," post to `ukcrypto` mailing list (June 5, 2000), archived at `http://www.cs.ucl.ac.uk/staff/ I.Brown/archives/ukcrypto/` and `http://www.chiark.greenend. org.uk/mailman/listinfo/ukcrypto`.

[501] "Minister Backs Phone Crime Initiative," *Lewisham Community News*, at `http://www.lewisham.gov.uk/templates/community/ commdetails.cfm?file=2000071200.txt`.

[502] CC Lin, WC Lin, "Extracting Facial Features by an Inhibiting Mechanism Based on Gradient Distributions," in *Pattern Recognition*, v 29 no 12 (Dec 1996), pp 2079–2101.

[503] R Linde, "Operating Systems Penetration," *National Computer Conference*, AFIPS (1975), pp 361–368.

[504] JPMG Linnartz, "The 'Ticket' Concept for Copy Control Based on Embedded Signalling," *Fifth European Symposium on Research in Computer Security* (ESORICS 1998), Springer LNCS, v 1485, pp 257–274.

[505] JPMG Linnartz, M van Dijk, "Analysis of the Sensitivity attack against Electronic Watermarks in Images," in [59], pp 258–272.

[506] B Littlewood, "Predicting Software Reliability," in *Philosophical Transactions of the Royal Society of London*, A327 (1989), pp 513–527.

[507] WF Lloyd, *Two Lectures on the Checks to Population*, Oxford University Press (1833).

[508] Lockheed Martin, "Covert Surveillance Using Commercial Radio and Television Signals," at `http://silentsentry.external.lmco.com`.

[509] L Loeb, *Secure Electronic Transactions—Introduction and Technical Reference*, Artech House (1998), ISBN 0-89006-992-1.

[510] PA Loscocco, SD Smalley, PA Muckelbauer, RC Taylor, SJ Turner, JF Farrell, "The Inevitability of Failure: The Flawed Assumption of Security in Modern

Computing Environments," in *20th National Information Systems Security Conference;* proceedings published by NIST (1998), pp 303–314.

[511] WW Lowrance, "Privacy and Health Research," Report to the U.S. Secretary of Health and Human Services (May 1997).

[512] M Ludwig, *The Giant Black Book of Computer Viruses*, American Eagle Publishers (1995), ISBN 0-929408-10-1.

[513] AP Lutzker, "Primer on the Digital Millennium—What the Digital Millennium Copyright Act and the Copyright Term Extension Act Mean for the Library Community," Association of Research Libraries, at http://www.arl.org/info/frn/copy/primer.html.

[514] M Lyu, *Software Reliability Engineering*, IEEE Computer Society Press (1995), ISBN 0-07-039400-8.

[515] B Macq, "Special Issue: Identification and Protection of Multimedia Information," *Proceedings of the IEEE*, v 87 no 7 (July 1999).

[516] W Madsen, "Airline Passengers to Be Subject to Database Monitoring," in *Computer Fraud and Security Bulletin* (Mar 1997), pp 7–8.

[517] W Madsen, "Crypto AG: The NSA's Trojan Whore?" in *Covert Action Quarterly* (Winter 1998), at http://www.mediafilter.org/caq/cryptogate/.

[518] W Madsen, "Government-Sponsored Computer Warfare and Sabotage," in *Computers and Security*, v 11 (1991), pp 233–236.

[519] M Maes, "Twin Peaks: The Histogram Attack on Fixed-Depth Image Watermarks," in *Proceedings of the Second International Workshop on Information Hiding* (1998), Springer LNCS, v 1525, pp 290–305.

[520] K Maguire, "Muckraker Who Feeds Off Bins of the Famous," in *The Guardian* (July 27, 2000), at http://www.guardianunlimited.co.uk/Labour/Story/0,2763,347535,00.html.

[521] S Maguire, *Debugging the Development Process*, Redmond, WA: Microsoft Press, ISBN 1-55615-650-2 (1994), p 50.

[522] D Maio, D Maltoni, "Direct Gray-Scale Minutiae Detection in Fingerprints," in *IEEE Transactions on Pattern Analysis and Machine Intelligence*, v 19 no 1 (Jan 1997), pp 27–40.

[523] L Marks, *Between Silk and Cyanide—A Codemaker's War 1941–1945*, New York: HarperCollins (1998), ISBN 0-68486780-X.

[524] D Martin, "Internet Anonymizing Techniques," in ;login: Magazine, (May 1998); at http://www.usenix.org/publications/login/1998-5/martin.html.

[525] B Masuda, "Reducing the Price of Convenience," *International Security Review*, no 82 (Autumn 1993), pp 45–48.

[526] M Matsui, "Linear Cryptanalysis Method for DES Cipher," in *Advances in Cryptology—Eurocrypt 93*, Springer LNCS, v 765, pp 386–397.

[527] M Matsui, "New Block Encryption Algorithm MISTY," in *Fourth International*

Workshop on Fast Software Encryption (1997), Springer LNCS, v 1267, pp 54–68.

[528] Gospel according to St. Matthew, Chapter 7, verse 3.

[529] R Matthews, "The Power of One," in *New Scientist* (Oct 7, 1999), pp 26–30; at `http://www.newscientist.com/ns/19990710/thepowerof.html`.

[530] V Matyás, "Protecting the Identity of Doctors in Drug Prescription Analysis," in *Health Informatics Journal*, v 4 nos 3–4 (Dec 1998), pp 205–209.

[531] D Mazières, MF Kaashoek, "The Design, Implementation, and Operation of an Email Pseudonym Server," in *Proceedings of the 5th ACM Conference on Computer and Communications Security* (1998), `http://www.pdos.lcs.mit.edu/~dm`.

[532] J McCormac, "*European Scrambling Systems—The Black Book,*" version 5, Waterford University Press, Ireland (1996), ISBN 1-873556-22-5.

[533] D McCullagh, "U.S. to Track Crypto Trails," in *Wired* (May 4, 2000), at `http://www.wired.com/news/politics/0,1283,36067,00.html`; statistics at `http://www.uscourts.gov/wiretap99/contents.html`.

[534] D McCullough, "A Hook-up Theorem for Multi-Level Security," in *IEEE Transactions on Software Engineering*, v 16 no 6 (June 1990), pp 563–568.

[535] K McCurley, Remarks at IACR General Meeting, *Crypto 98*, Santa Barbara, CA: (Aug 1998).

[536] AD McDonald, MG Kuhn, "StegFS: A Steganographic File System for Linux," in [613], pp 463–477.

[537] G McGraw, EW Felten, *Java Security*, New York: John Wiley & Sons, Inc. (1997), ISBN 0-471-17842-X.

[538] I McKie, "Total Vindication for Shirley McKie!" (June 23, 2000), at `http://onin.com/fp/mckievindication.html`.

[539] J McLean, "The Specification and Modeling of Computer Security," in *Computer*, v 23 no 1 (Jan 1990), pp 9–16.

[540] J McLean, "Security Models," in *Encyclopedia of Software Engineering*, New York: John Wiley & Sons, Inc. (1994).

[541] J McLean, "A General Theory of Composition for a Class of 'Possibilistic' Properties," in *IEEE Transactions on Software Engineering*, v 22 no 1 (Jan 1996), pp 53–67.

[542] J McNamara, "The Complete, Unofficial TEMPEST Information Page," at `http://www.eskimo.com/~joelm/tempest.html`.

[543] B McWilliams, "Sex Sites Accused of Gouging Visitors with Phone Scam," in `InternetNews.com` (Apr 7, 2000), at `http://www.internetnews.com/bus-news/print/0,,3_337101,00.html`.

[544] AJ Menezes, PC van Oorschot, SA Vanstone, *Handbook of Applied Cryptography*, CRC Press (1997); ISBN 0-8493-8523-7; also available online at `http://www.cacr.math.uwaterloo.ca/hac/`.

[545] CG Menk, "System Security Engineering Capability Maturity Model and Evaluations: Partners within the Assurance Framework," in *19th National Information Systems Security Conference* (1996), pp 76–88.

[546] J Mercer, "Document Fraud Deterrent Strategies: Four Case Studies," in *Optical Security and Counterfeit Deterrence Techniques II* (1998), IS&T (The Society for Imaging Science and Technology) and SPIE (The International Society for Optical Engineering), v 3314, ISBN 0-8194-2754-3, pp 39–51.

[547] TS Messergues, EA Dabish, RH Sloan, "Investigations of Power Analysis Attacks on Smartcards," in *USENIX Workshop on Smartcard Technology;* proceedings published by USENIX (1999), ISBN 1-880446-34-0, pp 151–161.

[548] CH Meyer and SM Matyas, *Cryptography: A New Dimension in Computer Data Security*, New York: John Wiley & Sons, Inc. (1982).

[549] R Meyer-Sommer, "Smartly Analyzing the Simplicity and the Power of Simple Power Analysis on Smartcards," in *Workshop on Cryptographic Hardware and Embedded Systems* (2000); Springer LNCS, v 1965, ISBN 3-540-41455-X, pp 78–92.

[550] J Micklethwait, A Wooldridge, *The Witch Doctors—What the Management Gurus Are Saying, Why It Matters and How to Make Sense of It*, New York: Random House (1997), ISBN 0-7493-2645-X.

[551] A Midgley, "R.I.P. and NHSNet," post to ukcrypto mailing list (July 1, 2000), archived at http://www.cs.ucl.ac.uk/staff/I.Brown/archives/ukcrypto/.

[552] J Millen, "A Resource Allocation Model for Denial of Service Protection," in *Journal of Computer Security*, v 2 nos 2–3 (1993), pp 89–106.

[553] B Miller, "Vital Signs of Security," in *IEEE Spectrum* (Feb 1994), pp 22–30.

[554] ML Miller, IJ Cox, JA Bloom, "Watermarking in the Real World: An Application to DVD," in *Sixth ACM International Multimedia Conference* (1998); workshop notes published by GMD—Forschungszentrum Informationstechnik GmbH, as v 41 of GMD Report, pp 71–76.

[555] K Mitnick, Congressional testimony, as reported by Associated Press (Mar 3, 2000); see also http://www.zdnet.com/zdnn/stories/news/0,4586,2454737,00.html and http://news.cnet.com/category/0-1005-200-1562611.html.

[556] B Moghaddam, A Pentland, "Probabilistic Visual learning for Object Representation," in *IEEE Transactions on Pattern Analysis and Machine Intelligence*, v 19 no 7 (July 1997), pp 696–710.

[557] F Mollet, "Card Fraud Nets Esc6 billion," in *Cards International* (Sept 22, 1995), p 3.

[558] E Montegrosso, "Charging and Accounting Mechanisms" (3G TR 22.924, v 3.1.1), from Third-Generation Partnership Project, at http://www.3gpp.org/TSG/Oct_status_list.htm.

[559] R Morris, "A Weakness in the 4.2BSD UNIX TCP/IP Software," Bell Labs

Computer Science Technical Report no. 117 (Feb 25, 1985); at `http://www.cs.berkeley.edu/~daw/security/seq-attack.html`.

[560] R Morris, Invited talk, *Crypto 95*.

[561] R Morris, K Thompson, "Password Security: A Case History," in *Communications of the ACM*, v 22 no 11 (Nov 1979), pp 594–597.

[562] DP Moynihan, *Secrecy—The American Experience*, New Haven, CT: Yale University Press (1999), ISBN 0-300-08079-4.

[563] P Mukherjee, V Stavridou, "The Formal Specification of Safety Requirements for Storing Explosives," in *Formal Aspects of Computing*, v 5 no 4 (1993), pp 299–336.

[564] T Mulhall, "Where Have All the Hackers Gone? A Study in Motivation, Deterrence, and Crime Displacement," in *Computers and Security*, v 16 no 4 (1997), pp 277–315.

[565] S Mullender (ed), *Distributed Systems*, Addison-Wesley (1993), ISBN 0-201-62427-3.

[566] JC Murphy, D Dubbel, R Benson, "Technology Approaches to Currency Security," in *Optical Security and Counterfeit Deterrence Techniques II* (1998), IS&T (The Society for Imaging Science and Technology) and SPIE (The International Society for Optical Engineering), v 3314, ISBN 0-8194-2754-3, pp 21–28.

[567] E Murray, "SSL Server Security Survey," at `http://www.meer.net/~ericm/papers/ssl_servers.html`.

[568] K Murray, "Protection of Computer Programs in Ireland," in *Computer Law and Security Report*, v 12 no 3 (May/June 1996), pp 57–59.

[569] RFH Nalder, *History of the Royal Corps of Signals*, Royal Signals Institution (1958).

[570] Napster, `http://www.napster.com`.

[571] M Nash, R Kennett, "Implementing Security Policy in a Large Defense Procurement," in *12th Annual Computer Security Applications Conference*, San Diego, CA (Dec 9–13, 1996); proceedings published by the IEEE, ISBN 0-8186-7606-X; pp 15–23.

[572] National Information Infrastructure Task Force, "Options for Promoting Privacy on the National Information Infrastructure" (Apr 1997), at `http://www.iitf.nist.gov/ipc/privacy.htm`.

[573] National Institute of Standards and Technology, archive of publications on computer security, `http://csrc.nist.gov/publications/history/index.html`.

[574] National Institute of Standards and Technology, "Common Criteria for Information Technology Security," Version 2.0/ISO IS 15408 (May 1998), `http://www.commoncriteria.org`.

[575] National Institute of Standards and Technology, "Data Encryption Standard (DES)," FIPS 46; Draft FIPS 46-3, incorporating upgrade to triple DES, at `http://csrc.nist.gov/encryption/`.

[576] National Institute of Standards and Technology, "Security Requirements for Cryptographic Modules" (Jan 11, 1994), at `http://www.itl.nist.gov/fipspubs/0-toc.htm#cs`.

[577] National Institute of Standards and Technology, "SKIPJACK and KEA Algorithms," (June 23, 1998), at `http://csrc.nist.gov/encryption/skipjack-kea.htm`.

[578] National Institute of Standards and Technology, "Escrowed Encryption Standard," FIPS 185 (Feb 1994).

[579] National Institute of Standards and Technology, "SCSUG Smart Card Protection Profile" (draft, v 2.0, May 2000), at `http://csrc.nist.gov/cc/sc/sclist.htm`.

[580] National Research Council, *Cryptography's Role in Securing the Information Society*, National Academy Press (1996), ISBN 0-309-05475-3.

[581] National Research Council, *For the Record: Protecting Electronic Health Information*, National Academy Press (1997), ISBN 0-309-05697-7.

[582] National Security Agency, "The NSA Security Manual," at `http://www.cl.cam.ac.uk/ftp/users/rja14/nsaman.tex.gz`.

[583] P Naur, B Randell, "Software Engineering—Report on a Conference," NATO Scientific Affairs Division, Garmisch (1968).

[584] R Neame, "Managing Health Data Privacy and Security," in [29], pp 225–232.

[585] GC Necula, P Lee, "Safe, Untrusted Agents Using Proof-Carrying Code," in *Mobile Agents and Security*, ISBN 3-540-64792-9, pp 61–91.

[586] RM Needham, "Denial of Service: An Example," in *Communications of the ACM*, v 37 no 11 (Nov 1994), pp 42–46.

[587] RM Needham, "Naming," in [565], pp 318–327.

[588] RM Needham, "The Hardware Environment," in *Proceedings of the 1999 IEEE Symposium on Security and Privacy*, IEEE Computer Society Press, p 236.

[589] RM Needham, MD Schroeder, "Using Encryption for Authentication in Large Networks of Computers," in *Communications of the ACM*, v 21 no 12 (Dec 1978), pp 993–999.

[590] P Neumann, *Computer-Related Risks*, Addison-Wesley (1995), ISBN 0-201-55805-X.

[591] J Newton, "Countering the Counterfeiters," in *Cards International* (Dec 12, 1994), p 12.

[592] J Newton, "Organised Plastic Counterfeiting," Her Majesty's Stationery Office (1996), ISBN 0-11-341128-6.

[593] Nuclear Regulatory Commission, `www.nrc.gov`.

[594] AM Odlyzko, "The History of Communications and Its Implications for the Internet," at `http://www.research.att.com/~amo/doc/networks.html`.

[595] AM Odlyzko, "Smart and Stupid Networks: Why the Internet Is Like Microsoft,"

ACM netWorker (Dec 1998), pp 38–46, at `http://www.acm.org/networker/issue/9805/ssnet.html`.

[596] N Okuntsev, *Windows NT Security*, R&D Books (1999), ISBN 0-87930-473-1.

[597] R Oppliger, *Internet and Intranet Security*, Artech House (1998), ISBN 0-89006-829-1.

[598] Organization for Economic Cooperation & Development, "Guidelines for the Protections of Privacy and Transborder Flow of Personal Data," OECD Doc. No C(80)58 (1981), at `http://www.oecd.org//dsti/sti/it/secur/prod/PRIV-EN.HTM`.

[599] J Osen, "The Cream of Other Men's Wit: Plagiarism and Misappropriation in Cyberspace," in *Computer Fraud and Security Bulletin* (Nov 1997), pp 13–19.

[600] S Pancho, "Paradigm Shifts in Protocol Analysis," in *Proceedings of the 1999 New Security Paradigms Workshop*, ACM (2000), pp 70–79.

[601] DJ Parker, "DVD Copy Protection: An Agreement At Last? Protecting Intellectual Property Rights in the Age of Technology," in *Tape/Disc Magazine* (Oct 1996), `http://www.kipinet.com/tdb/tdb_oct96/feat_protection.html`.

[602] DJ Parker, *Fighting Computer Crime—A New Framework for Protecting Information*, New York: John Wiley & Sons, Inc. (1998), ISBN 0-471 16378-3.

[603] B Patterson, letter to *Communications of the ACM*, v 43 no 4 (Apr 2000), pp 11–12.

[604] LC Paulson, "Inductive Analysis of the Internet Protocol TLS," in *ACM Transactions on Computer and System Security*, v 2 no 3 (1999), pp 332–351; also at `http://www.cl.cam.ac.uk/users/lcp/papers/protocols.html`.

[605] TP Pedersen, "Electronic Payments of Small Amounts," in *Security Protocols* (1996), Springer LNCS, v 1189, pp 59–68.

[606] A Perrig, "A Copyright Protection Environment for Digital Images," Diploma thesis, École Polytechnique Fédérale de Lausanne (1997).

[607] P Pesic, "The Clue to the Labyrinth: Francis Bacon and the Decryption of Nature," in *Cryptologia*, v XXIV, no 3 (July 2000), pp 193–211.

[608] R Petersen, "UCITA Update," at `http://www.arl.org/info/frn/copy/petersen.html`.

[609] I Peterson, "From Counting to Writing," MathLand Archives, `http://www.maa.org/mathland/mathland_2_24.html`.

[610] FAP Petitcolas, RJ Anderson, MG Kuhn, "Attacks on Copyright Marking Systems," in *Proceedings of the Second International Workshop on Information Hiding* (1998), Springer LNCS, v 1525, pp 219–239.

[611] FAP Petitcolas, RJ Anderson, MG Kuhn, "Information Hiding—A Survey," in *Proceedings of the IEEE*, v 87 no 7 (July 1999), pp 1062–1078.

[612] H Petroski, *To Engineer Is Human*, New York: Barnes and Noble Books (1994), ISBN 1-56619502-0.

[613] A Pfitzmann, *Proceedings of the Third International Workshop on Information Hiding* (1999), Springer LNCS, v 1768.

[614] B Pfitzmann, "Information Hiding Terminology," in *Proceedings of the First International Workshop on Information Hiding* (1996), Springer LNCS, v 1174, pp 347–350.

[615] GE Pickett, "How Do You Select the 'Right' Security Feature(s) for Your Company's Products???," in *Optical Security and Counterfeit Deterrence Techniques II* (1998), IS&T (The Society for Imaging Science and Technology) and SPIE (The International Society for Optical Engineering), v 3314, ISBN 0-8194-2754-3, pp 52–58.

[616] RL Pickholtz, DL Schilling, LB Milstein, "Theory of Spread-Spectrum Communications—A Tutorial," in *IEEE Transactions on Communications*, v TC-30 no 5 (May 1982), pp 855–884.

[617] RL Pickholtz, DB Newman, YQ Zhang, M Tatebayashi, "Security Analysis of the INTEL-SAT VI and VII Command Network," in *IEEE Proceedings on Selected Areas in Communications*, v 11 no 5 (June 1993), pp 663–672.

[618] D Polak, "GSM Mobile Network in Switzerland Reveals Location of Its Users," in *Privacy Forum Digest*, v 6 no 18 (Dec 31, 1997), at `http://www.vortex.com/privacy/priv.06.18`.

[619] Politech mailing list, at `http://www.politechbot.com/`.

[620] B Pomeroy, S Wiseman, "Private Desktops and Shared Store," in *Computer Security Applications Conference*, Phoenix, AZ (1998); proceedings published by the IEEE, ISBN 0-8186-8789-4, pp 190–200.

[621] B Preneel, PC van Oorschot, "MDx-MAC and Building Fast MACs from Hash Functions," in *Advances in Cryptology—Crypto 95*, Springer LNCS, v 963, pp 1–14.

[622] RS Pressman, *Software Engineering: A Practitioner's Approach*, New York: McGraw-Hill (5th ed, 2000), ISBN 0-073-65578-3.

[623] G Price, "The Interaction between Fault Tolerance and Security," Technical Report no 214, Cambridge University Computer Laboratory.

[624] WR Price, "Issues to Consider When Using Evaluated Products to Implement Secure Mission Systems," in *Proceedings of the 15th National Computer Security Conference*, National Institute of Standards and Technology (1992), pp 292–299.

[625] H Pringle, "The Cradle of Cash," in *Discover*, v 19 no 10 (Oct 1998); at `http://www.discover.com/oct_issue/cradle.html`.

[626] C Prins, "Biometric Technology Law," in *The Computer Law and Security Report*, v 14 no 3 (May/Jun 1998), pp 159–165.

[627] D Pritchard, *The Radar War—Germany's Pioneering Achievement 1904–1945*, Wellingborough (1989), ISBN 1-85260-246-5.

[628] The Privacy Exchange, `http://www.privacyexchange.org/`.

[629] Public Lending Right (PLR), at `http://www.writers.org.uk/guild/Crafts/Books/PLRBody.html`.

[630] Public Record Office, "Functional Requirements for Electronic Record Management Systems," (Nov 1999), at `http://www.pro.gov.uk/recordsmanagement/eros/invest/reference.pdf`.

[631] Rain Forest Puppy, "Issue Disclosure Policy V1.1," at `http://www.wiretrip.net/rfp/policy.html`.

[632] W Rankl, W Effing, *Smartcard Handbook*, New York: John Wiley & Sons, Inc. (1997), ISBN 0-471-96720-3; translated from the German *Handbuch der Chpkarten*, Carl Hanser Verlag (1995), ISBN 3-446-17993-3.

[633] ES Raymond, "The Case of the Quake Cheats," (Dec 27, 1999), at `http://www.tuxedo. org/~esr/writings/quake-cheats.html`.

[634] ES Raymond, "The Cathedral and the Bazaar," at `http://www.tuxedo.org/~esr/writings/cathedral-bazaar/`.

[635] ES Raymond, "The Magic Cauldron," (June 1999), at `http://www.tuxedo.org/~esr/writings/magic-cauldron/magic-cauldron.html`.

[636] SM Redl, MK Weber, MW Oliphant, *GSM and Personal Communications Handbook*, Artech House (1998), ISBN 0-89006-957-3.

[637] MG Reed, PF Syverson, DM Goldschlag, "Anonymous Connections and Onion Routing," in *IEEE Journal on Special Areas in Communications*, v 16 no 4 (May 1998), pp 482–494.

[638] C Reiss, "Mystery of Levy Tax Phone Calls," *The Evening Standard* (July 5, 2000), p 1; also at `http://www.thisislondon.com/`.

[639] MK Reiter, "A Secure Group Membership Protocol," in *IEEE Transactions on Software Engineering*, v 22 no 1 (Jan 1996), pp 31–42.

[640] MK Reiter, MK Franklin, JB Lacy, RA Wright, "The Omega Key Management Service," in *3rd ACM Conference on Computer and Communications Security* (1996), pp 38–47.

[641] M Reiter, AD Rubin, "Anonymous Web Transactions with Crowds," in *Communications of the ACM*, v 42 no 2 (Feb 1999), pp 32–38.

[642] J Reno, `http://www.cnn.com/2000/US/05/25/security.breaches.01/index.html`.

[643] MA Rice, AJ Sammes, *Command and Control: Support Systems in the Gulf War*, Brassey's (1994), ISBN 1-8575 3-015-2.

[644] D Richardson, *Techniques and Equipment of Electronic Warfare*, Salamander Books, ISBN 0-8601-265-8.

[645] LW Ricketts, JE Bridges, J Miletta, *EMP Radiation and Protective Techniques*, John Wiley & Sons, Inc. New York (1975), ISBN 0-471-010403-6.

[646] M Ridley, "The Red Queen: Sex and the Evolution of Human Nature," New York: Viking Books (1993), ISBN 0-1402-4548-0.

[647] V Rijmen, *The block cipher Rijndael*, at `http://www.esat.kuleuven.ac.be/~rijmen/rijndael/`.

[648] RL Rivest, A Shamir, "PayWord and MicroMint: Two Simple Micropayment Schemes," in *Security Protocols* (1996), Springer LNCS, v 1189, pp 69–87.

[649] RL Rivest, A Shamir, L Adleman, "A Method for Obtaining Digital Signatures and Public-Key Cryptosystems," in *Communications of the ACM*, v 21 no 2 (Feb 1978), pp 120–126.

[650] AR Roddy, JD Stosz, "Fingerprint Features—Statistical Analysis and System Performance Estimates," in *Proceedings of the IEEE*, v 85 no 9 (Sept 1997), pp 1390–1421.

[651] DE Ross, "Two Signatures," in `comp.risks`, v 20.81: `http://catless.ncl.ac.uk/Risks/20.81.html`.

[652] M Rowe, "Card Fraud Plummets in France," *Banking Technology* (May 1994), p 10.

[653] WW Royce, "Managing the Development of Large Software Systems: Concepts and Techniques," in *Proceedings IEEE WESCON* (1970), pp 1–9.

[654] A Rubin, "Bugs in Anonymity Services," bugtraq (Apr 13, 1999); at `http://www.securityportal.com/list-archive/bugtraq/1999/Apr/0126.html`.

[655] HH Rubinovitz, "Issues Associated with Porting Applications to the Compartmented Mode Workstation," in *ACM SIGSAC*, v 12 no 4 (Oct 1994), pp 2–5.

[656] RA Rueppel, *Analysis and Design of Stream Ciphers*, Springer-Verlag (1986), ISBN 0-387-16870-2.

[657] RA Rueppel, "Criticism of ISO CD 11166 Banking: Key Management by Means of Asymmetric Algorithms," in *Proceedings of 3rd Symposium of State and Progress of Research in Cryptography*, Rome: Fondazione Ugo Bordoni (1993), pp 191–198.

[658] R Ruffin, "Following the Flow of Funds," in *Security Management* (July 1994), pp 46–52.

[659] J Rushby, B Randell, "A Distributed Secure System," in *IEEE Computer*, v 16 no 7 (July 1983), pp 55–67.

[660] D Russell, GT Gangemi, "Computer Security Basics," Chapter 10: *TEMPEST*, O'Reilly & Associates (1991), ISBN 0-937175-71-4.

[661] DR Safford, DL Schales, DK Hess, "The TAMU Security Package: An Ongoing Response to Internet Intruders in an Academic Environment," in *USENIX Security 93*, pp 91–118.

[662] JD Saltzer, MD Schroeder, "The Protection of Information in Computer Systems," in *Proceedings of the IEEE*, v 63 no 9 (Mar 1975), pp 1278–1308.

[663] RG Saltman, "Assuring Accuracy, Integrity, and Security in National Elections: The Role of the U.S. Congress," in *Computers, Freedom, and Privacy* (1993); at `http://www.cpsr.org/conferences/cfp93/saltman.html`.

[664] T Sammes, B Jenkinson, *Forensic Computing—A Practitioner's Guide*, Springer (2000), ISBN 1-85233-299-9.

[665] P Samuelson, "Copyright and Digital Libraries," in *Communications of the ACM*, v 38 no 4 (April 1995).

[666] P Samuelson, "Intellectual Property Rights and the Global Information Economy," in *Communications of the ACM*, v 39 no 1 (Jan 1996), pp 23–28.

[667] P Samuelson, "The Copyright Grab," at `http://uainfo.arizona.edu/~weisband/411_511/copyright.html`.

[668] D Samyde, JJ Quisquater, "S.E.M.A. Electromagnetic Analysis," *presented at the rump session of Eurocrypt 2000*.

[669] RS Sandhu, S Jajodia, "Polyinstantiation for Cover Stories," in *Computer Security—ESORICS 92*, LNCS, v 648, pp 307–328.

[670] SANS Institute, "Consensus List of the Top Ten Internet Security Threats," v 1.22 (June 19, 2000); at `http://www.sans.org/`.

[671] G Sandoval, "Glitches Let Net Shoppers Get Free Goods," in *CNET News.com* (July 5, 2000); at `http://news.cnet.com/news/0-1007-200-2208733.html`.

[672] PF Sass, L Gorr, "Communications for the Digitized Battlefield of the 21st Century," in *IEEE Communications*, v 33 no 10 (Oct 1995), pp 86–95.

[673] M Schaefer, "Symbol Security Condition Considered Harmful," in *Proceedings of the 1989 IEEE Symposium on Security and Privacy*, pp 20–46.

[674] RR Schell, "Computer Security: The Achilles' Heel of the Electronic Air Force?" in *Air University Review*, v 30 no 2 (Jan-Feb 1979), pp 16–33.

[675] RR Schell, PJ Downey, GJ Popek, "Preliminary Notes on the Design of Secure Military Computer Systems," Electronic Systems Division, Air Force Systems Command (Jan 1, 1973), MCI-73-1; at `http://seclab.cs.ucdavis.edu/projects/history/papers/sche73.pdf`.

[676] DL Schilling, *Meteor Burst Communications: Theory and Practice*, New York: John Wiley & Sons, Inc. (1993), ISBN 0-471-52212-0.

[677] DC Schleher, *Electronic Warfare in the Information Age*, Artech House (1999), ISBN 0-89006-526-8.

[678] D Schmandt-Besserat, *How Writing Came About*, University of Texas Press (1996); ISBN 0-29277-704-3, `http://www.dla.utexas.edu/depts/lrc/numerals/dsb1.html`.

[679] ZE Schnabel, "The Estimation of the Total Fish Population in a Lake," in *American Mathematical Monthly*, v 45 (1938), pp 348–352.

[680] PM Schneider, "Datenbanken mit genetischen Merkmalen von Straftätern," in *Datenschutz und Datensicherheit*, v 22 (June 1998), pp 330–333.

[681] B Schneier, *Applied Cryptography*, New York: John Wiley & Sons, Inc. (1996); ISBN 0-471-12845-7.

[682] B Schneier, "Why Computers Are Insecure," in `comp.risks` v 20.67; at `http://catless.ncl.ac.uk/Risks/20.67.html`.

[683] B Schneier, *Secrets and Lies: Digital Security in a Networked World*, New York: John Wiley & Sons, Inc. (2000); ISBN 0-471-25311-1.

[684] B Schneier, D Banisar, *The Electronic Privacy Papers—Documents on the Battle for Privacy in the Age of Surveillance*, New York: John Wiley & Sons, Inc. (1997); ISBN 0-471-12297-1.

[685] M Schnyder, "Datenfluesse im Gesundheitswesen," in *Symposium für Datenschutz und Informationssicherheit*, Zuerich (Oct 1998).

[686] RA Scholtz, "Origins of Spread-Spectrum Communications," in *IEEE Transactions on Communications*, v TC-30 no 5 (May 1982), pp 822–854.

[687] MD Schroeder, "Cooperation of Mutually Suspicious Subsystems in a Computer Utility," MIT PhD Thesis (Sept 1972); also available as Project MAC Technical Report MAC TR-104, `http://hdl.handle.net/ncstrl.mit_lcs/MIT/LCS/TR-104`.

[688] CJ Seiferth, "Opening the Military to Open Source," in *COTS Magazine* (Nov-Dec 1999), at `http://www.rtcgroup.com/cotsjournal/cotsj111200/cots111200.html`.

[689] CJ Seiferth, "Adoption of Open Licensing," in *COTS Magazine* (Nov-Dec 1999), at `http://www.rtcgroup.com/cotsjournal/cotsj111200/cots111200.html`.

[690] R Senderek, "Key-Experiments—How PGP Deals with Manipulated Keys," at `http://senderek.de/security/key-experiments.html`.

[691] D Senie, "Changing the Default for Directed Broadcasts in Routers," RFC 2644, at `http://www.ietf.org/rfc/rfc2644.txt`.

[692] A Shamir, "How to Share a Secret," in *Communications of the ACM*, v 22 no 11 (Nov 1979), pp 612–613.

[693] MI Shamos, "Electronic Voting—Evaluating the Threat," in *Computers, Freedom, and Privacy* (1993); at `http://www.cpsr.org/conferences/cfp93/shamos.html`.

[694] CE Shannon, "A Mathematical Theory of Communication," in *Bell Systems Technical Journal*, v 27 (1948), pp 379–423, 623–656.

[695] CE Shannon, "Communication Theory of Secrecy Systems," in *Bell Systems Technical Journal*, v 28 (1949), pp 656–715.

[696] C Shapiro, H Varian, *Information Rules*, Boston: Harvard Business School Press (1998), ISBN 0-87584-863-X; see `http://www.inforules.com`.

[697] D Sherwin, "Fraud—The Unmanaged Risk," in *Financial Crime Review*, v 1 no 1 (Fall 2000), pp 67–69.

[698] PW Shor, "Algorithms for Quantum Computers," in *35th Annual Symposium on the Foundations of Computer Science* (1994); proceedings published by the IEEE, ISBN 0-8186-6580-7, pp 124–134.

[699] O Sibert, PA Porras, R Lindell, "An Analysis of the Intel 80x86 Security Architecture and Implementations," in *IEEE Transactions on Software Engineering*, v 22 no 5 (May 1996), pp 283–293.

[700] GJ Simmons, "The Prisoners' Problem and the Subliminal Channel," in *Proceedings of CRYPTO '83*, Plenum Press (1984), pp 51–67.

[701] GJ Simmons, "How to Insure That Data Acquired to Verify Treaty Compliance Are Trustworthy," in *Proceedings of the IEEE*, v 76 no 5 (1988); reprinted as a chapter in [702]).

[702] GJ Simmons (ed), *Contemporary Cryptology—The Science of Information Integrity*, IEEE Press (1992), ISBN 0-87942-277-7.

[703] GJ Simmons, "A Survey of Information Authentication," in [702], pp 379–439.

[704] GJ Simmons, "An Introduction to Shared Secret and/or Shared Control Schemes and Their Application," in [702], pp 441–497.

[705] GJ Simmons, invited talk at the *1993 ACM Conference on Computer and Communications Security*, Fairfax, VA (Nov 3–5, 1993).

[706] GJ Simmons, "Subliminal Channels: Past and Present," in *European Transactions on Telecommunications*, v 5 no 4 (July/Aug 1994), pp 459–473.

[707] GJ Simmons, "The History of Subliminal Channels," in *IEEE Journal on Selected Areas in Communications*, v 16 no 4 (April 1998), pp 452–462.

[708] DR Simon, "Anonymous Communication and Anonymous Cash," in *Advances in Cryptology—Crypto 96*, Springer LNCS, v 1109, pp 61–73.

[709] WA Simpson, "Electronic Signatures Yield Unpleasant Surprises," (June 23, 2000), at http://cryptome.org/esigs-suck.htm.

[710] A Sipress, "Tracking Traffic by Cell Phone Maryland, Virginia to Use Transmissions to Pinpoint Congestion," in *The Washington Post* (Dec 22, 1999), p A1, at http://www.washingtonpost.com/.

[711] KS Siyan, J Casad, J Millecan, D Yarashus, P Tso, J Shoults, *Windows NT Server 4—Professional Reference*, New Riders Publishing (1996).

[712] SP Skorobogatov, "Low Temperature Remanence in Static RAM" (*to appear*).

[713] Smartcard Developer Association, http://www.scard.org/gsm/.

[714] "Plastic Card Fraud Rises in the UK," in *Smart Card News*, v 6 no 3 (Mar 1997), p 45.

[715] RE Smith, "Constructing a High-Assurance Mail Guard," in *17th National Computer Security Conference* (Oct 11–14, 1994), Baltimore, MD; proceedings published by NIST, pp 247–253.

[716] RM Smith, "Problems with Web Anonymizing Services," (Apr 15, 1999), at http://www.tiac.net/users/smiths/anon/anonprob.htm.

[717] SP Smith, H Perrit, H Krent, S Mencik, JA Crider, MF Shyong, LL Reynolds, *Independent Technical Committee Review of the Carnivore System—Draft report*, U.S. Department of Justice Contract No. 00-C-0238 IITRI, CR-022-216 (Nov 17, 2000), at http://cryptome.org/carnivore.rev.htm.

[718] S Smith, S Weingart, "Building a High-Performance, Programmable Secure Coprocessor," IBM Technical report RC 21102, available at http://www.ibm.com/security/cryptocards/.

[719] Peter Smulders, "The Threat of Information Theft by Reception of Electromagnetic Radiation from RS-232 Cables," in *Computers & Security*, v 9 (1990), pp 53–58.

[720] A Solomon, "A Brief History of PC Viruses," in *Computer Fraud and Security Bulletin* (Dec 1993), pp 9–19.

[721] A Solomon, Seminar given at Cambridge University Computer Laboratory (May 30, 2000).

[722] P Sommer, "Intrusion Detection and Legal Proceedings," in *Recent Advances in Intrustion Detection* (RAID) (1998), at `http://www.zurich.ibm.com/ ~dac/Prog_RAID98/Full_Papers/Sommer_text.pdf`.

[723] South West Thames Regional Health Authority, "Report of the Inquiry into the London Ambulance Service" (1993), at `http://www.cs.ucl.ac.uk/staff/ A.Finkelstein/las.html`.

[724] E Spafford, "The Internet Worm Program: An Analysis," in *Computer Communications Review*, v 19 no 1 (Jan 1989), pp 17–57.

[725] EH Spafford, "OPUS: Preventing Weak Password Choices," in *Computers and Security*, v 11 no 3 (1992), pp 273–278.

[726] "Tip von Urmel," in *Spiegel Magazine*, no 38 (Sept 11, 1995).

[727] J Spolsky, "Does Issuing Passports Make Microsoft a Country?" at `http://joel.editthispage.com/stories/storyReader$139`.

[728] "Your Car Radio May Be Revealing Your Tastes," in *St. Petersburg Times* (Jan 31, 2000), at `http://www.sptimes.com/News/013100/Technology/ Your_car_radio_may_be.shtml`.

[729] T Standage, *The Victorian Internet*, Phoenix Press (1999), ISBN 0-75380-703-3.

[730] F Stajano, personal communication with the author.

[731] F Stajano, RJ Anderson, "The Resurrecting Duckling: Security Issues in Ad-Hoc Wireless Networks," in *Security Protocols—7th International Workshop*, Springer LNCS, v 1796, pp 172–182.

[732] F Stajano, RJ Anderson, "The Cocaine Auction Protocol—On the Power of Anonymous Broadcast," in [613], pp 434–447.

[733] WA Steer, "VideoDeCrypt," at `http://www.ucl.ac.uk/~ucapwas/vdc/`.

[734] P Stein, P Feaver, *Assuring Control of Nuclear Weapons*, University Press (1987) quoted in [92].

[735] J Steiner, BC Neuman, JI Schiller, "Kerberos: An Authentication Service for Open Network Systems," in *USENIX* (Winter 1988); version 5 in "RFC 1510: The Kerberos Network Authentication Service (V5)"; at `http://sunsite.utk.edu/net/security/kerberos/`.

[736] N Stephenson, *Snow Crash*, New York: Bantam Doubleday Dell (1992), ISBN 0-553-38095-8.

[737] FA Stevenson, "Cryptanalysis of Contents Scrambling System," at `http://www.derfrosch.de/decss/`.

[738] DR Stinson, *Cryptography—Theory and Practice*, CRC Press (1995); ISBN 0-8493-8521-0.

[739] "Watching Them, Watching Us—UK CCTV Surveillance Regulation Campaign," at `http://www.spy.org.uk/`.

[740] R Strehle, *Verschlüsselt—Der Fall Hans Bühler*, Werd Verlag (1994), ISBN 3-85932-141-2.

[741] K Stumper, "DNA-Analysen und ein Recht auf Nichtwissen," in *Datenschutz und Datensicherheit*, v 19 no 9 (Sept 1995), pp 511–517.

[742] Suetonius (Gaius Suetonius Tranquillus), *Vitae XII Caesarum, translated into English as History of Twelve Caesars*, by Philemon Holland, 1606; Nutt (1899).

[743] D Sutherland, "A Model of Information," in *9th National Computer Security Conference (1986)*, pp 175–183.

[744] L Sweeney, "Weaving Technology and Policy Together to Maintain Confidentiality," in *Journal of Law, Medicine, and Ethics*, v 25 nos 2–3 (1997), pp 98–110.

[745] S Tendler, N Nuttall, "Hackers Run Up £1m Bill on Yard's Phones," in *The London Times* (Aug 5, 1996); at `http://www.the-times.co.uk/`.

[746] K Thompson, "Reflections on Trusting Trust," in *Communications of the ACM*, v 27 no 8 (Aug 1984), pp 761–763; at `http://www.acm.org/classics/sep95/`.

[747] J Ticehurst, "Barclays Online Bank Suffers Another Blow" (Aug 11, 2000), at `http://www.vnunet.com/News/1108767`.

[748] AZ Tirkel, GA Rankin, RM van Schyndel, WJ Ho, NRA Mee, CF Osborne, "Electronic Watermark," in *Digital Image Computing, Technology, and Applications* (DICTA 93) McQuarie University (1993), pp 666–673.

[749] JW Toigo, *Disaster Recovery Planning for Computers and Communication Resources*, New York: John Wiley & Sons, Inc. (1996), ISBN 0-471-12175-4.

[750] C Tomlinson, *"Rudimentary Treatise on the Construction of Locks,"* (1853) excerpt at `http://www.deter.com/unix/papers/treatise_locks.html`.

[751] Transactional Records Access Clearinghouse, "TRACFBI," at `http://trac.syr.edu/tracfbi/index.html`.

[752] M Trombly, "VISA Issues 10 'Commandments' for Online Merchants," in *Computerworld* (Aug 11, 2000), at `http://www.computerworld.com/cwi/story/0,1199,NAV47_STO48487,00.html`.

[753] JD Tygar, BS Yee, N Heintze, "Cryptographic Postage Indicia," in *Concurrency and Parallelism, Programming, Networking, and Security*, Springer-Verlag, (Dec 1996), pp 378–391, at `http://buffy.eecs.berkeley.edu/~tygar/recommend.html`.

[754] R Uhlig, "BT Admits Staff Could Have Fiddled System to Win Concorde Trip," in *The Daily Telegraph* (July 23, 1997), at `http://www.telegraph.co.uk:80/`.

[755] ukcrypto mailing list, at `http://www.chiark.greenend.org.uk/mailman/listinfo/ukcrypto`.

[756] Underwriters' Laboratories, `http://www.ul.com`.

[757] J Ungoed-Thomas, A Lorenz, "French Play Dirty for £1bn Tank Deal," in *The Sunday Times* (Aug 6, 2000), p 5.

[758] United Kingdon Government, "e-commerce@its.best.uk," at `http://www.e-envoy.gov.uk/2000/strategy/strategy.htm`.

[759] United States Code—U.S. Federal Law, online for example at `http://www4.law.cornell.edu/uscode/`.

[760] United States Court of Appeals, District of Columbia Circuit, *United States Telecom Association v. Federal Communications Commission and United States of America*, No. 99-1442 (Aug 15, 2000), at `http://pacer.cadc.uscourts.gov/common/opinions/200008/99-1442a.txt`.

[761] United States Senate Select Committee on Intelligence, *CIA Office of Inspector General Investigations Staff Report on the Improper Handling of Classified Information by John M. Deutch*, 106th Congress, at `http://intelligence.senate.gov/igreport.pdf`.

[762] UPI newswire item, Oklahoma distribution (Nov 26, 1983), Tulsa, OK.

[763] L van Hove, "Electronic Purses: (Which) Way to Go?" in *First Monday*, v 5 no 7 (June 2000), at `http://firstmonday.org/issues/issue5_7/hove/`.

[764] P van Oorschot, M Wiener, "Parallel Collision Search with Application to Hash Functions and Discrete Logarithms," *Second ACM Conference on Computer and Communications Security*; proceedings published by the ACM, ISBN 0-89791-732-4, pp 210–218.

[765] R van Renesse, *Optical Document Security* (2nd ed), Artech House (1997), ISBN 0-89006-982-4.

[766] R van Renesse, "Verifying versus Falsifying Banknotes," in *Optical Security and Counterfeit Deterrence Techniques II* (1998), IS&T (The Society for Imaging Science and Technology) and SPIE (The International Society for Optical Engineering), v 3314, ISBN 0-8194-2754-3, pp 71–85.

[767] H van Vliet, *Software Engineering—Principles and Practice*, 2nd ed, New York: John Wiley & Sons, Inc. (2000), ISBN 0-471-97508-7.

[768] R van Voris, "Black Box Car Idea Opens Can of Worms," in *Law News Network* (June 4, 1999), at `http://www.lawnewsnetwork.com/stories/A2024-1999Jun4.html`.

[769] G Vanneste, J Degraeve, "Initial Report on Security Requirements," in [56].

[770] HR Varian, *Intermediate Microeconomics—A Modern Approach*, 5 ed, New York: W. W. Norton (1999), ISBN 0-393-97370-0.

[771] HR Varian, "Managing Online Security Risks," in *The New York Times* (June 1, 2000); at `http://www.nytimes.com/library/financial/columns/060100econ-scene.html`.

[772] V Varadharajan, N Kumar, Y Mu, "Security Agent-Based Distributed Authorization: An Approach," in *20th National Information Systems Security Conference;* proceedings published by NIST (1998), pp 315–328.

[773] S Vaudenay, "FFT-Hash-II Is Not Yet Collision-Free," in *Laboratoire d'Informatique de l'Ecole Normale Supérieure report LIENS-92-17.*

[774] W Venema, "Murphy's Law and Computer Security," in *USENIX Security 96*, pp 187–193.

[775] B Vinck, "Security Architecture" (3G TS 33.102 v 3.2.0), from *Third-Generation Partnership Project*, at `http://www.3gpp.org/TSG/Oct_status_list.htm`.

[776] B Vinck, "Lawful Interception Requirements"(3G TS 33.106 v 3.0.0), from *Third-Generation Partnership Project*, at `http://www.3gpp.org/TSG/Oct_status_list.htm`.

[777] VISA International, "Integrated Circuit Chip Card—Security Guidelines Summary," version 2 draft 1 (Nov 1997).

[778] A Viterbi, "Spread-Spectrum Communications—Myths and Realities," in *IEEE Communications Magazine*, v 17 no 3 (May 1979), pp 11–18.

[779] PR Vizcaya, LA Gerhardt, "A Nonlinear Orientation Model for Global Description of Fingerprints," in *Pattern Recognition*, v 29 no 7 (July 1996), pp 1221–1231.

[780] D Wagner, B Schneier, J Kelsey, "Cryptanalysis of the Cellular Message Encryption Algorithm," in *Advances in Cryptology—Crypto 95*, Springer LNCS, v 1294, pp 527–537.

[781] D Wagner, "Cryptanalysis of Some Recently Proposed Multiple Modes of Operation," in *Fifth International Workshop on Fast Software Encryption* (1998), Springer LNCS, v 1372, pp 254–269.

[782] DA Wagner, SM Bellovin, "A 'Bump in the Stack' Encryptor for MS-DOS Systems," in *Proceedings of the Internet Society Symposium on Network and Distributed System Security* (1996); proceedings published by the IEEE, ISBN 0-8186-7222-6, pp 155–160.

[783] D Wagner, I Goldberg, M Briceno, "GSM Cloning," at `http://www.isaac.cs.berkeley.edu/isaac/gsm-faq.html`; see also `http://www.scard.org/gsm/`.

[784] D Wagner, B Schneier, "Analysis of the SSL 3.0 Protocol," in *Second USENIX Workshop on Electronic Commerce* (1996), pp 29–40; at `http://www.counterpane.com`.

[785] M Waldman, AD Rubin, LF Cranor, "Publius: A Robust, Tamper-Evident, Censorship-Resistant, Web Publishing System," in *9th USENIX Security Symposium* (2000), pp 59–72.

[786] M Walker, "On the Security of 3GPP Networks," invited talk at Eurocrypt 2000, at `http://www.ieee-security.org/Cipher/ConfReports/2000/CR2000-Eurocrypt.html`.

[787] G Walsh, "Review of Policy Relating to Encryption Technologies" (1996), at `http://www.efa.org.au/Issues/Crypto/Walsh/`.

[788] KG Walter, WF Ogden, WC Rounds, FT Bradshaw, SR Ames, DG Shumway, "Models for Secure Computer Systems," Case Western Reserve University, Report No. 1137 (July 31, 1973, revised Nov 21, 1973).

[789] KG Walter, WF Ogden, WC Rounds, FT Bradshaw, SR Ames, DG Shumway, "Primitive Models for Computer Security," Case Western Reserve University, Report No. ESD–TR–74–117 (Jan 23, 1974); at `http://www.dtic.mil`.

[790] E Waltz, *Information Warfare—Principles and Operations*, Artech House (1998), ISBN 0-89006-511-X.

[791] W Ware, "Security Controls for Computer Systems: Report of Defense Science Board Task Force on Computer Security," Rand Report R609-1, The RAND Corporation, Santa Monica, CA (Feb 1970); at `http://csrc.nist.gov/publications/history/index.html`.

[792] SD Warren, LD Brandeis, "The Right to Privacy," *Harvard Law Review*, series 4 (1890), pp 193–195.

[793] M Weaver, "Developer Tortured by Raiders with Crowbars," *Daily Telegraph* (Oct 31, 1997).

[794] W Webb, "High-Tech Security: The Eyes Have It," in *EDN* (Dec 18, 1997), pp 75–78.

[795] SH Weingart, "Physical Security for the μABYSS System," in *Proceedings of the 1987 IEEE Symposium on Security and Privacy*, IEEE Computer Society Press, pp 52–58.

[796] SH Weingart, SR White, WC Arnold, GP Double, "An Evaluation System for the Physical Security of Computing Systems," in *Sixth Annual Computer Security Applications Conference* (Dec 3–7, 1990), Tucson, AZ; proceedings published by the IEEE (1990), pp 232–243.

[797] L Weinstein, "IDs in Color Copies—A PRIVACY Forum Special Report," in *Privacy Forum Digest*, v 8 no 18 (Dec 6, 1999), at `http://www.vortex.com/privacy/priv.08.18`.

[798] C Weissman, "Security Controls in the ADEPT–50 Time-Sharing System," in *AFIPS Conference Proceedings*, v 35, 1969 Fall Joint Computer Conference, pp 119–133.

[799] C Weissman, "BLACKER: Security for the DDN, Examples of A1 Security Engineering Trades," in *Proceedings of the 1992 IEEE Symposium on Security and Privacy*, pp 286–292.

[800] G Welchman, *The Hut Six Story*, New York: McGraw-Hill (1982), ISBN 0-07-069180-0.

[801] A Westfeld, A Pfitzmann, "Attacks on Steganographic Systems," in *Proceedings of the Third International Workshop on Information Hiding* (1999), Springer LNCS, v 1768, pp 61–76.

[802] AF Westin, "Data Protection in the Global Society" (1996 conference report), at `http://www.privacyexchange.org/iss/confpro/aicgsberlin.html`.

[803] A Whitten, "Why Johnny Can't Encrypt: A Usability Evaluation of PGP 5.0," in *Eighth USENIX Security Symposium*, proceedings ISBN 1-880446-28-6, pp 169–183.

[804] MV Wilkes, RM Needham, *The Cambridge CAP Computer and Its Operating System*, Elsevier North Holland (1979).

[805] J Wilkins, *Mercury; or the Secret and Swift Messenger: Shewing, How a Man May, with Privacy and Speed Communicate His Thoughts to a Friend at Any Distance*, London: Rich Baldwin (1694).

[806] FW Winterbotham, *The Ultra Secret*, New York: Harper & Row (1974).

[807] K Wong, "Mobile Phone Fraud—Are GSM Networks Secure?" in *Computer Fraud and Security Bulletin* (Nov 1996), pp 11–18.

[808] CC Wood, "Identity Token Usage at American Commercial Banks," in *Computer Fraud and Security Bulletin* (Mar 1995), pp 14–16.

[809] JPL Woodward, "Security Requirements for System High and Compartmented Mode Workstations," Mitre MTR 9992, Revision 1 (1987); also published by the Defense Intelligence Agency as document DDS-2600-5502-87.

[810] B Wright, "The Verdict on Plaintext Signatures: They're Legal," in *Computer Law and Security Report*, v 14 no 6 (Nov/Dec 1994), pp 311–312.

[811] B Wright, *The Law of Electronic Commerce: EDI, Fax and Email*, New York: Little Brown (1991); 4th ed, (with supplement) 1994.

[812] JB Wright, "Report of the Weaponization and Weapons Production and Military Use Working Group," Appendix F to the Report of the Fundamental Classification Policy Review Group, U.S. Department of Energy Office of Scientific and Technical Information (1997), `http://www.osti.gov/opennet/app-f.html`.

[813] MA Wright, "Security Controls in ATM Systems," in *Computer Fraud and Security Bulletin* (Nov 1991), pp 11–14.

[814] P Wright, *Spycatcher—The Candid Autobiography of a Senior Intelligence Officer*, Australia: William Heinemann (1987), ISBN 0-85561-098-0.

[815] JX Yan, A Blackwell, RJ Anderson, A Grant, "The Memorability and Security of Passwords—Some Empirical Results," University of Cambridge Computer Laboratory Technical Report no 500; at `http://www.cl.cam.ac.uk/ftp/users/rja14/tr500.pdf`.

[816] JX Yan, S Early, R Anderson, "The XenoService—A Distributed Defeat for Distributed Denial of Service," Third Information Survivability Workshop (Oct 2000), at `http://www.cl.cam.ac.uk/users/rja14/`.

[817] T Ylönen, "SSH—Secure Login Connections over the Internet," in *USENIX Security 96*, pp 37–42.

[818] KS Yoon, YK Ham, RH Park, "Hybrid Approaches to Fractal Face Recognition Using the Hidden Markov Model and Neural Network," in *Pattern Recognition*, v 31 no 3 (1998), pp 283–293.

[819] G Yuval, "Reinventing the Travois: Encryption/MAC in 30 ROM Bytes," in *Fourth International Workshop on Fast Software Encryption* (1997), Springer LNCS, v 1267, pp 205–209.

[820] MC Zari, AF Zwilling, DA Hess, KW Snow, CJ Anderson, D Chiang, "Personal Identification System Utilizing Low Probability of Intercept (LPI) Techniques for Covert Ops," in *30th Annual IEEE Carnahan Conference on Security Technology* (1996), pp 1–6.

[821] Zero Knowledge Systems Inc., `http://www.zeroknowledge.com/`.

[822] MW Zior, "A Community Response to CMM-Based Security Engineering Process Improvement," in *18th National Information Systems Security Conference* (1995), pp 404–413.

[823] M Zviran, WJ Haga, "A Comparison of Password Techniques for Multilevel Authentication Mechanisms," in *The Computer Journal*, v 36 no 3 (1993), pp 227–237.

Index

A

A3/A5/A8 algorithms, 77, 99,
    357–358, 359, 362
access codes. *See* passwords
    capabilities, 54, 58, 59–60, 126
    See also public key
        certificates
access controls, 1, 51–61, 62–64,
    65–71. *See also*
        censorship; copyright;
        security policies;
        specific applications
    access control lists (ACLs),
        54, 55–58, 59–60, 170.
        See also public key
        certificates
    access control matrices,
        53–55. *See also* lattice
        model
    access triples, 54, 56–57
    ADEPT-50, 143–144
    attacks, 57, 65–70
    cryptography and, 59
    failures, 69–70
    granularity, 60–61
    mandatory/discretionary,
        142, 150
    ORBs, 61
    principle of least privilege, 69
    proof-carrying code, 61

sandboxing, 61, 62
security policies and, 52–53,
    54, 55
as security targets, 11
separation of duty, 166, 187,
    189–191
access tokens, 229, 285–286
accessory control protocols,
    16–17, 408–409, 474–475
account master files, 188
ACID (atomic, consistent,
    isolated, durable)
    transactions, 118–119
Acorn Risc Machine (ARM).
    See ARM processors
Addamax, 148
additive stream ciphers, 99
address forgery attacks, 373
Address Resolution Protocol
    (ARP), 370
ADEPT-50 access control,
    143–144
adhesive, tamper-evident,
    252–253
Advanced Encryption Standard
    (AES) algorithm, 91,
    93–94
    banking, 78
aggregation attacks, 156–157,
    168, 170–171, 172, 174

aggregation of targets, 223n
Airborne Warning and
    Control System
    (AWACS), 331
airport security, 216, 255
alarms. *See* burglar alarms
alias band structures, 247
American-Arab
    Anti-Discrimination
    Committee, 387
Ames case, 182
Amulet. *See* ARM processors
annual loss expectancy (ALE),
    511–512
anomaly detection, 385
anonymity, 10, 443–445. *See also*
    inference controls;
    privacy
    abuse of, 444–445, 449–450
    in business systems, 166
    in census data, 162, 173–176
    in medical systems, 7, 166,
        181–183
    in military systems,
        156–157, 174
anonymous remailers, 332, 414,
    445, 447–448
    attacks, 383, 443–444
answering machine attacks,
    350, 351